INTRODUCTION TO
» » » » Logic « « « «

Paul Herrick
Shoreline Community College

New York (
OXFORD UNIVERSITY PRESS

Oxford University Press, Inc., publishes works that further Oxford University's
objective of excellence in research, scholarship, and education.

Oxford New York
Auckland   Cape Town   Dar es Salaam   Hong Kong   Karachi
Kuala Lumpur   Madrid   Melbourne   Mexico City   Nairobi
New Delhi   Shanghai   Taipei   Toronto

With offices in
Argentina   Austria   Brazil   Chile   Czech Republic   France   Greece
Guatemala   Hungary   Italy   Japan   Poland   Portugal   Singapore
South Korea   Switzerland   Thailand   Turkey   Ukraine   Vietnam

For titles covered by Section 112 of the US Higher Education Opportunity Act,
please visit www.oup.com/us/he for the latest information about pricing and alternate formats.

Published by Oxford University Press, Inc.
198 Madison Avenue, New York, New York 10016
http://www.oup.com

Library of Congress Cataloging-in-Publication Data

Herrick, Paul William.
  Introduction to logic / Paul Herrick.
    p. cm.
  Includes index.
  ISBN 978-0-19-989049-1 (alk. paper)
  1. Logic—Textbooks. I. Title.
  BC108.H435 2013
  160—dc23
                    2012002896

Contents

Unit Four: Predicate Logic   467

To the Instructor

This textbook was written with the fully online student and the independent learner in mind. The explanations are more thorough, more "from the ground up" than usual; the examples and applications are more numerous; and the relations between each unit are carefully explained to make the text an interconnected whole. In short, much of the explanatory work one would ordinarily do in the classroom is provided within this text. In addition, optional appendices, sidebars, and interludes take the interested student beyond the introductory level, offering food for thought as well as opportunities for advanced research not usually available in the introduction to logic text.

Not that this book is unsuitable for the face-to-face class. I am confident it will serve both populations of students very well. I plan to use this text in the classroom as well as in my fully online logic classes. The fact that this book was written with the online learner in mind means less content will need to be explained in the classroom, leaving more time for discussion and practice.

I hope that the addition of an integrated history track running from the beginning to the end of the book adds realism, gives a personal touch, and makes it a little more fun to teach as well as to learn logic. In this text, the history of logic is not confined to occasional sidebars; it is built into the content. Logical theory unfolds historically, as a story starting in ancient Athens and reaching undreamed of heights in the late twentieth century. I hope you will agree that historical context not only adds personality to a course that can be pretty dry if you let it be, it also makes the logic course more interesting. Many of the great logicians of history were interesting characters, and the conceptual problems they sought to solve were serious ones. In short, I have tried to present logic as a human endeavor and not merely as a collection of techniques.

Some of the material in this book appeared in an earlier textbook that I wrote, *The Many Worlds of Logic*, first published in 1993. Oxford University Press published the second edition of that book. This new book covers everything treated in *Many Worlds* and more. The difference between my earlier book and this book stems from two intervening experiences. First, in the 12 years since the second edition of *Many Worlds* appeared, I have been teaching fully online logic classes every quarter, in addition to face-to-face logic classes. It was my experiences as an online logic teacher that inspired me to begin this textbook. My online students, and their struggles to learn logic in a fully online environment, inspired me to aim for a text with explanations so crystal clear, so thorough, so from the ground up, that the independent online student would find in the text all he or she needs to fully master the subject outside the traditional classroom.

Second, at some point I became convinced that the history of logic adds real-world context as well as a wonderful human element to the introductory logic course. Most of us move through the subject in a roughly historical order anyway. After laying down fundamental concepts, we often progress from Aristotelian to truth-functional to predicate logic, perhaps visiting informal and inductive logic along the way. I have found that adding historical context as the course proceeds takes very little class time while adding the nice touches already mentioned. The history of logic is more interesting than many might initially suppose. With this new text I plan to teach logic as a fascinating, human story unfolding over time, as well as a body of important technical information with applications to every area of human thought. The two approaches—the historical and the technical—do not have to be kept separate. They are intertwined in this book.

Every quarter, one or two students always ask about advanced logic. What comes next in logical theory? What sort of class can I take if I want to study more logic? I am sure you have been asked the same questions. In the past, I have recommended Hunter's *Metalogic* and Mates's *Elementary Logic*. With this new textbook I will no longer have to send the student off to a university library. Accessible, nontechnical appendices on metalogic, Gödel, Turing, and logic and computing will now mean that the student who seeks to go beyond the introductory level has a place to start—right here in this textbook.

Students also often ask questions like these: Why does logic have to be so technical? What is the point of all of this really abstract stuff? What difference does it all make anyway? I am sure you have been asked these or similar questions, perhaps even in front of the class. I hope that the nontechnical appendix on logic and computing, and the applications of logic to real-world issues within the text, will help you answer those who call into question the very worth of logic as an academic subject.

The experiences I've had teaching logic in the classroom for a little over 30 years have all gone into this book. It is my hope that this book will allow you to take a somewhat novel approach in your logic course while covering all the standard material as before, in the usual order and as rigorously as ever.

The following are suggestions for organizing various compact units within a single logic course.

1.   A comprehensive unit on traditional Aristotelian syllogistic logic alone, without any mention of the modern or Boolean approach, can be taught with Chapters 7 and 8. Chapter 9 adds Venn diagrams, the Boolean interpretation of universal statements, and the story of the nineteenth-century revolution in categorical logic.

2.   All the standard concepts of truth-functional logic can be taught, without any modern symbols and without a modern formal language, in plain English, using Chapters 10 and 11 alone. This is logic much as it would have been taught on the painted porch in ancient Athens, complete with truth-functional sentences, operators, and valid argument forms. Modern truth-functional logic, with horseshoes, triple bars, an artificial language, and all the rest, only begins in Chapter 12. Chapters 10 and 11 thus provide an intuitive, natural-language-based foundation for the rest of the truth-functional logic unit.

3.   Some of us like to teach truth tables, and others skip them in favor of natural deduction. The unit on truth-functional logic can be handled in either way: with or without truth tables and with or without natural deduction.

    a.   Skip truth tables. Teach the basics (Chapters 10–13), pass over truth tables altogether, and go straight to natural deduction (Chapters 18–22). The natural deduction chapters contain no tables and do not presuppose them.

    b.   Skip natural deduction. Teach the basics, then truth tables, and stop before natural deduction begins by selecting only Chapters 10 through 17.

4.   A course in critical thinking, covering all the standard topics, can be taught with this text if the material in the text is supplemented with references to current events, online research, and so on. Unit One not only covers all the basic concepts of logic, including a section on how to build a good argument, it also contains an appendix on critical thinking, introduces Socrates and the Socratic method, and includes numerous arguments for discussion and analysis. Unit Five covers definitions, the informal fallacies, the standard forms of inductive reasoning, and probability theory, with applications in law, science, debate, hypothesis testing, and many other topics usually treated in the critical thinking class. In addition, elementary treatments of categorical and truth-functional logic are easy to include in a critical thinking course using Chapters 7 and 8 as a compact unit in categorical logic and Chapters 10 and 11 as a short introduction to truth-functional arguments.

5.   A rigorous treatment of modern predicate logic limited to monadic predicates can be taught using Chapter 23 (translation with only monadic predication) and Chapter 26 (natural deduction with only monadic predicates). Of course, add the other chapters in the unit for a comprehensive treatment all the way to identity.

6.   Students in search of advanced topics can be sent to appendices and interludes in the text that treat the philosophy of logic, computers and logic, Gödel and Turing, and metalogic. Some of this material might be useful for independent study and extra credit projects.

7.   Students in search of multicultural aspects of logical theory will definitely want to read the wonderful and fascinating appendix by Professor Mark Storey (Bellevue College, Bellevue, WA), on classical Indian logic. One interesting extra credit project would be to compare and contrast classical Greek and classical Indian logical theory.

8.   Finally, a short but robust unit on elementary modal logic, covering translation, S5 natural deduction, and applications to several famous modal arguments, can be taught using Chapter 35 alone. My previous textbook spread modal logic across two chapters. This text condenses the subject into one, which is more appropriate for an introductory textbook, I think.

In addition, interspersed throughout the text you will find summaries of many classic philosophical arguments, ready for logical analysis and evaluation, representing philosophy of religion, the free will issue, the mind–body problem, epistemology, metaphysics, ethics, and political philosophy. These can be used as homework problems or as topics for discussion; they can also serve as material for extra credit projects with instructions such as these: Summarize the argument in your own words, translate it into a formal language of your choice, prove it valid using natural deduction or give an argument for the claim that it is invalid, defend it against the strongest objection you can think of, state an objection of your own, rewrite the argument to improve it, and so on. There is much to be learned applying precise logical techniques to meaningful philosophical arguments.

In short, I have tried to make the book flexible and suited for a variety of different logic courses and teaching styles. Throughout, I have written with both teachers and students in mind.

To the Student

Welcome to logic! You are about to study a subject that will expand your thinking and stretch your mind in ways you never imagined. After you complete a course in logic, you will never look at an argument the same way again. The successful student of logic is less likely to fall prey to logical fallacies designed to manipulate rather than enlighten. He or she is also more likely to be the author of sound arguments that relate important matters to truth rather than illusion. Logic might be so general that it seems to be about everything, but it is also so general that it *applies* to everything.

If you take it seriously, logic class will contribute to the development of important intellectual skills, including the following:

1. Precise thinking. Accurately apply words and instructions in technical contexts.
2. Systematic thinking. Draw connections and stay with the program.
3. Information processing. Efficiently handle complex information.

These intellectual abilities are important requirements in almost every occupation and field of thought today. Logic class therefore helps you prepare for almost any subject or line of work, from computing, education, law, business, science, health care, and medicine, to auto mechanics, engineering, and city planning.

I wish to offer some advice. First, each section of a logic course builds on previous sections. Therefore, if you fail to understand one section, you will probably not understand later sections. Don't fall behind!

Second, logic courses emphasize problem solving. With most people, problem solving is a skill that only develops with practice. Your instructor can show you exactly how to solve logic problems in class, but if you do not practice solving problems on your own, you might do poorly on tests, and you could come away from the course with little understanding.

Third, read the text carefully, line by line. Logic is a very precise, technical subject. The "devil is in the details," so to speak. Misreading or misunderstanding a technical definition or a precise instruction can throw everything off when you go to apply it, resulting in major errors in the end.

Fourth, take notes as you read the text. Summarize the main ideas in your own words. Make colorful flash cards for key ideas! Writing things down is a good way to cement your understanding and also helps when it comes time to review for a test or quiz.

Finally, test your understanding every step of the way by doing the exercises in the text and by taking the quizzes and self-tests available online. In logic class, especially at the beginning, a student sometimes thinks he or she understands the material when in reality he or she does not understand it at all. Taking a self-test usually catches the error . . . and leads to a better score in the end.

Other Benefits

The study of logic will also help you develop your critical thinking skills. Critical thinking can be briefly defined as the application of rational, reality-based standards of evaluation to your own beliefs and values. A critical thinker continually asks these questions: Are my core beliefs really true? Or am I just fooling myself? Are the values I live by truly good? Are my actions morally right? Or do I need to make some changes? Our feelings and desires come and go and often lead us astray. Just because I *feel* like doing something at the moment does not make it the right thing to do. Just because I *want* to believe something does not make it true or in correspondence with reality. Sometimes what we feel like doing is the wrong thing to do. Sometimes we want to believe something, but it is just not true. A belief is worthy of acceptance only when we have sufficient evidence to believe that it is true, in other words, only when we have good reason to believe it is reflective of reality. There is widespread agreement among those who study ethics that the best values to live by are not those we just "feel" like adopting or "want" to adopt at the moment. Rather, the best values to live by are those we have the best reason to believe really are right or good. Since at least the days of the ancient Greek philosopher Socrates (470–399 BC), whom you will meet in this book, philosophers have argued that an "examined life"—a life continually tested by critical thinking—is the best life a human being can live. The study of logic and critical thinking go hand in hand.

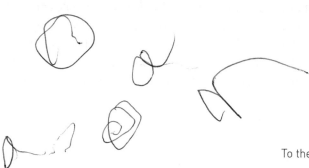

Acknowledgments

A textbook is never the work of one person; it is always a collaborative effort. This book is certainly no exception. I am grateful to all who have contributed their expertise and talent.

First, I am grateful to the group of logic professors selected by Oxford University Press to review the manuscript. The seven reviewers studied the manuscript carefully and made many suggestions for improvement, offered many of their own insights into the subject and into the teaching of the subject, and gave me many new ideas. Their comments greatly improved every chapter of the text. I sincerely thank (in alphabetical order) Dr. Steven Duncan, Bellevue College; Dr. Brian Glenney, Gordon College; Dr. Andrew Jeffery, Green River Community College; Dr. John Messerly, my colleague at Shoreline Community College; Professor Paul Pardi, Seattle Pacific University and Green River Community College; Professor Mark Storey, Bellevue College; and Dr. Peter Westmoreland, University of Florida.

I am also indebted to S. Marc Cohen, Professor of Philosophy, University of Washington, for the valuable comments that he wrote after reviewing the historical sections of this book. His expertise and suggestions improved the book in many places. I deeply appreciate his advice and help. Needless to say, any errors that remain are my own. In addition to class-testing the manuscript of this book while it was in production, Mark Storey graciously double-checked the Selected Answers. Mark also took the time to discuss with me just about every section of this book. His thoughtful comments were helpful and are deeply appreciated. Professor Catherine Roth (Spokane Falls Community College) also class-tested the manuscript while it was in production, and I want to thank her for her valuable comments.

I have also learned so much over the years from the many informal discussions of logical theory and its applications that I have had with Professors Bob Kirk, Robert Coburn, Robert Richman, Laurence BonJour, Larry Stern, Tom Kerns, S. Marc Cohen, Doug Cannon, Richard Purtill, Shawn Mintek, Liz Unger, Brad Rind, Steve Layman,

Raymond Bradley, Norman Swartz, Mitch Erickson, Sandy Johanson, Andrew Jeffery, Steven Duncan, Art DiQuattro, Richard McClelland, George Goodall, Richard Kopcinsky, Richard Curtis, Dan Howard-Snyder, and Jeff Clausen. I have learned so much in conversations with colleagues in philosophy that I want to acknowledge their contribution; many of their insights into logic have been incorporated into this book. I also have learned a great deal from the logic texts that I used in the classroom over the years, including the excellent texts by Hurley, Copi, Kahane, Gustafson and Ulrich, Baum, Bradley and Scwartz, Carney and Scheer, and Bonevac.

In addition, I have learned so much from the students who have taken my classes over the years that I feel a large debt of gratitude to them as well. Many students have helped me spot errors in my thinking. Many others have shared valuable insights from which I have learned much. Still others have asked questions that have helped me find better ways to explain the concepts of logical theory. What I have learned from these and other students has made this a better book.

I also want to record a very special note of thanks to the copyeditors for this book, Teresa Horton and Karen Olson. Thank you for your excellent work. I am also very grateful to my editor at Oxford University Press, Robert Miller, for his solid support, wise advice at crucial times, and encouragement in this project. I also sincerely thank the assistant editor, Kristin Maffei, and production editor, Shelby Peak, for their invaluable help as well. It has been wonderful to work with all of the people at Oxford University Press. Finally, for her constant support and encouragement, I want to thank my wife, Joan.

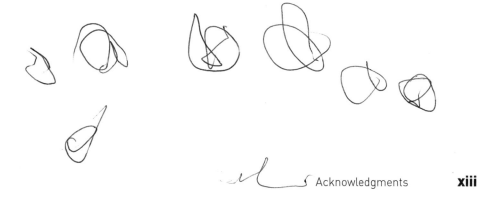

Unit
1

The Fundamental Concepts
of Logic

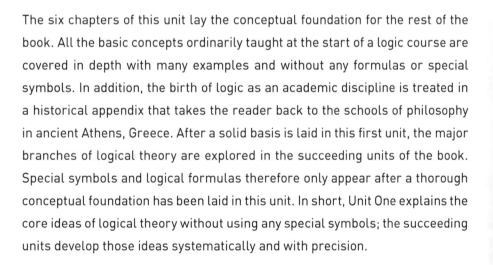

The six chapters of this unit lay the conceptual foundation for the rest of the book. All the basic concepts ordinarily taught at the start of a logic course are covered in depth with many examples and without any formulas or special symbols. In addition, the birth of logic as an academic discipline is treated in a historical appendix that takes the reader back to the schools of philosophy in ancient Athens, Greece. After a solid basis is laid in this first unit, the major branches of logical theory are explored in the succeeding units of the book. Special symbols and logical formulas therefore only appear after a thorough conceptual foundation has been laid in this unit. In short, Unit One explains the core ideas of logical theory without using any special symbols; the succeeding units develop those ideas systematically and with precision.

1 What Is Logic? « « « « « «

We are almost always reasoning about something or other. You reasoned when you got up this morning and thought about what to do today. Every day you form new beliefs on the basis of reasoning about things you have experienced. Separating truth from falsehood, learning about the world, and putting your knowledge to use all call for reasoning. **Logic**, as an academic subject, is the systematic study of the standards of correct reasoning. The principles of logic are guides to correct reasoning, just as the principles of arithmetic are guides to correctly adding, subtracting, multiplying, and dividing numbers, the principles of photography are guides to taking good photos, and so on. Whereas psychology studies our reasoning as it actually is, with all of its errors and flaws, logic is concerned with the principles our reasoning should follow if it is to be correct, or good, reasoning. You can improve your reasoning by studying the principles of logic, just as you can improve your numerical abilities by studying the principles of mathematics. Because correct reasoning can be applied to any subject matter whatsoever, the number of potential applications of logical theory is practically unlimited. But what exactly is reasoning, anyway?

Reasoning occurs when you conclude one thing on the basis of something else, in other words, when you draw a conclusion on the basis of evidence. For example, you see thick, dark clouds rolling in and conclude that it is probably going to rain, or you hear the cat meowing and conclude that it is likely he is hungry. Essentially, in an act of reasoning, the mind moves from evidence to a conclusion based on that evidence. Albert Einstein was reasoning when he derived the special theory of relativity from observations he and others had made concerning the speed of light. Charles Darwin was reasoning when he proposed his theory of evolution as the best explanation of facts about the way species have changed over time. You reasoned when you decided whether or not to study logical theory. Can you think of additional examples of reasoning? Here are a few more:

- You listen to a politician's speech and conclude that he will *not* get your vote.
- After reading an editorial in the newspaper, you change your mind on an issue.
- You hear your car's engine making a strange noise and decide to take it into the shop.

In each case you are going from evidence to a conclusion based on that evidence. This is reasoning.

Obviously, reasoning is something we do all the time. But isn't it just as obvious that *not* all reasoning is correct, or good, reasoning? How do you rate the quality of the reasoning in the following examples?

1. Smith meets Jones at a party and learns that Jones is a vegetarian. Based only on this information, Smith concludes that Jones *must* be a Buddhist!
2. In biology class, Jan puts her reasoning into a three-step argument: "Since (1) all tapirs are mammals, and (2) all mammals are warm-blooded, it follows with certainty that (3) all tapirs are warm-blooded."
3. On a math test, Pat reasons, "First, all squares have four equal sides. Second, it is given that figure ABCD has four sides. So, figure ABCD *must* be a square."

Looking at these examples, isn't it pretty clear that not all acts of reasoning are equally correct? Sometimes our reasoning shines, but other times—like Smith's and Pat's reasoning here—it is not as good as it could be. What do you think is wrong with the reasoning in Examples 1 and 3?

The fact that some reasoning certainly appears to be flawed suggests that there are independent standards of correct, or good, reasoning. There are rules in mathematics that tell us how to add, subtract, multiply, and divide correctly. Satellites are sent into the right orbits on the basis of the principles of physics. Chemical compounds are analyzed on the basis of the principles of chemistry. Doesn't it seem plausible to suppose that there are also principles of good, or correct, reasoning? This is what logic, as an academic subject, seeks to discover and is all about: the principles of correct reasoning.

Logic Class . . . in 335 BC

Logicians have certainly had enough time to discover principles of correct or good reasoning. Logic was first taught as an academic subject in the universities of ancient Athens, Greece, during the fourth century BC, making it one of the oldest of all academic subjects. Logic class was one of the core or "general education" requirements in the universities of Europe during the Middle Ages. In the seventeenth century, during the rise of modern science, every college student took logic as a graduation requirement. Today the study of logic remains part of the curriculum in colleges and universities around the world. So you might think of it this way: You are about to learn a subject that has been studied since ancient times, when scholars wrote books on papyrus, people kept time with sundials, and professors wore togas to class.[1]

One reason logic class has remained a core requirement of a higher education is that logical theory contains principles that can help you reason more accurately no matter what subject you are reasoning about, making it an all-purpose "tool-kit" for your mind.

Some people suppose that logical theory, because it is so abstract, has few or no practical applications. On the contrary. One example is probably sitting in front of you right now: Each of the tiny electric circuits inside a digital computer is constructed so that it follows certain very exact rules. Those rules, which open and close the circuits or "logic gates" that make up the brains of a computer, start with the rules of logic expressed in symbolic form. But the digital computer is only the latest in a series of amazing applications of logical theory that all began when a *logician* in the Middle Ages designed a hand-cranked machine theoretically capable of computing the correct sequence of reasoning for a certain class of logical arguments. This mechanical forerunner of the modern computer worked by following rules of logic programmed into it in the form of precisely aligned gears, cogs, and turning wheels. The computer and other practical applications of logic are explained in this book, as we follow the development of our subject from its beginning in ancient Greece to its continued relevance as a guide to good reasoning, and effective computing, in the twenty-first century.

Major Divisions of Logical Theory

Formal vs. Informal Logic

Formal logic studies the abstract patterns or forms of correct reasoning. Here the focus is on *form* rather than *content*, that is, on the logical structure of reasoning apart from what it is specifically about. Since ancient times, logicians have used special symbols and formulas, similar to those used in mathematics, to record the abstract logical forms they have discovered. This is why formal logic is sometimes also called symbolic logic and mathematical logic.

Informal logic studies the nonformal aspects of the reasoning process that cannot be accurately translated into abstract symbols. This is why informal logic for the

---

[1] Actually, contrary to the impression left by the movie *Animal House*, the ancient Greeks did not wear togas; they wore a toga-like garment called a *chiton*. The toga was Roman.

most part eschews special symbols and formulas. In this division of logical theory, the focus is reasoning expressed within everyday language.

Deductive vs. Inductive Logic

Logicians divide all reasoning into two very broad categories. **Deductive reasoning** aims to show that a conclusion *must* be true. The underlying claim in a case of deductive reasoning is that the reasoning *conclusively* proves the conclusion is true. Put another way, the goal of deductive reasoning is to establish a conclusion with *certainty*. Here is a brief example of deductive reasoning: "Tiny Tim played the ukulele. Anyone who plays the ukulele is a musician. Thus, Tiny Tim was a musician." **Deductive logic** is the study of the standards of correct deductive reasoning.

Inductive reasoning aims to show *not* that the conclusion *must* be true, but only that the conclusion *probably* is true. The underlying claim in a case of inductive reasoning is that the conclusion is *likely* or *probably* true but not certainly true. (For now, by "probably" let us mean "more than 50% likely.") In other words, the goal of inductive reasoning is to establish a conclusion based on probability, not complete certainty. Here is a simple example of inductive reasoning: "It has been raining in Seattle for a solid week, and the sky is still full of rain clouds; therefore, *probably* it will rain tomorrow." **Inductive logic** is the study of the methods for evaluating inductive reasoning.

This book is a comprehensive introduction to both deductive and inductive reasoning. As you might have guessed, the deductive branch of logic lends itself more to purely formal symbolism and resembles mathematics in many ways, while the inductive branch of logic is more informal in nature and is more easily expressed in the words of ordinary language. Thus, deductive and formal (or "symbolic") logic almost totally overlap, whereas inductive logic and informal logic overlap quite a bit, except for the branch of inductive reasoning known as probability theory, which is very mathematical and thus very formal in nature, as you will see.

The Plan of This Book

Logic has a reputation as an abstract and difficult academic subject, but it does not have to be so. To help make this ancient and perhaps daunting subject less abstruse, this book takes a somewhat novel approach: We are going to proceed in a historical manner and in small, easy-to-digest steps, in shorter than usual chapters. After all the basic concepts of logical theory have been presented, in this unit, our journey through the many worlds of logic will begin with a stop at categorical logic, the first specialized branch of logic to be formalized and transmitted in written form. This body of principles is more than 2,300 years old and is still in use. The end of our trip will be a look at some of the major twentieth-century developments in logical theory—discoveries that have revolutionized our understanding of the reasoning process. Applications to real-life arguments along the way will help you learn these wonderful ideas.

As we proceed, we will also look at some of the individuals who have made important contributions to logical theory, starting with the founder of logic as an academic subject, the ancient Greek philosopher Aristotle.

Finally, in keeping with the historical nature of our approach, we will ask: What *use* is all this logical theory? What difference has it made in the real world? How has it affected human history? In search of answers, we will look at world-changing applications of logical theory, starting with the invention of the first mechanical computer in the Middle Ages by a logician. Other applications of logical theory covered in this book might surprise you: from the logical theory that was used at Bletchley Park, England, during World War II to crack Hitler's secret "Enigma" code and save tens of thousands of Allied lives, to the millions of tiny "logic gates" in your cell phone that enable it to contact and communicate with one particular phone out of a hundred million on the other side of the country, to the algorithm-driven logic circuits built into everything today from guitar amps to TV sets to the engine inside the car you drive or the bus you ride.

Exercise 1.1   We usually do not understand a concept well until we can articulate it in our own words. Answer these questions to demonstrate your understanding of the main ideas of this chapter.

1. How is logic defined in this chapter?
2. What is reasoning?
3. What is deductive reasoning?
4. What is inductive reasoning?
5. How does deductive reasoning differ from inductive reasoning?
6. What is the focus in the branch of logic known as formal logic?
7. How does formal logic differ from informal logic?
8. Some people argue that because logic is so abstract it has few "real-world" applications. This is a challenge to the usefulness of logical theory. Explain the reply to this challenge that is offered in this chapter.

Exercise 1.2   The following questions give you an opportunity to apply what you have learned in this chapter.

1. Find an example of reasoning that interests you, in a newspaper editorial, magazine article, website, and so on, and summarize it in your own words.
2. Identify and explain an example of poor reasoning from your own life. How did you discover that your reasoning was not so good? Did you test it in some way?

3. Identify and explain an example of good reasoning from your own life. How do you know that your reasoning is good? Did you substantiate it in some way?

4. Discuss: When reasoning is done well, the consequences can be wonderful. Witness the many life-saving and life-enhancing advances in medicine and technology made during the twentieth century alone. However, when reasoning goes astray, the consequences can be horrible. Witness just the horrendous wars of the twentieth century.

Appendix 1   The Birth of Logical Theory

Logic, as an academic subject, was born in the city of Athens, in the country we now call Greece, in the fourth century BC, when an individual named **Aristotle** (384–322 BC) wrote the first known treatise devoted to the systematic, theoretical study of reasoning. Aristotle was one of those persons the ancient Greeks called *philosophers* (from the Greek words *philein* for love and *Sophia* for wisdom; literally, "lovers of wisdom"). Four additional works of logical theory followed. Thus, in five highly original (and extremely complex) treatises, collectively known to history as the "Organon" (Greek for "tool," as in "tool of thought"), Aristotle gave reasoning its first systematic treatment preserved in written form and earned the title that history has given him: founder of logic. Aristotle wrote the first logic textbook in history![2] In his excellent and widely used text *Elementary Logic*, Benson Mates writes:

> [W]e can say flatly that the history of logic begins with the Greek philosopher Aristotle. . . . Although it is almost a platitude among historians that great intellectual advances are never the work of only one person (in founding the science of geometry Euclid made use of the results of Eudoxus and others; in the case of mechanics Newton stood upon the shoulders of Descartes, Galileo, and Kepler; and so on), Aristotle, according to all available evidence, created the science of logic absolutely ex nihilo.[3]

Aristotle: Life and Times

Aristotle was born in 384 BC, in the Greek colony and seaport of Stagirus, Macedonia. His father, who was court physician to the King of Macedonia, died when Aristotle was young, and the future founder of logic went to live with an uncle. When

---

[2] The name *Organon* ("tool") was applied to Aristotle's logical works after his death by an editor, but it reflects Aristotle's claim that logic is an all-purpose tool of thought, a guide to the precise thinking that is needed if we want to attain solidly proven truth on *any* subject.

[3] Benson Mates, *Elementary Logic*, 2nd ed. (New York: Oxford University Press, 1972, p. 206).

Aristotle was 17, he was sent to Athens to study at Plato's Academy, the first university in Western history. Here, under the personal guidance of the great philosopher **Plato** (427–347 BC), the young Aristotle embarked on studies in every organized field of thought at the time, including mathematics, physics, cosmology, history, ethics, political theory, and musical theory. But Aristotle's favorite subject in college was the field he eventually chose as his area of concentration: the subject the Greeks had only recently named philosophy.

Aristotle to his uncle: "Unc, I'm going to major in philosophy." Uncle of Aristotle: "But Ari, there are no jobs in that field. How are you going to make a living?"

Philosophy Class, 366 BC

Philosophy, as the Greeks practiced it, was a new, cutting-edge field of study when Aristotle entered Plato's Academy in Athens. Later in his life, Aristotle would write the very first history of philosophy, tracing the discipline back to its origin in another Greek colony, the bustling harbor town of Miletus on the west coast of Asia Minor. Aristotle's historical research has subsequently proven accurate, for it was indeed there, during the early part of the sixth century BC, that **Thales of Miletus** (625–546 BC) first rejected the customary Greek myths of Homer and Hesiod, with their exciting stories of gods, monsters, and heroes proposed as explanations of how the world and all that is in it came to be, and offered instead a radically new type of explanation of the world, one that would later be named philosophy. At issue was the right way to answer a certain type of *question*.

Every society in history has asked certain extremely fundamental questions about the universe and about human existence, questions such as these: Where did the universe come from? Why does it exist? Where do we come from, and where are we going? Do the gods exist? Does one supreme God exist? What happens at death? How do we separate reality from illusion? What is truth? Do we have free will? What is freedom? How do we know things? What is the best way, all things considered, for a human being to live? What is justice?

Every ancient society developed colorful stories called **myths**, passed orally from generation to generation, one purpose of which was to answer fundamental questions such as these. By offering explanations of the world, the ancient myths responded to the universal human need to place things in an overall context, in short, the human need to make sense of our existence.

However, for Thales and the first Greek philosophers, the traditional myths had one major defect: Although they contained interesting *stories*, no reasoning or tangible evidence was ever offered to substantiate those stories. No myth-maker ever said, after presenting his myth, "And here is my evidence; here are the reasons why I believe my stories are really true." Thales asked the critical question: "But then why believe them?"

In place of unsupported myth, Thales proposed a radically new type of answer to the fundamental questions: a **rational explanation** of the universe and of human existence, that is, an explanation of the universe based solely on observable evidence and unassisted reason alone, independent of unsubstantiated myth, unquestioned power, or unexamined tradition. By presenting this new type of explanation, Thales basically said, "Here is my theory, and here are the reasons why I think it is true. Decide for yourself whether or not you think the evidence supports my theory."

Thales did something else that is also worthy of note because it would also play a role in the eventual birth of logic itself: He put his reasoning into written form and passed the result around for critical comments and debate.[4] Thus began an ongoing *dialectic*, as the Greeks called it, a self-sustaining process of *critical thinking* in which (a) one person proposes a theory backed by observable evidence and independent reasoning; (b) in response, another person steps up to offer a *criticism* of the first argument, an opposing argument also based on observation and independent reasoning; and (c) the first person either defends his theory, revises it, or rejects it, based on independent observations and unassisted reasoning alone, without reliance on unsubstantiated myth, unjustified authority, or tradition.

Thus was born the discipline the Greeks came to call **philosophy**, "the love of wisdom." Parallel movements away from unexamined custom, unbacked myth, and unquestioned authority, and toward critical thinking were occurring, or would soon be occurring, in other regions of the world, most notably in India and China.

Aristotle Gets a Genius Idea: A Subject Whose Object of Study Is Reason Itself

It is easy to imagine Aristotle as a young student at Plato's Academy studying and debating the many arguments and counterarguments of the Greek philosophers, favoring one theory one day, another theory the next, as college students often do when they are making up their minds about fundamental issues. It was probably while he was studying this exciting dialectic of argument and counterargument that Aristotle first got the seed idea for a new academic subject that would one day be called logic. The new field of thought would be devoted to the systematic study of the standards of reasoning itself. Not reasoning *about* some specific subject matter, just reasoning itself. This would be a metalevel subject, one aimed ultimately at discovering the general principles of good, or correct, reasoning that govern all logical inferences, no matter what specific subject matter they are applied to.

---

[4] Unfortunately, none of his writings survived; we know of his work through the testimony of later philosophers, including Aristotle. See Patricia F. O' Grady, *Thales of Miletus, The Beginnings of Western Science and Philosophy* (Burlington, VT: Ashgate Publishing Company, 2002.)

But just what are the general principles of correct reasoning? As Aristotle would later remark, in founding his new subject there was no previous work to build on. Where to start and how to proceed were questions he would have to resolve on his own as he developed the subject from scratch. In a rare personal comment, Aristotle wrote:

> In the case of rhetoric [the study of persuasive speech], there were many old writings to draw upon, but in the case of logic we had absolutely nothing at all . . . until we had spent much time in laborious research.[5]

By the second century AD, an independent tradition of logical theory, bearing similarities to the logic of Aristotle, had arisen in India. For an introduction to classical Indian logic, also called Hindu logic, written by my colleague, Mark Storey, see Appendix A at the back of the book.

Glossary

Aristotle Greek philosopher and author of the first published treatises of logical theory in recorded history. Generally considered the founder of logic as an academic subject.

Deductive logic The study of the standards of correct deductive reasoning.

Deductive reasoning Reasoning that aims to show that a conclusion *must* be true.

Formal logic The study of the abstract patterns or forms of correct reasoning.

Inductive logic The study of the standards of correct inductive reasoning.

Inductive reasoning Reasoning that aims to show that a conclusion is *probably* true although not certainly true.

Informal logic The study of the nonformal aspects of correct reasoning.

Logic The systematic study of the standards of correct reasoning.

Myths Unsubstantiated stories, originally passed down orally from generation to generation, offered as explanations of the world and of things within it.

Philosophy The discipline that asks fundamental questions about the world and our place in it and attempts to answer those questions on the basis of unassisted reasoning and observable evidence alone, independent of unsubstantiated myth, unexamined tradition, and unquestioned authority or power.

Plato Greek philosopher, Aristotle's teacher, and founder of the first university in Western history, the Academy.

Rational explanation An explanation backed by one or more reasons to believe it is true.

---

[5] See Richard McKeon, ed., *The Basic Works of Aristotle*, (New York: Random House, 1941, page 212). The quote is from the closing paragraph of Aristotle's *On Sophistical Refutations*.

Reasoning The mental process that occurs when you conclude something on the basis of something else.

Thales of Miletus Generally considered the founder of philosophy, Thales was the first person in recorded history to reject the traditional myths of his society and to offer in their place a radically new kind of explanation of the world, one based on unassisted reasoning and observable evidence, independent of unbacked myth, unquestioned custom, or unexamined authority. In addition, Thales put his reasoning in writing and passed it around for debate and rational discussion.

2 Let's Have an Argument! « « « « « « «

We have seen that logic, as an academic subject, is "the systematic study of the standards of correct reasoning" and that reasoning is what we do when we "conclude something on the basis of something else." However, we can't study what goes on inside someone's mind—thoughts alone are too intangible. The object of study must be something we can get our hands on, so to speak, something we can examine and analyze together. Reasoning, and the standards by which it can be judged, only become tangible enough for academic study when they are put into words. This is why the concept of an argument is the starting point of logical theory.

Essentially, an **argument**, as the term is used in logic and in academic subjects generally, is reasoning that has been put into words. In other contexts, the word *argument* might mean people yelling at each other or having an angry dispute. But in academic and intellectual contexts, argument refers just to reasoning put into words. Once reasoning has been expressed in words, we can all study it together. This is why Aristotle's system of rules for correct reasoning, the first system of logic in history to be published in written form, begins with the concept of an argument. Let us follow the founder of our subject and begin by taking a closer look at this idea, the first of the core concepts of logic.

What Is an Argument?

A **definition** is an explanation of the meaning of a word or phrase, and a **precise definition** is a detailed explanation of a word's meaning. Precise definitions are needed at the beginning of any systematic study or else we won't agree on exactly what it is we are talking about. This is why the concept of an argument, so fundamental to logical theory, must be defined in more detail before we go any further.

Let us begin with an observation. Reasoning, no matter what subject matter it is applied to, always moves from evidence to a conclusion. Thus every argument breaks down into two parts.

- Part 1. One or more statements, called premises, offering evidence for, or reasons in support of, the truth of a further statement, called the conclusion.
- Part 2. The conclusion whose truth is said to be supported by the premise or premises.

Notice that an argument, as defined here, has one or more premises but exactly one conclusion. So, if a passage contains more than one conclusion, then it contains more than one argument.

Examples are always helpful when learning a new concept. The following argument offers two premises in support of its conclusion:

1. All whales are mammals.
2. No mammal is a fish.
3. Therefore, no whale is a fish.

The conclusion seems to be well supported by the premises. Do you agree? Compare this argument:

1. Not one of Ann's pets is a dog.
2. No dog is a reptile.
3. Thus, not one of Ann's pets is a reptile.

What's wrong with the reasoning here? Does the conclusion logically "follow" straight from the premises? In other words, if the premises are true, must the conclusion be true? Or is the information provided by the premises insufficient for the purpose at hand? Suppose the premises are true. Is it *possible*, granting just the premises, that Ann has a pet lizard, a pet turtle, or a pet snake? In later chapters we will see exactly why this argument is *not* a case of good reasoning.

Arguments are part of the currency of everyday life. You present an argument every time you offer one or more reasons (premises) in support of the truth of a further statement; others present arguments to you every time they present one or more reasons in support of a claim. You have undoubtedly stated (and heard) thousands of arguments in your lifetime, and you will surely state (and hear) thousands more.

Truth and Falsity

You probably noticed that the words *true* and *false* appeared in our detailed definition of an argument. Aristotle realized that the precise definition of an argument presupposes we know what the words *true* and *false* mean when they are applied to statements. That is why he included a definition of truth and falsity in one of his logic textbooks. Here is one way to state the definition of truth first proposed by Aristotle: A statement is **true** if it corresponds to, or accurately describes, reality; it is **false** if it does not.

Aristotle's account of truth and falsity is called the **correspondence theory of truth** because it defines truth as the correspondence between a statement and the reality it purports to describe. Embedding this in our definition of an argument, we can now say more fully: An argument is one or more statements, called premises, offered as reason to believe that a further statement, called the conclusion, is true, that is, corresponds to reality.

Premise and Conclusion Indicator Words

You will learn a great deal more about the nature of an argument if you carefully examine the following arguments, each named so that we can refer to it more easily.

The Coffee Argument

All coffee is made from coffee beans. All coffee beans contain natural oils. Anything made from something containing natural oils must contain oils. Therefore, every cup of coffee contains oils.

This is an argument because it offers one or more reasons to believe that a conclusion is true. The first three sentences offer the evidence, the reasons to believe the conclusion is true or in correspondence with reality. These are the premises. The last sentence contains the conclusion, the truth of which is asserted on the basis of the premises. In addition to the premises and conclusion, this argument contains another element worth noting: the word *therefore*. This word is neither a premise nor a part of the conclusion. Its job is simply to announce that the conclusion is about to be given. For this reason, it is called a *conclusion indicator word*.

Conclusion Indicator Words

A **conclusion indicator** can be defined as any word that, in the context of an argument, flags the conclusion. Do you see the way in which the reasoning in the coffee argument "flows," or moves, from the premises to the conclusion and how it substantiates or supports the truth of the conclusion? Thus:

Premise One:	All coffee is made from coffee beans.
Premise Two:	All coffee beans contain natural oils.
Premise Three:	Anything made from something containing natural oils also contains natural oils.
Conclusion Indicator:	Therefore
Conclusion:	Every cup of coffee contains natural oils.

Does this argument seem to you to be a good piece of reasoning? Here is one desirable feature of this argument: *If* the premises are true, then the conclusion *must* be true. In other words, if the premises are true, then the conclusion cannot possibly be false.

Some Typical Conclusion Indicators

therefore	this shows that	this implies that	thus
hence	consequently	in conclusion	which means that
so	it follows that	accordingly	this entails that
ergo	this demonstrates that	as a result	we may conclude that

If someone is presenting an argument and uses one of these words or phrases, you naturally expect a conclusion to follow.

The Snow in Seattle Argument

In all of recorded history, it has never snowed in Seattle, Washington, in the month of August. Thus, it will not snow in Seattle next August.

In this argument, the first sentence is the premise and the second sentence is the conclusion. Notice that this argument has only *one* premise. (Recall that an argument has *one or more* premises, plus exactly *one* conclusion.) This time the conclusion indicator word is *thus*:

Premise:	In all of recorded history, it has never snowed in Seattle, Washington, in August.
Conclusion Indicator:	Thus
Conclusion:	It will not snow in Seattle next August.

Does the reasoning in this argument seem correct to you? Here is one attractive feature of this argument: *If* the premises are true, then the conclusion, although not completely certain, is *very probably true*. This argument does not conclusively establish its conclusion; that is, it does not guarantee its conclusion or show that its conclusion *must* be true. However, its premises, if true, make its conclusion *probable*, don't they? That's worth something, isn't it? (For now, let us define probable as more than 50% likely.)

Contrast the previous argument with the following one, which appears to claim more than it delivers.

The Survey Argument

To estimate how many people believe that animals have rights, we surveyed 25 people coming out of a meeting of People Endorsing the Rights of Animals. Everyone surveyed said they believe that animals have rights. Consequently, everybody in the world believes in "animal rights."

The placement of the conclusion indicator *consequently* tells us that the last sentence is the conclusion and the first two sentences are the premises. Now, *if* the premises were to be true, would that information make it reasonable to believe the conclusion is true? Is this a good argument? Or is the reasoning flawed? Is there a gap in this argument?

Premise Indicator Words

Notice that the word *since* appears twice in the following argument.

The Zombie Argument

Since all zombies are mindless slaves, and since all mindless slaves lack free wills of their own, it follows necessarily that all zombies lack free wills of their own.

This little word, *since*, is not properly part of the premises; rather, it is serving as a **premise indicator**, defined as any word that, in the context of an argument, indicates or flags a premise.

Premise indicator:	Since
Premise One:	All zombies are mindless slaves.
Premise Two:	All mindless slaves lack free wills of their own.
Conclusion Indicator:	It follows that
Conclusion:	All zombies lack free wills of their own.

When you are presenting an argument, carefully placed indicator words will help your audience follow the "flow" of your reasoning.

Exercise 2.1   Each of the following passages contains one or more arguments. Identify or list the premises, conclusions, and indicator words in each passage.

1. Statistics show that it is safer to fly than to drive. Therefore, if you are traveling across the country this summer, your chance of surviving the trip will be higher if you fly than if you drive.

2. Since no weapons of mass destruction were found, and because eliminating the threat of weapons of mass destruction was the main reason for the war, and since the other reasons given were all inadequate, it follows that the war in Iraq was morally unjustified.

3. Weapons of mass destruction were not the only rationale for the Iraq war. The war was conducted for a number of additional morally sufficient reasons, at least six of which were substantiated. For instance, Saddam Hussein had a long history of harboring and supporting international terrorists such as Carlos the Jackal, Abu Nidal, and Abu Abbas. Moreover, each of the additional reasons satisfied the traditional criteria for "just war." Thus, the Iraq war was morally justified.

4. Saint Thomas Aquinas says that an argument based on authority is never a good argument. And he is a great philosopher. Therefore, an argument based on authority is never a good argument.

5. Because it takes a worried man to sing a worried song, and since Joe is a very worried man, Joe could sing this worried song very well.

6. God is said to be all-powerful, all-good, and all-knowing. But if an all-powerful, all-good, all-knowing being were to create a world containing sentient creatures, that being would not allow *any* of its creatures ever to suffer and there would be no suffering. For good is opposed to evil, and suffering is an evil. God would know about any evil if it arose, God would

have the power to end any evil if it arose, and God would oppose any evil that might arise. The upshot is that if God exists and created this world, it contains no suffering at all. Since the world is full of massive amounts of suffering, it follows that God, understood as an all-powerful, all-good, all-knowing being who created the world, does not exist.

7. God, understood as an all-powerful, all-good, all-knowing being who created the universe, would allow suffering if God had a morally sufficient reason for allowing it. After all, a good and loving parent will sometimes allow a child to suffer when the suffering is a necessary step toward a greater good in the future that outweighs and completely overshadows the suffering, making it all good in the end. But if God has morally sufficient reasons for allowing suffering, those reasons are probably far beyond our ken, likely involving future goods the greatness of which we cannot even conceive at the present time. God's reasons would be no more available to us than the mature reasons of an adult are available to a little child. Therefore, we cannot know for sure that a good, all-powerful, all-knowing God would never, under any conditions, allow any suffering.

8. Thought can be fully explained in terms of the neurophysiological functioning of the cells in the brain. For instance, the firing of neurons can be correlated with the onset of the thought that $1 + 1 = 2$, that today is Tuesday, that it is wrong to lie, and so on. The functioning of our mind thus appears to be nothing more than the functioning of our brain. It would seem to follow that our mind is the same thing as our physical brain, and not a separate immaterial thing.

9. Thought cannot be fully explained in terms of the neurophysiological functioning of the cells of the brain; science has not even come close to accomplishing this. It may be true that science has found a correlation between (a) the occurrence of thoughts, and (b) events happening in the brain. However, the mere fact that two things are correlated does not show that they are one and the same thing. In addition, consciousness has at least two properties that physical mechanisms such as brains do not possess. First, conscious mental states possess underived intentionality or "aboutness"; but nothing purely physical or material can possess underived intentionality. Second, there is "something it is like" to be *in* a conscious mental state, whereas there is not "something it is like" to be an atom, a molecule, or a purely material object. Consequently, mind and brain are two different things, not one and the same thing.

10. According to the moral theory known as simple ethical egoism (from *ego*, the Latin word for *I*) the only moral obligation anyone has is this: Do

whatever you really *want* to do at the moment. However, if everyone followed this principle, the result would be not only chaotic but morally horrific. Social life would turn into a war of all against all, human relations would disintegrate, and life would be hellish. If a theory has absurd implications, that is a good reason to reject the theory. Therefore, simple ethical egoism is an absurd theory of ethics.

11. If simple ethical egoism is true, then it would follow that it is morally acceptable for someone to make a living robbing little old ladies who just cashed their meager Social Security checks (if that is what the robber wants to do at the moment). But upon careful reflection on all the facts of the matter, including the interests of everyone involved, robbing little old ladies clearly seems morally wrong. Therefore, simple ethical egoism has an absurd consequence and is thus a false theory.

12. Simple ethical hedonism (from *hedon*, the Greek word for *pleasure*) is the view that the only moral obligation is this: "Do whatever brings you pleasure at the moment." But if simple ethical hedonism is true, then it follows that if someone takes pleasure in robbing little children who are selling lemonade on their neighborhood sidewalk in the summer, then doing so is morally acceptable. But upon cool reflection on all the facts of the matter and on the interest of everyone involved, this is clearly morally outrageous, even monstrous. So, simple ethical hedonism has absurd implications and is therefore a false theory of morality.

13. All differences in income and wealth between people are due solely to luck. Nobody deserves something if it is due solely to luck that they have it. Therefore, all differences in income and wealth are undeserved, in particular, the poor do not deserve to be poor and the rich do not deserve to be rich.

14. Nobody deserves something if it is due solely to luck that they have it. When communism finally arrives at some point in the distant future, those *lucky enough* to be alive at the time will all be guaranteed by the state a roughly equal income and wealth. Thus, under communism, nobody will deserve what they have, as it will ultimately be a matter of luck that they happen to live in a communist society and are given the equal baskets of goods (income and wealth) they are given.

15. Differences in income and wealth between people are not due solely to luck; they are due to a combination of luck and choice. Nobody deserves something if it is due *solely* to luck that they have it, but someone might deserve something if he or she recognized a chance opportunity, acted on it, and then worked hard, made smart choices, and produced some-

thing of value through a combination of both chance and choice without violating anyone's rights in the process. By its nature, life for contingent, situated beings such as we are is almost always a combination of choice and chance, luck and meritorious effort. Therefore, it is not true that all differences in income and wealth are undeserved; some are deserved on the basis of choices made.

16. Justice is giving each person what he or she morally deserves. Each person is equally morally deserving of well-being. Only wealth and income can guarantee well-being. Therefore, justice requires an equal distribution of wealth and income for everyone.

17. According to moral relativism, there are no moral universals; nothing is morally wrong universally, across all societies. But the institution of slavery is certainly morally wrong no matter where it occurs. Honor killing is also clearly morally wrong no matter where it occurs. Consequently, there are known moral universals and moral relativism is a false theory of morality.

18. What is considered right and wrong varies from society to society. Therefore, there is no basis, independent of the morals of a given society, for an act to be right or wrong.

19. Eating all your meals at a fast-food restaurant does not automatically make you gain weight. For if an ordinary person went to a fast-food joint three times a day for a year, and ate one small breakfast sandwich every morning, one small hamburger for lunch each day, and one small hamburger for dinner, and nothing else, he or she would *lose* weight.

20. The universe has many parts, and the parts are arranged in an unlikely structure that functions in a systematic way that makes life possible. Thus, the universe is similar in form to a watch or some other functioning mechanism, for in both cases, we see many parts systematically and intricately arranged so as to function in a certain way.

21. Similar effects usually have similar causes. An intelligent designer is usually found to be the cause of an orderly mechanism such as a watch. Therefore, because the universe is similar in form to an intelligently designed mechanism, the cause of the universe is probably also an intelligent designer, albeit one great enough to design the whole universe.

22. The universe is not really very much like a mechanism such as a watch. For one reason, vast swaths of it are chaotic. Ergo, we do not have any good reason to believe that the universe was put together by a super-duper intelligent designer.

Exercise 2.2   In each case, is the expression a premise or a conclusion indicator?

1.	Thus	7.	Hence
2.	Since	8.	Inasmuch as
3.	Ergo	9.	As indicated by
4.	Because	10.	Accordingly
5.	For	11.	Seeing that
6.	Therefore	12.	So

Arguments and Skyscrapers

We commonly use architectural metaphors when describing arguments. For example, we say that the conclusion is "based on" the premises, or that it is "supported by," or "grounded in," the premises, and so on. The premises are the argument's "foundation," the conclusion "rests" on the premises, the premises are the "basis" of the argument, and so on. These common expressions suggest the image of a building with its upper floor supported by the floors below, with these in turn based ultimately on the structure's concrete foundation.

Arguments are analogous, or similar, to buildings. For example, just as a building's top floor remains in place only as long as the levels under it provide adequate support, so the conclusion remains either proven or "rationally justified" only if the premises of the argument give it adequate logical support. Like the top story of a building, which ultimately rests on the building's foundation, an argument's conclusion ultimately rests logically on the argument's premises. Thus, from a purely logical perspective, your conclusion is only as reasonable as your premises make it.

Logical theory investigates the many ways in which the premises of an argument may support, or fail to support, the conclusion, in other words, the many ways a conclusion can follow from or not follow from the premises. When the premises provide adequate reasons or evidence for the conclusion, that is, when the premises give us good reason to believe that the conclusion is true, we sometimes say the conclusion is "justified" by the premises. Alternatively, in such a case, we might say that the conclusion "follows logically from the premises."

Recognizing Arguments

If we had always seen everything through green-tinted glasses, so that green was the only color we had ever experienced, would we have a word for green? Would we be consciously aware that everything is the same color? This is a great philosophical question. Whatever the right answer is, it is probably true that we don't fully understand what something *is* until we can distinguish it from what it is *not*. We have been talking about arguments—reasoning put into words. However, not every use of words constitutes an argument; words can obviously be used for many other purposes. A basic logical skill, therefore, is the ability to distinguish an argument from something that is not an argument. Let's consider some examples.

Sometimes we use language simply to describe something, and when we do so, we are not presenting an argument. For example, "The possum is a cute little mammal with a skinny little tail, beady eyes, and short hair." This is a description, not an argument. It is not an argument because (at least within the context) nobody is offering one or more premises in support of a conclusion; that is, nobody is offering one or more reasons to believe that a conclusion is true. To be an argument, a passage must contain two distinct parts: one part offers evidence and consists of one or more premises; the other part is the conclusion drawn from, or based on, the premise or premises.

Sometimes we use language to express our feelings, and when we do so, we are not always presenting an argument. For example, suppose at a lavish, posh dinner party, Joe drops a casserole of macaroni and cheese on the kitchen floor and says, "Darn it!" His words do not constitute an argument: Joe is not offering one or more premises in an attempt to establish a conclusion as true.

This really happened:

At 5 a.m. on the morning of April 19, 1775, 77 "Minutemen" under the command of Captain Parker lined up on the village green in Lexington, Massachusetts, to oppose the approaching British army. Most of the men were farmers. Just as the sun was coming up, 700 British soldiers commanded by Lieutenant Colonel Francis Smith arrived at the green. Outnumbered 10 to 1, Captain Parker gave the order: "Stand your ground men; don't fire unless fired upon; but if they mean to have a war, let it begin here." At this moment, a British major stepped forward and shouted, "Lay down your arms, you damned rebels!" A moment later, a single shot rang out—nobody knows who fired it or even where it came from—and all hell broke loose. The rest, as they say, is history.

That is a *story*, not an argument. The preceding paragraph is not an argument because a conclusion is not being drawn based on evidence. The following passage raises an interesting question in connection with the preceding story:

Among the men lined up in parade formation at Lexington green on the morning of April 19, 1775, was a man named Prince Estabrook, the only African-American member of the Lexington Minutemen. But Estabrook was a slave at the time. Which raises an intriguing question: Why did he risk his life for the Patriot cause? If they lost, he would likely be hung by the British, along with all the rest, as a traitor. On the other hand, if they ultimately prevailed, Estabrook would likely remain a slave. What was in it for him?

What a fascinating question! But a question is not an argument, for premises are not being offered in support of the truth of a conclusion. This passage, like the one before it, does not present an argument.

Other nonargumentative uses of language include the following:

- Giving commands ("Stand your ground, men.")
- Making requests ("May I have another glass of grog?")
- Making promises ("I promise to be there.")

Stories, commands, questions, and so on are not arguments because no evidence is being offered in support of a conclusion. The lesson is clear: Be careful not to confuse arguments with things that are not arguments. Essentially, in the case of an argument—but not in the case of a nonargument—someone is offering one or more reasons to believe that a statement is true.

> **Lesson:** A group of statements constitutes an argument only when it contains one or more reasons offered in support of the truth of a conclusion.

Exercise 2.3   Which of the following passages contain an argument, and which do not? If a passage does not contain an argument, what does it contain? What would you call it?

1. I think Seattle has the best fish and chips in the country.
2. The two oldest fish and chips establishments in Seattle are Ivar's (founded in 1938) and Spud's (founded in 1935).
3. If Socrates died, then either he died when he was living, or when he was dead. But he couldn't have died when he was living, for he was not dead when he was living. But he couldn't have died when he was dead, for when he was dead he had already died. Therefore, Socrates never died. But this same reasoning can be applied to anyone. Therefore, nobody has ever died. (From the ancient Greek skeptic, Sextus Empiricus.)
4. Skepticism is the claim that nobody can ever *know* anything. Knowledge is impossible, claims the skeptic. However, in saying that skepticism is true, the advocate of skepticism is claiming to *know* at least one thing, namely, that skepticism is true. Therefore, to assert skepticism is to contradict oneself; skepticism is therefore a self-contradictory viewpoint.

5. What you have not lost you still have. But you have not lost horns. Therefore, you have horns!

6. You know your best friend. But that man who walked by you with a hood over his head was your best friend, and you didn't know him. Therefore, you don't really know your best friend.

7. Know thyself.

8. A certain man is exactly as thirsty as he is hungry. Placed equidistantly between food and water, he will only make a move if he chooses one over the other. But he will only choose one over the other if he has a sufficient reason to do so. He will only have a sufficient reason to do so if one of the two is closer than the other. The man will die. (From Aristotle)

9. Ying's Drive-In has the best fried rice in Seattle.

10. In 1938, to promote his newly opened aquarium located on the Seattle waterfront, Ivar Haglund staged a wrestling match between an octopus named Oscar and a washed-up prizefighter named "Two-Ton Tony" Galento. (The name was not due to his weight but to the excuse he once gave to his manager for being late to a fight: "I had two tons of ice to deliver on my way here.") The historic match actually took place on the Seattle waterfront, in a large tub of water, in front of a rowdy crowd and many cameras.

11. According to the philosophical view known as determinism, everything that happens is caused to happen by all that has already gone before, in such a way that everything that happens, when it happens, must inevitably happen, meaning nothing can ever happen otherwise than it does. In other words, the course of events is fixed from the beginning of time if there was a beginning, or from all eternity if there was no beginning.

12. All aardvarks are mammals. All mammals are warm-blooded. Therefore, all aardvarks are warm-blooded.

13. One day, Elaine went to get some soup at the "Soup Nazi" shop. However, because she didn't follow the proper procedure when she placed her order, the Soup Nazi told her, "No soup for you."

14. Watch out for the wild illy-pies! (Illy-pies are mythical beasts said to inhabit the wilds of the Pacific Northwest.)

15. Go directly to jail. Do not pass go. Do not collect $200.

Enthymemes

People often leave something out when they present an argument. They start with point A and they get to point B, but somewhere along the way there is a gap! This is not always a bad thing. Sometimes the item left out is information so obvious and uncontroversial it does not need to be stated. The item is "common ground." Occasionally the conclusion of an argument is left unstated so that the audience can draw the conclusion for themselves. However, occasionally the missing item is an important step in the reasoning process that has been overlooked—information required if the argument is to successfully establish its conclusion. An **enthymeme** is an argument that is missing one or more premises or a conclusion. (*Enthymeme* is derived from a Greek word meaning "have in mind," which is appropriate, because an enthymeme leaves unstated something we have in mind.)

The following short argument is an enthymeme: "All chemists are scientists, so Miss Hathaway must be a scientist." The unstated premise in this case, assuming the arguer intends the argument to be a good one, is obviously "Miss Hathaway is a chemist." Notice that without the unstated premise, the argument has a gap. It only becomes a case of good reasoning when we add the missing premise.

The ability to spot an enthymematic argument—to be aware when there is a gap in someone's reasoning—is obviously an important logical skill. However, so is the ability to fill in a gap in someone's argument, or to help them fill in the gap.

The Principle of Charity

When others present enthymematic arguments, human kindness bids us to fill in the blanks, or to help them fill in the blanks, before we assess their reasoning. But a concern for the truth also urges the same thing. For when we help someone plug a gap in their reasoning, we help them make their argument as good as it can be. Only then do we give them a fair shot at convincing us of something we might not already know—something we might very well *need* to know. In helping each other avoid enthymemes, we help each other in the search for truth.

When we help someone fill in the gaps in their argument, it is therefore best to follow the **principle of charity**, which says that when you must attribute a premise or a conclusion to someone's enthymematic argument, add something that helps make their case as reasonable as it can be. Don't attribute something that is ignorant or illogical. In short, assume the other person is trying to make a reasonable case and interpret their argument in its best light. Following the principle of charity in this way is sure to have surprising consequences at least some of the time if you have an open mind: The other person might just have a good point. They might just have something to teach you.

Exercise 2.4   Follow the principle of charity as you fill in the missing parts in these enthymemes.

1. I have owned three XYZ brand lawnmowers and all three have run poorly. I noticed this year's model hasn't changed a bit.
2. The annual gathering is wonderful every time Joe attends. Next year's gathering promises to be a wonderful one again.

3. The new subatomic particle just discovered is like an electron in many different ways. So, it will probably be found to have a negative electric charge.

4. Every time the Beatles play at the Cavern Club, the joint is standing room only. Ergo, I bet it will be jam-packed next Saturday night.

5. The XYZ energy drink contains too much caffeine for me—one bottle keeps me up all night. I therefore am not going to try the new ABC energy drink.

6. I have loved every one of Mickey Rooney's movies. I am thus sure I will love the movie we will be watching tomorrow, "Girl Crazy."

7. Candidate Smith has been taking huge amounts of money from lobbyists and he has given no evidence he can think critically and independently. For this reason I don't think he would make a good U.S. senator.

8. Stevens Pass usually has a lot of snow in January and heavy snow can make the trip difficult. I conclude that your trip across the pass is likely to be a difficult one.

9. All Scotsmen are frugal. So I suppose you are frugal.

10. Formed in 1965, the Daily Flash was one of Seattle's first folk-rock bands. Therefore, one of Seattle's first folk-rock bands is still performing.

11. Little Bill and the Blue Notes is one of the premier blues bands of the Pacific Northwest. Therefore, the Pacific Northwest has at least one major band that has been together since the mid-1950s.

Diagramming Arguments

It can be hard to follow the reasoning in a complex newspaper or magazine editorial. When someone is making an in-depth case for their view, they may state many different premises before reaching a conclusion. Sometimes authors string together a sequence of arguments and the connections from one argument to the next are not always obvious. When such things happen, it can be helpful to diagram the argument or arguments. An argument diagram charts the "flow" of the reasoning when a complex case is being made. Consider the following passage, containing just one argument:

Two witnesses identified Joe as the man they saw at the scene of the crime. One of the witnesses is a very trustworthy individual. Additionally, Joe's business card was found at the scene of the crime. Did you know he markets ice cubes over the Internet? I can't imagine there's that much money in that. Finally, fingerprints matching Joe were found at the scene of the crime. Therefore, Joe probably committed the crime.

To produce a diagram showing the flow of the reasoning in this argument, begin by distinguishing those sentences that are part of the argument from those that are not. A sentence that is neither a premise nor a conclusion does not contribute to the flow of thought and is not properly part of the argument. It is in a sense unnecessary padding. In everyday life we often include superfluous elements when we make a case for something we believe. This is not a problem unless the extra baggage makes it hard to follow the reasoning.

Next, assign a number to each premise and to the conclusion, ignoring the superfluous sentences that are not technically part of the argument:

> ❶ Two witnesses identified Joe as the man they saw at the scene of the crime. ❷ One of the witnesses is a very trustworthy individual. ❸ Additionally, Joe's business card was found at the scene of the crime. Skip: Did you know he markets ice cubes to Alaska over the Internet? Skip: I can't imagine there's that much money in that. ❹ Finally, fingerprints matching Joe's were found at the scene of the crime. Therefore, ❺ Joe probably committed the crime.

When two premises work together to provide support for the conclusion, indicate this by joining their corresponding numbers with a + sign. When two premises work together, each depends on the other to help make the point in favor of the conclusion. Call such premises joint premises. When two premises do not refer to each other or depend on each other in some way, then their numbers are not joined by a plus.

Finally, use downward arrows to mark the support conferred on the conclusion by the premises. Put another way, use downward arrows to mark the flow of the reasoning from the premises to the conclusion:

Our diagram indicates that premises 1 and 2 work together to support the conclusion, sentence 5, whereas premises 3 and 4 confer their support independently of one another.

This was a relatively simple case of reasoning. In longer passages, the reasoning can be more convoluted. Usually, in a longer passage, two or more arguments are being presented, not just one argument. In such a case, the arguments are linked together and the reasoning is coursing through them like water through a series of pipes. How can arguments be linked together like pipes? Argument A links to argument B when the conclusion of A becomes a *premise* in B, and is used to support the conclusion of B, as in this example, which has already been numbered:

❶ All cats are mammals. ❷ Moreover, all mammals are warm-blooded. Therefore, ❸ all cats are warm-blooded. ❹ But all warm-blooded creatures have hearts. Therefore, ❺ all cats have hearts.

This passage contains two separate arguments. The first argument starts with statements 1 and 2 and reaches its conclusion at statement 3. The second argument "borrows" statement 3 from the first argument, where it served as a conclusion, and uses it as a premise; thus the second argument runs from statements 3 and 4 to *its* conclusion at 5. When the conclusion of one argument becomes a premise in the next argument in this way, we diagram the relationship as follows:

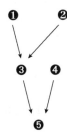

This diagram says that 1 and 2 support the conclusion, 3, which in turn becomes a premise alongside 4 supporting the final conclusion, statement 5. Two arguments, two rivers of reasoning, flow to the final destination, statement 5.

In some cases, a passage will contain a cascade of arguments, with the reasoning flowing through them the way water flows down a waterfall. The conclusion of the first argument in the chain becomes a premise in the next argument, and so on, until one final conclusion is reached.

In some cases, one or more premises will be given, and then *two* separate conclusions will be drawn from the same premises, producing two separate lines of reasoning: two arguments starting from the same base. There are two cases to consider: (a) two conclusions are drawn from a pair of conjoint premises, and (b) two conclusions are drawn from a pair of independent premises. The two diagrams would look like this, assuming two arguments sharing two premises each:

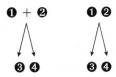

Notice that in each case, we technically have two arguments, not one. In the first case, the arguments share conjoint premises (numbered 1 and 2); in the second case the shared premises are independent. The two conclusions are numbered 3 and 4. Time to sum up. To diagram a passage:

1. Number the premises and the conclusion, skipping any superfluous or "extra baggage" statements.
2. Decide which premises work together and which work independently. Using the plus sign, join the numbers for the dependent premises. The hermit premises will be left on their own.
3. If a passage contains more than one argument, locate the junction where the conclusion of one argument becomes a premise of the next argument.
4. Map the argument or arguments in the passage by placing the numbers according to the structure of the argument, with downward arrows marking the flow of the reasoning.

Exercise 2.5   Diagram the following arguments.

1. In order for something to come into existence, it must first be *possible* that it come into existence. If absolutely nothing were to exist, then possibilities would not exist, since a possibility is a "something," not an absolute nothing. Therefore, it is impossible that something can come into existence out of sheer, absolute nothingness. Therefore, anything that *begins* to exist has a cause. We know from scientific cosmology that the material universe began to exist a finite time ago. Therefore, the material universe has a cause. The cause is always greater than the effect and always precedes the effect. Therefore, the cause of the universe is a supernatural being whose existence precedes the creation of time, matter, and space.

2. The self is not at all "self-made." Success and failure in all spheres of life, and the resulting socioeconomic differences between people, are never due to alleged "choices" made or to differential exercises of something called "free will." Rather, human behavior is *fully* caused by genes and external social conditions. Thus, nobody can ever rightly claim "credit" for anything he or she has done, and nobody can ever rightly be blamed for anything he or she does. That is, nobody ever deserves praise or blame for anything they do. Therefore, nobody ever really deserves anything at all. Therefore, all differences in income and wealth are undeserved. Therefore, those conservative social policies that are justified on the basis of the claim that success and failure in life, and the resulting income and wealth differentials, are the "just deserts" of differential exercises of free will, or of the different choices people make in life, are unjustified. Everyone deserves an equal share of all income and wealth created. However, wealth and in-

come can only be equalized by the state, by state redistribution of wealth. Thus, government should redistribute wealth and income until it is all equally shared.

3. The person who made the argument in 2 was fully caused to reason that way by his genetics and social conditions. But we have no good reason to believe that genetics and social conditions are a guarantee of truth or justice, or that they inherently tend to take us to the truth or to justice. Indeed, the arguer in the preceding example claims that genetics and existing social conditions are untamed and unjust on their own. Therefore, the preceding argument contradicts itself: If we accept its premises as true, then we have no good reason to believe that the argument is a good argument, in other words, we have no good reason to believe its conclusion is true.

4. According to Protagorean relativism, believing something true makes it *true for you* and there's nothing more to truth than that. In particular, there is no further basis for saying that one person's believed truth is better or more true than that of another. Each person's truth is equally true or real; everyone is right about everything. However, this view has absurd consequences. First, it implies that everyone is infallible. In addition, the doctrine makes a claim about how truth *really* is. But a claim about how truth really is, is a nonrelative claim, for it claims to be a truth that all ought to accept if they want to be realistic. Thus, if relativism is true, then there exists at least one nonrelative truth, namely, the claim that relativism is true, in which case relativism is false. So if relativism is true, then it is false. These are all good reasons to reject Protagorean relativism!

5. It is true right now that tomorrow at noon you will either eat a hamburger for lunch or you will *not* eat a hamburger for lunch. If it is true right now that tomorrow at noon you will eat a hamburger for lunch, then tomorrow at lunch you *must* eat a hamburger—you cannot do otherwise—for the truth cannot be changed. On the other hand, if it is true right now that tomorrow at noon you will *not* eat a hamburger for lunch, then tomorrow you will not eat a hamburger for lunch and will not be able to do otherwise (for the truth cannot be changed). If someone does something, and he or she could not have done otherwise at the time, then he or she does not act of his or her own free will. Therefore, tomorrow at lunch, no matter what you do, you will not be acting of your own free will. But this same reasoning can be applied to every future moment in time, and to each future action, for each person. Therefore the future has already been determined and nobody will ever exercise something called "free will."

6. Every event in the universe, including the occurrence of each and every human action, is caused to occur by the sum total of all immediately preceding

events. If event A causes event B, then once A happens B must happen; B is inevitable. Thus, nothing can ever happen otherwise than the way it does happen. It follows that whenever a person performs an action, no matter how deliberate and self-aware the person is at the time, the person could not have done anything other than exactly what he or she did. But if, in a particular situation, a person does something, and the person could not have done otherwise, then that person did not act freely in that situation. In addition, if a person, on a particular occasion, performs an action, and the person could not have done otherwise, then the person is not morally responsible for his or her action and deserves neither praise nor blame, reward nor punishment for what he or she has done. Therefore, nobody has free will, nobody is ever responsible for what they have done, and nobody ever deserves praise or blame, reward or punishment. In short, free will and moral responsibility simply do not exist.

7. The only theory capable of explaining free will is agent causation theory. On this theory, free will is hypothesized as the power of a rational being to cause an action, for instance, to move the body or mind in a certain way, without being caused to cause by preceding events. In other words, it is the power to be an uncaused cause of one's own actions, a "first cause" of motion. Only if human beings have the "contra-causal" power hypothesized by agent causation theory, the power to truly originate an action, instead of serving as a mere conduit for external forces, do humans have real free will. But the thesis that humans have free will is the only way to make sense of our evident moral responsibility, and of our moral experience in general. Therefore, humans probably have free will, and agent causation theory is likely a true account of what free will is.

8. Change is impossible. If something comes into being, either it comes from something that already is, or it comes from something that is not. If it comes from something that already is, it would already exist (and did not come into being). It is impossible that something could come into being from something that does not exist. Therefore, change is impossible. (From the ancient Greek philosopher Parmenides.)

9. Every truth about the past is necessary. (In other words, the past is over, settled, fixed, it cannot be changed.) What logically follows from the necessary is also necessary. (It is a law of modal logic that only the necessary follows from the necessary.) The future follows necessarily from the past. Given past conditions, what happens next must happen next. Therefore, nobody has free will. (From Diodorus, ancient Greek logician.)

10. Let C be the conjunction of all contingently true propositions. Thus, C is a conjunction with trillions of conjuncts, each expressing a contingent fact

about the world. Call C the "great big conjunctive fact"or "GBCF." What *explains* the truth of GBCF? What accounts for the fact that GBCF is true? No contingent statement can explain itself. So, no wholly contingent statement could fully account for the truth of the GBCF, for any contingent statement would be one of the conjuncts of the GBCF. Everything is either contingent or necessary. Therefore, the only thing that could account for the fact that GBCF is true would be something that is necessary. Everything that exists or is the case has an explanation, known or unknown. Therefore, something necessary, a necessary being, exists and is the cause or explanation for the fact that GBCF is true.

11. What *explains* the truth of the GBCF? What accounts for the fact that it is true? No contingent statement can explain itself or account for its own truth. So, no wholly contingent statement could fully account for the truth of GBCF, for any contingent statement would be one of the conjuncts of C. Every statement is either contingent or necessary. No necessary statement could account for the fact that GBCF is true, for that which is contingent never logically follows from that which is necessary. Therefore, there can be no ultimate explanation for the fact that GBCF is true. GBCF is simply a brute fact—a fact with no explanation at all.

Make Your Case! Four Steps to Building a Good Argument

Anyone who is good at analyzing or breaking down an argument has acquired a valuable logical skill. We are always in a better position to evaluate something when we have identified its parts and can see how they fit together. However, the ability to construct a good argument of one's own, from scratch, is also an important logical skill.

Step 1. Start with "Common Ground"

When you reason with other people, you *hope*. Specifically, you hope that once they understand your premise or your premises, they will, on that basis, come to believe that your conclusion is *true*. But what if they don't accept your premises as true? In that case, they probably will not accept your conclusion, because your conclusion is based on your premises. Your argument won't even get off the ground! It follows that if you want to reason effectively with another person, you should begin with premises that you and the other person both accept as true. Otherwise, you might be wasting everybody's time.

Statements accepted by all sides to an argument can be called **common ground**. Start your argument on common ground if you want to be effective when you reason with others. For example, in his 5,000-page treatise, *Summa Theologica* ("Sum of Theology"), Thomas Aquinas (1224–1274), one of the greatest philosophers of the Middle Ages, summarized five different arguments for the existence of God.

Aquinas's first argument begins with the following simple premise: "Some things are in motion." Now, before you say, "Well, duh!" notice what Aquinas is doing: He is starting his argument with a premise that is sure to be *common ground*! It was supposed to be obvious!

Step 2. *State* Your Case

An argument, as you will recall, is one or more statements, called premises, offered in support of a further statement, called the conclusion. What is a statement? A **statement**, as logicians use the term, is simply a claim that is either true or false. Thus, the premises and the conclusion of an argument are always claims that are either true or false. We typically make a statement by writing or otherwise asserting a **declarative sentence**, which can be defined as a sentence expressing a claim that is either true or false. Thus, an argument will typically be expressed with declarative sentences. The following sentences are all declarative:

1. Tiny Tim sang "Tiptoe Through the Tulips."
2. The colleges that constitute Oxford University contain over 100 libraries.
3. There are real mountains on the Moon.

Of course, not all sentences are declarative; that is, not all sentences express claims that are either true or false. Consequently, constructing an argument out of declarative sentences requires knowing the difference between those sentences that are declarative and those that are not. Because we often understand something better when it is placed in contrast with things it is not, let us distinguish five different types of sentences:

1. A **declarative sentence** expresses a claim that is either true or false.
2. An **imperative sentence**, such as "Close the door!" expresses a command. Because commands are neither true nor false, imperative sentences are not declarative. If someone said to you, "Close the door," you would not reply, "That's true."
3. An **interrogatory sentence**, such as "What time is it?" expresses a question. Because questions are neither true nor false, this type of sentence is not declarative. If someone asked you, "What time is it?" it would be odd to say, "That's true!"
4. An **exclamatory sentence**, such as "Ouch!" is used to express an emotion or a feeling; exclamatory sentences are obviously neither true nor false.
5. A **performative sentence** is used to perform an action, for instance, to make a promise ("I promise to be good"), to name something ("I christen this 'The Good Ship Lollipop'"), to wed someone ("I do"), and so on. Such sentences

are neither true nor false, although they can be sincere or insincere, appropriate or inappropriate, rude or polite, legal or illegal, and so on.

When constructing an argument, you should normally use declarative sentences to express your reasoning. There are exceptions, but they are best avoided. For instance, in the midst of an argument, people sometimes use an imperative, interrogative, or exclamatory sentence as a rhetorical way of expressing something that they would otherwise say with a declarative sentence. For example, while speaking in support of a piece of legislation, a politician might say, "Does anyone in the audience really want to allow children to go hungry in this country?" That sentence is, of course, a question, and *considered strictly as a question*, it is neither true nor false (and therefore cannot technically be part of an argument). But in the context of the speech, the statement is obviously a rhetorical way of asserting as a premise this declarative sentence: "It is morally wrong to allow children to go hungry."

So, an argument can contain nondeclarative sentences as long as they are understood as rhetorical ways of expressing what could otherwise be put in declarative form. Nevertheless, when stating an argument, it is best to be direct and stick with declarative sentences, for the following reason: When you present someone with an argument, you are asking for mental work on their part. It takes effort to follow someone's line of reasoning. And just as it takes more effort to grasp what someone is trying to say when the person is not being direct, when the person is "beating around the bush," or his or her meaning has to be interpreted, it usually takes more effort to follow someone's reasoning when the argument contains rhetorical sentences that need to be translated into declarative claims before they function as true (or false) premises. Choose sentences that effectively and *directly* express your truth claims!

Step 3. Use Indicator Words to Mark the "Flow" of Your Reasoning

Have you ever been listening to someone presenting an argument and all of a sudden you become aware that you are not following his or her reasoning? You are not sure which statements are premises and which is the conclusion. You feel lost. This is one reason why argument indicator words were invented. As you recall, a conclusion indicator word or phrase, when used in the context of an argument, signals that a conclusion is about to be given. Premise indicators, as you know, are words or expressions used in an argument to indicate that a premise is about to be given. Use indicator words to clarify your reasoning, to mark the way. Help your audience follow your argument!

Step 4. Support Your Conclusion

As you construct an argument, keep in mind that your ultimate goal is to provide adequate logical support for your conclusion. Construct your argument accordingly, supplying premises that adequately back up, support, or justify your conclusion. The following argument certainly seems to do just this:

1. An action is morally permissible if it harms nobody.
2. Brushing your teeth with baking soda harms nobody.
3. Therefore, brushing your teeth with baking soda is morally permissible.

The two premises of this argument support the conclusion in the following very precise sense: *If* the premises are all true, then the conclusion *must* be true. In other words, the premises are related to the conclusion in such a way that it would be impossible for the conclusion to be false *if* the premises are all true. Thus, if you know that the premises are all true, then you can be *certain* that the conclusion is true. In other words, the truth of the premises would *guarantee* the truth of the conclusion. However, consider the following argument:

1. The average teenager grows two inches per year.
2. Teenager A is two inches shorter than teenager B.
3. Therefore, it must be that A is one year younger than B.

The reasoning is faulty because, based only on the information provided in the premises, and nothing more, it is possible that the premises are true and the conclusion is false. Thus, even if we were to know *for certain* that the premises are true, it would not follow from that alone that the conclusion *must* be true; the conclusion might nevertheless be false. For all we know, A might be older than B! In this case, the premises provide little or no support for the conclusion. Broken reasoning makes this a defective argument. Do you agree?

Thus we see again that not all arguments are created equal: Some arguments provide solid, logical support for their conclusions; others do not. There are good arguments, and there are bad ones; there is good reasoning and bad reasoning. This question therefore arises: Are there general principles we can follow to make our arguments better? Is there a principled way to distinguish good from bad reasoning when we evaluate the arguments that others present to us? How can we make sure that the arguments we present to others are good? When we reason with others, how can we ensure that our conclusion has adequate justification or support? This is where the next chapter picks up the thread.

Exercise 2.6   Demonstrate your understanding by answering these questions in your own words.

1. What is an argument?
2. What is a premise?
3. What is a conclusion?
4. How is truth defined in this chapter?

5. What is a declarative sentence?
6. What is an interrogative sentence?
7. What is an imperative sentence?
8. What is an exclamatory sentence?

WRITING MODULE: STATE YOUR CASE!

Part One. Pick a topic that you feel passionate about. Perhaps something to do with politics, morality, or religion, but anything that really matters to you.

Part Two. State your viewpoint on the matter, as clearly and precisely as you can. This is your conclusion.

Part Three. In approximately one page, back up your conclusion with one or more premises. Keep in mind that your argument will be more successful if your premises start with "common ground." So, think about your audience, think about what common ground you share, and then choose your premises accordingly. Give your readers sufficient reason to believe that your claim is *true*. Make your case!

Appendix 2.1 Logic and Critical Thinking

The words "logic" and "critical thinking" are often used in the same context, and the question arises, What is the relationship between the two? We have already defined logic. Critical thinking is best explained by first drawing a distinction between two types, or levels, of thinking. Most of the time we notice things, come to believe things, draw conclusions, make decisions, and so on, in the usual way. Call this "level one" thinking. However, sometimes we take a step back and think *about* our usual thinking, evaluating it on the basis of independent standards. Call this "level two" thinking. When we evaluate our usual thinking on the basis of rational, reality-based standards, we are engaging in critical thinking. Critical thinking is thus one kind of level two thinking.

A critical thinker continually asks himself or herself questions such as these: I believe such and such, but do I have any good evidence or reason to believe that such and such is really true, that is, in correspondence with reality? Or am I in the grips of an illusion? Do my beliefs rest on good evidence? Or do I believe these things due to factors I've never really thought about, factors perhaps having nothing to do with truth? In short, are my beliefs rooted in reality? Or are they rooted in some motive unrelated to actuality?

A critical thinker also asks: Are my core values truly reflective of justice? Or am I only fooling myself? Am I doing the morally right thing, or am I only rationalizing bad behavior? Am I leading the best life I can, all things considered? Or are there some areas in need of improvement?

When someone makes a controversial claim, a critical thinker asks: What's your evidence? That is, what reason do we have to believe this is actually true? When others urge a plan of action, a critical thinker asks: Is this the morally right thing to do? Or is it merely serving my, or someone else's, purely egocentric needs, which may or may not be morally right?

The relation between logic and critical thinking can now be stated. Logic is the systematic study of the standards of good reasoning, whereas critical thinking is concerned with the *application* of those standards to our beliefs and values. No analogies are perfect, but the relation between logic and critical thinking is a little like the relation between arithmetic and accounting. Arithmetic is the study of the abstract principles of correct adding, subtracting, multiplying, and dividing; accounting teaches you how to *apply* those principles to your finances in order to keep an accurate set of books.

Some people say that they do not trust reason and do not rely on it as a guide to truth or justice. To someone who takes such a position, one wants to ask: What are your core beliefs and values based on, if not evidence and reasoning? Are your core beliefs and values based on feelings? On desires? On emotions? On needs? But none of these is *by itself* indicative of truth or reality. For example, just because someone "feels" that all people of a certain skin color are morally and intellectually inferior does not make it true that they are. Just because someone "wants" to believe that their nation is the greatest on earth and has never done anything wrong does not make it so. Wants, desires, emotions, hopes, and so on, may be involved in our search for truth, but they can lead us astray when cut free from the oversight of reason and sober reflection based on evidence and rational argument.

I have heard a pragmatist say, "I don't trust reason. I base my beliefs and values on what *works*." In response, one wants to ask: But don't we use our reason to figure out not only what works but what works *best*? By the way, "works" *for whom*? Works is a pretty relative term. Slavery worked pretty well for slave owners, though not for those enslaved. Moreover, why suppose that truth or justice is simply what "works"? Doesn't this pragmatist's claim require justification or back up before it is believable? But what could justify the claim other than good reasons to believe it is true?

Some folks argue that since reasoning can be biased it therefore cannot be trusted. However, as philosopher Robert Nozick pointed out, the very notion of "biased reasoning" implies the existence of an *un*biased reason that serves as a standard against which biases in reasoning are detected.

Why Critical Thinking Is Needed

We believe things for all sorts of reasons, not all of them connected firmly to reality. Sometimes we believe something simply because believing it makes us feel better, although we may not be aware of it. But just because it "feels good" to believe something doesn't make it true or right. Sometimes what makes us feel good is not really right or good. Or we adopt a view because it promotes our self-interest, although we may not realize that this is the only basis for our belief. There may be times when self-interest and morality coincide, but surely there are times when they do not. Sometimes we hold a view due to pure prejudice, without a careful look at all the facts. Other beliefs may be rooted in fears, unconscious wishes ("wish fulfillment"), hatred, anger, or bigotry. But none of these things is by itself indicative of truth or reality. Sometimes we hold a belief merely because an authority tells us to, without looking at the evidence or testing the reliability of the authority. However, authorities are not always right. Finally, we may adopt a belief or value just because everyone else believes it, and it is easier to go with the group ("groupthink") than to think for ourselves. But the group is not always right.

The problem with believing things and adopting values solely on the basis of feelings, desires, inclinations, pure self-interest, prejudice, wish-fulfillment, fear, bigotry, groupthink, and so on, is that none of these is an adequate basis for supposing a belief is really true or that a value is truly moral. Critical thinkers try to assess their beliefs and values from a more realistic standpoint and with total honesty. Everyone has the potential to think critically. It may require "thinking for yourself." It may require an honest look in the mirror. It may require following the evidence wherever it leads, even when it leads to something one does not want to believe. Or it may mean all of the above.

Level 1 thinking: "All redheaded people are idiots!"

Level 2 thinking: "Wait a minute. Do I actually have any good evidence for this belief?" (No.)

It's Not All Negative

Many people, when they hear the term critical thinking, suppose that it is a completely negative activity involving nothing more than criticizing everything—tearing down rather than building up. Nothing could be further from the truth. The word *critical* in critical thinking means "fine-tuned" or "careful;" it does not entail being against everything or arguing with anyone who tries to tell you something. Just as a "critical care" nurse must be extremely alert and careful (a slight error could cost someone his or her life), a critical thinker is alert to the many ways that beliefs and values may fail to relate to reality and, with that in mind, carefully and deliberatively decides what to believe and how to live on the basis of good reasons, on the basis of "rational, reality-based standards."

Socrates

The ancient Greek philosopher Socrates (479–399 B.C.) is considered one of the founders of critical thinking as a rigorous intellectual discipline because he was among the first figures in recorded history to practice critical thinking in a disciplined and systematic way. Socrates became convinced that many people *think* they know what they are talking about when in reality they do not have the foggiest idea. They think they have the truth, when in reality they are deluded. He also saw that many people *believe* that they are doing the right thing, but in reality their actions are unjust and they are in a state of denial.

A lesser person, upon discovering this general fact about human nature, might have walked around town angrily telling people, "Wake up! Shed your illusions! Straighten out your lives!" A more authoritarian approach would have been to force the truth on everyone. Such methods were not for Socrates. His respect for the dignity and freedom of the individual was so great that he refused to simply tell people what to believe. His method was to ask people questions. However, not just any questions. Socrates asked carefully chosen questions designed to cause the other person to look in the mirror and critically evaluate his or her own beliefs and values on the basis of rational, reality-based standards. Today we call his form of honest self-examination the "Socratic method."

Glossary

Argument One or more statements, called premises, offered as reasons or evidence in support of the truth of a further statement, called the conclusion.

Common ground In an argument, statements accepted by all sides.

Conclusion In an argument, the statement that the premises are said to support or justify.

Conclusion indicator A word or expression used in the context of an argument to signal the presence of the conclusion.

Correspondence theory of truth The theory which claims that truth is the correspondence of a statement with reality.

Declarative sentence A sentence typically used to make a claim about the world and thus to express something that is either true or false.

Definition An explanation of the meaning of a word or phrase.

Enthymeme An argument that is missing one or more premises or a conclusion.

Exclamatory sentence A sentence expressing an emotion or feeling.

Falsity The property a statement or proposition has when it does not correspond to reality.

Imperative sentence A sentence expressing a command.

Interrogatory sentence A sentence expressing a question.

Performative sentence A sentence the utterance of which performs an action.

Precise definition A detailed explanation of the meaning of a word or phrase.

Premise In an argument, a statement offered as evidence in support of the truth of the conclusion.

Premise indicator A word or expression used in the context of an argument to indicate that a premise is about to be given.

Principle of charity When you must attribute a premise or a conclusion to someone's enthymematic argument, add something that helps make the person's case as reasonable as it can be.

Socratic method Asking another person carefully chosen questions designed to cause the person to look in the mirror and evaluate his or her beliefs and values on the basis of rational, realistic standards.

Statement A claim that is either true or false.

Truth The property a statement or proposition has when it corresponds to reality.

3 The Two Basic Types of Argument « « « « « «

Aristotle was the first in recorded history to notice a sharp distinction between two very different types of reasoning and to write about it. Sometimes we reason like this:

1. All wasps have stingers.
2. This insect is a wasp.
3. Therefore, it is certain that this insect has a stinger.

Here the underlying claim is that *if* the premises all are true, then the conclusion ("this insect has a stinger") is *certainly* true. This argument aims to show *conclusively* that its conclusion is true! But other times we reason like this:

1. Joe has eaten a Dick's Deluxe burger for lunch every day for the past year.
2. So, it is very probable, although it is not certain, that he will have a Dick's Deluxe burger for lunch tomorrow.

This argument makes a weaker claim: If the premises are true, then the conclusion, that Joe will have a Dick's Deluxe burger for lunch tomorrow, although not certain, *probably* is true. (Remember that for the time being, by probably we mean more than 50% likely.) Following Aristotle, logicians call the first type of reasoning above **deduction** and the second type **induction**. Every argument falls into one, or the other, of these two general categories of reasoning, making the distinction between deduction and induction one of the core ideas of logical theory. Let's now have a closer look at what might be Aristotle's most fundamental logical discovery.

What Is a Deductive Argument?

A **deductive argument** is an argument which aims to show that its conclusion *must* be true if its premises all are true. Put another way, the underlying claim, in the case of a deductive argument, is that it is impossible for the conclusion to be false if the premises all are true. A deductive argument thus aims to establish its conclusion with complete certainty, in such a way that the conclusion is *guaranteed* to be true if the premises all are true. In a deductive argument, the aim is to show *conclusively* that the conclusion is true and cannot possibly be false.

Examples of Deductive Reasoning

The following short arguments are meant to be cases of deductive reasoning. Examine each one closely to sharpen your understanding of this important logical idea.

1. All bats are mammals. But no mammals are birds. So, it must be that no bats are birds.
2. Some pets are cats. But all cats are mammals. So, it necessarily follows that some pets are mammals.
3. If it is raining, then the lawn is wet. But it is raining. Therefore, certainly the lawn is wet.
4. Either we will eat burritos or we will eat fried rice. We will not be eating burritos. Therefore, necessarily we will eat fried rice.

Notice that deductive arguments have an air of definiteness, of confidence, a "my conclusion cannot possibly be false" attitude. They aim for certainty, for conclusive proof, for a guarantee of truth, and nothing less.

What Is an Inductive Argument?

An **inductive argument** aims to show that if its premises all are true, then although its conclusion is not certain to be true it is *probably* or *likely* true. Put another way, the underlying claim, in the case of an inductive argument, is that it is unlikely that the conclusion is false if the premises all are true. Inductive arguments thus aim to establish their conclusions with probability, or likelihood, but not with complete certainty. An inductive argument does not attempt to guarantee its conclusion, nor does it attempt to show that it is conclusively true; however, it aims to show that we have good reasons to accept the conclusion as probably true nevertheless, despite the lack of complete certainty.

In a court of law, for example, the prosecutor does not argue that the defendant *must* be guilty; he or she argues only that the defendant is *probably* guilty. (In civil cases, the claim is that it is more likely that the accused is guilty than that he or she is not guilty; in criminal cases, the claim is that the defendant is guilty "beyond a reasonable doubt.") Arguments in court are typically inductive.

Examples of Inductive Reasoning

Examine the following arguments, each intended as an inductive argument, for a better grasp of this type of reasoning.

1. It has been sunny for 10 days in a row. There are no clouds in the sky. So, probably it will be sunny tomorrow.
2. Joe hasn't had a drink in 10 years. So, it is likely that he won't drink at the party tonight.
3. We randomly interviewed 600 students at Green River Community College, and 400 of them said they drink coffee in the morning. Therefore, it is probable that two-thirds of the student population there drink coffee in the morning.
4. For years Joe and Pete have not gotten along well on the job. Therefore, it is likely that if we put Joe and Pete on the same project, they will not get along well.
5. We left the fish out on the table last night after dinner. Nobody in the house ate any overnight. Orangie, the cat, loves fish. It is reasonable to suppose Orangie ate the leftover fish last night.

Notice that whereas deductive arguments have an air of certainty, confidence, and conclusiveness, inductive arguments have an air of uncertainty and incompleteness. While a deductive argument claims, explicitly or implicitly, that its conclusion *must* be true, and with certainty, an inductive argument claims, explicitly or implicitly, that if its premises all are true, then its conclusion is probable although not completely certain.

How to Tell the World That Your Argument Is Deductive (or Inductive)

Is the following argument deductive? Or is it inductive?

1. Sodium and chlorine always react together to produce a salt.
2. Therefore, when I mix sodium and chlorine, the product will be a salt.

Does the author intend the premise as a guarantee that the conclusion is true? In other words, is the author claiming that the conclusion *must* be true if the premises are true? Or is the premise intended to be a reason to believe the conclusion is probable but less than certain, or in other words, that the conclusion is *likely* to be true but not certain to be true? The answer is that we cannot tell for sure. The argument's wording does not make it clear which form of reasoning, deductive or inductive, the author intends!

Consider this argument:

1. Every spider ever observed so far has eight legs.
2. Joe is a spider.
3. So, Joe has eight legs.

Is this argument deductive or inductive? Is the author claiming the conclusion *must* be true if the premises are true? Or is he or she only claiming the premises make the conclusion *probable* but not certain? Again, there is no way to tell for sure because the author does not explicitly (i.e., in words) say which form of reasoning is intended. Like the previous argument, this argument is not as clear as it could be.

If you are presenting an argument and you want to make it obvious to everybody that your reasoning is deductive, insert a word or phrase into the conclusion indicating the deductive claim, namely, the claim that the conclusion *must* be true if the premises are true. Phrases such as "it *necessarily* follows that," "it *must* be that," "it cannot be otherwise," and "it is therefore *certain* that" typically signal the presence of deductive reasoning. Additionally, single words such as *necessarily, certainly,* and *must,* when used appropriately in an argumentative context, also signal that deductive reasoning is present.

Deductive Indicator Words

Words or phrases that indicate the presence of deductive reasoning are called **deductive indicator words**. The following is a partial list of commonly used deduction indicators:

it must be that	it is certain that	necessarily
absolutely	conclusively	undeniably
definitely	surely	certainly
for sure		

"But My Argument Is Inductive!"

If you want to make it clear to everybody that your reasoning is inductive and not deductive, then insert a word or phrase indicating the presence of the inductive claim, namely, the claim that if the premises are true, then the conclusion is probably or likely true, although not certain. Phrases such as "it's probably true that," or "it's likely that," or "it's plausible to suppose that," or "one can safely conclude that," or "it is therefore reasonable to suppose" usually suffice to signal the presence of inductive reasoning. In addition, single words such as *probably* or *likely* also indicate the presence of induction when inserted in the conclusion.

Inductive Indicator Words

Words or phrases that signal inductive reasoning are called **inductive indicator words**. The following is a partial list of commonly used induction indicators:

it is likely that	statistically	probably
it is probable that	it is plausible to suppose that	
the most reasonable conclusion to draw is		most likely
it's not certain but the most likely conclusion is		usually
the best explanation is	You can bet that	

Back to the Drawing Board

Let's go back to the earlier arguments that were missing deductive and inductive indicator words. Here they are again with indicator words added in italics:

1. Sodium and chlorine always react together to produce a salt.
2. Therefore, in a moment, when I mix sodium and chlorine, the product will *necessarily* be a salt.

1. Every spider ever observed so far has eight legs.
2. Joe is a spider.
3. So, it is *highly probable* that Joe has eight legs.

Do you see the difference an indicator word or phrase can make? Now it is clear that the first argument is deductive and the second is inductive.

Further Examples

The indicator words shown in bold in the following arguments make it crystal clear that the reasoning is deductive:

1. The three interior angles of every Euclidean triangle sum to exactly 180 degrees.
2. Triangle ABC is Euclidean.
3. In triangle ABC, angle A is 60 degrees and angle B is 60 degrees.
4. Therefore, the remaining angle, C, **must** be 60 degrees.

1. All aardvarks are mammals.
2. All mammals have lungs.
3. Therefore, **necessarily**, all aardvarks have lungs.

1. All squares have four sides.
2. All squares have four equal angles.
3. So, it is **certain** that all squares have four sides and four equal angles.

1. They either ate hamburgers or hot dogs.
2. They did not eat hamburgers.
3. Thus, based on this information, it is **guaranteed** that they ate hot dogs.

Similarly, the bold indicator words in the following arguments make it crystal clear that the reasoning is inductive:

1. It has been snowing for six days in a row and the sky is still full of snow clouds.
2. Therefore, **probably** it will snow tonight.

1. Ed is a lifelong Democrat.
2. Thus, it is **likely** he will vote for the Democratic candidate in the next presidential election.

1. Ed is the only person in the house who will eat meatloaf.
2. Therefore, it is **reasonable to suppose** he is the one who ate all the leftover meatloaf sometime late last night.

1. Almost all cats love cream.
2. Orangie is an ordinary cat.
3. Therefore, it is **plausible** to suppose that Orangie is going to love this cream.

Exercise 3.1   In each case, is the argument intended as deductive or inductive?

1. The sign says "Closed." So, most likely the establishment is not open.
2. All certified financial consultants have to pass a test. She is certified, so it must be that she passed the test.

3. The figure has four equal sides and four equal angles, so it necessarily follows that it is a square.

4. The substance is an acid, so certainly it can turn blue litmus paper red.

5. "Each snow crystal contains about a quintillion water molecules, and these molecules can be arranged in countless numbers of ways. Of course, no one can prove it, but it is quite likely that every snowflake is unique."–Scott Camazine, *The Naturalist's Year*.

6. Dr. Frasier Crane, Seattle's most popular radio psychologist, will be broadcasting from the event, so I'll bet a lot of people will be there.

7. The Soup Nazi is frowning, so most likely he is unhappy.

8. According to the theory known as psychological hedonism, pleasure is the sole motive of every human action. We never do anything except to get pleasure. However, honest self-examination reveals that pleasure accompanies actions but is not always the motive of action. Sometimes we do things for the sake of other people, for the sake of their welfare, or for the sake of a cause larger than us, and not for the pleasure it will bring us. The pleasure we might feel after accomplishing our goal is only an unintended by-product of our action, not what we were after in the first place. It follows that very probably psychological hedonism is false.

9. A zombie is a being that acts exactly as if it is conscious, but in reality it has no conscious mental experiences at all. It is operating on automatic pilot, so to speak. Since it acts exactly as if it is conscious, while lacking a conscious mind, there is absolutely no way to truly know whether anyone around you, even your best friend, is really conscious or if, instead, he or she is in reality a robotic zombie programmed by mad scientists or evil aliens pulling the strings from behind the curtains.

10. Everything has a cause. The universe is a thing. Therefore, the universe has a cause. This could only be God. Therefore, God must exist.

11. If everything has a cause, and if God exists, then God has a cause. This would be something prior to God that created God—that brought God into existence. But according to those who believe in God, God does *not* have a cause. Therefore, the previous argument certainly contains a contradiction!

Why Label Arguments Deductive or Inductive?

When we label an argument inductive, we are calling attention to a very important aspect of the argument, namely, this: The author is *not* trying to prove the conclusion with complete certainty; that is, he or she is *not* trying to guarantee that the conclusion *must* be true. Rather, the author is only trying to show that the conclusion is probably or likely true.

On the other hand, by indicating that an argument is deductive, we alert the reader to the deductive claim—that the conclusion *must* be true if the premises are true. This reminds the reader that the ultimate goal of the argument is to show conclusively, with certainty, and not merely with a high degree of probability or likelihood, that the conclusion is true.

Why does it matter whether an argument is perceived as deductive or inductive? It matters because the standards by which we judge deductive arguments are very different from the standards by which we judge inductive arguments. Because the standards differ, the first thing we need to know about an argument, before we judge it or evaluate it, is whether its reasoning is deductive or inductive. Only then will we know which standard to apply: a deductive standard, or an inductive standard of evaluation. What are these "standards" by which we judge or evaluate deductive and inductive arguments? They are the topic of the next two chapters.

Using Structural Features of an Argument to Decide Whether It Is Deductive or Inductive

Although deductive and inductive indicator words make it abundantly clear to which category our reasoning belongs, the sad fact of the matter is that in everyday life, people rarely use deductive and inductive indicator words to signal the nature of their reasoning. Deductive and inductive indicator words are usually found only in academic contexts, not in ordinary conversation. Suppose, as is usually the case, that an argument has no words indicative of deduction or induction. How do we decide whether it is intended as a deductive or as an inductive argument? In such cases, an argument can usually be classified as deductive or inductive based on the general pattern or form of reasoning that it embodies.

An **argument form** is a general pattern of reasoning that many different arguments, about many different subjects, can follow. A number of argument forms are commonly associated with deductive reasoning, whereas certain other common argument forms usually indicate that an induction argument is being given. We will examine these forms in depth later in this book. However, a brief, introductory explanation of each pattern can often be enough to place an argument into the proper category.

Common Forms of Deductive Reasoning

If an argument follows one of the general patterns listed below, it is probably meant to be interpreted as a deductive argument.

Mathematical Arguments. In this type of argument, the conclusion is derived from the premises using precise mathematical principles or calculations. For example:

1. Rectangle A is 10 inches high by 5 inches wide.
2. Rectangle B is 5 inches high by 5 inches wide.
3. The area of a rectangle is found by multiplying its width by its height.
4. Therefore, the area of rectangle A is twice that of rectangle B.

Definitional Arguments. The conclusion of a definitional argument is said to follow from the premises on the basis of the definition of a key word or phrase. For example:

1. "Jaywalking" is defined as "crossing a street outside of a marked crosswalk and not at a corner."
2. Herman Snodgrass crossed the street outside of a marked crosswalk and not at a corner.
3. Therefore, Mr. Snodgrass engaged in jaywalking.

This form of reasoning is very frequently employed in law, when judges must decide whether a particular law does, or does not, apply in a particular case; but it is employed in many other contexts as well.

The Categorical Syllogism. In the *Prior Analytics*, the first published textbook of deductive reasoning, Aristotle introduced the word "syllogism" and used it to refer to arguments whose conclusions were claimed to follow "necessarily" (as he put it) from their premises. Although the word will be given a fuller meaning in Unit Two, for now a syllogism can be loosely defined as a deductive argument.

The premises and conclusion of a *categorical* syllogism are always sentences that relate two categories of things by asserting that all, none, or some, of one category, either belongs to, or does not belong to, a second category. Here are four examples of such sentences:

1. All turtles are reptiles.
2. No cats are birds.
3. Some cats are pets.
4. Some cats are not pets.

We interpret the first to be saying that all the members of the turtle category belong to the reptile category. The second says that no members of the cat category belong to the bird category. The third says that some members of the cat category belong to the pet category, and the fourth says that some members of the cat category do not belong to the pet category. Now, here is an argument composed of such sentences:

1. All dogs are mammals.
2. No mammals are plants.
3. So, no dogs are plants.

The presence of statements like these, linked together into a categorical syllogism, is a good indicator that you have a case of deductive reasoning on your hands. Biologists love categorical syllogisms.

Hypothetical Syllogism. A **hypothetical sentence**, also called a conditional, is a sentence of the form, "If P then Q," with P and Q each standing in for a sentence that will be embedded inside the conditional. This form for a sentence, called a *sentence form*, is a general structure or pattern that a particular sentence can follow. To illustrate, begin with the form, "If P then Q." Now replace P with the sentence "It is raining" and replace Q with the sentence "The picnic will be cancelled." The result, called a *substitution instance* of the form, is: "If it is raining, then the picnic will be cancelled." This sentence is called a "substitution instance" of the form because sentences were substituted for the letters in the form. Now, in a hypothetical syllogism, two conditional sentences are linked together, forming a chain of reasoning, and then a conclusion is drawn, as in the following example.

1. If the battery is dead, then the car won't start.
2. If the car won't start, then we'll be late to the meeting.
3. Therefore, if the battery is dead, then we'll be late to the meeting.

We reason this way all the time, don't we? If this, then this. But if this, then this. Therefore, if this, then this. If an argument follows this form, it is probably intended as a deductive argument.

Disjunctive Syllogism. A disjunction is a sentence of the form "P or Q." Substituting "Today is Tuesday" for P and "Today is Wednesday" for Q produces the following substitution instance of the form: "Today is Tuesday or today is Wednesday." The sentence that replaces the P is called the left disjunct, and the sentence substituted for the Q is called the right disjunct. A **disjunctive syllogism** begins with a disjunction and then draws a conclusion after denying the truth of one of the disjuncts. For example:

1. We'll eat at Dick's Drive-In or we'll eat at Spud's Fish and Chips.
2. We will *not* eat at Dick's Drive-In.
3. Therefore, we will eat at Spud's.

If someone's reasoning takes this form, it is probably deductive. We reason this way all the time, don't we? And not just about fast food.

Modus Ponens. This often-employed form of argument begins with a conditional ("If P, then Q") sentence and reaches its conclusion by asserting or "affirming" the "if" part of that conditional. The following argument follows the modus ponens form:

1. If it is sunny, then we'll cut the grass.
2. It is sunny.
3. Therefore, we'll cut the grass.

The unusual name modus ponens is Latin for "mode of affirmation." The term was invented by logicians during the Middle Ages and remains the standard name, all over the world, for this form of reasoning. The name modus ponens earns its keep by reminding the initiated that the second premise *affirms* the "if" part of the first premise. We'll study this important deductive argument form in depth in Unit Three.

Modus Tollens. Like modus ponens, this common pattern of reasoning begins with a conditional ("If P then Q") sentence. However, modus tollens (Latin for "mode of denying") reaches its conclusion by denying the "then" part of the conditional. The following argument follows the modus tollens form:

1. If the store is open, then the lights will be on.
2. The lights are not on.
3. Therefore, the store is not open.

The name of this argument form also goes back to the schools of logic that dotted Europe in the Middle Ages, and it remains the universally recognized name today. We'll also examine this very important form of deductive reasoning in depth in Unit Three.

Common Forms of Inductive Reasoning

If an argument follows one of the following patterns, it is probably intended as an inductive argument.

Prediction Arguments. In this type of argument, a claim about the future is made, based on information about the past. In short, we reason from past to future. For example:

1. It has been raining for seven days straight and the sky is cloudy.
2. Therefore, it will be rainy tomorrow.

We reason this way all the time, don't we? This pattern of inductive reasoning is arguably a component every time we plan for the future.

Analogical Arguments. This type of argument begins by asserting that two things, call them X and Y, have many features in common. This establishes an analogy (similarity) between X and Y. Next, an additional feature of X is identified—something not known to *not* be possessed by Y. The conclusion is that Y probably has this feature as well, on the grounds that X and Y have many other features in common. For instance:

1. Monkeys and humans have similar hearts.
2. Drug X cures heart disease in monkeys.
3. Therefore, drug X will cure heart disease in humans.

A great deal of medical research follows this form. We also reason this way when we buy a car, as you will see in Unit Five. If someone's reasoning follows this form, it is probably inductive.

Generalization From a Sample. In this type of argument, the premises present information about a sample of a larger group. The conclusion then projects that information onto the larger group.

1. We randomly sampled 10% of the widgets produced on assembly line 1, and fewer than 1% were defective.
2. Therefore, fewer than 1% of *all* widgets produced on assembly line 1 are defective.

This very common form of inductive reasoning is also explored in more depth in Unit Five.

Arguments From Authority. This type of argument concludes that something is true on the grounds that an authority on the matter says it is true. For instance:

1. Professor Jones is a recognized authority on nuclear energy.
2. Professor Jones says that living near a nuclear power plant does not increase one's risk of cancer.
3. Therefore, living near a nuclear power plant does not increase one's risk of cancer.

In many areas of life these days, things are so complicated and knowledge is so built up, that we have no choice but to rely on expert authority. The trick is to pick your experts wisely. This issue is discussed in more detail in Unit Five.

Inference to the Best Explanation. This type of argument begins by citing facts in need of explanation. Ideally, all potential explanations that are plausible based on what we know are then examined. Next, on the basis of commonly used standards of comparison, one of these explanations is judged the best explanation; that is, as the account that makes the best sense of the facts in question. The conclusion is drawn: This explanation is probably the correct or true explanation. Here is an example.

1. The suspect's fingerprints were found at the crime scene.
2. No other fingerprints were found at the crime scene.
3. The suspect's alibi did not check out.
4. The missing jewelry was found in the suspect's car, with his fingerprints on it.
5. The best overall explanation of the facts is that the suspect is the culprit.
6. Therefore, the suspect likely did it.

This form of inductive reasoning is often used in crime scene investigation, in courts of law, and in science. It is also a staple of commonsense, everyday reasoning as well, as we will see in Unit Five.

Cause and Effect Reasoning. Sometimes we reason from the effect back to the cause of the effect, as in the following argument:

1. This can of soda pop has lost its fizz.
2. Experience shows that leaving a pop can open for a period of time causes it to lose its fizz.
3. Therefore, someone probably left this can of pop open for a period of time.

Other times, we reason from cause to effect, as in this example:

1. Experience shows that mixing baking soda and vinegar causes foam.
2. Therefore, if you mix that baking soda and vinegar, you will probably get foam.

Here is a philosophical version of cause-and-effect reasoning:

1. Everything so far observed has a cause.

2. The universe is a thing.
3. Therefore, the universe probably has a cause.

But philosophers and theologians are not the only ones who reason this way. Auto mechanics reason from cause to effect and from effect to cause every time they diagnose what's wrong with your car. Plumbers and electricians couldn't fix your broken toilet or get your lights working again without engaging in cause-and-effect reasoning.

Hypothesis Testing

The following two forms of argument are frequently employed in science as well as in everyday life to test hypotheses.

1. If hypothesis H is true, then we may expect to observe phenomenon P.
2. P is not observed.
3. Therefore, hypothesis H is not true.

1. If hypothesis H is true, then we may expect to observe phenomenon P.
2. P is observed.
3. Therefore, hypothesis H is true.

In the opening premise of this argument form, a prediction is derived from a hypothesis—a prediction about what we can expect to observe *if* the hypothesis is true. When the prediction comes true, this counts as evidence in support of the truth of the hypothesis. When the prediction fails to come true, this counts as evidence against the truth of the hypothesis. In the following example, the evidence supports the hypothesis that a car has a dead battery:

1. If the car has a dead battery, then when you turn the key, there will be no click.
2. There was no click when I turned the key.
3. Therefore, the battery is probably dead.

In the next example, the evidence goes against the hypothesis that the truck is out of gas:

1. If the truck is out of gas, then the gas gauge will be below empty.
2. The gas gauge is *not* below empty.
3. Therefore, the truck is probably not out of gas.

Exercise 3.2   In each case, is the argument intended as deductive or inductive? Cite the structure that supports your verdict.

1.   Angle A is larger than angle B, and angle B is larger than angle C, so angle C is smaller than angle A.

2.   Either we will have cabbage hamburgers for dinner, or we will have peanut-buttered hot dogs. We won't be having the hot dogs. So, we will eat the cabbage hamburgers for dinner.

3.   My car just quit on me in the middle of the freeway. The gas gauge has been on empty for the past 10 miles. Everything else seems fine. My car ran out of gas.

4.   All zombies are mindless robots. All robots lack free will. So, zombies lack free will.

5.   The K-man hasn't worked in over two years. So, he won't be working tomorrow.

6.   It rarely rains in Seattle in August, so Charlie will have sunny weather for his picnic next August in Seattle.

7.   If it rains, the picnic will be cancelled. It is raining, so the picnic will be cancelled.

8.   If it rains, then the concert is cancelled. If the concert is cancelled, then nobody will be playing music. Therefore, if it rains, then nobody will be playing music.

9.   By definition, what you are doing is theft. But theft is morally wrong. Therefore, you are doing something morally wrong.

10.   Dr. Smith says that drinking that stuff is bad for your health and he is an acknowledged expert on health drinks. So, that drink is not healthy.

11.   Three witnesses saw Joe crash his car into the parked car, and none of them knew Joe or each other. In addition, a video camera caught the whole thing. Joe crashed into the parked car.

12.   Substance X causes tremors in rats. But rats have many similarities to humans. So, substance X will cause tremors in humans.

13.   If the substance is an acid, then it will react with this chemical. The substance does not react with this chemical. Therefore, the substance is not an acid.

14. If Smith's hypothesis about gravity is true, then here is what should happen when you run the test in the lab: You should get a reading between 1 and 2 on the dial. (Later) We ran the test and the dial reading was 1.5. Therefore, Smith's hypothesis is true!

Glossary

Argument form A general pattern or structure of reasoning that many different arguments, about many different subjects, can follow.

Categorical sentence A sentence asserting that all, none, or some of one category of things either belong to or do not belong to another category of things.

Deductive argument An argument that claims, explicitly or implicitly, that if the premises are true, the conclusion must be true, which is to claim that it would be impossible for the conclusion to be false if the premises were all to be true.

Deductive indicator words Words or phrases that indicate the presence of deductive reasoning.

Disjunctive syllogism An argument that begins with a disjunction and then draws a conclusion after denying the truth of one of the disjuncts.

Hypothetical or conditional sentence A sentence of the form, "If P then Q," where P and Q each stand in for a sentence that will be embedded inside the conditional.

Inductive argument An argument that claims, explicitly or implicitly, that if the premises are true, it is probable that the conclusion is true, although the conclusion might nevertheless be false.

Inductive indicator words Words or phrases that indicate the presence of inductive reasoning.

Syllogism A deductive argument.

4 How to Evaluate a Deductive Argument ‹‹ ‹‹

What Is a Valid Argument?

As we have seen, a deductive argument aims to establish its conclusion *conclusively*, in such a way that its conclusion *must* be true if its premises all are true. If a deductive argument succeeds in its aim, that is, if it indeed does establish its conclusion in this way, we call it a **valid deductive argument** (or a **valid argument** for short). It follows that a valid argument has this feature: its conclusion *must* be true if its premises all are true. A deductive argument is invalid if it is not valid. It follows that an **invalid deductive argument** has this feature: it is *not* the case that its conclusion must be true if its premises all are true. Consider the following categorical argument:

1. All aardvarks are mammals.
2. All mammals have hair.
3. Therefore, necessarily, all aardvarks have hair.

The presence of the deductive indicator word *necessarily* makes it clear that this is a deductive argument and represents the claim that *if* the premises are true, then the conclusion *must* be true. Suppose the premises are indeed true. Must the conclusion be true, as claimed? The answer is clearly yes. If the premises all are true, then the conclusion must be true. This argument is therefore a *valid* argument.

Lesson: A valid argument is a deductive argument that has the following feature: *If* its premises all are true, then its conclusion *must* be true.

When learning an abstract idea, it can help to hear it explained in more than one way. The following are other ways logicians have defined validity, all amounting to the same thing in the end:

- A valid argument is such that its premises, if true, guarantee the truth of its conclusion.
- In the case of a valid argument, the conclusion must be true if the premises all are true.
- In a valid argument, the conclusion follows necessarily from the premises.
- A valid argument is one in which if the premises are true then the conclusion must be true.
- In a valid argument, the premises and conclusion are related in such a way that it is not possible the premises are true and the conclusion is false.

Examples of Valid Deductive Arguments

Examine the following valid arguments to deepen your understanding of this core logical idea.

1. Every time it rains, without any exception, the roof gets wet.
2. It is raining right now.
3. Therefore, necessarily, the roof is getting wet right now.

1. All shrews are nocturnal.
2. All shrews are mammals.
3. Therefore, certainly at least some mammals are nocturnal.

1. If we go to Portland, then we will visit Powell's Bookstore.
2. If we visit Powell's, then we will buy a book.
3. Accordingly, if we go to Portland, then surely we will buy a book.

1. Only stamp collectors live in the Turnigan Arms apartments.
2. Luke Pavement lives in the Turnigan Arms apartments.
3. So, Luke Pavement must be a stamp collector.

1. All members of the ABC hockey team live in Colorado.
2. Luke Pavement is a member of the ABC hockey team.
3. So, Luke Pavement must live in Colorado.

1. The computer is either a PC or a Mac.
2. It is not a PC.
3. So, it must be a Mac.

1. If Elaine places her order incorrectly, the Soup Nazi won't serve her.
2. If he refuses to serve her, she won't bring home any mulligatawny soup.
3. Therefore, necessarily, if Elaine places her order incorrectly, she won't bring home any mulligatawny soup.

These arguments are all deductively valid because, in each case, *if* the premises are true, then the conclusion *must* be true.

Can an Argument Be "True"?

Upon being introduced to the terminology of logical theory, some students begin applying the concept of truth to arguments, calling arguments true and false. This is a mistake. As our terms have been defined, there is no such thing as a true or a false argument. There are true and false *statements*, true and false *premises*, true and false *conclusions*, but truth is not the sort of thing that can be predicated of an argument. Of course, arguments can be valid or invalid, and later we will see that they can also be "sound" or "unsound"; but an argument is never true or false.

Validity and Possibility

As we have seen, a valid argument has this feature: If its premises all are true, then its conclusion *must* be true. Let us think about the word *must* for a moment. "Must be so" means "cannot possibly be otherwise." It follows that in the case of a valid deductive argument, it would *not be possible* that the premises all are true and yet the conclusion is *false*. Saying, "If the premises are true, then the conclusion *must* be true" is logically equivalent to saying, "If the premises are true, then it is *not possible* the conclusion is *false*." It follows that validity can also be defined this way: A valid argument has the following feature: It would not be possible that the premises are all true and yet the conclusion is false. To put it another way, an argument is valid if and only if it is not possible for its premises all to be true while its conclusion is false.

Notice that in each of the previous sample arguments, it is not possible that the premises all are true and yet the conclusion is false. Naturally, because each one is a *valid* argument!

INTERLUDE

Defining Possibility

We have been speaking of possibilities. But what exactly are we talking about here? In everyday life, the word *possibility* has no definite, generally agreed-on meaning. The word is used loosely and in many different ways. (Some things are physically possible but not legally possible, some moves are possible in baseball but not in basketball, and so on.) In logic the word is given a very definite meaning, albeit a very broad and inclusive one: As far as logic is concerned, anything whatsoever counts as **logically possible**, no matter how unlikely, no matter how far-fetched or implausible, no matter how bizarre or unorthodox, no matter how much it cuts against the status quo, as long as it is not self-contradictory, that is to say, as long as it is not a self-contradiction and does not imply a self-contradiction. Logic thus employs the broadest available meaning of the word *possible*. The following statements count as logically possible because although they are extremely unlikely, they are simply not self-contradictory.

- Someone paid $1 million for an ordinary hot dog the other day before a game at Yankee Stadium.
- A guy named "Lucky" won the New York State Lottery 100 times in a row for a total of $100 million.

These extremely unlikely scenarios are logically possible simply because they are not self-contradictory. Of course, this raises the question: What exactly is a self-contradiction? Formally speaking, an explicit self-contradiction is any statement of the form "P and it is not the case that P," where P is a variable standing in for a declarative sentence. Here are examples:

- Joe is 16 and it is not the case that Joe is 16.
- Today is Monday and it is not the case that today is Monday.
- The car is a Chevrolet and it is not the case that the car is a Chevrolet.

Notice that in each of these self-contradictions, the sentence that replaces the P on the left side of the contradiction ("Joe is 16," "Today is Monday," etc.) is *the very same statement* as the statement that replaces the P on the right side. A self-contradiction starts by asserting a declarative statement ("Joe is 16," "Today is Monday," etc.). Next, the word *and* conjoins this to the rest of the contradiction. But the rest of the contradiction is the *negation* of the statement originally asserted ("it is not the case that Joe is 16," "it is not the case that today is Monday," etc.). Thus, a self-contradiction starts by asserting something, but then retracts the original assertion, leaving nothing really asserted in the end, and thus nothing to be true! Self-contradiction is a paradigm case of the logically impossible, and for good reason.

Invalid Deductive Arguments

Consider this argument:

1. Ann and Bob are cousins.
2. Bob and Chris are cousins.
3. Therefore, necessarily, Ann and Chris must be cousins as well.

The presence of deductive indicator words (*necessarily*, *must*) makes it amply clear that this is a deductive argument: The arguer is claiming that the conclusion must be true if the premises are true. The claim is not that the conclusion *may* be true, or that the conclusion is *probably* true. No, the claim is that the conclusion *must* be true if the premises are true. However, not all claims are true. Is it the case that the conclusion *must* be true if the premises are true? Of course not!

Why not? For the following reason: Even if both premises are true, it is possible that the conclusion is false. How could this be? Here is one way. Given only the information contained in the premises, it is possible that Ann and Chris are sisters, not cousins. Thus, even if the premises are true, it is still possible that the conclusion is false; the premises do not make it certain the conclusion is true. Put another way, the premises do not guarantee the truth of the conclusion. This is therefore an invalid argument. Let us highlight this by expressing it in a few different ways:

- An invalid argument is a deductive argument that has this feature: It is *not* the case that if its premises all are true, then its conclusion *must* be true.
- An invalid argument has this feature: If its premises all are true, its conclusion might nevertheless be false.
- In the case of an invalid argument, it is possible the premises all are true when the conclusion is false.

Examples of Invalid Arguments

Examine the following arguments carefully to better understand deductive invalidity.

1. Fred is a senior in high school.
2. Jan is a junior in high school.
3. So, Fred must be older than Jan.

1. Whenever Ann goes swimming, Bob goes swimming.
2. Ann won't swim today.
3. Thus, it necessarily follows that Bob won't swim today.

1. Banya is a friend of Jerry's.
2. George is a friend of Jerry's.
3. Therefore, it necessarily follows that Banya is a friend of George's.

In each of these arguments, the implicit claim is that if the premises are true then the conclusion *must* be true. But that claim is incorrect in each case, because in each case it is possible that the premises all are true although the conclusion is nevertheless *false*. That is why each is invalid!

Valid or Invalid? How Do You Decide?

In future chapters you will learn extremely precise methods that can be used to test deductive arguments for the presence of validity or invalidity. Many of these methods are so exact they resemble methods used in mathematics and computer science. For the time being, while we are yet becoming familiar with the basic ideas of logical theory, it is possible to perform an **intuitive test** for validity or invalidity. (In this context, the word *intuitive* means using common sense rather than fancy technical rules and exact mathematical procedures.)

An Intuitive Test for Validity

Step 1. Assume (for the sake of argument) that the premises all are true.

Step 2. Ask the following question: If (hypothetically) the premises are true, is it *possible* the conclusion is false? That is, are there any possible circumstances, no matter how unlikely, bizarre, or unusual, in which the premises would all be true while the conclusion is false?

Step 3. If the answer is "no," then the argument is valid. If the answer is "yes," then the argument is invalid.

Let us apply the intuitive test to the following argument.

1. Every member of the Seattle Tiny Tim fan club plays the ukulele.
2. Lorraine and Sue live in Seattle and play the ukulele.
3. Therefore, Lorraine and Sue belong to the Seattle Tiny Tim fan club.

We begin by assuming the premises are true. Now, assuming the premises are true, is it *possible* that the conclusion is false? (Answer this for yourself before moving on.) Certainly it is. Isn't it *possible* that, although all the members of Seattle's Tiny Tim fan club play the ukulele, not all who play the ukulele belong to the Tiny Tim fan club of Seattle? And isn't it possible that Lorraine and Sue are among those ukulele players who do *not* belong to the club? This easily conceivable possibility shows that the argument is invalid.

It is extremely important to notice something here: We classified this argument as invalid without knowing whether its premises are actually true or not. We did not know whether it is really true or false that "Lorraine and Sue live in Seattle and play the ukulele." We proceeded without this information, simply by considering possibilities. Thus, two questions were kept separate:

1. Are the premises true?
2. Is the argument valid or invalid?

We answered the second question without having answered the first question. The information we might have uncovered by answering 1 would not have contributed in any way to answering 2. And, of course, the reverse is also true. The two questions are thus logically independent.

Now consider the following argument:

1. Frasier is taller than Niles.
2. Niles is taller than Mr. Crane.
3. So, Frasier must be taller than Mr. Crane.

This is obviously deductive because of the presence of the word *must*. Is the argument valid or invalid? First, we assume the premises are true. Next, we ask this: Is it possible the premises are true but the conclusion is false? Is there any possibility of this, no matter how unlikely or remote? Clearly not! If the premises are true, then the conclusion *must* be true too. The argument is therefore valid. Incidentally, are the premises true? That's a completely separate issue! To answer that question, we would have to measure the members of the TV show *Frasier*. In most cases, pure logical theory alone is insufficient to determine whether the premises of an argument are really true or not—sometimes things like measuring tapes and investigations of the world are necessary. However, we decided that this argument is valid without measuring the heights of the actors, that is, without even knowing whether the premises are, or are not, true.

Exercise 4.1   Which of the following deductive arguments are valid and which are invalid?

1. Since some Chevrolets are purple and some Chevrolets are trucks, it necessarily follows that Chevrolet makes at least some purple trucks.
2. No cat is a reptile. No reptile is a splurp. So, no cat is a splurp.
3. The United States House of Representatives has more members than there are calendar days in a leap year. Therefore, at least two members of the House must have the same birthday.

4. Father Flanagan's Boys Town is located in Nebraska. Nebraska is located in the United States. So, Boys Town must be located in the United States.

5. Every member of the Progressive Labor Party has studied the writings of Chairman Mao. Bob studied the writings of Chairman Mao. So, Bob must be a member of the Progressive Labor Party.

6. Listening to loud music always ruins your hearing. Joe is hard of hearing. Therefore, Joe must have been listening to loud music.

7. The Monterey Pop Festival (1967) featured some of the greatest bands of the 1960s. The Beatles did not perform at Monterey. So, the Beatles must not have been among the greatest bands of the 1960s.

8. The Monterey Pop Festival featured some of the greatest bands of the 1960s. Big Brother and the Holding Company performed at Monterey. So, Big Brother and the Holding Company must have been one of the greatest bands of the 1960s.

9. Only Hell's Angels live in the Brentwood Apartments. Hank belongs to the Hell's Angels. Therefore, Hank must live in the Brentwood Apartments.

10. All rodents are mammals. All mice are rodents. So, necessarily, all mice are mammals.

11. Figure A has four equal sides. Therefore, figure A must be a square.

12. All the members of the Ohio Southpaw Club are left-handed. Joe is left-handed. So, Joe must be a member of the Ohio Southpaw Club.

13. Every member of Tacoma's legendary Little Bill and the Bluenotes has been elected to the Northwest Blues Hall of Fame. Dick Curtis is a member of Little Bill Engelhart's group. Therefore, Dick Curtis must have been elected to the Northwest Blues Hall of Fame.

14. Every member of Little Bill and the Bluenotes has been elected to the Northwest Blues Hall of Fame. Legendary guitarist Billy Stapleton has been elected to the Northwest Blues Hall of Fame. Therefore, Billy must be a member of Little Bill's group.

15. Terry Lauber is a legendary Northwest composer, singer, and guitarist. Therefore, Lauber must be a member of the Seattle musician's union.

16. Every member of the Seattle rock band The Daily Flash is a terrific musician. Steve Lawlor is a terrific musician. Therefore, Steve Lawlor must be a member of The Daily Flash.

17. All the members of the Ohio Southpaw Club are left-handed. Joe is a member of the Ohio Southpaw Club. So, Joe must be left-handed.

18. When a nonmetallic element forms more than one oxide, the oxide containing the most oxygen gives the strongest acid. Sulfur is a nonmetallic element and forms two oxides: sulfuric and sulfurous acid. Sulfuric acid

contains more oxygen than sulfurous acid. Therefore, sulfuric acid is certainly stronger than sulfurous acid.

19. Table salt is formed from a strong acid and a strong base. Any substance formed from a strong acid and a strong base produces a neutral solution when dissolved in water. A neutral solution will neither turn red litmus paper blue nor blue litmus paper red. Therefore, if red litmus paper is dropped in a solution composed of salt dissolved in water, it surely will not turn blue. (This and the previous example are adapted from the Lionel Porter Chemical Company, Chemcraft Home Experiment Manual, 1951.)

20. If Ann swims, then Bob swims. But Bob is not swimming today. Therefore, Ann must not be swimming today.

21. *The Wizard of Oz* debuted August 25, 1939. All movies are filmed before they debut. Therefore, *The Wizard of Oz* must have been filmed before August 25, 1939.

22. If an all-powerful, all-knowing, all-good, absolutely perfect God were to create a world, it would make an absolutely perfect world. In a perfect world, there would be no suffering (such as cancer, war, etc.), there would be no crime (such as rape, kidnapping, etc.), and there would be no natural disasters (such as hurricanes, floods, etc.). The people in it would all be perfectly good (there would be no sinners, no crimes, etc.). The world we live in is obviously not perfect. It is full of diseases, wars, crimes, natural disasters, and people who do terrible things. Therefore, this world was not made by an all-powerful, all-knowing, all-good, absolutely perfect God.

Show Me It Is Invalid: The Method of Counterexample

Suppose a friend presents a deductive argument and believes it is valid, although the argument actually is invalid. Your friend insists the argument is valid; but he is totally deluded. How can you show your friend that his or her argument is invalid? One way is called the **method of counterexample**. Recall that a deductive argument claims that *if* its premises are true, then its conclusion must be true. A **counterexample to a deductive argument** is a description of a possible situation or circumstance in which the premises of the argument would all be true although the argument's conclusion would be false. When you present a counterexample to someone's deductive argument, you help them see one way in which the premises of their argument could be true although their conclusion is false, which shows them that their argument is invalid.

For instance, suppose someone proposes the following deductive argument and insists it is valid:

1. Ann is Jane's biological mother.
2. Ann is married to Tom.
3. Therefore, Tom *must* be Jane's biological father.

The presence of the word *must* signals that this is a deductive argument. But the following counterexample shows that this argument is invalid: Supposing the premises are true, it is still *possible* that Ann gave birth to Jane before having met Tom. Perhaps Ann married Tom after Jane had already grown up and gone off to college. This *possibility* shows that it is at least possible the premises of the argument are true although the conclusion is false. This is a counterexample and it shows that the argument is invalid.

Look back at the previous argument involving Frasier, Niles, and Mr. Crane. Can you describe a counterexample to that argument? Try to describe a situation in which the premises of that argument would be true while its conclusion is false. You cannot, for the argument is valid. There is no such thing as a counterexample to a deductively valid argument!

Exercise 4.2   Go back to the problems in Exercise 4.1 and specify a counterexample for each of the invalid arguments.

Enter Truth: Sound Arguments

Suppose we know that a particular deductive argument is valid. Does it follow that its conclusion is true? As we have seen, the answer is no. An argument need not have true premises in order to qualify as valid. To say that an argument is deductively valid is only to say that *if* its premises are true, then its conclusion must be true. Some valid arguments have true premises, and some have false premises. We have seen examples of both types of cases.

This is why we usually want to know more than whether an argument is valid or invalid. We usually also want to know whether the premises and conclusion are *true*, that is, that they correspond to, or accurately describe, reality. Truth is the ultimate goal of reasoning, or should be if it is not. So, we are looking for more than deductive validity in our deductive arguments: We are looking for truth. A **sound argument** has these two properties:

1. It is deductively valid.
2. Its premises are all true.

In short, a sound argument is a valid argument with premises that are all true.

Suppose an argument is sound. Must its conclusion be true, or might it be false? Break it down: Because any sound argument is valid, it follows that *if* the premises are true, the conclusion *must* be true. Furthermore, the premises of a sound argument are all true. It follows that the conclusion of any sound argument must be true as well. Thus, every sound argument is valid, has true premises, and on account of that has a true conclusion. Because truth is, or should be, the ultimate goal of arguing, it is soundness, rather than mere validity, that we are ultimately interested in when we evaluate deductive arguments.

Lesson: Sound = valid reasoning + all true premises

Caution: Valid Does *Not* Mean True!

Outside of logic class, we often use the words "valid" and "true" interchangeably, as when we say, "You are making a valid point there," or "Your complaint is valid," and so on. This is probably why some students, on first being introduced to the terminology of logic, confuse or mix together the meanings of valid and true. Now, it might be that in everyday life valid means true, but not so in logic! As we have defined our terms, "valid" does *not* mean the same as "true." An argument is valid when it is the case that its conclusion must be true if its premises all are true. On the other hand, a statement is true when it corresponds to reality (otherwise it is false). Thus, validity pertains to arguments, truth pertains to statements. In logic, validity and truth are two very different concepts.

This raises an extremely important yet potentially confusing point: If you reflect on the definition of validity, you will notice that an argument's validity has nothing to do with whether or not its premises are actually true. When we say that a particular argument is valid, we are *not* saying that its premises are true, nor are we saying that its conclusion is true. This is very important. All we are saying is this: *If* its premises are true then its conclusion must be true. It is not required that an argument actually have true premises and a true conclusion to be valid. It follows that in some cases an argument will be valid even though it has false premises and a false conclusion! Study the following examples carefully to reinforce this important point.

The "Rum" Argument: False Premises, False Conclusion, Yet Valid!

1. All people who drink coffee also drink beer.
2. All people who drink beer also drink rum.
3. So, necessarily, all people who drink coffee also drink rum.

The word *necessarily* indicates that this is a deductive argument. Notice that the premises of this argument are false and so is the conclusion. Every statement in this argument is false. Nevertheless, this is a valid argument! It is valid because if, hypothetically, the premises were to be true, then the conclusion would have to be true as well; in other words, it would not be possible for the premises to all be true while the conclusion is false. That is what makes the rum argument a valid argument. This illustrates the point that it is possible for an argument to qualify as valid even though its premises are false and its conclusion is false. Again, true premises are not required for an argument to qualify as valid. Valid does not mean true!

Of course, in many cases, an argument is valid and it also has true premises and a true conclusion. This is the usual case.

The "Dog" Argument: True Premises, True Conclusion, and Valid to Boot

1. All dogs are mammals.
2. No mammals are reptiles.
3. So, certainly no dogs are reptiles.

This argument is valid and it also happens to have true premises, which is nice. Unlike the rum argument, the dog argument is **sound** in addition to being valid.

How to Lose a Million Dollars: True Premises, True Conclusion, but Invalid!

The next argument requires some set up. First, suppose that Joe knows two things:

1. Ann and Bob are cousins.
2. Bob and Chris are cousins.

Second, suppose that Ann and Chris actually are cousins but Joe does **not** know this. One day Joe finds himself a contestant on the popular **Logic Time** TV show and the first question is worth $1 million. The announcer asks, "Are Ann and Chris cousins?" Joe answers, "Yes." This happens to be the correct answer, but before he can collect his $1 million, he must provide solid logical proof that they are indeed cousins. "That's simple," Joe says. "Here is the argument." Now Joe writes this on the board:

1. Ann and Bob are cousins.
2. Bob and Chris are cousins.
3. Therefore, it *must* be that Ann and Chris are cousins!

That's $1 million down the drain. (Can you explain why?) Notice that this argument has true premises and a true conclusion, but its reasoning is invalid. The reasoning is invalid because the premises do not conclusively prove the conclusion. It is **not** the case that if the premises are true then the conclusion **must** be true, for it is at least possible the premises are true and the conclusion is false. This example shows that true premises are not sufficient by themselves to make an argument valid. In this case, true premises and a true conclusion do not add up to validity!

Caution: Invalid Does *Not* Mean False!

It is equally important to keep the following point in mind: When we say that an argument is invalid, we are *not* saying that its premises are false, nor are we saying that its conclusion is false. In some cases, an argument will be invalid even though its premises are true and its conclusion is true. No lie! Consider the following example.

The Mountain Argument: True Premises, True Conclusion, Yet Invalid

1. The state of Washington has mountains.
2. The state of Oregon has mountains.
3. California borders Oregon.
4. Therefore, California must have mountains, too.

That one certainly gets the gong. If someone knew nothing about the state of California, the premises of this argument would not conclusively prove that it contains mountains! Of course, in other cases, an argument will have false premises and a false conclusion, and it will be invalid, as in the next example.

The Canada Argument: False, False, False, and Invalid to Boot

1. Canada is south of Mexico.
2. Mexico is north of Alaska.
3. Therefore, the population of Mexico is greater than the population of China.

However, it is important to keep in mind that the mere fact alone, that an argument has false premises and a false conclusion, does not mean that the argument is deductively invalid. False premises combined with a false conclusion is not what makes an argument invalid. Some arguments have false premises and a false conclusion and yet are *valid* (recall the rum argument). It will pay to keep the following in mind:

- The mere fact that a deductive argument has all true premises and a true conclusion does *not* make it a valid argument.
- The mere fact that a deductive argument has false premises and a false conclusion does *not* make it an invalid argument.
- In some cases a deductive argument can have false premises and a false conclusion and yet nevertheless be valid.
- In some cases a deductive argument can have true premises and a true conclusion and yet nevertheless be invalid.

How Not to Make One of the *Worst* of All Logical Errors

Aristotle thought that one of the all-time worst errors in reasoning is this: To pass from truth to falsity in a single act of reasoning, that is, to start out with all true premises and end in a false conclusion. How can you minimize the chance of committing this error? Make sure your deductive arguments are valid! But how do you do that? How do you know for sure that your deductive arguments are really valid? The answer is this: There are standards, templates of correct reasoning, which, if obeyed, ensure that your deductive arguments are valid. You will learn the first of these logical templates in the next unit.

Exercise 4.3   The following questions allow you an opportunity to demonstrate your understanding.

1. Can an argument be true or false? Explain.
2. Can a valid argument contain false premises? Back up your answer with an example of your own creation.
3. Can a valid argument have a false conclusion? Back up your answer with an example of your own creation.
4. Can an invalid argument contain true premises? Back up your answer with an example of your own creation.
5. Can an invalid argument have a true conclusion? Back up your answer with an example of your own creation.
6. What is the *only* combination of truth and falsity with respect to premises and conclusion that a valid argument cannot possibly have?

Two Ways an Argument Can Go Wrong

It follows, from all that has been said so far, that there are two ways an argument can go wrong. First, an argument might have flawed reasoning. In a deductive argument, this would be reasoning that is invalid. Second, an argument might have one or more false premises. If the argument is deductive, false premises would automatically make the argument unsound. As we have seen, an argument could have faulty reasoning but true premises, and an argument could have good reasoning but false premises.

> **Lesson:** An argument can go wrong in two completely different ways: (a) flawed reasoning; or (b) one or more false premises.

An Ineffective Way to Criticize an Argument

Many people believe that the proper way to criticize an argument is to argue for the opposite of the argument's conclusion. For example, if an argument concludes that justice is equality of outcomes, they might object by arguing that justice is not outcome equality. However, this is not an effective way to criticize an argument. Let us see why. Suppose Joe presents an argument for the conclusion such and such is the case, and in response Jane presents an argument for the conclusion that such and such is *not* the case. The result is simply a logical standoff. He says tomato, she says tom-ah-to. The problem is that neither argument *engages* the reasoning of the other. There is no dialogue here, no dialectic. This conflict is going nowhere. There is a better way to engage the reasoning of another person.

Two Ways to Effectively Criticize an Argument

There are two ways to effectively criticize an argument. The first way is to produce an argument against one of the *premises* of the target argument. This would be an argument whose conclusion is the claim that one of the premises of the target argument is false. The second way to effectively critique or object to an argument is to show that the argument's reasoning is flawed. If the argument is deductive, this would involve showing that the reasoning of the target argument is invalid. How do you show someone his or her reasoning is flawed? In subsequent chapters you will learn many practical and effective methods for accomplishing this important logical task.

> **Lesson:** There are two completely different ways to effectively criticize an argument: (a) Argue that a premise is false, and (b) argue that the reasoning is flawed.

Exercise 4.4   Which of the following statements are true and which are false?

1. Some deductive arguments have true premises and yet they are invalid.
2. Some deductive arguments are invalid and yet they have a true conclusion.
3. A deductive argument can have false premises and a false conclusion and yet be valid nevertheless.

4. Some sound arguments have false premises.

5. All sound arguments have true premises and are also valid.

6. Some sound arguments are invalid.

7. All invalid arguments have false premises.

8. If the premises of a deductive argument are all true and the conclusion is true, then the argument must be deductively valid.

9. If the premises of a deductive argument are all false and the conclusion is false, then the argument must be deductively invalid.

10. An argument can be invalid and yet have a true conclusion.

11. Some invalid arguments have true premises.

12. All valid arguments have true premises.

Appendix 4.1   Fun with Logic!

Solving Brainteasers Using Deductive Reasoning

Do you like brainteasers? If you do, then you will probably enjoy the logic puzzles invented by the philosopher and logician Raymond Smullyan. One way to solve logic puzzles such as the ones created by Professor Smullyan is to start out by developing a grid or table that systematically shows all the logical possibilities. After that is complete, you find the solution by eliminating, on logical grounds, all the possibilities except one, which will inevitably be the only solution. Solving Smullyan's brainteasers is thus an exercise in deductive reasoning.

The Magical Island of Knights and Knaves

Each of the following problems is adapted from Raymond Smullyan's classic *What Is the Name of This Book?* (New York: Touchstone, 1986). For each problem, you are to imagine that you have been transported to a mysterious island, the Island of Knights and Knaves. Every inhabitant of this island is either a knight or a knave. Every knight always tells the truth and every knave always lies. Unfortunately, knights and knaves cannot be distinguished in terms of appearance; they can only be distinguished by applying deductive reasoning to what they say! In each case, explain your reasoning.

Exercise 4.5   Knights and Knaves

1. The Strange Case of the Silent One in Red
Late one night, you come across three strangers, one dressed in black, one in white, and one in red. The one in red remains silent, but the other two speak:

Black: All of us are knaves.
White: Exactly one of us is a knight.

What are these individuals? Knights? Knaves? Which is which?

2. Tall Guy and Short Guy Puzzle

One morning, two individuals present themselves to you. One is very tall and the other is very short. The tall one says, "I am a knave and/or Shorty here is a knight." Now, with only that statement to go on, what are these two individuals? Is the tall one knight or knave? Is the short one knight or knave?

3. Three Weird-Looking Dudes

Three individuals approach you. The first says, "The second one is a knave." The second says, "The first and third are of the same type." What kind of being is the third?

4. The Case of the Mysterious Circler

One evening you come across an individual who slowly circles around you and quietly says, "Either I am a knave or 2 + 3 = 5." What is he? Knight or knave?

5. The "Either I Am a Knight or I Am Not a Knight" Gas Attendant

You stop for gas and the attendant says, "Either I am a knight or I am not a knight." What is he?

6. The Case of the Mysterious Guard

You approach an old fort and the guard standing in front says, "I am a knight and I am not a knight." What is he?

7. Could Anyone Here Say That?

Is the following event possible? An inhabitant of the island speaks the words "I am a knave."

8. Two Cautious Guys

Two strange-looking individuals cautiously approach you. The first says, "Neither of us is a knight." The second is silent. What are they?

Exercise 4.6   Recall that an enthymeme is an argument that is missing a premise or a conclusion. This exercise will deepen your understanding of validity and of enthymemes. Each of the following is an enthymematic deductive argument missing a premise. In each case, add a premise so as to make the argument valid.

1. All reptiles are cold-blooded, so your pet is cold-blooded.
2. If Ann swims today, Bob will swim today. So, Bob will swim today.

3. We will either take our bikes or we will walk. So, we'll be walking.

4. The universe exists. Therefore, the universe has a cause.

5. Human thoughts are not spatial objects. Therefore, human thoughts are not physical objects.

6. Each human thought is an existent entity. Therefore, each human thought has a location in space.

7. All human actions have causes. So, no human action is an act of free will.

8. Spiders are not insects, for insects have six legs.

9. Ed must be unhappy, for he is scowling.

10. That is a particle of matter. Therefore, it has mass.

11. Ann lives in Las Vegas. So, Ann lives in Nevada.

12. Liberace was a great pianist. Therefore, Liberace was a great musician.

Glossary

Counterexample to a deductive argument A description of a possible situation in which the premises are true and the conclusion is false (which shows that the argument is not deductively valid).

Intuitive test A test based on common sense.

Invalid deductive argument A deductive argument that has the following feature: It is possible its premises all are true and its conclusion is false.

Logically Possible Any state of affairs, circumstance, statement, etc., no matter how improbable, that is not self-contradictory.

Method of counterexample Show that an argument is invalid by presenting a counterexample to the argument.

Self-contradiction A statement of the form "P and it is not the case that P," where P is a variable standing in for a declarative sentence.

Sound argument A deductive argument that is valid and that also has true premises.

Valid deductive argument A deductive argument that has the following feature: If the premises all are true, the conclusion must be true.

5 How to Evaluate an Inductive Argument « « «

What Is a Strong Argument?

Recall that an inductive argument aims to show that *if* its premises all are true, then its conclusion, although not certain to be true, is *probably* true. If an inductive argument succeeds in its aim, we call it a **strong argument**. A strong argument is thus an argument in which the conclusion is *probably* true, although not certainly true if its premises all are true. Put another way, a strong argument has this key feature: If its premises all are true, then its conclusion is probable, although not certain. An inductive argument that is not strong is said to be a **weak inductive argument**. A weak inductive argument is therefore an inductive argument in which it is not the case that if its premises all are true then its conclusion is probably true.

> **Lesson:** A *strong argument* is an inductive argument that has the following feature: *If* its premises all are true, then its conclusion is *probably* true, although not certain.

When learning an abstract idea, it can help to hear it explained in more than one way. The following are other equivalent ways logicians have defined inductive strength:

- A strong argument is such that its premises, if true, make the truth of its conclusion probable although not certain.
- In the case of a strong argument, the conclusion is probably true, although not certain, if the premises all are true.
- In a strong argument, the conclusion follows with probability, although not with certainty, from the premises.

- In a strong argument, the premises and conclusion are related in such a way that it is improbable that the premises all are true while the conclusion is false.

Examples

Consider the following argument:

1. Every day for the past year, Jones has had three cheeseburgers for lunch.
2. He is about to eat lunch today.
3. Therefore, he will probably eat three cheeseburgers.

The presence of the word *probably* signals that this is an inductive argument, thus an argument claiming that if the premises are true then the conclusion is probably true although not certain. Suppose that the premises of the argument are indeed true. Based on that, is the conclusion *probably* true? The answer is "yes," isn't it? The premises really do support the conclusion in the sense that if the premises are true, then on account of that the conclusion is indeed probably true. The conclusion is not certain, it is not established conclusively, as in a valid argument, but the information contained in the premises does make the conclusion likely or probable, doesn't it? This is a strong argument. Now consider this argument:

1. I've known three people from New York, and all three were Catholic.
2. The Stern brothers are from New York.
3. Therefore, the Stern brothers are very likely Catholic.

The phrase "very likely" tells us this is an inductive argument. The underlying claim is thus: If the premises are true, then the conclusion is probable. However, is the claim correct in this case? If the premises are true, does that information alone make the conclusion "very likely" to be true? What do you think? This is surely a weak argument. In the case of a weak inductive argument, the truth of its premise or premises would not be enough to make its conclusion probably true. That is, even if, hypothetically, the premises were to be true, that alone would *not* make its conclusion probably true.

Examine the following arguments to strengthen your understanding of this important concept. Each of these is a strong argument:

1. The Chugiak Mountains surrounding Anchorage, Alaska, are known as a haven for dense swarms of mosquitoes in the summer months.
2. Indeed, the mosquito has been named the Alaska state bird.
3. Therefore, when we go hiking in the Chugiaks this summer, we will probably suffer numerous mosquito bites.

1. It is illegal to own a lion within the city limits.
2. Most people are law-abiding.
3. Therefore, when we go for a walk in the city today, it is unlikely we will be attacked by a lion.

1. Tiny Tim was a great musician who created wonderful music that appeals to almost everyone.
2. A new CD of previously unreleased material is coming out next year.
3. Therefore, it will probably contain wonderful music that will appeal to almost everyone.

In contrast, each of the following arguments would seem to be rather weak:

1. I have visited Washington, DC twice.
2. Both times, it was raining when I arrived.
3. Both trips were in January.
4. Therefore, when I travel to Washington, DC next August, it will probably be raining when I arrive.

1. We interviewed three people at random and two of them said they are voting for Smith for governor.
2. Therefore, we predict that Smith will probably be elected governor.

1. The last two Christmases in Seattle have been rainy ones.
2. Therefore, the next Christmas in Seattle will be rainy.

1. I've owned two Fords—both pickup trucks—and they were both mechanically sound.
2. I am about to buy my first Ford sedan.
3. It will probably also be mechanically sound.

Enter Truth: Cogent Arguments

If an inductive argument is strong, and, in addition, it has all true premises, then we call it a **cogent argument**. (Some logicians use the term "sound inductive argument" instead of "cogent argument.") Thus, a cogent inductive argument has two properties:

1. It is strong.
2. Its premises are all true.

Must its conclusion be true as well? Not necessarily! The conclusion of a cogent argument will be *probably* true, of course, but that does not make it certain to be true. Here are two cogent arguments:

1. The past 25 years it has snowed at least once a year in Nome, Alaska.
2. Therefore, it is highly probable that it will snow at least once next year in Nome.

1. The sun has risen every morning for the past 200 years.
2. Therefore, it will probably rise tomorrow morning.

In each case, there is a true premise, but no absolute guarantee on the conclusion!

Shifting gears, although the following inductive argument is strong, it is not cogent because it has a false premise:

1. It has been snowing every day in Seattle for the past 50 years.
2. The sky is full of snow clouds right now.
3. Therefore, it very probably will snow in Seattle tomorrow.

This argument is strong because *if* its premises were to be true, in that case its conclusion would be highly probable. However, at least one of its premises is false, which means it does not rise to the level of being a cogent argument. In addition to being strong, an inductive argument must also have all true premises to qualify as cogent!

Lesson: Cogent = strong reasoning + all true premises

Caution: Strong Does Not Mean True!

Suppose an inductive argument is strong. Does it follow from that fact alone that its premises are true? No, it does not. Remember that in logic, strong does *not* mean true. Strong is a term that applies to inductive arguments when they have this feature: *If* the premises of the argument all are true, then the conclusion *probably* is true, although the conclusion is not certain to be true.

Thus, when we say that a particular inductive argument is strong, we are *not* saying that its premises are true, nor are we saying that its conclusion is true. We are only saying that *if* its premises are true, then its conclusion is probably true (although less than certain). An inductive argument's strength thus has nothing directly to do with whether or not its premises are actually true.

The Snow in Dallas Argument: False Premises
and False Conclusion, but Strong!

Indeed, an inductive argument can have false premises and a false conclusion and yet still qualify as strong. Here is an example:

1. It has been snowing in Dallas, Texas, for 60 days straight.
2. Today in Dallas, Texas, the sky is completely full of snow clouds, and the temperature is 25 degrees, perfect for snow.
3. Therefore, it will probably snow in Dallas today, October 28, 2011, although it is not certain.

This example illustrates the fact that true premises and a true conclusion are *not* required for an inductive argument to be a strong one.

Of course, in many cases an inductive argument is strong, and in addition it also has true premises and a conclusion that is very probably true as well, which is nice, as in the following example.

The Sunrise Argument: True Premises, True Conclusion, and Strong

1. The sun has risen and set every day in recorded history.
2. That's a lot of days.
3. Therefore, the sun will probably rise and set tomorrow as well.

Lesson: Be careful not to confuse cogent with strong.

Caution: Weak Does Not Mean False!

Consider next this feature of induction. When we say that an argument is inductively weak, we are *not* saying that its premises are false, nor are we saying that its conclusion is false. Some inductively *weak* arguments have true premises and a true conclusion, such as this one.

The Burrito Argument: True Premises, True Conclusion, but Weak!

1. Yesterday, Jack had a burrito for lunch.
2. Jack worked 10 hours today.
3. Therefore, Jack will probably have a burrito for lunch tomorrow, too.

Let us suppose Jack did eat a burrito for lunch yesterday and he loved it. Let us grant the claim that he worked 10 hours today. Let us also suppose, independently of the information in the argument, that tomorrow Jack will order a burrito for lunch. Nevertheless, the reasoning in this argument, from the premises to conclusion, is really *weak*, isn't it? Given only the information contained in the premises—on the basis of that alone—we do not have a very good reason to suppose the conclusion is going to be true. It seems that an argument can have true premises and even a true conclusion and nevertheless be weak. It will pay to keep the following points in mind.

- The fact that an inductive argument has all true premises and a true conclusion does not alone make it a strong argument.
- The fact that an inductive argument has false premises and a false conclusion does not alone make it a weak argument.
- In some cases an inductive argument can have false premises and a false conclusion and yet nevertheless be strong.
- In some cases an inductive argument can have true premises and a true conclusion and yet nevertheless be weak.

How Not to Make One of the *Worst* of All Logical Errors—Again

As you will recall, Aristotle thought that one of the all-time worst errors in reasoning is passing from truth to falsity in an argument: starting out with true premises and ending with a false conclusion. How does one minimize the chance of committing this error in an inductive argument? Make sure your inductive arguments are as strong as possible! But how does one do that? How does one know for sure whether or not one's inductive arguments are strong? There are standards, principles of reasoning that, if obeyed, ensure that your inductive reasoning is as strong as it can be. We examine these standards in Unit Five.

Exercise 5.1   Which of the following statements are true and which are false?

1. All inductively strong arguments have all true premises.
2. Some cogent arguments have false premises.
3. Some inductive arguments have true premises and yet they are weak.
4. Some inductive arguments are weak and yet they have a true conclusion.
5. An inductive argument can have false premises and a false conclusion and yet be strong.
6. Some cogent arguments are weak.
7. If the premises of an inductive argument are all true, and the conclusion is true, then the argument must be inductively strong.

8. If the premises of an inductive argument are all false, and the conclusion is false, then the argument must be inductively weak.

9. If the premises of an inductive argument are all true, and the conclusion is true, then the argument must be cogent.

10. If the premises of an inductive argument are all false, then the argument must not be cogent.

Exercise 5.2   Assume each of the following arguments is inductive. In each case, is the argument strong or weak?

1. The bank robber accidentally left behind his checkbook. He also dropped his wallet which contained his driver's license. Both items were traced to Joe Doakes, who was trying to hide $10,000 in his coat when the police arrived. The bank robber escaped with $10,000 but was also covered with red dye when the dye pack exploded. Joe Doakes was found to be covered with red dye. The obvious conclusion is that Joe robbed the bank.

2. Exercising daily helps prevent heart attacks. Don exercises daily. Therefore, Don will probably never suffer a heart attack.

3. It was sunny in Seattle yesterday for the first time in four weeks. Therefore, it will probably be sunny in Seattle all next week.

4. Ed is walking the 12 miles to downtown. He just left five minutes ago. He walks at an ordinary pace. Therefore, probably he has not arrived yet.

5. Few cats are orange colored. I hear a cat meowing across the street. The cat meowing is probably not orange.

6. A Purdue University study found that rats consumed many more calories and put on weight when they were fed artificial sweeteners before meals. The sweeteners were found to cause powerful urges to eat—urges the rats could not control. The study was repeated five times, with the same results each time. But humans and rats have similar digestive systems. Therefore, artificial sweeteners probably increase weight in humans as well.

7. Planets have been discovered orbiting many stars. The stars found with orbiting planets all have in common six characteristics. No star lacking planets has been found to have all six characteristics. A new star has been discovered and it has all six characteristics. It is probable that the new star has planets.

8. One thousand coffee drinkers selected randomly from all walks of life, from all ages, and from spots all around the city, were interviewed and 10% said they add sugar to their coffee. Therefore, probably 10% of the city's coffee drinkers add sugar to their coffee.

9. Eight people at the Army recruiting center were interviewed and all of them said they believe the war is justified. Therefore, probably everyone believes the war is justified.

10. Polar bear attacks on humans have been increasing over the past several years in certain parts of the Arctic. Scientists studying the attacks have discovered only one common variable present in each case: The animals had been disturbed by certain specific noises emanating from large cargo airplanes and scientific research stations. Moreover, these specific noises do not seem to be present in areas where the attacks are not increasing. Therefore, the attacks are probably caused by the disturbances in question.

Deduction and Induction Contrasted

Deductive reasoning and inductive reasoning have some features in common. In both types of reasoning, the aim is to adequately support the conclusion, that is, to provide adequate reason to believe the conclusion is true. Both types of reasoning base the conclusion on one or more premises. But there are also big differences between the two types of reasoning. The most important is this: Deductive validity does not come in degrees, but inductive strength does. Validity is an all-or-nothing matter. A deductive argument is either valid or it is invalid; there is no middle ground. Thus, it can never be the case that one deductive argument is more valid than another, or that one deductive argument is less valid than another. On the other hand, inductive strength comes in degrees; it is not an all-or-nothing affair, for some inductive arguments are stronger than others, and some are weaker than others.

Exercise 5.3 Assume each of the following arguments is inductive. In each case, state a premise that, if added, would make the argument stronger. Then state a premise that, if added, would make the argument weaker.

1. At the crime scene, the police found these items belonging to the suspect Jones: his phone (apparently dropped during the confusion), his coat with his name in it, and his car keys. Therefore, Jones probably did it.

2. At the crime scene, the police found no direct evidence that Jones was present; however, an eyewitness identified Jones from a police lineup. Unfortunately, the witness had been extremely inebriated at the time the crime was committed.

3. Since moving into the neighborhood a week ago, we have heard loud rock music every night coming from the corner house. Therefore, tonight we will probably hear loud rock music coming from the corner house.

4. Joe has eaten lunch at Grinders Hot Sands every day for the past week. Each time, he orders the meatball grinder and a whack-whack salad. So, he will probably have the same thing today.

5. Tiny Tim is one of Lorraine's favorite artists. She owns every one of his records and CDs. A new CD of unreleased material is coming out tomorrow, titled *Long Live Tiny Tim*. Lorraine will probably buy it.

6. Baby, the cat, loves tuna and she rarely turns down food. Therefore, when we put this tuna out for her, she will likely gobble it up.

7. It has been raining for six days straight. Therefore, it will probably rain tomorrow.

8. We interviewed 20 people at the coffee shop, and 10 of them said they believe in UFOs. Therefore, probably half the population believes in UFOs.

9. The price of gas usually goes up when there is serious trouble in the Middle East. A very large demonstration was held in Libya today and a number of demonstrators were killed. Therefore, the price of gas will probably go up.

10. The weather has been unusually dry. Therefore, the orange crop will probably be smaller than usual this year.

Glossary

Cogent argument An inductive argument that is strong and that also has true premises.

Strong argument An inductive argument that has the following feature: If the premises are true, the conclusion is probably true; that is, the truth of the premises would make the conclusion probable.

Weak inductive argument An inductive argument that has the following feature: The truth of all the premises would not make the conclusion probable.

6

Logical Relations and Concluding Matters « « « « « « « « «

Many logic teachers will skip this chapter, opting instead to cover the logical relations later in the book where they are explored in exquisite detail as we visit the different specialized branches of logic. Other teachers will make this chapter part of the course base. It's all good, either way one goes!

So far we have been concerned with the logical properties of arguments: validity, invalidity, strength, weakness, soundness and cogency. But in everyday life, we use our power of reasoning to do more than just evaluate arguments. We also use reason to determine whether or not our beliefs stand in *logical conflict*. Reasoning is again employed when we have to decide what is *implied* by something we believe. We also use reason to determine whether or not one statement is logically *equivalent* to another. Finally, we reason when we decide whether something is *necessarily* so, or only *contingently* so. Each of these fundamental logical concepts is related to validity and invalidity and thus to the proper evaluation of arguments.

When Claims Conflict

Logical Consistency

Two or more statements are **logically consistent** if there is any possibility, no matter how unlikely, remote, or improbable, that they are all true. Consider the following two statements:

1. Abraham Lincoln ate three pieces of cherry pie on his 13th birthday in 1822.

2. John F. Kennedy ate three pieces of cherry pie on his 13th birthday in 1930.

Is it *possible* both of these statements are true? Of course it is *improbable* that both are true, but we are not concerned here with probability. The question is this: Is it *possible* that both statements are true? Certainly it is. Therefore, the two statements are logically consistent. Recall that in logic, something counts as logically possible as long as it does not contain or imply a self-contradiction. There is no contradiction in these two statements being true; therefore, it is possible they both are true, and therefore they are logically consistent.

It is very important to note this: It is not required, for two or more statements to be consistent, that they are all actually true. The statements might all be true, they might all be false, and it could be that one is false. All that is required is the *possibility* that they are all true. Thus, whether two or more statements actually are true or false has no bearing on their consistency. The mere possibility that two or more statements are true is all it takes for the statements to be consistent!

Logical Inconsistency

Two or more statements are **logically inconsistent** if it is not possible they are all true. Suppose Maxine has long believed that Ringo Starr is the only drummer the Beatles ever had. One day she learns that Pete Best was the drummer for the Beatles before Ringo joined the group. Maxine's two beliefs about the history of the Beatles now stand in logical conflict: They cannot both be true. To remain consistent, Maxine must give up at least one of her (inconsistent) beliefs.

It is important to note this important fact: It is not required, for two or more statements to be inconsistent, that they are all false. All that is required is that it is not possible all of the statements are true. In the following example, the statements are inconsistent even though one is *true*:

1. Kobe Bryant is over 30 years old.
2. Kobe Bryant is under 30 years old.

Application: Courts of Law

Why do trial attorneys ask witnesses in the courtroom so many questions? One reason has to do with logical consistency. Attorneys know that if the witness is making up a false story, it is likely that under intense questioning he will forget some of the earlier details he has given and will contradict himself. If the witness contradicts himself, then his testimony is inconsistent. But if his statements are inconsistent, then not all of his statements are true, which means at least one of his statements must be false. That means he is not telling "the whole truth and nothing but the truth." Suddenly the witness has no credibility; the cross-examination "tripped him up." The test of consistency plays a big role in the courtroom, but we also use the consistency test in everyday life, don't we? Can you think of examples?

The Dreaded Socratic "Elenchus"

As we have seen, the ancient Greek philosopher Socrates (470–399 BC) was famous for asking people lots of questions, but not just any questions. The Socratic method consisted in asking people questions carefully chosen to cause them to look in the mirror and evaluate their own core beliefs and values in terms of rational, realistic standards. The argument format known as the **Socratic elenchus** was an important part of the Socratic method. Typically, an elenchus begins with Socrates asking someone the following question:

"So you say X?"

After the other person replies, "Yes, Socrates, I believe X is true!" Socrates says, "But you also believe statement Y, don't you?"

Now Y is a statement everyone knows is true because it is well-supported by evidence, so the other person admits that, yes, he does indeed believe that Y is true. Socrates then shows that statements X and Y are logically *inconsistent*. They cannot both be true! It follows, of course, that at least one of them *must* be false. The other person now has a choice to make, assuming he wants to be consistent: Give up belief X, or give up belief Y. If belief Y is much more solidly grounded in reality than belief X, then the logical choice is obvious.

Relation to Deductive Validity

How do consistency and inconsistency relate to validity? Suppose argument A is deductively valid: It is not possible that the premises all are true, yet the conclusion is at the same time false. It follows that the truth of its premises is *inconsistent* with the falsity of its conclusion. In general, if an argument is deductively valid, then the falsity of its conclusion is logically inconsistent with the truth of its premises. That's how consistency relates to validity. Here is a brief example:

1. All hamsters are cute.
2. Horatio is a hamster.
3. Therefore, Horatio is certainly cute.

It would be inconsistent to assert the premises of this argument and then to deny the conclusion. That is, it would be inconsistent to assert all three of the following statements:

1. All hamsters are cute.
2. Horatio is a hamster.
3. But it is false that Horatio is cute.

Because this is a valid argument, one cannot agree with the premises and deny the conclusion and remain logically consistent. On pain of inconsistency, if you agree with the premises then you must accept the conclusion. That's a valid argument for you; they are always like that.

Exercise 6.1   In each case, are the sentences consistent or inconsistent?

1. Some hamsters are pets. Some hamsters are not pets.
2. Some hamsters are pets. It is false that some hamsters are pets.
3. No hamsters are pets. At least one hamster is not a pet.
4. No hamsters are pets. Some hamsters are pets.
5. All hamsters are pets. Some hamsters are not pets.
6. Someone is 21. Someone is 44.
7. Nobody is 21. Nobody is 66.
8. Everybody is 77. Nobody is over 60.
9. Somebody is 10. Nobody is older than 100.
10. Joe believes it is Friday. It is Thursday.
11. Jan believes that action X is morally right. Action X is not morally right.
12. The Earth is perfectly flat. The Earth is round.
13. $1 + 1 = 2. 1 + 1 = 4$.
14. Someone believes that $1 + 1 = 2$. Someone believes that $1 + 1 = 88$.
15. Someone is older than 21. Someone is younger than 12.
16. Someone won a million-dollar lottery 10 times in a row. Someone won $10 million at the Tulalip Casino—10 days in a row.

Exercise 6.2   Are statements A and B logically consistent? Or are they logically inconsistent? Back up your answer with an argument.

(1) A. The universe was created by an all-good, all-powerful, all-knowing, loving God.
     B. The universe contains large quantities of suffering and moral evil.
(2) A. Income and wealth are unequally distributed.
     B. Social justice exists.
(3) A. Every event is completely determined by antecedent conditions.
     B. Human beings have free will.

Implication

One statement **implies** a second statement when the following is the case:

If the first statement is true, then the second one *must* be true.

In other words, it would not be possible that the first statement is true but the second is false. For example, the statement "Maria is 21" implies the statement "Maria is older than 10." The first statement implies the second because *if* the first is true, then the second *must* be true. Examine the following examples to clarify this important logical idea in your mind. In each case, the first statement implies the second one:

1: Jose is 21 years old.	2: Jose is not a teenager.
1: Sue is 13.	2: Sue is a teenager.
1: Ed is 40.	2: Ed is older than 30.
1: Julio is 16.	2: Julio is under 21.
1: Margarita is 30.	2: Margarita is legally an adult.

Notice that in each example, although the first statement implies the second, the reverse does not hold: The second statement does not imply the first. In each of the following examples, the first statement does not imply the second because it is possible the first is true and the second is false:

1: Julio is rich.	2: Julio is materialistic.
1: Julio is religious.	2: Julio is Catholic.
1: Julio is Hindu.	2: Julio lives in India.
1: Julio is French.	2: Julio lives in Paris.
1: Julio is married.	2: Julio has six children.
1: Julio has three sons.	2: Julio is married.

Implication and Falsity

It is extremely important that you understand the next point. A statement P can imply a statement Q even when both are actually false. For example:

P: Joe Blow is exactly 110 years old.
Q: Joe Blow is over 100 years old.

Suppose Joe Blow is only 40 years old. Both statements are false, yet it is still the case that the first statement logically *implies* the second. Thus, one statement can imply a second even though both are *false*.

Implication and Sets of Statements

A group ("set") of several statements can also imply a given statement. Formally, a group of statements implies a further statement if and only if the further statement *must* be true if all the members of the group are true. Consider this group of three statements:

1. All accountants working at the XYZ company have MBA degrees.
2. Maria is an accountant.
3. Maria works at the XYZ company.

If all the members of this group of statements are true, then the following statement must also be true:

4. Maria has an MBA degree.

In other words, the group of statements 1, 2, and 3 implies the further statement 4.

Relation to Deductive Validity

How does implication relate to validity? Suppose argument A is deductively valid. It follows that its premises, considered as a group of statements, logically imply its conclusion, for this is just to say that if the premises of argument A all are true, then the conclusion of the argument must be true too. In general, the premises of a valid argument will always logically imply the argument's conclusion. That's how implication relates to validity.

Application: Socrates, Implication, and Finding Truth

Implication is "truth-preserving." This means that if we start with a statement already known to be true, call it P, and then we consider a further statement that is logically *implied* by the initial statement P, the further statement *must* also be true. In other words, implication can never take us from truth to falsity; if we start with truth, implication takes us only to further truth.

How does this relate to you? If you are interested in finding the truth, no matter what it is, then you will not turn a blind eye to the logical implications of those things you already know to be true. If you are sure that X is true, and then you discover that X logically implies Y, then you will accept Y as true as well. The result is more truth, of course, which is always a good thing.

It was this concern for truth, and the relation logical implication has to it, that led Socrates to one of his most enduring principles: When engaged in honest reasoning, follow the argument wherever it leads, even if it leads to a conclusion you do not want to believe. If an argument is deductively valid, then it logically implies its conclusion. To dismiss the argument merely because it has a conclusion you do not want to hear is to flee from the truth. To follow the argument to its logical conclusion is to attain more truth (if the premises are indeed true). And in the long run, more truth will always be a good thing, or so argued Socrates.

Using Implication to Ferret Out Falsehood

Suppose you believe that statement P is true although you are not certain it is true. Now suppose after investigating the matter you discover two things:

(a) Statement P logically implies statement Q.

(b) Statement Q is false.

It logically follows that statement P *must* be false. Here is why. If P implies Q, then it is not possible that P is true and Q is false. If Q is false, and if P implies Q, then P *must* be false too, as it is not possible that P is true while Q is false. Here is the general principle: If you believe that a statement P is true, and then you discover that P logically implies Q and that Q is false, then you ought to conclude that P is false as well. An understanding of implication can thus help us uncover falsehood.

Exercise 6.3   In each case, does P imply Q? Yes or no?

1. P: Jim is 21. Q: Jim is older than 20.

2. P: Someone is 21. Q: Someone is older than 12.

3. P: Jim is 99. Q: Someone is 99.

4. P: Someone is 99. Q: Jim is 99.

5. P: Someone is older than 44. Q: Someone is younger than 35.

6. P: Figure A has four equal sides and four equal angles. Q: Figure A is a square.

7. P: Jan could not have done otherwise than what she just did. Q: Jan is not morally responsible for what she just did.

8. P: The number n is an even number. Q: The number n is divisible by 2.

9. P: Jan is a millionaire. Q: Jan is a Republican.

10. P: Jan is a Buddhist. Q: Jan was born in India.

11. The universe has a cause. God exists.

12. Figure A has four equal sides. Figure A is a square.

13. Number n is divisible by 2. Number n is even.

14. Pat is a human being. Pat has human rights.

15. Doing X increases the total amount of happiness in the world. Doing X is morally required.

16. All members of the XYZ club are members of the ABC club. All members of the ABC club are members of the XYZ club.

17. The mind has a property that the brain does not have. The mind is not the brain.

18. The temperature is over 80 degrees. The temperature is over 70 degrees.

Logical Equivalence

Two statements are logically equivalent if and only if they imply each other. In other words, **equivalence** is a logical relation that holds between two statements P and Q when P implies Q and Q implies P. The following two statements are equivalent:

P: Paul is taller than Ringo.
Q: Ringo is shorter than Paul.

These two statements are equivalent because they imply each other. If one is true, then the other must be true, too, and vice versa. It follows that if two statements are equivalent, then it is not possible that they ever differ as to truth and falsity.

Notice that two statements can be equivalent even though both are false. For instance, the following two statements are equivalent even though both are false:

P: Dennis Rodman is shorter than Danny DeVito.
Q: Danny DeVito is taller than Dennis Rodman.

Of course, two statements can be both true and equivalent at the same time as well. For instance:

P: Al Gore is older than Barack Obama.
Q: Barack Obama is younger than Al Gore.

Each of the following pairs of statements is a pair of logically equivalent statements. Notice that in each case, the two statements will always match insofar as truth and falsity are concerned:

P: Sue is married to Ron.   Q: Ron is married to Sue.
P: Sue is taller than Ron.   Q: Ron is shorter than Sue.
P: Sue is exactly as old as Ron.   Q: Ron is exactly as old as Sue.
P: Joe is older than Pete.   Q: Pete is younger than Joe.
P: Sue is 33.   Q: Sue is older than 32 but younger than 34.
P: Ed is the same height as Ann.   Q: Ann is the same height as Ed.
P: Some cats are pets.   Q: Some pets are cats.

Application: Use Equivalence to Fix an Argument

Suppose you present a valid, or a strong, argument to someone, but that person does not understand one of your premises. One solution is to replace the problem premise with a logically equivalent statement that makes more sense to the person. If the replacement statement is equivalent to the statement it replaces, then the argument must remain valid (or strong) after the replacement, for switching one statement for its equivalent cannot affect the validity or strength of an argument.

Here is an analogy. Suppose Kim's old Chevy is running well. If a mechanic removes the carburetor and replaces it with an identically functioning carburetor, then the car will be running well after the replacement, right? Similarly, if you remove a poorly stated premise from a valid or strong argument and replace it with a statement that is an improvement, the argument will remain valid (or strong) if the replacement is logically equivalent to the statement taken out.

Relation to Deductive Validity

How does equivalence relate to validity? Suppose argument A is deductively valid. Suppose you remove a premise from argument A and replace it with a logically equivalent statement. Argument A must remain valid—if the replacement sentence is equivalent to the sentence replaced. In general, when you replace one sentence in a valid argument with a logically equivalent sentence, the argument remains valid. Likewise, of course, if you replace one sentence in an inductively strong argument with a logically equivalent sentence, the argument remains exactly as strong as it was before.

Exercise 6.4   In each case, are the two statements P and Q logically equivalent?

1. P: Jim is 21.   Q: Jim is older than 20 and less than 22.
2. P: Someone is 21.   Q: Someone is older than 20.
3. P: Jim is 99.   Q: Someone is 99.
4. P: Someone is 99.   Q: Someone is 89.
5. P: Someone is older than 44.   Q: Someone is 44.
6. P: Figure A has four equal angles.   Q: Figure A is a square.
7. P: Jan likes Pete.   Q: Pete likes Jan.
8. P: Number n is an even number.   Q: Number n is divisible by 2.
9. P: Jan is a millionaire.   Q: Jan is a Republican.
10. P: Jan is a Buddhist.   Q: Jan was born in India.
11. P: Figure A is a square.   Q: Figure A has four sides.
12. P: Pat is at least as old as Jane.   Q: Jane is at least as old as Pat.
13. P: Pat is the same age as Jane.   Q: Jane is the same age as Pat.
14. P: Joe is happy.   Q: Joe is not angry.

Necessity vs. Contingency

Since ancient times, philosophers and mathematicians have distinguished two different "modes" of truth and falsity. Consider the Pythagorean theorem, which was discovered in about 525 BC: The sum of the squares of the legs of a right triangle equals the square of the hypotenuse. Ancient mathematicians noticed something interesting about this mathematical truth: It is impossible to consistently suppose that it is false. That is, if we try to conceive it as false, we contradict ourselves! We inevitably land in a self-contradiction. But that which is self-contradictory is a paradigm of the impossible. Hence, it is *impossible* that the Pythagorean theorem is false. In everyday life, if something cannot possibly be otherwise than it is, we say that it is *necessarily* so. Therefore, because the Pythagorean theorem cannot possibly be false, it is *necessarily true*.

Now contrast the Pythagorean theorem with a mundane truth: "Seattle's Space Needle has an observation deck." This is true, but we can easily imagine it false. That is, we can consistently think of a possible circumstance in which the statement ("Seattle's Space Needle has an observation deck") would have been false. We can think of this without any self-contradiction at all. For instance, the Space Needle could have been built with a small zoo instead of an observation deck. (Keep in mind that in logic, something counts as logically possible, no matter how improbable or bizarre, so long as it is not self-contradictory.)

In everyday discourse, we generally use the term *contingent* to mean "depends on" and thus to indicate dependency. For example, we can say that the sale of a house is contingent on the payment of all liens against the property. A **contingent statement** is therefore one whose truth or falsity depends on (is contingent on) changing circumstances. In some circumstances, the statement would be true, and in other circumstances it would be false. The statement about the Space Needle is thus *contingent*, for its truth or falsity is contingent on circumstances. Unlike necessary truth, a contingent statement varies as to truth and falsity from circumstance to circumstance; its truth or falsity is not permanently set.

Thus we see that there are two modes or types of truth: necessary truth and contingent truth. More formally:

- A statement is **contingently true** if it is true but could have been false. Its truth and falsity thus vary from circumstance to circumstance. A statement is **contingently false** if it is false but could have been true.
- A statement is **necessarily true** if it is true in all possible circumstances and false in none. A necessary truth is absolute in the sense that its truth cannot possibly vary from circumstance to circumstance. A statement is **necessarily false** if it is false in all possible circumstances and true in none.

Some examples might help bring these ideas into focus. The following statements (given their standard meanings) are all necessarily true:

- Nothing is red all over and green all over at the same time.
- If today is Tuesday, then today is not Monday.
- Every Euclidean triangle has three sides.

- Every Euclidean square has four equal angles.
- If X is heavier than Y, and Y is heavier than Z, X must be heavier than Z.

In each of these cases, if the statement is given its usual meaning, then it cannot possibly be false, that is, there are no consistently describable circumstances in which it would be false. The following are examples of statements that are necessarily false:

- Jan and Pat are each older than the other.
- Pat is 30, and it's not the case that Pat is 30.
- Some circles are square.
- There is a man who is older than all men.
- Some Euclidean triangles have seven sides.
- Every Euclidean square has seven equal angles.

Notice that in each of these cases, there is no possibility, that is, there is no consistently describable state of affairs, no matter how remote or unlikely, in which the statement (given its standard meaning) would be true. Each of the following is a logically contingent statement:

- Red Delicious apples are on average selling for 59 cents a pound.
- President Abraham Lincoln ate an apple on his 12th birthday.
- Rita works as a meter maid.
- The Beatles first appeared on the *Ed Sullivan Show* in February 1964.
- Dick's Drive-In was founded in Seattle in April 1954.

In each case, there are possible circumstances in which the statement would be true, and there are possible circumstances in which the statement would be false.

Relation to Deductive Validity

How do necessity and contingency relate to validity? Suppose argument A is valid: If its premises all are true, then its conclusion *must* be true. This means that if the premises are true, then it is not a mere contingent matter that the conclusion is true. In other words, the conclusion doesn't just randomly happen to be true as well; rather, if the premises are true then it *cannot* be otherwise than that the conclusion is true, too. In other words, it is *necessary* that if the premises are true then the conclusion is true.

Exercise 6.5   In each case, is the statement necessarily true, necessarily false, or contingent?

1. $2 + 2 = 4$
2. Starbucks stock is at $20 today.

3. $2 + 4 = 99$

4. All bachelors are unmarried.

5. All bachelors are males.

6. If A is taller than B, and B is taller than C, then A is taller than C.

7. All triangles have three angles.

8. Some triangles have five sides.

9. If the roof leaks every time it rains and it is raining, then the roof is leaking.

10. *The Wizard of Oz* was filmed in Culver City, California, at the MGM Studios.

11. Judy Garland was born in Grand Rapids, Minnesota.

12. If a figure is a square, then it has four sides.

13. Nobody is 150 years old.

14. It snows a lot in Fairbanks, Alaska.

15. The Beatles played 297 nights at the Cavern Club in Liverpool, England.

Ideals of the Well-Formed Intellect

We associate ideals with each type of human activity. Let's reflect for a moment on the ideals we associate with the activity of reasoned discussion. Two ideals suggest themselves right away. They are presented here only as food for thought, to start you thinking.

Ideal 1: Be "intellectually honest." When trying to make your mind up on a controversial matter of importance, carefully examine the supporting evidence and arguments offered by all the contending points of view on the matter, and do so with as open a mind as possible. Initially, be sympathetic to each view under consideration and open to all that it has to offer. Otherwise, you may be forming your beliefs after considering only *part* of the evidence.

Ideal 2: Be respectful. In the midst of serious discussion, people sometimes get angry, defensive, hostile, or even mean-spirited when their viewpoint is challenged. We have all been guilty of this at one time or another. You can't control someone else's reactions, but you can control your own by always striving to treat others in conversation with the same respect and understanding you want them to show to you. This might mean many different things, but it certainly includes listening attentively to the other person's point of view, and with an open mind. The other person might just have something to teach you. Because it can be hard to express yourself when discussing serious matters, respecting the other person might sometimes require that you help them make their point, before you consider whether the point they are making is on track or not. In return, the other person might help you, too.

What's Next?

This concludes our "cook's tour" of the fundamental concepts of logic. The rest of this book makes all of these ideas more definite, more precise, and more *applicable*. This is in essence what logical theory does to earn its keep: It starts with a set of fundamental ideas, expressed in everyday language, and then it probes them in depth, clarifying the concepts and placing them into a system that can be applied to any subject matter. In addition, whenever it is feasible, logical theory *automates* these ideas, thus making it possible for a programmed machine to apply them to solve a problem. We'll also look at this aspect of logical theory when we examine the relationship between logic and the digital computer.

We have seen that validity is the standard by which logical theory judges deductive arguments as good or bad. But when we create a deductive argument, how do we know whether it is indeed valid or invalid? How can we know with precision? We take up this topic in the next chapter, when we examine the first formal templates of valid reasoning ever discovered: the rules for valid arguments formulated by Aristotle 2,300 years ago and still in use today.

Appendix 6.1   *Logical* Paradoxes?

Do you like paradoxes? If not, you might not want to read this appendix. If you do, proceed with caution! The paradoxes of modern physics are well known: the clock and twin paradoxes of relativity theory, quantum theory's paradox of Schrodinger's cat, and so on. It turns out that logical theory has its own paradoxes—conundrums every bit as puzzling (and intellectually exciting) as the paradoxes that bedevil modern physics.

Paradoxes of Validity

Suppose all you know about a certain deductive argument is that it has a necessarily true conclusion. Paradoxically, it follows *from this fact alone* that the argument must be valid—regardless of whether the premises are true or false and regardless of whether or not the premises are even about the conclusion. This follows from the standard definition of validity going back to Aristotle. For example, because the following deductive argument ends in a necessary truth, it is automatically valid, even though its premises are false and even though they have nothing to do with the conclusion:

1. The Earth is perfectly flat.
2. The Moon orbits the Earth.
3. Therefore, certainly all triangles must have three sides.

Remember that an argument is valid if it is not possible that the premises all are true and the conclusion is false. Look at this argument closely. It is not possible the premises all are true and the conclusion is false. This is because it is not possible the conclusion is false. Therefore, this argument is valid! In general, if the conclusion of a deductive argument is *necessarily* true, then it will not be possible that the conclusion is ever false. In this case it is not possible that the conclusion is false and the premises are true. It follows that any such argument is always valid!

> **Paradox.** A deductive argument is automatically valid if its conclusion is necessarily true, even if its premises have nothing to do with its conclusion.

Next, suppose a deductive argument contains a self-contradictory *premise*. Paradoxically, it follows from this fact alone that the argument must be valid, regardless of whether the other premises are true or false, and regardless of whether the conclusion is true or false. For example, the following argument contains a self-contradictory premise:

1. The Earth is one year old, and the Earth is not one year old.
2. Therefore, all squares have only three sides.

This argument is valid, even though the premise has nothing to do with the conclusion! Here is why. An argument is valid when it is not possible that the premises are all true and the conclusion is false. But if a premise is self-contradictory, then it is not possible that that premise is ever true, in any circumstance. If so, then the following combination is not possible in this case: The premises *all* are true and the conclusion is false. Therefore, the argument is valid. Because the preceding argument has a self-contradictory premise, it must be valid.

> **Paradox.** A deductive argument is automatically valid if one of its premises is self-contradictory or necessarily false, even if the conclusion has nothing to do with the premises.

These curious aspects of validity strike most of us as paradoxical. Yet they are purely logical consequences of the established definition of validity. Just as physicists wrestle with paradoxical consequences of relativity theory and quantum mechanics, logicians wrestle with paradoxes that arise from within pure logic itself. One might suppose that there is a simple solution to the paradoxes of validity: Alter the definition of validity so that the paradoxes no longer arise. It seems like this would be an easy fix. However, logicians have found that the definition cannot be altered without creating new paradoxes that take the place of the old.

Of course, these conundrums only arise in unusual circumstances—when an argument has a necessarily true conclusion or a self-contradictory premise. Most arguments in real life do not have necessarily true conclusions or necessarily false premises. But this does not take the bite out of the paradox. In Unit Six, we look at some of the solutions logicians have proposed—solutions that would soften or even eliminate the paradoxes associated with validity and with other aspects of modern logical theory.

The paradoxes associated with validity are part of the reason why validity *alone* is not all we want in a good deductive argument. Validity is a good thing: It is good when it is not possible the conclusion is false *if* the premises are all true. But ultimately we want more than mere validity: We want truth as well. In other words, we want our deductive arguments to be *sound*. Only when we have a *sound* deductive argument can we be certain we have a true conclusion. And truth is always a good thing!

Question. Suppose two premises of a deductive argument contradict each other. It follows from this fact alone that the argument must be valid. Can you explain why such an argument is automatically valid?

Paradoxical Aspects of Equivalence and Inconsistency

If two sentences are both self-contradictory, then it follows that they are inconsistent (because they cannot both be true). However, it also follows that they are equivalent (because their truth values will always match in every circumstance). Inconsistent yet equivalent! Paradox. Of course, this paradox only arises in the case of necessary statements, not contingent ones. But a paradox it is, nonetheless. The fascinating logic of necessary truth and falsity is probed and unraveled, at least partially, in the chapter on modal logic in Unit Six.

Glossary

Consistency Two or more statements are consistent if and only if it is possible they are all true together.

Contingent statement A statement is contingent if there are possible circumstances in which it would be true and there are possible circumstances in which it would be false.

Contingently true (or false) statement A statement that is true (or false) but contingent.

Equivalence Two statements are equivalent if and only if they imply each other. If two statements are equivalent, then it is impossible that they ever differ in terms of truth and falsity.

Implication One statement implies a second statement if and only if there is no possibility that the first statement is true and the second is false. A group of statements implies a further statement if and only if no possible situation exists in which all the statements in the group are true and in which the further statement is false.

Inconsistency Two or more statements are inconsistent if and only if it is impossible that all of the statements are true together.

Intellectual honesty Intellectually honest people look as objectively as possible at *all* the plausible views on an issue, and at the evidence for each view, before making up their minds; in so doing they attempt to take into account all the facts, not just some of the facts. In the end, intellectually honest people follow the evidence where it leads, even if it leads to a conclusion they do not want to believe.

Necessarily false A statement is necessarily false if and only if it is false and could not possibly have been true; that is, no possible circumstances exist in which it is or would be true.

Necessarily true A statement is necessarily true if and only if it is true and could not possibly have been false; that is, no possible circumstances exist in which it is or would be false.

Socratic elenchus The method of questioning used by Socrates to show someone that his or her beliefs stand in logical conflict.

Unit 2

Categorical Logic

Categorical logic was the first of the specialized branches of logical theory systematically developed in writing and taught in the college classroom; it remains an important part of the logic curriculum today. Amazingly, the fundamental principles have changed very little since they were first formulated in ancient Athens by the Greek philosopher Aristotle (384–322 BC). Although he was starting from scratch with no previous discoveries to build on, Aristotle produced an impressive body of principles that have withstood the test of time well. For producing the first comprehensive system of logic in written form that has survived intact, Aristotle has been called the founder of logic.

It has long been traditional to teach this branch of logical theory first in an introductory logic course, after surveying the fundamentals of the subject. Following tradition, we introduce it here, at the start of our travels through the major specialized branches and many worlds of logical theory.

7 Logic Takes Form «« «« «« ««

Categorical Logic Version 1.0

Product Description

- Lead designer: Aristotle
- Company: The Lyceum, Athens, Greece
- Release date: Approximately June 1, 335 BC
- Distinctions:
  - First deductive system of logic
  - First use of logical variables
  - First system of formal logic
- Advertisement: As valid today as it was on its launch day

The system of **categorical logic** developed by Aristotle is the study of arguments composed of sentences that state relationships between categories of things. Essentially, each of the sentences in a standard categorical argument relate one category of things to another category of things by asserting that all, some, or none of one category of things, either belong to or do not belong to another category of things. The following argument is an example that might even have been used in class by Aristotle himself:

1. All Greeks are human beings.
2. All Spartans are Greeks.
3. Therefore, all Spartans are human beings.

In this argument, the terms *Greeks*, *human beings*, and *Spartans* refer to groups or categories of things, while the words *all* and *some* specify the quantities of things in those categories. The first premise of this argument indicates that all the members of the "Greeks" category belong to the category of human beings, the second premise says that all members of the "Spartans" category belong to the Greek category, and so on.

We reason about categories of things, and about the relations between categories of things, all the time in everyday life. This type of reasoning is also prevalent in the law, where legal rules are carefully written to apply to all the members of one category of things but to no members of another category, only to some members of a further category, and so on, and in the sciences, when relations between various categories of things must be stated with great precision.

The Mathematical Model

Mathematics was a required subject when Aristotle, at the age of 17, entered Plato's Academy to study philosophy. Plato (427–347 BC), Aristotle's teacher, valued the precision, certainty, and systematic nature of mathematical theory and tried to pass on to his students a respect for that type of thinking. The rigorous style of Aristotle's logical treatises makes it clear that he shared his teacher's love of precise thought. The new subject of logic, as Aristotle envisioned it from the beginning, would be as exact and as certain as mathematics. This meant several things:

1.   Begin with precise definitions for all important terms. The Greek mathematicians had learned that reasoning can be sidetracked and can even become completely derailed if the words in use are not defined with sufficient precision. A good definition clearly explains the meaning of a term or phrase to remove vagueness and ambiguity as much as possible. A word is **vague** if it has borderline cases. These are cases where it is not clear whether the word applies or does not apply. For example, the words *rich* and *poor* are vague as they are ordinarily used. A word with borderline cases is said to have "fuzzy boundaries of application." Reasoning with vague words can be like playing catch with balls of cotton—it is hard to get a firm hold on anything. A word or term is **ambiguous** when it can be interpreted in two or more ways: It has two or more meanings, and we are not sure which is intended. Ambiguity can also short-circuit a reasoning process, especially when a word is used with one meaning in one phase of an argument and then with a different meaning in another place. Consequently, the ability to construct good definitions is an important logical skill. This is why Unit Five contains a chapter on the "art" of defining words.

2.   Solve problems in an analytic way. Mathematicians usually solve a big problem by breaking it down into a series of smaller problems that they solve first. That is *analysis* (from the Greek word *analytikos* meaning "to break something down into its parts"). An analytical methodology is used in just about every subject today, from physics, chemistry, and biology to grammar, economics, and psychology to medi-

cine, nursing, climatology, and auto mechanics. We employ an analytic approach all the time in everyday life as well.

3.   Prove it. For the Greek mathematicians, this meant establishing discoveries on the basis of systematic deductive reasoning starting with premises that are certain.

4.   Organize results precisely on tables, charts, and in figures.

The stage was set. Aristotle would begin the subject of categorical logic by breaking the act of reasoning down into its constituent elements. Everything would be rigorously defined. Results would be proven with the precision of mathematics. Finally, the results would be assembled in handy charts and tables. A deductive system for pure reason itself!

All of this might not sound out of the ordinary today, immersed as we are in systematic thinking, but Aristotle's seed idea for a systematic science of logic was amazing and truly revolutionary in its own day. The deductive logical system of Aristotle, developed at a time when almost all people around the world based their lives on myth and superstition, ranks as one of the most seminal ideas in all of human history.

Sentences

Aristotle held that every declarative sentence can be translated without loss of essential meaning into a sentence stating that all, some, or none, of the members of one category of things either belong to, or do not belong to, a second category of things. It followed that any deductive argument whatsoever, about any subject matter, can be translated into the type of argument studied in his system of categorical logic. Therefore, if a deductive system could be produced for all such arguments, that would constitute a deductive system for all possible deductive arguments, telling us with precision which arguments are valid and which are not. Moreover, the system would be *complete* in the sense that any valid argument, no matter how complex, could in principle be proven valid within the system. We would then have a detailed roadmap for all valid reasoning. The first step was the logical analysis of the sentences making up the premise and conclusions of categorical arguments.

There are four basic ways to construct a sentence of a categorical argument:

1.   State that *all* the members of one given category *belong to* a second category; for example, "All cats belong to the category of mammals," or simply, "All cats are mammals."

2.   State that *none* of one category *belongs to* a second category; for example, "No cats belong to the category of fish," or simply, "No cats are fish."

3.   State that *some* of one category *belong to* a second category; for example, "Some cats belong to the category of pets," or simply, "Some cats are pets."

4. State that *some* of one category do *not belong* to a second category; for example, "Some cats do not belong to the category of pets," or simply, "Some cats are not pets."

Any sentence constructed in one of these four ways shall be called a "categorical sentence." Let's now analyze the four ways of constructing a categorical sentence, one by one.

All___ are___

Our example of this form is, "All cats are mammals." Aristotle broke this type of categorical sentence down into four elements:

1. The quantifier: "All"
2. The subject term: "cats"
3. The copula: "are"
4. The predicate term: "mammals"

All	**cats**	**are**	**mammals.**
↑	↑	↑	↑
quantifier	subject term	copula	predicate term

The *subject term* of a sentence states what the sentence is about. The *predicate term* says something about the subject. The subject term in this case (*cats*) refers to a category or "class" of things—the category of cats. A **class** is a group of things that have a specified characteristic in common. For example, the category of cats consists of all things that have in common the characteristic of being a cat. The predicate term (*mammals*) also denotes a category or class—in this case the class of mammals.

The word *all* is called a **quantifier** because it tells us the quantity of things in the subject category—the category named in the subject of the sentence—that are said to belong to the predicate category, that is, the category named in the predicate. The word *are* is called the **copula** because it joins, or "couples," the subject to the predicate. In this case the quantifier (*All*) teams up with the copula (*are*) to assert that all the members of the subject category belong to the predicate category, which is to say, in this case, that every cat is *included within* the mammal category. But what does *included within* mean?

A member of category A is *included within* category B if the member of A is also a member of B. If every member of category A also belongs to category B, then we can say that category A is included within category B. For instance, the category of cats is included within the category of mammals, the category of roses is included within the category of plants, and so on.

Thus, the sentence "All cats are mammals" asserts that all the members of the subject category (cats) are included within the predicate category (mammals), which is to say that every cat belongs to the mammal category. In short, "Every cat is a mammal."

No____ are____

Our example of this, the second way to form a categorical sentence, is "No cats are fish." This sentence asserts that no member of the subject category (cats) belongs to the predicate category (fish), which is to say that all the members of the subject category are *excluded* from the predicate category. In general, a member of category A is excluded from category B if the member of A is not a member of B, that is, does not belong to B.

No	**cats**	**are**	**fish.**
↑	↑	↑	↑
quantifier	subject term	copula	predicate term

The word *No* counts as a quantifier because it states the quantity of things in the subject category that also belong to the predicate category, namely, the quantity zero.

Some____ are____

"Some aardvarks are pets" asserts that some members of the subject category (aardvarks) are included within the predicate category (pets). But what exactly does the word *some* mean? This seemingly innocent little word turns out, on close inspection, to be ambiguous. A definition is needed to make things more precise. Two interpretations are possible:

1. *Some* means "one or more but not all."
2. *Some* means "one or more," that is, at least one.

Aristotle chose the second meaning. Thus, in standard categorical logic, the word **some** means "one or more," which means the same as "at least one."

Some	**aardvarks**	**are**	**pets.**
↑	↑	↑	↑
quantifier	subject term	copula	predicate term

This sentence says that at least one aardvark is a pet.

Some____are not____

"Some aardvarks are not pets" says that some (one or more) members of the subject class are not included in the predicate class, that is, one or more aardvarks do not belong to the class of pets.

Some	**aardvarks**	**are not**	**pets.**
↑	↑	↑	↑
quantifier	subject term	copula	predicate term

Sentence Forms

And Aristotle Said, "Let the Forms Be Separate from the Content."

In the beginning, Aristotle was in search of principles so general they could be applied to any and all possible arguments, no matter what the subject matter. Because no such principles had ever been formulated or even attempted, he would have to invent an entirely new logical concept and a way to express it in print. The new concept was the concept of logical form; the key to expressing it in writing was a symbol we now call a variable. To convey the basic idea, consider this question: What do the following sentences have in common?

1. All dogs are mammals.
2. All snakes are reptiles.
3. All robins are birds.

Although each is about a different subject matter, these sentences all share a common structure. This common structure is called the **logical form** of the three sentences, and the three sentences are called *substitution instances* of that form. The form in this case is represented by the following expression:

All **S** are **P**

where the boldfaced, capitalized **S** and **P** are variables ranging over terms, or nouns, that stand for categories of things. In this formula, the **S** stands in for the subject term of a categorical sentence, and the **P** stands in for the predicate term. The three English sentences, "All dogs are mammals," "All snakes are reptiles," and "All robins are birds," are thus *substitution instances* of the logical form "All **S** are **P**."

Here is a precise definition of this important concept: A categorical sentence counts as a *substitution instance* of a corresponding form if the sentence can be generated from the form by substituting the terms of the sentence for the variables in the form, making no other changes. Starting with the form "All **S** are **P**," for example, if we substitute "dogs" for **S**, and if we substitute "mammals" for **P**, the result is "All dogs are mammals," which shows that "All dogs are mammals" is a substitution instance of the form "All **S** are **P**." We might also say that "All dogs are mammals" *instantiates* the form "All **S** are **P**." (More loosely we could simply say that the sentence in question "fits" the form.) Notice that the logical form is an abstract structure with no content, a pattern that can be instantiated by many different sentences, about many different subject matters.

The Four Categorical Sentence Forms

With the idea of a logical form precisely defined, we can now specify a form for each kind of categorical sentence.

1. Some categorical sentences assert that all of the subject class is included in the predicate class; that is, every member of the subject class is a member of the predicate class. For example, "All Athenians are Greeks." The logical form in this case is "All **S** are **P**."

2. Some categorical sentences assert that all members of the subject class are excluded from the predicate class; that is, no member of the subject class belongs to the predicate class. For example, "No Persians are Greeks." The logical form in this case is "No **S** are **P**."

3. Some categorical sentences assert that some of the subject class is included in the predicate class; that is, some members of the subject class are members of the predicate class. For example, "Some Greeks are Spartans." The logical form is "Some **S** are **P**."

4. Some categorical sentences assert that some of the subject class is excluded from the predicate class. For example, "Some Greeks are not Spartans." The logical form is "Some **S** are not **P**."

Standard Form

In everyday English we say things in many different ways, and there are many different ways to say a single given thing. Logical theory needs a little more uniformity. Let us say that a categorical sentence of English is in *standard form* if it precisely instantiates one of the four categorical forms just identified. Thus, it begins with one of the identified quantifiers ("All," "No," or "Some"); its subject and predicate terms are names of categories of things (such as "Greeks," "mammals," or "students who are majoring in classical studies in college"); its copula is either "are" or "are not"; and it contains no other elements. Thus, "Some Greeks are Spartans" is in standard form, but the sentence "Many Greeks are Spartans" is not. (Change the word "Many" to "Some" and the latter sentence *is* in standard form.) The sentence "All cats are mammals" is in standard form, but the sentence "Every cat is a mammal" is not. (Change the word "Every" to "All" and the latter sentence *is* in standard form.)

Quantity and Quality

Two further properties of logical forms must be defined before our system is ready to serve its ultimate purpose: proving categorical arguments valid. Aristotle discovered that every categorical sentence has a *quantity* and a *quality*. The quantity is **universal** if the sentence makes a claim about *every* member of the subject term category, and the quantity is **particular** if the sentence makes a claim about *some* members of the category denoted by the subject term.

Thus, a sentence such as, "All snakes are reptiles" is a universal sentence, as it makes a claim about *every* member of the subject category. But a sentence such as "No birds are mammals" is also universal, for it, too, makes a claim about every member of its subject category, namely, that every bird is *not* a mammal. In contrast, statements such as "Some cats are pets" and "Some cats are not pets" are obviously particular because they talk about *some* of the subject category.

The quality is *affirmative* if the copula affirms membership in the predicate category, and the quality is *negative* if it denies membership in the predicate group. For example, "All aardvarks are mammals" is affirmative, as the copula tells us the members of the subject category are included within the predicate category. "Some cats are pets" is also affirmative, for it, too, says members of the subject group belong to the predicate group. However, the sentence "Some cats are not pets" is negative, since the copula denies membership in the predicate category ("Some cats do not belong to the pet category"). Thus:

Quantity: Universal ("All" or "No") or Particular ("Some")
Quality: Affirmative ("are") or Negative ("are not")

Putting This All Together

1. Sentences of the form "All **S** are **P**" are both universal and affirmative. They are therefore **universal affirmative sentences**.

2. Sentences of the form "No **S** are **P**" are both universal and negative. These are **universal negative sentences**.

3. Sentences of the form "Some **S** are **P**" are both particular and affirmative. These are **particular affirmative sentences**.

4. Sentences of the form "Some **S** are not **P**" are both particular and negative. These are **particular negative sentences**.

During the Middle Ages, when most of the cutting-edge research in logical theory was conducted in the cathedral schools of Europe, Latin was the universal language of scholarship. It has become customary since the Medieval period to label the two affirmative forms A and I (from the first two vowels of the Latin word *affirmo*, which means "I affirm"), and to label the two negative forms E and O (from the two vowels in the Latin word *nego*, which means "I deny"). Thus:

Type	Quantity/ Quality	Logical Form
A	Universal Affirmative	All **S** are **P**
E	Universal Negative	No **S** are **P**
I	Particular Affirmative	Some **S** are **P**
O	Particular Negative	Some **S** are not **P**

Notice that the content of the various categorical sentences has dropped away, and our focus is now on pure logical forms alone: form without content. Aristotle was the first to see that it is the *logical form* that makes an argument valid or invalid, not its content, as we will see shortly. It is now time to apply all of this.

Exercise 7.1   For each sentence that follows: (a) Is the sentence an A, E, I, or O sentence? (b) State the quantity and quality.

1. All adult male Spartans are highly trained soldiers.
2. No Athenian citizens are Spartans.
3. Some Athenians are not philosophers.
4. No students of Socrates are professional sophists.
5. Some Athenians are farmers.
6. All philosophers are logicians.
7. No Spartan warriors are philosophers.
8. All logicians at Aristotle's school are philosophers.
9. All priests who work for the Oracle at Delphi are professionals.
10. No hoplites serving in the Athenian infantry are logic teachers.

Arguments

Three Types of Categorical Reasoning

Recall that an argument has one or more premises and exactly one conclusion. Any argument composed solely of categorical sentences is a **categorical argument**. Aristotle divided categorical arguments into three fundamental kinds.

1. An **immediate inference** is an argument composed of exactly one premise and one conclusion immediately drawn from it. Here is a one-premise argument or immediate inference:

1. All Spartans are brave persons.
2. So, some brave persons are Spartans.

2. A **mediate inference** is an argument composed of two categorical premises and exactly one conclusion, in which the reasoning from the first premise to the conclusion is "mediated" by passing through a second premise. This type of argument is called a *categorical syllogism*. The reasoning passes from the premise to the conclusion via the *mediation* of a second premise. For example:

1. All goats are mammals.
2. All mammals are animals.
3. Therefore, all goats are animals.

We will define the categorical syllogism much more precisely (and oh will it be precise!) in Chapter 8, when we learn to systematically evaluate mediate inferences.
3. Categorical reasoning can also take place in a sorites. What's this? A **sorites** is a chain of interlocking mediate inferences leading to one conclusion in the end. (The accent is on the second syllable, so-*ri*-tes, and the plural and singular forms of the word are the same.) Thus, a sorites is a sequence of categorical syllogisms that have been connected like links in a chain, with the conclusion of the first argument serving as a premise in the next argument, and so on up the line, until a final conclusion is reached. Here is a sorites:

1. All Spartans are warriors.
2. All warriors are brave persons.
3. All brave persons are strong persons.
4. Therefore, all Spartans are strong persons.

In the usual case, as in this one, the first two premises logically imply a conclusion—a third statement—that is left unstated. This third statement, although unexpressed, is then used as a premise in the next argument in the chain. The unexpressed conclusion, when combined with the next statement in the chain, logically supports another conclusion, which is also left unstated. Now the second conclusion becomes an unexpressed premise in the next argument in the chain, combining with the fourth statement in the sorites to support another conclusion, which is then carried over as a premise in the next argument, and so on, until the final conclusion in the sorites is reached. Thus a sorites is an enthymematic argument. This will all be explained in more depth, and we will look at many examples, when we evaluate sorites in the next chapter.

Aristotle held that any argument, categorical or otherwise, can be translated without loss of essential logical meaning into one of these three structures of categorical reasoning: either into a categorical argument that makes an immediate inference, or into one that reaches its conclusion through the mediation of a second premise, or into a sorites. As Aristotle envisioned it, categorical logic would be complete as well as systematic: Its methods would be capable of handling all logically possible arguments—no matter what the subject matter, and no matter what the length.

Evaluating One-Premise Arguments

Aristotle's Square of Opposition

With preliminary definitions complete, the next step is the evaluation of immediate inferences—arguments having only one premise. This will consume the rest of this chapter. The evaluation of mediated inferences, including the chain arguments known as sorites, is our focus in the next chapter.

Aristotle developed two methods for determining validity and invalidity for one-premise arguments. One method employs a logical device known as the Square of Opposition, and the second method involves a set of logical "laws" for categorical sentences: the laws of conversion, obversion, and contraposition. Best to take these one at a time. We begin with the square.

Loading Up the Square

Recall that in a one-premise argument, or immediate inference, a statement is inferred immediately from a single premise. The logic of immediate inferences, which we are about to explore, was first systematized by Aristotle in his *De Interpretatione*, in a discussion listing all the known logical relationships that could possibly obtain among the four types of categorical sentences (A, E, I, and O). In the Middle Ages, Aristotle's discoveries were compiled, supplemented, and placed in a table that has come to be known as the Traditional Square of Opposition. Because the original blueprint stems from Aristotle, I call this Aristotle's **Square of Opposition**. It would be hard to exaggerate the historical significance of this logical device: It was the first general-purpose algorithm in logical theory; it was also the inspiration for the world's first mechanical computer. (See Appendix D, on computers and logic, at the back of the book, for more information on this.) As usual, certain definitions are required first.

Contradiction

Two statements are **contradictories** if and only if they cannot both be true at the same time *and* they also cannot both be false at the same time. It follows that in all possible situations, if one is true, the other *must* be false and vice versa. The two will always be opposite in terms of truth and falsity. For example, "Plato is 80" and "Plato is not 80."

Contrariety

Two statements are **contraries** if and only if they cannot both be true at the same time (in the same circumstance), but it is logically possible both are false. For example, "Plato is 80" and "Plato is 46."

Subcontrariety

Two statements are **subcontraries** if and only if they cannot both be false (at the same time in the same circumstance), but it is logically possible that both are true. For example, "Some goats are pets" and "Some goats are not pets."

Subalternation

One statement P is a *subaltern* of another statement Q if and only if P must be true if Q is true. Subalternation is also sometimes called *subimplication*. For example, "Plato is older than 70" is a subaltern of "Plato is 80."

Superalternation

One statement P is a *superaltern* of another statement Q if and only if P must be false if Q is false. Superalternation is also sometimes called *superimplication*. For example, "Plato is older than 70" is a superaltern of "Plato is older than 60."

Aristotle's Square of Opposition: "A Computer on Paper"

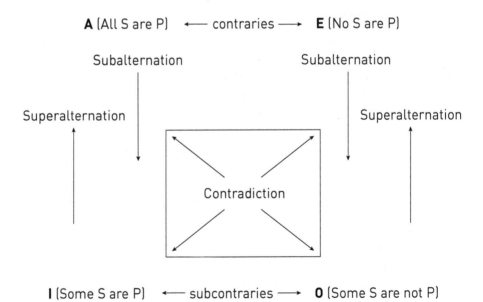

A (All S are P) ⟵ contraries ⟶ **E** (No S are P)

Subalternation   Subalternation

Superalternation   Superalternation

Contradiction

I (Some S are P) ⟵ subcontraries ⟶ **O** (Some S are not P)

Interpreting the Square

The Arrows for Contradiction

The first arrow for contradiction tells us that an A statement and its corresponding O statement will always be contradictories. The second arrow tells us that an E statement always contradicts its corresponding I statement. Let's test the first arrow: Is the A statement "All Macedonians are Greeks" contradictory to the corresponding O statement "Some Macedonians are not Greeks"? Is it possible both are true at the same time? Is it possible both are false at the same time? The answer is no twice, of course. They are indeed contradictories, as the table predicts. The two arrows for contradiction thus indicate:

> If an A statement is true, the corresponding O statement is false, and if an A statement is false, the opposing O statement is true. Also, if an O statement is true, the corresponding A statement is false, and if an O statement is false, the opposing A statement is true.

> If an E statement is true, the corresponding I statement is false, and if an E statement is false, the corresponding I statement is true. Also, if an I statement is true, the corresponding E statement is false, and if an I statement is false, the corresponding E statement is true.

For example, if the A statement, "All citizens of Miletus are Greeks," is true, then the corresponding O statement is false, namely, "Some citizens of Miletus are not Greeks." If the O statement, "Some Greeks are not citizens of Athens," is true, then the corresponding A statement is false, namely, "All Greeks are citizens of Athens." And if the E statement, "No citizens of Miletus are Persians," is true, then the corresponding I statement is false, namely, "Some citizens of Miletus are Persians." Finally, if the I statement, "Some citizens of Miletus are Persians," is true, then the corresponding E statement is false, namely, "No citizens of Miletus are Persians." Do these examples ring true to you?

The Arrow for Contrariety

This arrow indicates that an A sentence and its corresponding E sentence will always be contraries. Let's test this claim by comparing the A sentence "All Athenians are Greeks" with the corresponding E statement "No Athenians are Greeks." Are they contraries? Is it correct to say that they cannot both be true at the same time but that both might be false at the same time? Certainly! Thus:

> Corresponding A and E statements cannot both be true but can both be false. So, if an A statement is true, the corresponding E statement is false; and if an E statement is true, the corresponding A statement is false.

For example, the A statement, "All Spartans are Greeks," and the corresponding E statement, "No Spartans are Greeks," cannot both be true at the same time, although it is possible both are false. (Under what conditions would both be false?)

The Arrow for Subcontrariety

This arrow tells us that an I sentence and its corresponding O sentence will always be subcontraries. Let's test this claim by comparing the I sentence "Some Ionians are Greeks," and its corresponding O sentence "Some Ionians are not Greeks." Is it possible both are true? Is it possible both are false? These two statements are subcontraries because they cannot both be false but it *is* possible both are true. Thus:

> Corresponding I and O statements cannot both be false, but both may be true. So, if an I statement is false, the corresponding O statement is true; and if an O statement is false, the corresponding I statement is true.

For example, the I statement, "Some Ionians are Greeks," and the corresponding O statement, "Some Ionians are not Greeks," cannot both be false at the same time, although it is possible both are true. (Under what conditions would both be true?) Keep in mind that *some* means just "one or more."

Subalternation

The two subalternation arrows point downward (the direction a submarine goes when it dives). The principles associated with these arrows can be expressed more efficiently if we use the concept of a truth-value. When a sentence is true, let us say it has the **truth-value** of true, and when a sentence is false, let us say it has the truth-value of false. Thus, we will speak here of two truth-values: truth and falsity. Now, the arrows for subalternation may be interpreted as follows.

Left side downward arrow: This arrow says that if an A statement is true, then the corresponding I statement *must* be true. However, when an A statement is false, nothing logically follows with respect to the truth-value of the corresponding I statement. The arrow "shuts down" in this case. That is, if the A statement is false, then the corresponding I statement might be true, but then again it might be false.

Right side downward arrow: This arrow says that if an E statement is true, then the corresponding O statement *must* be true. However, when an E statement is false, nothing logically follows with respect to the truth-value of the corresponding O statement. The arrow shuts down in this case. That is, if the E statement is false, then the corresponding O statement might be true, and might be false.

For example, if the A statement "All hoplites are brave persons" is true, then the corresponding I statement must be true as well, namely, "Some hoplites are brave persons." And if the E statement, "No men over the age of 65 are hoplites" is true, then the corresponding O statement, "Some men over the age of 65 are not hoplites," must be true as well.

However, if all we know is that the A statement, "All Ionians are Greeks" is false, then the truth-value of the corresponding I statement, "Some Ionians are Greeks," is up in the air. We cannot know whether it is true or false from only the information given. With only the information at hand, it might be true and it might be false. Likewise, suppose we know that the E statement, "No Ionians are Greeks," is false. Based on this information alone, we cannot know whether the corresponding O statement, "Some Ionians are not Greeks," is true or false.

Here is one way to picture this: The subalternation arrows only take in and transmit truth. Furthermore, they only take truth in at the top and they only transmit it to the bottom. However, they refuse to take in falsity; they close if the top statement is false.

The Precise Meaning of "Undetermined"

Thus, there are two cases where the subalternation arrows shut down and refuse to transmit information:

> If an A statement is known to be false, nothing can be concluded as to the truth-value of the corresponding I statement. In this case, we say that the truth-value of the corresponding I statement is *undetermined*. This means that given just the assumption at hand—that the A statement is false—we cannot, from that information alone, determine the truth-value of the corresponding I statement.

> If an E statement is known to be false, nothing can be concluded as to the truth-value of the corresponding O statement. We cannot know, with just the information at hand, whether the corresponding O statement is true or false. The O statement's truth-value in this case is also undetermined.

So, suppose that all we know is this: The E statement, "No Athenians are poets," is false. What logically follows, regarding the corresponding O statement, "Some Athenians are not poets", according to subalternation? Nothing. The corresponding O statement could be true, but then again it could be false. If the E statement in this case is false, then it is false that no Athenian is a poet. Therefore, one or more Athenians is a poet. However, based on this information alone, it *might* be that all Athenians are poets, in which case it would be false that some are not. But it *might* be that some are poets and some are not, in which case the corresponding O would be true. Thus, given only the information that the E is false, the corresponding O might be true, but then again it might be false. The truth-value of the O statement in this case is undetermined.

Superalternation

These arrows point upward (the direction in which Superman flies) and are interpreted as follows.

Left side upward arrow: This arrow indicates that if an I statement is false, then the corresponding A statement *must* also be false. However, when the I statement is true, the arrow is silent regarding the corresponding A statement.

Right side upward arrow: This arrow indicates that if an O statement is false, then the corresponding E statement must also be false. However, when the O statement is true, the arrow is silent regarding the corresponding E statement.

In other words, the superalternation arrows only take in and transmit falsity. For example, if the I statement, "Some Persians are Athenians," is false, then the corresponding A statement must be false as well, namely, "All Persians are Athenians." If the O statement, "Some Persians are not poets," is false then the corresponding E must be false as well: "No Persians are poets." Furthermore, these arrows only take falsity in at the bottom; they shut down if truth is fed into their open end.

> If an I statement is known to be true, nothing can be concluded as to the truth-value of the corresponding A statement. In this case, the truth-value of the A statement is undetermined.

> If an O statement is known to be true, nothing can be concluded as to the truth-value of the corresponding E statement; the truth-value of the corresponding E in this case is undetermined.

For example, if all we know is that some Persians are poets, nothing logically follows with respect to the truth-value of "All Persians are poets." The corresponding A statement might be true, but then again it might be false, given only the information at hand. Likewise, if all we know is that some Persians are not poets, nothing logically follows regarding the truth-value of the corresponding E statement, "No Persians are poets." The truth-value of the E statement in this case is undetermined; it is up in the air, given only the information at hand.

In Sum

The following sums up all the logical relations displayed on Aristotle's Square of Opposition:

1.   If an A statement is assumed true, then the corresponding E statement is false, the corresponding I is true, and the corresponding O is false.

2. If an E statement is assumed true, then the corresponding A is false, the corresponding I is false, and the corresponding O is true.

3. If an I statement is assumed true, then the corresponding E is false, the corresponding A is undetermined, and the corresponding O is undetermined.

4. If an O statement is assumed true, then the corresponding A is false, the corresponding E is undetermined, and the corresponding I is undetermined.

5. If an A statement is assumed false, then the corresponding E is undetermined, the corresponding I is undetermined, and the corresponding O is true.

6. If an E statement is assumed false, then the corresponding A is undetermined, the corresponding I is true, and the corresponding O is undetermined.

7. If an I statement is assumed false, then the corresponding A is false, the corresponding E is true, and the corresponding O is true.

8. If an O statement is assumed false, then the corresponding A is true, the corresponding E is false, and the corresponding I is true.

Here is a table for handy reference:

Assumption	This implies
1. A is true	E is false, I is true, O is false
2. E is true	A is false, I is false, O is true
3. I is true	E is false, A is undetermined, O is undetermined
4. O is true	A is false, E is undetermined, I is undetermined
5. A is false	E is undetermined, I is undetermined, O is true
6. E is false	A is undetermined, I is true, O is undetermined
7. I is false	A is false, E is true, O is true
8. O is false	A is true, E is false, I is true

Exercise 7.2

Part I

For each of the following pairs of statements, specify whether the two statements are contradictories, contraries, or subcontraries.

1. All Athenians are Greeks.   No Athenians are Greeks.
2. Some Athenians are Greeks.   Some Athenians are not Greeks.
3. All Athenians are Greeks.   Some Athenians are not Greeks.
4. No Athenians are Greeks.   Some Athenians are Greeks.

Part II

1. State the contradictory of "All Greeks are religious."
2. State the contradictory of "No Greeks are religious."
3. State the contradictory of "Some Greeks are religious."
4. State the contradictory of "Some Greeks are not religious."
5. State the contrary of "All Greeks are religious."
6. State the contrary of "No Greeks are religious."
7. State the subcontrary of "Some Greeks are religious."
8. State the subcontrary of "Some Greeks are not religious."

Evaluating Inferences Using the Square

Aristotle's Square of Opposition can be used as a "paper computer" to precisely determine whether a one-premise categorical argument is valid or invalid. After entering a truth-value at one spot on the square, we look at another spot to find our answer. In a sense, the table "computes" the answer for us.

Suppose a one-premise categorical argument contains only standard form A, E, I, or O sentences, negations of such sentences, or both. The *negation* of a categorical sentence is the sentence with the prefix "It is not the case that" added to it. (We may also use the prefix "It is false that" to form the negation of a sentence.) Thus, the negation of "All Spartans are Greeks" is "It is not the case that all Spartans are Greeks." The argument is evaluated as follows:

1. Assume the premise is true and enter the corresponding truth-value into the square at the appropriate spot.
2. Follow the appropriate arrow to determine the corresponding truth-value of the conclusion.
3. If the conclusion is true, then the argument is valid. Otherwise, the argument is invalid.

For example, consider the following immediate inference:

1. All reptiles are cold-blooded.
2. Therefore, it is false that some reptiles are not cold-blooded.

The premise is an A statement, so we enter a T (for "true") in the Square of Opposition at the A statement's spot. The conclusion of the argument states that the corresponding O statement is false. We look at the Square, and sure enough, it tells us that the corresponding O statement is false. The argument is thus valid.

Let's test the following one-premise argument:

1. No cats are birds.
2. So, some cats are not birds.

The premise is an E statement, so we enter a T in the Square at the E statement slot. The conclusion of the argument states that the corresponding O statement is true. The Square tells us that the corresponding O statement is true. This argument is also valid.

Test the Square all you want. It works flawlessly every time. Why does it work? The logical relations represented in the table, among the four forms of the categorical sentences, are *necessary* relations. This means that when the table indicates that a conclusion is true given that a premise is true, the conclusion *must* be true if the premise is true, a sure sign that an argument is valid. Thus, we see that by entering a value at one spot and then looking at another spot, we can determine with precision whether a one-premise argument is valid or invalid. The Square of Opposition thus functions like a computer—a computer made of paper! It has no moving parts, and it is primitive, no doubt, but it is a computing device nevertheless.

HOW ARISTOTLE'S SQUARE INSPIRED THE BIRTH OF THE COMPUTER

We have seen that Aristotle's Square of Opposition can be used to compute the truth-value of one statement given the truth-value of another. Mathematicians call this type of procedure an algorithm. An *algorithm* is a problem-solving procedure that has the following properties:

1. It consists of a finite number of discrete steps.
2. Each step is so precisely defined that no creativity is required, just "blindly" following a rule.
3. A definite answer is guaranteed at the end of the procedure if the steps are followed exactly.

Many logicians maintain that every algorithm can at least in principle be implemented (followed) by a machine, but this has not been strictly proven for all cases. At any rate, Aristotle's Square of Opposition was the first large-scale, general-purpose algorithm in the history of logic. This might help explain why the first person in history to design a mechanical computer was an Aristotelian logician. Inspired by Aristotle's Square of

(continued)

Opposition, Raymond Lull (1232–1315), a medieval logician who was also a Catholic priest, designed a computing machine consisting of two rotating disks, each inscribed with symbols for categorical propositions. The disks were aligned in such a way that one could turn a dial and see which statements validly follow from a given statement. Although it was extremely rudimentary, Lull's basic idea underlies the modern digital computer. For the first time in history, someone had conceived of a machine that takes inputs of a certain sort and then, on the basis of rules of logic, computes an exact answer, which is then read off some other part of the device. Some historians of computer science have called Lull the founder of computer science. We usually associate computing with mathematics; perhaps this is why it is interesting that the first designs in history for machines that compute were designs for mechanical devices that would operate according to the exact laws not of mathematics but of logic.

Exercise 7.3   Use the Square of Opposition to answer the following questions. To simplify things, abbreviate the negation of a sentence by prefixing to it "False:" rather than "It is false that." Thus, the negation of "All Spartans are Greeks" can be abbreviated by writing "False: All Spartans are Greeks" rather than the longer "It is false that all Spartans are Greeks."

1. Assuming "All Spartans are Greeks" is true, what can be inferred about the truth or falsity of the following? Is the statement true, false, or undetermined?
   a. No Spartans are Greeks.
   b. Some Spartans are Greeks.
   c. Some Spartans are not Greeks.

2. Assuming "All Spartans are Greeks" is false, what can be inferred about the truth or falsity of the following? True, false, or undetermined?
   a. No Spartans are Greeks.
   b. Some Spartans are Greeks.
   c. Some Spartans are not Greeks.

3. Assuming "No Spartans are Greeks" is true, what can be inferred about the truth or falsity of the following? True, false, or undetermined?
   a. All Spartans are Greeks.
   b. Some Spartans are Greeks.
   c. Some Spartans are not Greeks.

4. Assuming "No Spartans are Greeks" is false, what can be inferred about the truth or falsity of the following? True, false, or undetermined?

   a. All Spartans are Greeks.

   b. Some Spartans are Greeks.

   c. Some Spartans are not Greeks.

5. Assuming "Some Spartans are Greeks" is true, what can be inferred about the truth or falsity of the following? True, false, or undetermined?

   a. All Spartans are Greeks.

   b. No Spartans are Greeks.

   c. Some Spartans are not Greeks.

6. Assuming "Some Spartans are Greeks" is false, what can be inferred about the truth or falsity of the following? True, false, or undetermined?

   a. All Spartans are Greeks.

   b. No Spartans are Greeks.

   c. Some Spartans are not Greeks.

7. Assuming "Some Spartans are not Greeks" is true, what can be inferred about the truth or falsity of the following? True, false, or undetermined?

   a. All Spartans are Greeks.

   b. No Spartans are Greeks.

   c. Some Spartans are Greeks.

8. Assuming "Some Spartans are not Greeks" is false, what can be inferred about the truth or falsity of the following? True, false, or undetermined?

   c. All Spartans are Greeks.

   b. No Spartans are Greeks.

   c. Some Spartans are Greeks.

Exercise 7.4   Use the Traditional Square of Opposition to decide if the following one-premise arguments are valid or invalid.

1. It is false that no Spartans are diplomats. So, some Spartans are diplomats.
2. All Spartans are diplomats. So, it is false that no Spartans are diplomats.
3. No Spartans are lovers of peace. So, some Spartans are not lovers of peace.
4. It is false that some Spartans are cowards. So, no Spartans are cowards.
5. All Spartans are loud. So, some Spartans are loud.
6. It is false that some Spartans are poets. So, it is false that all Spartans are poets.

7. It is false that some Spartans are not athletes. So, it is false that no Spartans are athletes.

8. It is false that all Athenians are hairy. So, it is true that some Athenians are hairy.

9. Some Athenians are not poets. So, no Athenians are poets.

10. It is not the case that no Athenians are brave. Therefore, some Athenians are brave.

11. Some Athenians are not citizens. Thus, not all Athenians are citizens.

12. No Athenians are Spartans. So, some Athenians are Spartans.

13. No Athenians are Spartans. So, all Athenians are Spartans.

14. All Spartans are warriors. Consequently, some Spartans are not warriors.

15. Some Macedonians are kings. So, it is false that no Macedonians are kings.

16. Some Macedonians are artists. So, all Macedonians are artists.

Another Way to Test Immediate Inferences: The Laws of Conversion, Obversion, and Contraposition

We have learned how to use the Square of Opposition to test immediate inferences for validity. Aristotle discovered another method for evaluating immediate inferences. One categorical sentence can be transformed into another one by applying certain exact logical operations or algorithms to the first categorical sentence. The results of these operations provide the basis for a set of principles, or laws, governing many different immediate inferences. Aristotle discovered the first several of these laws, and logicians following him discovered the rest. The laws governing conversion, obversion, and contraposition are especially useful.

How to Create the Converse of a Categorical Statement

If you start with a standard A, E, I, or O categorical sentence and switch the subject and predicate terms—without making any other changes—the result is the **converse** of the original sentence. For example, if we begin with "All cats are pets," the converse is "All pets are cats." Here are further examples:

Statement	Converse
A: All bats are mammals.	All mammals are bats.
E: No dogs are cats.	No cats are dogs.
I: Some politicians are poets.	Some poets are politicians.
O: Some politicians are not poets.	Some poets are not politicians.

In general:

Statement	Converse
A: All S are P.	All P are S.
E: No S are P.	No P are S.
I: Some S are P.	Some P are S.
O: Some S are not P.	Some P are not S.

Recall from Chapter 6 that two statements are logically equivalent if they imply each other, which is to say that in all situations they have matching truth-values. In a case of two equivalent statements, if one is true, the other will be true, and if one is false, the other will be false. Now, every time you form the converse of an E statement, the result will be logically equivalent to its converse. Likewise, every time you form the converse of an I statement, the result will be logically equivalent to its converse. Converting an E or an I statement thus *always* produces a logically equivalent statement.

- An E statement is logically equivalent to its converse.
- An I statement is logically equivalent to its converse.

However, converting an A or an O statement does not always result in an equivalent sentence. For instance, the A statement "All bats are mammals" is true, although its converse, "All mammals are bats," is false. In general, converting an A or an O statement is not guaranteed to produce an equivalent statement. This gives us the following logical law in two parts.

The Law of Conversion

- The converse of an E statement validly follows from the original statement.
- The converse of an I statement validly follows from the original statement.

To say that the converse "validly follows" from the original statement is to say that if the original statement is true, then the converse *must* be true as well. In other words, the original statement *implies* its converse. For example:

- E: No mammals are fish. Converse: No fish are mammals. The converse in this case validly follows from the original E statement.
- I: Some mammals are pets. Converse: Some pets are mammals. The converse in this case validly follows from the original I statement.

How to Create the Obverse of a Categorical Statement

If you perform the following two operations on a categorical statement, the result is called the **obverse** of the original statement:

1. Change the quality (without changing the quantity).
2. Replace the predicate term with its term complement.

The quality of a categorical sentence is always either affirmative or negative, so if you change the quality, then you change the sentence from affirmative to negative or from negative to affirmative. The **complement of a category or class C** is the class consisting of all those things that do not belong to C. For example, the complement of the class of cars is the class of all noncars; the complement of the class of mammals is the class consisting of all nonmammals (i.e., all things that are not mammals), and so on. The **term complement** is the term denoting the class complement. The term complement is formed by adding or subtracting the prefix *non* (or some equivalent) to the term. So, the term complement of cars is noncars, the term complement of cats is noncats, the term complement of nonbirds is birds, and so on.

A class and its complement constitute a pair of *mutually exclusive* classes (nothing is a member of both classes); they also constitute a pair of *jointly exhaustive* classes (anything whatsoever is a member of one or the other).

Let us now obvert the A statement "All Athenians are Greeks." Two steps are required:

1. We change the quality without changing the quantity. So we change the statement from the affirmative to the negative: All Athenians are *not* Greeks. But this is not in proper form. To say that all Athenians are not Greeks is to say that no Athenians are Greeks. So, at this stage, the sentence becomes "No Athenians are Greeks."
2. Next, we replace the predicate term with its term complement: The sentence becomes "No Athenians are non-Greeks."

Next, let us produce the obversion of "Some Greeks are Athenians."

1. We change the quality from affirmative to negative: Some Greeks are not Athenians.
2. We replace the predicate with its term complement: Some Greeks are not non-Athenians.

Notice that *not* is part of the copula and *non* is part of the predicate. Here are further examples:

Statement	Obverse
No Greeks are Persians.	All Greeks are non-Persians.
Some hoplites are farmers.	Some hoplites are not nonfarmers.

In general:

Statement	Obverse
A: All S are P.	No S are non-P.
E: No S are P.	All S are non-P.
I: Some S are P.	Some S are not non-P.
O: Some S are not P.	Some S are non-P.

Obversion and Equivalence

Notice that in each case above, if one of the statements is true, its obverse is true, and if one is false, its obverse is false. Therefore, every time you form the obverse of an A, E, I, or O statement, the result will be equivalent to the original statement. Notice also that if you obvert a categorical statement twice, and then cancel out any double negatives that result, you will end up back where you started, with your original statement. The result is another law governing a class of logical inferences.

The Law of Obversion

The obverse of any categorical statement validly follows the original statement.

For example:

- A: All bats are mammals. Obverse: No bats are nonmammals. The obverse validly follows from the original A statement.
- E: No mammals are fish. Obverse: All fish are nonmammals. The obverse validly follows from the original E statement.
- I: Some mammals are pets. Obverse: Some mammals are not nonpets. The obverse validly follows from the original I statement.
- O: Some bats are not pets. Obverse: Some bats are nonpets. The obverse validly follows from the original O statement.

How to Create the Contrapositive of a Categorical Statement

If you perform the following two operations on a categorical statement, the result is the **contrapositive**.

1. Switch the subject and predicate.
2. Replace each term with its term complement.

If we begin with "All Athenians are Greeks," the two steps are:

1. Switch subject and predicate: All Greeks are Athenians.
2. Replace terms with complements: All non-Greeks are non-Athenians.

For example, beginning with the O statement "Some cats are not pets," the contrapositive is formed in these two steps:

1. Switch subject and predicate: Some pets are not cats.
2. Replace terms with complements: Some nonpets are not noncats.

Contraposition and Equivalence

Every time you form the contrapositive of an A statement, the result will be equivalent to the original statement. Similarly, an O statement and its contrapositive will be logically equivalent in every case. However, not so for E and I statements. The converse of an E statement will not in every case be equivalent to the original, and the converse of an I statement will not always be a statement that is equivalent to the original. Thus:

- An A statement is logically equivalent to its contrapositive.
- An O statement is logically equivalent to its contrapositive.

This gives us another law of logical inference:

The Law of Contraposition

- The contrapositive of an A statement validly follows from the original statement.
- The contrapositive of an O statement validly follows from the original statement.

For example:

- A: All cats are mammals. Contrapositive: All nonmammals are noncats. The contrapositive in this case validly follows from the original statement.
- O: Some mammals are not cats. Contrapositive: Some noncats are not nonmammals. The contrapositive in this case validly follows from the original statement.

The laws of conversion, obversion, and contraposition, and the Square of Opposition, constitute a powerful system of logic for evaluating immediate inferences.

In Sum

Statement	Converse	
A: All S are P.	All P are S.	
E: No S are P.	No P are S.	(equivalent)
I: Some S are P.	Some P are S.	(equivalent)
O: Some S are not P.	Some P are not S.	

Statement	Obverse	
A: All S are P.	No S are non-P.	(equivalent)
E: No S are P.	All S are non-P.	(equivalent)
I: Some S are P.	Some S are not non-P.	(equivalent)
O: Some S are not P.	Some S are non-P.	(equivalent)

Statement	Contrapositive	
A: All S are P.	All non-P are non-S.	(equivalent)
E: No S are P.	No non-P are non-S.	
I: Some S are P.	Some non-P are non-S.	
O: Some S are not P.	Some non-P are not non-S.	(equivalent)

Exercise 7.5   Instructions in context.

1. For each of the following statements, construct the converse and state whether the converse is equivalent or not to the original statement.
   a. All Athenians are Greeks.
   b. No Athenians are Greeks.
   c. Some Athenians are Greeks.
   d. Some Athenians are not Greeks.

2. For each of the following statements, construct the obverse and state whether the obverse is equivalent or not to the original statement.
   a. All Persians are subjects of the "King of kings."
   b. No Persians are subjects of the "King of kings."
   c. Some Persians are subjects of the "King of kings."
   d. Some Persians are not subjects of the "King of kings."

3. For each of the following statements, construct the contrapositive and state whether the contrapositive is equivalent or not to the original statement.
   a. All politicians are honest persons.
   b. No politicians are honest persons.
   c. Some politicians are honest persons.
   d. Some politicians are not honest persons.

Exercise 7.6   Use the Square of Opposition plus the laws of conversion, obversion, and contraposition to determine whether the following are valid or invalid.

1. Some Athenians are not noncitizens. Thus, not all Athenians are citizens.

2. All Athenians are non-Spartans. So, some Athenians are not non-Spartans.

3. No Athenians are Spartans. So, no Athenians are non-Spartans.

4. Spartans are nonwarriors. Consequently, some Spartans are nonwarriors.

5. Some Macedonians are not nonkings. So, it is false that no Macedonians are kings.

6. Some Macedonians are not nonartists. So, no Macedonians are nonartists.

7. It is false that no Spartans are diplomats. So, some Spartans are not nondiplomats.

8. No Spartans are nondiplomats. So, it is false that no Spartans are diplomats.

9. All Spartans are nonlovers of peace. So, some Spartans are not lovers of peace.

10. It is false that some Spartans are not noncowards. So, no Spartans are cowards.

11. All Spartans are loud persons. So, some Spartans are not nonloud persons.

12. It is false that some Spartans are not nonpoets. So, it is false that all Spartans are poets.

13. It is false that some Spartans are not athletes. So, it is false that no Spartans are athletes.

14. It is false that no Athenians are nonhairy. So, it is true that some Athenians are hairy.

15. Some Athenians are not poets. So, all Athenians are nonpoets.

16. It is not the case that no Athenians are brave. Therefore, some Athenians are not nonbrave.

Reality Check: Translating Common Sentences of English into Standard Categorical Form

You probably noticed that the categorical sentences in this chapter all sound sort of stiff and rigid. "Some cats are mammals," "Some dogs are pets," "No cats are reptiles," and so on. The common feature, of course, is that each exactly fits one of the four standardized forms, "All S are P," "No S are P," and so on. We don't speak this way in ordinary life. On a hot summer day, Joe down at the corner store might say, "Flies are a problem this time of year," but he is never going to say, "All flies are bugs that are a problem this time of year." Thus, we note a discrepancy between the stuffy language forms we have been using and the forms of speaking in everyday life. There is a reason for this discrepancy. The English language is flexible, which means that in most cases it allows us to say something in many different ways. However, this flexibility raises a problem for a logical theory that aims to be systematic and universal. If we want to formulate precise rules that hold universally, we must specify them so that they apply to specifically identified sentences fitting a limited number of exact forms. It is possible to formulate rules that fit any sentence, no matter what its form, but given the incredible variety of English sentences (or sentences in any other language, for that matter), rules that would apply to any sentence in any form would be rules so incredibly complex as to be practically useless. Sentences in standardized forms have the virtue of being clearer, have a more precise meaning, and are freer of emotional overtones. It is easier to reason about such sentences.

To make matters as precise as possible, a categorical sentence is in *standard form* if the following are true:

1. It begins with a quantifier, and the quantifier is either *All*, *No*, or *Some*.
2. The subject term (designating the subject class) appears next, and it always designates or names a class or category of things (*cats*, *mammals*, etc.).
3. The copula (relating the subject and predicate terms) appears next and is either the word *are* or the words *are not*.
4. The predicate term (designating the predicate class) appears last, and it always names or designates a class or category of things.

Few sentences in everyday English fit this fairly rigid standard format, but most sentences in everyday English can be translated into this format without loss of essential logical meaning. There are eight cases to consider.

Sentences with Nonstandard Predicates

The subject and predicate terms of a standard categorical statement must each be a noun or other term that denotes a class or category of things. For example, the sentence "Some roses are red" is not in standard form, for its predicate term is an adjective (*red*), and adjectives do not by themselves name groups of things (they denote characteristics of things). In everyday life, we often state categorical sentences containing only adjectives as their predicate terms, but this is easy to fix. If the predicate term in a categorical sentence is only an adjective, we can change the adjective to a noun or a noun-like expression referring to a class or category of things. If we rewrite "Some roses are red" as "Some roses are red flowers," then the sentence fits the standard form, for *red flowers* denotes a class of things. In general, then, if a statement has an adjectival predicate, replace this predicate with a term designating the class of all objects of which the adjective may truly be predicated. Study the following examples closely:

Nonstandard	Standard
All tigers are carnivorous.	All tigers are carnivorous animals.
All deer are fleeing the fire.	All deer are things that are fleeing the fire.
All students are striking.	All students are persons who are striking.
Some aardvarks are cute.	Some aardvarks are cute animals.
All cars are metallic.	All cars are metallic things.

Sentences with Missing and Nonstandard Quantifiers

A categorical sentence in standard form begins with a quantifier, either *All, No,* or *Some.* Therefore, an ordinary sentence such as "Mammals are animals" or "A dog is in the room" are not in standard form. The problem, of course, is that these sentences are missing a quantifier. But this can easily be fixed. We can translate these sentences into standard form by simply adding a quantifier to each one. But which quantifier? We think about what the author probably intends, and then we add the quantifier the author probably intended.

Usually, a universal quantifier is intended when a quantifier is left unstated in a sentence such "Mammals are animals." Why? It is a matter of common sense that *all* mammals are animals. Following the principle of charity, we assume the author possesses common sense, and we suppose she meant "All mammals are animals." We therefore rewrite the sentence and place the universal quantifier *All* at the front.

Similarly, it is a matter of common sense that there are hundreds of millions of dogs in the world. So when someone says, "A dog is in the room," we assume the author has common sense and we do not interpret the sentence as saying that *all* dogs are in the room. How could you fit 250 million dogs in one room? We add the existential quantifier and rewrite the sentence as "Some dogs are in the room." Of course, the predicate of this sentence needs work. Best to render the sentence: "Some dogs are animals that are in the room." Here are some further examples:

Nonstandard	Standard
A tiger is a mammal.	All tigers are mammals.
A fish is not a mammal.	No fish are mammals.
Emeralds are green.	All emeralds are green things.
A whale is a beautiful creature.	All whales are beautiful creatures.
A protestor is holding a sign.	Some protesters are persons holding signs.

The context and our general or commonsense knowledge of the world thus play a role when translating sentences into standard form.

Recall that in logic the word *some* means "at least one" or "one or more." Many ordinary sentences start with *most, few,* and *at least one,* rather than the word *some.* Such sentences need to be rewritten with the quantifier *some* replacing nonstandard quantifiers such as *most, many, few,* and so on. Any quantity less than *All* is best translated as *Some.*" Thus:

Nonstandard Quantifier	Standard Interpretation
Most cats are cute.	Some cats are cute animals.
Few aardvarks are handsome.	Some aardvarks are handsome animals.
At least one platypus is cute.	Some platypuses are cute animals.
Several pigs are smart.	Some pigs are smart animals.
Many bears are timid.	Some bears are timid animals.
There are bears in the woods.	Some bears are animals in the woods.
A tiger roared.	Some tigers are animals that roared.

Missing or Nonstandard Copulas

Recall that the copula connects (couples) the subject and predicate terms. In standard form, the only copulas allowed are the words *are* and *are not*. Consider the sentence "All mice eat cheese." This sentence obviously is meant to express a universal affirmative statement. However, the sentence does not contain *are* or *are not*, so we need to supply a proper copula. To place this sentence into standard form, we rewrite the predicate term so as to preserve the sense of the original sentence but also so that the sentence uses the copula *are*. When we do this, the sentence (in standard form) becomes "All mice are cheese-eaters." In other words, all mice belong to the category of cheese-eating creatures. Similarly, "All hens lay eggs" takes standard form once we supply the copula *are* and make suitable adjustments: "All hens are egg-laying animals."

There are many other nonstandard ways to couple subjects and predicates in a categorical sentence. Such sentences must be rewritten so that they contain *are* or *are not*. In general, we do this by moving the verb into the predicate and adding the proper copula at the same time. For example, "Some dogs shake hands" should be rewritten "Some dogs are animals that shake hands." And "Some persons who go to college will become educated" can be rewritten as "Some persons who go to college are persons who will become educated." Similarly, "Some dogs bite" needs to be rewritten as "Some dogs are animals that bite." The nonstandard "All ducks swim" becomes "All ducks are animals that swim." Finally, "Some birds fly south for the winter" can be rewritten as "Some birds are animals that fly south for the winter." Study these examples carefully to see the way sentences are translated from ordinary English into standard categorical form without loss of meaning.

Time and Tense

Sentences in standard categorical form are always stated in the present tense. Thus, when we supply a proper copula, we must always supply the present tense of the verb. For example, "Some Democrats will be elected" is about the future. The sentence therefore needs to be rewritten in the present tense: "Some Democrats are persons who will be elected." Likewise, "Some Democrats were technocrats" is about the past and needs to be restated in the present tense. The sentence becomes "Some Democrats are technocrats." Keep in mind that when you add a copula, always supply the plural *are*, or *are not*. Thus, "No dog is a cat" needs to be rewritten "No dogs are cats," and so on.

Translating Singular Statements

We often reason about one specifically identified individual thing, rather than a group of things, and in such cases we express our reasoning with singular statements. A *singular statement* makes an assertion about one specifically identified entity or thing. For instance, "Aristotle is a logician," "Plato is a teacher," "The tallest man in Athens is also a soldier." A singular statement in standard form begins with a *singular term*, which can be defined as "a word or phrase that refers to one specifically identified thing," and concludes by saying something about that which the singular term designates. Two types of singular terms will concern us here. A *proper name* refers to one specifically identified thing by naming it (John F. Kennedy, Barack Obama, etc.). A *definite description* refers to one specifically identified thing by describing it in a definite way. "The tallest building in town," "the oldest man on earth," and "the first house on the left" are all definite descriptions in a particular context.

Can a logic that was designed for categorical talk about *groups* of things handle singular sentences that begin with singular terms? The answer, surprisingly, is yes. The strategy will be to treat the singular term in a singular sentence as if it designates a one-member class or category of things. In other words, a singular term will be interpreted as a term that refers to all the members of a class that has only *one* specific member. In addition, the concept of quantitative identity will be employed.

When we say, "Clark Kent is Superman," we mean that the individual named Clark Kent is one and the same person as the individual named Superman. In other words, they are one and the same person, not two different persons. Similarly, the Island of Formosa is the same as the nation of Taiwan. In other words, Formosa and Taiwan are one and the same thing, not two different things. Now, when we say that X and Y are identical in the *quantitative* sense, we mean that they are in reality one and the same thing, not two different things.

In contrast, if two different coffee cups look exactly alike, we might call them "identical" cups, but we do not mean that they are one and the same cup. They are two different cups. They simply look alike; in other words, they have the same qualities. This form of identity is called *qualitative* identity.

Now, let us translate the sentence "Aristotle is a logician." Using the concept of quantitative identity, and forming an artificial class consisting of just one person, we say: "All persons *identical to Aristotle* are persons who are logicians." The subject class is thus "persons identical to Aristotle," which means "all persons who are one and the same person as Aristotle." Because Aristotle is the only person who is identical to Aristotle, this is a class of one. Aristotle is in a class by himself! (In Unit Four, we will meet one of the logical laws of identity, the principle that each thing is identical to itself.)

Adverbs

Sentences containing temporal and spatial adverbs need some work before they fit one of the standard forms. Basically, temporal adverbs (*when, whenever, anytime, always*, etc.) need to be translated into times, and spatial adverbs (*where, everywhere, anywhere*, etc.) must be translated into places. For example, "Aristotle always paces back and forth when he lectures" translates into "All times in which Aristotle lectures are times he paces back and forth." Similarly, "Plato is never unreasonable" goes into standard form as "No times in his life are times Plato is unreasonable." Likewise, "Socrates is always questioning people" needs to be rewritten as "All times of his life are times Socrates is questioning people."

Continuing the same pattern with spatial adverbs, "Nowhere on earth is there a unicorn" translates as "No places on earth are places where there is a unicorn." Likewise, "Nowhere on Earth is there a perfect pizza" can be rewritten "No places on earth are places where there is a perfect pizza." A sentence such as "Illie pies live in the woods of the Pacific Northwest" becomes "Some places in the woods of the Pacific Northwest are places in which illie pies live." Similarly, the sentence "Love is everywhere" translates as "All places in the world are places where there is love."

Conditional Sentences

The standard form for a conditional sentence is "If _____, then _____," where the blanks are filled in with declarative sentences. For instance, "If Aristotle lectures, then Zorba will snore," or "If the Persians launch a sea attack, then they will lose." In a conditional sentence, the *antecedent* is the part introduced by the word *If* and the *consequent* is the part introduced by the word *then*. Conditional sentences get their name from the fact that the antecedent states a condition needed for the truth of the consequent.

Conditional sentences obviously fit none of the four standard forms that a categorical sentence can take. However, they are easily translated into standard categorical form. The trick is to think of a conditional sentence as a universal sentence making a claim (in the consequent) about all the items referred to by the antecedent. Specifically, a conditional sentence is interpreted as attributing the property expressed in the consequent to each and every item denoted by the antecedent. For example, consider "If it's a mouse, then it's a mammal." This is best interpreted as attributing the property of being a mammal to each and every mouse. Accordingly, "If it's a mouse, then it's a mammal" goes into standard form as "All mice are mammals." Similarly, "If it is a mouse, then it is not a reptile" becomes "No mice are reptiles."

Exclusive Statements

Exclusive sentences attribute a characteristic exclusively to the members of one group of things; for example, "None but the brave are free" or "Nobody can do the shingaling like me." Exclusive sentences can be very difficult to translate properly. Let us think about what "None but the brave are free" means. It is best to interpret this so that it is a universal claim. Is it saying that all brave people are free people? Or is it saying that all free people are brave people? On reflection, the most plausible interpretation is "All free persons are brave persons." For when we say, "None but the brave are free," we are *not* claiming that all brave people are free (surely there might be some brave people who are not free); we are saying that the only people who are free are people who are also brave. Thus, the sentence seems to be saying *not* that each and every brave person is free, but that each and every free person is a brave person. Notice that when we translate an exclusive sentence, "None but the As are Bs," we reverse the subject and predicate, place it into a universal affirmative form, and say "All Bs are As."

Consider "Only logic students are invited to the reception at the Lyceum." This, too, is exclusive and translates in a similar way. The claim is *not* that all logic students are invited; rather, the claim is that all who are invited are logic students. Thus the translation: "All persons invited to the reception at the Lyceum are logic students." Likewise, a sentence such as "Only elected officials will attend the meeting" says that all who will attend the meeting will be people who are elected officials. Consequently, "Only elected officials will attend the meeting" becomes "All persons who will attend the meeting are elected officials." Again, notice that we reversed the subject and predicate when we translated from ordinary English to standard form.

A sentence beginning with "The only" (instead of just "only") is typically *not* an exclusive sentence. For instance, "The only food available is Greek food" is best interpreted as saying that "All available meals are Greek meals." Likewise, the sentence "The only people invited were logicians" becomes "All persons invited are logicians." Thus, when it appears at the start of a sentence, the expression "The only" typically translates simply as "All."

Exceptive Statements

Consider this sentence: "All except truckers are happy with the new regulations." How shall we translate this? On analysis, the sentence is saying two things: (a) All nontruckers are happy with the new regulations, and (b) no truckers are happy with the new regulations. Consequently, the sentence can be translated, "All nontruckers are persons who are happy with the new regulations, and no truckers are persons who are happy with the new regulations." Generally, a sentence of the form "All except As are Bs" translates as two separate sentences conjoined by *and*, with one type taking the form "All non-As are Bs," and the other the form "No As are Bs."

Exercise 7.7   Instructions in context.

1. Translate the following undisciplined statements into perfectly formed A statements.

    a. A drop of seawater is salty.

b. A virtuous person accepts criticism calmly and rationally.

c. Teenagers are naturally a little rebellious.

d. If that is a spear, then it is an instrument of war.

e. Whoever worships regularly at the temple of Athena is religious.

f. Truly religious people are charitable.

g. A moral person is a rational person.

h. A rational person is a moral person.

i. Olives are a good source of cooking oil.

j. Only the rational are truly free.

k. Wherever he goes, a cloud of gloom hangs over him.

l. None but students of logic were admitted to the toga party.

m. It's always raining.

n. Human beings are hard-wired to be selfish in all that they do.

2. Translate the following loosely put statements into exact E statements.

a. A cowardly person is not a rational person.

b. An irrational person does not accept criticism calmly.

c. A self-realized person is not an irrational person.

d. If that person is a Spartan, then he is not an Athenian.

e. Whoever hurts innocent people is not a rational person.

f. Criminals are not charitable.

g. A person who is a user is not a moral person.

h. A thief is not a moral person.

i. Rocks are not a good source of cooking oil.

j. Persians do not make good infantrymen.

k. A professional wrestler is not someone you want to mess with.

l. Students of logic were not admitted to the toga party.

m. If it's raining, then it is not a good day for an outdoor lecture.

n. Human beings are not naturally selfish.

o. Human beings are not selfish.

p. No one who is a student is rich.

3. Translate the following wildly formed statements into precise I statements.

a. There are moral warriors.

b. Most kings are tyrants.

c. Some kings are tolerant.

d. Many warriors are religious.

e. Several citizens voted.

f. A few philosophers drink wine.

g. There have been some old philosophers.

h. Several people saw smoke.

i. Sometimes it rains.

j. There are some sacred places.

4. Translate the following flabbily stated statements into precise O statements.

a. There are dishonest politicians.

b. There are philosophers who aren't logicians.

c. Most logicians are not astronomers.

d. There are some old philosophers.

e. Many logicians don't own a spear and suit of armor.

f. Most logicians aren't rich.

g. There have been philosophers who cannot read music.

h. Sometimes it doesn't rain.

i. Some places are not sacred.

j. Some logicians have never studied at Plato's Academy.

Glossary

Affirmative sentence A sentence that affirms class membership.

Ambiguous Having two or more meanings.

Categorical Argument An argument composed of categorical sentences.

Categorical Logic The study of arguments that are composed of categorical sentences.

Categorical sentence A sentence asserting that all, or some, of one category of things either belong to or do not belong to another category of things.

Class A collection of objects having a specified characteristic in common.

Complement of a class The class consisting of all those things outside the class.

Contradictories Two statements are contradictories if and only if they cannot both be true and they cannot both be false. In all possible situations, if one is true, the other is false.

Contrapositive The sentence that results if you perform the following two operations on a categorical sentence: 1. Switch the subject and predicate. 2. Replace each term with its term complement.

Contraries Two statements are contraries if they cannot both be true, but might both be false. If two statements are contraries, at least one is false.

Converse of a sentence The sentence that results if we switch the subject and predicate terms in a categorical sentence.

Copula A word that links the subject term with the predicate term.

Immediate inference An argument composed of exactly one premise and one conclusion immediately drawn from it.

Logical equivalence Two statements are logically equivalent if they imply each other, which is to say that in all situations they have matching truth-values.

Logical form of an argument An abstract logical structure that many arguments, about many different subjects, may have in common.

Logical form of a sentence An abstract logical structure that many sentences may have in common.

Mediate inference An argument composed of two categorical premises and one conclusion, in which the reasoning from the first premise to the conclusion is "mediated" by passing through a second premise.

Negative sentence A sentence in which class membership is denied.

Obverse of a sentence The sentence that results if you perform the following two operations on a categorical sentence: 1. Change the quality (without changing the quantity) from affirmative to negative or negative to affirmative. 2. Replace the predicate term with its term complement.

Particular Pertaining to one or more members of a category.

Particular affirmative sentence Categorical sentence asserting that some of the members of one category of things belong to a second category of things.

Particular negative sentence Categorical sentence asserting that some of the members of one category of things do not belong to a second category of things.

Particular sentence A categorical sentence that makes a claim about some of the class denoted by the subject term.

Quantifier A word such as *all* or *some* that specifies a quantity for the subject term of the sentence.

Singular statement A sentence that makes an assertion about a specifically identified entity or thing.

Some One or more; that is, at least one. Another way to put this: one or more, possibly all.

Sorites A series of four or more categorical statements with one of the statements designated as the conclusion and the rest designated as premises.

Square of Opposition A table representing the logical relations between corresponding categorical statements.

Subcontraries Two statements that cannot both be false, but that might both be true. If two statements are subcontraries, at least one is true.

Term complement The term denoting the class complement.

Truth-value The value a sentence has when it is true or false. When a sentence is true, it has the truth-value of true and when a sentence is false, it has the truth-value of false.

Universal Pertaining to all the members of a category.

Universal affirmative sentence A categorical sentence asserting that all the members of one category of things belong to a second category of things.

Universal negative sentence A categorical sentence asserting that none of the members of one category of things belong to a second category of things.

Universal sentence A categorical sentence that makes a claim about every member of the class denoted by the subject term.

Vague Having fuzzy boundaries of application.

8 The Categorical Syllogism « « « « « « « «

What Is a Categorical Syllogism?

We have been evaluating immediate inferences—arguments that draw a conclusion immediately from one single premise. In a mediate inference, a conclusion is inferred from one premise through the mediation of a second premise. A *mediate inference* is thus a two-premise argument. Aristotle held that every mediate inference can be translated without loss of meaning into a *categorical syllogism*, which he defined precisely as an argument that has all the following properties:

1. It is composed of exactly two premises and one conclusion, all categorical statements.
2. Each sentence in the argument contains exactly two terms—no more, no less.
3. The argument as a whole contains exactly three different terms, each appearing exactly twice in the argument.
4. No term appears twice in the same sentence.

The following argument is a categorical syllogism:

1. All whales are swimmers.
2. All whales are mammals.
3. Therefore, some mammals are swimmers.

The three terms are *whales*, *swimmers*, and *mammals*. Notice that, given the definition of a categorical syllogism (hereafter, "syllogism" for short), each term appears in only two of the syllogism's sentences.

It was Aristotle who first discovered that what makes a syllogism valid, when it is valid, is not its content; that is, what it is about. Rather, what makes it valid is its form or logical structure—something that has nothing intrinsically to do with the subject matter at all, or indeed with *any* particular subject matter. The logical form is a purely logical structure—"pure" in the sense of being "unsullied" by direct contact with objects of the material world. If categorical logic is to be comprehensive and exact, a form must be specified for every possible type of categorical syllogism. All 256 types, as it turns out.

Logical Form for Categorical Syllogisms

Middle, Major, and Minor Terms

The term appearing in both premises (and thus not in the conclusion) is called the **middle term**. The predicate term of the conclusion is called the **major term**. The term appearing as the subject of the conclusion is the **minor term**. The **major premise** is the premise containing the major term, and the **minor premise** is the premise containing the minor term. In the following example, *animals* is the major term, *snakes* is the minor term, and *pets* is the middle term.

1 All pets are animals.
2. Some snakes are pets.
3. So, necessarily, some snakes are animals.

Standard Form

Let us say that a categorical syllogism is in **standard form** if the major premise is listed first, followed by the minor premise, and finally the conclusion.

Figure

Aristotle next divided syllogisms into three groups called figures. An overlooked fourth figure was later added to the system by his successor at the Lyceum, Theophrastus (371–287 BC), the second head of the school. A syllogism written in standard form (and thus with the major premise listed first) is placed into one of the four figures according to the following schema:

- Figure 1: In syllogisms of this figure, the middle term appears in the major premise as a subject term and in the minor premise as a predicate term.
- Figure 2: In syllogisms of this figure, the middle term appears as the predicate term in both premises.
- Figure 3: In syllogisms of this figure, the middle term appears as the subject term in both premises.

- Figure 4: In syllogisms of this figure, the middle term appears as the predicate term in the major premise and as the subject term in the minor premise.

Notice that the figure of a categorical syllogism is determined by the placement of its middle term and by nothing else. One way to remember the four figures is to keep in mind the following diagram. In the table, S stands for the minor term, P stands for the major term, and M stands for the middle term. The minor term is assigned S because it is the subject of the conclusion, the major term gets P because it is the predicate of the conclusion, and the middle term gets M for "middle."

	Figure 1	Figure 2	Figure 3	Figure 4
Major Premise:	MP	PM	MP	PM
Minor Premise:	SM	SM	MS	MS
Conclusion:	SP	SP	SP	SP

Some people remember the figures by noticing that the arrangement of the Ms on the chart resembles the outline of a collar on a shirt. Can you see the collar in the chart?

Mood and Complete Logical Form

The **mood of a categorical syllogism** is indicated by listing the A, E, I, or O type for each of its three sentences. The **logical form of a categorical syllogism** is then specified by listing the syllogism's mood followed by the figure it belongs to, assuming the syllogism starts with its major premise. Consider the following syllogism:

1. No aardvarks are birds.
2. Some aardvarks are happy.
3. Therefore, some happy things are not birds.

The mood is EIO because the major premise is an E statement, the minor premise is an I statement, and its conclusion is O. The arrangement of the middle term (*aardvarks*) places this syllogism in Figure 3. The logical form is thus EIO-3. Make sure you see why the following syllogism has an AEE-4 form:

1. All S are M.
2. No M are P.
3. So, No S are P.

Substitution Instance of a Form

If we substitute *cats* for the variable S, and if we substitute *mammals* for the variable M, and if we replace P with *birds*, the result is a *substitution instance* of the form:

1. All cats are mammals.
2. No mammals are birds.
3. So, no cats are birds.

Each argument form has an infinite number of potential substitution instances, naturally, because argument forms are abstract blueprints that many different arguments, about many different topics, can instantiate or fit.

> The **logical form** of a syllogism in standard form is specified by listing the syllogism's mood followed by the figure to which it belongs.

Exercise 8.1   Instructions in context.

1. Rewrite each syllogism in standard form and name the mood and figure.
    a. All logicians are philosophers. No philosophers are zombies. So no logicians are zombies.
    b. Some logicians are poets. Some poets are artists. So some logicians are artists.
    c. No mammals are fish. Some fish are brown. So some mammals are not brown.
    d. Some logicians are not poets. All poets are courageous. So no logicians are courageous.
    e. No philosophers are zombies. Some zombies are ugly creatures. So no philosophers are ugly creatures.
    f. Some philosophers are logicians. All logicians are logical individuals. So all philosophers are logical individuals.
    g. All philosophers are self-questioning individuals. All self-questioning individuals are improvable individuals. So all philosophers are improvable individuals.
    h. Some logicians are not teachers to be feared. All geometers are teachers to be feared. So some logicians are not geometers.
2. In the preceding problems, identify the major, minor, and middle terms.

3. Construct a syllogism in the mood EIO, Figure 2.
4. Construct a syllogism in the mood EAE, Figure 1.
5. Construct a syllogism in the mood AII, Figure 1.
6. Construct a syllogism in the mood AEE, Figure 3.
7. Construct a syllogism in the mood IAI, Figure 4.
8. Construct a syllogism in the mood OAO, Figure 3.
9. Construct a syllogism in the mood AOO, Figure 3.

Evaluating Categorical Syllogisms Using Rules of Validity

Distribution Defined

One of the methods Aristotle devised for determining whether a categorical syllogism is valid or invalid involves a set of rules governing the "distribution" of terms and positive (affirmative) and negative claims within a categorical syllogism. What is a distributed term? A term appearing in a syllogism is said to be a **distributed term** if it is being used in the syllogism to make a claim about every member of a given category. There are four cases to consider.

1. In an A (universal affirmative) sentence, the subject term is distributed because it is being used to say something about every member of the category to which it refers. However, the predicate term is not being used to say something about every member of the predicate category, and so the predicate term of an A sentence is not distributed. For example, the A sentence "All cats are mammals" claims that every member of the cat category belongs to the mammal category. The subject term is thus distributed because it is being used to say something about every member of the category to which it refers. However, the sentence does not say that every mammal is a cat. The predicate term (mammals) is therefore not distributed because it is not being used to say something about every member of the category to which it refers.

2. In an E (universal negative) sentence, the subject term is distributed because it is being used to say something about every member of the category to which it refers. Likewise for the predicate term. Therefore, both terms are distributed in an E sentence. For example, consider the E sentence "No cats are birds." The claim is that every member of the cat category does *not* belong to the bird category. The subject term is thus distributed because it is being used to say something about every member of the category to which it refers. The predicate term is also distributed because it is being used to say something about every member of the predicate category (*birds*), namely, that each member is not a cat.

3.   It is obvious that neither term is distributed in the I sentence "Some **S** are **P**." For example, in the I sentence "Some cats are pets," no claim is being made about all cats and no claim is being made about all pets.

4.   The situation is not as clear in the case of the O form "Some **S** are not **P**," for example, "Some horses are not pets." The subject term is obviously not distributed, as it is not being used in this case to say something about all horses. However, is the predicate term distributed? It does not appear to be, at least at first glance. However, on closer inspection, the predicate term (*pets*) is being employed to say something about the entire category to which it refers (*pets*), for the sentence says that at least one horse is such that it cannot be found anywhere in the *entire category* of pets. The predicate term of an O sentence thus is distributed. In sum:

	Subject Term	Predicate Term
A	D	U
E	D	D
I	U	U
O	U	D

where D signifies "distributed" and U means "undistributed."

The Four Traditional Rules of Validity for Syllogisms

We are now ready for the four rules of validity governing categorical syllogisms, formulated by Aristotle and his successors. If a syllogism satisfies all the rules, it must be valid; if it does not satisfy them all, it must be invalid. The rules are complete in the sense that they allow us to determine, for any possible syllogism, whether or not it is valid. The rules also correspond well to common sense, in that the results they yield agree with our commonsense judgments of validity and invalidity for syllogisms. Here is one way to state the traditional rules of validity for categorical syllogisms:

A syllogism is valid if, and only if, all the following conditions are met:

1.   The middle term is distributed in at least one premise.
2.   If either term is distributed in the conclusion, it is also distributed in a premise.
3.   The syllogism does not contain two negative premises.
4.   If one premise is negative, then the conclusion is negative; if the conclusion is negative, then one premise is negative.

Associated Fallacies

A fallacy is an error in reasoning. If a syllogism violates the first rule, the syllogism is said to commit the *fallacy of undistributed middle*. Here is an example:

1. All philosophers are writers.
2. All artists are writers.
3. So, all artists are philosophers.

Recall that the predicate term of an A statement is undistributed. When we say that all Spartans are Greeks, we are not saying something about *all Greeks*. Because the middle term, *writer*, is not distributed in either premise, this argument violates rule 1. Intuitively, does this syllogism seem invalid to you?

If a syllogism violates rule 2, the fallacy is the *fallacy of illicit major* if the major term is distributed in the conclusion but is not distributed in the major premise. The mistake is the *fallacy of illicit minor* if the minor term is distributed in the conclusion but is undistributed in the minor premise. Here is a syllogism that commits the illicit major fallacy:

1. All cats are mammals.
2. All calicos are cats.
3. So, no calicos are mammals.

Recall that the predicate term of an E statement is distributed whereas the predicate term of the A statement is not. Notice that the major term *mammals* is distributed in the conclusion but not in the major premise, premise 1. With obviously true premises and an obviously false conclusion, this is a fallacy no doubt.

This syllogism commits the illicit minor fallacy:

1. All artists are idealists.
2. All idealists are passionate people.
3. So, no passionate people are artists.

This violates the rule because the minor term (*passionate people*) is distributed in the conclusion but not in the minor premise. Does this syllogism seem invalid to you?

If a syllogism violates rule 3, the fallacy is the *fallacy of exclusive premises*. Here is an example:

1. No poets are logicians.
2. No logicians are ice cube salesmen.
3. Therefore, no poets are ice cube salesmen.

A syllogism that violates the fourth rule is said to commit either *the fallacy of drawing a negative conclusion from affirmative premises* or else the *fallacy of drawing an affirmative conclusion from a negative premise*. Here is an example of each, in order:

1. All mammals are warm-blooded creatures.
2. All dogs are warm-blooded creatures.
3. So, no dogs are mammals.

And:

1. No reptiles are mammals.
2. No birds are mammals.
3. Therefore, some birds are reptiles.

The four traditional rules of validity for categorical syllogisms are *sound* (this means only valid syllogistic forms pass the test) and *complete* (this means all valid syllogistic forms pass the test), although a rigorous proof of this claim is beyond the scope of our discussion. The student of logic seeking to become the next Aristotle is encouraged to give it a try.

Of the 256 logical forms for categorical syllogisms, only these 24 do not violate any of the traditional rules:

Figure 1	Figure 2	Figure 3	Figure 4
AAA	EAE	IAI	AEE
EAE	AEE	AII	IAI
AII	EIO	OAO	EIO
EIO	AOO	EIO	AAI
AAI	EAO	AAI	AEO
EAO	AEO	EAO	

Exercise 8.2   If you are looking for something to do on a rainy afternoon, go back to Exercise 8.1 Part 1 and determine which syllogisms are valid by checking the mood and figure against the list of valid syllogistic forms.

Exercise 8.3   Test these syllogisms for validity using the rules of validity for syllogisms. For each syllogism, also list the mood and figure.

1. Some logicians are lawyers. All lawyers are extemporaneous speakers. So some extemporaneous speakers are logicians.

2. All chariot racers are musicians. Some chariot racers are soldiers. Therefore, some musicians are soldiers.

3. All philosophers are lovers of truth. No lovers of truth are closed-minded people. Thus, no philosophers are closed-minded people.

4. All goats are cute. All small mammals are cute. So all small mammals are goats.

5. Some musicians are not poets. All musicians are happy persons. Therefore, some happy persons are not poets.

6. No soldiers are rich. No rich persons are poets. So no soldiers are poets.

7. No logicians are musicians. All musicians are artists. Consequently, no artists are logicians.

8. Some politicians are idealistic persons. No idealistic persons are scientists. So some scientists are not politicians.

9. No scientists are poets. Some scientists are logicians. Therefore, some logicians are not poets.

10. Some actors are sculptors. Some poets are not actors. So some poets are not sculptors.

11. No A are B. All C are A. So no C are B.

12. All A are B. All A are C. So some C are B.

13. Some A are B. All C are B. So some C are A.

14. All A are B. No B are C. Therefore, some C are A.

15. All A are B. All A are C. Thus, all C are B.

16. All A are B, because all A are C and all B are C.

17. No A are B. Therefore, some C are B, because no A are C.

18. Some A are B. Some A are C. So some B are C.

19. Some A are not B, because some A are not C, and all C are B.

20. No A are B, so no C are A because all B are C.

21. All M are P. No S are M. So no S are P.

22. All P are M. Some S are M. So some S are P.

23. All P are M. All S are M. Consequently, all S are P.

24. Some M are not P. Some S are M. Therefore, some S are not P.

25. No M are P. All M are S. So some S are not P.

26. No A are B. No C are B. So no C are A.

27. No H are G. All F are G. So no F are H.

28. No H are G. Some F are G. So some F are not H.

29. Some G are not H. No F are G. So some F are not H.

30. Some H are G. Some F are G. Therefore, some F are H.

INTERLUDE

Medieval Game Show: "Name That Argument!"

In the Middle Ages, logicians teaching in the cathedral schools of Europe assigned these Latin names to the 15 syllogisms first proven valid by Aristotle:

Figure 1 *(MIDDLE TERM IS THE SUBJECT TERM IN THE MAJOR PREMISE, PREDICATE TERM IN THE MINOR PREMISE.)*

Name	Logical Form	Details
Barbara:	AAA-1:	All M are P; all S are M. So, all S are P
Celarent:	EAE-1:	No M are P; all S are M. So, no S are P
Darii:	AII-1:	All M are P; some S are M. So, some S are P
Ferio:	EIO-1:	No M are P; some S are M. So, some S are not P

Figure 2 *(MIDDLE TERM IS THE PREDICATE TERM IN BOTH PREMISES.)*

Name	Logical Form	Details
Cesare:	EAE-2:	No P are M; all S are M. So, no S are P
Camestres:	AEE-2:	All P are M; no S are M. So, no S are P
Festino:	EIO-2:	No P are M; some S are M. So, some S are not
Baroco:	AOO-2:	All P are M; some S are not M. So, some S are not P

Figure 3 *(MIDDLE TERM IS THE SUBJECT TERM IN BOTH PREMISES.)*

Name	Logical Form	Details
Darapti:	AAI-3:	All M are P; all M are S. So, some S are P.
Disamis:	IAI-3:	Some M are P; all M are S. So, some S are P.
Datisi:	AII-3:	All M are P; some M are S. So, some S are P.
Felapton:	EAO-3:	No M are P; all M are S. So, some S are not P.
Bocardo:	OAO-3:	Some M are not P; all M are S. So, some S are not P.
Ferison:	EIO-3:	No M are P: some M are S. So, some S are not P.

After Aristotle's death, his successors at the Lyceum studied syllogisms in the overlooked fourth figure and proved the following forms valid:

Figure 4 *(MIDDLE TERM IS THE PREDICATE TERM IN THE MAJOR PREMISE AND THE SUBJECT TERM IN THE MINOR PREMISE.)*

Name	Logical Form	Details
Bramantip:	AAI-4:	All P are M; all M are S. So some S are P.
Camenes:	AEE-4:	All P are M; no M are S. So no S are P.
Dimaris:	IAI-4:	Some P are M; all M are S. So some S are P.
Fesapo:	EAO-4	No P are M; all M are S. So some S are not P.
Fresison:	EIO-4:	No P are M; some M are S. So some S are not P.

Reducing the Number of Terms

Imagine that "Don the Difficult," a logic student known for making everything more difficult than it needs to be, offers the following syllogism and insists it is valid:

1. All cats are nonreptiles.
2. Some turtles are reptiles.
3. Thus, some noncats are not nonturtles.

The difficulty is apparent: This syllogism has six different terms! It is not in standard form. Recall that a syllogism in standard form contains only three different terms, each appearing exactly twice. Because our rules are constructed only for syllogisms in standard forms, this syllogism cannot be treated as presently written. However, Don the Difficult has caused a problem where a problem need not exist. Using the laws of conversion, obversion, and contraposition, the number of terms in a syllogism like this one can easily be reduced to a manageable number without losing any of the meaning of the original syllogism.

Step 1. The law of obversion, second clause, tells us that the following two statements are equivalent:

No S are P   All S are non-P.

It follows that if we replace the first premise of Don's syllogism with the following sentence, the meaning and logic of the argument will remain unchanged:

No cats are reptiles.

So we swap out "All cats are nonreptiles," replacing it with "No cats are reptiles."

Step 2. It looks like Don was just messing with us on the conclusion. For the law of contraposition (fourth clause) tells us the following two statements are equivalent:

Some S are not P   Some non-P are not non-S.

This time we swap out "Some noncats are not nonturtles" for "Some turtles are not cats." The result, the "reduced" syllogism, carries the same essential meaning, and the same logical form, and has only three terms:

1. No cats are reptiles.
2. Some turtles are reptiles.
3. Some turtles are not cats.

Our rules can now be applied, and the syllogism can be proven valid or invalid, as the case may be. Is it valid?

In general, given a syllogism containing too many terms, it is sometimes possible to use the rules of conversion, obversion, and contraposition to reduce the number of terms to three and thus to render the syllogism manageable, without loss of essential logical meaning. A word of caution is in order, however. To avoid any loss of essential meaning, use the laws so that you never replace a sentence with anything but an equivalent sentence. Thus, only use conversion on E and I statements, and only use contraposition on A and O statements. Obversion, of course, produces an equivalent when used on any sentence.

Merging Synonyms

After learning that we reduced the number of terms in his syllogism to three, Don the Difficult gives us another syllogism. No term *complements* in this one, but there are too many terms nevertheless:

1. All who have doctor of philosophy degrees are eggheads.
2. No persons with PhDs are soothsayers.
3. Therefore, no soothsayers are eggheads.

It only takes a moment of reflection to see that the number of terms in this argument (four) can also be reduced without loss of essential meaning, and by a process logically similar to that used on Don's first "difficult" syllogism. However, instead of using the equivalence rules of conversion, obversion, and contraposition, we'll simply use our understanding of ordinary language. It is a matter of common knowledge that the PhD degree and a "doctor of philosophy degree" are one and the same thing. The two terms are synonymous. It follows that Don's syllogism won't lose any meaning at all if we "merge the synonyms" and render the original argument this way:

1. All who have PhD degrees are eggheads.
2. No persons with PhD degrees are soothsayers.
3. Therefore, no soothsayers are eggheads.

The syllogism is now in standard form, with three terms each used twice, and our methods can now be applied. Is this a valid syllogism? Don was again being difficult. But his difficulties are easily surmounted, using a little common sense, combined with a little logical theory and perhaps a dictionary.

Exercise 8.4   **Part A.** The following syllogisms are not in standard form. Reduce the number of terms to three in each syllogism. **Part B.** Which are valid and which are invalid?

Syllogism 1

1. All wealthy Athenians are voters.
2. No rich Athenians are slaves.
3. Therefore, no voters are slaves.

Syllogism 2

1. All nonwealthy Athenians are nonvoters.
2. No nonrich Athenians are nonslaves.
3. Therefore, no nonvoters are nonslaves.

Syllogism 3

1. No soldiers are cowards.
2. No warriors are weepers.
3. Therefore, no weepers are cowards.

Syllogism 4

1. All soldiers are nonweepers.
2. No weepers are logicians.
3. Therefore, no soldiers are logicians.

Syllogism 5

1. Some nonfarmers are not nonpoets.
2. All farmers are logicians.
3. Some logicians are poets.

Syllogism 6

1. All morally just people are happy people.
2. All happy people are kind people.
3. All morally good individuals are kind people.

Syllogism 7

1. No logicians are bad neighbors.
2. No bad neighbors are harmonious individuals.
3. So, some well-integrated individuals are logicians.

Syllogism 8

1. All highly moral persons are well-integrated persons.
2. No career criminals are harmonious persons.
3. So, no criminals for life are highly moral persons.

Syllogism 9

1. All logicians are nonpoets.
2. All poets are idealistic persons.
3. All logicians are nonidealistic persons.

Syllogism 10

1. Some nonphilosophers are not nonlogicians.
2. Some nonlogicians are Sophists.
3. All philosophers are non-Sophists.

Aristotle's Deductive System

We have seen how to use rules to establish validity and invalidity for categorical syllogisms. Aristotle also pioneered a second method for proving syllogisms valid: He discovered how to prove arguments valid using a deductive system similar in many respects to an axiom system such as geometry. Unfortunately, Aristotle's original system is so cumbersome, so difficult to use, that it is seldom employed in logic today and is rarely covered in an introductory logic course. For this reason, we'll look only briefly into its overall workings here; the actual nuts and bolts of the system will be left to Appendix 8.1 at the end of this chapter. As usual, some exact definitions are required at the start.

Aristotle defined a **perfect categorical syllogism** as "one which needs nothing other than what has been stated to make plain what necessarily follows." A syllogism is *imperfect* if it needs either one or more propositions, which are the necessary consequences of the terms set down but have not been expressly set down by the premises." A perfect syllogism, in other words, is one that is self-evidently valid: Its validity is grasped immediately, directly, in an unmediated act of rational understanding, without relying on any *previously* proven propositions.

Aristotle chose four perfect syllogistic forms from the first figure as the basis of his system. Here they are, along with the names assigned during the Middle Ages:

Barbara:	(AAA-1)	All M are P; all S are M. So all S are P.
Celarent:	(EAE-1)	No M are P; all S are M. So no S are P.
Darii:	(AII-1)	All M are P; some S are M. So some S are P.
Ferio:	(EIO-1)	No M are P; some S are M. So some S are not P.

For illustration, here is one of Barbara's infinitely many substitution instances:

1. All mammals are warm-blooded.
2. All goats are mammals.
3. Therefore, all goats are warm-blooded.

Barbara, Celarent, Darii, and Ferio would be the logical bedrock of the system, the logical patterns on the basis of which all else would be proven. The basic principles of a deductive system are not themselves proven on the basis of still deeper levels in the system; rather, they are the basis for proving everything else. Some people find this problematic. The system seems to rest on nothing, they say. However, as Aristotle noted, every system of thought has to start somewhere, every system must have rock-bottom "primitives," or fundamentals. (Could a computer function if *every* circuit in it would not open or close until operated on by a *prior* circuit?) If every valid logical form had to be proven valid using forms of reasoning that had *already* been proven valid on the basis of prior forms of reasoning that had already been proven valid on the basis of prior forms of reasoning already proven valid, and so on without end, the process would go on forever, and nothing would ultimately be proven. Life is too short. The perfect syllogisms that form the basis of Aristotle's deductive system all seem self-evidently valid.

Two Methods of Deductive Proof

Aristotle devised two different ways to prove syllogisms valid on the basis of the perfect syllogisms: Proof by Reduction and Proof by Contradiction. One preliminary definition will be required. A syllogistic form is a **valid argument form** if every substitution instance of the form is a valid argument.

Proof by Reduction

In a **Proof by Reduction**, a valid argument form is proven valid through a series of step-by-step inferences, each of which is "necessary" (Aristotle's term) or "deductively valid" (today's term), culminating in a step that "reduces" the form in question to one of the four perfect syllogisms. When a form was proven valid in this way, it was said to have been "reduced to a perfect syllogism." Essentially, reducing an argument form A to a perfect syllogism B showed that if the perfect syllogism, B, is valid then the form A must be valid. But B is self-evidently valid. Therefore, it follows that form A must be valid. The overall reasoning in a Proof by Reduction would therefore be:

1. Syllogism form A reduces to syllogism form B.
2. Therefore, if B is valid, then A must be valid.
3. But B is a perfect syllogism; it is thus valid.
4. Therefore, syllogism form A must be valid.

For example, using this method, Aristotle showed that Camestres (AEE-2) reduces to Celarent, which shows that Camestres is a valid argument form. A sample Proof by reduction can be found in Appendix 8.1 at the end of this chapter.

Proof by Contradiction

In a *proof by contradiction*, a syllogistic form is proven valid using the forms of reasoning in the perfect syllogisms by showing that we contradict ourselves if we suppose that an instance of the form could have true premises with a false conclusion. The overall reasoning would be this, for some syllogistic form x:

1. Assuming the perfect syllogisms are valid, we contradict ourselves if we accept the premises but deny the conclusion, in the case of a syllogism of form x.
2. Therefore, in the case of a syllogism of this form, it is self-contradictory, and hence impossible, that the premises all are true but the conclusion is false.
3. Therefore, syllogistic form x is valid.

As stated previously, Aristotle's axiom-like deductive system is very difficult to use; for this reason it is consigned to Appendix 8.1 at the end of this chapter, where it waits for those souls brave enough to attempt it.

Thus did Aristotle systematize logic, producing in effect a periodical table of all valid categorical argument forms—a veritable tower of inference rules resting on a rock-solid base of seemingly self-evident principles. A towering achievement for the fourth century BC.

DEDUCTIVE AND AXIOMATIC SYSTEMS COMPARED

Aristotle's deductive system resembles in many ways an axiom system. An **axiom system** is an organized collection of propositions in which some statements (called "theorems") are deduced from others (called "axioms"), on the basis of precise definitions and strict deductive reasoning. The axioms are not themselves deduced or proven; rather, they are the starting points of the system. They are the basis for proving everything else. In most axiom systems, the axioms are asserted as "self-evident" or necessarily true. The starting points of Aristotle's deductive system are valid argument *forms* rather than necessarily true statements that might be called axioms. His system is therefore not, strictly speaking, an axiom system; the analogy is not exact. However, each of the perfect syllogisms in Aristotle's system can be converted into a corresponding statement that is self-evidently true. Here is the axiom-like statement for Barbara: If every A is B, and every B is C, then every A is C. A few years after the death of Aristotle, the Greek mathematician Euclid (c. 325–c. 265 B.C.) created the first formal axiom system in history. Starting with 5 axioms asserted as self evident, combined with a number of precise definitions, and using valid deductive reasoning, Euclid deduced 13 *volumes* of theorems, providing strict proofs for nearly all the truths that had been discovered in Greek mathematics. The first axiom system in history is still in use and carries its original Greek name: *geometry*. The first formal axiom system for logic would not be developed until the 19th century A.D. You will meet this logical creation in Unit Three.

Metalogic . . . in the Fourth Century BC

There is much more to Aristotle's complete theory of logic. For example, he also did research on the theoretical properties of whole logical systems. For instance, he investigated the question: What is the smallest possible set of valid argument forms that would be sufficient for proving all valid arguments valid? In taking up such questions, he initiated a higher level branch of logic, one that in effect studies the "logic of logical systems." Today this extremely abstract field of study is called *metalogic* (from the Greek word *meta* meaning "after" or "about") because it is the logical study of systems of logic. See Appendix B at the back of the book, and Appendix C on Kurt Gödel, for some of the fascinating discoveries that have been made in this branch of logic in recent years.

Which Forms Are Invalid? The Method of Counterexample

As we have seen, Aristotle proved valid forms of reasoning valid on the basis of a deductive system. Invalid forms, however, required a different method. Invalid forms were shown to be invalid by the *Method of Counterexample*. As you know, a *counterexample* to an argument form is a substitution instance of the form having obviously true premises and a false conclusion. Producing a counterexample to a form shows that not all arguments with that particular form are valid arguments, which proves that the form is not a valid form. For example, consider this categorical argument form:

1. All **S** are **P**.
2. Some **P** are **M**.
3. So, some **S** are **M**.

Substituting *cats* for **S**, *mammals* for **P**, and *dogs* for **M** produces the following substitution instance:

1. All cats are mammals.
2. Some mammals are dogs.
3. So, some cats are dogs.

The premises are obviously true, but the conclusion is clearly false. This shows that not all arguments following this form are valid, as this is an instance of the form and yet this is an invalid argument. The form is thus not a valid form. This English argument is a counterexample to the argument form before it and proves that the form is invalid. One by one, Aristotle proved many of the invalid categorical forms invalid by supplying a counterexample for each.

Exercise 8.5   Use the method of counterexample to show that the following argument forms are invalid forms:

1. No S are P. No P are M. So no S are M.
2. Some S are P. No P are M. So some M are S.
3. Some S are P. Some P are M. So some S are M.
4. All S are P. All P are M. So all M are S.
5. Some S are P. All S are M. So all P are M.
6. Some S are P. No M are P. So some M are S.
7. No S are P. No P are M. So no M are S.
8. Some S are P. Some P are M. So some M are S.

9. No S are P. All P are M. So no S are M.

10. Some S are not P. Some P are not M. So some S are not M.

Criticizing an Argument Using the Method of Logical Analogy

Aristotle's method of counterexample suggests a commonsense way to show that a categorical argument is *formally invalid*, that is, that it instantiates an invalid form. Produce an argument that has exactly the same logical form as the original argument (the "target" argument) but that also has obviously true premises and a false conclusion. Because the second argument is obviously invalid, and because it displays the same logical form as that displayed by the target argument, the form in question must not be a valid form. The target argument is thus a substitution instance of an invalid logical form. The target argument is *formally* invalid. This method is called *refutation by logical analogy* because it involves producing a logically *analogous* argument that has true premises and a false conclusion. This strategy is also called *refutation by counterexample* because the logically analogous yet invalid argument is offered as a *counterexample* to the target argument.

For example, suppose someone argues the following: "All whales are mammals, and all whales are swimmers, so all mammals are swimmers." To show that this argument follows an invalid form, we produce an argument with the same form and that also has true premises and a false conclusion. First, the logical form of this argument is:

All As are Bs, and all As are Cs, so, all Bs are Cs.

Here is an argument with this form:

All cats are mammals, and all cats are feline, so, all mammals are feline.

Because this argument has obviously true premises and a false conclusion, it is invalid. Thus, the form in common is an invalid form (because one of its substitution instances is invalid). This second argument is thus a counterexample and shows that the first argument is formally invalid.

We use this method in everyday life, usually launching it with a phrase such as, "That's like saying. . . ." For example, suppose someone argues, "Some politicians are dishonest, for some dishonest people are famous and some politicians are famous." In everyday life (as opposed to logic class) you might naturally reply, hopefully in a respectful tone of voice, "But that is like arguing, 'Some cats are dogs, for some dogs are pets and some cats are pets.'" Hopefully, after seeing the analogy, the other person will reevaluate his or her argument. Now *that* is critical thinking!

Exercise 8.6   State a refutation by logical analogy for each of the following arguments and argument forms.

1. Some people are selfish, and some people are philosophical, so some people are selfish and philosophical.
2. All Spartans are fast runners. Some horses are fast runners. So some horses are Spartans.
3. All logicians are deliberative persons. Some deliberative persons are clumsy people. Therefore, some clumsy persons are logicians.
4. Some advocates of democracy are philosophers. No tyrants are advocates of democracy. So some philosophers are tyrants.
5. No farmers are tyrants. No tyrants are democrats. Therefore, no farmers are democrats.
6. No logicians are impulsive persons. Some artists are impulsive persons. Therefore, some artists are logicians.
7. All politicians are animals. Some pets are animals. So some pets are politicians.
8. All politicians are animals. Some pets are animals. So some politicians are pets.
9. All politicians are animals. Some animals are pets. So some pets are politicians.
10. Some A are B. All C are A. So some C are B.
11. All A are B. Some C are not A. Therefore, all C are not B.
12. No A are B. All A are C. Therefore, no C are B.
13. All A are B. Some B are C. So some C are A.
14. Some A are B. Some B are C. So some A are C.

Enthymemes Again

Recall from Unit One that an *enthymeme* (from the Greek word for "have in mind") is an argument that is missing one or more premises or a conclusion. When we present a line of reasoning to others we sometimes intentionally leave out either a premise or the conclusion either because the premise is obvious or because the conclusion is one we want our audience to draw on its own. However, when we need to prove an enthymematic argument valid with precision, the missing parts must be added. For example, consider the following argument:

1. All aardvarks are mammals.
2. So all aardvarks are warm-blooded.

This argument is invalid as it stands, but only because the arguer has left a premise unstated. If the suppressed premise is added—"All mammals are warm-blooded"—the argument becomes a complete categorical syllogism, and a valid one as well.

As we have seen, when we add a suppressed premise to an enthymeme, it is good to follow the principle of charity, which advises: When you must fill in a gap in someone's reasoning, fill in the hole in such a way as to make their argument as strong or as reasonable as possible. Don't assume they are being illogical. So, when presented with an incomplete categorical syllogism, assume the enthymematic arguer is trying to be logical. Search for a statement that, when added, closes the hole. If necessary, look for a premise that connects any terms not yet related so as to produce a valid syllogism with true premises. For a simple example, suppose Joe argues:

All Spartans are Greeks, for all Spartans are Hellenes.

Now, Joe's argument is invalid as it stands. But it is obviously enthymematic. If we add a single premise, "All Hellenes are Greeks," the argument becomes valid:

All Spartans are Greeks, for all Spartans are Hellenes and all Hellenes are Greeks.

Notice that we added a premise that not only completes the argument, but makes it valid and sound. We did this because we are assuming Joe is being logical; that is, we are assuming he would not knowingly advance an invalid argument. We could have added this premise to his argument, in which case his argument would be invalid: "No Hellenes are Greeks." However, the principle of charity advised us to suppose instead that Joe is a reasonable guy who would leave unstated only a reasonable premise.

Exercise 8.7   In the following enthymemes, supply missing premises or missing conclusions in such a way that the result in each case is a valid argument.

1.   All tyrannies oppress their citizens. Therefore, the city-state of Alexia oppresses its citizens.
2.   Anyone who sympathizes with the Spartans is a traitor. So Demetri is a traitor.
3.   Some mammals live in the water, since whales live in water.
4.   You owe taxes only if you are a citizen. Therefore, you are not a citizen.
5.   Only Greeks are allowed to enter the race. Therefore, you are not allowed to enter the race.
6.   Because all goats are mammals, all goats are animals.

7. All Athenian citizens owe military service in time of war. It is a time of war.

8. All shrews are mammals. So, all shrews have hair.

9. Some cats are pets. So, some mammals are pets.

The Sorites: Evaluating a Pile of Arguments

So far we have learned how to evaluate single-premise (immediate inference) arguments and two-premise (mediate inference) arguments called categorical syllogisms. The final form of mediated inference treated in the Aristotelian syllogistic is the sorites, which we have already defined. Recall that a *sorites* (from the Greek word *soros* for "pile" or "heap") is a series of four or more interlocking categorical statements, with one designated the conclusion and the rest designated premises. In a sorites, two premises are given, after which a conclusion is drawn but left unstated. The unstated conclusion is then used as an unstated premise in the next categorical syllogism in the chain, which in turn draws a conclusion in the same way, and so on, until a final conclusion is drawn. The following argument is a sorites:

1. All goats are mammals.
2. All mammals are animals.
3. No plants are animals.
4. Therefore, no plants are goats.

Like a categorical syllogism, a sorites is composed of categorical statements; however, it is not a categorical syllogism; rather, it is an enthymematic chain of multiple categorical syllogisms. Thus, the methods of the previous sections cannot be directly applied. However, this does not mean the sorites is beyond our reach. We can reason through a sorites step-by-step, writing down the unstated conclusions as we go. After reaching the final conclusion, we can reconstruct the individual syllogisms in the chain, revealing the path the reasoning takes as it runs from the first premise of the sorites to the final conclusion, through the mediation of several syllogisms along the way. The methods we already have in hand can then be applied individually to each syllogism in the chain.

For example, in the immediately preceding sorites, from the first two premises:

1. All goats are mammals.
2. All mammals are animals.

We may validly conclude:

All goats are animals.

We have deduced an "intermediate conclusion" from the first two premises. Now, if we combine this intermediate conclusion with the next premise of the sorites, namely:

3. No plants are animals.

It validly follows that:

4. No plants are goats.

But this is the conclusion of the sorites. The reasoning is now complete. This sorites was a chain of only two categorical syllogisms, but all sorites function in essentially this way. One syllogism is joined to the next one by an intermediate, unexpressed conclusion that serves as an unexpressed premise in the next syllogism in the chain, and so on until a final conclusion is reached. Hence the name: A sorites is a heap (soros) of conclusions.

Let us say that a sorites is in standard form if it satisfies the following conditions:

1. All statements are standard-form categorical statements.
2. Each term occurs twice.
3. The predicate term of the conclusion appears in the first premise.
4. Every statement up to the conclusion has a term in common with the statement immediately following.

More Formally

As we have seen, a sorites is really a chain of distinct arguments. Just as a chain is only as strong as its weakest link, a sorites is only valid if each syllogism in the chain is valid; if even one syllogism in the series is invalid, the whole sorites is invalid. This suggests an obvious way to evaluate a sorites when it is in standard form:

1. Pair together two premises that have a term in common and derive an intermediate conclusion. This conclusion should have a term in common with one of the unused statements in the sorites.
2. Pair together these two statements and draw a conclusion from this second pair.
3. Repeat this procedure until all the premises have been used. The resulting conclusion is the conclusion of the sorites.
4. Evaluate each individual syllogism. If each one is valid, the sorites is valid. If even one syllogism in the chain is invalid, the sorites is invalid because a chain is only as strong as its weakest link.

Exercise 8.8   If necessary, rewrite each sorites that follows in standard form. In each case, is the sorites valid or invalid?

1. All logicians are sane persons. All jurors are sane persons. No logicians are whimsical persons. So, jurors are whimsical persons.
2. Some philosophers are logicians. All logicians are analytical individuals. All philosophers are introspective individuals. So, some introspective individuals are analytical individuals.
3. All athletes are healthy persons. No philosophers are happy people. Healthy people are happy people. Therefore, no athletes are philosophers.
4. No soldiers are politicians. Some politicians are doctors. All doctors are healers. Therefore, some soldiers are not healers.
5. All logicians are temperate persons. Some poets are logicians. All poets are artists. So, some artists are temperate persons.
6. All dogs are mammals. All mammals are animals. All animals are ensouled creatures. Therefore, all dogs are ensouled creatures.

Exercise 8.9   Assume each of the following is an already symbolized sorites. If necessary, rewrite each in standard form and assess for validity.

1. Some S are D. All D are A. All S are G. Therefore, some G are A.
2. All A are B. Some C are A. All C are D. So some D are B.
3. All A are B. Some C are A. All C are D. So some D are not B.
4. All A are B. No C are B. All D are C. So no D are A.
5. All A are B. Some C are not D. No B are D. So no A are C.
6. All A are B. No C is B. All D are C. So no D are A.

Concluding Matters

Aristotle on Logic and Truth

Aristotle defined logic concisely as the study of "what follows from what." This is consistent with the way we have defined logic in this study (as "the systematic study of reasoning"). However, Aristotle did not present logic as an abstract tool that could be used to prove anything one wants to believe. Aristotle held that logical theory is an intellectual tool that we use properly only when we use it to discover *truth*. The proper goal of reasoning, Aristotle, believed, was not, as many seem to think, merely to win the argument, or to get your way, or to attain power. Rather, as Aristotle saw it, the goal of reasoning is to find the truth, meaning to bring our thoughts and words into correspondence with reality. Thus for Aristotle, every valid form of reasoning, from Barbara to Fresison, serves as a logical blueprint, or guide, for correct reasoning, but ideally for reasoning aimed at real truth.

The deductive system Aristotle designed for logical theory, so precise, so well-knit together, so sweeping in its scope, was a remarkable accomplishment. It was also a virtual blueprint for a logical computer, a blueprint that would one day result in just such a machine. It also placed logic on a foundation as solid as the axiomatic foundation of mathematics developed by Euclid. Scholars who study the history of ideas say that the development of the first complete theoretical system of logic in human history, during the fourth century BC, in the little backwater civilization of Greece, was an astonishing intellectual achievement, one of many that set the Greeks apart from the rest of the ancient world at the time.

Appendix 8.1   Aristotle's Deductive System

Proof by Reduction

Recall that in a proof by reduction, an argument form is proven valid by "reducing" it to a perfect syllogism. In the first example, we prove the Figure 2 form *Camestres* valid by reducing it to Celarent. This is Camestres:

> All P are M. No S are M. So no S are P.

Here is an English *instance* of this form:

> All lions are mammals. No snakes are mammals. So no snakes are lions.

Step 1

We begin the reduction by noting that the second premise of Camestres is an E statement. The Law of Conversion assures us that the converse of this premise will be equivalent to the original premise. Thus, if we replace premise 2 (No S are M) with its converse (No M are S), the validity of the syllogism will not be affected. If the reasoning was valid before the replacement, it will be valid after. (Analogously, if we take a carburetor out of a perfectly functioning car and replace it with a *mechanically equivalent* carburetor, the car runs perfectly after the replacement.)

This gives us: All P are M. No M are S. So no S are P.

Step 2

The two premises now match the premises of one of the axioms, namely, the perfect syllogism Celarent. Because Celarent is a perfect syllogism, we know its form of reasoning is valid. Reasoning in accord with the Celarent form, we therefore deduce from this:

No P are S.

Step 3

We apply the Law of Conversion again, replacing No P are S with:

No S are P.

But this is the conclusion of Camestres. Thus, Camestres must be valid if Celarent is valid. But Celarent is a perfect syllogism. Therefore, Camestres must be valid.[1]

In general, to prove a syllogism valid in Aristotle's system, simply use the rules of conversion, obversion, or contraposition as needed, and the forms of reasoning of the four perfect syllogisms, and reduce the syllogism in question to a perfect syllogism.

Proof by Contradiction (Indirect Proof)

Recall that in a proof by contradiction, also called an indirect proof, a syllogistic form is proven valid by showing that we contradict ourselves if we suppose the conclusion is false although the premises are true. Logicians during the Middle Ages named this method of proof "Reduction per *Impossibile*" (Latin: "Reduce it to the impossible") because this form of proof works by showing that the corresponding position is contradictory and thus should be rejected. This form of proof was also called "Reductio ad Absurdum." In this example we prove the form *Baroco* valid indirectly, in a proof by contradiction.

Step 1

Baroco: All P are M. Some S are not M. So some S are not P.

We begin by assuming the contradictory of the conclusion. The conclusion is "Some S are not P," so the contradictory, according to the Square of Opposition, is:

All S are P.

---

[1] I am indebted to Professor Robin Smith's article on Aristotle's logic in the *Stanford Encyclopedia of Philosophy* for this and the next example.

Step 2

Next we add this to premise 1:

1. All P are M.
2. All S are P.

Step 3

Lines 1 and 2 match the premises of the Barbara syllogism, one of our valid argument forms. Thus, from lines 1 and 2, reasoning in accord with Barbara, we deduce:

All S are M.

But this is the contradictory of the other premise of Baroco, "Some S are not M." This shows that if one premise of Baroco is true and the contradictory of the conclusion is true, then the other premise of Baroco must be false. This shows that we contradict ourselves if we assert both premises of Baroco while also asserting the denial or contradictory of the conclusion. This in turn shows that it would be impossible for the premises of Baroco to be true while the conclusion is false. This means Baroco is valid. We have proven Baroco valid by Reduction per Impossibile, via the Barbara form.

In general, to prove a higher figure form valid by Reduction per Impossibile:

1. Assume one premise and then assume the *contradictory* of the conclusion.
2. Using a pattern of reasoning from a valid first-figure form, derive the contradiction of the *other* premise.
3. It follows that the form in question must be valid, assuming the following self-evidently valid principle: If the contradictory of a sentence Q necessarily follows from a sentence P and the contradictory of a sentence R together, then R necessarily follows from P and Q together.

Employing both the Proof by Reduction and the Proof by Contradiction, Aristotle produced the first deductive system of logic in history.

Glossary

Axiom system An organized collection of propositions in which some statements (called "theorems") are deduced from others (called "axioms"), on the basis of definitions and strict deductive reasoning.

Categorical syllogism An argument that contains three categorical statements; the statements contain three different terms altogether, each statement contains two different terms, and no two statements contain the same two terms.

Counterexample A circumstance in which the premises of an argument are true while the conclusion is false.

Distributed term A term within a categorical statement is said to be "distributed" if the statement makes an assertion about every member of the class denoted by the term.

Figure of a categorical syllogism A specification of the pattern of placement, inside the syllogism, of the syllogism's middle term. Four possible patterns of placement exist, and therefore four figures.

Formally invalid argument An argument that displays an invalid form.

Formally valid argument An argument that displays a valid form.

Logical form of a categorical syllogism The syllogism's general logical structure, expressed by listing the syllogism's mood and figure.

Major premise The premise containing the major term.

Major term The conclusion's predicate term.

Middle term The term appearing in both premises (and thus not in the conclusion).

Minor premise The premise containing the minor term.

Minor term The term appearing as the subject of the conclusion.

Mood of a categorical syllogism Something that is specified by listing in order the type—A, E, I, or O—of each of the syllogism's categorical statements when it is expressed in standard form.

Perfect syllogism A syllogism in the first figure that is self-evidently valid.

Proof by Contradiction Proving a syllogistic form valid by showing that we contradict ourselves if we suppose that an instance of the form could have true premises with a false conclusion.

Proof by Reduction Proving an argument form valid by reducing it to a perfect syllogism.

Standard form A categorical syllogism in which the major premise is written first, the minor premise is written second, and the conclusion is written last.

Valid argument form An argument form all of whose instances are valid.

9 Categorical Logic Version 2.0 « « « « « « «

Boole, Venn, and the Nineteenth-Century Revolution in Categorical Logic

In an essay written near the end of the eighteenth century, the great German philosopher Immanuel Kant (1724–1804) expressed an opinion that was representative of the thinking of his day. Kant mused that almost nothing important had been added to logical theory since the time of Aristotle and predicted that nothing of consequence in the field was left to discover. Since Aristotle, logic "has not advanced a single step, and is to all appearances a closed and completed body of doctrine." In addition, Kant wrote, "there are but few sciences that can come into a permanent state, which admits of no further alteration. To these belong logic and metaphysics."[1]

Kant and others at the time could not have foreseen it, but a number of sweeping, revolutionary advances in mathematics and logic would take place during the nineteenth century. Even greater changes would occur in both fields during the twentieth century—changes that would shake the foundations of both subjects and push logical and mathematical thought to frontiers nobody could have imagined. Some of these discoveries are recounted in the final chapter of this book and in the appendices at the end of the book.

The modern revolution in logical theory began around the middle of the nineteenth century when the brilliant British mathematician and logician George Boole (1815–1864) demonstrated two things. First, Aristotle's system of categorical logic rests on a certain assumption regarding the existence of things. Second, this "existential" assumption is not necessarily true, nor is it required for logical theory. As usual, we proceed step-by-step.

---

[1]Susan Haack, *Deviant Logic, Fuzzy Logic* (Chicago: University of Chicago Press, 1996), p. 27.

To Be or Not to Be

The traditional Square of Opposition summarized all known logical relationships among the various corresponding categorical sentence forms. Forms, as you know, are abstract—a step away, in a sense, from existence. In this sense, as we have seen, the traditional square is all form and no content. Reflecting on the formal nature of the square, Boole wondered on what assumptions, if any, regarding the actual *existence* of things, is the square based? In addition, he asked, Are these assumptions about existence warranted? The traditional Square of Opposition, he discovered, rests on the assumption that all the subject terms of categorical statements refer to actually existing things. Yet this existential assumption, as it is called, is by no means a necessary requirement of logic. A perfectly consistent system of logical principles can be constructed without it. Which raises this question: Is the existential assumption warranted?

The assumption brought to light by Boole is also known in logic as the **Aristotelian assumption**, the traditional assumption, and the assumption of existential import. Boole showed two things: (a) The Aristotelian, or existential, assumption can be dropped without any contradictory results, and (b) big changes follow with respect to the laws of categorical logic if the assumption is dropped. In addition, he argued, the changes that follow are not absurd or logically undesirable at all, for they make logical theory more relevant to everyday reasoning, and they also bring it closer into line with the practices of modern science. Boole proceeded to develop a new system of categorical logic, one that drops the existential assumption. Is the new system acceptable? Before we decide, some definitions will streamline the discussion and make matters more precise.

A statement is said to have **existential import** if it cannot be true unless its subject term refers to one or more actually existing things. So a statement with existential import makes a claim about one or more actually existing things, and the statement is not true unless the one or more things denoted by its subject term actually exist. A statement *lacks* existential import if its subject term does not refer to one or more actually existing things. Such a term is an "empty" term.

The statement "All unicorns are magical flying creatures" lacks existential import because unicorns do not actually exist. We say that the subject term in this case (*unicorns*) names an **empty class** because the category it refers to or denotes does not contain any actually existing entities. In contrast, the statement "Some cats are pets" has existential import because at least one cat exists. The term *cats* is thus not an empty term.

The question can now be put this way: Is the Aristotelian assumption warranted for categorical logic? Should the information in the Square of Opposition presuppose that the subject terms refer to actually existing things? That no subject terms are empty? Let us begin with particular statements. It is clear and not controversial that *particular statements* (of the form "Some **S** are **P**" or "Some **S** are not **P**") have existential import. Such statements are never true unless their subject terms refer to actually existing things. That is common sense, so there is nothing to debate there.

However, universal statements ("All **S** are **P**" or "No **S** are **P**") are another matter entirely. When we assert a universal statement, do we *always* assume that the subject term refers to existing things? We do not. For instance, a teacher writes in her syllabus, "All students who receive an A on each of their tests are students who will receive an A for the course." She means it, but her statement does not presuppose that there actually will be any students who receive an A on each of their tests. It might be that the top student will receive all As except for one B. The statement is made, but there is no assumption that the subject term refers to actually existing individuals. Another teacher might say, "No late papers are eligible for extra credit." He means it, too, but his statement does not assume there are, or will be, any late papers. Perhaps everyone will get everything in on time this quarter. The point is that at least sometimes in everyday talk we assert an A or an E statement without assuming that the subject term refers to things that actually exist.

Furthermore, modern mathematical physics contains universal statements that lack existential import. Galileo proved formulas about bodies moving on frictionless surfaces, but no frictionless surfaces actually exist (or even can exist). Einstein discovered one of his most important theories, the Special Theory of Relativity, by asking himself, "What would happen if a material body were to travel at the speed of light?" Yet a body traveling at the speed of light is a physical impossibility; no body actually has, or ever will do so, for it would violate the laws of physics. Einstein's hypothetical lacks existential import.

The Existential vs. the Hypothetical Viewpoints

When we interpret a categorical sentence in such a way that we presuppose its subject term denotes or refers to actually existing things, we are taking the **existential viewpoint** (also called the Aristotelian or traditional viewpoint) with respect to the sentence. If we do not presuppose that the subject term denotes or refers to actually existing things when we interpret a sentence, we are taking the **hypothetical viewpoint** (also called the Boolean or modern viewpoint). Thus, a universal statement can be interpreted from either the Aristotelian, or the Boolean, standpoint, by assuming that the subject term either does, or does not, refer to actually existing things. (Remember that *particular* statements always presuppose the existential or Aristotelian standpoint.)

Let's try to make some sense of the hypothetical standpoint. Suppose someone asserts a universal sentence and the sentence is about things that do not exist. For instance, someone says, "All unicorns are white animals." This is easily interpreted on the basis of the hypothetical standpoint. From the hypothetical standpoint, to say, "All unicorns are white animals," is merely to claim, "If there ever were to be any unicorns (and we are not saying that there are), then they would all be white animals." That makes sense, doesn't it? Similarly, assuming the hypothetical viewpoint, to say that "All vampires are bloodsuckers" is to just say that vampires (*if* they were to exist) would be bloodsuckers. Similarly, taking the hypothetical standpoint, to say that all werewolves are hairy is just to say that werewolves (*if* they were to exist) would be hairy creatures. We speak this way all the time—without assuming that werewolves, unicorns, and vampires actually exist.

Notice that this *hypothetical* way of interpreting an A statement (e.g., reading "All unicorns are white animals" as "If a unicorn ever were to exist, then it would be a white animal") does *not* force us to accept the truth of the corresponding I statement, which would be the claim that some unicorns actually exist. In other words, if we interpret the A statement in this hypothetical way, then we should not infer that the corresponding I statement is true. Thus, from "All unicorns are white animals" (interpreted hypothetically), it does not logically follow that "Some unicorns are white animals" is true. The A statement, interpreted hypothetically, does *not* imply the corresponding I statement. But that's good! We want to be able to say that all unicorns are white animals, meaning that *if* a unicorn were to exist, it would be white, without being committed to saying that one of those fabled creatures actually exists.

Similarly, assuming the hypothetical standpoint, "All vampires are bloodsuckers" does not imply that any vampires actually exist, rather, it just implies that vampires (*if* they were to exist) would be bloodsuckers. Likewise, to say that all werewolves are hairy does not imply that werewolves actually exist, it is just to say that werewolves (*if* they were to exist) would be hairy creatures. Notice that it does not follow from either of these statements, interpreted hypothetically, that vampires or werewolves actually exist. Thus, it seems that from the hypothetical standpoint, the A statement does *not* imply the corresponding I statement.

Nevertheless, in normal, everyday conversation, when we assert universal (A or E) statements, we usually assume (consciously or not) that the subject terms refer to things that actually exist. Most of the time when we utter A or E statements, we are talking about existing things like dogs, cats, or students. This might be why for so many centuries only the existential viewpoint was considered in categorical logic. This also might be why it makes such immediate and intuitive sense to argue that, for example, if all dogs are animals, it must then be the case that some dogs (i.e., at least one) are animals. In such contexts, if an A statement is true, then the corresponding I statement must be true, too. This is, of course, an inference licensed by the Traditional Square. From the Aristotelian viewpoint, if an A statement is true, the corresponding I statement *must* be true, too.

Logical Relativity? The Modern Square of Opposition

We have seen what happens, however, when we assert an A statement, and it is about things that do *not* exist. Assuming the hypothetical viewpoint, if the A statement is true, it does *not* logically follow that the corresponding I statement must be true. Keep in mind that an I statement *always* has existential import. Thus, an I statement does not follow from its corresponding A statement, assuming the hypothetical viewpoint with respect to the A statement. A shadow of logical relativity looms: From the Aristotelian standpoint, the A statement implies the corresponding I statement. However, from the Boolean or hypothetical standpoint, the A statement does not imply the corresponding I statement. Likewise, from the Aristotelian standpoint, the E statement implies the corresponding O statement, per the Traditional Square of Opposition; not so from the Boolean or hypothetical standpoint. (Pause and verify this for yourself before moving to the next point.)

The bottom line, then, for using the existential or hypothetical viewpoints, is this: If the terms of a universal categorical statement refer to things that either do not exist or that we do not wish to assume exist, then we interpret the sentence from the hypothetical or Boolean viewpoint; that is, as saying that *if there were to be an S*, then it would belong to such and such a group, and so on. On the other hand, if the terms of a categorical statement refer to something everyone in the conversation believes exists, then we assume the Aristotelian or existential viewpoint (because that will be what is normally meant by the arguer).

For example, if an argument is about astronomers and logic students, then unless we have reason to believe otherwise, we should assume that the arguer knows such things exist and that he is asserting the A or E statements with existential import. However, if an argument is about unicorns, griffins, particles that travel faster than the speed of light, and so on, then we should assume that the arguer does not intend his statements to be interpreted with the Aristotelian or existential assumption, and we would assume the hypothetical viewpoint when interpreting the *universal* statements. (Keep in mind that particular sentences always have existential import.)

A set of apparent problems might arise but are easily dealt with. Sometimes it is not clear what an arguer intends by an A or E statement. Does she present it from an existential or a hypothetical viewpoint? If you are talking with the person, you can ask her, "Are you assuming that the terms of your premises refer to existing things?" If she answers, you know how to interpret her claims. Of course, some benighted people actually do believe in unicorns and vampires. In such cases, we might make them happy by interpreting their A or E claims (about unicorns and vampires) using the existential viewpoint. Their argument might turn out to be valid, but the premise in question will be false given this interpretation (although they might think it is true). If you do not have the opportunity to determine what the arguer believes regarding the existence of the things referred to by the terms of his argument, you have no choice but to rely on your understanding of the context. Finally, if you are completely unable to determine if some arguers believe in the existence of the things referred to by the subject terms of their premises, you can always assess the argument using the existential viewpoint, and then again using the hypothetical viewpoint. (Both methods are explained below.) If the argument comes out valid only one way, then in charity assume the arguer intended that interpretation. If the argument is valid both ways, then its logic is good regardless of the viewpoint taken. If it comes out invalid both ways, then the argument is invalid *absolutely*. More on this in a moment.

As we have seen, the Traditional Square of Opposition presupposes the existential viewpoint; it rests on the Aristotelian assumption that the categorical statements under consideration all have existential import. The square must be drastically altered if we take the hypothetical rather than the existential viewpoint for universal statements. When we drop the Aristotelian assumption and take the hypothetical viewpoint, we must draw a new square of opposition. The new figure, called the **Modern Square of Opposition**, loses most of the arrows in its quiver.

The Modern Square of Opposition

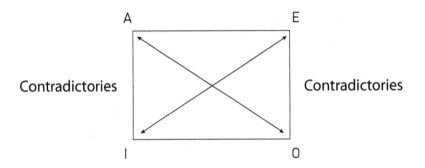

Only the arrows for contradiction remain; the modern table appears to be just a shell of its former self. Assuming the hypothetical viewpoint and the modern square, we can no longer validly infer an I statement from the corresponding A; we can no longer derive an O statement from the corresponding E; an A statement and its corresponding E are no longer automatically contraries, an I and its corresponding O are no longer automatically subcontraries; and so on around the board. A shell of its former self indeed.

Thus, given an A statement and the assumption that it is true, we can infer that the corresponding O statement is false, for the contradiction of a statement is always opposite in truth value. Given an A statement and the assumption that it is false, we can infer that the corresponding O statement is true. Given an E statement and the assumption that it is true, we can infer that the corresponding I statement is false. Given an E statement and the assumption that it is false, we can infer that the corresponding I statement is true, and so on around the table. We simply follow the arrows!

Exercise 9.1　Using the Modern Square of Opposition, state the relations (if any) that obtain between the following sentences:

1. All Victorian logicians are Englishmen. No Victorian logicians are Englishmen.

2. All Victorian logicians are Englishmen. Some Victorian logicians are not Englishmen.

3. All Victorian logicians are Englishmen. Some Victorian logicians are Englishmen.

4. Some Victorian logicians are Englishmen. Some Victorian logicians are not Englishmen.

5. Some Victorian logicians are Englishmen. No Victorian logicians are Englishmen.

6. Some Victorian logicians are not Englishmen. No Victorian logicians are Englishmen.

The Rules for Valid Syllogisms Again

In the previous chapter, four rules were presented for determining the validity of syllogisms. If a syllogism satisfies all four, it was said, then the syllogism must be valid; if it does not, then it must be invalid. However, now that the Aristotelian assumption has been brought to the surface, a qualification can be added. A syllogism that satisfies those four rules of distribution is guaranteed to be valid on the Aristotelian assumption. To guarantee that a syllogism is valid from the hypothetical or Boolean viewpoint, we must add the following rule to the previous four rules:

5. The argument cannot have two universal premises and a particular conclusion. In other words, if both premises are universal, the syllogism cannot have a particular conclusion.

To be valid from the Boolean standpoint, a syllogism must satisfy all five rules of distribution. A categorical syllogism that satisfies all four rules and violates only rule 5 is valid from the existential viewpoint but is invalid from the hypothetical viewpoint. If a Boolean syllogism (i.e., one interpreted from the hypothetical standpoint) violates this last rule, it is guilty of the "existential fallacy." The following syllogism, interpreted from the hypothetical standpoint, commits this fallacy:

1. All mammals are warm-blooded.
2. All aardvarks are mammals.
3. So, some aardvarks are warm-blooded.

John Venn and His Famous Circles

Another revolutionary development in nineteenth-century logic was the discovery, by the English logician and philosopher John Venn (1834–1923), of a radically new way to show that a categorical syllogism is valid. Venn's method allows us to visually represent the information content of categorical sentences, in such a way that we can actually see the relations between the sentences of a syllogism. This, in turn, allows us to determine validity and invalidity visually, simply by looking at a diagram. When matters get extremely complex, it is always nice when we can draw a picture. This was an enormous leap forward for logical theory.

A **Venn diagram** is a set of overlapping circles, with each circle standing for a category or class of things, and with the circles arranged so as to display the logical relationships between the categories represented. A Venn diagram for a single categorical statement has two overlapping circles, one standing for the category named by the subject term and one representing the category named by the predicate term, producing four distinct areas or regions. To illustrate, consider "All As are Bs." For clarity, we shall adopt the convention of numbering each region from the left side.

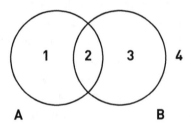

The A circle represents all the things in the universe that are A, while the B circle represents all the things that are B. If the As are aardvarks, the A circle represents all aardvarks; if the Bs are brown things, then the B circle represents all the things that are brown, and so forth. Thus:

Region 1 represents things that are A but not B.
Region 2 represents things that are both A and B.
Region 3 represents things that are B, but not A.
Region 4 (the area outside the circles) represents everything that is neither A nor B.

Next, information is entered into a Venn diagram in three ways: We shade an area to indicate that the area is empty. (Note that in many math contexts using Venn diagrams, shading means the opposite; i.e., that the quadrant is full.) We place an X in an area to say that the area contains at least one thing. An X is thus used for particular statements, as the X makes a claim about a thing actually existing, whereas shading just tells where things would not be. If two areas have been defined and we know that something exists in one of the two areas but we do not know which of the two areas contains the item, then we straddle the line, that is, we place the X directly on the line separating the two areas.

Venn Diagrams for Particular Statements

As we have seen, it is common sense that particular statements always have existential import. A particular statement is only true when its terms refer to one or more actually existing things. It follows that the Venn diagrams for particular statements will be the same whether we assume the Aristotelian or the hypothetical viewpoint. Using obvious abbreviations (A for "aardvarks," etc.), here is the Venn diagram for the I statement "Some aardvarks are mammals":

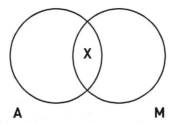

You might find it helpful to imagine all the aardvarks in the universe rounded up and rooting around for ants inside the first circle—the A circle. Likewise, imagine all the mammals in the universe collected and resting inside the second circle—the M circle. The X indicates that there is at least one aardvark existing in the part of the aardvark region that overlaps with the mammal region. That is, some aardvarks are mammals. Notice that we did *not* put an X in region 3. Independent of the diagram, we might know that there are creatures in region 3—there are mammals that are not aardvarks—but the I statement does not tell us this, and we wish to diagram *only* the information the statement gives, and nothing more. Region 3 therefore gets no X.

The following is the Venn diagram for the O sentence "Some cats are not pets":

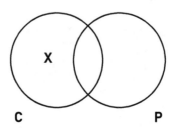

Region 1 represents things that are cats but not pets, region 2 represents cats that are pets, and region 3 represents pets that are not cats. The X tells us there is at least one thing "inside" area 1.

Venn Diagrams from the Aristotelian Standpoint

On the Aristotelian assumption of existential import, the Venn diagrams for the two universal categorical sentence forms look like this:

All cats are mammals:

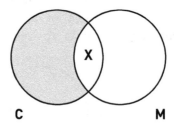

The shading in region 1 tells us that nothing is in region 1. The area is empty. This tells us there are no Cs in the part of the C region that lies outside the M circle. In other words, no cats exist outside the mammal circle: No cats are nonmammals. The X in region 2 tells us that at least one thing exists in that region. So there is at least one cat (and it is a mammal). In addition, it follows there is at least one mammal (and it is a cat). Region 3 has no shading and no X. This does not mean that nothing exists in that region—it just means we have no information about the region. For all we know, it might or might not be populated. All we know, based on the information content of the sentences, as represented on the diagram, is that all the cats are located in the overlap with the mammal circle. In short, all cats are mammals. Next:

No cats are mammals:

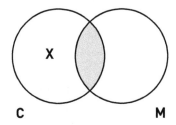

The X in region 1 tells us that at least one thing exists in that area. So there is at least one thing that is a cat. (This records the Aristotelian assumption.) The shading in region 2 tells us that nothing is in region 2. The area is empty. There are no Cs in that region, and there are no Ms in that region. In other words, no cats exist in the part of the cat circle that overlaps with the mammal circle. (This is false, of course, but our method can diagram false statements as well as true ones.) Thus, the diagram tells us that no cats are mammals.

Venn Diagrams from the Boolean Standpoint

The Venn diagram for the A statement "All cats are mammals," when it is given a hypothetical (or Boolean) interpretation, looks like this.

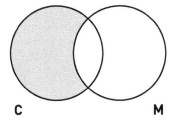

All cats are mammals.

Because the assumption of existential import has been dropped, no X was added to the circle for the subject category *cats*. No X was needed in the cat circle because we were not assuming that the category referred to by the subject term *cats* has any actual members; that is, we were not assuming that any cats actually exist. Recall that on the hypothetical or **Boolean interpretation,** an A statement such as "All cats are mammals" is understood as saying, "Nothing is a cat and not a mammal." Region 1 is where cats that are not mammals would be, if any such creatures were to exist. It is shaded, indicating there are no such creatures. Thus, there are no cats that are not mammals. This is fine, for this is all we mean, on the Boolean interpretation, when we say, "All cats are mammals." If we wanted to make a universal claim about cats, but did not wish (for whatever reason) to assume that cats exist, this is what we'd mean and how we'd do it. In most everyday conversations, however, it's only when we are talking about nonexisting or hypothetical things (e.g., unicorns or that billion dollars you'd love to have drop out of the sky and into your lap) that our intended meaning is best interpreted by others as coming from the hypothetical viewpoint.

Because the preceding diagram no longer has an X, the diagram no longer explicitly asserts the existence of any entity. It only tells us where there are *not* entities. Specifically, this Venn diagram tells us there is nothing in the part of the C circle outside the M circle—no member of C is outside M. That is all it says; it does not say that any existing thing is both C and M. The overlapping area might have members, or it might be empty. Based only on the information content of the premises, looking only at the diagram, we simply do not know. In other words, the diagram tells us where there are no members of C, but it does not say any C actually exists. It is neutral (or noncommittal) on the existence of Cs. If there is a C, we can tell from the diagram where it will be, but we can't tell from the diagram whether or not there actually are any Cs. We call this Boolean interpretation the *hypothetical viewpoint* because of its hypothetical or "if–then" nature.

On the Boolean interpretation, the corresponding universal negative or E statement in this case is "Nothing is a cat and a mammal," or "No cats are mammals." The Venn diagram for this universal negative, using the Boolean interpretation, looks like this:

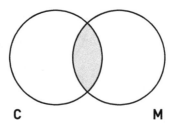

C   M

No cats are mammals.

In sum, on the Boolean interpretation, the Venn diagrams for the four categorical forms indicate the following:

A: No members of S are outside P.
E: No members of S are inside P.
I: At least one S exists and it is a member of P.
O: At least one S exists and it is not a member of P.

Remember that the Aristotelian and Boolean standpoints agree on the interpretation and diagramming of I and O statements; they only differ with respect to the A and E statements.

Venn-Testing Immediate Inferences

Once you understand how to draw a Venn diagram for a categorical statement, it's relatively easy to assess immediate inferences (one-premise arguments) as either valid or invalid. Examples of immediate inferences include the following:

1. No cats are fish.
2. Thus, no fish are cats.

1. Some birds are parrots that fly high in the sky.
2. Thus, some birds are not parrots that fly high in the sky.

1. All sharks are fish.
2. Thus, some fish are sharks.

Because some immediate inferences might include negated statements (e.g., "It is false that all dogs are cats," or "It is not the case that some dogs are not animals"), let's adopt the following convention: Instead of writing "It is false that," "It is not the case that," and the like, we shall just write "False:" Thus, for the immediately preceding two examples, we'd abbreviate them as "False: All D are C" and "False: Some D are not A." Now, the following is the procedure for using Venn diagrams to test immediate inferences for validity.

The Venn Diagram Test for Immediate Inferences

1. Abbreviate the argument, consistently replacing each term with a single capital letter, retaining the quantifier and copula of each statement. Example: "No wolves are goats" is abbreviated "No W are G." By convention we will place the conclusion last. (As usual, we use a letter that reminds our audience of the term being abbreviated—A for "ants," C for "cats," etc.)
2. Draw two overlapping circles aligned horizontally, one for each of the two terms, to form three distinct regions.
3. Label the circles using your two chosen capital letters. Use the subject term of the premise for the left circle, and the predicate term of the premise for the right circle.

4. Enter the information for the premise in accordance with the assumption at hand, either the Aristotelian or the Boolean interpretation.
   a. If the subject term of the premise refers to existing things, then, if you've already shaded one region of the left circle, place an X in the other region (thereby presenting the existential viewpoint); *or*
   b. If the subject term of the premise refers to things that do *not* exist or that the arguer does not wish to assume exist, then you are finished (thereby presenting the hypothetical viewpoint).
5. The test for validity for Venn diagrams is as follows:

An immediate inference made up of categorical statements is valid if, when the information from the premise has been entered into the diagram, visual inspection of the diagram reveals that the information content of the conclusion is represented as well. In other words, by diagramming the premise we have also diagrammed the information found in the conclusion.

This shows that the information contained in the conclusion is already present in the premise. This in turn means that it would be impossible for the premise to be true and the conclusion false—a sure sign that an argument is valid.

6. The test for invalidity for Venn diagrams follows:

An immediate inference made up of categorical statements is invalid if, when we have diagrammed the premise, information must be added to the diagram to represent the information content of the conclusion.

If the diagram for the premise does not contain all the information in the conclusion, it is possible for the premise to be true and the conclusion false. In this case, the argument is invalid.

Let us apply our new procedure to a real argument.

1. All big dogs are animals.
2. Thus, some big dogs are animals.

Step 1: We abbreviate the argument, placing the conclusion last.

1. All B are A.
2. Some B are A.

Steps 2 and 3: We draw two circles and label them using the premise's subject term for the left circle and the premise's predicate term for the right circle.

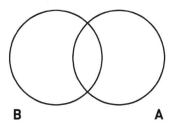

Step 4: We diagram the information found in the premise. Before we enter the information required for the existential assumption, we have this:

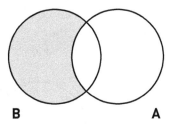

Next, we know that big dogs exist, so we look at the left circle (where big dogs are to be found) and see that region 1 is shaded. So, because big dogs do indeed exist, they must exist in region 2. We thus place an existential X in 2, thereby incorporating the existential viewpoint warranted by our knowledge that big dogs exist.

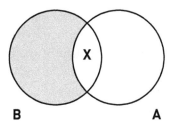

Step 5: We now ask ourselves: Is the information content of the conclusion represented in this diagram? That is, does the diagram say (perhaps among other things) what the conclusion says? In this case, the conclusion says that there is a B that is also an A. Thus, the conclusion says that an X should be found in region 2. Because we do see an X in region 2, the argument is valid. There is enough information in the premise to absolutely guarantee the conclusion, assuming the existential viewpoint.

Another example can't hurt.

1. No unicorns are happy hamsters.
2. Thus, some unicorns are not happy hamsters.

In symbols:

1. No U are H.
2. Some U are not H.

First, we draw two overlapping circles, label them according to the terms of the premise, and diagram the information found in the premise. To begin with, because the premise is universal and about unicorns, we know we'll shade a region of circle U. Because the premise tells us that no U are H, that is, that all U are outside the H circle, we know that if there are any U, they will all be in region 1. But shading tells us where things are not, so we shade region 2 to ensure that no U are in the H camp.

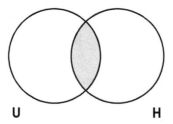

Next, because "unicorns" is the subject term of the premise, and unicorns do not exist, then Step 4 tells us not to place an existential X anywhere. Now, to complete the assessment, we look at the information provided by the diagram and ask if it already conveys the information content of the conclusion. The conclusion says "Some U are not H." This claim would call for an X in region 1. Because we do not see an X in region 1, the argument is invalid.

Here is yet another example, and again about mammals.

1. It is false that some cats are mice.
2. Thus, no cats are mice.

This argument is abbreviated as follows:

1. False: Some C are M.
2. No C are M.

Diagramming "False": Swap an X for Shading and Shading for an X

Steps 1 through 4 guide us as we draw the two circles, label them appropriately, and diagram the premise information. But how do we diagram negated statements like "False: Some C are M"? Fortunately, it's easy. Imagine what the statement would look like without the "False:" In this case it would be "Some C are M." Imagine how you would diagram that. In this case you'd place an X in region 2. The trick now is simply to swap the X for shading, keeping the marking in the same area. So the correct diagram for "False: Some C are M" would have shading (and not an X) in region 2.

Because abbreviating a statement beginning with "False:" is new, let's pause and consider two more examples of negated statements. Consider "False: All A are B." First we ignore the "False:" for a moment and represent "All A are B," assuming the two-circle diagram has the left circle labeled A. Here we would shade region 1. So to abbreviate "False: All A are B," we place an X in region 1 instead of the shading.

Consider "False: Some G are not J." Ignoring the "False:" for a moment, we recognize that the diagram "Some G are not J" would need an X in region 1. To diagram "False: Some G are not J," we would simply place shading in region 1 instead of the X. That's it!

The idea of swapping an X for shading, or shading for an X, in order to record the negation of a sentence, should make intuitive sense. A statement such as "Some A are B" requires that we place an X in region 2. That X means that something exists in region 2. The negation of that statement (i.e., "False: Some A are B") says that it is false that there is something in region 2. To diagram that, we simply place shading in region 2 (instead of an X).

We can now diagram the premise ("False: Some C are M") of our preceding argument. We briefly ignore the "False:" in the premise and note that we must place an X in region 2 to diagram "Some C are M." However, taking account of the "False," we do the opposite and *shade* region 2 to accurately diagram "False: Some C are M."

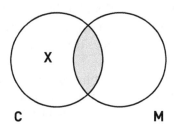

Because cats (the subject term of the premise) exist, we are warranted in taking the existential viewpoint. We thus look at the left circle and see that one of its two regions is shaded. The existing cats must, therefore, be in the unshaded area of circle C. We thus place an X in region 1. The premise now has two pieces of information: The

X in region 1 tells us that there are cats that are not mice, and the shading in region 2 tells us that there are no cats that are mice (and, *by conversion*, that there are no mice that are cats). That is more than enough information to guarantee what the conclusion says: No cats are mice. The argument is therefore valid. Here is one more example.

1. Some tooth fairies are winged creatures.
2. Thus, it is not the case that no winged creatures are tooth fairies.

We abbreviate the argument and provide a diagram of the premise.

1. Some T are W.
2. F: No W are T.

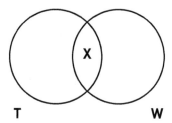

The subject term is "tooth fairies," and as we all know, tooth fairies do not exist. So we take the hypothetical viewpoint and do not assume the existence of these generous beings. Moreover, even if tooth fairies did exist, there is no shading in the left circle, so there would still be no place for us to place an existential X. We are thus finished diagramming.

Considering the conclusion ("False: No W are T"), we ignore momentarily the "False:" and see that for "No W are T" we would expect to see shading in region 2 conveying this information. But because this is actually a "False:" or negated statement, we imagine the opposite: an X in region 2. In the preceding diagram we do indeed see an X in region 2. Therefore, this final example is a valid argument.

Exercise 9.2 Go back to Exercise 7.4 in Chapter 7 and test the one-premise arguments there for validity using Venn diagrams. In each case, use common sense to choose either the Aristotelian or the Boolean interpretation. State which interpretation you chose.

Venn-Testing Categorical Syllogisms

Recall that a categorical syllogism has two premises and a conclusion. A set of three interlocking Venn circles can be drawn to represent the information content and logical structure of an entire categorical syllogism. Once the diagram is drawn, we can determine, just from a visual inspection of the circles, whether or not the argument is valid. The first step is to set the circles up correctly. In the following example, S stands for the minor term, P stands for the major term, and M stands for the middle term. The circle labeled S represents the category of things referred to by the minor term, circle P represents the category of things referred to by the major term, and circle M represents the category of things referred to by the middle term.

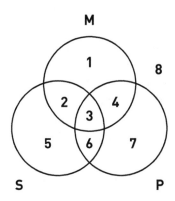

To represent all the logical possibilities, the Venn circles must overlap to form the seven different areas numbered by convention shown here. Each of these areas, starting in order from the top, and dropping down and moving from left to right as one would read an English text, represents a different class of things:

Area 1: Anything here is an M, but not an S, and not a P.

Area 2: Anything here is an S, an M, but not a P.

Area 3: Anything here is an S, a P, and an M.

Area 4: Anything here is a P, an M, but not an S.

Area 5: Anything here is an S, but not an M, and not a P.

Area 6: Anything here is an S, a P, but not an M.

Area 7: Anything here is a P, but not an S, and not an M.

Area 8: Things out here would be neither P, S, nor M.

Once your circles are in place, the following general procedure allows you to test a categorical syllogism for validity. It's an easy technique, but be careful with step 7, as it has some very specific demands.

The Venn Diagram Test for Categorical Syllogisms

1. Abbreviate the argument, replacing (consistently) each term with a single capital letter and retaining the quantifier and copula of each statement.

(Example: "Some gems are not green rubies": Some G are not R.) By convention we place the conclusion last.

2. Draw three overlapping circles, one for each term, to form seven distinct regions.

3. Label the circles using the three capital letters chosen (use the predicate term of the conclusion for the lower right circle, the subject term of the conclusion for the lower left circle, and the middle term for the middle circle).

4. Enter the information for both premises and stop. Thus, enter only the information for the premises. Do not enter information for the conclusion. If the argument contains a universal premise, enter its information first. If the argument contains two universal premises or two particular premises, either premise can be entered first. This step requires a decision: Are you taking the Aristotelian standpoint, or the Boolean? It is up to you. However:

   a. When placing an X in an area, if one part of the area has been shaded, place the X in an unshaded part.

   b. When placing an X in an area, if a circle's line runs through the area, place the X directly on the line separating the area into two regions. In other words, the X must "straddle" the line, hanging over both sides equally. An X straddling a line means that, for all we know, the individual represented by the X might be on either side of the line, or on both sides; in other words, it is not known which side of the line the X is actually on.

   c. Look at the two circles standing for the subject terms of your premises. If these terms refer to existing things, then if there is only *one* region unshaded in either or both circles, place an X in that unshaded region (thereby presenting the existential viewpoint). If these terms refer to things that do not exist or that the arguer does not wish to assume exists, then you are finished (thereby presenting the hypothetical viewpoint) and can go to the next step.

5. Use the following tests to determine if the argument is valid or invalid.

(i) A categorical syllogism is valid if, when the information from only the two premises has been entered into the diagram, visual inspection of the diagram reveals that the information content of the conclusion is represented as well. In other words, by diagramming only the premises, we have also diagrammed the information found in the conclusion.

This shows that the information contained in the conclusion is already present in the premises. In a sense, the premises "contain" all the information presented in the conclusion. This in turn means that it would be impossible for the premises to be true and the conclusion false—a sure sign that an argument is valid.

(ii) A categorical syllogism is invalid if, when we have diagrammed the information content of the premises, information must be added to the diagram to represent the information content of the conclusion.

If the diagram for the premises does *not* contain all the information in the conclusion, it is possible for the premises to be true and the conclusion false; that is, the conclusion could be false even though the premises are true. In this case, the argument is invalid.

Let us begin with an example, the Barbara (AAA-1) syllogism:

1. All mammals are warm-blooded creatures.
2. All aardvarks are mammals.
3. Therefore, all aardvarks are warm-blooded creatures.

Our first step is to abbreviate the argument, placing the conclusion at the bottom:

1. All M are W.
2. All A are M.
3. All A are W.

Second, we draw the three overlapping circles. For step 3 we label the circles:

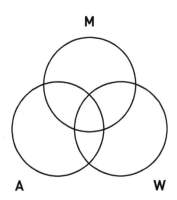

The subject term of the conclusion, A, is at the lower left. The predicate term of the conclusion, W, is at the lower right. The middle term, M, is above and to the middle.

Because both premises are universal, we can enter them into the diagram in either order. Let us enter the shading for the major premise first. This premise tells us that all M are W. That is, no M are not W. In terms of the diagram, this indicates that all of the M circle that is outside the W circle is empty. Therefore, the part of the M circle that is outside the W circle must be shaded to indicate that it is empty.

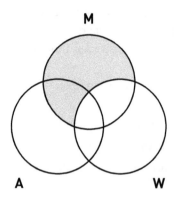

We are assuming here that at least one mammal exists; however, we must wait to enter an X for this assumption until we diagram the shading for the next premise.

Next, we enter into the diagram the information from the other premise, "All A are M." This premise asserts that all aardvarks belong to the class of mammals. That is, all of the members of the A circle are inside the M circle. To enter this information, we must shade the part of the A circle that lies outside the M circle, indicating that this area is empty.

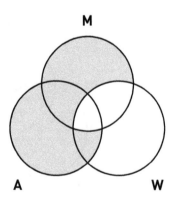

We are assuming there are aardvarks. So, with the shading completed we look to see if either circles M or A have only one region unmarked. We note that circle A has only one region unmarked: region 3. Because we know that aardvarks exist, we record the existential viewpoint by placing an X in region 3, the only region on our diagram that can hold them.

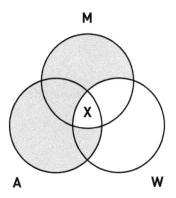

The terms represented by the other two circles also happen to refer to existing things. However, for circle M, there are two unmarked regions, and the premises do not tell us which region or regions contain mammals; and for circle W there are three unmarked regions, and the premises do not tell us which regions contain warm-blooded creatures. It would be guesswork on our part to place an X in a region in these cases. As it happens, if we placed one or more Xs on lines in these cases, it would not alter the final assessment of the argument as valid or invalid anyway.

The preceding diagram represents the information contained in the premises. We purposely do not enter the information from the conclusion.

Finally, we inspect the diagram to see if the information in the conclusion is already represented in the diagram of the premises. If it is, then the conclusion cannot possibly be false if the premises are true, which means the argument is valid. The conclusion "All A are W" indicates that all members of the class of A are also members of the class of W. That is, nothing in the A circle is not also in the W circle. And that is, indeed, exactly what our diagram indicates, for all sections of the A circle outside the W circle have been shaded. Nothing more would need to be added to our diagram to have it also represent the conclusion. The information content of the conclusion is already present in the premises. The conclusion would have to be true if the premises are true, and the argument is therefore valid.

Let us test another categorical syllogism.

1. Some farmers are not happy individuals.
2. No happy individuals are greedy individuals.
3. So, some greedy individuals are farmers.

We again begin by abbreviating the argument.

1. Some F are not H.
2. No H are G.
3. Some G are F.

Next, we draw and label three overlapping circles.

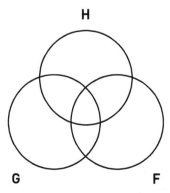

The next step is to enter the information from the second premise because it is the only one of the two that is universal. The premise tells us that no member of the H circle is a member of the G circle. Consequently, we shade the part of the H circle that lies inside the G circle.

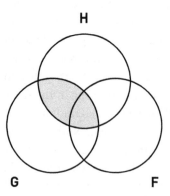

Next, the first premise indicates that some F are not H. To record this information, we place an X inside the F circle but outside the H circle. However, we must avoid any shaded areas, for these areas are supposed to be empty. Where do we place our X? The remaining region is divided into two parts, and the premises do not indicate which of the two parts contains the X. In this case, we place the X squarely on the line between the two parts. We "straddle the fence," so to speak. This indicates that, given the information in the premises, we *do not know* to which of the two areas X belongs.

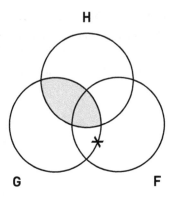

To record the Aristotelian assumption, we place an X inside the unshaded part of the H circle, indicating the existence of at least one happy person. Note that the first X took care of the assumption of at least one farmer. Because the remaining part of the H circle is divided into two parts, we place this X on the line dividing the parts.

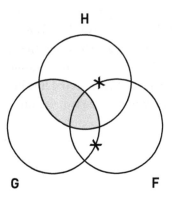

Now, the conclusion claims that some greedy individuals are farmers, but the diagram of the premises does not guarantee this at all. The information content of the conclusion is not "contained" within the diagram of the premises. It is therefore possible that the premises are true and the conclusion is false. The syllogism is invalid.

Let us diagram another syllogism that has already been abbreviated. We'll assume that the terms refer to things that exist.

1. All C are G.
2. Some G are S.
3. Therefore, some S are C.

After drawing and labeling three overlapping circles, we diagram the universal premise first. It indicates that all members of the C class also belong to the G class. In terms of our diagram, this is to say that all members of the C circle are also inside the G circle; the area of the C circle that lies outside the G circle is therefore empty and is shaded.

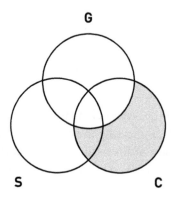

Next, the remaining premise indicates that at least one member of the G class is a member of the S class. We therefore place an X in a spot within the G circle that is also within the S circle. However, the area we are interested in is divided into two regions (2 and 3), and our premises do not tell us in which region to place our X. In such a case, we place the X on the line between the two areas. This indicates that we do not know to which of the two regions the X belongs.

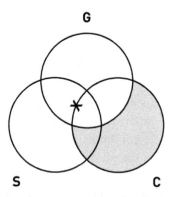

This completes step 6 of our procedure. We recall our assumption for this example that the terms refer to existing things, so moving to step 7, we consider the C and G circles to see if either has only one region unmarked (i.e., one region without shading or clearly containing an X). C has two such unmarked regions, and G has four such regions. Thus, even though the argument's subject terms refer to existing things, we do not add an additional X. We are done diagramming.

For step 8, we note that the information conveyed by the conclusion (Some S are C) is not represented in the diagram. Given just the information in the premises, the conclusion is not guaranteed. This argument is therefore invalid.

Here is another example. Consider the following syllogism of the EIO-3 form, again abbreviated for us, and again assuming each term refers to existing things.

1. No S are F.
2. Some S are R.
3. Some R are not F.

After drawing the three circles and labeling them according to our convention, we diagram the universal premise. In terms of our diagram, this premise tells us that no members of the S circle are also inside the F circle. We therefore shade the part of the S circle that is inside the F circle.

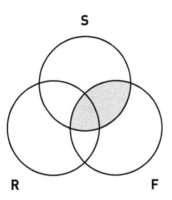

To diagram the next premise, we must place an X inside a part of the S circle that is also a part of the R circle.

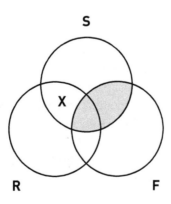

We have completed step 4. For step 5 recall that we assumed for this example that the subject terms from the premises refer to existing things. There is no circle, however, that has only one quadrant unmarked, so we are finished. The information conveyed by the conclusion (Some R are not F) is indeed represented by this diagram of the premises (the X in region 2 represents an example of an R that is not an F). The argument is thus valid.

We can't have too many examples. Consider the following syllogism: We can conclude that some leprechauns are not rainbow hunters, because all leprechauns are seekers of fortune, and no seekers of fortune are rainbow hunters. Notice that the first sentence is the conclusion of the argument. Step 1 looks like this:

1. All L are S.
2. No S are R.
3. Some L are not R.

Next, we draw and label our circles. No matter which premise we diagram first, the diagram looks like this:

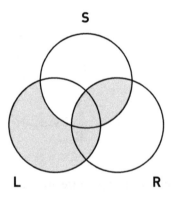

The next step asks us to note whether the subject terms of the premises refer to existing things, and in this case they do not: "Leprechauns," found in the first premise, do not exist. Unless we have reason to believe the person who offered this argument believes in leprechauns, we are warranted in taking the hypothetical viewpoint. In doing so, we will not even consider placing any additional existential Xs in the diagram. We thus now have a diagram conveying the information from the premises, assuming the hypothetical viewpoint. The diagram does not contain the information conveyed by the conclusion (Some L are not R), for if it did we would expect to see an X in the L circle but outside the R circle (i.e., in 2, or 5, or both). The argument is thus invalid.

Here is yet another example. This one is abbreviated, and we'll again assume for the sake of illustration that all terms refer to existing things.

1. Some A are K.
2. Some K are not C.
3. Some C are not A.

We draw three circles, label them, and note that because both premises are particular, it really does not make any difference which we diagram first. The diagram will look the same either way.

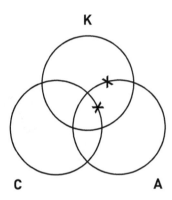

Diagramming the first premise, we wanted to place an X in the area where the A and K circles overlap, but noted that a line cut that area into two quadrants. We thus placed the X right on the line, straddling both sides, indicating that the premise only tells us that there is something in region 3, region 4, or both. We just don't know which side of the line the X is actually on, and so we "hedge our bets" by placing the X "on the fence" so to speak (to mix metaphors). Diagramming the second premise, we wanted to place an X in the K circle but outside the C circle, but again noted that a line cut the area into two regions, 1 and 3. We thus placed the X straddling the line dividing 1 and 3. All the terms refer to things that exist (as we stipulated earlier), but the A and K circles both have more than one region unmarked. So, we are finished diagramming. The information we see here does not convey the content of the conclusion, for we do not see an X confidently placed anywhere inside the area that is C but not A. The argument is thus invalid.

Finally, here is one more example.

1. Some abominable snowmen are icy personalities.
2. No icy personalities are cheerful chaps.
3. Thus, some cheerful chaps are abominable snowmen.

In symbol, this is:

1. Some A are I.
2. No I are C.
3. Some A are C.

Next we draw and label our circles and then diagram the premises. We begin with the universal.

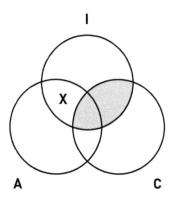

Abominable snowmen do not exist. (If the person offering the argument believes they do, then you can assess the argument from the existential viewpoint; a better strategy, however, might be to point out the person's confusion, even though it would be *really* cool if such creatures were indeed roaming the higher altitudes.) At any rate, given that abominable snowmen do not exist, we do not place an additional existential X in the diagram. Now we see that the information found in the conclusion is indeed found in the diagram; there is a big fat X in region 4, somewhere in the two-region area where A and C overlap. The argument is thus valid.

Remember that Venn diagrams do not tell us if arguments are deductively sound or unsound; they only tell us if arguments are valid or invalid. In the preceding case, the first premise is false, as it is not the case that there exists an abominable snowman. The argument is valid, but it is deductively unsound.

Exercise 9.3   Go back to Exercise 8.3 in Chapter 8 and test the syllogisms there for validity using Venn diagrams. In each case, use common sense to choose either the Aristotelian or the Boolean interpretation. State which interpretation you chose.

Exercise 9.4   Go back to the "Medieval Game Show" Interlude in Chapter 8 and construct a Venn diagram for each form.

Venn-Testing Sorites

Recall that a *sorites* is a series of four or more interlocking categorical statements, with one designated the conclusion and the rest designated premises. A sorites is in standard form if it meets the following conditions:

1. All statements are standard-form categorical statements.
2. Each term occurs twice.
3. The predicate term of the conclusion appears in the first premise.
4. Every statement (except the last) has a term in common with the statement immediately following.

A sorites can be tested with Venn diagrams by the following procedure.

1. Place the sorites in standard form.
2. Deduce a conclusion from the first two premises, and test the resulting syllogism with a Venn diagram. The conclusion deduced here is the first "intermediate conclusion"—it will become a *premise* in the next syllogism in the chain.
3. Using the first intermediate conclusion and the third premise in the sorites, deduce the next intermediate conclusion and test the resulting syllogism with a Venn diagram.
4. Test each syllogism in order within the sorites.
5. If each syllogism in the chain is valid, the sorites is valid. If even one syllogism in the chain is invalid, the sorites is invalid.

Let us now apply this to the following symbolized sorites:

1. No B are C.
2. Some D are C.
2. All A are B.
4. Therefore, some D are not A.

First, we place the sorites into standard form:

1. All A are B.
2. No B are C.
2. Some D are C.
4. Therefore, some D are not A.

The first two premises logically imply the following intermediate conclusion:

No A are C.

This sorites thus breaks down into the following two syllogisms:

1. All A are B.
2. No B are C.
3. Therefore, no A are C.

And:

1. No A are C.
2. Some D are C.
3. Therefore, some D are not A.

Now we draw the Venn diagrams for these two syllogisms. If both syllogisms are valid, the sorites is valid. If one or more of the constituent syllogisms is invalid, the sorites is invalid. The two diagrams follow:

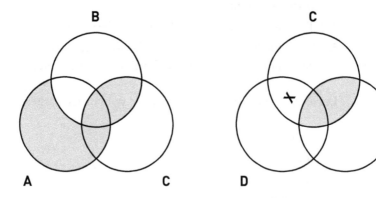

Because both syllogisms in the chain are valid, the sorites as a whole is valid!

Let's try another.

1. All C are D.
2. All A are B.

3. All B are C.
4. Therefore, all D are A.

In standard form this sorites becomes:

1. All A are B.
2. All B are C.
3. All C are D.
4. Therefore, all D are A.

Now, from the first two premises, we can deduce the following intermediate conclusion:

All A are C.

This sorites therefore breaks down into the following two syllogisms:

1. All A are B.
2. All B are C.
3. So, all A are C.

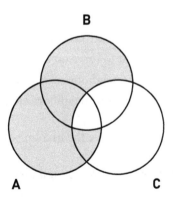

And:

1. A are C.
2. All C are D.
3. So, all D are A.

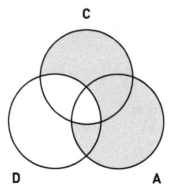

C

D   A

The two Venn diagrams above show that although the first syllogism is valid, the second syllogism in the chain is invalid; this sorites is therefore invalid.

Alice in Sorites Land

Charles Lutwidge Dodgson (1832–1898) was a logician, mathematician, Oxford University professor, and deacon in the Anglican church who wrote children's books in his spare time. You might know him by his pseudonym, Lewis Carroll, or by the two books he wrote under that name: *Alice's Adventures in Wonderland* and its sequel, *Through the Looking Glass*. Less well known is the fact that Dodgson also wrote a symbolic logic textbook! The following sorites is adapted and slightly modernized from his *Symbolic Logic*, a beautiful Victorian-era logic text still in print and readily available online.[2]

1. All persons who are sane are persons who can solve symbolic logic problems.
2. All persons fit to serve on a jury are persons who are sane.
3. None of your neighbors can solve symbolic logic problems.
4. Thus, none of your neighbors are persons who are fit to serve on a jury.

From 1 and 2 we derive the first unexpressed intermediate conclusion:

2* All persons fit to serve on a jury are persons who can solve symbolic logic problems.

Next, from 2* and 3, this validly follows:

None of your neighbors are persons who are fit to serve on a jury.

---

[2] See *Mathematical Recreations of Lewis Carroll: Symbolic Logic and Game of Logic. Two Books Bound as One.* (New York: Dover Publications, 1958).

Carroll's sorites is now seen to be composed of two syllogisms interlocked:

1. All persons who are sane are persons who can solve symbolic logic problems.
2. All persons fit to serve on a jury are persons who are sane.
2* All persons fit to serve on a jury are persons who can solve symbolic logic problems.

2* All persons fit to serve on a jury are persons who can solve symbolic logic problems.
3. None of your neighbors can solve symbolic logic problems.
4. Thus, none of your neighbors are persons who are fit to serve on a jury.

Notice the way the reasoning cascades through both syllogisms down to the conclusion in the end. Using the method of Venn diagrams, which dates to the period of Professor Dodgson's life, both syllogisms can be *seen* to be valid; thus, the sorites as a whole is valid! This is one nice thing about the method developed by Professor Venn: It allows you to actually *see* the validity or invalidity.

Exercise 9.5   The following syllogisms are from Lewis Carroll's *Symbolic Logic*, originally published in 1896. Using the method of Chapter 8, translate each into standard form. Then test for validity using Venn diagrams. Reduce the number of terms if necessary. In each case, which standpoint are you assuming? Boolean or Aristotelian?

1

1. No son of mine is dishonest.
2. People always treat an honest man with respect.
3. No son of mine ever fails to be treated with respect.

2

1. All cats understand French.
2. Some chickens are cats.
3. Some chickens understand French.

3

1. All diligent students are successful.
2. All ignorant students are unsuccessful.
3. All diligent students are learned.

4

1. All soldiers are strong.
2. All soldiers are brave.
3. Some strong men are brave.

5

1. None but the brave deserve the fair.
2. Some braggarts are cowards.
3. Some braggarts do not deserve the fair.

Exercise 9.6 The following sorites are from Lewis Carroll's *Symbolic Logic.*. Using the method of Chapter 8, translate each into standard form. Each is missing the conclusion. In each case, add a conclusion and then test for validity using Venn diagrams. Reduce the number of terms if necessary. In each case, which standpoint are you assuming? Boolean or Aristotelian?

1

1. All the policemen on this beat have supper with the cook.
2. No man with long hair can fail to be a poet.
3. Amos has never been in prison.
4. Our cook's cousins all love cold mutton.
5. None but policemen on this beat are poets.
6. None but her cousins ever sup with the cook.
7. Men with short hair have all been in prison.

2

1. I greatly value everything that John gives me.
2. Nothing but this bone will satisfy my dog.
3. I take particular care of everything that I greatly value.
4. This bone was a present from John.
5. The things of which I take particular care are things I do not give to my dog.

3

1. All babies are logical.
2. Nobody is despised who can manage a crocodile.
3. Illogical persons are despised.

4

1. My saucepans are the only things I have that are made of tin.
2. I find all your presents very useful.
3. None of my saucepans are of the slightest use.

5

1. No potatoes of mine that are new have been boiled.
2. All my potatoes in this dish are fit to eat.
3. No boiled potatoes of mine are fit to eat.

6

1. No ducks waltz.
2. No officers ever declined to waltz.
3. All my poultry are ducks.

7

1. No terriers wander among the signs of the zodiac.
2. Nothing that does not wander among the signs of the zodiac is a comet.
3. Nothing but a Terrier has a curly tail.

8

1. All puddings are nice.
2. This dish is a pudding.
3. No nice things are wholesome.

9

1. Mike Gardner is well worth listening to on military subjects.
2. No one can remember the Battle of Waterloo unless he is very old.
3. Nobody is really worth listening to on military subjects unless he can remember the Battle of Waterloo.

10

1. All hummingbirds are richly colored.
2. No large birds live on honey.
3. Birds that do not live on honey are dull in color.

11

1. All members of the House of Commons have perfect self-command.
2. No M.P. who wears a coronet should ride in a donkey race.
3. All members of the House of Lords wear coronets.

12

1. Showy talkers think too much of themselves.
2. No really informed people are bad company.
3. People who think too much of themselves are not good company.

13

1. Promise breakers are untrustworthy.
2. Wine drinkers are very communicative.
3. A man who keeps his promises is honest.
4. No teetotalers are pawnbrokers.
5. One can always trust a very communicative person.

14

1. Animals that do not kick are unexcitable.
2. Donkeys have no horns.
3. The buffalo can always toss one over a gate.
4. No animals that kick are easy to swallow.
5. No hornless animal can toss one over a gate.
6. All animals are excitable except buffaloes.

Exercise 9.7   In these problems, Carroll asks his readers to derive a conclusion from each pair of premises. Translate each into standard form, add a conclusion, and then test for validity using Venn diagrams. In each case, which standpoint are you assuming? Boolean or Aristotelian?

1

1. Those who are not old like walking.
2. You and I are young.

2

1. Your course is always honest.
2. Your course is always the best policy.

3

1. Some who deserve the fair get their deserts.
2. None but the brave deserve the fair.

4

1. Sugarplums are sweet.
2. Some sweet things are liked by children.

5

1. John is in the house.
2. Everybody in the house is ill.

6

1. Umbrellas are useful on a journey.
2. What is useless on a journey should be left behind.

7

1. Audible music causes vibrations in the air.
2. Inaudible music is not worth paying for.

8

1. No Frenchmen like plum pudding.
2. All Englishmen like plum pudding.

9

1. No portrait of a lady that makes her simper or scowl is satisfactory.
2. No photograph of a lady ever fails to make her simper or scowl.

10

1. All pale people are phlegmatic.
2. No one looks poetical unless he is pale.

11

1. No one who exercises self-control fails to keep his temper.
2. Some judges lose their tempers.

12

1. Some pictures are not first attempts.
2. No first attempts are really good.

13

1. Some lessons are difficult.
2. What is difficult needs attention.

14

1. Pigs cannot fly.
2. Pigs are greedy.

15

1. No bride cakes are wholesome.
2. What is unwholesome should be avoided.

16

1. No military men write poetry.
2. None of my lodgers are civilians.

17

1. Dictionaries are useful.
2. Useful books are valuable.

18

1. A prudent man shuns hyenas.
2. No banker is imprudent.

19

1. All wasps are unfriendly.
2. No puppies are unfriendly.

20

1. No idlers find fame.
2. Some painters are not idle.

21

1. No monkeys are soldiers.
2. All monkeys are mischievous.

22

1. No wheelbarrows are comfortable.
2. No uncomfortable vehicles are popular.

23

1. No frogs are poetical.
2. Some ducks are unpoetical.

24

1. Every eagle can fly.
2. Some pigs cannot fly.

Exercise 9.8 For even more practice, go back to Exercise 8.8 in Chapter 8 and test the sorites there for validity using Venn diagrams. In each case, use common sense to choose either the Aristotelian or the Boolean standpoint. State which standpoint you choose in each case.

Glossary

Aristotelian assumption (assumption of existential import) The assumption underlying the Aristotelian Square of Opposition, that the categorical statements under consideration all have existential import.

Boolean interpretation The interpretation of categorical sentences that was developed by George Boole and that dispensed with the assumption of existential import for universal sentences.

Empty class A class in which no entities of that category exist.

Existential import A categorical statement is said to have "existential import" if its subject term refers to a class that is not empty; that is, the subject term refers to actually existing entities. (A statement lacks existential import if its subject term refers to a class that is empty.)

Existential viewpoint (or "standpoint") The viewpoint presupposing that the subject terms of the categorical sentences under consideration designates actually existing things.

Hypothetical viewpoint (or "standpoint") The viewpoint that does not presuppose that the subject terms of the categorical sentences under consideration designate actually existing things.

Modern Square of Opposition The square of opposition that results when the Aristotelian assumption is dropped. The arrows for contradiction are all that remain.

Venn diagram A drawing of overlapping circles designed to represent the information contained within one or more categorical statements, with each circle representing a class denoted by a term and each circle labeled for the class it denotes.

Unit 3

Truth-Functional Logic

Aristotle might be the founder of logic as an academic discipline, but it was the Stoic philosophers who gave the subject its actual name. At the research institute founded by Aristotle, the Lyceum, the subject apparently had no formal title. After the death of Aristotle, his logic texts were bundled together as a unit known only as the "organon" or "tool of thought." Early in the third century BC, logicians in the Stoic school of philosophy, also located in Athens, Greece, named the subject after the Greek term *logos* (which could mean "word," "speech," "reason," or even "the underlying principle of the cosmos"). You will meet some of the Stoic philosophers and logicians in this unit. In the previous unit, we explored categorical logic: the first specialized branch of logic to be worked out and published, the branch systematized by Aristotle. In this unit, we explore the second field of logic to be systematized, published, and taught as an academic discipline—a branch of logic discovered not by Aristotle, but by the philosophers who actually gave the subject its name.

Truth-functional logic, the subject of this unit, is the most fully developed branch of logic today. This fascinating field has so many real-world applications that it is hard to know where to begin when explaining them. Whether or not we are aware of it, we try to obey the laws of this branch of logic every time we create a truth-functional argument—which is often, because this is an extremely common type of reasoning. Students of computer science study this branch of logic because the logic of truth-functions forms the basis of their field: The circuits, or logic gates, inside every digital computer are built so that when the electricity flows, it automatically obeys the laws of truth-functional logic. Yet the logic of truth functions was first worked out on a colorful porch across from the marketplace in ancient Athens, early in the third century BC! You will understand this and more by the end of this book.

In the first two chapters of this unit, we will travel back in time, at least in our minds, and you will experience a sudden immersion into the second school of logic to form in ancient Greece. You will be exposed to the subject much as a student of the day would have experienced it sitting on the famous painted porch (*stoa poikile*) across from the agora, the marketplace of Athens. Not only is the logic of the ancient Stoic school fascinating in its own right, and not only is it the precursor to modern logic as well as computer science, but the Stoics also had cool names, which makes it all the more fun to join in their life and thought, if only for a few chapters. This will be an "express version" of Stoic logic, the principles of which are as valid today as when they were first discovered.

In addition to imparting a sense of history, this sudden immersion into the ancient context will yield another fruit: When we move to the modern "upgrades" that have been made to the Stoic system, it will become apparent why they were made! So, let us now tour the field of truth-functional logic, from its roots in ancient Athens all the way to its completion in the twentieth century.

10 Think Like a Stoic! « « « «

Truth-Functional Logic Version 1.0

The Birth of Truth-Functional Logic

Truth-functional logic was discovered and first systematized by logicians associated with the Stoic school of philosophy, in Athens, in the early third century BC. The Stoics are thus the founders of truth-functional logic. The "porch philosophers" started their school of philosophy on a painted porch, or *stoa*, in the marketplace of ancient Athens (hence their colorful name), approximately a generation after the death of Aristotle. Stoic philosophy is fascinating. The Stoics argued that reason (*logos*) is the underlying basis of the *cosmos*—the Greek term for the universe understood as a systematically ordered whole. This Stoic idea helped pave the way for the emergence of physical science. The Stoics also developed philosophical arguments for the existence of God and for a comprehensive system of ethical principles. The best life, argued the Stoics, is a life lived in accord with right reason. The Stoics are best known for their philosophy of ethics, which included the seed idea for the modern doctrine of universal human rights. Every human being, they argued, contains a spark of the divine reason, or logos, that pervades the universe and keeps the system in balance. At a time in history when slavery was universally accepted as natural, the Stoics alone argued that slavery is morally wrong.

A department of logic was inaugurated by Chrysippus, the third head of the Stoa, who became one of the most prolific logicians of history. Said to have written 700 books, 300 of them on logical theory alone, Chrysippus is generally considered the greatest logician of antiquity after Aristotle. However, from the start, the philosophers and logicians of the Stoa faced some stiff competition.

Across town was Plato's Academy, the first university in Western history, located in the Grove of Academus (hence its name). In a garden in another suburb of Athens was the school of philosophy founded by Epicurus. Of course, Athens was also home to the university and scientific research institute founded by Aristotle a few years before, the Lyceum. It was here that Aristotle had written the first logic textbooks in recorded history. Thus, by the time the Stoics appeared on the scene, an active community of logicians at Aristotle's Lyceum dominated the field of logic, conducting research in every area of the subject, or *almost* every area. The Stoic philosophers were also interested in logical theory, and in the course of their research stumbled on something the great Aristotle, and all of his students, had completely missed. Something big, too, for the Stoic discovery opened the door to a whole new field of logical research. The Stoics discovered the "truth-function." As usual, we proceed in small steps.

History Note

The Stoic school of philosophy was founded in Athens in the early third century BC by Zeno of Citium (335–263 B.C.), a student of the famous Megarian logicians Diodorus Cronus (d 307 BC), Philo of Megara, and Stilpo of Megara (380–300 BC). The Megarian school of logic had been founded in the neighboring city-state of Megara by Euclid of Megara (430–360 BC), a student of Socrates. It was the Megarians who launched the original seed idea for truth-functional logic, but the school was defunct by the time Zeno opened his philosophy shop on the painted porch. The competition that subsequently developed between the Stoic logicians and the logicians of Aristotle's school resembles in some ways the rivalry today between Microsoft and Apple. The difference between the two approaches to logical theory can be likened to the difference between the PC and Mac operating systems. Whereas Aristotle broke the reasoning process down into terms (dogs, mammals, etc.) and quantifiers (all, some, etc.), the Stoics broke reasoning down into whole sentences linked by sentence operators (and, or, not, and if). The principles of Aristotle's term logic can be translated into the principles of Stoic sentence logic using logical algorithms, but the transfer is clumsy and difficult, which raises this question: Is there a bigger system that encompasses both systems of logic? The answer is yes. It was discovered in 1879 by a German mathematician named Gottlob Frege. Modern predicate logic, which generalizes and combines categorical and truth-functional logic, is the subject of Unit Four.

Declarative Sentences

In standard logical fashion, Stoic logic begins with precise definitions of all key ideas. A *sayable* is "a meaning." A *self-complete sayable* is "a meaning that can be expressed in a complete sentence." Five kinds of complete sentences are distinguished. In modern terms, these are as follows:

1. Questions, or "interrogative" sentences; for example, "What time is it?"
2. Commands, or "imperative" sentences; for example, "Close the door!"
3. Exclamations, or "exclamatory" sentences; for example, "Ouch!"
4. Performatives; for example, "I promise," "I declare this a holiday," and "I thee wed."
5. Declarative sentences; for example, "Carbon is an element."

The Stoics noted that of these five types of sentences, only declarative sentences (which they called *assertibles*) are capable of expressing something that is either true or false. Because an argument is composed of sentences that are either true or false, a properly stated argument contains only assertibles—declarative sentences. From this point on, when we speak of sentences, let us assume that we have in mind *declarative* sentences.

Exercise 10.1   Is the sentence declarative, imperative, interrogative, performative, or exclamatory? Or none of the above?

1. Ugh.
2. That's so easy a caveman could do it.
3. Does anyone know what time it is?
4. $1 + 1 = 23$
5. Everybody line up in alphabetical order according to height. (Diva Espresso)
6. Man is the only animal who sets a trap, baits it, and then steps in it.
7. I dream of giving birth to a child who will ask, "Mommy, what was war?"
8. I do not want to be a passenger in my own life.
9. There is no objective truth; there are only points of view.
10. The sentence "There is no truth; there are only points of view" is self-contradictory.
11. Yuck!
12. Every human being has a right to equal concern and respect.
13. That is no way to treat a human being.

14. Beware of Greeks bearing gifts.
15. This sentence is false.
16. The Stoic school is sponsoring a public debate tonight.
17. Do you want to know a secret?
18. Hurry up and wait!
19. I name this ship *The Cape Falcon*.
20. In 480 BC, approximately 180,000 Persian troops invaded the tiny land of the Greeks.

Simple, Compound, and Embedded Sentences

A **compound sentence** is any sentence that contains one or more sentences and one or more sentence operators. (We'll define the term *sentence operator* in a moment.) This sentence is compound: "Aristo is home and Stilpo is home." A sentence within a compound sentence is called an **embedded sentence**, or a **component sentence**. The sentence "Aristo is home and Stilpo is home" thus contains two embedded or component sentences within it, namely, "Aristo is home," and "Stilpo is home." A **simple sentence** is any sentence that is not compound. Thus, "Aristo is home" is simple, as is the sentence "Stilpo is home."

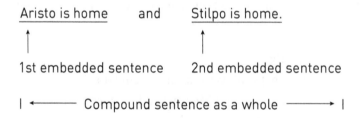

Study the following additional examples carefully.

Examples

Compound: "Today is the festival of Dionysius and tonight we'll have a big toga party."

Embedded sentences: "Today is the festival of Dionysius."
"Tonight we'll have a big toga party."

Compound: "The harvest will be good or the goddess Demeter will be blamed."
Embedded sentences: "The harvest will be good."
"The goddess Demeter will be blamed."

Compound: "If today is the festival of Dionysius, then much wine will be served."
Embedded sentences: "Today is the festival of Dionysius."
"Much wine will be served."

Compound: "It is not the case that tonight is the Delphic festival."
Embedded sentence: "Tonight is the Delphic festival."

History Note

Some of the ancient logicians were interesting characters. For instance, Zeno, who was from Cyprus, did not make himself very popular when, upon arriving in Athens, he proposed to reform the Greek language before he had even learned to speak it! Zeno is said to have died at the age of 98 by holding his breath. According to legend, Diodorus finally committed suicide because he couldn't solve a logical puzzle Stilpo had given him. (Now that's taking logic seriously!) Chrysippus (ca. 280–205 BC), the founder of Stoic logic, is supposed to have written to his fellow Stoic Cleanthes, "Just send me the theorems; I'll find the proofs for myself." One of the old sayings was, "If there is any logic in Heaven, it is that of Chrysippus." According to Diogenes, Chrysippus wrote 311 books on logic. Incidentally, Cleanthes has been described as a "poverty-stricken prize fighter who came to Athens and entered Zeno's school, became its head, transmitted Zeno's doctrines without change, and eventually starved himself to death at the age of 99."

Sentence Operators

Because a compound (of anything) is formed out of one or more parts, a binding agent must exist to hold the parts of the compound together. Concrete, for example, is a composite substance formed out of rocks, sand, and other materials, with cement (a chemical first used for construction in ancient Greece and Rome) serving as the binding agent. Compound sentences are no exception to the rule. Inside every compound sentence sits a "sentence operator" performing the same role in the sentence that cement performs inside concrete. A **sentence operator** (also called a **sentence connective**) is a word or phrase that forms a compound sentence out of one more sentences. Let's start with two separate sentences, each simple:

Philo hates goat cheese.

Stilpo puts olive oil on everything.

Next, let us bind these sentences into a compound using the connecting word *and*:

Philo hates goat cheese *and* Stilpo puts olive oil on everything.

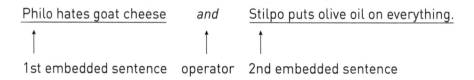

The word *and* is serving here as a sentence operator, for it binds the embedded sentences into a whole. It is important to note that *and* does not always serve in such a capacity. For example, *and* is not serving as an operator in the following sentence, "Stilpo's favorite meal is bread and butter," for it is not joining two sentences together. However, when we use the word *and* to join two sentences together into a compound sentence, the word *and* is functioning as a sentence operator (or sentence connective), forming a compound sentence out of that which it "operates on" (or "connects to").

The word *or* can also be used as a sentence operator. Start with two separate sentences:

1. Today is the festival of Dionysius.
2. Today is the festival of Demeter.

If we join these using the word *or* we get: "Today is the festival of Dionysius *or* today is the festival of Demeter." *Or* is an often-used compound sentence former.

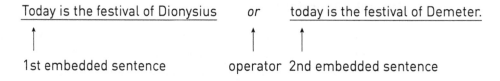

The word "if" is often combined with "then" to join two sentences into a compound, as in the following example: "If Stilpo the Stoic is lecturing on the Logos, then Philo will be in attendance." Notice that we sometimes suppress the word "then" and just write: "If Stilpo the Stoic is lecturing on the Logos, Philo will be in attendance." Saves space.

An operator that joins two sentences into a compound is called a **dyadic** or **two-place** operator. Thus, the compound sentence formers *and* and *or* and "If-then" are dyadic operators.

Not all sentence operators, however, are dyadic. Suppose we start with just one simple sentence:

Wine will be served.

Next, let us prefix to this the phrase: "It is not the case that":

It is not the case that wine will be served.

This sentence is compound, even though it only contains *one* embedded sentence. Recall the definition of compound. This sentence is compound because it contains "one or more" sentences and "one or more operators." The embedded sentence is "Wine will be served." Thus the expression "It is not the case that" is serving here as a sentence-forming operator, since it was used to form the compound out of "one or more" simpler sentences (in this case, out of the single simple sentence "Wine will be served").

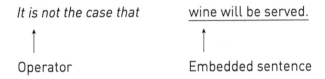

An operator that operates on just *one* sentence to form a compound is called a **monadic** or **one-place operator**. The compound sentence former "It is not the case that," often abbreviated in the form of the word *not*, is thus a monadic operator or connective.

> **Note:** Some compound sentences contain only *one* component sentence.

Exercise 10.2 Is the sentence simple or compound? If it is compound, list any embedded sentences and the operator or operators.

1. Stilpo bought a goat.
2. If Cleanthes lectures on the porch, then everyone will attend.
3. Either Blipo will sing or Flipo will play the lyre.
4. Cleanthes has achieved complete Stoic serenity.
5. It is not the case that Chrysippus will lecture on the porch tonight.
6. If it is daytime, then it is not the case that Stilpo is lecturing.
7. It is daytime or it is not daytime.

8. Blipo is eating olives or Stilpo is eating olives.
9. If Aristo eats an olive, Blipo eats an olive.
10. It is not the case that Cleanthes is home.
11. If war with Persia is averted, many lives will be saved.
12. Blipo is a Stoic sage.
13. The Pythagoreans do not eat beans and they drink a lot of wine.
14. Olive oil has many uses and chick peas are a good side dish.
15. The ancient Greeks ate more fish than meat.
16. Persephone is the daughter of the goddess Demeter.
17. Demeter is the goddess of the harvest.
18. Demeter was the sister of Zeus and she was the daughter of Gaia.
19. If Posiedon is angry, there may be an earthquake.
20. The Stoics argued that the good life results when destructive emotions are brought under control by reason.
21. The Stoics produced a number of philosophical arguments for the claim that God exists.
22. According to the Stoics, free will and universal determinism are logically compatible.
23. Socrates argued that the soul is absolutely simple and he concluded from this that the soul is an immaterial entity.
24. The Stoics argued that all human beings, all the world over, are morally equal and they also argued that all human beings contain within a spark of divinity.
25. According to some of the Stoic philosophers, life is a play, the world is the stage, and each person has an assigned role to play; your duty is to play your part to the best of your abilities.

Naming the Operators

Elementary Stoic logic is concerned with four sentence operators in particular, and with the compound sentences they can form:

- And
- Or
- Not
- If

Let us examine and name each of these "compound sentence formers" and the compound sentences they form, one by one.

"And"

When two sentences are joined together using *and*, the resulting compound is called a *conjunction* and the word *and* is serving as a sentence operator (called the *conjunction operator*). The first embedded sentence is called the *left conjunct* and the second is called the *right conjunct*. Thus:

"Aristo is home   and   Bilpo is home."

↑   ↑   ↑

1st embedded sentence   operator   2nd embedded sentence
(left conjunct)   (conjunction operator)   (right conjunct)

.... Conjunction as a whole ....

"Or"

When two sentences are joined together using "or," the resulting compound is called a *disjunction* and the word "or" is serving as a sentence operator (called the *disjunction operator*). The first embedded sentence is called the *left disjunct* and the second is called the *right disjunct*. Thus:

"Aristo is home   or   Bilpo is home."

↑   ↑   ↑

1st embedded sentence   operator   2nd embedded sentence
(left disjunct)   (disjunction operator)   (right disjunct)

.... Disjunction as a whole ....

"If"

When two sentences are joined together using "if," the resulting compound is called a *conditional* and the word "if" is serving as a sentence operator (called the *conditional operator*). The first embedded sentence is called the *antecedent* and the second is called the *consequent*. For example, "If Aristo is home, Bilpo is home":

"If   Aristo is home,   Bilpo is home."

↑   ↑   ↑

Conditional operator   1st embedded sentence   2nd embedded sentence
                          (antecedent)   (consequent)

.... Conditional as a whole ....

"Not"

When we prefix "It is not the case that" to a sentence, the result is a compound sentence called the *negation* of the original sentence. The words "It is not the case that" are serving as a compound sentence forming operator (called the *negation operator*) because they form a compound sentence out of "one or more" simpler sentences. For example, "It is not the case that Baristo is home":

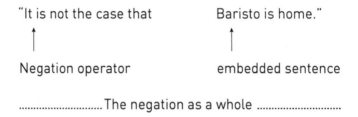

"It is not the case that   Baristo is home."

Negation operator   embedded sentence

.............................The negation as a whole ....

Abbreviating a Negation. In English we often abbreviate a negation by simply placing the word *not* in the verb. Thus, instead of saying, "It is not the case that Baristo is home," we can simply say, "Baristo is not home." It is customary in Stoic logic to abbreviate a negation such as "It is not the case that Baristo is home" by writing, Not: Baristo is home. This just means "Baristo is not home," which in turn abbreviates, "It is not the case that Baristo is home."

Sentence	Abbreviated Negation of Sentence
Zeno is teaching on the stoa.	Not: Zeno is teaching on the stoa.
The Sun is a god.	Not: the Sun is a god.
Socrates is questioning Plato.	Not: Socrates is questioning Plato.

Now we can present each operator in the form of a single word:

- And   (the conjunction operator)
- Or   (the disjunction operator)
- Not   (the negation operator)
- If   (the conditional operator)

With our initial definitions complete, we can now define each type of compound sentence quite concisely:

- Conjunction: Two sentences joined by *and*.
- Disjunction: Two sentences joined by *or*.

- Negation: A sentence prefixed with *not*.
- Conditional: Two sentences joined by *if*.

Exercise 10.3   List the operator or operators in each sentence:

1. If Glopo achieves serenity now, Calista will achieve serenity now.
2. Bipo is studying logic or Clipo is studying logic.
3. Cleanthes has achieved serenity now and Blipo has achieved serenity now.
4. It is not the case that Aristo has achieved total Stoic serenity.
5. If Blopo proves the law of noncontradiction, it is no longer an axiom.
6. Calista is studying propositional logic or Arista is studying categorical logic.
7. Aristo claims he has proved his conclusion and Blipo claims he has not.
8. It is not the case that Glopo has proved that relativism is false.
9. Blopo has proved skepticism false or Blopo has proved he is a fool.
10. Aristotle is the founder of categorical logic and Chrysippus is the founder of truth-functional logic.
11. Plato argues that the soul is separate from the body and Aristotle argues that the soul is the form of the body.
12. The Stoics argued that moral principles are universal and they also argued that moral principles are knowable by pure reasoning.
13. The philosophers of the hedonist school argued that the attainment of the higher pleasures is the goal of life and they also argued that there is no life after death.
14. If every proposition is true or false now, then what will come to be has already been determined.
15. If each person contains within himself or herself an equal spark of divine reason, then each person is intrinsically valuable.

Truth-Values and Truth-Functions

It is finally time to bring truth into the picture. A special terminological convention will greatly simplify the wording in the explanations to follow. If a sentence expresses the truth, instead of simply calling it true, we shall sometimes say that it has the *truth-value* of true. Similarly, if a sentence expresses a falsehood, we shall sometimes say that it has the truth-value of false. Thus we shall be speaking of two truth-values: truth and falsity. Stoic logic, like Aristotelian logic, is a *bivalent* (two-valued) system.

The Stoic logicians were the first to notice that inside certain compound sentences there is a *functional* relationship between the truth-values of the embedded sentences and the truth-value of the compound as a whole. Let us proceed in small steps.

Definition of Function

Essentially, a **function** is a rule that relates one set of values to another set of values. Suppose that every time Blipo (who is a very big man) attends the local festival of Dionysius, he drinks five glasses of wine with every loaf of olive bread that he eats. The following function describes his festive behavior:

$$y = 5x$$

where y is the number of glasses of wine he drinks and x is the number of loaves of bread he consumes. Thus, a *functional relationship* exists between the number of glasses of wine Blipo drinks and the number of loaves of bread he consumes. The function, or rule, $y = 5x$, relates wine numbers to bread numbers.

Definition of Truth-Function

Functions can be named after the values they tie together. Thus, a numerical function is a rule relating one set of numerical values to another set of numerical values, a culinary function would be a rule relating food values to drink values, and so on. Thus, a **truth-function** is simply a rule relating one set of truth-values to another set of truth-values. But where do sets of truth-values, and the rules relating them, exist? Inside certain kinds of compound sentences. This was the Stoics' big discovery!

The Conjunction Function

We have already met the conjunction operator and the conjunction sentences it forms. Consider again a conjunction such as, "Aristo is home and Blipo is home." Let us assume that this conjunction is being used to assert that both conjuncts are true and nothing more. The Stoics noticed something logically interesting going on inside this type of sentence. They noticed that there is a *functional relationship* between the truth-values of the embedded sentences and the truth-value of the compound sentence as a whole. Here is one way to state that functional relationship:

> When the left conjunct ("Aristo is home") is true, and the right conjunct ("Blipo is home") is true, then the compound sentence as a whole ("Aristo is home and Blipo is home") is automatically true. In every other case—when one of the conjuncts is false and when both conjuncts are false—the compound as a whole is automatically false.

There is nothing mysterious here; this is common sense. Furthermore, this relationship exists inside *any* conjunction asserting just that both conjuncts are true. The Stoics had uncovered a functional relationship between the truth-value of the parts and the truth-value of the whole in the case of such a conjunction. However, there is more. Much more important, they also discovered that this functional relationship is a key unlocking a whole new type of logical argument—one that (as I said) had totally eluded the great Aristotle! Here is another way to state the function for conjunction:

- When both conjuncts are true, the compound as a whole is true.
- When the left conjunct is true and the right conjunct is false, the compound as a whole is false.
- When the left conjunct is false and the right conjunct is true, the compound as a whole is false.
- When the left conjunct is false and the right conjunct is false, the compound as a whole is false.

These four clauses define a function because they constitute a "rule relating one set of values to another set of values." This function is called a **truth-function** because it relates one set of truth-values to another set of truth-values. Because this rule pertains specifically to conjunctions it is called the "conjunction function." Perhaps you have heard of it.

Some Aristotelian logicians made fun of the Stoics, calling the logic of truth-functions a "useless form of reasoning." If the Stoics had only known that the logic they were discovering would one day govern the circuits of the digital computer, they could have replied, "Wait about 2,000 years and you'll see what this logic can do: It will change the world."

In Logic, You Can't Have Too Many Definitions!

So that we know *exactly* what we are talking about, a few more definitions are in order. A sentence operator is a **truth-functional operator** if the truth-value of the compound that it forms is a function of the truth-value or values of the component or component sentences within the compound. A compound sentence formed by a truth-functional operator is a **truth-functional compound sentence**. Thus, a truth-functional compound sentence is a compound sentence whose truth-value is a function of the truth-value or values of its component or components. When we use *and* to form a conjunction and the conjunction asserts that both conjuncts are true and nothing more than this, the word *and* is being used as a truth-functional operator and the conjunction is a **truth-functional conjunction**. From this point on, let us assume that each conjunction mentioned is a truth-functional conjunction.

Are there other truth-functions? Yes, the Stoics discovered a number of others. They also discovered that a very common type of reasoning uses these little logical machines to regulate the flow of reasoning and to channel it so as to produce a valid argument in the end. The Stoic logicians had discovered the truth-functional *argument*. We shall turn to this very important idea in a moment, after we define the rest of the Stoic truth-functions.

The Disjunction Function

We are already familiar with the disjunction operator and the compound sentences it forms. A disjunction is the compound sentence that results when two sentences are joined together by the word *or*. The Stoics were the first logicians to discover that the word *or* can be used as a truth-functional operator and to build on this fact. However, the word *or* can be used in two different ways, to express two different meanings, and so a distinction must be drawn before we proceed. Sometimes we use *or* to join two sentences together, asserting that one or the other *but not both* are true. To use a modern example, when the restaurant menu says, "Choice of soup *or* salad," everyone knows this means you can choose one or the other, but not both. This is the *exclusive* or.

However, we sometimes use *or* to assert that one or the other *or both* of two disjuncts are true. This is the *inclusive* or. Suppose a restaurant generously lets you choose soup or salad *or both* for the same price; this invokes the inclusive *or*.

Exclusive or: One or the other is true *but not both*.

Inclusive or: One or the other is true *or both* are true.

When we join two sentences together using an exclusive *or*, the disjunction is an *exclusive disjunction*. When we use an inclusive *or* the compound is an *inclusive disjunction*. Both types of disjunction are truth-functional, as we shall see, for the truth-value of the disjunction as a whole, whether it is inclusive or exclusive, is a strict function of the truth-values of the components. The following rule defines the truth-function for the inclusive or.

- An inclusive disjunction is only false when both disjuncts are false; it is true in every other case.

This is the rule for the exclusive or:

- An exclusive disjunction is only true when one of the two disjuncts is true; it is false in every other case.

From this point on, when we use the word *or* as a sentence operator, let us assume the disjunction is inclusive. The exclusive or will be ignored for the time being. (Remember, this is the "express" version of Stoic logic.) Thus, the rule for inclusive *or* will serve as our disjunction function:

- When both disjuncts are true, the disjunction as a whole is true.
- When the left disjunct is true and the right disjunct is false, the disjunction as a whole is true.
- When the left disjunct is false and the right disjunct is true, the disjunction as a whole is true.
- When the left disjunct is false and the right disjunct is false, the disjunction as a whole is false.

The Negation Function

We have seen that the phrase "It is not the case that" is a compound sentence forming operator (called the negation operator), for it forms a compound sentence out of that to which it attaches. The Stoics were the first to notice and build on the truth-functional nature of this operator. Suppose we start with a simple sentence, "Chrysippus is the third head of the Stoa." When we prefix to this "It is not the case that," we form the denial, or negation, of the original sentence, namely: "It is not the case that Chrysippus is the third head of the Stoa." The following rule defines the truth-function for negation:

A negation is always opposite in truth-value to the sentence negated.

In other words:

- If the sentence negated is true, then the negation as a whole is false.
- If the sentence negated is false, then the negation as a whole is true.

But you already knew this. The negation function is part of common sense. For example, if we begin with "Athens is a city," then the negation is "It is not the case that Athens is a city." In this case, the sentence negated ("Athens is a city") is true, which makes its negation false. If we begin with "Athens is a continent," the negation is "It is not the case that Athens is a continent." In this case, the sentence negated ("Athens is a continent") is false, which makes its negation true. That is simple common sense.

The Conditional Function

Recall that a conditional is a compound sentence composed of two sentences joined by the word *if*, with the first embedded sentence called the antecedent and the second called the consequent. The first three operators studied by the Stoics posed no conceptual problems at all. The truth-functions for *and*, *not*, and *or* are simply their commonsense meanings spelled out with precision. However, the exact meaning of *if* was another matter entirely. It was not clear which truth-function accurately expresses the meaning of *if* when the word is ordinarily used to form a compound out of two simpler sentences. Indeed, logicians still debate the matter today, more than 2,000 years later!

The Stoics had two theories to build on. Earlier, Philo of Megara (fourth century BC) had proposed associating the following function with the conditional operator:

> A conditional is always false when its antecedent is true and its consequent is false; in all other cases, it is true.

A conditional interpreted in terms of this truth-functional rule is called a Philonian conditional, in honor of Philo. (In modern truth-functional logic it is called a material conditional, as we shall see.) Philo's proposal—to designate any conditional as true as long as it does *not* have a true antecedent with a false consequent—is a very inclusive, open-minded, easy-going way to interpret conditional sentences. In essence, Philo is saying this: Let's just call *any* conditional true, no matter what it says, and not argue about it, except in one definite case: when the antecedent is true and the consequent is false. In that *one* case, when the antecedent is true and the consequent is false, let us say that the conditional is false. Commonsense reasoning agrees with Philo on one point: In ordinary, everyday contexts, we always call a conditional "false" when the antecedent is true and the consequent is false. There are no exceptions to this part of his rule. A Philonian conditional is thus a conditional interpreted on the basis of the following truth function:

- When the antecedent and the consequent are true, we'll call the conditional true.
- When the antecedent is true and the consequent is false, the conditional is false.
- When the antecedent is false and the consequent is true, we'll call the conditional true.
- When the antecedent and the consequent are false, we'll call the conditional true.

These four clauses specify what logicians called the truth-conditions for the Philonian conditional—the conditions under which such a conditional is true (or false).

The second theory of the conditional was proposed by Philo's teacher, the Megarian logician Diodorus Cronus. Because this second account is not truth-functional, it cannot be fully expressed as a line-by-line truth function. Let us put it this way:

A conditional is true only when it is *not possible* that the antecedent is true and the consequent is false; it is false otherwise.

It is much tougher for a conditional sentence to be true on this, the Diodoran interpretation. That is, the truth-conditions for a Diodoran conditional are stricter—more limited—compared to the truth-conditions for the Philonian conditional. Thus, in modern logic, an "if–then" sentence interpreted as suggested by Diodorus is called a strict conditional.

Apparently the Megarian logicians debated the meaning of *if* so intensely that the controversy spilled out into the streets, for an ancient commentator, Callimachus, wrote, "Even the crows on the roof are cawing about the nature of the conditional!"

Stoic truth-functional logic chose to go with the easy-going, more inclusive Philonian interpretation of the conditional sentence. Thus, following Philo, Stoic truth-functional logic assigns the following truth-function to the conditional operator *if*:

- A conditional is only false when the antecedent is true and the consequent is false; the conditional is true in every other case.

Let us call a conditional whose truth-conditions are given by this truth-function a truth-functional conditional. Such a compound could also be called a Philonian conditional, of course, in honor of its discoverer, Philo, the logician known as "the dialectician." We examine the logic of the Philonian conditional in this unit. The logic of the strict conditional will not be taken up until Unit Six, when we enter a most intriguing branch of our subject, indeed, the branch of logic where most of the cutting-edge work in the subject is currently taking place: modal logic.

What's Next?

We have now identified four kinds of compound sentences and four truth-functions. What are we going to do with this knowledge? We are going to learn how truth-functions regulate the flow of reasoning inside arguments. Ultimately, this will lead to a very precise method for assessing a certain class of arguments, called truth-functional arguments, for validity. The next chapter begins the process.

Exercise 10.4   Is the compound sentence true or false?

1. The left conjunct is true and the right conjunct is true.
2. The left conjunct is true and the right conjunct is false.
3. The left conjunct is false and the right conjunct is true.
4. The left conjunct is false and the right conjunct is false.
5. The left disjunct is true and the right disjunct is true.
6. The left disjunct is true and the right disjunct is false.
7. The left disjunct is false and the right disjunct is true.
8. The left disjunct is false and the right disjunct is false.
9. The antecedent is true and the consequent is true.
10. The antecedent is true and the consequent is false.
11. The antecedent is false and the consequent is true.
12. The antecedent is false and the consequent is false.
13. The embedded sentence in the negation is true.
14. The embedded sentence in the negation is false.

Glossary

Component (or embedded) sentence A sentence that is a part of a compound sentence.

Compound sentence A sentence that contains one or more sentences and one or more operators.

Dyadic operator A connective that joins together two sentences to form a compound sentence.

Embedded sentence *See* Component sentence

Exclusive *or* The *or* that asserts that one or the other but not both disjuncts are true.

Function A rule that relates one set of values to another set of values.

Inclusive *or* The *or* that asserts that one or the other or both disjuncts are true.

Monadic operator A connective that is joined to just one sentence to form a compound sentence.

Sentence operator A word or phrase that can be connected to one or more sentences to produce a compound sentence.

Simple sentence A sentence that does not contain one or more shorter sentences and does not contain one or more sentence operators.

Truth-function A rule that relates one set of truth-values to another set of truth-values.

Truth-functional compound sentence A compound sentence with the following feature: the truth-value of the compound as a whole is a function of the truth-values of the components.

Truth-functional operator An operator that forms a truth-functional compound sentence when attached to one or more component sentences.

11 Truth-Functional Logic Version 1.1 «« «« «« «« «

Stoic Logic Takes Form

A **truth-functional argument** is any argument whose validity is due to the arrangement of the truth-functional operators (*and, or, if, not*) within it and nothing else. In other words, the validity (or invalidity) of a truth-functional argument is not a function of content (of what the argument is about), nor is it a function of the state of the world or of specific facts; rather, the validity of the argument is determined solely by the way the truth-functions inside it are arranged or put together. This is why, as you will see (starting in Chapter 12) that an argument's internal truth-functions can be mapped out in symbols, and the validity or invalidity of the argument can be determined by the arrangement of the symbols, with the precision of mathematics and without reference to the content of the argument. If one of these arguments were a machine, its truth-functions would be little internal logical circuits directing the flow of reasoning the way circuits direct the flow of electricity. Inside a *valid* truth-functional argument, of course, truth-functions direct the flow of reason so that *if* the premises are true, the conclusion *must* be true. Here is a truth-functional argument:

1. If Aristo is home, Ballisades the logician is home.
2. If Ballisades the logician is home, Cristo is home.
3. But Aristo is home.
4. Therefore, Cristo must be home.

Notice that this argument is a combination of sentences standing on their own and embedded sentences joined by truth-functional sentence operators, and nothing else, all related in the form of premises leading to a conclusion. You will see many more truth-functional arguments before this unit has concluded.

Argument Forms

Two more ideas must be firmly in place before we proceed. The first is the concept of an argument form. Consider the following argument:

Argument 1

1. If Aristo is teaching, Blopo is listening.
2. Moreover, Aristo is teaching.
3. Therefore, Blopo is listening.

Compare this with the following argument:

Argument 2

1. If Cleanthes is swimming, Diogenes is swimming.
2. Moreover, Cleanthes is swimming.
3. Therefore, Diogenes is swimming.

Although these arguments are about different subjects and different Stoic logicians, they share a common structure, pattern, or form. Argument Structure 1, shown next, is one way to represent, in writing, the abstract structure or pattern that these two arguments have in common. The annotated blanks serve as placeholders in the form marking where the individual sentences of each argument can be placed.

Argument Structure 1

1. If (embedded sentence 1) then (embedded sentence 2).
2. Moreover (embedded sentence 1).
3. Therefore (embedded sentence 2).

Argument 1 can be reproduced by plugging its embedded sentences into the appropriate blanks in Argument Structure 1. The first embedded sentence is "Aristo is teaching." The second embedded sentence is "Blopo is listening." If we substitute "Aristo is teaching" for the blanks marked "embedded sentence 1" in Argument Structure 1, and if we substitute "Blopo is listening" for the blanks marked "embedded sentence 2," we convert the abstract pattern of Argument Structure 1 into Argument 1:

1. If (Aristo is teaching), then (Blopo is listening).
2. Moreover (Aristo is teaching).
3. Therefore (Blopo is listening).

In this sense, Argument 1 "fits" or follows Argument Structure 1. Ditto for Argument 2, placing "Cleanthes is swimming" into the appropriate blanks and then doing the same for "Diogenes is swimming":

1. If (Cleanthes is swimming), then (Diogenes is swimming).
2. Moreover (Cleanthes is swimming).
3. Therefore (Diogenes is swimming).

Do you see the way in which Arguments 1 and 2 both "fit" the common pattern or form of reasoning in Argument Structure 1? (Make sure you see this before you move on.)

The abstract pattern in Argument Structure 1 is called the "logical form" of Arguments 1 and 2, and Arguments 1 and 2 are called "substitution instances" of the corresponding argument form. (The Stoics called argument forms *argument modes*.)

Argument Form and Substitution Instance Precisely Defined

Let us define an **argument form** as an abstract pattern of reasoning that many arguments, about many different subjects, may follow or share in common. A specific argument is a **substitution instance of an argument form** if it is possible to generate the argument from the argument form by consistently substituting sentences for the blanks or placeholders in the argument form. If an argument is a substitution instance (or "instance" for short) of a form, we can say the argument "instantiates" the form.

How to Show That a Particular Argument Is an *Instance* of a Form

We can confirm that Argument 1 is a substitution instance of the corresponding argument form (expressed as Argument Structure 1) in the following way. Starting with the argument form, place the first embedded sentence, "Aristo is teaching," into the first blank. Next, place the second embedded sentence, "Blopo is listening," into the second blank. Notice the way the blanks act as *placeholders* for sentences. In the next line of the form, place "Aristo is teaching" in the blank. Finally, place "Blopo is listening" in the last placeholder. If you did this, even if only in your mind, you generated Argument 1 from the corresponding argument form. This shows that Argument 1 is a substitution instance of the form. (This exercise also shows that Argument Structure 1 is the logical form of Argument 1.)

The Stoics' Favored Placeholders: Numbers

The Stoics used numbers (rather than annotated blanks) as placeholders when writing out argument forms. Thus, they would have written Argument Structure 1 this way:

1. If the 1st, the 2nd.
2. Moreover, the 1st.
3. Therefore, the 2nd.

Here the terms *1st* and *2nd* are serving as placeholders marking where embedded sentences may be placed to produce a substitution instance of the form. In a sense, they serve as "stand-ins" for sentences that could take their place. Today, placeholders inside forms are called variables. A *variable* is a symbol standing for anything from a designated group of things. The group of things is called the variable's *domain*, and the variable is said to "range" over its domain. By serving as a placeholder for objects in its domain, the variable represents all the objects in its corresponding domain. You are probably familiar with the variables used by mathematicians, letters such as x, y, and z. Mathematical variables usually serve as placeholders for numbers. For example, the commutative law of addition uses x and y as variables ranging over the domain of all real numbers:

$$x + y = y + x.$$

Assuming the domain of real numbers, this sentence says, for any real number x, and any real number y, x added to y equals y added to x. Call these variables *numerical* variables. In logic, variables usually serve as placeholders for sentences and are called *sentence* variables. The Stoic numbers, 1st, 2nd, and so on, were thus serving as sentence variables.

In a sense, the abstract argument form is the skeleton of an argument. Once it is "fleshed in" with real content—with a substitution instance—you have a real argument. Notice that the argument skeleton is all form and no content; whereas the substitution instance contains content and is about a definite subject matter. The Stoic argument form immediately preceding can be understood as abbreviating:

1. If (the 1st embedded sentence), (the 2nd embedded sentence).
2. Moreover, the 1st embedded sentence is true.
3. Therefore, the 2nd embedded sentence is true.

Many arguments in everyday life instantiate this pattern of reasoning. The Stoics were very fond of this argument form. They were also very fond of this one:

1. It is not the case that both the 1st and the 2nd.
2. But the 1st.
3. Therefore, not the 2nd.

For instance:

1. It is not the case that both Ari is home and Bari is home.
2. But Ari *is* home.
3. Therefore, it is not the case that Bari is home.

In more colloquial terms, Ari and Bari are not both home. But Ari is home; so Bari must be out of the house.

Exercise 11.1 **Part A.** Consider the following argument forms, written with numbers in Stoic fashion. For each form, state which of the following numbered arguments is an instance of the corresponding form. Note: Not all of the numbered arguments below are valid arguments.

Form 1

1. If the 1st, the 2nd
2. But not: the 2nd
3. Therefore not: the 1st

Form 2

1. If the 1st, the 2nd
2. But not: the 1st
3. Therefore not: the 2nd

Form 3

1. If the 1st, the 2nd
2. Moreover the 1st
3. Therefore, the 2nd

Form 4

1. If the 1st, the 2nd
2. If the 2nd, the 3rd.
3. Therefore, if the 1st, the 3rd

Form 5

1. The 1st or the 2nd
2. But not the 1st
3. Therefore, the 2nd

Form 6

1. If the 1st, the 2nd
2. But the 2nd
3. Therefore, the 1st

Form 7

1. Not both the 1st and the 2nd
2. But the 1st
3. Therefore not: the 2nd

Arguments

1.

    1. If Ari swims then Bari swims.

    2. But Bari swims.

    3. Therefore, Ari swims.

2.

    1. If Ari swims then Bari swims.

    2. If Bari swims then Cristo swims.

    3. Therefore, if Ari swims, then Cristo swims.

3.

    1. If Ari swims then Bari swims.

    2. But not: Bari swims.

    3. Therefore, not: Ari swims.

4.

    1. If Ari swims then Bari swims.

    2. But not: Ari swims.

    3. Therefore, not: Bari swims.

5.

    1. If Blopo offers a sacrifice to the gods, then Flopo offers a sacrifice.

    2. If Flopo offers a sacrifice, then Glopo offers a sacrifice.

    3. Therefore, if Blopo offers a sacrifice to the gods, then Glopo offers a sacrifice.

6.

    1. Ari swims or Bari swims.

    2. Not: Ari swims.

    3. Therefore, Bari swims.

7.

    1. If Ari swims, Bari swims.

    2. Ari swims.

    3. Therefore, Bari swims.

8.

1. If Stilpo swims, Glipo swims.
2. But not: Glipo swims.
3. Therefore, not: Stilpo swims.

9.

1. It is not the case that both Bari is teaching and Cristo is teaching.
2. But Bari is teaching.
3. Therefore, it is not the case that Cristo is teaching.

10.

1. Ari swims or Bari swims.
2. But not: Ari swims.
3. Therefore, Bari swims.

11.

1. If Cristo achieves a state of apatheia, then he will be free of all anxiety.
2. Moreover, Cristo has achieved a state of apatheia.
3. Therefore, Cristo is free of all anxiety.

12.

1. It is not the case that both the olives are ripe and the olives are green.
2. Moreover the olives are ripe.
3. Therefore, it is not the case that the olives are green.

Exercise 11.1 **Part B** For each of the seven argument forms above, create an original argument of your own, about something that interests you. Make sure that each of your arguments is a substitution instance of the corresponding argument form. Is your argument valid?

Abbreviating Arguments

As you know, arguments can be short and sweet, but they can also be long and complicated. (They can also be long and boring, but we dare not go there in this book.) From this point on, to save space, and also to make future calculations more manageable, it will be helpful to institute a very elementary system of abbreviation. Recall that the validity of a truth-functional argument is not determined by its content—what it is about. Rather, its validity is determined solely by the abstract arrangement of its truth-functional operators. This means that when we are evaluating a truth-functional argument for validity, the content drops away and all we need to inspect is the structural arrangement of the operators. It follows that we will not miss anything logically crucial if we abbreviate an argument by replacing each embedded sentence with a capital letter that reminds us of the sentence it replaces. Once the content drops away, leaving the operators in place, we can focus just on the structural arrangement of the operators. We also save space. The abbreviation process will be so simple that a few examples should suffice. To abbreviate an argument, we simply replace each component sentence with a capital letter that reminds us of the sentence it is replacing.

Argument	Abbreviation
1. If it is autumn, the days are shorter.	1. If A, D
2. It is autumn.	2. A
3. Therefore, the days are shorter.	3. Therefore, D
1. Glopo is home or Hopo is home.	1. G or H
2. But it is not the case that Glopo is home.	2. But not: G
3. Thus, Hopo is home.	3. Thus, H
1. Aristo is home and Blobbo is home.	1. A and B
2. If Aristo is home, Cristo is home.	2. If A, C
3. So, Blobbo and Cristo are home.	3. So, B and C
1. It's not the case that both Cristo sings and Dio sings.	1. Not both: C and D
2. But Cristo sings.	2. But C
3. Thus it is not the case that Dio sings.	3. Thus not: D
1. If it is day, it is light outside.	1. If D, L
2. It is not the case that it is day.	2. Not: D
3. Thus it is not the case that it is light outside.	3. Thus, not: L

Exercise 11.2   Abbreviate the following arguments, choosing obvious letters of abbreviation (e.g., A for "Aristo walks," B for "Blipo sings," C for "Cristo talks," etc.).

1. If it is winter, it is cold. If it is cold, we will not be swimming. If we will not be swimming, then the race is cancelled. It is winter. Therefore, the race is cancelled.

2. If it is winter, it is cold. If it is cold, we will not be swimming. If we will not be swimming, then the race is cancelled. It is cold. Therefore, the race is cancelled.

3. If it is summer, it is cold. But it is not cold. If it is not summer, then the time is not right for a race. It is not summer. Therefore, the time is not right for a race.

4. If it is spring, flowers are in bloom. Flowers are in bloom. Thus, it is spring.

5. If it is spring, flowers are in bloom. It is spring. So, flowers are in bloom.

6. It is night or it is day. But it is not night. Therefore, it is day.

7. If Blopo is home, Flopo is home. But it is not the case that Flopo is home. Therefore, it is not the case that Blopo is home.

8. If Blopo is home, Flopo is home. But it is not the case that Blopo is home. Therefore, it is not the case that Flopo is home.

9. If Aristo is home, it is night. If it is night, it is quiet. If it is quiet, it is peaceful. Therefore, if Aristo is home, it is peaceful.

10. If Aristo is home, it is night. If it is night, it is quiet. If it is quiet, it is peaceful. Therefore, if it is peaceful, Aristo is home.

11. If it is fall, the general mood is romantic. If the general mood is romantic, it is not the case that both the temperature is cold and the weather is dry. It is fall. And the temperature is cold. If the weather is dry, then it is time for action. Thus, it is time for action.

12. If it is summer, the atmosphere is carefree. It is not the case that both it is summer and the atmosphere is somber. If it is not the case that the atmosphere is somber, then it is summer.

13. If it is autumn then the general atmosphere is romantic. But it is not autumn. So the general mood is not romantic.

14. Winter has a melancholy temper and spring has an invigorating temper. So, if it is Easter, then the temper is invigorating.

Why So Many Definitions?

Why does logic require so many definitions? And why do those definitions have to be so technical? If we try to communicate using undefined terms with imprecise meanings, the result will be confusion. Definitions and terminology are crucial to every field of thought, which is why the early part of just about any course of study involves the introduction of terminology.

Four Valid Forms of Reasoning

The last element we need in place before we ascend to the summit of the Stoic system is the concept of a valid argument form and the four valid forms that constitute the basis of the Stoic system. An argument form is a **valid argument form** if every instance of the form is a valid argument. If your reasoning is an instance of a valid form, then it must be valid reasoning. Valid argument forms are thus guides to valid reasoning (no matter what subject matter you are reasoning about) just as the addition table is a guide to correct adding (no matter what stuff you are counting). The Stoics identified quite a number of valid argument forms; we shall examine only four. Remember, this is the "express" version of Stoic logic. One could spend *years* studying the whole system. Life is short.

Modus Ponens

The Stoics had no agreed on name for the first valid argument form in their system. Today this argument form is universally referred to by a Latin name it was assigned in the Middle Ages, when research in logic was almost all conducted in that language: *modus ponens* (Latin for "method of affirmation"). Let us commit a small historical anachronism and use the universally established name, modus ponens. The medieval name is not only used by everybody in logic today, but it is more interesting than the alternative, which would be Form 1. We have already encountered this argument form; indeed, it is a staple of everyday reasoning. The Stoics expressed it this way:

1. If the 1st, the 2nd.
2. Moreover, the 1st.
3. Therefore: the 2nd.

The Stoics gave this argument as an instance of this form:

1. If it is day, it is light outside.
2. It is day.
3. Therefore, it is light outside.

As a student on the painted porch, you probably would have seen the following argument offered as an instance as well:

1. If Dion walks, Dion is in motion.
2. But Dion walks.
3. Therefore, Dion is in motion.

Using D for "Dion walks" and M for "Dion is in motion," the abbreviation would be:

1. If D, M
2. But D
3. Therefore, M

Caution: Modus Ponens Differs from This Fallacious Form!

It is very important that you not confuse the modus ponens pattern of reasoning, which is valid, with another pattern of reasoning that looks deceptively similar to it but that is not valid. Consider this reasoning:

1. If Stilpo is sick, logic class is cancelled.
2. Logic class is cancelled.
3. Therefore, Stilpo is sick.

Abbreviated, this is:

1. If S, L
2. L

Therefore:

3. S

The pattern of reasoning here is *not* the same pattern as modus ponens. Do you see the difference? (If you do not see the difference, compare the patterns carefully and note exactly where they differ before continuing.) This last argument embodies an *invalid* form of reasoning. It is possible the conclusion of the argument is false *even if both premises are true*. If you do not see this, consider the following counterexample:

> Perhaps the premises are both true. But in addition, perhaps Stilpo is not sick at all. Perhaps he is just fine and class was cancelled because of bad weather. In this case, the premises would both be true and the conclusion would be false.

This counterexample helps us see the possibility that the premises are true and yet the conclusion is false. That is the defining feature of an invalid argument. The argument is surely invalid. This error in reasoning is so frequently committed that it has been given a name. Logicians call it the fallacy of affirming the consequent. (Recall that a fallacy is an error in reasoning.) To avoid fallacious reasoning, note carefully the difference between modus ponens, which is a valid form of reasoning, and affirming the consequent, which is not.

Modus ponens	Fallacy of affirming the consequent
1. If the 1st, the 2nd	1. If the 1st, the 2nd

2. The 1st   2. The 2nd

3. Therefore the 2nd   3. Therefore the 1st

The name of the associated fallacy derives from the fact that the second premise *affirms* the consequent of the first premise.

Modus Tollens

The second valid form on the Stoic list is universally known today by a Latin name also assigned in medieval times: *modus tollens* ("method of denial"). For the sake of continuity in our studies, let us use the well-known name, the modus tollens argument form:

1. If the 1st, the 2nd
2. But Not: the 2nd
3. Therefore Not: the 1st

The following argument was often offered in the Stoa as an instance of this form:

1. If it is day, then it is light outside.
2. It is not the case that it is light outside.
3. Therefore, it is not the case that it is day.

Many people, when they first consider the modus tollens argument form, think it is an invalid form of reasoning. It might look invalid at first glance, but on reflection, it can be seen to be as valid as the modus ponens form. Consider this instance of modus tollens:

1. If it is July, then it is summer.
2. But it is not summer.
3. Then it is not July.

Does this seem valid? If the premises are true, must the conclusion be true? Certainly!

Caution: Modus Tollens Differs from This Fallacious Form!

It is important that you not confuse the modus tollens pattern of reasoning, which is valid, with another inference pattern that looks eerily similar to it but that is not valid. Consider this reasoning:

1. If Aristo is swimming, then Bloppo is swimming.
2. It is not the case that Aristo is swimming.
3. Therefore, Bloppo is not swimming.

Abbreviated, this is:

1. If A, B
2. Not A

Therefore:

3. Not B

Although it might look valid at first glance, this is an invalid argument. If you doubt this, here is a counterexample: Isn't it *possible*, from only the information given, that Bloppo is swimming *alone*? Certainly it is, given only the information presented in the premises. Thus, it is possible that the premises of this argument are true but the conclusion is false, making this an invalid argument. This error in reasoning is so frequently committed that it has been given a name, the fallacy of denying the antecedent. (The name derives from the fact that the second premise denies the antecedent of the first premise.) Carefully note the way in which this fallacy differs from the modus tollens pattern. Modus tollens is a valid form of reasoning, denying the antecedent is not.

Modus tollens   The fallacy of denying the antecedent

1. If the 1st, the 2nd   1. If the 1st, the 2nd
2. But Not: the 2nd   2. Not: the 1st
3. Therefore Not: the 1st   3. Therefore Not: the 2nd

Here is another instance of modus tollens:

1. If Basilides the Stoic is on the porch, then Poleman is on the porch.
   (this is the 1st)   (this is the 2nd)
2. Not: Poleman is on the porch.
       (this is the 2nd)
3. Therefore Not: Basilides the Stoic is on the porch.
       (this is the 1st)

Exercise 11.3   For each argument form, create an original argument of your own about something that interests you. Make sure that each of your arguments is a substitution instance of the corresponding argument form. Is your argument valid or invalid?

1. Modus ponens
2. Modus tollens

3. Affirming the consequent
4. Denying the antecedent

Disjunctive Syllogism

The third valid form on the Stoic list is universally known today by the name it was given in the modern period: disjunctive syllogism. (The name derives from the fact that the argument is a syllogism—a deductive argument—and that it starts with a disjunction.) Following precedent, we'll continue with the modern name, the disjunctive syllogism argument form:

1. The 1st or the 2nd
2. But Not: the 1st
3. Therefore: the 2nd

Here is an instance:

1. We'll have green olives or we'll have black olives.
2. It is not the case we'll have green olives.
3. Therefore, we'll have black olives.

Here is another instance:

1. Stilpo is on the porch lecturing or Cleanthes is on the porch lecturing.
2. But Stilpo is not on the porch lecturing.
3. Therefore, Cleanthes is on the porch lecturing.

Make sure that you understand why each preceding argument is an instance of the corresponding form before you move on.

The "Not Both" Form

The fourth valid form on the Stoic list has no universally established modern name. Let us call it the "not both" form. It was written this way on the painted porch:

1. Not both: the 1st and the 2nd
2. But the 1st is true.
3. Therefore: Not the 2nd.

This form should seem valid immediately. Suppose you know that it is not the case that Aristo and Blopo are both home. They are not both home. Now you learn that Aristo *is* home. Certainly it follows that Blopo is *not* home. Yes?

Here are additional examples of the valid "not both" form of reasoning:

1. It is not the case that both: the animal is a mammal and the animal is a fish.
2. The animal is a mammal.
3. Therefore, it is not the case that the animal is a fish.

1. It is not the case that both: Stilpo is wrestling an octopus and Chrysippus is wrestling an octopus.
2. But Stilpo is wrestling an octopus.
3. Therefore, it is not the case that Chrysippus is wrestling an octopus.

1. It is not the case that both Aratus is lecturing and Dardenus is lecturing.
2. But Aratus is lecturing.
3. Therefore, it is not the case that Dardenus is lecturing.

Make sure that you understand why each of the preceding arguments is an instance of the corresponding form before you move on.

What's the Point?

Let us recall the point of all of this. If an argument instantiates a valid argument form, then the argument must be valid, for every instance of a valid argument form is a valid argument. Valid argument forms are thus templates for valid reasoning. They are guides to valid reasoning just as the addition table is a guide to correct addition. Valid reasoning is a good thing, as are valid argument forms.

History Note

The Stoic school went into decline after the death of Chrysippus. By the first century AD, the categorical logic studied at Aristotle's school had eclipsed the truth-functional logic of the Stoics, which was by now largely forgotten. The main manuscripts of Stoic logic were apparently lost in someone's attic and rotted away over the centuries. As a result of the demise of Stoic logic, very little original research would be conducted in truth-functional logic for almost 2,000 years. The history of logic records a few scattered discoveries here and there, made by a few notable logicians in Europe in the Middle Ages, but nothing monumental happens until the late nineteenth century, when an unknown logician comes out of nowhere and revolutionizes logical theory—to a large extent by rediscovering and building upon the forgotten logic of the Stoics, as we shall see shortly.

Exercise 11.4   Identify each abbreviated argument as an instance of modus ponens, modus tollens, disjunctive syllogism, or the not both form. If the argument is not an instance of one of these valid forms, answer "Not an instance."

1.
   1. If A, B
   2. Not: B
   3. Therefore, not A

2.
   1. A or B
   2. Not A
   3. Therefore, B

3.
   1. If A, B
   2. Moreover, A
   3. Therefore, B

4.
   1. If A, B
   2. Not: A
   3. Therefore, not B.

5.
   1. A or B
   2. Moreover, A
   3. Therefore, B

6.
   1. If A, B
   2. Moreover, B
   3. Therefore, A

7.
   1. Not both: A and B
   2. But A
   3. Therefore, not B

8.
   1. Not both A and B
   2. Not A
   3. Therefore, not B

9.
   1. A or B
   2. Not A
   3. Therefore, not B

10.
   1. If D, E
   2. Not: E. Thus not D

Where Do We Go From Here?

The discovery of truth-functional argument forms was not the only accomplishment of the Stoic school. The Stoic logicians also pioneered a new method of logical proof. Recall that Aristotle developed the first deductive system for logic. Aristotle proved arguments valid on the basis of the argument forms present in a set of "perfect" syllogisms each member of which was asserted as valid without proof. The Stoic system went beyond the system of Aristotle in several ways. First, it contained explicitly stated "rules of inference." A rule of inference (or "inference rule") is a rule for drawing correct inferences from premises, no matter what the premises are about. Second, the Stoic system covered truth-functional arguments, thus argument forms not recognized in the system of Aristotle. Today we call the type of proof invented by the Stoics "natural deduction." Remember proofs in geometry class? Those are very much like the natural deduction proofs of the Stoics.

However, the Stoic system of natural deduction suffered from a number of deficits that would not be repaired until the late nineteenth century. To learn the original Stoic system of deduction now, and then later the modern upgrade, would involve us in unnecessary duplication of effort. For this reason, it is best at this point in the story to thank the Stoics kindly and jump ahead 2,200 years, to 1879, the year that an obscure German mathematician discovered how to improve the Stoic system and bring it into the modern age. The biggest piece of the puzzle, missing from the Stoic system of deduction—and from the deductive system of Aristotle as well—was a fully formal logical language. What is this? The next chapter picks up that thread of the story. Truth-functional logic is about to become as precise as mathematics.

Exercise 11.5   These questions will allow you to apply what you have just learned.

1. In a newspaper, magazine, website, or book you are reading, find an argument that can be construed as an instance of one of the four valid argument forms identified above. Name the form, quote the argument, abbreviate the argument, and cite your source.

2. For each of the four valid argument forms, create an original substitution instance, in English. For each substitution instance, state an accurate abbreviation.

Glossary

Argument form An abstract pattern of reasoning that many arguments can follow or share in common. Argument forms are all form and no content.

Substitution instance of an argument form A specific argument is a substitution instance of an argument form if it is possible to generate the specific argument from the abstract argument form by substituting sentences for the blanks or placeholders in the argument form.

Truth-functional argument Any argument whose validity is due to the arrangement of its truth-functional operators and nothing else.

Valid argument form An argument form every substitution instance of which is a valid argument.

12 Truth-Functional Logic Version 2.0 « « « «

The Invention of Formal Languages in the Nineteenth Century

Have you ever wondered, "What is the relationship between mathematics and logic?" What, if anything, is the common factor? During the nineteenth century, logicians and mathematicians were hotly debating this question. Some argued that mathematics is entirely based on logic. Others argued that logic is based entirely on pure math. According to the one school of thought, logic is a branch of math and can be deduced from a set of purely mathematical axioms. According to the other side, math is really just a branch of logic and can be derived from an axiom base of purely logical principles alone.

Gottlob Frege (1848–1925), a professor of mathematics at a German university, known to few people outside his profession, had an opinion on the issue. He had a hunch that mathematics is, in reality, just a branch of logic. After receiving his doctorate in mathematics in 1873, he spent years trying to rigorously prove that all of mathematics is reducible to pure logical axioms alone; in other words, that math is a logical outgrowth of pure logic itself. To prove his theory, which is known as **logicism**, Frege sought to construct an axiom system that would have the following properties: (a) All the axioms and initial definitions would be drawn from pure logic alone, with no mathematics present in the foundation; and (b) all of mathematics could be logically deduced, step by step, from the axioms alone, using precisely defined rules of logical inference, with the help of purely logical definitions. The resulting proof would show that *all* mathematical truths are contained in the theorems of the system. Logic is the trunk of the tree; math is the branches.

However, two roadblocks stood in the way—basically the same roadblocks that had prevented the Stoics from completing their project of perfecting truth-functional logic over 2,000 years before. In the 1870s, a general theory of mathematical proof, containing precise, rigorously defined rules of inference, simply did not exist. This made it impossible to rigorously prove even the truths of elementary arithmetic on the basis of logical axioms and definitions alone, without any gaps, "without any guesswork" as Frege put it, let alone anything beyond that.

The second and most significant roadblock concerned language. Frege found that even the most elementary theorems of arithmetic could not be *accurately* expressed within the existing language of logic at the time. The problem stemmed from the fact that the logic of the day was all expressed within a *natural* language. A **natural language**, as opposed to a "formal" language, is one that is normally learned at birth and that serves as a general tool of communication. German, English, French, and Spanish are natural languages. A **formal language**, on the other hand (also called an artificial language), is created by a group of people to communicate a specialized and restricted body of ideas. Musical notation is a good example. Mathematics, electronics, and computer science also use formal languages. Formal languages usually employ specially defined symbols (for example, ♪, ⊃, ≡) that allow us to simplify the expression of complex ideas.

Special symbols serve another purpose as well. The words of a natural language often carry emotional overtones that can sidetrack the reasoning process. Natural language words can also have vague or ambiguous meanings. Roughly, the meaning of a word is *vague* if it has "borderline cases"—situations where it is not clear whether the word does or does not apply. A word is *ambiguous* in a context if it can be interpreted in two or more different ways. The presence of vagueness and ambiguity can short-circuit any reasoning process. When information is translated into the special symbols of a formal symbolic language, many of these pitfalls can be avoided.

Frege realized that before he could prove his thesis, that math is a branch of logic, he would have to develop a rigorous theory of proof, one more rigorous than anything existing at the time. The new theory of proof, he decided, would be based on the Stoic system. However, Frege also realized that before the new theory could even be formulated, he would have to improve on the existing language of logic. The first step in Frege's grand project would therefore be the construction of a new, symbolic logical language, also based on the Stoic system. In 1879, Frege rolled out the new system, the first update of Stoic logic in 2,000 years. Unfortunately, the formal language devised by Frege, for the expression of complex logical ideas, was so cumbersome, so hard to read and use, that logicians today have abandoned it in favor of simpler and more effective formal logical languages that accomplish the same thing. We begin with one such formal language commonly found in introductory logic textbooks today.[1]

The Formal Language "TL"

Any language, formal or natural, can be specified in terms of a syntax and a semantics. The **syntax** of a language consists of its vocabulary and its rules of grammar. The vocabulary is the elements we can use to construct expressions in the language and the grammar is the rules stating how to construct properly formed expressions. The **semantics** for a language assigns meanings to the properly formed expressions of the language.

The formal logical language to be presented here shall be called **TL** (for "truth-functional language"). Whereas the syntax of a natural language such as English contains hundreds of rules and takes years to learn, the syntax of TL consists of three simple rules and a small number of vocabulary items and can be learned in a few minutes.

Syntax of TL

Vocabulary

Sentence constants:	A, B, C, . . . Z	
Sentence operators:	Name	Operator
	Tilde	~
	Wedge	v
	Ampersand	&
	Horseshoe	⊃
	Triple bar	≡
Grouping indicators:	( ) [ ] { }	

Rules of Grammar

Where **P** and **Q** are variables ranging over sentences of TL:

Rule 1. Any sentence constant standing alone is a sentence of TL.
Rule 2. If **P** is a sentence of TL, then ~**P** is a sentence of TL.
Rule 3. If **P** and **Q** are sentences of TL, then (**P** v **Q**), (**P** & **Q**), (**P** ⊃ **Q**), and (**P** ≡ **Q**) are sentences of TL.

---

[1] The formal languages commonly used in logic textbooks today are modeled after the formal logical language first developed by Bertrand Russell and Alfred North Whitehead in their monumental *Principia Mathematica*, published in three volumes between 1910 and 1913.

Any expression that contains only items drawn from the vocabulary of TL, and that can be constructed by a finite number of applications of any of rules 1 to 3, is a sentence or **well-formed formula** ("wff") of TL. Nothing else counts as a well-formed formula of TL.

How to Apply the Rules of Grammar

The rules are simple to apply, and a few examples should suffice. Following rule 1, the letter G, for example, standing all by itself, counts as a sentence of TL. Likewise, the letter B, standing all by itself, is a sentence of TL according to rule 1. The letter A, standing alone, counts as a well-formed formula of TL by rule 1, as does the letter Z, and so on, for each individual constant in the vocabulary.

Rule 2 tells us that if we start with a sentence of TL and apply a tilde to the left side of that sentence, the result is also a sentence of TL. Thus, by rule 2, if G is a sentence of TL, which it is, then ~G is also a wff of TL. Likewise, if A is a sentence of TL, which it is, then ~A is a sentence of TL as well, according to rule 2. Because E is a sentence of TL, ~E is a well-formed formula as well, by this rule, and so on.

Rule 3 says that if we take *two* sentences of TL, stand them next to each other, and place & between them while wrapping the whole in parentheses, the result is a sentence of TL. For instance, if we start with B, which is a wff of TL by rule 1, and then we place next to it E, which is also a sentence of TL by rule 1, and then we place & in between and wrap with parentheses, the result is also a sentence or wff of TL: (B & E).

Likewise, rule 3 tells us that if we start with two sentences of TL and place the wedge (v) between them and wrap it, the result is also a sentence or well-formed formula of TL. For instance, start with A, place B next to it, place the wedge in between, and wrap: (A v B). Likewise for ⊃ and ≡:

- Start with E, place G next to it, place the horseshoe in between and wrap: (E ⊃ G).
- Start with O, place W next to it, place the triple bar in between and wrap: (O ≡ W).

It follows, of course, that if we start with (A ⊃ B), which is a wff according to rule 3, and if we place next to it (O ≡ W), which is a wff according to rule 3, and if we place & between these two formulas and then wrap, the result is also a well-formed formula according to rule 3:

[(A ⊃ B) & (O ≡ W)]

Finally, it follows that if we start with this well-formed formula and slap a tilde on its left, the result is well-formed according to rule 2, which says that if we add a tilde to the left of a well-formed formula the result is a well-formed formula:

~ [(A ⊃ B) & (0 ≡ W)]

In this way, an infinite number of well-formed formulas of TL can be generated from the vocabulary of TL on the basis of just three simple rules of grammar. Sometimes a great many things can come out of something seemingly so very small!

Monadic vs. Dyadic Operators Again

Recall from Chapter 10 the distinction between monadic and dyadic sentence operators: A **monadic operator** hooks to one sentence, a **dyadic operator** joins two sentences into a compound. Notice that the tilde (~) is the only monadic operator of TL: It is properly applied only to one sentence. (Of course, the sentence to which it is applied may be simple or compound.) The other operators of TL are all dyadic, for they link two sentences together into a compound, one sentence on each side.

Computer Languages and TL: The Importance of Being Well-Formed

It is extremely important that the formulas of TL that you create are properly formed, that is, that they strictly obey the rules of grammar of TL. If your formulas are not well-formed according to the rules of grammar of TL, then you will be sure to make errors in later chapters when you apply symbolic logical techniques and rules to your malformed formulas. This is due to the fact that the rules we are about to learn are written so that they apply only to well-formed expressions. Computers face a similar problem: A computer running a particular program only accepts information that is presented in certain predefined formats. If the information going into the computer is not well-formed according to the rules of grammar of the programming language, then the computer outputs "syntax error," or something like that, and refuses to execute the instruction.

This brings up a related point. TL, and the other logical languages that you will learn later in this book, are very similar to computer programming languages. Both logical languages and computer programming languages include symbolic vocabularies and precise rules of grammar, and both types of language are carefully designed to communicate complex ideas with precision. This is why many schools believe that learning a logical language such as TL is good preparation for learning a computer programming language.

How Can I Know That It Is Well-Formed?

A formula is a well-formed formula of TL if it can be created out of the vocabulary items of TL by applying one or more of the rules of grammar of TL one or more times. Consequently, if you can create a formula out of nothing but the vocabulary items of TL, using the rules of grammar of TL, then you know the formula is well-formed. For example, consider this expression:

~(~A v ~B)

We can show that this is a wff of TL with the following line of reasoning. The sentence constant A, all by itself, is a wff of TL according to rule 1 of TL's grammar. (Rule 1 tells us that any sentence constant by itself is a wff.) Of course, B is also a wff according to rule 1. Consequently, ~A is a wff according to rule 2, and ~B is also a wff according to rule 2. (Rule 2 says that if we prefix ~ to a wff, the result is also a wff.) Therefore, if we join these two wffs together using v, and wrap with parentheses, the result, (~A v ~B), is a wff according to rule 3. (Rule 3 says that if we join two wffs together with a dyadic operator and enclose the whole in parentheses, the result is a wff.) Finally, if we apply a tilde to this, producing ~(~A v ~B), the result is a wff according to rule 2 because we have merely applied a tilde to the left side of a wff.

Exercise 12.1 The purpose of this exercise is to cause you to experiment with the vocabulary and rules of grammar of TL. Choose sentence constants and operators, apply the rules exactly, and build your own formulas! At this point, do not be concerned with the meanings of your formulas, just be concerned that your formulas are well-formed. In short, be concerned only with syntax, not with semantics.

1. Following the rules of grammar of TL "to the t," create a wff that contains at least one tilde, one horseshoe, and two sentence constants.
2. Following the rules of grammar of TL, create a wff that contains at least one ampersand, one tilde, and three sentence constants.
3. Following the rules of grammar of TL, create a wff that contains at least one tilde, one horseshoe, one triple bar, and four sentence constants.
4. Following the rules of grammar of TL, create a wff that contains at least one of each operator, and six sentence constants.

Abbreviatory Rule

Consider the wff [(A v B) & (E v J)]. As you will see shortly, if no tilde has been applied to the outermost parentheses of a completed formula, the outer parentheses are actually redundant—they add no new information to the formula. Consequently, the outermost parentheses on a completed wff may be dropped without any loss of information—if they are not encumbered by a tilde. When outer parentheses are dropped, formulas become easier to read. Consequently, let us add the following helpful "abbreviatory" rule:

- You may drop the outer parentheses on a completed wff when they are not encumbered by a tilde.

When we drop the outer parentheses on a completed wff, we are in effect abbreviating the formula with no loss of meaning. So, using this "abbreviatory" rule, we can do the following:

(A v B)	may be simplified to	A v B
[(A v B) & C]	may be simplified to	(A v B) & C
[(G & J) v (E & S)]	may be simplified to	(G & J) v (E & S)

Notice that while you may drop the outer parentheses on a formula such as [(A v B) & C], you are *not* allowed to drop the outer parentheses on the formula ~ [(A v B) & C], for in the second case, the outer parentheses are encumbered by the tilde on the left.

Syntax Error!

If a formula cannot be constructed out of the vocabulary of TL, following the rules of grammar of TL, then the formula is not a wff of TL. Here are some examples.

Expression	Reason this is not a wff
AB v G	TL's grammar does not allow two constants side by side with nothing between them.
A ~ H	TL's grammar does not allow you to place just a tilde between two constants.
H &v E	TL's grammar does not allow two operators side by side with nothing in between.
G & S~	TL's grammar does not allow a tilde to dangle on the right.
P v **Q**	TL's vocabulary does not include variables such as the bold **P** or the bold **Q**.
A v B & C	This expression needs a pair of parentheses (according to rule 3).
A (B v C)	This expression needs a dyadic operator between the A and the first parenthesis.
~ &B	The rules do not allow you to apply a tilde directly to a dyadic operator.

Exercise 12.2   Which of the following are well-formed formulas (wffs) of TL and which are not?

1. (A & ~B) v (~E & ~H)
2. ~(A v S) & [(H v B) v S]

3. ~[~(~A v ~S)~(H v G)]

4. A v (B v C) v E

5. ~(~H & R)

6. R v S v (B & G)

7. H & ~(P & S)

8. ~(~S v ~G)

9. ~(A & B) v (v S v G)

10. A & (~& R v G)

11. HELLO THERE!

12. R & ~ ⊃ H

13. (~A v B) & ~(H v S)

14. G

15. AB

16. ~[~(A v B) v ~E] v ~S

Metalanguage and Object Language

When we use one language to talk about a second language, the first language is called the **metalanguage** and the language being talked about is called the **object language**. Thus, in Spanish 101, if the teacher speaks in English *about* a Spanish sentence, in that context English is the metalanguage and Spanish is the object language. We have used the English language to define TL. Thus, TL, our artificial logical language, is in this context the object language and English, the language we use to talk about the object language, is the metalanguage.

A **constant** is a symbol standing for one specified thing. Our system uses capital letters as **sentence constants**—constants abbreviating, or standing for, specified sentences. In contrast, a variable is a symbol standing for anything from a group of things. When we stated the syntax for TL, we used boldfaced capital letters **P**, **Q**, **R**, and **S** as variables ranging over sentences of TL. These variables belong to the metalanguage, English. They do not belong to TL for the vocabulary of TL contains no variables. Because our variables belong to the metalanguage, and because they range over linguistic entities—sentences of TL—they are called **metalinguistic variables**.

What Will We Do with All of This?

Now that we have it, what do we do with it? We will use TL the way any formal language is used: to simplify the expression of complex ideas. TL will also function as a logical tool, a logical scalpel if you will, which we will use to dissect and surgically analyze real arguments. But as usual, we must proceed in small steps.

How to Use TL Sentence Constants

Recall that a sentence constant is a letter that abbreviates a specifically identified sentence. If we let A abbreviate "Alice is home," then A is serving as a sentence constant. TL uses capital letters A through Z as sentence constants. We use constants to abbreviate two kinds of sentences. Recall that a *compound sentence* is any sentence that contains one or more sentences and one or more operators, whereas a *simple sentence* is any sentence that is not compound. "Ann is home and Bob is home" is a compound sentence, whereas "Bob is home" is a simple sentence. A sentence contained within a compound sentence is called a sentence *component* (it can also be called an *embedded sentence*). Now, given the compound sentence "Ann is home and Bob is home," we can use the sentence constant "A" to abbreviate the component sentence "Ann is home," and the constant "B" to abbreviate the second component, "Bob is home." The result: In place of "Ann is home and Bob is home," we now can write "A and B." The difference is 5 characters versus 21, which saves space and is simpler to write. Notice that "A" abbreviates a simple sentence in this case, as does B.

Here are some representative abbreviations, based on examples drawn from a book written by a logician who lived at the same time Frege was inventing truth-functional logic version 2.0. We analyzed sorites from this logician's book in the last unit: *Alice in Wonderland*, by Oxford University logic professor Charles Dodgson, better known by his pseudonym, Lewis Carroll. In each case, the sentence components have been replaced by sentence constants.

Sentence	Abbreviation with Sentence Constants
1. Alice is a mile high.	A
2. The white rabbit wears white gloves and carries a large fan.	W and C
3. If everybody minded their own business, the world would go around much faster than it does.	If E, W
4. The King of Hearts is on the throne or the Queen of Hearts is on the throne.	K or Q
5. It is not the case that the hatter's hat is his own.	It is not the case that H

Keep in mind that in the abbreviation, each letter represents a complete sentence or sentence component. For example, in the abbreviation of 2, W abbreviates the full sentence "The white rabbit wears white gloves" and C abbreviates "The white rabbit carries a large fan." In 5, the H abbreviates the whole embedded sentence, "The hatter's hat is his own," and so on. In other words, the H in the last example does not merely represent the subject of the sentence, "the hatter's hat," it represents the whole sentence component, "The hatter's hat is his own."

How to Use the TL Operators

To begin with:

- The ampersand (&) shall stand for any truth-functional conjunction operator.
- The wedge (v) shall stand for any truth-functional (and inclusive) disjunction ("or") operator.
- The horseshoe (⊃) shall stand for any truth-functional conditional operator.
- The tilde (~) shall stand for any truth-functional negation operator.
- The triple bar (≡) shall stand for any truth-functional biconditional operator.

Now, once we substitute the appropriate TL operators for the English operators in the five preceding examples, the sentences are fully symbolized and the translation from English to TL is complete:

Sentence	Complete Abbreviation
1. Alice is a mile high.	A
2. The white rabbit wears white gloves and carries a large fan.	W & C
3. If everybody minded their own business, the world would go around much faster than it does.	E ⊃ W
4. The King of Hearts is on the throne or the Queen of Hearts is on the throne.	K v Q
5. It is not the case that the hatter's hat is his own.	~ H

A Note on the Triple Bar

You probably noticed that the triple bar operator (≡) is a new addition—it did not appear in the Stoic system. Standing in for the English language biconditional operator, which is usually expressed with the words "if and only if," the triple bar symbol was introduced in modern times to handle logical issues associated with modern science and mathematics. When we use "if and only if" to join two sentences together, as in "The deal closes *if and only if* both parties sign the papers," the sentence thus formed is compound and the words "if and only if" are serving as a dyadic sentence operator. Most people have never actually used this sentence connective, as it is employed mainly in law, math, logic, and other technical subjects. In these fields, "if and only if" is typically used in a way that is closely related to the ordinary conditional operator. By convention, to say something like, "The deal closes *if and only if* both parties sign the papers" is the same as saying, "If the deal closes then both parties sign the papers and if both parties sign the papers then the deal closes." In general, then, a sentence of the form "**P** if and only if **Q**" is equivalent to one of the form "If **P** then **Q** and if **Q** then **P**." This type of sentence is called a biconditional because it contains two conditionals within itself.

History Note

The wedge (∨) is due to Whitehead and Russell's *Principia Mathematica* (1913). The tilde originated as a modified letter "n" during the nineteenth century. The use of the ampersand (&) for conjunction started with the German mathematician and logician David Hilbert in 1928. The horseshoe was used in logic as early as 1816, although not for the truth-functional meaning of "if, then."

Exercise 12.3   Using obvious abbreviations, symbolize the following sentences in TL.

1. If it is not the case that all Victorian-era logicians are philosophers, then it is not the case that some Victoria-era logicians are mathematicians.

2. Either it is not the case that Professor Smith is a logician or it is not the case that Professor Smith is a metaphysician.

3. Stamp collectors are encouraged to attend the meeting and coin collectors are *not* encouraged to attend the meeting.

4. Everyone is welcome at meetings of the London Anti-Logic League and it is not the case that everyone is welcome at meetings of the London Anti-Logic League.

5. Either Professor Smith is a novelist or it is not the case that he is a logician.

6. It is not the case that Professor Dodgson is a member of the London Anti-Logic Society, and it is not the case that Professor Dodgson collects bugs.

7. The meeting of the London Pro-Logic Society will be called to order if and only if all members are present.

8. It is not the case that the meeting of the London Society of All Who Are Neither Pro-Logic Nor Anti-Logic will be held as usual tonight.

9. If it is not the case that everyone is welcome at meetings of the London Anti-Logic League then it is the case that everyone is welcome at meetings of the London Anti-Logic League.

10. Everyone is welcome to attend the meetings of the London Tolerance League and nobody is allowed to attend the meetings of the London Intolerance League.

Alternative Symbols

Logicians can be a finicky about some things. Some logicians favor using the ampersand for conjunction, as in "A & B," but many others prefer the raised dot symbol, thus writing "A · B" instead. Likewise, some logicians prefer using the horseshoe for conditional sentences, writing "A ⊃ B." Others, however, prefer to symbolize a conditional using the arrow, writing "A → B" instead. Those who use the arrow for "if, then" usually symbolize the biconditional ("if and only if") operator using the double or two-headed arrow, as in: A ↔ B. It's all good either way. You say tomato, I say tom*ah*to.

Alternative English Operators

Two of our operators have common substitutes in English worth noting and worth allowing. When we join two sentences together to form a truth-functional conjunction, we usually use the word *and*. It is just natural to say, "Ann is home *and* Bob is home." However, a number of other words are commonly used as conjunction operators in place of *and,*; for example, *but, however, nevertheless, although, having said that,* and *moreover*. Here are examples, with the alternative conjunction operators italicized:

Alice is hungry; *however*, she is not eating.
The Eaglet is a bird, *but* it is talking.
The Duchess is royalty, *although* you wouldn't know it.
The Hatter is mad; *having said that*, he is a good hatter.
It is Tuesday; *nevertheless*, school is not in session.

Sentences like these will all be treated as conjunctions. We normally use one of these alternative conjunction operators when the conjunction is surprising; for example, "She is 18 years old but she has a master's degree." So let us lay it down: The ampersand can be used as a stand-in for *any* word or phrase serving as a truth-functional conjunction operator, in other words, as an operator joining two sentences together asserting that both are true and nothing more.

Similarly, in place of the phrase "it is not the case that," we sometimes form a negation by simply placing the word *not* in the verb, writing, for example, "Joe is not home" instead of the longer but equivalent statement "It is not the case that Joe is home." Other phrases that also serve as a negation operator include "It is false that . . . ," "I deny that . . . ," and "It is not true that . . . ."

Let it be said that the tilde (~) stands for any word or phrase serving as a negation operator, including "not," "it is false that," "I deny that," and so on.

We now have two levels of abbreviation:

Level One: Replace sentences with sentence constants.
Level Two: Replace sentence operators with their corresponding symbols.

In addition, here is an example of the biconditional operator:

The Dormouse speaks *if and only if* he is allowed. $D \equiv A$

Further examples might be helpful.

Alice is *not* two miles high.	~A
The Knave of Hearts steals tarts *but* he is a nice guy.	K & H
The Mock Turtle is lonely, *however*, he is happy.	M & H
A Lobster Quadrille is delightful, *although* it is tiring.	L & T
It is false that pigs can fly.	~P
The Dormouse is sweet, *nevertheless*, he is a squeaky little rodent.	D & S

Lesson: Look for English operators and trade them in for TL operators.

Table 12.1 summarizes the five truth-functional sentence operators.

TABLE 12.1   Truth-Functional Sentence Operators

Symbol	Name	Stands for	English
&	Ampersand	Conjunction operator	and, but, nevertheless, however . . . although
~	Tilde	Negation operator	It is not the case that, not, it is false that, I deny that
v	Wedge	Disjunction operator	Or
⊃	Horseshoe	Conditional operator	If, then
≡	Triple bar	Biconditional operator	If and only if

Exercise 12.4   Using obvious abbreviations, symbolize the following sentences in TL. Represent each English operator with its corresponding TL operator.

1. If the White Rabbit is not home, then Alice will not have lunch today.
2. Alice is not asleep but the King is trying to be very quiet nevertheless.
3. The quadrille is a difficult dance although it is fun once you learn it.
4. Everyone is welcome at meetings of the London Anti-Logic Society; however, some people are more welcome than other people.
5. Either Queen Victoria is not a novelist or it is false that she is a professional logician.
6. The Mad Hatter is a complex character; nevertheless, he can be a lot of fun.
7. Although all the members of the London Pro-Logic society were present, the meeting ended an hour earlier than usual.
8. All the members of the Liverpool Anti-Logic Society attended the annual meeting of the Liverpool Pro-Logic Society; however, this year none of the usual brawls were reported to the police.
9. Either Professor Mintek is not a collector of old logical positivism memorabilia or Professor Mintek is not a metaphysician.
10. Stamp collectors are not encouraged to attend the meeting and coin collectors are encouraged to attend the meeting.
11. Everyone is welcome to attend the meetings of the London Anti-Logic League but nobody is welcome to attend the meetings of the London Anti-Logic League.
12. Professor Duncan is not a member of the International Metaphysical Cartel although he is a member of the International Epistemological Cartel.
13. The weekly meeting of Philosophers on Holiday will not be held in the usual place tonight but it will be back at the usual spot next week.
14. If everyone is not welcome at meetings of the London Anti-Intolerance League then it is not the case that the London Anti-Intolerance League is really tolerant.
15. Everyone is welcome to attend the meetings of the London Tolerance League however nobody is welcome at the meetings of the London Intolerance League.

How to Use Parentheses

Logic and mathematics face a common problem. Consider the following expression:

$$3 \times 4 + 7 = ?$$

Without assuming an order of operations, what is the answer? The problem is that without an order of operations, this formula can be interpreted in two very different ways:

Interpretation 1:   Multiply 3 times 4, and then add 7 to this.
Interpretation 2:   Add 4 and 7, and then multiply this by 3.

Thus the expression $3 \times 4 + 7$ is ambiguous; it can be interpreted in two or more different ways. Mathematicians use parentheses to *disambiguate* the sentence. To represent Interpretation 1, they write:

$$(3 \times 4) + 7 = ?$$

To represent Interpretation 2, they write:

$$3 \times (4 + 7) = ?$$

Modern truth-functional logic faces a similar problem. As you know, an operator joins one or more sentences into a compound. Thus, every operator "hooks" to or applies to one or more sentences. But sometimes it is not obvious what parts of a compound sentence an operator is "operating" on. Consider this sentence and an abbreviation in TL that uses only sentence constants and operators, with no parentheses:

Alice is home and Bob is home or Cat is home. Abbreviation: A & B v C

There are two ways to interpret this sentence:

Interpretation 1:   Alice and Bob are home (pause here) *or* Cat is home.
Interpretation 2:   Alice is definitely home, and in addition, Bob or Cat is home too.

The original sentence, like the mathematical expression $3 \times 4 + 7 = ?$, is ambiguous; it can be interpreted in two different ways. Assuming the original sentence is true, the two interpretations would mean two very different things:

Interpretation 1:   On this interpretation, it is possible that Cat is home alone. It is also possible that Alice and Bob are the only ones there and Cat is gone.
Interpretation 2:   On this interpretation, we know for sure that Alice is home, but we aren't sure about the other two. It is possible Alice is there alone, and it is also possible Alice is there with just Bob; it is also *possible* Ann is there with just Cat.

We have seen that ambiguity can sidetrack a reasoning process. Logic, like mathematics, needs a way to disambiguate the expressions on which it operates. And logic, like mathematics, uses parentheses to do so. In TL we shall use parentheses to disambiguate complex sentences such as this one. To represent Interpretation 1, we write:

Interpretation 1:   (A & B) v C

The parentheses indicate that the ampersand joins A to B, and they also say that this unit as a whole is joined via the wedge to C. To represent Interpretation 2, we shall write:

Interpretation 2:   A & (B v C)

In this case the parentheses tell us that the wedge joins B to C, and that this unit as a whole is conjoined by the ampersand to A.

Scope and Main Operator

Before we go any further, two new terms will be very helpful. The **scope of an operator** is the operator itself and what it applies to or joins together. We use parentheses to indicate the scope of an operator when needed. The parentheses in the formula for Interpretation 1 earlier tell us that the ampersand applies to, and thus joins together, only the A with the B. In contrast, the parentheses in the formula expressing Interpretation 2 tell us that the wedge (the disjunction operator) applies to, and thus joins together, only the B with the C.

In the first interpretation, the scope of the ampersand is thus "given by" the parentheses. The ampersand's scope is underlined here:

(A & B) v C

In the second interpretation, the scope of the wedge is given by the parentheses. The wedge's scope is underlined here:

A & (B v C)

In Interpretation 1, the scope of the wedge thus spans the entire formula, as indicated by the underlining here: (A & B) v C. In Interpretation 2, it is the scope of the ampersand that spans the entire formula, as indicated by the underlining here: A & (B v C).

The **main operator** is the connective with the largest scope. The scope of the main operator will always span the entire formula. This is the purpose of parentheses: We use parentheses to specify the scope of our truth-functional operators, just as mathematicians use parentheses to specify the scope of *their* operators (addition, subtraction, multiplication, etc.).

Scope of first tilde:	[~A & ~ E] & J
Scope of second tilde:	[~A & ~ E] & J
Scope of first ampersand:	[~A & ~ E] & J
Scope of second ampersand	[~A & ~ E] & J
Main operator: Second ampersand	

Exercise 12.5   Identify the main connective in each of the following.

1. ~ (A & S) & ~ (G v B)
2. (A v B) v (H & ~ S)
3. ~ [~ (A v B) v (E & **F**)]
4. ~ A v B
5. ~ (~ A v ~ B) & E
6. [(A v B) v C] v (~ S & G)
7. A v ~ (H v B)
8. D ⊃ (~H v ~ J)
9. B ≡ ~ (J ⊃ E)
10. [(B & ~K) ⊃ (G ≡ U)] ⊃ D
11. ~ ~ (A v B) ≡ (~~L & K)
12. ~{ [(~A v ~I) & ~O] ⊃ [~(G ≡ D) v I]}
13. ~~~L
14. ~~~~~O

Translating From English to TL: The "Three-Step" Program

When we translate a sentence or an argument into symbols, we produce an *abbreviation* of the sentence or argument, just as a musician abbreviates a song when he translates it into sheet music or a mathematician abbreviates a line of reasoning when she translates it into mathematical notation. A compound English sentence goes into symbols in three steps.

Step 1. Consistently replace each component sentence within the compound with a sentence constant. It is best to choose a constant that reminds us of the sentence it abbreviates (thus "A" for "Alice swims," "B" for "Bob swims," etc.).

Step 2. Replace each English truth-functional operator with its TL *avatar*.

Step 3. When necessary, use parentheses to tell your reader which sentence components are affected by which operators; in other words, to indicate the parts of a sentence an operator joins together or applies to.

In the next chapter, we will delve more deeply into the logic of compound sentences.

Exercise 12.6   Translate the following sentences from English to TL, choosing obvious abbreviations.

1. If rabbits have watches and rabbits wear coats, then Alice is in another world indeed and the universe truly does have multiple levels of reality.

2. It is not the case that the King and the Queen are both home at the same time, although one might be home.

3. If either the Duck or the Eaglet wins the race, then Alice will cheer.

4. Both the King and the Queen are not home.

5. Neither the King nor the Queen is home.

6. The King and the Queen are both not home.

7. Either the caterpillar with the hookah in his mouth is not home or the dormouse is not home; however, Alice is home.

8. If one side of the mushroom makes you grow taller and the other side makes you grow shorter, then sitting on the mushroom is not recommended.

9. The race will be held if and only if either the King or the Queen oppose it.

10. The mouse is not home and the duck is not home; however, either Alice or the Mad Hatter is home.

11. The mouse is not home or the duck is not home; nevertheless, the party will be held as scheduled.

12. If the mouse is not home and the duck is not home, then Alice will be sad.

13. It is not the case that if Alice eats the mushroom then she will experience an alternative reality.

14. If Alice eats the mushroom then it is not the case that she will either experience an alternative reality or return home.

15. If both the King and the Queen are not home, then either the race will not be held or the quadrille dance will not be held.

16. The following is simply not the case: If Alice sings, then the Mad Hatter will go home.

Glossary

Artificial or formal language A language created by a group of people to communicate a specialized and restricted body of ideas.

Biconditional operator The dyadic truth-functional operator typically expressed in English with the words "if and only if."

Constant A symbol standing for a specifically identified item.

Dyadic operator An operator that joins together two sentences.

Logicism The claim that all of mathematics can be logically deduced from statements of pure logic.

Main operator or connective The operator or connective of greatest scope.

Metalanguage A language being used to talk about another language.

Metalinguistic variable A variable ranging over the sentences of a language.

Monadic operator An operator that applies to one sentence.

Natural language A language usually learned at birth and serving as a general tool of communication.

Object language A language being talked about from the standpoint of a corresponding metalanguage.

Scope of an operator The operator plus that which it operates on or joins together.

Semantics The theory of meaning for a language. The semantics for a language assigns meanings to the well-formed expressions of the language.

Sentence constant A symbol standing for a specified sentence.

Syntax The vocabulary and rules of grammar of a language.

TL The name of the formal language used in this text to represent truth-functional logical properties and logical relationships.

Well-formed formula (wff) An expression composed only of elements drawn from the vocabulary of TL and formed according to the rules of grammar of TL.

From English to TL « « «

Techniques for Great Translations

Translating sentences and arguments from English into TL requires an understanding of English grammar, as well as an ability to spot the logically relevant divisions inside compound sentences. This chapter presents techniques that could help you with this important task: translating reasoning from English to TL. After reasoning has been translated into our formal language, very precise methods of evaluation can be applied to the formulas, and exact solutions to various logical problems can easily be found—as you will see in the chapters to come.

Translating "Not Both _____ and _____"

Let us begin with the following sentence:

It is not the case that Ann is home and Bob is home.

As this sentence is written, it is ambiguous. Because it can be interpreted in more than one way, it cannot be accurately translated into TL. The sentence is ambiguous because it is not clear whether the negation operator applies just to "Ann is home," or to the whole conjunction, "Ann is home and Bob is home." Here are two interpretations of this ambiguous sentence, each written differently to clarify the claim being made:

Interpretation 1: It is not the case that Ann is home, but Bob *is* home.

Notice the comma added. The comma divides the sentence in half. By dividing the sentence after "Ann is home," the comma tells us that the "It is not the case that" operator applies only to the part about Ann being home. On this interpretation, the sentence says Ann is not home, but Bob is home. This implies that if you go to their house, you will see Bob, but you won't see Ann. Ann is gone.

Interpretation 2: It is not the case that both of them are home together.

Notice the placement of the word *both*, called a *coordinating phrase*. Placed after the negation operator, its purpose is to group the following two component sentences together as a unit. Now the "It is not the case that" operator applies *not* to the part about Ann being home, but to the claim that both of them are home together. What is being *denied* is the claim that both of them are home at the same time, together. On this interpretation, the sentence implies that if you go to their house, you will *not* see the both of them there together. You might see Ann there alone; you might see Bob there alone; you might see nobody home; but you won't see *the both of them* together. Bottom line: The sentence tells us that Ann and Bob are not both home together. Other than that, it does not tell us who *is* home.

Once the sentence has been disambiguated, it is ripe for translation. We now have two sentences where we formerly had one. These go directly into TL:

Interpretation 1

It is not the case that Ann is home, but Bob is home.   ~A & B.

Comment.   The tilde always applies to that which is to its immediate right. In this case, the tilde applies only to the A (symbolizing "Ann is home"). Corresponding to this, the negation operator in the English sentence applies only to the part about Ann being home.

Interpretation 2

It is not the case that both Ann and Bob are home.   ~(A & B)

Comment.   Just as the word *both* directs the force of the negation operator onto the claim that both are home together (in the English sentence), the parentheses direct the force of the tilde onto the A and B grouped together as a unit, making it clear that what is being denied is not that Ann is home, but rather that the both of them are home *together*. The tilde no longer applies to the A alone, it applies to the parentheses that join the A and B together. These two very different meanings have two very different symbolizations.

Unlike our previous example, the following sentence is not ambiguous at all; it is ripe for translation:

Both Ann and Bob are not home.

Notice that the word *both* appears first and that it groups Ann and Bob together as a unit, and the negation operator comes later in the sentence, *after* Ann and Bob have been grouped together. In addition, in this sentence, Ann and Bob share the same verb phrase ("are not home"). This is very important. Because they share the verb phrase, the *not* in the verb applies to each of them equally. Thus, this sentence is logically equivalent to:

Ann is not home and Bob is not home.

What is the sentence telling us? That both Ann and Bob are gone. Both are not home. In other words, nobody is home (assuming they are the only ones who might be there). If we enter their house, we will not see Ann, and we will not see Bob. Nobody is home in this case! Consequently, when we symbolize the sentence, "Both Ann and Bob are not home," the A and the B each get their own tildes, after which the two are conjoined:

~A & ~B.

Notice how this meaning differs from the meaning of "It is not the case that both Ann and Bob are home." Let us now compare the two:

Ann and Bob are *not both* home: ~(A & B)

If you go to their house, you *might* find Ann home alone (with Bob gone), you might find Bob home alone (with Ann gone); maybe nobody will be home. What you will *not* find is both of them home together. Notice that in this case, the *not* comes before the *both*. Next:

Both Ann and Bob are *not* home: ~A & ~B

If you go to their house, you will find that *both* are gone. Nobody will be home. Notice that in this case, *both* comes before *not*. A slight change in wording can make a world of difference in meaning!

Consider this sentence:

It is not the case that either Ann is home or Bob is home.

This sentence has two major parts: (a) a negation operator, and (b) a disjunction, "Ann is home or Bob is home." Notice the placement of the word *either* in this sentence. This is a coordinating phrase helping group the two sentences following it into a disjunction. The word *either* helps us see that the negation operator is applied to the disjunction as a whole, and not just to the A alone. Consequently, we first symbolize the disjunction inside the sentence, "Ann is home or Bob is home," using the formula A v B. To keep this unit intact, we wrap it in parentheses, producing (A v B). After this, we apply a tilde to the disjunction as a whole, just as the English negation operator is applied to the disjunction as a whole. To do this, we place the tilde on the left, directing its full force onto the parentheses:

~(A v B).

Remember that tilde applies to whatever sits to its immediate right. The parentheses in this case indicate that the tilde applies to the disjunction as a whole, and not just to the A.

Recall that when we use the word *or* we mean the *inclusive* disjunction ("one or the other or both") unless otherwise specified. Now that we have introduced the word *either*, as a disjunction indicator, a new issue arises. Many people use the word *either* only when indicating an *exclusive* disjunction ("one or the other but not both"). However, the rule is not hard and fast. In logic we may, if we choose to, use *either* to indicate simply any disjunction—inclusive or exclusive—and that is what we shall do.

The word *neither*, combined with *nor*, is a contraction of "It is not the case that either." Thus, the following two symbolized sentences assert the same thing and are thus logically equivalent:

It is not the case that either Ann or Bob is home.   ~(A v B)
Neither Ann nor Bob is home.   ~(A v B)

Either _____ Is Not or _____ Is Not

Suppose someone says, "Ann or Bob is not home." Because Ann and Bob share the same verb phrase ("is not home") in this sentence, the verb is applied to each equally, and thus each equally owns the "not." In other words, the negation splits in two and applies to each side of the disjunction. This sentence is therefore an abbreviated way of saying with more words, "Ann is not home or Bob is not home." Let us now analyze the latter sentence. The sentence is a disjunction, obviously. In addition, each disjunct contains a negation operator. Therefore, when we symbolize it, we disjoin the two sentences, using the wedge, and then we apply a tilde to each one separately, indicating that each side gets the negation operator: ~A v ~ B.

Swapping *and* for *or* and Vice Versa

Recall that two sentences are logically equivalent if and only if they cannot possibly ever differ in truth-value. This means that in any situation, if one is true, then the other is true, and if one is false then the other is false. (The two sentences therefore imply each other.) Most languages possess at least two ways to convey an idea. Let us think about the sentences we have just symbolized, looking for equivalencies. To begin with, notice that instead of saying "Ann and Bob are not both home," in symbols ~(A & B), someone could just as well say instead, "Ann is not home or Bob is not home." In symbols, this is ~A v ~B. Now, aren't these two sentences just two ways of saying the same thing? After all, if they are *not both* home, then at least one of them is gone, and so either Ann is gone or Bob is gone, or both are gone. The two sentences are thus logically equivalent.

Sentences 1 and 2 Are Equivalent

1. Ann and Bob are *not both* home.   ~(A & B)
2. Ann is not home or Bob is not home.   ~A v ~B.

Suppose someone says, "Both Ann and Bob are not home." In symbols, this is ~A & ~B. However, doesn't the following sentence say the same thing: "It's not the case that either Ann or Bob is home," in other words, "Neither Ann nor Bob is home." In symbols this is ~(A v B). Now, if both are not home, then neither of them is home, and vice versa. The two sentences are therefore logically equivalent ways of saying one and the same thing.

Sentences 1, 2, and 3 Are Equivalent

1. Both Ann and Bob are not home.   ~A & ~B.
2. It's not the case that either Ann or Bob is home.   ~(A v B).
3. Neither Ann nor Bob is home.   ~(A v B).

Here is a point needing emphasis. Notice, in the preceding examples, that when *both* comes before *not*, and thus operates on *not*, as in "*Both* Ann and Bob are *not* home," the word *both* functions to distribute *not* onto each of the subjects equally. If both are not home, then Ann is not home *and* Bob is not home. Each letter gets its own *not*. However, when *not* comes before *both*, and thus when *not* operates on *both*, as in "Ann and Bob are *not both* home," the change is dramatic. In this case, *not* does not distribute onto each subject. If Ann and Bob are not both home, it does *not* follow that Ann is not home and Bob is not home. It does not follow that each letter gets its own tilde.

English	Symbols
It is not the case that both Ann and Bob will go.	~ (A & B)
Ann and Bob will not both go.	~ (A & B)
Both Ann and Bob will not go.	~ A & ~B
Ann and Bob both will not go.	~ A & ~ B
It is not the case that either Ann or Bob will go.	~ (A v B)
Neither Ann nor Bob will go.	~ (A v B)
Either Ann or Bob will not go.	~ A v ~ B

Exercise 13.1   Using obvious abbreviations, translate the following sentences from English to TL. In your translation, assign each English operator its TL equivalent.

1. Neither Professor Dodgson nor Professor Frege is in the office today.

2. Either Professor Erickson is not a metaphysician or Professor Payne is not a student of Kripke's.

3. Neither Dana nor Annika is interested in symbolic logic.

4. Professor Dodgson and Professor Storey both will not be teaching logic today.

5. It is not the case that Professor Duncan will not be delivering a major lecture today on the metaphysical and theological implications of symbolic logic and it is not the case that the lecture will not be open to the public.

6. It is not the case that all logicians are mathematicians and it is not the case that all logicians are communists.

7. Professor DiQuaatro is not a metaphysician but he respects the philosophical work of some philosophers of religion.

8. It is not the case that either Professor Duncan or Professor Payne will be lecturing today on the nature of scientific inference.

9. Either Professor Storey will be lecturing today on the philosophy of naturism or he will not be lecturing today on the philosophy of naturism.

10. It is not the case that either Professor DiQuattro will be presenting a philosophical argument against the existence of God or Professor Cohen will be presenting an argument for the existence of God.

11. Either the members of the philosophy club will not hold their debate today or the members of the International Metaphysical Cartel will not hold their meeting today.

12. Both Professor Storey and Professor Duncan are not teaching this hour.

The "Laws" of Grouping in English

As you have seen, the rules of English grammar help us decide where to put our parentheses when we symbolize complex sentences. We have already been taking our cues from some of these grammatical rules when deciding where a sentence "breaks." It is now time to highlight the most important of these "grouping" rules. Three are especially useful.

1. Use commas to divide sentences into parts and thus to limit the reach of an operator, as in the following example:

   Ann went home and Bob went home, but Ed stayed. In symbols: (A & B) & E

   In this case, the comma grouped the A and B parts together as one unit, and the parentheses recorded this.

2. Group things together by having two subjects share the same verb, as in the following example:

   Ed swam and Ann and Bob stayed home. In symbols: E & (A & B)

   The fact that Ann and Bob (figuratively speaking) "shared" the verb ("stayed home") put the A and B together. The parentheses recorded the fact.

3. Use coordinating phrases such as *both* and *either* to group things together, as in the following examples:

   Both Ann and Bob swam and Ed did not swim. In symbols: (A & B) & ~E
   Either Ann swam or if Ed swam then Bob swam. In symbols: A v (E ⊃ B)
   Both Ann and Dave jogged although it was raining. In symbols: (A & D) & R

Examine the following samples closely for more guidance on this matter.

English	Symbolic Translation
Both Ann and Bob are home, but Ed is not home.	(A & B) & ~E
Either Ann or Ed is home; however Julie is not home.	(A v E) & ~J
It is not the case that if Ed swims then Jan swims.	~(E ⊃ J)
If it is not the case that Ed swims, then Jan will swim.	~E ⊃ J
If Ed does not swim, then Jan does not swim.	~E ⊃ ~J

Notice the way the commas in each of these sentences guided the placement of the parentheses and operators.

Exercise 13.2   Imagine a mythical, ethereal reunion of bygone 1960s rock groups, and symbolize the following sentences in TL. Use obvious abbreviations and make sure that each English operator is assigned its TL equivalent. The bands are about to take the stage.

1. The Animals will do three songs and the Beatles will do six songs, or the Doors will do four songs.

2. The Animals will do three songs, and the Beatles will do six songs or the Doors will do four songs.

3. Either the Yardbirds will perform two songs and the Beach Boys will do five songs, or Santana will perform three numbers.

4. The Jefferson Airplane will do three songs, or the Grateful Dead and the Byrds will play.

5. Donovan will do a song and either Cream will perform or Otis Redding will perform.

6. Jimi Hendrix will perform, and the Beach Boys and the Grateful Dead will perform.

7. Ike and Tina Turner won't both sing.

8. Grace Slick and Janis Joplin both will not do encores.

9. Grace Slick and Janis Joplin will not both do encores.

10. The Lovin' Spoonful will not perform an extra song but the Moody Blues will perform an extra song.

11. Both the Rolling Stones and Procol Harem will perform but Creedence Clearwater Revival will not play.

12. Either the Monkees or the Rolling Stones will not perform.

13. Either Canned Heat performs or Moby Grape performs, or The Young Rascals and Buffalo Springfield perform.

14. Neither the Wailers nor the Sonics will perform, but the Bards and the Natural Gas Company will perform.

15. Either the Association or The Dave Clark Five have not performed, or Tiny Tim and Janis Ian both have not been up.

Exciting philosophy lectures will be delivered during the concert:

16. Professor DiQuattro will be lecturing as usual on the philosophy of Karl Marx and he will answer any and all questions as well; however, it is not the case that if Professor Rind attends then DiQuattro's lecture will be expanded to include a refutation of Austrian capital theory and an attack on Nozick's theory of human rights.

17. If Professor Dodgson is giving a lecture on logic in east London tonight then neither Pam nor Susan will be home.

18. Either Professor Erickson is not a metaphysician or Professor Payne is not a student of Kripke's; however, neither professor is a lover of sloppy reasoning.

19. Although neither Dana nor Annika is interested in symbolic logic; both are interested in cell biology.

20. Neither Professor Dodgson nor Professor Storey will be teaching logic today; however, Professor Steven Duncan will be delivering a major lecture on the metaphysical and theological implications of symbolic logic.

21. It is not the case that all logicians are mathematicians and it is not the case that all logicians are communists; nevertheless, if you attend the University of London you will encounter at least one communist mathematician who is a logician.

22. Professor DiQuatro is not a metaphysician but he respects the philosophical work of some philosophers of religion and believes that their arguments are worthy of consideration.

23. Neither Professor Duncan nor Professor Payne will be lecturing today on the nature of scientific inference; however, Professor Storey will be lecturing on the philosophy of naturism, and he always generates an interesting discussion.

24. Professor DiQuattro will be presenting a philosophical argument against the existence of God; both Professor Duncan and Professor Goodal will be questioning his premises.

Translating Conditionals

It is time to begin tackling more complex sentences. Conditional sentences present some of the most difficult cases for translation; consequently, a little time invested in this area could pay big dividends later on. Consider the following two conditionals: "If it's sunny, then we will jog" and "We will jog if it's sunny." Both say exactly the same thing, don't they? In English, we usually place the antecedent ("it's sunny") first, as in the first of the two. However, we sometimes place the antecedent second, as in the second of the two. In each case, the antecedent is always introduced with the word *if*. Because the two sentences, "If it's sunny, then we will jog" and "We will jog if it's sunny," amount to the same claim, both should be symbolized the same way: with S ⊃ J.

When translating conditionals, keep two points in mind:

- In English, the antecedent is typically introduced by the word *if*.
- In our logical symbolism, the abbreviated antecedent is always placed to the *left* of the horseshoe.

Suppose we wish to represent the following sentence in our logical symbolism:

If Elaine orders soup and Jerry orders soup, then either George orders soup or Newman orders soup.

The first thing to notice is that everything in this sentence from *if* to *then* forms a logical unit: It is the antecedent of a conditional. If we let E stand for "Elaine orders soup" and J stands for "Jerry orders soup," this part is symbolized with (E & J). Second, everything from *then* to the end forms another unit: This is the consequent of the conditional. Using obvious abbreviations, this part is symbolized with (G v N). The word *then* appears between these two units, of course, and gets traded in for a horseshoe. So, we place a "horse" between (E & J) and (G v N) to get:

(E & J) ⊃ (G v N)

This sentence was symbolized in the following three steps:

1. If E and J then either G or N.
2. If (E & J) then (G v N).
3. (E & J) ⊃ (G v N).

For another example, suppose an insurance company has the following policy: "If you accumulate an accident and a ticket on your record, your insurance will be cancelled." In other words:

If you have an accident and you have a ticket, then your policy will be cancelled.

Let's symbolize this sentence. Notice that the comma breaks the sentence into two parts. Using obvious abbreviations, and placing the parentheses based on the placement of the comma, the symbolization is

(A & T) ⊃ C

Let us now think about what this implies. This logically implies that *if* you have an accident, you had better be on guard, for then it will follow that *if* you get a ticket, then your insurance will be cancelled. In other words:

If you have an accident, then if you get a ticket then your policy will be cancelled.

Notice that in this sentence, the comma divides the sentence after the word *accident*. Also, the second part of the sentence, the part after *accident*, is itself compound, and therefore must be enclosed in parentheses. Furthermore, each *then* will need a horseshoe. The symbolization of this sentence is thus:

A ⊃ (T ⊃ C)

Lesson: A sentence symbolized (A & T) ⊃ C logically implies one symbolized A ⊃ (T ⊃ C).

Suppose a country has the following law:

A person has the right to vote if and only if the person is an adult and the person is also a citizen.

It follows that:

Bart has the right to vote if and only if Bart is an adult and Bart is also a citizen.

Notice that the sentence divides in half at the "if and only if" operator. The half of the sentence to the right of the "if and only if" is clearly a conjunction of "Bart is an adult" and "Bart is a citizen." To symbolize this, we must give the "if and only if" a triple bar, and we enclose the conjunction on the right side in parentheses. In symbols, using obvious abbreviations, we get B ≡ (A & C).

Representing Necessary and Sufficient Conditions

When a jet crashes, investigators from the Federal Aviation Administration are called in to track down the likely cause. When these investigators track down causes, the procedures they use are often based on a set of principles first formulated by the British philosopher John Stuart Mill (1806–1873) in his *System of Logic* published in 1843. We do not examine these principles, now known as Mill's methods, until Unit Five. However, here we take a brief look into the way cause-and-effect statements can be symbolized within truth-functional logic.

When scientists search for causes, they seek to discover the conditions under which a specific effect will occur and the conditions under which it will not. A key question of causal reasoning is therefore this: Under which conditions will the effect occur and under which conditions will the effect be absent? Philosophers have found it illuminating to analyze causes in terms of underlying or antecedent conditions, and specifically in terms of two types of antecedent or underlying conditions: necessary conditions and sufficient conditions.

- A condition N is called a **necessary condition** for an event E just in case event E is not possible without N. In other words, in the absence of condition N, E cannot occur. Another way to put this is: Condition N must be present if E is to occur. For example, the presence of oxygen is a necessary condition for the operation of a typical gasoline engine, reaching the age of 18 is currently a necessary condition for voting, and a bachelor's degree is usually a necessary condition for entering graduate school.
- A condition S is called a **sufficient condition** for an event E just in case S is all that is required for E to occur. In other words, once S occurs, E is certain to occur. For example, jumping into Seattle's most famous lake, Green Lake, is sufficient for getting wet, for jumping into a lake is all that is required for getting wet. Once you jump in Green Lake, it is certain you will be wet. A sufficient condition for an effect E has the following feature: When the sufficient condition is present, E *must* occur.

Notice that although gasoline is *necessary* for a gasoline engine to run, it is not *sufficient*, for some engines will not run even though they have a full tank of gasoline. (The engine might be broken, the spark plug might not be sparking, oxygen might not be present, etc.) Notice also that although jumping in Green Lake is *sufficient* for getting wet, it is not *necessary*, for there are other ways to get wet besides jumping in a lake. (One could take a shower, jump in the ocean, etc.)

> N is a necessary condition for effect E if and only if the following is true:
> E will not be present unless N is present; or
> In the absence of N, E will not be present; or
> Without N, E won't occur.
>
> S is a sufficient condition for effect E if and only if the following is true:
> If S is present, E will occur.
> If S is present, E is certain to occur.
> In presence of S, E is certain to occur.

In logic, statements about necessary and sufficient conditions are naturally treated as conditional sentences. (After all, they are about *conditions*.) Consequently, statements of necessary and sufficient conditions are typically symbolized with horseshoes. Suppose we want to symbolize this sentence:

Gasoline is necessary for the engine's operation.

We need to paraphrase this sentence slightly. If we let G abbreviate "The engine's fuel tank contains gasoline" and if O abbreviates "The engine will operate," we could try to abbreviate this sentence by placing the statement about the necessary condition in the antecedent of a conditional:

G ⊃ R

This says, "If the engine's fuel tank has gasoline, then the engine will operate." It is obvious that this way of representing a necessary condition is incorrect. The mere presence of gasoline alone does not guarantee that a gas engine will run. However, if we place the symbol for the necessary condition in the consequent, the symbolism seems correct:

R ⊃ G

This indicates that if the engine is running, then it has gasoline in it. This seems right, for if a gasoline engine is running, it must have gasoline in it. However, it is not the case that if a gasoline engine has gas in it, then it *must* run.

Next, suppose we want to symbolize

Jumping in Green Lake is sufficient for getting wet.

First, to allow this to fit into our symbolism, we have to slightly rewrite the sentence. Let W abbreviate "You are wet" and let J abbreviate "You jumped into Green Lake." We could try placing the sufficient condition in the consequent, so to speak, as follows:

W ⊃ J

The formula says: If you are wet, then you jumped into Green Lake. This is obviously incorrect. The mere fact that someone is wet doesn't imply that she or he jumped into Seattle's Green Lake. Clearly, the way to symbolize a claim about a sufficient condition is to represent the sufficient condition in the antecedent:

J ⊃ W

This indicates that if you jumped into Green Lake you are wet. This seems true.

"Here Comes the Sun"

A useful mnemonic device for remembering this is the word SUN. Start with the capitalized word SUN. Now, picture the U pointing to the right so that it looks like this: S ⊃ N. Next, let S represent "sufficient condition" and let N represent "necessary condition." The word SUN now reminds you that a sufficient condition is represented in the antecedent of a conditional, and a necessary condition is represented in the consequent!

A few additional examples follow:

Sam's win is a necessary condition for Ed's win.

S: Sam wins.
E: Ed wins.
In symbols: E ⊃ S

Joe's entry is a sufficient condition for Joe's winning the prize.

J: Joe enters the contest.
W: Joe wins the prize.
In symbols: J ⊃ W

The presence of water is a necessary condition for the chemical reaction to occur.

W: Water is present.
C: The chemical reaction occurs.
In symbols: C ⊃ W

The presence of chemicals x and y is a sufficient condition for the release of heat.

C: Chemicals x and y are present.
H: Heat is released.
In symbols: C ⊃ H

Translating Other Conditional Sentences

Translating "Only If"

Necessary conditions are sometimes introduced using the connective "only if." For example, suppose a group of coal miners is trapped deep inside a mine shaft and the rescue crew is about to search for survivors. The following statement would be true:

Human life is present *only if* oxygen is present.

On the standard interpretation of such a sentence, the words *only if* introduce a necessary condition, and the necessary condition is necessary for that which is referred to in the statement to the left of the *only if*. Thus, the sentence, "Human life is present only if oxygen is present" means "Oxygen is a necessary condition for human life."

Generalizing this point, a statement of the form "**P** only if **Q**" typically says that **Q** is a necessary condition for **P**. Thus, the earlier statement of a necessary condition, "Gasoline is necessary for the engine to run," could also be rendered as "The engine will run *only if* it has gasoline." Since the necessary condition is represented in the consequent, the preceding sentence should be symbolized E ⊃ G, where E abbreviates "The engine runs" and G abbreviates "The engine has gasoline."

To return to our earlier sentence, "Human life is present only if oxygen is present," that sentence is saying that oxygen is necessary for human life. It therefore goes into symbols as

H ⊃ O

where H abbreviates "Human life is present" and O abbreviates "Oxygen is present."

Note that it would certainly be incorrect to symbolize this sentence the other way around, that is, as O ⊃ H. This symbolization indicates: "If oxygen is present, then human life is present." But the mere presence of oxygen does not guarantee the presence of human life. So, in general, a statement fitting the general form "**P** only if **Q**" must be symbolized as **P** ⊃ **Q**. Earlier, it was noted that the lone word *if* typically introduces the antecedent, which is always symbolized to the left of the horseshoe. A statement of the form "**P** *only if* **Q**" is an exception to this general rule.

Translating "Unless"

Suppose that medics have arrived at the scene of a car accident and one of the medics says, "The victim will die unless he gets a blood transfusion." The simplest way to translate this sentence into TL is to translate *unless* as an inclusive *or*: "The victim will die *or* he gets a blood transfusion." In TL, using obvious abbreviations, this is obviously D v B. Many logicians translate *unless* as an inclusive *or*.

However, we might also interpret this sentence in a more complicated way, although the result is logically equivalent in the end. The medic could also be interpreted as saying, "The victim will die *if he does not* get a blood transfusion." In other words, "If the victim does not get a blood transfusion, then the victim will die."

With D abbreviating "The victim will die," and with B abbreviating "The victim gets a blood transfusion," this sentence is symbolized ~ B ⊃ D. In general, understood in this way, the word *unless* serves to introduce a necessary condition: "P unless Q" says that Q is a necessary condition for ~P. Notice that when the medic says, "The victim will die unless he gets a blood transfusion," he does *not* mean:

If the victim gets a transfusion, then he will surely live.

Perhaps (unfortunately) the victim will get a transfusion but then will die from other complications. The medic is merely indicating that the blood transfusion is *necessary* but *not sufficient* for the victim's survival. If this is right, then a sentence such as "Bob will quit unless Ann gets a raise" could go into symbols as $\sim$A $\supset$ B. However, as we will see in Chapter 20, $\sim$A $\supset$ B is logically equivalent to A v B. Thus, we can translate "A unless B" either way: simply as A v B, as we did in the beginning, or in the more complicated way, as $\sim$A $\supset$ B. Both ways are right!

"Provided That"

The phrase "provided that" generally functions inside a conditional sentence the same way the word *if* functions. Normally, the word *if*, when used all by itself (and thus not attached to *only*), serves to introduce the antecedent. Thus, a sentence of the form "Provided that P . . . Q," means the same as "If P . . . Q." In symbols, P $\supset$ Q. Likewise, a sentence of the form "P provided that Q" would mean the same as a corresponding sentence of the form "P if Q," which means the same as one of the form "If Q then P," which in turn goes into symbols: Q $\supset$ P.

Thus, "Joe swims provided that Ann swims" translates as if it had been written "Joe swims *if* Ann swims," thus as A $\supset$ J (given that J stands for "Joe swims" and A stands for "Ann swims"). On the other hand, "Provided that Ann swims, Joe swims" translates as if it had been written "If Ann swims, then Joe swims," which in symbols is, of course, A $\supset$ J.

For additional practice, consider the following sentences:

Provided that the rental car is returned, the VISA surcharge will be refunded.

Letting R abbreviate "The rental car is returned," and letting V abbreviate "The VISA surcharge will be refunded," this sentence is abbreviated R $\supset$ V.

Next:

Provided that Joe has a ticket, he may attend the concert.

In symbols, using obvious abbreviations, this is J $\supset$ A.

New Light on "If and Only If"

In light of our discussion of necessary and sufficient conditions, we can now make new sense of a sentence of the form "**P** if and only if **Q**," for example, "Ann swims if and only if Sue swims." Recall that a sentence of the form "**P** if and only if **Q**" (in symbols: **P** $\equiv$ **Q**) is equivalent to one of the form "If **P** then **Q** and if **Q** then **P**" (in symbols: (**P** $\supset$ **Q**) & (**Q** $\supset$ **P**)). Recall also that the sufficient condition is represented in the antecedent and the necessary condition is represented in the consequent of a conditional. Understood in this way, a sentence of the form "**P** if and only if **Q**" asserts that **Q** is both a necessary and sufficient condition for **P** *and* that **P** is both a necessary and sufficient condition for **Q**. To return to our preceding example, "Ann swims if and only if Sue swims," says that Ann's swimming is both a necessary and sufficient condition for Sue's swimming and vice versa, that Sue's swimming is both a necessary and sufficient condition for Ann's swimming, or in symbols, A ≡ S.

Where Do We Go From Here?

The next step, of course, is putting our formal language to use. After sentences and arguments have been translated from a natural language such as English into TL, extremely precise methods can be applied to test arguments for validity and sentences for various logical properties, and these methods are as precise as any in mathematics. In addition, computer circuits can be designed to function in certain predefined ways, reasoning can be broken down into its basic elements, and many fascinating logical problems, in many areas of thought, can be solved with precision. None of this would be possible if formal logical languages, such as TL, had never been developed.

| Step 1 | Step 2 | Step 3 |

Translate from English ⟶ Apply exact methods ⟶ Precise Answers
into TL

    At this point, with our formal language in hand, there are actually three directions we can go. Some logicians proceed from here, with TL in place, to the truth-table analysis of sentences and arguments. Using truth tables, which are explained in the next chapter, we can show arguments valid and invalid and we can test sentences for various logical properties—with mathematical precision. However, other logicians go from where we are now, with TL in hand, straight to modern natural deduction proofs of validity, skipping truth-table analysis entirely. Still other logicians cover both truth-table analysis and proofs.

    Truth-table analysis, discovered in the 1920s, is a "bottom-up" method for evaluating sentences and arguments. Because it is more mechanical and algorithmic, the truth-table approach is less intuitive, less like everyday reasoning. Modern natural deduction is a "top-down" method of evaluation. Deduction is less machine-like, more creative, and very much like the reasoning we actually employ in everyday life. You will understand these things and more by the end of this unit. You might see why some logicians prefer truth tables, whereas others prefer natural deduction proofs, and perhaps why some logicians teach both methods!

From the Language TL

To Tables   To Proofs
(Chapters 14–17)   (Chapters 18–22)

Or to both!

Exercise 13.3   This time the concert is artists from 1930s Harlem, from the Big Band era, and from the 1950s.

1. If Fats Domino performs one song, then either Jerry Lee Lewis or the Big Bopper will perform one song.
2. If both Buddy Holly and Little Richard perform, then Chuck Berry will perform.
3. Either Cab Calloway will perform or if Duke Ellington performs, then Ella Fitzgerald will perform.
4. If Ethel Waters performs and either Louis Armstrong or Lena Horne performs, then Mel Torme will sing.
5. If it is not the case that Bill "Bojangles" Robinson will be there, then either Cab Calloway or Duke Ellington will not be there.
6. Either Benny Goodman's band or Glenn Miller's orchestra will perform if Lena Horne will not be available.
7. It is not the case that if Nat King Cole performs, then ticket prices will be raised.
8. If Johnny Mathis sings, then it's not the case that Frank Sinatra or Johnny Ray will miss the show.
9. Elvis Presley and Patsy Cline will sing if and only if admission is free and the performance is not televised.
10. If Elvis Presley and Ricky Nelson perform, then neither the Brothers Four nor the Drifters will perform.
11. Provided that Joe buys a ticket, Joe will be admitted to the concert.
12. The concert is in San Francisco only if the concert is in California.
13. Bill Haley and the Comets will perform provided that Richie Valens performs.

14. If either Buddy Holly or the Kingston Trio perform, then it will not be the case that many people will leave the concert early and the promoters will lose money.
15. This is not the case: If Frankie Avalon performs then people will walk out.

At the concession stand . . .

16. This hot dog will taste good only if ketchup and mustard are both present.
17. Ann will order a Dick's Deluxe burger if and only if Bob and Sue both order Deluxes.
18. Relish is necessary for this to be a good hamburger.
19. It is not the case that mayonnaise is necessary for this to be a good hamburger.
20. To get a ticket in this town all you need to do is go 80 mph in front of the schoolhouse when school is in session.

Exercise 13.4.   Advanced Translations

Symbolize the following sections of State of Washington, Initiative Measure 1163:

1. If any provision of this act or its application to any person or circumstance is held invalid, the remainder of this act or the application of the provision to other persons or circumstances is not affected.
2. If an agreement of distributorship is terminated, canceled, or not renewed for any reason other than for cause, failure to live up to the terms and conditions of the agreement, or a reason set forth in RCW 19.126.030(5), the wholesale distributor is entitled to compensation from the successor distributor for the laid-in cost of inventory and for the fair market value of the terminated distribution rights.

Appendix 13.1   Medieval Logic

As we have seen, the Stoic school of logic went into decline after the third century BC. Little of note happened in logical theory until the Middle Ages, when a great revival of learning in all fields of thought occurred. Benson Mates, a historian of logic, has written:

> [T]he history of logic does not consist of a gradual development leading from Aristotle down to modern times. Instead, there are three high points, each of relatively short duration, which are separated by long periods of decline. The

first of these peaks occurred in the third and fourth centuries B.C., the second from the twelfth to the fourteenth centuries, and the third began in the late nineteenth century, and, according to the optimists, is at present in full swing.[1]

We have examined the first "peak" in detail—the emergence of the Aristotelian and Stoic schools of logic in Athens during the fourth and third centuries BC. We are about to move to the third peak, the beginning of modern logic in the nineteenth century, certainly the highest vantage point yet attained on the mountain of logical theory. However, the medieval period should not be passed over in complete silence. During this period a number of important logicians made fascinating discoveries and produced extremely interesting work. The interested student is advised to consult a history of logic for the details.[2] In the short space available here, let us look briefly at some of the theorems you might have studied, if you had been a student in a medieval logic class. Professor Mates lists a number of interesting theorems proved by medieval logicians, including the following. P, Q, and R are variables ranging over declarative sentences:

1. $(P \supset Q) \supset (\sim(P \supset R) \supset \sim (Q \supset R))$
2. $(Q \supset R) \supset (\sim(P \supset R) \supset \sim (P \supset Q))$
3. $(P \,\&\sim Q) \supset \sim(P \supset Q)$
4. $\sim P \supset \sim(P \,\& \,Q)$
5. $\{P \,\& \,[(P \supset Q) \,\& \,(Q \supset R)] \,\} \supset R$
6. $(P \supset Q) \supset [(Q \supset \sim R) \supset (P \supset \sim R)]$
7. $(P \supset Q) \supset [(P \,\& R) \supset (Q \,\& \,R)]$
8. $[(P \,\& \,Q) \supset R] \supset [\sim R \supset (\sim P \,v \sim Q)]$
9. $[(P \,\& \,Q) \supset R] \supset [(P \,\&\sim R) \supset \sim Q]$

Glossary

Necessary condition Condition N is a necessary condition for an event E just in case event E is not possible without N; that is, in the absence of condition N, E cannot occur.

Sufficient condition A condition S is a sufficient condition for an event E just in case S is all that is required for E to occur; that is, once S occurs, E will occur.

---

[1] Benson Mates, *Elementary Logic*, 2nd ed. (New York: Oxford University Press, 1972, page 217).

[2] The standard work is William Kneale and Martha Kneale, *The Development of Logic*. (Oxford: Clarendon Press, 1962).

14 Truth-Table Analysis
Part 1 «« «« «« «« «« «« «« «« «« ««

Truth Tables for the Operators

Recall from Chapter 10 that a *sentence operator* is a word or phrase that forms a compound sentence out of one or more sentences. As we have seen, the Stoics discovered that an amazing number of arguments are formed just out of sentences joined together by a small number of sentence operators, now called truth-functional operators, and that such arguments are actually the stuff of most everyday reasoning. They also saw that the validity of this new type of argument—the truth-functional argument—does not depend on content, i.e., on what the sentences of the argument are about; rather, it depends only on the formal or structural arrangement of the operators within the argument. As in the logic of Aristotle, validity in the Stoic system is a matter of *form* rather than *content*.

Truth-table analysis is a mechanical way of evaluating truth-functional arguments and the sentences out of which such arguments are composed. The Stoics had the seed idea, but it was not developed systematically and in a robust way until the late nineteenth and early twentieth centuries, by the logicians Charles Sanders Peirce (1839–1914), Emil Post (1897–1954), and Ludwig Wittgenstein (1889–1951). As usual, some preliminary definitions are required before the action can begin.

Truth Tables for the Operators

Recall that a *function* is a rule that relates one set of values to another set of values. A function is a *truth-function* if the values it relates are truth-values. A sentence operator is *truth-functional* if the compound sentence that it forms is a truth-functional compound sentence. A compound sentence is a truth-functional compound if its truth-value is a function of the truth-value of its component or components. Five truth-functional operators have been defined so far, and five corresponding truth-functional compound sentences. However, each function has been specified in English. It is also possible to define each truth-function on a device called a truth table. A **truth table** is a table that displays a functional correspondence between two sets of truth-values. Let us begin with the truth-function associated with the conjunction operator.

When we use a conjunction operator (*and, but, although,* etc.) to join two sentences into a compound asserting that both sentences (conjuncts) are true and nothing more, the conjunction as a whole is true if both conjuncts are true; otherwise it is false. In other words:

- If both conjuncts are true, then the conjunction as a whole is true.
- If the left conjunct is true and the right conjunct is false, then the conjunction is false.
- If the left conjunct is false and the right conjunct is true, then the conjunction is false.
- If both conjuncts are false, then the conjunction as a whole is false.

This information can be more compactly displayed in a truth table as follows:

Let **P** and **Q** be variables ranging over all declarative sentences.
Let & represent a conjunction operator joining **P** and **Q**.

P	Q		P	&	Q
T	T			T	
T	F			F	
F	T			F	
F	F			F	

Truth Table for Conjunction

Here is how to interpret this table: Rows are horizontal and columns are vertical. **T** and **F** stand for true and false, respectively. Row 1 of this table (the only row containing three **T**s) indicates that when the left conjunct **P** is true and the right conjunct **Q** is true, the compound as a whole, represented by **P & Q**, is in that case true. The second row says that when the left conjunct is true and the right conjunct is false, the compound as a whole is in that case false. The third row says that when the left conjunct is false and the right conjunct is true, the compound as a whole is false, and so on. You can remember this table if you keep in mind just one idea: A conjunction is only true when both conjuncts are true; it is false in every other case.

Notice that the four rows of the table cover every possible combination of truth-values that could be assigned to the two component sentences **P** and **Q**. In other words, between them the four rows list all possible truth-value assignments for the components of the compound. The truth table for conjunction displays the relationship between the truth-values of the parts and the truth-value of the whole for *any* truth-functional conjunction.

Recall that a disjunction is *exclusive* if it asserts that one or the other *but not both* disjuncts are true; and that a disjunction is *inclusive* if it asserts that one or the other *or both* disjuncts are true. Recall also that when we use the word *disjunction* we mean the inclusive kind, unless otherwise specified. The truth table for the truth-functional, inclusive disjunction, is shown here.

P	Q		P	v	Q
T	T			T	
T	F			T	
F	T			T	
F	F			F	

Truth Table for Inclusive Disjunction

Row 1 says that when the left disjunct (**P**) is true and the right disjunct (**Q**) is true, then the compound as a whole, represented by (**P v Q**), is true. The second row tells us that when the left disjunct is true and the right disjunct is false, the compound as a whole is still true. The third row says that when the left disjunct is false and the right disjunct is true, the compound is true, and so on. Notice that one idea sums up the whole table: An inclusive disjunction is only false when both of its disjuncts are false; it is true in all other cases.

Recall that we normally form a negation by prefixing the operator "It is not the case that" (or an equivalent phrase) to a sentence. A negation is true when the sentence negated is false, and a negation is false when the sentence negated is true. This is common sense, of course. The truth table for negation sums it up nicely in two rows.

P		~	P
T		F	
F		T	

Truth Table for Negation

As we have seen, truth-functional logic assigns to the horseshoe operator the truth-function first identified by Philo of Megara more than 2,000 years ago: When the antecedent is true and the consequent is false, the conditional is false; it is true in every other case. Philo was more farsighted than he could ever have imagined. Of the 14 two-valued truth-functions that exist, none works better, for the purpose served, than the one chosen by Philo. The truth table for the Philonian, or truth-functional, conditional follows:

P	Q		P	⊃	Q
T	T			T	
T	F			F	
F	T			T	
F	F			T	

Truth Table for the Conditional

Notice that one idea sums up the whole table: A truth-functional conditional is false only when its antecedent is true and its consequent is false; otherwise it is true. In truth-functional logic, a conditional sentence whose truth conditions are understood in terms of this table is called a **material conditional**.

The Modern Addition: The "Biconditional" Truth-Function

As we have seen, to cope with certain complexities arising out of modern science and philosophy, in the twentieth century, logic added a new truth-function to the list, the truth-function for the "biconditional" operator.

The truth table for "**P** if and only if **Q**" logically follows from the truth table for the horseshoe, although this cannot be demonstrated until the principles of truth-table analysis have been presented in the next chapter. The table for the biconditional assigns **T** to the compound as a whole when the components are both true, it also assigns **T** to the compound when the components are both false, and it assigns **F** to the compound in the other two cases. Thus:

P	Q		P	≡	Q
T	T			T	
T	F			F	
F	T			F	
F	F			T	

Truth Table for Biconditional

Notice that one idea sums up the whole table: A truth-functional biconditional is true only when its components have matching truth-values; otherwise it is false. In truth-functional logic, a biconditional sentence whose truth conditions are understood in terms of this table is called a **material biconditional**.

A Summary of the Truth-Functions

A conjunction (**P** & **Q**) is only true when both conjuncts are true, otherwise it is false.
A disjunction (**P** v **Q**) is only false when both disjuncts are false, otherwise it is true.
A negation (~**P**) is always opposite in truth-value to the sentence negated.
A material conditional (**P** ⊃ **Q**) is only false when the antecedent (**P**) is true and the consequent (**Q**) is false, otherwise it is true.
A material biconditional (**P** ≡ **Q**) is only true when both sides match in truth-value.

What do we do with all of this? We use it to make bigger and ever bigger truth tables. The first step is to learn how to calculate the value of a compound formula from the values of its sentential components.

Exercise 14.1   Refer to the truth tables and complete the following sentences.

1. If the left conjunct is true and the right conjunct is false, the conjunction as a whole is . . .
2. If the left conjunct is false and the right conjunct is false, the conjunction as a whole is . . .
3. If the left conjunct is true and the right conjunct is true, the conjunction as a whole is . . .
4. If the left disjunct is true and the right disjunct is false, the disjunction as a whole is . . .

5.   If the left disjunct is false and the right disjunct is false, the disjunction as a whole is . . .

6.   If the left disjunct is true and the right disjunct is true, the disjunction as a whole is . . .

7.   If the antecedent is true and the consequent is false, the conditional as a whole is . . .

8.   If the antecedent is false and the consequent is false, the conditional as a whole is . . .

9.   If the antecedent is true and the consequent is true, the conditional as a whole is . . .

10.   If the left component of a biconditional sentence is true and the right component is false, the biconditional as a whole is . . .

11.   If the left component of a biconditional sentence is false and the right component is false, the biconditional as a whole is . . .

12.   If the left component of a biconditional sentence is true and the right component is true, the biconditional as a whole is . . .

Using the Tables to Calculate the Value of a Compound Sentence

The development of formal logical languages in the twentieth century allowed logicians to turn logic in a more mathematical direction. Part of that movement involved adding methods of exact calculation to logical theory. Recall that the *scope of an operator* (*and, or*, etc.) occurring in a sentence is "the operator itself along with the part of the sentence that the operator applies to or links together." For example, consider the following formula:

(H v S) ⊃ (A & B)

In this formula, the scope of the ampersand (&) on the right is the (A & B) part of the formula. (The parentheses around the "A & B" part tell us this.) The scope of the wedge (v) on the left is the (H v S) part. (The parentheses indicate this.) By a process of elimination, the scope of the "horse" (⊃) is thus the whole formula.

Next, recall that the *main operator* of a sentence is the operator of largest scope. This will always be the scope spanning the entire formula, of course. In the preceding formula, the horseshoe (⊃) is therefore the main connective (or main operator). The main operator will therefore always be the operator whose scope spans the entire sentence. The truth-value determined by the main operator will always be the truth-value for the compound as a whole. This will become clearer as we work through several examples.

The Replacement Method

We employ the **replacement method** to calculate the truth-values of compound sentences based on the values assigned to the parts. This method gets its name from the fact that it involves *replacing* parts of formulas with truth-values as we calculate the value of a whole formula.

Let us begin with the sentence ~A & B. Suppose arbitrarily that the truth-value of A is false (**F**) and the truth-value of B is true (**T**). The truth-values are assigned just for the sake of illustration, as there is no meaning to the assignment. Now, given this assignment of truth-values to the parts of the formula ~A & B, what is the truth-value of the formula ~A & B as a *whole*? At step 1, to keep track of our calculations, we copy the formula, making no change in it, except that we insert an **F** in place of A and we insert a **T** in place of B. This reminds us that A is assigned false and that B is assigned true. (Keep in mind that we assigned **F** to A, we did not assign **F** to the ~A.)

Start: ~A & B
Given: A is assigned **F**, B is assigned true **T**
Step 1:   ~**F** & **T**

When we put an **F** in place of A and a **T** in place of B, this is just a "bookkeeping" device that records the fact that A has been assigned the truth-value **F** and that B has been assigned the truth-value **T**.

Next, in ~A & B, the negation sign applies only to that part of the compound to its immediate right. So, in the formula at step 1, when we calculate the value, we must apply the tilde only to the **F** to its immediate right. The negation truth table tells us that when a tilde applies to a component with a truth-value of **F**, the compound gets the truth-value of **T**. In short, ~**F** produces **T**. Therefore, at step 2 we replace the ~**F** with **T**:

Step 2:   **T** & **T**

Now we see that the ampersand actually joins a unit that is **T** with a unit that is also **T**. According to the truth table for the &, when & joins true with true, the compound is assigned true. So, at step 3 we replace the **T** & **T** with **T**:

Step 3:   **T**

Because the ampersand is the main operator, its value is the value of the compound as a whole. So, we have reached the truth-value of the compound as a whole: true. Notice that we calculated the smallest scoped operator first.

Let's look at a slightly more complex example. Suppose someone symbolizes an English sentence with the formula ~(A & B). Furthermore, let us assign **F** to A and **T** to B. (This is the same as saying that A is false and B is true.) Before we begin the calculation, we note that the tilde applies to the parenthesis to its immediate right. The tilde does not apply just to A alone. Thus the tilde applies to the conjunction (A & B) as a whole. Here are the steps:

Formula: ~(A & B)

Given: A is **F**, B is **T**

Step 1: ~(**F** & **T**)

At step 1, we look at the (**F** & **T**) *part* of the ~(**F** & **T**). The truth table for conjunction tells us that when & joins a false statement to a true statement, the whole is false. In other words, **F** "anded" to **T** produces **F**. So, at the next step, we replace just the (**F** & **T**) part with **F**:

Step 2: ~(**F**)

Notice that we replaced only the (**F** & **T**) part with **F**. The tilde on the outside carried down. Next, because a tilde applied to a false produces a compound with the truth-value of true, we replace the ~**F** with **T**:

Step 3: **T**

The value of the compound, given the values assigned to the parts, is thus true.

Now for a complex example: If A is assigned **F** and B is assigned **T**, what is the truth-value of this wff: (A & ~B) v (A v B)?

Formula: (A & ~ B) v (A v B)

Given: A is **F**, B is **T**

Step 1: (**F** & ~ **T**) v (**F** v **T**)

We begin our calculations with the connectives of smallest scope. The smallest scope possible is a tilde applied to a single atomic component with no intervening bracket. This is the ~**T** inside the first parenthesis at step 1, and so we begin by calculating that. A tilde applied to a **T** produces an **F**, and so the ~**T** is replaced by an **F**:

Step 2: (**F** & **F**) v (**F** v **T**)

Moving on, we evaluate the function of next largest scope (and if there is a tie, the order doesn't matter). Here, we evaluate the (**F** v **T**) component. The truth table for the wedge tells us that a false component disjoined to a true component produces a true compound; that is, **F v T** is true. We replace the **F v T** with a **T**:

Step 3: (**F & F**) v (**T**)

The function of next largest scope is the (**F & F**) component. The truth table for & tells us that a false component conjoined to a false component yields a false compound. Thus, we replace the (**F & F**) with an **F**:

Step 4: (**F**) v **T**

Finally, the remaining formula is calculated. According to the truth table for inclusive disjunction, a disjunction with a false left side and a true right side is always true. So:

Step 5: **T**

This is the final truth-value. The formula as a whole is true, given the initial values assigned. Remember that the final value, the value for the compound as a whole, is always the value determined by the main operator—the operator of greatest scope—and the main operator is always the last operator to be evaluated.

Notice the way in which the truth-values "flow" from the atomic components down through the structure and emerge at the end from the main operator. Notice also that as we calculate the truth-values, we move from the inside to the outside, starting with the functions of smallest scope and graduating in stages to larger functions, until we reach the function of greatest scope, the main operator—the operator whose influence spans the whole.

Naming Compound Sentences

You already know by now that logicians like precision. They also like to name things. Truth-functional compound sentences are named in terms of their main operators:

- If the main operator of a sentence is a conjunction operator, the sentence is a **conjunction**. For example, the following sentence is a conjunction: (A v B) & (E v H).
- If the main operator is a disjunction operator, the sentence is a **disjunction**; for example, (A & B) v (E & S).
- If the main operator is a negation operator, the sentence is a **negation**; for example, ~(A & H).

- A **conditional** is any sentence whose main operator is a horseshoe; for example, (A & H) ⊃ F.
- If the main operator is the triple bar, the sentence is a **biconditional**; for example, (A v D) ≡ (E & S).

Exercise 14.2 Assume that A is true, B is false, and C is true. Determine the truth-value in each case.

1.	A & B	7.	~(A v B) & C
2.	~(A v B)	8.	A & (B v C)
3.	~ A & ~B	9.	~A v ~B
4.	~A & B	10.	(A v B) v C
5.	~(A & B)	11.	A v (B v C)
6.	(A & B) v C	12.	(A & B) & C

Exercise 14.3 Assume A, B, and E are each true, and determine truth-values for the following:

1.	A ⊃ B	9.	~A ⊃ (~B & ~E)
2.	B ⊃ A	10.	~E ⊃ ~(A ≡ B)
3.	~B ⊃ ~A	11.	(A & B) ⊃ E
4.	(A ⊃ B) ⊃ E	12.	~(A & B) ⊃ ~ E
5.	A ⊃ (B ⊃ E)	13.	(A & B) ≡ (A & E)
6.	A ⊃ (B & E)	14.	A ≡ E
7.	A ⊃ (B ≡ E)	15.	E ≡ A
8.	(A ⊃ B) ⊃ (B ⊃ A)	16.	(~A & ~B) ⊃ ~E

Exercise 14.4 Letting A, B, E, and G stand for true sentences, while I, O, K, L, and U stand for false sentences, determine the value of the following formulas:

1. ~~ {~[~[(~A v ~B) ⊃ ~(E & ~G)] ≡ ~[~(~ I v ~O) ⊃ (~K & ~L)] } ⊃ ~~[~(G ≡ U) & (I ⊃ O)]
2. {~[~(A & B) ⊃ ~(E ⊃ ~G)] ⊃ ~[(~ I ⊃ ~O) & (~K v ~L)] } ⊃ [~(G ⊃ U) & (I ⊃ O)]

Exercise 14.5 Refer to the problems in Exercise 14.2. In each case, is the formula a conjunction, disjunction, negation, conditional, or biconditional?

Exercise 14.6 Refer to the problems in Exercise 14.3. In each case, is the formula a conjunction, disjunction, negation, conditional, or biconditional?

Appendix 14.1   Test Your Brain with Truth-Functional Puzzles

Remember when you solved "equations with unknowns" in math class? Truth-functional logic has a similar exercise. Suppose that P and Q are sentences whose truth-values are unknown. Let A and B stand for sentences whose truth-value is true, and suppose C and D stand for sentences whose truth-value is false. Given only this partial information, can you determine the truth-values of the following formulas anyway?

1.	C & P	8.	(A v P) v (P v Q)
2.	P v A	9.	(D & P) & (P & Q)
3.	P v ~P	10.	(Q ⊃ P) ⊃ (D ⊃ P)
4.	Q & ~Q	11.	(P & ~P) ⊃ (Q v Q)
5.	P ⊃ A	12.	(P v P) ⊃ ~(Q & ~Q)
6.	D ⊃ Q	13.	~[(P & ~P) ⊃ (Q v Q)]
7.	P ≡ ~P		

Hint. Let us solve the first problem together. Using only the incomplete information given, what is the value of (C &P)? We know that C is false but we do not know the truth-value of P. That is, P's value is completely unknown. The first thing to notice is that the formula in question is a conjunction. A glance at the conjunction truth table, the table for &, reminds us that a conjunction is *only* true when both conjuncts are true. In every other case, the conjunction is false. When we look at formula 1, C & P, we can see that it is not the case that both conjuncts are true (because we know that C is false). Therefore, even though we do not know the value of P, we can deduce, using purely deductive reasoning, that the value of the formula as a whole *must* be false.

Consider formula 2: P v A. The first thing to notice is that this formula is a disjunction, an *or* statement. We do not know the value of P, but we do know that A is true. Looking at the truth table for *or*, the disjunction table, we note that a disjunction is only false when both sides are false. In all other cases, an *or* statement is true. Because we know the A in this case is true, we see that the disjunction as a whole *must* be true, as one side of the disjunction is true (the A side) and one side true is enough to make a disjunction true. Again, by purely deductive reasoning, we can see that even though we do not know the value of P, the disjunction P v A *must* be true—simply on the grounds that the A is true.

All 10 of the "missing piece" problems shown, and many more like them, can be solved using purely deductive reasoning and a knowledge of the respective truth tables (the tables for &, v, ~, etc.). You can do it!

Exercise 14.7   Determine truth-values for problems 1–13 above, even though each formula contains an unknown.

Back to the Island of Knights and Knaves

Recall the "Knights and Knaves" problems from Unit One. On the mysterious island of knights and knaves, all you know is that knights always tell the truth and that knaves always lie. Unfortunately, the inhabitants of this dreadful place cannot be distinguished on the basis of outward appearances. Nevertheless, using strict deductive reasoning, what can be deduced in each of the following cases? What is A? What is B? Knight or knave?

1. B is silent but A says: "We are not both knaves." Later on, A says, "1 + 1 = 8."
2. B is silent but A says, "We are not both knights." Later on, A says, "1 + 1 = 2."
3. B is silent but A says, "We are both knaves." Later on, A says, "1 + 1 = 8."
4. B is silent but A says, "We are both knights." Later on, A says, "1 + 1 = 2."
5. B is silent but A says, "Neither of us is a knight." Later on, A says, "1 + 1 = 8."
6. B is silent but A says, "Neither of us is a knave." Later on, A says, "1 + 1 = 2."
7. A says: "C is a knave."
    B says: "Either A or C is a knave."
    C says: "If I am a knave the other two are, too."
8. A says: "B is a knight."
    B says: "We all are knaves."
    C says: "The other two are knaves."
9. A says: "We are not all knaves."
    B says: "A is a knave."
    C says: "If A is a knight then B is."
10. A says: "I am a knight or I am not a knight."
    B says: "I am a knight and I am not a knight."

Glossary

Biconditional A formula in which the connective is a biconditional operator.

Conditional A formula in which the main connective is a conditional operator.

Conjunction A formula in which the main connective is a conjunction operator.

Disjunction A formula in which the main connective is a disjunction operator.

Material conditional A conditional sentence whose truth conditions are given by the truth table for the horseshoe.

Negation A formula in which the main connective is a negation operator.

Replacement method A method for calculating the truth values of compound sentences by replacing parts of the formula with truth values assigned to those parts.

Truth table A table that displays a functional correspondence between two sets of truth-values.

15 Truth-Table Analysis Part 2 « « « « « « « « « «

Testing Sentences for Logical Status

Beginning in the early twentieth century, building on the achievements of the German logician Frege, logicians discovered that a truth-table display has many interesting uses within logical theory. Indeed, the introduction of truth-table analysis was a great advance in logical theory. Amazingly, the new insights were all just a logical outgrowth of the original logical system of the Stoics—the inventors of the world's first truth tables for compound sentences within logical arguments. As usual, we build the new methods in discrete stages, with definitions, step by step.

Let us begin with the English sentence "Ann is home or Ann is not home." In TL this is of course symbolized: A v ~A. What is the truth-value of the compound as a whole? "Well," someone might say, "it depends on the values of the components." Let's consider the possibilities. There are only two: (a) A is assigned true, and (b) A is assigned false. Beginning with the first, if A has the truth-value **T**, then (using the replacement method):

$$A \text{ v} \sim A$$
$$\mathbf{T} \text{ v} \sim\mathbf{T}$$
$$\mathbf{T} \text{ v } \mathbf{F}$$
$$\mathbf{T}$$

The compound is thus true on this truth-value assignment. Turning to the second possibility, if A has the truth-value **F**, then:

$$A \text{ v} \sim A$$
$$\mathbf{F} \text{ v} \sim\mathbf{F}$$
$$\mathbf{F} \text{ v } \mathbf{T}$$
$$\mathbf{T}$$

The compound remains true. It is true on both truth-value assignments. No matter what value A is assigned, the formula as a whole is true.

Constructing a Truth Table for a Formula

The two preceding calculations take up a lot of space. Both possibilities—worked out earlier using the replacement method—can be more compactly displayed in a truth table as follows. First, on top of a table, we write the formula we are evaluating (A v ~A). Under this we fill in all the possible truth-values the letter or letters (the atomic components) might be assigned. In this case, the formula only has one atomic component, namely A, and so there are two possible truth-value assignments :

A	v	~	A
T			T
F			F

The first row is the case where A is assigned **T**, and the second row is the case where A is assigned **F**. Notice that only two truth-value assignments exist for this formula. (Remember that rows are horizontal and columns are vertical.)

We are ready to "populate" the table, that is, to fill in the values under the connectives. The first thing to notice is that the smallest scoped connective is the tilde (because it only applies to the A). When calculating the value of a formula on a row, we always start with the smallest scoped connective. If there is a tie, then the order does not matter. Therefore, applying the rule for negation (as specified in the negation table) to the tilde, we apply the tilde to the A on each row, writing the resulting values directly under the tilde in the third column from the left, column 3, which is now numbered for ease of reference:

A	v	~	A
T		F	T
F		T	F
1	2	3	4

In row 1, the ~A part was assigned **F** because the truth table for negation tells us that whenever **P** is true, ~**P** is false. That is, if **P** is true, and we apply a tilde to it, the resulting compound is false. Thus, if A is true on a row then ~A is false on that row. On row 2, the ~A was assigned **T** (in column 3) because the A was assigned F and the negation table tells us that ~A is always opposite in truth-value to A. The column under the tilde is now complete. Next we calculate the truth-value of the remaining connective, the wedge, row by row, placing our values directly under the wedge in column 2:

A	v	~	A
T	T	F	T
F	T	T	F

The value under the wedge was determined by comparing the values, row by row, in columns 1 and 3 (counting columns from the left). For example, in row 1, A is assigned **T** at column 1. On the other side of the wedge, the "~A" part is assigned **F** at column 3. The value of the wedge (column 2) is thus determined by comparing the **T** on its left, at column 1, with the **F** on its right, at column 3. The table for disjunction tells us that when a wedge joins a **T** to an **F**, the whole is **T**. In other words, when the P part is true and the Q part is false, the P v Q as a whole is true.

On each row of this table, the truth-values were calculated just as they were in the "replacement method" diagrams earlier, except that truth-values were entered horizontally along a row of the table. The completed table tells us that if A is assigned **T**, then the formula A v ~A is true, and if A is assigned **F** then the formula A v ~A is still true.

The column of truth-values directly under the main operator (in this case the wedge) is called the **final column**. Thus, in the preceding table, column 2 is the final column. The values in the final column, appearing under the main connective, give the value for the formula as a whole on each row.

Next, let us consider a slightly more complex formula:

$$(A \& B) \text{ v } {\sim}A$$

The table for the formula must list all the different combinations of truth-values that could possibly be assigned to the atomic components of the formula. In this case the formula has two components: A and B. We already know that there are only four possible combinations of truth-values that could be assigned two at a time to the two components A and B, and so we have only four possible truth-value assignments to consider:

1. Perhaps A is true and B is true.
2. Perhaps A is true and B is false.
3. Perhaps A is false and B is true.
4. Perhaps A is false and B is false.

These four possibilities are displayed as follows, with the formula to be evaluated written across the top of the table:

(A	&	B)	v	~	A
T		T			T
T		F			T
F		T			F
F		F			F

Next, we must calculate the value of the formula in each row, row by row, for each assignment of truth-values. To calculate the value of the formula on a row, we start with the value of the smallest scope connective in the compound. (If there is a tie, then the order of calculation does not matter.) The smallest scoped connective in this compound is the tilde attached to the A. So we calculate the ~A part first, row by row, placing the result in column 5. We have erased all but the truth-values in use to clarify the operation at this step:

(A	&	B)	v	~	A
				F	T
				F	T
				T	F
				T	F
1	2	3	4	5	6

The columns have again been numbered for ease of reference. To calculate the values in the column under the tilde (column 5), we applied tilde to the values under the A on the right (column 6). That is how column 5 was populated. Thus, in accordance with the truth table for negation, when the A in line 6 is **T**, the ~A in line 5 is **F**, and so on.

The ampersand (&) is the connective of next biggest scope, so we calculate that part next. The result populates column 2:

(A	&	B)	v	~	A
T	T	T		F	T
T	F	F		F	T
F	F	T		T	F
F	F	F		T	F

To calculate column 2, we simply joined the values in columns 1 and 3 using the ampersand and calculated with the truth table for conjunction in mind. The truth table for conjunction tells us that & is only assigned a T (at column 2) when both A and B have been assigned T. Thus, row by row, we looked at the value of A at column 1 and the value of B at column 3 and placed a T at column 2 under the & when A and B were both T on the row, and we placed an F in the other cases. For each row, we obeyed the truth table for & as if it was the law. That is how column 2 was filled in.

The wedge is the last connective to get our attention. By a process of elimination, it is obviously the connective of greatest scope, and thus it is the main connective. We calculate it next:

(A	&	B)	v	~	A
T	T	T	T	F	T
T	F	F	F	F	T
F	F	T	T	T	F
F	F	F	T	T	F
1	2	3	4	5	6

The value of the wedge (at column 4) on each row is determined by comparing the value at column 2 and the value at column 5 in accord with the truth table for disjunction (*or*). Make sure you understand why it is that the value at column 4 is determined by looking at the values in columns 2 and 5 before you go further. Following the rule for disjunction, when the value on a row at column 2 is T and the value on that row at column 5 is F, the value in column 4 is T, and so on. We follow the rule for disjunction as if it is the "law of the land."

The completed table shows how each combination of truth-values determines the truth-value of the compound as a whole. Remember that each row of a truth table represents a different truth-value assignment. That is, each row of a table represents a different possible combination of truth-values that could be assigned to the atomic components of the formula or formulas on top of the table. Between them, the rows of a table collectively represent all possible combinations of truth-values that could be assigned to the atomic components of the formula or formulas on top of the table.

Next, consider a slightly more complex formula:

$$\sim[(A \ \& \ B) \ \& \sim(A \ \& \ B)]$$

The table follows, with the columns numbered for purposes of reference:

~	[(A	&	B)	&	~	(A	&	B)]
T	T	T	T	F	F	T	T	T
T	T	F	F	F	T	T	F	F
T	F	F	T	F	T	F	F	T
T	F	F	F	F	T	F	F	F
1	2	3	4	5	6	7	8	9

Because the first and third ampersands tie for the title of "smallest scoped connective," their values can be calculated in either order. Remember, we normally start with the smallest scoped connective, but when two connectives tie, then the order of calculation doesn't matter. Thus, columns 3 and 8 are populated first. The next biggest scope is the second tilde. Thus, column 6 is filled in next. The ampersand has the next biggest scope, so column 5 is calculated next. By a process of elimination, this leaves the first tilde as the connective of greatest scope. The first tilde is thus the main connective. Thus, column 1 will be the last to be populated. Column 1 is therefore the final column. Remember, the final column is always the column under the main connective. The formula as a whole thus receives its overall value at column 1. Before you go any further, make sure you understand why the value at this column is determined by applying the tilde in column 1 to the values in column 5.

Eight-Row Tables

Suppose we have a formula containing three different atomic components:

$$(A \lor B) \supset C$$

How many different truth-value assignments are there for this formula? The formula contains three atomic components, namely A, B, and C. A fairly simple process of trial and error reveals only eight possible combinations of truth-values for three components considered three at a time:

Possibility 1   A is **T**, B is **T**, C is **T**

Possibility 2   A is **T**, B is **T**, C is **F**

Possibility 3   A is **T**, B is **F**, C is **T**

Possibility 4   A is **T**, B is **F**, C is **F**

Possibility 5   A is **F**, B is **T**, C is **T**

Possibility 6   A is **F**, B is **T**, C is **F**

Possibility 7   A is **F**, B is **F**, C is **T**

Possibility 8   A is **F**, B is **F**, C is **F**

The truth table for this formula begins with the following truth-value assignments and with the formula arrayed across the top:

(A	v	B)	⊃	C
T		T		T
T		T		F
T		F		T
T		F		F
F		T		T
F		T		F
F		F		T
F		F		F

The table now displays all the different combinations of truth-values that could be assigned to the atomic components of the formula arrayed on top of it. The rows of the table are now calculated starting with the values for the smallest scope connective first. The wedge is the smallest scoped connective, so we fill in the values under the wedge first:

(A	v	B)	⊃	C
T	T	T		T
T	T	T		F
T	T	F		T
T	T	F		F
F	T	T		T
F	T	T		F
F	F	F		T
F	F	F		F
1	2	3	4	5

The value of the wedge on each row was obtained by comparing the values on each row at columns 1 and 3—with the truth table for disjunction in mind, of course. For example, the truth table for disjunction tells us that when P is true and Q is true, then P v Q is true. So, for example, in row 1, because A is assigned **T** and B is assigned **T** in that row, we placed a **T** under the wedge in the row, the first cell of column 2. Column 2 was populated all the way down in that way, by following the truth table for disjunction (*or*).

Continuing, we calculate the value of the connective of next biggest scope, which happens to be the only remaining connective—the horseshoe. This is therefore the main connective:

(A	v	B)	⊃	C
T	T	T	T	T
T	T	T	F	F
T	T	F	T	T
T	T	F	F	F
F	T	T	T	T
F	T	T	F	F
F	F	F	T	T
F	F	F	T	F
1	2	3	4	5

The values for the horseshoe (column 4) were obtained by comparing the values at columns 2 and 5 in each row in accord with the table for the horseshoe. Before you go further, make sure you understand why the value at the horseshoe column is determined by looking at the values in columns 2 and 5. The horseshoe table tells us that a statement P ⊃ Q is false only when P is true and Q is false—in every other case P ⊃ Q is true. Thus, as we go down column 4 row by row, looking only at the value at columns 2 and 5, we assign F when column 2 has a **T** in it and column 5 has an **F**, and in every other case we assign **T**! We followed the table for horseshoe here as if our life depended on it. Now that you know how to fill in a truth table for a formula, let's see what truth tables can tell us.

Truth-Table Tests for Logical Status

Recall from Chapter 6 that every sentence is either necessarily true, necessarily false, or contingent. A sentence is necessarily true if it is true and cannot possibly be false. A necessarily false sentence is a sentence that is false and cannot possibly be true. A contingent sentence is one that is true in some possible circumstances, false in others.

If we specify whether a sentence is necessarily true, necessarily false, or contingent, we are specifying the sentence's *logical status*. Thus, the **logical status** of a single sentence is either necessarily true, necessarily false, or contingent. Just as a chemist has tests he or she can perform for the presence of various chemical properties, we shall see that the logician has tests that show the presence of various logical properties: "truth-table" tests!

The Tautology Test

Consider the following sentence:

It is not the case that both Annette is 40 years old and she is not 40 years old.

In TL, this is best symbolized as: ~ (A & ~ A). What is the truth-value of the compound as a whole? You might say that it depends on the truth-values assigned to A. Let us see. The truth table allows us to look at all the possible combinations of truth-values that could possibly be assigned and the inevitable results of each assignment. The connective of smallest scope is the second tilde from the left, so we calculate that first, placing the results in the column underneath it:

~	(A	&	~	A)
	T		F	T
	F		T	F

The values in column 4 all resulted from applying the negation to the values under the A in column 5. When A is assigned **T**, we enter an **F** for ~A at column 4. When A is assigned **F**, we enter a **T** for the ~A at column 4, and so on. That gave us column 4.

The ampersand has the next biggest scope. The values under the ampersand (column 3) will be determined by comparing the values in columns 2 and 4, with the truth table for conjunction in mind.

~	(A	&	~	A)
	T	F	F	T
	F	F	T	F

The first tilde is the last connective to be evaluated because it has the greatest scope.

~	(A	&	~	A)
T	T	F	F	T
T	F	F	T	F

The value of the first tilde (column 1) was determined by looking at the value of the &, with the rule of the negation table in mind. The negation table tells us that when the tilde is applied to something that is true, the result is false, and when the tilde applies to something that is false, the result is true. In this case, the tilde applies to something that is false in both rows, so this tilde gets a **T** on each row. The final column, in other words, is all Ts.

Notice that when we began, only two possibilities existed: A is true (row 1) and A is false (row 2). The table shows us two things: If A is true, the compound is true; if A is false, the compound is true. In both cases, the truth-value of the whole, at column 1, is **T**.

The sentence ~(A & ~ A) thus has an interesting logical property. On every row of its truth table, the formula computes **T** at the main operator. This indicates that the sentence is true in every possible circumstance; in no circumstance will it ever be false. In other words, this sentence is necessarily true.

In English grammar, a sentence that is true in all circumstances and false in none, is called a **tautology**. An example of a tautology is, "Wherever you go, there you are." The counterpart in truth-functional logic is a formula or sentence whose main connective is true on every row of its truth table; in other words, a formula whose final column is all **T**s. For if the final column is all **T**s, then the formula is true in all circumstances. In truth-functional logic, such a statement is also called a tautology.

The tautology test for single sentences follows:

To test a sentence for this logical property, we first place the sentence on top of a truth table. We then run the table and examine the final column when finished. If the final column is all **T**s, the sentence is a tautology; if the final column is not all **T**s, the sentence is not tautological. It is that simple!

The Contradiction Test

Imagine a chemist turned politician who is trying to please all sides and says, "Aluminum is an element and it's not the case that aluminum is an element." This politician is trying to get the pro-aluminum vote and the anti-aluminum vote. In symbols, using obvious abbreviations, this political profundity is A & ~ A. The truth table is shown here.

A	&	~	A
T	F	F	T
F	F	T	F

The final column of this table contains all **F**s. This indicates that the sentence has the truth-value false in every possible circumstance; in no possible circumstance is the sentence true. In other words, the sentence is necessarily false. In everyday life, a sentence like this, false in all possible circumstances, true in no circumstances, is called a contradiction. Similarly, in truth-functional logic, a sentence whose main connective shows false on every row of the truth table is a **contradiction**.

The test for contradictions follows.

To test a sentence for this logical property, we first place the sentence on top of a truth table. We run the table and examine the final column. If the final column is all Fs, the sentence is a contradiction; if the final column is not all Fs, the sentence is not contradictory. It is that simple!

The Contingency Test

In everyday life, something is contingent if it depends on something else. In truth-functional logic, a sentence is said to be **contingent** if the final column of its truth table contains at least one **T** and at least one **F**. The sentence is contingent because whether it is true or false depends on the row of the table under consideration, which means its truth or falsity depends on external circumstances. For example, take the sentence "Gilligan is homesick or the Skipper is not hungry." This goes into symbols as G v ~S, and the corresponding table shows a mix of **T**s and **F**s in the final column.

G	v	~	S
T	T	F	T
T	T	T	F
F	F	F	T
F	T	T	F

Because each row of a truth table represents a possible circumstance, a contingent sentence is thus one that is true in some circumstances and false in others. In the case of any contingent sentence, whether the sentence is true or false depends on (is contingent on) the circumstance or row of the table under consideration.

To test a sentence for this logical property, we first place the sentence on top of a truth table. We run the table and examine the final column. If the final column is a mix—in other words, if it has at least one **T** and at least one **F**—the sentence is a contingent. Otherwise, it is not contingent.

More Terminology

Definitions are the bread and butter of logic: You can never have too many. Tautologies are called **logical truths**. They are also said to be "logically true." The terms reflect the fact that they can be shown to be true using only the abstract procedures of logical theory—without investigating the physical world, without relying on facts about the material world, and without using our senses (seeing, hearing, tasting, smelling, etc.) to investigate the material world. Similarly, contradictions are called **logical falsehoods** and are said to be logically false, again, because they can be shown to be false using just the procedures of logic alone without investigating the physical world.

Exercise 15.1 Use truth tables to determine which of the following sentences of TL are tautological, which are contradictory, and which are contingent.

1. (A & B) ⊃ (A v B)
2. ~(A ⊃ A)
3. (A ⊃ B) ⊃ (~A v B)
4. (A ⊃ B) ⊃ (~ B ⊃ ~ A)
5. (A & B) ⊃ (A v E)
6. A ⊃ (A v B)
7. ~(A ≡ A)
8. ~A ⊃ A

9. A ⊃ ~A
10. A ≡ (A v B)
11. A v (B ⊃ B)
12. A ≡ ~A
13. A ≡ (A v A)
14. (A & B) ⊃ B
15. (A & B) ⊃ (~A ⊃ ~B)
16. [A ⊃ (B v C)] ≡ [(A ⊃ B) v (A ⊃ C)]

Testing Sentence Forms for Logical Status

As you know, a *sentence form* is an abstract structure that many sentences, pertaining to many different subject matters, can follow or instantiate. Consider the following three English sentences:

a. It will rain or it will snow.
b. Jan is from Michigan or Jan is from Arkansas.
c. It is not Wednesday or this is not Belgium.

Symbolized within TL, these become:

a. R v S

b. M v A

c. ~W v ~B

Notice that each consists of a left disjunct joined by a wedge to a right disjunct. In logic, this general pattern is expressed by writing:

$$P \text{ v } Q$$

where **P** and **Q** are variables ranging over sentences of TL. This expression, **P v Q**, represents the general pattern exhibited by the three preceding TL sentences. The expression **P v Q** is the form of the three TL sentences, and those three sentences are said to be *substitution instances* or *instantiations* of the form **P v Q**. A TL sentence will qualify as a substitution instance of a form if and only if the TL sentence can be generated from the form by substituting sentences of TL for the variables in the form and, in addition, making any necessary parenthetical adjustments. This will become clearer after we work through several examples.

Consider again the form **P v Q**. Suppose we abbreviate the English sentence "Jean attended the Monterey Pop Festival in 1967" with the letter J and "Chris attended the Monterey Pop Festival in 1967" with the letter C. If we begin with the form **P v Q** and replace **P** with the constant J and **Q** with the constant C, we generate the substitution instance:

$$J \text{ v } C$$

To record the replacements, let us write:

$$\textbf{P} / J$$
$$\textbf{Q} / C$$

Here, **P** / J simply indicates that each occurrence of the variable **P** was replaced by the constant J and **Q** / C indicates that every occurrence of the variable **Q** was replaced by the constant C.

If we return to the form **P v Q** and replace **P** with the TL formula A, and if we replace **Q** with the TL formula B, we generate a new substitution instance:

$$A \text{ v } B$$

To record the replacements, we write:

$$\textbf{P} / A$$
$$\textbf{Q} / B$$

Substitution instances can grow quite large. For instance, remaining with the same form, if we replace **P** with (A & B) and if we replace **Q** with (C v D), we generate the substitution instance (A & B) v (C v D).

To record the replacements, we write

$$\textbf{P} / \text{A \& B}$$
$$\textbf{Q} / \text{C v D}$$

Next, let us replace **P** with ~ (A & B) and **Q** with ~(A & E):

$$\text{~(A \& B) v ~ (A \& E)}$$

Again, we record the replacements by writing

$$\textbf{P} / \text{~(A \& B)}$$
$$\textbf{Q} / \text{~ (A \& E)}$$

Notice that when we go from the form to its instance, the connectives in the form carry down unchanged; only the *variables* are replaced with TL sentences. Thus, ~A ⊃ ~B is an instance of the form **P ⊃ Q**, but A ⊃ B is *not* an instance of the form ~**P ⊃ ~Q**. The instance can contain more connectives than the form, but never less.

Logical Status for Sentence Forms

A sentence form is a **tautological sentence form** if and only if every one of its substitution instances is a tautology. A sentence form is contradictory if and only if every substitution instance of the form is a contradiction. A sentence form is a **contingent sentence form** if and only if at least *some* of its substitution instances are contingent. Truth tables can also be used to test truth-functional sentence forms for logical status. We simply place the symbolized form across the top of the table and then conduct the test in the usual manner. The following table shows that the form **P v ~P** is tautological:

P	v	~	P
T	T	F	T
F	T	T	F

Notice that the final column shows all **Ts**. Thus, it would be impossible for any substitution instance of this form to be anything other than a tautology. Here is an

English substitution instance of this tautologous form: You are either who you say you are, or it is not the case that you are who you say you are.

The following table shows that the form **P & ~P** is contradictory.

P	&	~	P
T	F	F	T
F	F	T	F

Notice that the final column shows all Fs—a sure sign of a contradiction. It would be impossible for any substitution instance of this form to be anything other than contradictory. Here is an English substitution instance of this contradictory form: Today is Tuesday and it is not the case that today is Tuesday.

The following table indicates that at least some substitution instances of the sentence form **P ⊃ (P & Q)** will be contingent:

P	⊃	(P	&	Q)
T	T	T	T	T
T	F	T	F	F
F	T	F	F	T
F	T	F	F	F

Exercise 15.2 Test the following sentence forms for logical status. In each case, is the form tautologous, contradictory, or contingent?

1. **(P & Q) v (~P v ~Q)**
2. **(P v Q) & (~P & ~Q)**
3. **(P ⊃ Q) v (~P v Q)**
4. **(P ⊃ Q) & ~ (~Q ⊃ ~P)**
5. **(P ⊃ Q) v (P & ~ Q)**
6. **P v (Q v ~P)**
7. **Q ⊃ (P v ~P)**
8. **(P & ~P) ⊃ Q**
9. **(P & ~P) & Q**
10. **(P v ~P) v Q**
11. **P v (Q ⊃ P)**
12. **P & (Q ≡ P)**

Exercise 15.3   Suppose **P** is a tautology and **Q** is any sentence. What can we correctly conclude about the logical status of these corresponding formulas?

  1. ~P
  2. P v Q
  3. Q ⊃ P
  4. P ⊃ Q

Suppose **P** is a contradiction and **Q** is any sentence. What can we correctly conclude about the logical status of these corresponding formulas?

  5. ~P
  6. P & Q
  7. P ⊃ P
  8. P ⊃ Q

Suppose **P** and **Q** are both tautologies. What can we correctly conclude about the logical status of these corresponding formulas?

  9. P & Q
  10. P v Q
  11. P ⊃ Q
  12. P ≡ Q

Suppose **P** and **Q** are both contradictions. What can we correctly conclude about the logical status of these corresponding formulas?

  13. P & Q
  14. P v Q
  15. P ⊃ Q
  16. P ≡ Q

Exercise 15.4   Without using truth tables, determine in each case whether the sentence is tautologous or contradictory.

  1. {[(P v Q) & ~D] v B} v ~{[(P v Q) & ~D] v B}
  2. {[(P v Q) & ~D] v B} & ~{[(P v Q) & ~D] v B}
  3. ~{[(P v Q) & ~D] v ~[(P v Q) & ~D]} v {[(P v Q) & ~D] v ~[(P v Q) & ~D]}

Glossary

Contingent sentence (in truth-functional logic) A sentence with the following feature: The final column of its truth table shows at least one **T** and at least one **F**.

Contradiction (in truth-functional logic) A sentence with the following feature: The final column of its truth table shows all **F**s.

Final column In a truth table, the column of truth-values under the main operator.

Logical falsehood A sentence that can be known to be false using only the methods of logical theory—without investigating the physical world. (Such a sentence is said to be "logically false.")

Logical status The logical status of a sentence is either tautology, contradiction, or contingent.

Logical truth A sentence that can be known to be true using only the methods of logical theory—without investigating the physical world. (Such a sentence is said to be "logically true.")

Tautology (in truth-functional logic) A sentence with the following feature: The final column of its truth table shows all **T**s.

Truth-value assignment An assignment of truth-values to the letters of a formula or group of formulas.

16 Truth-Table Analysis Part 3 « « « « « « « « « «

Testing Arguments for Validity

The great German philosopher, mathematician, and logician Gottfried Wilhelm Leibniz (1646–1716) once wrote:

> I feel that controversies can never be finished, nor silence imposed on the Sects, unless we give up complicated reasoning in favor of simple calculation, words of vague and uncertain meaning in favor of fixed symbols. . . . When controversies arise, there will be no more . . . disputation between two philosophers than between two accountants. Nothing will be needed but that they should take pen in hand, sit down with their counting tables and . . . say to one another: Let us calculate.[1]

Leibniz hoped that once all our reasoning had been translated into exact symbols, and once we discovered ways to calculate logical conclusions by applying precise mathematical rules or "algorithms" to our reasoning, all human disagreements would finally come to an end, war would become obsolete, and there would be peace on Earth. What a grand idea! The next test, the validity test, although developed after his day, is certainly of a piece with the logical techniques Leibniz hoped would lead to the end of war and peace on Earth forever.

Testing an Argument for Validity

Recall that an argument is valid if and only if there is no possibility that its premises are true and its conclusion is false. In other words, if the premises are true, then the conclusion *must* be true. Consider the following argument:

---

[1] From the essay "On the Universal Science: Characteristic" in Paul Schrecker and Anne Martin Schrecker, ed. *Leibniz. Monadology and Other Philosophical Essays*. (New York: Macmillan, 1965, page 14.)

1. If Ann is swimming, then Bob is swimming.
2. Bob is not swimming.
3. Therefore, Ann must not be swimming.

In TL this is

1. A ⊃ B
2. ~B / ~ A

In this symbolized argument, the premises are numbered and the symbolized conclusion follows the slanted slash mark. Is this argument valid? To many people, the argument looks invalid at first glance. Perhaps you can see, intuitively, that it is indeed valid. However, a truth table can decide the issue in a precise way. The procedure involves three steps, each very exact.

Step 1. Create a truth table for the argument and place the symbolized version of the argument, in order, across the top of the table. Enter the possible truth-value assignments under the letters at this step as well. For the preceding argument, the result looks like this. (The parts of the argument have been labeled.)

First premise				Second premise			Conclusion	
A	⊃	B		~	B		~	A
T		T			T			T
T		F			F			T
F		T			T			F
F		F			F			F

Step 2. In each row, compute the truth-values of the premises and conclusion, circling or identifying the final values, that is, the values under the main connectives.

A	⊃	B		~	B		~	A
T	T	T		F	T		F	T
T	F	F		T	F		F	T
F	T	T		F	T		T	F
F	T	F		T	F		T	F

Step 3. This step has two instructions:

- If at least one row of the table shows a **T** under the main connective of each premise but shows an **F** under the main connective of the conclusion on that row, the argument on top of the table is an invalid argument.
- If the table contains no row showing all true premises and a false conclusion, the argument is valid.

Perhaps surprisingly, this argument is valid, for no row of the table shows the "all true premises—false conclusion" combination.

In short, to test an argument for validity, we create a truth table for the argument, we fill in the table, and then we look: If the table shows no row with all true premises and a false conclusion, then the argument is valid; if it has at least one row in which the premises all are true and the conclusion is false, the argument is invalid. That is all there is to it!

Next, consider an argument that looks similar to the previous argument:

1. If Ann is swimming, then Bob is swimming.
2. Ann is not swimming.
3. Therefore, Bob is not swimming.

In symbols, this is:

1. A ⊃ B
2. ~A / ~ B

Is this argument valid? To test it, we construct a truth table. The first step is to write the argument across the top of the table along with all the truth-values that could be assigned to each letter:

A	⊃	B		~	A		~	B
T		T			T			T
T		F			T			F
F		T			F			T
F		F			F			F

Next, we compute the truth-values of the premises and conclusion in each row. In other words, we populate the table. The values under the main connectives for the premises and conclusion on each row are filled in here:

A	⊃	B		~	A		~	B
T	T	T		F	T		F	T
T	F	F		F	T		T	F
F	T	T		T	F		F	T
F	T	F		T	F		T	F

Next we recall step 3: If at least one row of the table shows a **T** under the main operator of each premise but shows an **F** under the main operator of the conclusion, the argument on top of the table is an invalid argument. This argument shows the "all true premises–false conclusion" combination in the third row, so the argument is invalid. Did you notice that this argument is an instance of the fallacy of denying the antecedent?

The Validity Test

1. Place a symbolized argument across the top of the table.
2. Fill in the cells of the table.
   - If at least one row of the table shows a **T** under the main operator of each premise but shows an **F** under the main operator of the conclusion, the argument on top of the table is invalid.
   - If the table contains no row showing all true premises and a false conclusion, the argument on top is valid.

The Underlying Rationale

Consider the rationale underlying the truth-table test for validity. An argument is valid if there are no possible circumstances in which the premises are true and the conclusion is false. Each row of the table represents a collection of possible circumstances. Between them, the rows of a table represent all possible combinations of truth-values the argument's components might have. The truth table allows us, then, to see how the truth-values of the premises and conclusion vary across all possible circumstances. A row showing true premises and a false conclusion thus represents a possibility of true premises and false conclusion. If a table contains such a row, the argument represented on top of the table *can* have true premises and a false conclusion. If there is any possibility that the premises are true and the conclusion is false, an argument is invalid. If no row of a table shows all true premises with a false conclusion, we know that in no possible circumstance are the premises true and the conclusion false. If it is not possible for the premises to be true and the conclusion false, an argument is valid.

The tables are precise, and they sometimes keep us from making elementary errors. For example, the next argument seems valid to many people at first glance, but the truth table shows it to be invalid:

1. If Ann swims today, then Bob swims today.
2. Bob swims today.
3. So, Ann swims today.

In TL, this is

1. A ⊃ B
2. B / A

Notice row 3 of the argument's truth table:

A	⊃	B		B		A
T	T	T		T		T
T	F	F		F		T
F	T	T		T		F
F	T	F		F		F

In row 3, the premises are all true and the conclusion is false. Because each row is a possibility, this table shows us the possibility of true premises and a false conclusion, which in turn shows that the argument is invalid. This argument is an instance of the fallacy of affirming the consequent.

Here is a more complex example. Consider the following English argument:

1. Ann and Bob are not both swimmers.
2. Ann is a swimmer.
3. Therefore, Bob is not a swimmer.

In symbols, this is:

1. ~(A & B)
2. A / ~B

To begin with, we write the argument across the top of the table and place the truth-value assignments underneath the letters:

~	(A	&	B)		A		~	B
	T		T		T			T
	T		F		T			F
	F		T		F			T
	F		F		F			F

Next we compute the truth-values of the premises and conclusion on each row. We can start anywhere, so let's do ~B first.

~	(A	&	B)		A		~	B
	T		T		T		F	T
	T		F		T		T	F
	F		T		F		F	T
	F		F		F		T	F

Next to go are the values for the ampersand.

~	(A	&	B)		A		~	B
	T	T	T		T		F	T
	T	F	F		T		T	F
	F	F	T		F		F	T
	F	F	F		F		T	F

Finally come the values for the first tilde, which sums up the first premise as a whole.

~	(A	&	B)		A		~	B
F	T	T	T		T		F	T
T	T	F	F		T		T	F
T	F	F	T		F		F	T
T	F	F	F		F		T	F

Now we ask, in accord with step 3 of the validity test: Is there a row on which all the premises are true and the conclusion is false? Because the table contains no such row, the argument is valid!

The following argument might appear valid at first glance, but its truth table shows that it is actually invalid:

1. If Hank does not go swimming, then John will not go swimming.
2. Hank will go swimming.
3. So, John will go swimming.

In TL, this argument is

1. ~H ⊃ ~J
2. H / J

We begin the test as usual by setting up the table. We write the argument across the top and fill in the truth-value assignments underneath each letter.

~	H	⊃	~	J		H		J
	T			T		T		T
	T			F		T		F
	F			T		F		T
	F			F		F		F

Next, we populate the table:

~	H	⊃	~	J		H		J
F	T	T	F	T		T		T
F	T	T	T	F		T		F
T	F	F	F	T		F		T
T	F	T	T	F		F		F
1	2	3	4	5	6	7	8	9

Notice that the value at column 3 was derived by comparing the values at columns 1 and 4 according to the table for the horseshoe. Because row 2 shows true premises and a false conclusion, the argument is invalid. This argument in English appeared to be valid at first glance, but appearances in some cases can be deceiving.

Exercise 16.1 Test each of the following arguments for validity on a truth table. In each problem, the premises are numbered and the conclusion follows the slanted slash.

1.
   1. A v B
   2. B v C / A v C

2.
   1. A v B
   2. ~ A / ~ B

3.
   1. A ⊃ B / B ⊃ A

4.
   1. A ⊃ B /~A ⊃ ~B

5.
   1. A ⊃ B
   2. B ⊃ C / A ⊃ C

6.
   1. A ⊃ (B ⊃ C) / C ⊃ (B ⊃ A)

7.
   1. (A & B) ⊃ C / A ⊃ (B ⊃ C)

8.
   1. A ⊃ B / ~ B ⊃ ~A

9.
   1. A ⊃ B
   2. ~B / ~ A

10.
   1. ~A ⊃ ~B
   2. ~A / ~B

11.
   1. (A & B) ⊃ C
   2. ~C / ~A v ~B

12.
   1. A ⊃ B / ~A ⊃ ~B

13.

    1.   A v ~A

    2.   ~(B & ~B) / (A v B) & (~A & ~B)

14.

    1.   A v B

    2.   ~B v C

    3.   ~(A v C) / A & ~C

15.

    1.   A v B

    2.   C v ~B

    3.   A v C / ~A v ~C

Exercise 16.2   Symbolize the following arguments and then test each for validity in a truth table.

1. If Betsy takes Philosophy 110, then John will take Philosophy 110. John won't take Philosophy 110. So, Betsy won't take Philosophy 110.

2. If Plektus IV invades Ruritania, then the Ruritania Senate will flee. Plektus IV will not invade Ruritania. Therefore, the Ruritania Senate will not flee.

3. Either Herman will be home or Lillian will be home. Herman won't be home, therefore Lillian won't be home.

4. Gomez and Morticia won't both be home. But Morticia will be home. So, Gomez won't be home.

5. If either Granny or Jethro is home, then Mr. Drysdale will be happy. Mr. Drysdale won't be happy. So, Granny won't be home and Jethro won't be home.

6. It is not the case that both Kirk and Spock will beam down. If Kirk doesn't beam down, then McCoy will. If Spock doesn't beam down, then McCoy will. So, McCoy will beam down.

7. If Ralph wins the game, then Alice will be happy. If Alice will be happy, then Norton will be happy. So, if Norton will be happy, then Alice will be happy.

8. If either Ralph or Alice is home, then Norton will come in and make himself comfortable. Therefore, either Ralph is not home or Norton won't come in and make himself comfortable.

9. If Moe slaps Larry up the side of the head, then Larry slaps Curly up the side of the head and Curly slaps Moe up the side of the head. Moe will not slap Larry up the side of the head. Therefore, either Larry won't slap Curly up the side of the head or Curly won't slap Moe up the side of the head.

10. Either the sun will shine and there will be no wind, or the sun will shine and the race will be cancelled. The sun will shine and the race will not be cancelled. So there will be no wind.

11. If Moe slips then if Curly slips then Larry will slip. If Curly slips, then if Moe slips then Larry will slip. However, neither Curly nor Moe will slip. So Larry won't slip.

12. Dobie will be pleased if Maynard gets a job and saves some money. But if Maynard gets a job and doesn't like the job, then Dobie won't be pleased. Maynard will get a job only if he wants to. So Maynard won't both get a job and save some money.

Testing Argument Forms for Validity

Recall that an *argument form* is an abstract pattern of reasoning that many arguments, pertaining to many different subject matters, can follow or instantiate. As we have seen, modus ponens was a favorite among the Stoic logicians:

1. If **P** is the case, then **Q** is the case.
2. But **P** is the case.
3. Therefore, **Q** is the case.

For instance:

1. If Pyhro is debating Zeno tonight, then everyone will attend.
2. Pyhro is debating Zeno tonight.
3. Therefore, everyone will attend.

In truth-functional logic this general pattern of reasoning is expressed by writing:

1. $\mathbf{P} \supset \mathbf{Q}$
2. $\mathbf{P} / \mathbf{Q}$

where **P** and **Q** are variables ranging over sentences of TL. This expression is called an *argument form*, and any argument that follows it is called a *substitution instance* of the form. More precisely, an argument is a substitution instance of an argument form if and only if the argument can be generated from the form by substituting sentences of the argument for the variables in the form. When we substitute "Pyhro is debating Zeno tonight" for **P** and "Everyone will attend" for **Q**, we produce the argument and demonstrate that it is a substitution instance of the form in question, namely, modus ponens.

We have been using truth tables to test arguments for validity. Truth tables can also be used to test truth-functional argument *forms* for validity. After representing the form using variables, as we have done, we simply place the symbolized form across the top of the table and then conduct the test in the usual manner. Recall that an argument form is valid if and only if *every one* of its substitution instances is a valid argument. The following table shows that modus ponens is indeed a valid argument form:

P	⊃	Q		P	/	Q
T	T	T		T		T
T	F	F		T		F
F	T	T		F		T
F	T	F		F		F

The slanted slash signals the conclusion. Notice that no row shows true premises and a false conclusion. Thus, every substitution instance of this argument form will be a valid argument. The following table shows that modus tollens, another Stoic favorite, is also a valid form of reasoning:

P	⊃	Q		~	Q	/	~	P
T	T	T		F	T		F	T
T	F	F		T	F		F	T
F	T	T		F	T		T	F
F	T	F		T	F		T	F

Exercise 16.3 Use truth tables to show that these interesting Stoic argument forms are valid.

1.

   1. P ⊃ (P ⊃ Q)

   2. P / Q

2.

   1. P ⊃ P

   2. ~P ⊃ P/ P

3.

   1. P ⊃ Q

   2. P ⊃ ~Q / ~P

4.

   1. (P & Q) ⊃ R

   2. ~R

   3. P / ~Q

Exercise 16.4   Use truth tables to demonstrate the validity of the following argument forms:

1.

   1. P ⊃ Q

   2. Q ⊃ R / P ⊃ R

2.

   1. P v Q

   2. ~P / Q

3.

   1. P ⊃ Q

   2. R ⊃ S

   3. P v R / Q v S

4.

   1. P ⊃ Q

   2. R ⊃ S

   3. ~Q v ~S / ~P v ~ Q

   5. P ⊃ Q / ~Q ⊃ ~P

   6. P ⊃ Q / ~P v Q

   7. ~(P & Q) / ~P v ~Q

   8. ~(P v Q) / ~P & ~Q

   9. P v (Q & R) / (P v Q) & (P v R)

  10. P ≡ Q / (P ⊃ Q) & (Q ⊃ P)

Exercise 16.5   Test the following argument forms for validity using the truth-table method.

1.

   1. P ⊃ Q

   2. Q ⊃ R / R ⊃ Q

2.

   1. P ⊃ Q

   2. Q ⊃ R / R ⊃ P

3.

    1. **P ⊃ Q**

    2. **~P / ~Q**

4.

    1. **P ⊃ (Q & R)**

    2. **R / P**

5.

    1. **~P ⊃ (~Q & R)**

    2. **P v ~R / Q**

Truth-Functional and Categorical Logic Compared

If you read Chapter 9 in Unit Two, and learned how to test arguments for validity using Venn diagrams, you might have noticed, just now, a similarity between categorical and truth-functional logic. In modern categorical logic, we draw a Venn diagram for an argument and then populate it with information from the argument. After that, we can tell, just by looking at the diagram, whether the argument is valid or invalid. The test is visual. Similarly, in modern truth-functional logic, we draw a truth table for an argument, populate it with information from the argument, and then decide whether the argument is valid or invalid by simply looking at the table. Both tests are visual. Both tests are mechanical as well. Every part of logical theory is connected in various logical ways with every other part . . . making a lovely whole in the end.

Formal Semantics for Truth-Functional Logic

Using truth tables, a formal semantical theory for TL, covering the logical properties of sentences and arguments, can now be stated, and in very precise terms:

- A sentence of TL is a *truth-functional tautology* if and only if the final column of its truth table is all **Ts**.
- A sentence of TL is a *truth-functional contradiction* if and only if the final column of its truth table is all **Fs**.
- A sentence of TL is a *truth-functional contingency* if and only if the final column of its truth table contains at least one **T** and at least one **F**.
- An argument in TL is *truth-functionally valid* if and only if its truth table contains no row on which the premises all are true and the conclusion is false.
- An argument in TL is *truth-functionally invalid* if and only if its truth table contains at least one row on which the premises are all true and the conclusion is false.

Other Types of Validity

In this chapter, we have been examining arguments whose validity or invalidity depends on the various *truth-functional* relationships connecting the premises to the conclusion. These truth-functional relationships are revealed in the configuration of Ts and Fs in the argument's truth table. In later chapters, we will study arguments whose validity is due not to truth-functional relationships but to logical relationships of other types. For instance, in the next unit, we learn about arguments whose validity is due not to the arrangement of truth-functional operators but to the arrangement of objects called quantifiers. These arguments will be called quantificationally valid. The point is that at some point we will have to distinguish truth-functionally valid arguments from valid arguments of other types. For now, we shall simply say that an argument whose validity is established with the methods of truth-functional logic alone is a truth-functionally valid argument. An argument that is shown to be valid with a truth table is sometimes also said to be truth-table valid. Of course, all valid arguments, in all branches of logic, have the same basic logical property: If the premises are true, then the conclusion must be true; that is, it is not possible that the premises are true and the conclusion is false.

Reflections on Truth Tables

A **decision procedure**, also called an **algorithm**, is a problem-solving method with precisely specified steps, structured in such a way that a definite answer is guaranteed in a finite number of steps. In addition, following the steps of an algorithm must be a matter so precise and mechanical that no creativity or ingenuity is required. The rules for long division, for example, constitute a decision procedure or algorithm that most people learn in grade school.

The truth-table technique is a decision procedure. We test sentences and arguments for the various logical properties by filling in the Ts and Fs on a truth table, following definite rules. In this sense, truth-functional logic is mechanical or algorithmic. However, the use of the truth table as a decision procedure in logic has its limits. It cannot be applied to certain types of arguments, which we will examine in future chapters.

The truth-table tests are also an example of an **analytic method**. One way to understand something is to *analyze* it (from the Greek word *analytikos* meaning "to resolve into elements"). This involves breaking the subject down into its constituent parts and seeing how those parts fit together to constitute the whole. Imagine, for example, taking a watch apart and putting it back together to see how it works. The analytic method has been successful in numerous fields of thought, especially the physical sciences, where its application led to the discovery of photons, protons, neutrons, electrons, and various other subatomic particles.

Logic is fundamentally concerned with arguments, of course. In truth-functional logic we employ an analytic method when we break arguments down into their component parts and then study how those parts fit together on a truth table. The truth-table tests are thus analytic and algorithmic in nature.

Appendix 16.1   Advanced Techniques

Partial Tables

The following argument just "looks" invalid, doesn't it?

1. A ⊃ B
2. B ⊃ C
3. C ⊃ D
4. D ⊃ E / E ⊃ A

However, to show that this argument is invalid using a truth table would require a huge table with many, many rows. Indeed, the argument has five components, so the table would have 32 rows. It might take an hour to fill it all in. A far simpler way to show that this argument is invalid would be to employ a **partial truth table**.

Step 1. Draw a horizontal line and write the premises and conclusion of the argument across the top of it as follows:

1. A ⊃ B   2. B ⊃ C   3. C ⊃ D   4. D ⊃ E   / E ⊃ A

Step 2. Form the hypothesis that the argument is invalid. Recall that if an argument is invalid, it is *possible* that the premises are all true and the conclusion is false. Thus, if this argument is invalid, then there must be a consistent assignment of truth-values to the letters of the argument that makes the premises all true and the conclusion false. In accord with this, record the hypothesis by assigning **T** to the main operator of each premise and **F** to the main operator of the conclusion.

1. A ⊃ B	2. B ⊃ C	3. C ⊃ D	4. D ⊃ E	/ E ⊃ A
T	T	T	T	F

Step 3. Test the hypothesis by trying to fill in the rest of the truth-values, consistently, based on the hypothesis that the argument is invalid. In other words, try to assign values to the letters in such a way as to make the premises true and the

conclusion false. If it is possible to assign the truth-values in such a way that the premises are true and the conclusion is false, with no contradictory assignment of truth-values, then the hypothesis—that it is possible the premises are true and the conclusion is false—is verified. (A contradictory assignment of truth-values is an assignment that assigns **T** to a letter at one place on the table and then assigns an **F** to that same letter at another place on the table.) In this case, the argument must be invalid, for an argument is invalid if it is even *possible* that it has true premises and a false conclusion.

If it is not possible to consistently assign truth-values so as to make the premises all true and the conclusion false, then the hypothesis—that there is a truth-value assignment on which all the premises are true and the conclusion is false—is contradictory or impossible. If so, then it is *not* possible for the premises to be true and the conclusion false. This shows that the argument is valid.

Application

Let us now attempt to fill in the truth-values to make the conclusion false and the premises all true.

It is best to begin with the conclusion. If the conditional E ⊃ A is false (as assumed), then E must be assigned **T** and A must be assigned **F**, for a conditional is false only when its antecedent is true and its consequent is false. Thus, we place a **T** under the E and an **F** under the A:

1. A ⊃ B   2. B ⊃ C   3. C ⊃ D   4. D ⊃ E   / E ⊃ A
                                                           T F F

So far so good. Now, if we are going to be consistent, we must assign **T** to each occurrence of E up the line, and we must assign **F** to each occurrence of A throughout the rest of the argument:

1. A ⊃ B   2. B ⊃ C   3. C ⊃ D   4. D ⊃ E   / E ⊃ A
    F   T   T F F

From here, it is easy to assign values in such a way that the premises all are true and the conclusion is false. If we add that B is true, C is true, and D is true, that is, if we assign **T** to B, **T** to C, and **T** to D, the premises will all be true while the conclusion is false:

1. A ⊃ B   2. B ⊃ C   3. C ⊃ D   4. D ⊃ E   / E ⊃ A
    F T T   T T T   T T T   T T T   T F F

This "partial table" presents us with the possibility of the argument's premises being true while its conclusion is false. This, in turn, shows that the argument is invalid, for an argument is invalid if it is *possible* for it to have true premises and a false conclusion.

Let us now think about what we have done. In effect, we simply reproduced a single row from the argument's full truth table—a row on which the premises are all true and the conclusion is false. (That is why this is called a partial table.) In this case, that row is the row on which A is assigned **F**, and B, C, D, and E are each assigned **T**. Remember that an argument is invalid if its table has at least one row showing all true premises and a false conclusion.

Here's another way to understand this partial table. Recall that a *counterexample* to a deductive argument is a description of a possible circumstance in which the argument's premises would be true and its conclusion false. If there is a counterexample to an argument, the argument is invalid. To show someone that his argument is invalid, we can present or describe a counterexample to the argument. Our partial table in effect presents a counterexample to the argument, thus showing that the argument is invalid.

Let us consider the following argument:

1. A ⊃ B
2. B ⊃ C/ ~C ⊃ ~A

We place the argument across the top of a partial table:

A ⊃ B   B ⊃ C   ~C ⊃ ~A

Our hypothesis is this: The argument is invalid. In accord with this, we search for a truth-value assignment that makes the premises all true and the conclusion false:

A ⊃ B	B ⊃ C	~C ⊃ ~A
T	T	F

The only way the conclusion will be false will be if we assign F to C and T to A:

A ⊃ B	B ⊃ C	~C ⊃ ~A
T	T	F F T

Now, if we want the first premise to be true, we must assign **T** to B. However, if we do so, then the second premise will inevitably become false:

A ⊃ B	B ⊃ C	~C ⊃ ~A
T T T	T F F	T F F F T

We simply cannot change the values around to make the premises true and the conclusion false, for C has to be assigned **F** and A has to be assigned **T** if we want to make the conclusion false. This shows that it is impossible to consistently assign truth-values in such a way as to make the premises true and the conclusion false. This in turn shows that our hypothesis is false. It is not possible that this argument has true premises and a false conclusion. The partial table thus indicates that this argument, unlike the last one, is a valid argument.

The Partial Table Method Formalized

Let us now make this more formal.

Step 1. Across a horizontal line, write the premises and conclusion of the argument being assessed.

Step 2. Assign **T** to the main operator of each premise, and assign **F** to the main operator of the conclusion. This is the hypothesis to be tested.

Step 3. Try to fill in the rest of the truth-values consistently based on this hypothesis. If this cannot be done consistently, all across the table, then the argument is valid. If it is possible to consistently assign the truth-values in such a way that the premises are all true and the conclusion is false, with no contradictory assignment of truth-values, the argument is invalid.

The "Shortcut" Table

When you construct a truth table, you usually fill in every cell on every row. A computer would never do it that way, for filling in every cell would involve too much wasted effort. Instead, a computer would start at the upper right corner of the table and follow a path from there that reaches a decision point in the smallest possible number of steps. Consider the following "abstract" truth table:

A	B	X	X		X	X	X		X	X	X		X
T	T												
T	F												
F	T												
F	F												

Suppose the Xs represent the premises and conclusion of an argument spelled out along the top of the table. To make a decision in the smallest possible number of steps, a computer would start at the upper right corner of the table. If the value of the main connective of the conclusion, on row 1, is **F**, then it moves one step left on row 1 and computes the value of the last premise on row 1. However, if the value of the main connective of the conclusion, on row 1, is **T**, then it stops, moves down one row to row 2, and computes the value of the conclusion on row 2.

As it proceeds, it follows this rule: If the value of the conclusion on a row is **F**, then it moves one step left and computes the value of the last premise on that row. However, if the value of the main connective of the conclusion on a row is **T**, then it stops, moves down one row, and computes the value of the conclusion on the next row. If the value of a premise is **T**, then it moves one step left and calculates the next premise. If the value of a premise is **F**, then it stops, moves one row down, and computes the value of the conclusion on the next row. If the computer gets to the bottom of the table and *fails* to find an entire row showing all true premises and a false conclusion, then it stops and prints "valid." However, if the computer finds a row showing all true premises and a false conclusion, it stops at once and prints "invalid." If you fill in a table the way a computer would do the job, your table is a "shortcut" table. Think like a computer. In some contexts, it might save time and wasted effort!

Exercise 16.6   Each of the following arguments is invalid. In each case, symbolize the argument and then use a partial table to show that it is invalid.

1. If Sue has a hamburger, then if Joe will not have one, then Rita will have one. So, if Rita will have a hamburger, then Joe will not have one.
2. If Arnold quits his job, then Betty will quit her job. Arnold won't quit his job. So, neither Arnold nor Betty will quit.
3. If Pat goes swimming, then neither Quinn nor Rita will swim. If Rita doesn't go swimming, then Sue will swim, but Dolores won't swim. So, if Sue swims then Pat swims.
4. If Janet swims, then Bill will swim. Janet won't swim. So, Bill won't swim.
5. If Angie sings, then Randy will sing. If Randy sings, then either Chris or Pat will sing. If Pat sings, then Roberta will sing. Therefore, if Angie sings, then Roberta will sing.
6. Craig and Faith won't both order burritos. If Craig doesn't order a burrito, then Darla will order one. So, Darla and Faith will both order burritos.
7. Neither Ann nor Bob will order tacos but Chris and Darla will. If either Ann or Chris orders a taco, then Berta will order a burrito. So, if Berta orders a burrito, then Ann will order a taco.
8. Both Ann and Bob won't order French fries. If Bob doesn't order French fries, then either Chris or Darla will order fries. If Robert doesn't want to

eat, then Chris won't order fries, and neither will Darla. Either Robert will not want to eat or Chris will order fries.

9. If neither Ann nor Bubba orders the Bob's Brontosaurus Burger Bar Special Combo Plate, then Cherie and Zack will both be disappointed. If Cherie is disappointed, then she will order four hamburgers. So, if Ann orders the Bob's Brontosaurus Burger Bar Special Combo Plate, then Cherie won't order four hamburgers.

Exercise 16.7 Use partial truth tables to prove that each of the following symbolized arguments is invalid. In each case, the argument's symbolized premises are written first, and the symbolized conclusion appears after the slash mark.

1. A ⊃ (B v W)
    B ⊃ S / A ⊃ S

2. A ⊃ B
    W ⊃ S
    ~A v ~W / ~B v ~S

3. A v B
    A / ~B

4. ~(A & B)
    ~A / B

5. A ⊃ B
    B ⊃ W
    W ⊃ S
    S ⊃ H / H ⊃ A

6. A ⊃ B / B ⊃ A

7. ~(A & B) / ~A & ~B

8. ~(A v B) / ~ A

9. ~(A & B) / ~ A

10. A v B
    A / B

11. A ⊃ B
    W ⊃ B / A ⊃ W

12. A ⊃ B
    W ⊃ S
    B v S / A v W

13. ~A ⊃ ~B
    ~B ⊃ ~C / ~C ⊃ ~A

Exercise 16.8   Test these arguments for validity using partial tables.

1.
  1. A ⊃ (A & B)
  2. A ⊃ (C & D)
  3. (E v A) ⊃ D / (E v C) ⊃ B

2.
  1. A ⊃ (B ⊃ C)
  2. A ⊃ D
  3. (B ⊃ E) ⊃ (C ⊃ F)
  4. (~A & ~D) ⊃ (C ⊃ E)

3.
  1. ~D
  2. (~F v ~E) / ~C v ~B

Exercise 16.9   These questions allow you to demonstrate your understanding of some of the concepts we have been learning.

1. What do we mean when we say that an argument is a substitution instance of a truth-functionally valid argument form?
2. How would you explain to your neighbor the notion of an argument form?
3. Is it true that every instance of a valid argument form is valid? Explain.
4. In your own words, describe the method of partial truth tables.
5. In your own words, explain the method required to test an argument for validity on a truth table.
6. Suppose all you know is that an argument has inconsistent premises. Is the argument valid or invalid? Or is the answer impossible to determine from the information given? Explain.
7. Is it possible that an argument has inconsistent premises and is sound at the same time? Explain your answer.
8. What is an instance of an argument form?

Glossary

Analytic method A method that involves breaking a subject down into its constituent parts and seeing how those parts fit together to constitute the whole.

Decision procedure (or **algorithm**) A problem-solving method that has the following features: (a) the method has precisely specified steps; (b) following the steps is a matter of following exact rules, requiring no creativity or ingenuity; and (c) the method is guaranteed to give a definite solution in a finite number of those steps.

17 Truth-Table Analysis Part 4 « « « « « « « « « « «

Relations

The Equivalence Test

This is a short chapter. Some teachers will prefer not to cover this chapter—there is never enough time to cover *everything* in life (or in one logic class). Let us begin with the logical relation known as equivalence. Recall from Unit One, Chapter 6, that two sentences are *equivalent* just in case they imply each other. Put another way, two sentences are equivalent if and only if they never differ as far as truth and falsity are concerned. Thus, in all possible circumstances, if one is true, the other will be true, if one is false, the other will be false. Now consider the following two sentences:

1. It is not the case that either Aristo or Blipo is home.
2. Aristo is not home and Blipo is not home.

In TL, these become:

1. ~ (A v B)
2. ~A & ~ B

In Chapter 13 we decided, on a commonsense basis, that these two sentences are equivalent. Now we can show this precisely and formally on a truth table. Let us place both formulas side by side on a single table, and let us fill in the final column for each formula:

~	(A	v	B)		~	A	&	~	B
F	T	T	T		F	T	F	F	T
F	T	T	F		F	T	F	T	F
F	F	T	T		T	F	F	F	T
T	F	F	F		T	F	T	T	F

Notice that these two formulas have identical or matching final columns (columns 1 and 8). That is, on each row, the final values of the two formulas match. Whenever, on a row, one formula computes true, the other on that row also computes true; and whenever on a row one formula computes false, the other on that row computes false as well. When two formulas match in this way, they must be equivalent.

The Equivalence Test

If two formulas on top of a table have matching final columns, then they are equivalent. If the final columns do not match, then the formulas are not equivalent.

The Consistency Test

Recall from Chapter 6 that two sentences are *consistent* if it is possible both are true; they are inconsistent if it is not possible both are true. The truth-table test for consistency suggests itself right away. To test two truth-functional sentences for consistency, place them side by side on a table and fill in the cells row by row. If there is at least one row in which both are true, then the two sentences are consistent. If there is no row in which both are true, then the two sentences are inconsistent.

The Consistency Test

Given two formulas side by side on top of a table: If there is at least one row on which both are true, the two sentences are consistent. If there is no row on which both are true, the two sentences are inconsistent.

The Implication Test

Recall from Chapter 6 that one sentence P *implies* a second sentence Q if and only if it is not possible that P is true when Q is false. The truth-table test for implication could not be more straightforward: To test two truth-functional sentences for implication, place them side by side in a table and fill in the cells row by row. If there is no row on which the first is true and the second is false, then the first implies the second. If there is at least one row on which the first is true and the second is false, then the first does not imply the second.

> ### The Implication Test
>
> Given two formulas side by side on top of a table: If there is no row on which the first is true and the second is false, then the first implies the second. If there is at least one row on which the first is true and the second is false, then the first does not imply the second.

This concludes our application of the method of truth-table analysis to the logical relations. We now have a truth-table test for each of the logical relations defined in Unit One, Chapter 6. The truth-table method is now complete. In the next chapter, we take up the second important method of modern logic, natural deduction. As you will see, whereas truth tables are a "bottom-up" and algorithmic method of evaluation, natural deduction is a "top-down" and nonalgorithmic method. Truth tables are mechanical, but natural deduction is creative, as you will see if you study the next chapter.

Exercise 17.1 Use truth tables to determine, for each of the following pairs of sentences, whether the sentences are equivalent or not equivalent. Note that a comma separates the members of each pair.

1. ~(P v Q) , ~P & ~Q
2. ~ ~P , P
3. ~(P & Q) , ~ P v ~Q
4. ~(P v Q) , ~ P v ~ Q
5. ~(P & Q) , ~ P & ~ Q
6. P v Q , ~ (~ P & ~ Q)
7. ~(P & ~P) , (Q & ~ Q)
8. P & (Q v R) , (P & Q) v (P & R)
9. P ⊃ Q , Q ⊃ P

10. P ⊃ Q , (~Q ⊃ ~P)
11. P ⊃ Q , ~P v Q
12. ~(~ P v Q) , ~ (P & ~ Q)
13. ~(P ⊃ Q) , (~P ⊃ ~Q)
14. P & P , P
15. P v P , P

Exercise 17.2   Use truth tables to determine, for each pair of sentences in Exercise 17.1, whether the sentences are consistent or inconsistent. Note that a comma separates the members of each pair.

Exercise 17.3   Use truth tables to determine, for each pair of sentences in Exercise 17.1, whether the first sentence implies the second sentence or does not imply it.

Exercise 17.4   Using truth tables, determine whether the following pairs of formulas are equivalent or not equivalent:

1. Q ⊃ P   P ≡ (Q v P)
2. Q & P   (Q v P) & (P ⊃ Q)
3. Q v P   ~P ⊃ Q
4. (Q & P)   (Q v P) & (Q ⊃ P)
5. ~(Q & P)   ~Q v ~P
6. ~(Q ⊃ P)   ~Q ⊃ ~P
7. ~(Q v P)   ~Q v ~P
8. ~(Q ≡ P)   ~Q ≡ ~P

Exercise 17.5   Using truth tables, determine whether the formula on the left implies the formula on the right.

1. A   P v ~P
2. P & ~P   E
3. A   (A v P) ⊃ P
4. A ⊃ B   ~B ⊃ ~A
5. A v B   A ⊃ B
6. A ⊃ B   B ⊃ A
7. A ⊃ B   ~A ⊃ ~B
8. A ≡ B   ~A ≡ ~B

Exercise 17.6   True or false?

1. All tautologies are logically equivalent.
2. All contradictions are logically equivalent.
3. All necessary truths are logically equivalent.
4. Any two tautologies are logically consistent.
5. Any two contradictions are logically consistent.
6. Any two contingent statements are logically consistent.
7. Any two contingent statements are logically equivalent.
8. If **P** is a randomly selected tautology, and **Q** is a randomly selected tautology, **P** implies **Q**.

Exercise 17.7   In the previous chapter, we used truth tables to state a formal semantical theory for truth-functional logic . Our theory covered the logical properties of sentences (tautology, contradiction, and contingency) and the logical properties of arguments (validity and invalidity). Complete the theory by specifying semantical clauses for the relations, that is, for truth-functional consistency, inconsistency, implication, and equivalence.

18 Modern Truth-Functional Natural Deduction Part 1 « « « « ‹

The First Four Rules

The discovery of truth-functions and the construction of a system of logic based on that discovery was not the only accomplishment of the Stoics during the third century BC. As noted in Chapter 11, the Stoic logicians also pioneered a new method of logical proof, a method known today as **natural deduction**. The previous three chapters covered truth-table analysis. Natural deduction is a completely different method of logical demonstration. What exactly is natural deduction? Like almost everything else in logic, the explanation begins with careful definitions.

First, to *deduce* something is to conclude it on the basis of something else. For example, I see the dog pawing at the door, and I deduce that he wants to go outside. Second, you *infer* something, or draw an inference, when you reason to something on the basis of something else. For example, I hear a siren and infer that an emergency vehicle is approaching. Sometimes in everyday life, we arrive at a conclusion after making a series of step-by-step deductions. As you will see, natural deduction is a very similar process.

An **inference rule** is a rule telling you how to make an inference of a certain type. An **inference** always starts with one or more statements and stops at a single statement. Essentially, an inference rule states that from one or more statements of such and such a logical form, you may infer a corresponding statement of thus and so a form. The statements you start with are the *premises* of the inference; the statement you stop with is the *conclusion* of the inference.

An inference is a **valid inference** just in case any argument formed out of its premises and conclusion is a valid argument. Thus, in the case of a valid inference, if the premises of the inference are true, then the conclusion of the inference must be true. A **valid inference rule** has the following feature: When the rule is followed correctly, the result is always a valid inference. Thus, if an inference follows a valid inference rule, the conclusion of the inference must be true if the premise or premises of the inference all are true.

With these definitions in place, natural deduction can now be defined as a method of proof in which the conclusion of an argument is deduced from its premises via a series of inferences in such a way that each inference follows a specified rule of inference. A *natural deduction proof* for an argument is a sequence of statements, each of which is either a premise of the argument to be proved or follows from a premise of the argument via a rule of inference, or follows from one or more previous statements in the sequence via a rule of inference, with the last step in the sequence being the conclusion of the argument.

Why Is It Called Natural Deduction?

The method gets its name from the fact that it involves *deducing* a conclusion from a set of premises in a step-by-step fashion using certain *natural* patterns of reasoning. The patterns of reasoning in a natural deduction proof are "natural" in the sense that they resemble forms of reasoning we routinely make in everyday life without any special training in logical theory. An argument is given later for the following proposition: If a natural deduction proof exists for an argument, and the inference rules used are all valid rules of inference, then the argument must be valid.

Review: What Is a Logical Form?

The notion of logical form is a prerequisite for any understanding of natural deduction, and so a brief review might be helpful. What do the following sentences have in common?

1. Ann is home or Bob is home.
2. Joe jogs or Fred swims.
3. Betty swims or Jan swims.

These sentences share a common structure, namely, each is a disjunction. This common structure is called the *logical form* of the sentences. It is customary to represent it by writing:

$$\mathbf{P} \vee \mathbf{Q}$$

where **P** is a variable standing in for the left disjunct and **Q** is a variable standing in for the right disjunct. (We are following a long-established convention of using boldfaced capital letters as variables.) The expression **P v Q** is the logical form of the three sentences, and each of the three sentences is said to be a *substitution* *instance* of that form. The form describes the structure shared in common by the three instances.

Recall that an English sentence is a **substitution instance** of a logical form if the sentence can be generated from the form by substituting English sentences for the variables in the form and by replacing the connectives in the form with their English counterparts, making no other changes. For example, starting with the form **P v Q**, we replace **P** with the sentence "Ann is home," we replace v with *or*, and we replace **Q** with the sentence "Bob is home." This generates "Ann is home or Bob is home" and shows that the English sentence is a substitution instance of the form. More loosely, we can simply say that an instance "fits" its form. Notice that the logical form is "all form and no content." That is, it is an abstract structure that many different sentences, about many different subject matters, might instantiate or "fit."

Finally, an already symbolized English sentence, such as A v B, is a substitution instance of a form if the symbolized sentence can be generated from the form by replacing the variables in the form with symbolized sentences, making no other changes. For example, starting with the form **P v Q**, if we replace **P** with A and **Q** with B, then the resulting formula, A v B, is a substitution instance of the form **P v Q**. We are now ready for the inference rules that will form the heart of our system.

Modus Ponens

The first inference rule of our system was also the first rule of the original Stoic system. During the Middle Ages, logicians in the cathedral schools of Europe named this rule modus ponens (Latin for "method of affirmation"), and the medieval name is universally recognized by logicians today. You will probably notice that this rule conforms to the modus ponens form of argument introduced in Chapter 11. Here is one way to put the rule:

The Modus Ponens Rule (MP)

Where **P** and **Q** are variables ranging over declarative sentences:

1. Given a compound sentence of the form **P ⊃ Q**
2. Given the corresponding sentence **P**
3. You may infer the corresponding sentence **Q**

In English, suppose you are given some information in the form of a conditional sentence and then some additional information that is the antecedent of that conditional. From this you may infer the consequent of the conditional. For example, to go back to a Stoic context, suppose you are given the following two items of information:

1. If Aristo swims, then Blipo swims.
2. Aristo swims.

Modus ponens says that from these two lines of information you may deduce:

3. Blipo swims.

Notice that line 1 is a conditional sentence of the form **P ⊃ Q** and line 2 is the *antecedent* (the **P** part) of that conditional. Lines 1 and 2 of this inference thus correspond to the first two lines of the MP rule. The third line, "Blipo swims," corresponds to the conclusion of the rule, the inference to **Q**. Here is an example in TL:

1. Given: A ⊃ B
2. Given: A
3. Infer: B

In this case, the A ⊃ B on line 1 is an instance of the form **P ⊃ Q**, sentence A on line 2 corresponds to the **P** part of the **P ⊃ Q**, and sentence B on line 3 corresponds to the **Q** part of the **P ⊃ Q**.

Here are additional English-language applications of the MP rule:

Given: If Ann swims then Bob swims.
Given: Ann swims.
Infer: Bob swims.

Given: If Joe jogs then Kit will jog.
Given: Joe jogs.
Infer: Kit will jog.

Here are additional TL applications of the MP rule:

Given:	A ⊃ B	Given:	J ⊃ L	Given:	(A v B) ⊃ (L & H)
Given:	A	Given:	J	Given:	(A v B)
Infer:	B	Infer:	L	Infer:	L & H

Given:	~E ⊃ ~K	Given:	~O ⊃ (A & B)
Given:	~E	Given:	~O
Infer:	~K	Infer:	A & B

It is important to understand that the order in which the two premises appear does not affect the validity of the inference. This is an implicit assumption of each inference rule. Thus, the following are also correct applications of MP, even though the order in which the premises appear is different:

Given: A   Given: J
Given: A ⊃ B   Given: J ⊃ L
Infer: B   Infer: L

Before you move on, make sure you see why each of these is a proper application of the MP rule. We can abbreviate this rule as shown here.

The Modus Ponens Rule (Abbreviation)

P ⊃ Q
P
Infer Q

Using Modus Ponens to Prove an Argument Valid

Let us now use modus ponens to prove an argument valid. This will be our first natural deduction proof. Consider the following argument:

1. If Aristo swims, Blipo will swim.
2. If Blipo swims, Crisco will swim.
3. If Crisco swims, Delpho will swim.
4. But Aristo will swim.
5. Therefore, Delpho will swim.

Here is the abbreviation in TL:

1. A ⊃ B
2. B ⊃ C
3. C ⊃ D
4. A / D

The slash (/) shall mean "therefore" and indicates the conclusion of the argument. Thus, the numbered statements preceding the slash are the abbreviated premises and the sentence after the slash is the conclusion (abbreviated). This is a valid argument, although it might not be obvious that it is valid. Let's prove it.

We begin by looking for a pattern that corresponds to our rule. Look at lines 1 and 4. Bracket out the other lines and look only at 1 and 4:

1. A ⊃ B
4. A

These two lines correspond to the two premises of the modus ponens rule. The rule tells us that from two lines of information such as these, we can infer B. Thus, we apply the modus ponens rule to lines 1 and 4 and infer, from this information, B. In other words, we deduce B from If A ⊃ B and from A. To record our deduction, underneath line 4 we add this line:

5. B   MP 1, 4

The information written to the right of our inference ("MP 1, 4") is called the **justification** of the inference. The justification states the rule that was used and the lines the rule was applied to when deducing B on line 5. The justification says this: To deduce line 5 we applied the MP rule to lines 1 and 4. Here is another way to put it: The justification says, "We inferred line 5 on the basis of the MP rule applied to lines 1 and 4." Because MP is a valid rule of inference, this is a solid basis indeed.

Next, again looking for patterns that correspond to our rule, we notice that lines 2 and 5 also match the first two lines of the MP rule. Look at lines 2 and 5 alone:

2. B ⊃ C
5. B

In this case, MP tells us that from two lines like this, we can infer C. Following dutifully in the footsteps of the Stoics, we apply MP to lines 2 and 5 and deduce:

6. C   MP 2, 5

Again, the information to the right of the inference is the justification for the inference. The justification says this: We applied MP to lines 2 and 5, and that is why we inferred C on line 6. Next, looking for patterns that correspond to our rule, we see that modus ponens can be applied to lines 3 and 6. From lines 3 and 6 alone we deduce D, following MP strictly:

7. D   MP 3, 6

But this letter, D, is the conclusion of the argument. (Remember that the conclusion is the formula following the slanted slash.) Our proof is thus complete. Let us line up all our ducks in a row now:

1. A ⊃ B
2. B ⊃ C
3. C ⊃ D
4. A   / D
5. B   MP 1, 4
6. C   MP 2, 5
7. D   MP 3, 6

Look what we have done. We deduced the conclusion of the argument, namely, D, from the premises, namely, lines 1 through 4, by applying a valid rule of inference (modus ponens) at each step. This proves that the argument is valid.

Why This Proves Validity

Here is why our step-by-step deduction proves that the argument is valid. Recall that when you make an inference in accord with a valid rule of inference, that which you deduce must be true if what you applied the rule to is true. It follows that if the four premises all are true, then line 5 must be true (because it follows by a valid rule of inference from two of the premises, namely, lines 1 and 4 alone). But if lines 1 through 5 are all true, then line 6 must be true (because it follows by a valid rule of inference from lines 2 and 5 alone). But if line 6 is true, then line 7 must be true (as it follows by a valid rule of inference from lines 3 and 6). But line 7 is the conclusion of the argument. It follows that if the premises are all true, then the conclusion *must* be true. But this is just another way of saying that the argument is valid! Thus, the *prime principle of natural deduction*:

> If you deduce the conclusion of an argument from its premises, using only valid rules of inference, then the argument must be valid.

So, to recap: A natural deduction proof begins by listing the premises and the conclusion of an argument, with the premises numbered and the conclusion separated from the premises by a slanted slash. The conclusion is deduced from the premises step by step, by applying one or more rules of inference to the premises and usually also to information derived from the premises. Once the conclusion is deduced, the proof is complete. The conclusion of the argument is always the last line of a successful natural deduction proof.

Caution: Do Not Confuse MP with Affirming the Consequent!

When you apply MP to two lines of information to derive a third line, it is very important that the two lines correspond *exactly* to the requirements of the MP rule. This means that one *whole* line must be a conditional, and one *whole* line must be the *antecedent* of that conditional. The rules of a natural deduction system are supposed to be applied exactly as stated, for the goal of a natural deduction system is a precise and gap-free system of logical deduction. That goal will not be met unless the rules are applied exactly as they are intended. The following application of the MP rule is backward and consequently does not count as a correct application:

From:

1. If the teacher is sick, class is canceled.
2. Class is canceled.

We infer:

3. Therefore, the teacher is sick.

Abbreviated, this is:

1. $T \supset C$
2. C

Therefore:

3. T

This is not the modus ponens pattern! Do you see why it is not? This last argument is invalid; indeed, you probably noticed that it is an instance of the fallacy identified in Chapter 11 as affirming the consequent. Modus ponens cannot be correctly applied to the two lines immediately preceding, namely, $T \supset C$ and C. The rule simply does not apply in a situation like that.

Modus Tollens

The second rule of our system is the second rule of the original Stoic system. During the Middle Ages, this rule was named modus tollens (Latin for "method of denial"), and it is universally recognized by that name today. You will probably notice that it conforms to the modus tollens form of argument introduced in Chapter 11. Here is one way to put the second Stoic inference rule:

Where **P** and **Q** are variables ranging over declarative sentences:

1. Given a compound sentence of the form **P ⊃ Q**
2. Given the corresponding sentence ~**Q**
3. You may infer the corresponding sentence ~**P**.

In English, suppose you are given information in the form of a conditional sentence, and additional information that is the negation of the consequent of the conditional. From this you may validly infer the negation of the antecedent of the conditional. For example, suppose you are given the following information:

1. If it is spring, the songs of the birds fill the air.
2. It is not the case that the songs of the birds fill the air.

Modus tollens says that from these two lines of information you may infer:

3. It is not the case that it is spring.

Notice that line 1 is a conditional sentence, and line 2 is the negation of the consequent of that conditional. Lines 1 and 2 of this inference thus correspond to the first two lines of the MT rule, and the third line corresponds to the rule's concluding line. Here are further English-language instances, or applications, of the rule:

Given: If Ann swims then Bob swims.
Given: It is not the case that Bob swims.
Infer: It is not the case that Ann swims.

Given: If Joe jogs then Kit will jog.
Given: It is not the case that Kit jogs.
Infer: It is not the case that Joe jogs.

And here are some symbolic applications:

Given: A ⊃ B   Given: J ⊃ L
Given: ~B   Given: ~L
Infer: ~A   Infer: ~J

Given:	~E ⊃ ~K	Given:	~O ⊃ (A & B)
Given:	~ ~K	Given:	~(A & B)
Infer:	~ ~E	Infer:	~ ~O

Again, the order in which the premises appear does not affect the validity of the inference. Thus, the following are also correct applications of the MT rule:

Given:	~B	Given:	~L	Given:	~(J v K)
Given:	A ⊃ B	Given:	J ⊃ L	Given:	(G &O) ⊃ (J v K)
Infer:	~A	Infer:	~J	Infer:	~(G &O)

Before you move on, make sure you see why each of these is a proper application of the MT rule. We can abbreviate MT as shown next.

The Modus Tollens Rule (Abbreviation)

P ⊃ Q
~Q
Infer ~P

Caution. It is important that you apply MT correctly. The following is an incorrect application of the rule:

From:

1. If Ann is swimming, then Bob is swimming.
2. It is not the case that Ann is swimming.

Infer:

3. Bob is not swimming.

Abbreviated, this is:

1. A ⊃ B
2. ~ A

Infer:

3. ~ B

Can you explain why this inference is *not* a correct application of MT? Perhaps you recognize this pattern of reasoning from Chapter 11. It is an instance of the fallacy of denying the antecedent. MT is a valid rule of inference, but denying the antecedent is an *invalid* argument form. Be careful not to confuse the two!

Putting MT to Work

Let us now put modus tollens to work proving an argument valid. Consider the following argument:

1. If Aristo swims, Blipo will swim.
2. If Blipo swims, Crisco will swim.
3. If Crisco swims, Delpho will swim.
4. But it is not the case that Delpho will swim.
5. Therefore, it is not the case that Aristo will swim.

In TL:

1. $A \supset B$
2. $B \supset C$
3. $C \supset D$
4. $\sim D$ / $\sim A$

We begin by looking for the MT pattern. Look closely at lines 3 and 4. Ignore the other lines and focus only on these two lines:

3. $C \supset D$
4. $\sim D$

Do you see that these two lines correspond exactly to the first two lines of the modus tollens rule? The rule tells us that from two lines of information such as these, we can infer $\sim C$. Being dutiful Stoics, we apply modus tollens to lines 3 and 4 and infer, from this information, $\sim C$. In other words, we deduce $\sim C$ from $C \supset D$ and from $\sim D$. To record our deduction, underneath line 4 we add this line to the proof:

5. $\sim C$ MT 3, 4

The justification says: To deduce line 5, we applied the MT rule to lines 3 and 4. In other words, we inferred line 5 on the basis of the MT rule applied to lines 3 and 4. Because MT is a valid rule of inference, our inference is a valid one.

Next, look at lines 2 and 5:

2. B ⊃ C
5. ~ C

These two lines also correspond to the premise section of MT. In this case, MT tells us that from two lines like this, we can infer Not B. Thus, applying MT to lines 2 and 5, we deduce line 6:

6. ~ B   MT 2, 5

Next, notice that modus tollens can be applied to lines 1 and 6, for those two lines, by themselves, match the first two lines of the MT rule. Thus, from lines 1 and 6 alone we deduce ~A, following the MT rule:

7. ~ A   MT 1, 6

We have deduced the conclusion of the argument. Our proof is complete:

1. A ⊃ B
2. B ⊃ C
3. C ⊃ D
4. ~ D   / ~ A
5. ~ C   MT 3, 4
6. ~ B   MT 2, 5
7. ~ A   MT 1, 6

Follow the Rules!

It is important to keep in mind that the inference rules of a natural deduction system must be followed exactly as they are written. The user cannot change the rules, add to them, or invent new rules. The rules must be followed to the letter. The reason for such a strict "attitude" has to do with the goal of natural deduction: The goal is a system of thought that has two properties: (a) it is completely "gap-free," and (b) it is completely and precisely "rule-governed." In such a system, no gaps in the reasoning occur, and nothing takes place that does not exactly and precisely follow an articulated rule. In this way, no mistakes are possible if the system is followed correctly.

The following inference follows the modus tollens rule *exactly*:

From: ~A ⊃ ~B
From: <u>~~B</u>
Infer: ~~A

And there are no gaps in the reasoning either. However, although the following is a case of valid reasoning, the inference *violates* the modus tollens rule:

From: ~A ⊃ ~B
From: B
Infer: A

This inference violates the rule because it does not follow the rule exactly and strictly as the rule is written. Again for emphasis, this last inference happens to be a valid inference, but it is illegal in our system and is not allowed because it does not follow the rule. Here is the bottom line: The rules of a natural deduction system are to be followed as precisely and as faithfully as one follows the rules of arithmetic!

History Note

Modus ponens and modus tolllens can be found in the works of the fourteenth-century English philosopher and logician William of Ockham (1285–1349).

Disjunctive Syllogism

This inference rule did not actually appear in the original Stoic system, although the Stoics had a rule that was very similar. The disjunctive syllogism rule was added to the system sometime during succeeding centuries.

The Disjunctive Syllogism Rule (DS)

Where **P** and **Q** are variables ranging over declarative sentences:

1. Given a compound sentence of the form **P** v **Q**
2. Given the corresponding sentence ~ **P**
3. You may infer the corresponding sentence **Q**.

And:

1. Given a compound sentence of the form **P** v **Q**
2. Given the corresponding sentence ~ **Q**
3. You may infer the corresponding sentence **P**.

In English, suppose you are given some information in the form of a disjunction and then some additional information that is the negation of one of the disjuncts. From this you can validly infer the other disjunct. For instance, suppose you are given the following information:

1. Dinner will be hot dogs or dinner will be burgers.
2. Dinner will not be hot dogs.

Disjunctive syllogism says that from these two lines of information you can infer:

3. Therefore, dinner will be burgers.

This is self-evidently valid reasoning. Notice that line 1 is a disjunction, and line 2 is the negation of the left disjunct of the disjunction. Lines 1 and 2 of this inference thus correspond to the first two lines of the DS rule, whereas the third line matches the rule's conclusion.

This rule can be applied from either side, so to speak:

1. Dinner will be hot dogs or dinner will be burgers.
2. But dinner will not be *burgers*.
3. Therefore, dinner *will* be hot dogs.

Here are some English examples:

Given: We shall eat hamburgers or we shall eat hot dogs.
Given: It is not the case that we will eat hamburgers.
Infer: We will eat hot dogs.

Given: We will swim or we will jog.
Given: It is not the case that we will jog.
Infer: We will swim.

Here are some TL instances of this pattern of reasoning:

Given:	A v B	Given:	E v B	Given:	A v B	
Given:	~A	Given:	~E	Given:	~B	
Infer:	B	Infer:	B	Infer:	A	

Given:	O v ~W	Given:	~M v ~D	Given:	D v L	
Given:	~O	Given:	~ ~M	Given:	~L	
Infer:	~W	Infer:	~D	Infer:	D	

We can abbreviate this rule as follows:

The Disjunctive Syllogism Rule (Abbreviation)

P v Q		P v Q
~P	and	~Q
Infer Q		Infer P

The Tale of Chrysippus's Dog

Chrysippus, the third head of the Stoa and the greatest logician of antiquity after Aristotle, noted that even his dog follows the disjunctive syllogism rule. According to legend, Chrysippus was watching his dog chase a rabbit down a trail. When the trail forked in two directions, the dog took the first fork. After finding no scent, the animal immediately came back and raced full speed down the second path, proving that even a dog knows the DS rule.

Putting Disjunctive Syllogism to Work

The following abbreviated argument is valid:

1. $A \supset B$
2. $\sim B$
3. $A \vee C$
4. $C \supset \sim H / \sim H$

However, there might be those who doubt. The proof follows. Looking for patterns that match our rules, lines 1 and 2 immediately catch our attention. This is the MT pattern. Applying MT to lines 1 and 2 allows us to deduce the following line:

5. $\sim A$ MT 1, 2

The next pattern that jumps out is the similarity between lines 3 and 5 and DS. Do you see that lines 3 and 5 match the premise section of our new rule, DS? In this case, DS tells us that from lines 3 and 5 we can infer:

6. C   DS 3, 5

Finally, we notice that lines 4 and 6 instantiate the MP pattern. Applying MP to these two lines, we validly infer:

7. $\sim H$ MP 4, 6

Because this is the conclusion of the argument, our proof is complete. The argument has been proved valid.

Hypothetical Syllogism

Also given its current name during the Middle Ages, this was the third Stoic inference rule. Here is one way to express the hypothetical syllogism rule:

The Hypothetical Syllogism Rule (HS)

Where **P** and **Q** are variables ranging over declarative sentences:

1. Given a compound sentence of the form **P ⊃ Q**
2. Given the corresponding sentence **Q ⊃ R**
3. You may infer the corresponding sentence **P ⊃ R**.

For example:

Given: If Ann swims, then Bob swims.
Given: If Bob swims, then Jan will swim.
Infer: If Ann swims, then Jan will swim.

Given: If Joe is fired, then Sue will quit.
Given: If Sue quits, then Ned will bellow like an ox.
Infer: If Joe is fired, then Ned will bellow like an ox.

Given:	A ⊃ M	Given:	H ⊃ L	Given:	A ⊃ (B & C)	
Given:	M ⊃ K	Given:	L ⊃ O	Given:	(B & C) ⊃ E	
Infer:	A ⊃ K	Infer:	H ⊃ O	Infer:	A ⊃ E	

Given:	~A ⊃ ~M	Given:	~O ⊃ ~U	Given:	(A ⊃B) ⊃ X	
Given:	~M ⊃ ~K	Given:	~U ⊃ ~I	Given:	X ⊃ (H ⊃ N)	
Infer:	~A ⊃ ~K	Infer:	~O ⊃ ~I	Infer:	(A ⊃B) ⊃ (H ⊃ N)	

Because the order in which the premises appear does not affect the validity of the inference, the following also exactly follow the HS rule:

Given:	M ⊃ K	Given:	L ⊃ O
Given:	A ⊃ M	Given:	H ⊃ L
Infer:	A ⊃ K	Infer:	H ⊃ O

Make sure you understand why each of these is a correct application of HS before moving on. We can abbreviate this rule as follows:

The Hypothetical Syllogism Rule (Abbreviation)

$$P \supset Q$$
$$Q \supset R$$
$$\text{Infer } P \supset R$$

The following short proof employs only one rule, HS:

1. $A \supset B$
2. $B \supset C$
3. $C \supset D$
4. $D \supset E / A \supset E$
5. $A \supset C$ HS 1, 2
6. $A \supset D$ HS 5, 3
7. $A \supset E$ HS 6, 4

Putting the Rules to Work

Let us now put all our rules to work. Consider the following English argument:

1. If Ann swims, then Bob will swim.
2. If Bob swims, then it is not the case that Ed will swim.
3. If it is not the case that Ed will swim, then it is not the case that Joe will swim.
4. Ann will swim.
5. Either Joe will swim or it is not the case that Dave will swim.
6. If Kit swims, then Dave will swim.
7. Therefore, Kit will not swim.

Translated into TL, using obvious abbreviations, this becomes:

1. $A \supset B$
2. $B \supset {\sim}E$
3. ${\sim}E \supset {\sim}J$
4. A
5. $J \vee {\sim}D$
6. $K \supset D / {\sim}K$

The conclusion of this argument can now be "deduced" from the premises using the rules of inference introduced above.

Step 1. We begin by surveying the premises of the argument. We are looking for two premises that are structured in such a way that one of our inference rules would apply. We survey only the premises, not the conclusion: We do not want to apply a rule to the conclusion, for the conclusion is what we aim to eventually deduce from the premises. We are working with four inference rules, each of which applies to two specifically structured statements, so we are looking for two premises that instantiate, or "fit," one of our inference rule patterns.

Looking at premises 1 and 2, we see that they correspond to the pattern in the hypothetical syllogism rule. That is, the HS rule can be applied to these two statements and once applied allows us to infer a further statement. For the A ⊃ B on line 1 corresponds to the **P ⊃ Q** part of HS, and the B ⊃ ~E on line 2 corresponds to the **Q ⊃ R** part of the HS rule. HS says to infer from this the formula **P ⊃ R**, that is, the formula composed by writing the **P** part, then a horseshoe, then the **R** part. Thus, from lines 1 and 2:

1. A ⊃ B
2. B ⊃ ~E

HS allows us to deduce:

$$A \supset \sim E$$

Step 2. This first inference is recorded on the line below the premises, and its justification is written to the right, like this:

1. A ⊃ B
2. B ⊃ ~E
3. ~E ⊃~J
4. A
5. J v ~D
6. K ⊃D / ~K
7. A ⊃~E   HS 1, 2

The nice thing about a system of natural deduction is that every movement of thought is explained and justified. If someone wonders how an inference was made, or where it came from, the justification answers the question and logically justifies the "move." Have you ever been in an argument with someone when they made a wild statement, and you wondered, "Where did that come from?" This cannot happen in natural deduction!

Step 3. Looking at lines 3 and 7, we see that the HS rule can be applied again, this time to lines 3 and 7, which allows us to add the following inference to the sequence:

8. A ⊃ ~J   HS 7, 3

Next, we see that the MP rule can be applied to lines 4 and 8, which allows us to add the following inference to the line:

9. ~J   MP 4, 8

Next, looking at lines 5 and 9, we see that the DS rule can be applied, which allows us to make the following inference:

10. ~D   DS 5, 9

Next, we see that the modus tollens rule can be applied to lines 6 and 10:

11. ~K   MT 6, 10

Notice that this formula is the conclusion of the argument. Look what we have done. We deduced the conclusion of the argument from the premises, using the rules of inference and nothing more. In other words, we derived the conclusion by applying the inference rules to only the premises of the argument. For reasons that have already been given, this proves that the argument is *valid*. Our full proof looks like this:

1. A ⊃ B
2. B ⊃ ~E
3. ~E ⊃ ~ J
4. A
5. J v ~D
6. K ⊃ D / ~K
7. A ⊃ ~E   HS 1, 2
8. A ⊃ ~J   HS 7, 3
9. ~J   MP 4, 8
10. ~D   DS 5, 9
11. ~K   MT 6, 10

The next proof is different from the proof above, and yet it proves the same argument valid. This illustrates the fact that in all but the simplest cases, there is more than one way to construct a proof of an argument's validity:

1. A ⊃ B
2. B ⊃ ~E
3. ~E ⊃ ~J
4. A
5. J v ~D
6. K ⊃ D / ~K
7. B   MP 1, 4
8. ~E   MP 7, 2
9. ~J   MP 3, 8
10. ~D   DS 5, 9
11. ~K   MT 6, 10

Many Different Paths, One Ultimate Destination

This last point needs emphasis. In all but the simplest cases, there are many different ways to build a proof and prove an argument valid. One proof proceeds in one order, using this rule and that rule, whereas another proof builds in a completely different order, using different rules; yet both proofs reach the same conclusion in the end. As long as each proof follows the rules correctly, and as long as each proof reaches the conclusion in the end, both proofs *equally* prove the argument valid. Both win! Rarely is there ever just one correct way to build a proof.

You know that the ancient Stoic philosophers are the founders of truth-functional logic. Have you been wondering what else they discovered? What other ideas were contained in their philosophy? Here is the core of the Stoic philosophy in a nutshell: Plain observation reveals that the universe (Greek: *cosmos*) is an extremely complex, yet orderly, whole. What holds the cosmos together and keeps the parts all functioning smoothly? The best explanation for all of this (according to the Stoic argument) is the following hypothesis: An all-pervasive cosmic force organizes and balances everything in the universe according to a rational plan. Since it holds everything in balance according to a rational plan, this force is not mere raw power; it is rational in nature. Indeed, holding things in order according to a rational plan is just the sort of thing a rational mind does. This being is therefore a divine, reasoning intelligence. This is the *Logos* (Greek: reason) of the universe. Stoic ethics begins with the claim that each person, insofar as he or she is a rational being, contains a spark of the universal Logos. Furthermore, this spark of the divine is the basis of the *equal* dignity and *equal* intrinsic value of each individual. The Stoics were the first philosophers in history to argue for something closely resembling the modern idea of universal human rights. Finally, according to the Stoic argument, we find our natural place in the whole of what exists when we bring our wills into conformity with divine reason by using our own reason, our own spark of the divine, as best we can. The morally best life to live is thus to know what the Logos requires and then to conform our life to *that*. What a fascinating philosophy of life or worldview! Even more interesting are the complex arguments the Stoic logicians gave supporting their worldview.

The Stoics saw the emotions or passions (anger, sadness, happiness, etc.) and the appetites (desire for food, sex, etc.) as irrational, unruly, and potentially destructive forces in the soul that as often as not may be at war with what reason requires. Reason was thought to be special and preeminent on the grounds that it is the only part of the soul capable of criticizing and correcting both itself and the other parts in light of real truth. Being able to reason well, calmly and coolly, without distraction, was thus an essential part of the Stoic conception of the good life, or the morally best life a person might lead. This explains why the Stoics took logic class so seriously. Logic was not a mere academic exercise: It was the mental skill at the heart of living the best life possible. The character we all know as Spock, from the original *Star Trek* series of the 1960s, was modeled on the Stoic ideal. Watch Spock on any of the old episodes to see how a true Stoic sage would conduct himself if he were to be stationed on the starship USS *Enterprise* alongside Captain James T. Kirk . . . in the twenty-third century AD.

Definitions Again

A **natural deduction system** consists of two parts:

1. A formal logical language into which natural language arguments are translated.
2. Rules of inference, all of which are valid.

A valid argument in a natural language is proved valid within a system of natural deduction in two steps. First, the argument is translated into the formal logical language of the system. Second, the rules of the system are applied and a natural deduction proof of validity is constructed.

A **proof in a natural deduction system** is a sequence of statements in the formal language of the system, each of which is either a designated premise or follows from one or more premises in the sequence or follows from one or more previous statements in the sequence, by a deduction rule of the system, and in which the last statement in the sequence is designated the conclusion.

The name of our natural deduction system is **TD** (for "truth-functional deduction"). TD includes the language TL and all the truth-functional rules of deduction contained in this text.

Advice When Learning to Construct Proofs

Here is some advice when you are learning to construct proofs of validity for truth-functional arguments:

1. You have many examples of completed proofs. Study the examples and make sure you understand clearly each step in each sample proof.
2. When you begin a proof, scan the argument, looking for patterns in the premises corresponding to the patterns in the inference rules.
3. When you see a pattern in the premises corresponding to an inference rule, it is recommended that you make the inference per the appropriate rule, even if you are not sure where it will take you.
4. Practice makes perfect. The more proofs you try, the faster you get, and the better you get as well.
5. It is not required that you use every available inference rule in every proof. In other words, some proofs do not require using every available inference rule. Some proofs might require using only one rule!
6. It is not required that you use every premise in every proof, that is, that you apply inference rules to every premise. Some proofs do not use every premise; sometimes a premise is superfluous information not needed for the proof of validity. Some proofs might require using only one of the premises!

Examples of Things You *Cannot* Do with the Inference Rules

Each of the following inferences is an illegal application of one of the inference rules:

Given: A ⊃ B

Given: B

Infer: A   By MP (illegal)

Comment. Illegal! You cannot apply MP this way. This is an incorrect, backward application of the MP rule. This is an invalid inference! (Recall that this is an instance of the formal logical fallacy known as affirming the consequent.)

Given: A ⊃ B

Given: ~A

Infer: ~B   By MT (illegal)

Comment. Illegal move. You cannot apply MT this way because this does not follow the rule. This is also an invalid inference. (Recall that this is an instance of the formal logical fallacy known as denying the antecedent.)

Given: E ⊃ ~K

Given: K

Infer: ~E   By MT (illegal)

Comment. Illegal move. You cannot apply MT this way because this does not follow the rule exactly as the rule is written. MT requires that the second "given," the ~**Q** part, be *exactly* like the **Q** part of the If P then Q, except that it has a tilde added. These rules must be followed exactly as they are written; no alterations are allowed.

Given: A ⊃ B

Given: B ⊃ C

Infer: C ⊃ A   By HS (illegal)

Comment. Illegal move. You cannot apply HS this way because this does not follow the rule. This is an illegal, backward application of the rule. This would also be an invalid inference!

Given: A ⊃ B

Given: A ⊃ C

Infer: B ⊃ C   By HS (illegal)

Comment. Illegal move. You cannot apply HS this way because this does not follow the rule. In addition, of course, this would be an invalid inference.

Given: A v B

Given: ~A

Infer: ~B   By DS (illegal)

Comment. Illegal. This does not follow the DS rule. In addition, of course, this would be an invalid inference.

Given: A v B

Given: ~B

Infer: ~A   By DS (illegal)

Comment. Illegal. This does not follow the DS rule. In addition, of course, this would be an invalid inference.

Given: ~A v B

Given: A

Infer: B   By DS (illegal)

Comment. Illegal. This does not follow the DS rule. One must follow the inference rules exactly as they are written. One line must be the *negation* of the left disjunct of the other line. The negation of ~A would be ~~A.

Exercise 18.1   In each proof that follows, the conclusion is the formula following the slanted slash mark and the premises are the formulas appearing prior to the conclusion. These proofs are complete except that the justifications for the derived lines have not been filled in. Using the first four rules, supply a justification for each derived line by filling in the appropriate rules and line numbers.

1.
   1.   J ⊃ (I & R)
   2.   (I & R) ⊃ S
   3.   (J ⊃ S) ⊃ ~G
   4.   G v H / H
   5.   J ⊃ S
   6.   ~G
   7.   H

2.
   1.   J v ~(I v R)
   2.   S ⊃ ~J

3. H v S
4. ~H
5. ~(I v R) ⊃ A   / A
6. S
7. ~J
8. ~(I v R)
9. A

3.
 1. J ⊃ (S & I)
 2. ~ J ⊃ (B v R)
 3. ~ (S & I)
 4. (B v R) ⊃ (I v H) / I v H
 5. ~ J
 6. B v R
 7. I v H

4.
 1. S v ~ (H & S)
 2. S ⊃ G
 3. J ⊃ ~G
 4. M ⊃ (H & S)
 5. J / ~ M
 6. ~G
 7. ~ S
 8. ~ (H & S)
 9. ~ M

5.
 1. (H & S) ⊃ ~ (F v G)
 2. M v (H & S)
 3. M ⊃ R
 4. ~ R   / ~ (F v G)
 5. ~ M
 6. H & S
 7. ~ (F v G)

6.
 1. (H & G) ⊃ (F ⊃ R)
 2. J & I

   3.   A v ~ (F ⊃ R)

   4.   ~A / ~ (H & G)

   5.   ~ (F ⊃ R)

   6.   ~ (H & G)

7.

   1.   ~ H v ~ Z

   2.   ~ (S ≡ G) ⊃ (F v S)

   3.   ~ ~ H

   4.   ~ (F v S) ⊃ Z / ~ ~ (F v S)

   5.   ~ Z

   6.   ~ ~ (F v S)

8.

   1.   A ⊃ (J v S)

   2.   B ⊃ ~ J

   3.   S ⊃ (G ⊃ H)

   4.   H ⊃ R

   5.   A

   6.   B / G ⊃ R

   7.   J v S

   8.   ~ J

   9.   S

 10.   G ⊃ H

 11.   G ⊃ R

9.

   1.   (A & B) ⊃ ~ S

   2.   A & B

   3.   S v [H ⊃ (F ⊃ M)]

   4.   ~ M

   5.   H / ~ F

   6.   ~ S

   7.   H ⊃ (F ⊃ M)

   8.   F ⊃ M

   9.   ~ F

10.

   1.   ~ A

   2.   ~ A ⊃ [~ A ⊃ (E ⊃ A)] / ~ E

3. ~ A ⊃ (E ⊃ A)
4. E ⊃ A
5. ~ E

11.
1. A ⊃ B
2. B ⊃ R
3. (A ⊃ R) ⊃ G / G
4. A ⊃ R
5. G

12.
1. J
2. ~ G
3. J ⊃ (A ⊃ ~ B)
4. G v (~ B ⊃ E) / A ⊃ E
5. A ⊃ ~ B
6. ~ B ⊃ E
7. A ⊃ E

13.
1. (A & B) v (E ⊃ S)
2. G ⊃ E
3. ~ (A & B) / G ⊃ S
4. E ⊃ S
5. G ⊃ S

14.
1. A v E
2. ~ A
3. E ⊃ [~ A ⊃ (E ⊃ S)] / ·S
4. E
5. ~ A ⊃ (E ⊃ S)
6. E ⊃ S
7. S

15.
1. (S & E) ⊃ ~ G
2. H ⊃ (S & E)
3. (H ⊃ ~ G) ⊃ ~ R
4. ~ B ⊃ R / ~ ~ B

5. H ⊃ ~ G
6. ~ R
7. ~ ~ B

16.
1. H ⊃ S
2. S ⊃ ~ R
3. ~ B ⊃ F
4. (H ⊃ ~ R) ⊃ (L ⊃ ~ B) / L ⊃ F
5. H ⊃ ~ R
6. L ⊃ ~ B
7. L ⊃ F

17.
1. H
2. H ⊃ (F v S)
3. (F v S) ⊃ (H ⊃ B) / B
4. H ⊃ (H ⊃ B)
5. H ⊃ B
6. B

18.
1. A v (B ⊃ G)
2. G v ~ A
3. ~ G
4. G ⊃ R / B ⊃ R
5. ~ A
6. B ⊃ G
7. B ⊃ R

Exercise 18.2   Each of the following symbolized arguments is valid. Using our first four rules, provide a proof for each argument.

1.
1. (A & B) ⊃ S
2. H ⊃ R
3. (A & B) / S

2.
1. R v G

2. H & (J ⊃ I)
3. ~ G / R

3.
1. ~ (F ≡ S)
2. R v M
3. ~ (F ≡ S) ⊃ D / D

4.
1. ~ (A & B)
2. R ⊃ (A & B)
3. H / ~ R

5.
1. F ⊃ (H & B)
2. A ⊃ ~(H & B)
3. A / ~ F

6.
1. A v (B & C)
2. A ⊃ F
3. ~ (B & C) / F

7.
1. J v ~S
2. ~ J
3. S v G / G

8.
1. ~(A & B) v ~ (E ≡ F)
2. H ⊃ (A & B)
3. ~~(E ≡ F) / ~H

9.
1. F ⊃ S
2. S ⊃ G
3. (F ⊃ G) ⊃ M / M

10.
1. R ⊃ H
2. H ⊃ S
3. S ⊃ G
4. (R ⊃ G) ⊃ F / F

11.

    1.   ~ F ⊃ ~ S

    2.   ~ S ⊃ ~ G

    3.   (~ F ⊃ ~ G) ⊃ H / H

12.

    1.   B ⊃ (A & G)

    2.   R ⊃ B

    3.   [R ⊃ (A & G)] ⊃ S / S

13.

    1.   (H v B) ⊃ ~ (S ≡ F)

    2.   R ⊃ (H v B)

    3.   ~(S ≡ F) ⊃ I / R ⊃ I

14.

    1.   J ⊃ I

    2.   I ⊃ ~ R

    3.   J

    4.   A ⊃ ~ B

    5.   A

    6.   R v (B v S)

    7.   S ⊃ L / L

15.

    1.   A ⊃ (B ⊃ E)

    2.   A

    3.   ~ E / ~ B

16.

    1.   A ⊃ B

    2.   B ⊃ E

    3.   B ⊃ R

    4.   ~ R

    5.   B v A / E

17.

    1.   I v A

    2.   (I v A) ⊃ ~S

    3.   J ⊃ [J v (I ⊃ S)]

    4.   ~S ⊃ [S v (S v A)] / A

18.

    1.   A $\supset$ B

    2.   B $\supset$ W

    3.   ~ W

    4.   J $\supset$ I

    5.   S $\supset$ ~I

    6.   ~A $\supset$ (J v Z)

    7.   S / Z

Exercise 18.3   Each of the following English arguments is valid. Symbolize each argument in TL and then use natural deduction to prove each valid. Suggested abbreviations are provided.

1. If Ann goes swimming, then Bob will go swimming. Either Ann or Chris will go swimming. Bob won't go swimming. So, Chris will go swimming. (A, B, C)

2. If Ann goes swimming, then Bob will go swimming. If Bob goes swimming, then Chris will go swimming. But Chris won't swim. So, Ann won't swim. (A, B, C)

3. If either Ann or Bob is home, then it's the case that either Bob or Chris is home. Either it's the case that if Bob is home then Chris is home, or Ann is home. If it's the case that if Bob is home then Chris is home, then either Ann or Bob is home. Ann is not home. So, either Bob or Chris is home. (A, B, C)

4. If either Pat or Quinn works late, then Rita and Winona will work late. If it's the case that Herman is on vacation, then either Pat or Quinn will work late. So, if Herman is on vacation, then Rita and Winona will work late. (P, Q, R, W, H)

5. If Ralph tells Alice he's sorry, then Alice will be forgiving. If Norton has a talk with Ralph, then Ralph will tell Alice he's sorry. Alice will not be forgiving. So, Norton won't have a talk with Ralph. (R, A, N)

6. If Pat gets a ticket, then if Pat has an accident then Pat's insurance will be canceled. Pat's insurance won't be canceled. If Pat doesn't slow down, then Pat will get a ticket. Either Pat's insurance will be canceled or Pat won't slow down. So, Pat won't have an accident. (T, A, I, S)

7. Elroy won't go jogging. If Lulu jogs, then Chris will jog. Either Lulu will jog or Elroy will jog. Therefore, Chris will jog. (E, L, C)

8. If Donovan doesn't perform tonight, then either the Jefferson Airplane or Fever Tree will perform. Fever Tree will not perform. If the Jefferson Airplane

performs then Suzie will get to hear her favorite song. Donovan won't perform tonight. So, Suzie will get to hear her favorite song tonight. (D, J, F, S)

9. If it's the case that if Ann swims then Bubba will swim, then Chris will swim. Either Dave won't swim or Ann will swim. If it's not the case that Dave swims, then if Ann swims then Bubba will swim. Ann won't swim. So, Chris will swim. (A, B, C, D)

10. Ann and Bob won't both sing. Either Chris or Rob will sing or Mary will sing. If Lucy doesn't sing, then it's not the case that either Chris or Rob will. Either Ann and Bob will both sing or Lucy won't sing. Consequently, Mary will sing. (A, B, C, R, L, M)

11. If Wimpy eats a hamburger, then Popeye will eat another can of spinach. Either Olive Oyl will eat a peach or Popeye won't eat another can of spinach. Olive Oyl won't eat a peach so Wimpy won't eat a hamburger. (W, P, O)

12. Either Gilligan will show up for dinner or either Mr. Howell will be upset or Mrs. Howell won't show up for dinner. If Gilligan shows up for dinner, then Mr. Howell will be upset. Mr. Howell won't be upset. So, Mrs. Howell won't show up for dinner. (G, H, M)

13. If Moe makes a face, then Curly will make a face. If it's the case that if Moe makes a face then Larry won't make a face, then it follows that if Curly makes a face then the director will not be happy. If Curly makes a face, then Larry won't make a face. So, if Moe makes a face then the director will not be happy. (M, C, L, D)

14. Either Hogan bribes Schultz or if Schultz tells Klink then General Burkhart will find out. If it's the case that if Schultz tells Klink then General Burkhart will find out, then if General Burkhart finds out, then Hogan will get in big trouble. Hogan won't bribe Schultz. And Hogan won't get in big trouble. So, Schultz won't tell Klink. (H, S, B, T)

15. If Gilligan is late, then the Skipper will be worried about his little buddy. If the Skipper is worried about his little buddy, then the Skipper won't eat. If the Skipper won't eat, then Mrs. Howell will become concerned. If it's the case that if Gilligan is late then Mrs. Howell will become concerned, then the Professor will argue that Mrs. Howell's peace of mind is dependent on Gilligan's punctuality. So, the Professor will argue that Mrs. Howell's peace of mind is dependent on Gilligan's punctuality. (G, S, E, M, P)

Appendix 18.1   FAQ on Proofs

Question. Is it necessary to refer to, or use, every line in an argument when we prove it?

Answer. No, it is not. Some proofs will use only some of the premises of an argument; it is not required that you "use" every premise. Just like in everyday life, some arguments may have *superfluous* premises.

Question. Is it necessary to use every rule when we construct a proof?

Answer. No it is not. Notice that some of the proofs above employed only one rule.

Question. How do you know where to begin a proof? How do you get started?

Answer. You scan the premises looking for a pattern in the premises that corresponds to one of the rules of deduction. The four rules we are using at this time each require a match with two premises. So, you are looking for two premises (not necessarily next to each other) that match one of the rules. When you see two premises that correspond to one of the rules, you apply the rule and make the deduction (or "draw the inference"). After writing the additional line (recording your inference), you repeat the process over and over again, looking for patterns that correspond to the rules you are using. You stop when you have derived the conclusion as the last line of the proof.

Question. Suppose you attempt to prove an argument valid and do not succeed. You are not able to complete the proof. Does this prove that the argument is *invalid*?

Answer. No it does not. All it proves is that you started a proof and did not complete it. It *might* be that the argument is invalid, but it also might be that the argument is valid and you simply failed to discover the remaining steps in the proof. Natural deduction, as we are employing it, is used to prove arguments valid; it is not used to prove arguments invalid.

Question. Is there only one correct proof per argument? Is there only one correct order in which to proceed when constructing a proof?

Answer. No. Creating a proof is a little like washing a car or making a Greek salad. Just as there is more than one way to wash a car or make a Greek salad, there is (usually) more than one way to prove an argument valid. With the exception of short, simple arguments, there will usually be more than one order in which to build your inferences, and more than one way to use various rules to get to the conclusion. In many cases, there will be dozens of different ways to prove an argument valid—all correct proofs of the argument's validity. Here are two equally correct proofs of validity for the same argument:

1. $A \supset B$	1. $A \supset B$
2. $B \supset C$	2. $B \supset C$

3.	A		3.	A	
4.	D v C		4.	D v C	
5.	~D / C		5.	~D / C	
6.	C	DS 4,5	6.	B	MP 1,3
			7.	C	MP 2, 6

Glossary

Inference An inference is "drawn" when a person asserts a conclusion on the basis of one or more premises.

Inference rule A rule specifying that a conclusion of a certain form may be inferred when certain premises are given.

Justification (of an inference) In a proof, a citation of the rule used in drawing the inference and the lines to which the rule was applied.

Natural deduction method A method in which we deduce a conclusion from a set of premises through a series of valid inferences corresponding to more or less natural patterns of reasoning.

Natural deduction system A system consisting of (a) a formal language that can be used to symbolize information; and (b) a set of natural deduction rules that can be used to deduce conclusions from premises.

Proof in TD A sequence of sentences of TL, each of which is either a premise or an assumption or follows from one or more previous sentences according to a TD inference or replacement rule, and in which (a) every line (other than a premise) has a justification, and (b) any assumptions have been discharged. The conclusion of a proof is the last line of the proof.

TD The name of the truth-functional natural deduction system used in this book.

Valid inference An inference is a valid inference just in case the argument formed out of the premises and conclusion of the inference constitutes a valid argument.

Valid inference rule An inference rule that has the following feature: When the rule is followed, the result is always a valid inference.

Valid in TD An argument is valid in TD if and only if there exists a proof in TD whose premises are the premises of the argument and whose conclusion is the conclusion of the argument. (An argument is invalid in TD if and only if it is not valid in TD.)

19 Truth-Functional Natural Deduction Part 2 « « « « « « « « « «

Four More Inference Rules

There is no limit to the number of valid inference rules that can be formulated. During the twentieth century, a number of important rules were added to the system of truth-functional logic, including the four to be introduced in this chapter. However, as you will see, once we have formulated a certain number of valid rules, any additional rules are redundant, in the sense that the additional rules merely allow inferences already allowed by the original group of rules. For practical purposes, about 20 rules are all we will ever need. Here are four more valid rules of inference.

The Simplification Rule

The simplification rule (abbreviated "Simp"), summarized in the following box, is obviously a valid inference rule.

The Simplification Rule (Simp)

From a sentence of the form **P** & **Q**, you may infer the corresponding sentence **P**.

From a sentence of the form **P** & **Q**, you may infer the corresponding sentence **Q**.

In other words, given a conjunction, you can infer the left conjunct. And, given a conjunction, you can infer the right conjunct instead. It is your choice. You might even infer one conjunct in one inference, and then in a later inference in the same proof you might infer the other conjunct. Again, the choice is yours. For example, from A & B you can infer A. From A & B you can also infer B.

If you doubt the validity of this rule, reflect on the following reasoning: Surely if a conjunction **P & Q** is true, then the corresponding sentence **P** is true (the left conjunct) and the corresponding sentence **Q** is true (the right conjunct), for a conjunction is only true when both conjuncts are true!

We abbreviate this two-part rule as follows:

The Simplification Rule (abbreviation)

$$\frac{\textbf{P \& Q}}{\textbf{P}} \qquad \frac{\textbf{P \& Q}}{\textbf{Q}}$$

In each of the following examples, the simplification rule was applied to the first sentence, and the second sentence was deduced in accord with the rule.

1.	A & B	1.	(A v B) & (E v F)	1.	A & B
2.	A	2.	(A v B)	2.	B

Here is an English argument that instantiates simplification:

1. Ann is a swimmer and Bob is a jogger.
2. Therefore, Ann is a swimmer.

In TL, this is:

1. A & B / A

Let us look at a short proof employing simplification. The argument is simple, but it illustrates the rule:

1. A & B
2. A ⊃ E / E

The proof:

1. A & B
2. A ⊃ E / E
3. A   Simp 1
4. E   MP 2, 3

At line 3 we applied Simp to line 1 and pulled down (inferred) the A. At line 4, we applied MP to lines 2 and 3 and deduced E. Because E is the conclusion, the proof is complete at line 4, and the argument is proved valid.

The Conjunction Rule

The next rule, the conjunction rule, summarized in the following box, is obviously valid.

The Conjunction Rule (Conj)

From a sentence **P** and a sentence **Q**, you may infer the corresponding sentence **P & Q**.

For example, from A, and from B, you may infer A & B. If you doubt the validity of this rule, reflect on the following argument: Surely if a sentence **P** is true, and a sentence **Q** is true, then the conjunction of the two, **P & Q**, must be true as well, for a conjunction is always true when both conjuncts are true. We abbreviate the conjunction rule as follows:

Conjunction Rule (Abbreviation)

$$P$$
$$Q$$
$$\overline{P \ \& \ Q}$$

In each of the following examples, the conjunction rule was applied to the first two sentences and the third sentence was deduced in accord with the rule.

1.	A	1.	(A v B)	1.	~A
2.	B	2.	(E v F)	2.	~B
3.	A & B	3.	(A v B) & (E v F)	3.	~A & ~B

Here is an English argument that instantiates the conjunction pattern:

1. Ann is home.
2. Bob is home.
3. Therefore, Ann is home and Bob is home.

That is:

1. A
2. B / A & B

Here is a short proof that employs conjunction:

1. A
2. B
3. (A & B) ⊃ E / E
4. A & B   Conj 1, 2
5. E   MP 3, 4

On line 4, we applied Conj to 1 and 2 and inferred A & B. We simply stuck the A and the B together with an ampersand to generate line 4. Next, we applied MP to lines 3 and 4 and pulled down (inferred) E. This gave us line 5. Because E is the conclusion, the proof is complete at line 5 and the argument is proved valid.

The Addition Rule

The next rule, the addition rule, strikes many as invalid at first, but it is perfectly valid.

The Addition Rule (Add)

From a sentence **P**, you may infer the corresponding sentence **P** v **Q**, where **Q** is *any* well-formed sentence of TL.

That is, from a sentence **P**, one may infer the disjunction of **P** with any sentence **Q**. For example, from B, one may infer B v G; from B, one may infer B v ~U; from B, one may infer B v K; and so on. The addition rule will be abbreviated as follows:

Addition Rule (Abbreviation)

$$\frac{\mathbf{P}}{\mathbf{P} \text{ v } \mathbf{Q}}$$

In each of the following examples, we applied the addition rule to the first sentence and deduced the second sentence in accord with the rule.

1. A	1. A	1. (A & B)	1. J $\supset$ E	1. B
2. A v H	2. A v ~K	2. (A & B) v (H & S)	2. (J $\supset$ E) v W	2. B v R

Here is an English argument that instantiates the addition pattern:

1. Ann is home.
2. Therefore, Ann is home or Bob is home.

That is:

1. A / A v B

Here is a short proof employing addition:

1. A
2. (A v B) $\supset$ H   / H
3. A v B   Add 1
4. H   MP 2, 3

At line 3, we simply inferred A v B from line 1 by applying the addition rule to line 1. We took line 1, copied it onto line 3, added a wedge to the right, and added a formula of our choice, namely B. This gave us A v B on line 3. We then applied MP to 2 and 3 to prove line 4, namely H. Because this is the conclusion, the proof is finished, and the argument is proved valid.

> ### History Note
>
> The addition rule was first formulated by Robert Kilwardby, Archbishop of Canterbury from 1272–1277.

The Constructive Dilemma Rule

Consider the following argument:

1. If it rains, then the roof will get wet.
2. If it snows, then the lawn will get white.
3. It will either rain or snow.

So, certainly either the roof will get wet or the lawn will get white.

Does this inference seem intuitively valid to you? If we symbolize this English argument in TL, we have:

1. R ⊃ W
2. S ⊃ L
3. R v S / W v L

This TL argument is an instance of the following argument form:

1. **P ⊃ Q**
2. **R ⊃ S**
3. **P v R / Q v S**

A truth-table test would reveal this to be a valid argument form, although most people see intuitively that it is valid. This valid form of reasoning is reflected in the constructive dilemma rule, as summarized in the following box:

The Constructive Dilemma Rule (CD)

From a sentence of the form **P ⊃ Q**, and a sentence **R ⊃ S**, and a corresponding sentence **P v R**, you may infer the corresponding sentence **Q v S**.

In each of the following examples, we applied the constructive dilemma rule to the first three sentences and deduced the fourth sentence in accord with the rule.

1. A ⊃ B	1. H ⊃ (G & B)	1. R ⊃ S
2. E ⊃ F	2. S ⊃ (A & M)	2. H ⊃ G
3. A v E	3. H v S	3. R v H
4. B v F	4. (G & B) v (A & M)	4. S v G

Notice that the constructive dilemma rule requires the presence of three elements:

1. A conditional
2. Another conditional
3. A disjunction with a left disjunct that is the antecedent of the one conditional and a right disjunct that is the antecedent of the other conditional.

From this, you are permitted to infer a disjunction with a left disjunct that is the *consequent* of the one conditional and a right disjunct that is the *consequent* of the other conditional.

With CD, we now have eight valid inference rules to work with. Here are some examples of proofs using various combinations of these rules. Study them carefully.

1. A ⊃ H
2. (H v C) ⊃ (D & E)
3. A   / D
4. H   MP 1, 3
5. H v C   Add 4
6. D & E   MP 2, 5
7. D   Simp 6

At line 5, we used Add to derive H v C. In effect, we "added" C to H to produce the formula H v C. This in turn matched the antecedent of line 2, which allowed us to apply MP to lines 2 and 5 and infer or bring down D & E. We could have added any other TL sentence to H at line 5, but we chose C because, looking ahead, we saw that we needed the formula H v C to bring down the D & E by MP. Here is another proof:

1. F ⊃ L
2. (M ⊃ N) & S
3. N ⊃ T
4. F v M / L v T
5. M ⊃ N   Simp 2
6. M ⊃ T   HS 3, 5
7. L v T   CD 4, 1, 6

We were allowed to apply Simp to line 2 because the main connective of 2 is the ampersand. Remember that you may only apply Simp to a line when the main connective on the line is &. This allowed us to bring down the M ⊃ N, which in turn made possible the application of HS. Notice the application of the constructive dilemma rule to lines 1, 4, and 6. This rule is always hard to spot at first. Draw a "map" of this inference if you feel you need more familiarity with the way this little rule operates. Here is another proof for your consideration:

1. ~M & N
2. D ⊃ M
3. W & R

4. (~D & W) ⊃ A / A v O
5. ~M   Simp 1
6. ~D   MT 2, 5
7. W   Simp 3
8. ~D & W   Conj 6, 7
9. A   MP 4, 8
10. A v O   Add 9

Notice that the last line of the proof is an application of Add to line 9. The O that appears on line 10 does not appear anywhere in the proof prior to line 10, and so at line 9 it was apparent that the O would only enter the proof through an application of the addition rule.

History Note

The first systems of modern natural deduction were developed in 1934 by two logicians working independently of each other: the German logician Gentzen and the Polish logician Jaskowski.

Some Unsolicited Advice

When one is first learning to construct proofs, it is natural to wonder if there are mechanical rules that tell you how to begin and just what steps to take. After all, mechanical rules—decision procedures—tell us precisely how to construct a truth table. Well, we could formulate precise algorithms for the construction of proofs, but the rules would be extremely complex and almost impossible to follow. They would be harder to learn and to follow than the rules of inference themselves. Consequently, no practical set of step-by-step instructions exists that tells you precisely and mechanically how to construct any and every natural deduction proof. Constructing a proof is therefore something of an art, and building a proof requires a certain amount of creativity. Complicated proofs also require a certain amount of skill. Because skills typically improve with practice, you can expect your abilities to improve as you successfully complete more and more proofs.

The first step in learning to build proofs is this: Develop an ability to spot the inference rule patterns when you look at the premises of an argument. Once you spot a pattern, you apply the appropriate rule and deduce a line in the proof. Each time you deduce or "bring down" a sentence, a new pattern forms that enables you to apply another rule and bring down another sentence—if you spot the new pattern. This in turn will form a new pattern, making possible another step in the proof, and so on.

Eventually, this process of spotting patterns and making inferences should take you to the conclusion. Constructing a proof involves the very important mental skill of pattern recognition, a skill that develops only with practice.

The second step in learning to build proofs is to learn to apply the rules accurately. You must apply the rules precisely or else incorrect sequences of formulas may result. If you apply a rule incorrectly at, say, step 3 and bring down the wrong formula, this can throw off every subsequent step in your proof. (The same thing can happen when solving a math problem: A mistake at step 3 could throw off every subsequent step, leading to a totally wrong answer in the end.)

The third step in the process of learning to build proofs involves what former President George W. Bush once called "strategery." (Bush was not talking about natural deduction, however.) Learn to strategize. Someone who is good at strategy looks at an argument for a few minutes before beginning a proof and then plans in advance the steps that will likely lead to the conclusion. Strategy in logic is a skill that develops only after extended practice and only after one understands the natural deduction process. Chess players develop a similar ability: They are always looking several steps ahead, thinking about where they want to be and how they will get there. A good chess player is always several steps ahead of the game! We discuss proof strategy in the next section.

Ultimately, the best way to become skilled at constructing proofs is to practice them on your own. Most people find logic proofs a bit overwhelming at first. However, if you refuse to get discouraged, and if you put some effort into it, you will find that your ability to complete a proof increases with each one that you solve. Like most things in life, success requires effort.

Suggestions Concerning Strategy

1. If one of the lines in the proof is a conditional, try to find or derive the antecedent. When you have the antecedent, apply MP and derive the consequent of the conditional. Or, try to find or derive the negation of the consequent. When you have that, derive the negation of the antecedent through an application of MT.

2. If one of the lines is a disjunction, try to find or derive the negation of one of the disjuncts. This will allow you to apply DS, yielding the other disjunct as a new inference.

3. If your conclusion is a conjunction, try using the conjunction rule.

4. If the main connective is &, it might be wise to apply Simp and derive one of the conjuncts.

5. If you have a disjunction and can't apply DS, try to spot a CD pattern. This would require two conditionals that have as antecedents the two disjuncts

of the disjunction. CD would then allow you to infer the disjunction of the two consequents of the two conditionals.

6. If you have more than one conditional, watch for HS.

7. If you have two conditionals along with a disjunction, watch for CD.

8. If a letter or formula appears just once in the premises and doesn't link with anything else in the proof, it might be a "useless" component. Not every element of the premises must be used in the derivation of the conclusion.

9. If the conclusion contains an element not found in the premises, you will have to use add to get it into the proof.

10. Try to isolate a single letter on a line by itself. In many cases, if you can derive a single letter, or a single negated letter, you can use it to break down other, bigger lines in the proof.

Concluding Matters

The "Law of Noncontradiction"

Recall from Unit One that anything counts as "logically possible" except for that which is self-contradictory. An explicit self-contradiction is any statement of the form **P** & ~ **P**; for instance, A & ~A, B & ~B, and so on. As we have seen, a truth table can show that any statement of the form **P** & ~ **P** is necessarily false, that is, can't possibly be true. A philosophical argument can also be given for the same claim (see later). The principle that self-contradictions are impossible is called the law of noncontradiction (LNC). The LNC was formulated in ancient times by the world's first mathematicians and philosophers. Aristotle, the founder of logical theory, was aware that the LNC is presupposed by any consistent logical theory and indeed by any logically consistent theory about anything. All of our inference rules presuppose the LNC.

However, some logic students have a skeptical attitude toward the LNC. They balk at the claim and wonder why they should agree with it. Now that you understand the nature of a formal proof, you have the background to understand one important, purely logical consideration in support of the LNC: Suppose a reasoning process begins with a self-contradictory premise, no matter what the contradiction is. By applying the obviously valid rules of simplification, addition, and disjunctive syllogism, any and every arbitrarily chosen conclusion validly follows. For example, in the following proof, A abbreviates "Ann is 16" and B abbreviates "The Earth is perfectly flat":

1. A & ~ A / B

2. A   Simp 1

3. A v B   Add 2

4. ~A   Simp 1
5. B   DS 3, 4

Notice that this argument has one premise. The one premise is a self-contradiction. Assuming just one contradiction, it validly follows that the Earth is perfectly flat. But this proof would be valid no matter what sentence B abbreviates (and no matter what sentence A abbreviates). The lesson that follows is clear: In general, if someone accepts even one contradiction as true, then any and every sentence validly follows. In other words, if even *one* contradiction is true, then any and every sentence is true. The distinction between truth and falsity collapses in a heap. Every sentence is true; no sentence is ever false—if even one contradiction is true. More formally, where **P** is any sentence and **Q** is any sentence, the demonstration that every sentence follows from a self-contradiction looks like this:

1. **P & ~P / Q**
2. **P**   Simp 1
3. **P v Q**   Add 2
4. **~P**   Simp 1
5. **Q**   DS 3, 4

So, if even one self-contradiction is true, then it validly follows that the total population of China is exactly 17, it follows that it is true that the moon is made entirely of wax paper, it follows that it is true that the surface of the Earth is covered entirely by a layer of marshmallow crème, and so on. After reflecting on these considerations, perhaps you will agree that logically absurd consequences follow if we reject the law of noncontradiction and accept even *one* self-contradiction as true.

Exercise 19.1   Using any of the first eight rules, supply justifications for each inference.

1.
1. (A v B) ⊃ (G v S)
2. (G v S) ⊃ H
3. (H v S) ⊃ M
4. (A v E) ⊃ I
5. A & R / M & I
6. A
7. A v B
8. G v S
9. H

10. H v S
11. M
12. A v E
13. I
14. M & I

2.

1. H ⊃ S
2. B
3. R
4. (B & R) ⊃ ~ S
5. ~ H ⊃ Z / Z v I
6. B & R
7. ~ S
8. ~ H
9. Z
10. Z v I

3.

1. (H v J) ⊃ (S v W)
2. S ⊃ O
3. W ⊃ K
4. H / O v K
5. H v J
6. S v W
7. O v K

4.

1. A v B
2. C
3. [(A v B) & C] ⊃ ~ ~ I
4. S ⊃ ~ I
5. (~ S v H) ⊃ X / X v E
6. (A v B) & C
7. ~~I
8. ~ S
9. ~ S v H
10. X
11. X v E

5.

1. $(S \lor J) \supset {\sim}{\sim}Z$
2. ${\sim}Z \lor A$
3. K
4. $S \& G$
5. $A \supset M$
6. $O \supset N / M \lor N$
7. S
8. $S \lor J$
9. ${\sim}{\sim}Z$
10. A
11. $A \lor O$
12. $M \lor N$

6.

1. $J \& R$
2. $(J \lor {\sim}S) \supset I$
3. $(R \& I) \supset H / H \& J$
4. J
5. $J \lor {\sim}S$
6. I
7. R
8. $R \& I$
9. H
10. $H \& J$

7.

1. $J \supset I$
2. $J \lor R$
3. $R \supset (R \supset S)$
4. ${\sim}I / S \lor I$
5. ${\sim}J$
6. R
7. $R \supset S$
8. S
9. $S \lor I$

Exercise 19.2   Each of the following arguments is valid. Using any of the eight inference rules, supply proofs.

   1.
      1.   A ⊃ B
      2.   B ⊃ R
      3.   ~ R / ~ A & ~ B

   2.
      1.   (A v B) ⊃ G
      2.   A
      3.   G ⊃ S / S

   3.
      1.   (H & S) ⊃ ~ (F ≡ S)
      2.   B ⊃ (F ≡ S)
      3.   H
      4.   S / ~ B

   4.
      1.   A & (R ⊃ S)
      2.   S ⊃ I
      3.   (R ⊃ I) ⊃ O / O

   5.
      1.   B ⊃ (S v R)
      2.   S ⊃ J
      3.   R ⊃ G
      4.   H & B / J v G

   6.
      1.   H ⊃ ~ (S v G)
      2.   ~(R v W) ⊃ (S v G)
      3.   F & H
      4.   R ⊃ (J & A)
      5.   W ⊃ M
      6.   ~ M / ~W

   7.
      1.   H v ~ S
      2.   [(H v ~ S) v G] ⊃ ~M
      3.   M v R / R v X

8.

   1.   ~ F ⊃ ~ S
   2.   H & F
   3.   F ⊃ B
   4.   B ⊃ G / G

9.

   1.   F v B
   2.   [H & (F v B)] ⊃ ~ S
   3.   I & H / ~ S

10.

   1.   A ⊃ (J & S)
   2.   B ⊃ F
   3.   A
   4.   [(J & S) v F] ⊃ G / G

11.

   1.   (H v S) ⊃ D
   2.   (R v M) ⊃ I
   3.   (D & I) ⊃ ~ A
   4.   H & R / ~ A

12.

   1.   A v (B ⊃ C)
   2.   ~ A ⊃ (~ H ⊃ J)
   3.   ~ H v B
   4.   ~ A & I / J v C

13.

   1.   (A ⊃ B) & (A ⊃ C)
   2.   A
   3.   (B v C) ⊃ Z / Z

14.

   1.   (S ⊃ I) & (S ⊃ J)
   2.   (I v J) ⊃ G
   3.   H & S / G

15.

   1.   (A ⊃ B) & (S ⊃ I)
   2.   J ⊃ R
   3.   (A v J) & (S v E) / B v R

16.
1. ~I ⊃ (C ⊃ E)
2. (B v D) ⊃ [F ⊃ (G & Z)]
3. I v (B v D)
4. ~I & (C v F) / E v (G & Z)

17.
1. S ⊃ [J & (I v S)]
2. [J v (A & B)] ⊃ (~ N & ~ O)
3. S & Z / ~N & J

18.
1. (A & S) ⊃ Z
2. ~J ⊃ A
3. ~J ⊃ S
4. ~J & B / Z v I

19.
1. (W & X) ⊃ (Z ⊃ ~U)
2. (B v F) ⊃ (A v W)
3. (B v G) ⊃ (~A ⊃ X)
4. A v (B & Z)
5. ~A & (O ⊃ L)
6. U v (I & C) / C v ~L

20.
1. (~N v D) ⊃ (H ⊃ F)
2. N v H
3. (H v C) ⊃ (A ⊃ E)
4. ~N
5. (F v E) ⊃ (F ⊃ W) / H ⊃ W

Appendix 19.1 ▐ More Deduction Errors

Students are prone to certain common mistakes when they first learn to construct proofs. The following is a list of common errors.

Error

From: ~(A & B)
Deduce: ~A   by Simp (error)

Reason This Is an Error

You cannot apply Simp to a negated conjunction. You may only apply Simp to a line for which the *main* connective is &.

Error

From: $A \supset B$
And B
Deduce: A   by MP (error)

Reason This Is an Error

If you are to apply modus ponens to $A \supset B$, the second line in this case would have to be A, and then B would follow by MP. This is a backward MP!

Error

From: $A \supset B$
And ~A
Deduce: ~B   by MT (error)

Reason This Is an Error

If you are to apply modus tollens to $A \supset B$, the second line in this case would have to be ~B, and then ~A would follow by MT. This is a backward MT.

Error

From: A v B
And A
Deduce: B   by MP (error)

Reason This Is an Error

To apply MP here, the main connective must be a horseshoe, not a wedge.

Error

From: A v B
Deduce: A   by Simp (error)

You cannot apply Simp to a disjunction. You may only apply Simp to a line for which the *main* connective is &.

Error

From: A ⊃ B
Deduce: A   by Simp (error)

Reason This Is an Error

You cannot apply Simp to a horseshoe. You may only apply Simp to a line for which the *main* connective is &.

Error

From: A
Deduce: A & B   by Add (error)

Reason This Is an Error

When you apply add, you add a wedge and the wedge becomes the main connective, never the &. For example, from A, you could infer A v E, or you could infer A v ~O, and so on.

Remember the old saying, "Practice makes perfect." Good luck practicing the proofs!

20 Truth-Functional Deduction Part 3 « « « « «

Replacement Rules

A *replacement* rule is a special type of inference rule. The inference rules we have been using so far apply *only* to *whole* lines of proofs, never to parts of a line. For instance, if we are to apply modus ponens to two lines of a proof, one whole line must be of the form **P ⊃ Q** and another whole line must be simply the corresponding formula **P**. In contrast, replacement rules are a type of inference rule that may be applied to whole lines *or* to well-formed parts of lines in a proof. In addition, a replacement rule has you replace one thing with something else that is logically equivalent, while proving an argument valid.

Let us briefly consider the rationale underlying this new type of rule. Suppose we take a valid argument and remove one premise. Suppose that we next replace that premise by inserting a logically equivalent formula in its place. (Just as a mechanic might remove a car's carburetor and replace it with a mechanically equivalent carburetor.) Will the argument remain valid? (Will the car still run?) Certainly. Substituting one formula for another won't affect the argument's validity if the two interchanged formulas are logically equivalent. Now, suppose we take a valid argument, remove a *subformula* from within a premise, and replace the subformula with a logically equivalent formula. (A subformula within a formula is a well-formed formula that constitutes part of a bigger formula.) Will the argument remain valid? Clearly, it will remain valid. Substituting one subformula for another, when the two are logically equivalent, won't affect the argument's validity. This reasoning underlies the replacement rules that follow.

The Commutation Rule

Certainly any sentence **P** v **Q** is equivalent to the corresponding sentence **Q** v **P**. In a disjunction, the order of the two disjuncts doesn't affect the truth-value of the disjunction. And certainly any sentence **P** & **Q** will be equivalent to the corresponding sentence **Q** & **P**. The order of the conjuncts doesn't affect the truth-value of the conjunction. Our first replacement rule, the commutation rule, reflects these two logical truths and thus has two parts, as shown in the following box.

The Commutation Rule (Comm)

Anywhere in a proof, a formula **P** v **Q** may replace or be replaced by the corresponding formula **Q** v **P**.

Anywhere in a proof, a formula **P** & **Q** may replace or be replaced by the corresponding formula **Q** & **P**.

When we replace a sentence **P** v **Q** on a line with the corresponding sentence **Q** v **P** (e.g., we replace A v B with B v A), the replacement is made by rewriting the entire line, making the replacement as the line is being rewritten. Understand that this replacement operation can be performed on a whole line, or on a well-formed subformula within a line, at any point in a proof. This should become clear after some examples.

If we apply a replacement rule to an entire line, we simply rewrite the whole line, writing the replacement in place of the original line. For example, in the following proof, as we go from line 2 to line 3, the commutation rule is applied, and the entire line consisting of B v A is replaced with A v B and rewritten on 3:

1. (A v B) ⊃ E
2. B v A   / E
3. A v B   Comm 2
4. E   MP 1, 3

After A v B was derived at line 3, we applied MP to lines 1 and 3 to derive E.

On the other hand, if we apply a replacement rule to a *part* of a line—to a subformula within a line—we rewrite the whole line, making the replacement at the appropriate slot in the formula. In the following proof, as we go from line 1 to line 3, line 1 is rewritten in its entirety, but as it is being rewritten, the subformula A v B inside line 1 is replaced by the subformula B v A.

1. (A v B) ⊃ E
2. B v A / E

3. (B v A) ⊃ E   Comm 1
4. E   MP 2, 3

Notice that as we wrote in line 3, we rewrote all of line 1 and in the process re-placed A v B with B v A. Notice that whether we apply a replacement rule to part of a line, or to a whole line, and make a replacement, we bring down the entire line when we draw our inference.

In each of the following, the commutation rule is applied to a whole line. Specifi-cally, the second formula is derived from the first by comm:

1.	A v B	1.	A & B	1.	(E ⊃ F) v G	1.	(A & B) & E
2.	B v A	2.	B & A	2.	G v (E ⊃ F)	2.	E & (A & B)

However, in each of the following, the commutation rule is applied to a subfor-mula within the first line, and the second formula is derived from the first by comm:

1.	(H & R) v G	1.	(S v G) & F
2.	(R & H) v G	2.	(G v S) & F

In short, comm tells us that if the main operator is a wedge—or if it is an ampersand—we may reverse the order of the components without affecting the truth-value of the formula or subformula.

Math Connection

The commutation rule in logic reminds us of a similar rule in arithmetic, namely, the commutative rule of addition and multiplication:

$$a \times b = b \times a$$
$$a + b = b + a$$

There is an interesting logical connection between the logic and math versions of this rule. In the nineteenth century, British mathematicians George Boole (1815–1864) and Augustus De Morgan (1806–1871) were among the first to explore the re-lation between math and logic, developing an "algebraic logic" that is now part of the basis of computer science. Boolean algebra is a fascinating subject, but unfortunately, this is not the place to go into the matter further.

History Note

De Morgan's rule can be found in the works of the fourteenth-century English philosopher and logician William of Ockham (1285–1349).

The Association Rule

According to the association rule (assoc), any sentence (**P** v **Q**) v **R** is equivalent to the corresponding sentence **P** v (**Q** v **R**), and any sentence (**P** & **Q**) & **R** is equivalent to the corresponding sentence **P** & (**Q** & **R**). For instance, (A v B) v C is equivalent to A v (B v C), and (A & B) & C is equivalent to A & (B & C). In a triple disjunction or triple conjunction, the placement of the parentheses does not affect the truth-value of the whole. Therefore, the parentheses can be shifted and the truth-value will not be affected. This can easily be confirmed on a truth table.

> ### The Association Rule (Assoc)
>
> Anywhere in a proof, a formula (**P** v **Q**) v **R** may replace or be replaced with the corresponding formula **P** v (**Q** v **R**).
>
> Anywhere in a proof, a formula (**P** & **Q**) & **R** may replace or be replaced with the corresponding formula **P** & (**Q** & **R**).

In each case that follows, the second sentence was derived from the first by applying the association rule.

1. (A v B) v E	1. A & (B & E)	1. [(A & B) v (E & S)] v (G & H)
2. A v (B v E)	2. (A & B) & E	2. (A & B) v [(E & S) v (G & H)]

Here is a proof employing this new rule:

1. (A v B) v E
2. ~A & ~ B / E
3. A v (B v E)   Assoc 1
4. ~A   Simp 2
5. B v E   DS 3, 4
6. ~B   Simp 2
7. E   DS 5, 6

Notice that at line 3 we applied the association rule to line 1. This allowed us to shift the brackets to set things up for the application of DS on line 5.

It is crucial that you remember this. If a pair of parentheses has a tilde attached, the association rule cannot be applied. For example, in the following case, you may *not* apply association:

$$\sim(A \vee B) \vee E$$

So, assoc tells us this: If the operators are all ampersands or all wedges, we may shift the brackets without affecting the truth-value of the formula, provided that the parentheses or brackets to be shifted have no tildes applied to them.

Math Connection

The association rule in logic reminds us of a similar rule in arithmetic, namely, the associative rule for addition and multiplication:

$$(a \times b) \times c = a \times (b \times c)$$
$$(a + b) + c = a + (b + c)$$

As with commutation, there is an interesting logical connection between the logic and math versions of this rule, but this is not the place to enter the matter.

The Double Negation Rule

If Pat is not a non-Hindu, Pat is Hindu. If someone's tractor "ain't got no traction," that tractor has traction. In English, if one negation operator applies directly to another, the two cancel each other out and the result is as if neither of the two negation operators existed. The double negation rule in logic corresponds to ordinary English usage.

> ### Double Negation Rule (DN)
>
> Anywhere in a proof, a formula $\sim\sim$ **P** may replace or be replaced with the corresponding formula **P**.

Many students anticipate this rule long before it is presented. For example, we can apply double negation to replace $\sim \sim A \vee B$ with $A \vee B$. We can also use DN to replace $A \supset \sim \sim B$ with $A \supset B$.

Here is another way to put this rule: Anywhere in a proof, you may trade two tildes for zero tildes or zero tildes for two tildes, as long as the tildes are not separated by a parenthesis. In each of the following cases, the second sentence was derived from the first by an application of double negation.

1.	$G \supset \sim \sim H$	1.	$H \vee \sim \sim (R \supset G)$	1.	$\sim \sim (C \,\&\, E)$	1.	A
2.	$G \supset H$	2.	$H \vee (R \supset G)$	2.	$(C \,\&\, E)$	2.	$\sim \sim A$

It is important to note that the two tildes cannot be separated by a parenthesis when DN is applied. Thus, the following inferences are *not* allowed by DN:

From: ~(~A v B)   From: ~(~U & ~G)
Infer: A v B by DN (illegal)   Infer: U & ~G by DN (illegal)

In these two cases, the first tilde does not apply *directly* to the second tilde. Rather, the first tilde applies directly to the parenthesis that comes between the two tildes. Thus, DN may not be applied. In addition, the following common error is not licensed by DN:

From: ~(~A & ~B)

Infer: A & B by DN (illegal)

Again, DN does not operate "across" a parenthesis.

Here are two short proofs that require double negation:

1.   ~ ~ A ⊃ S   1.   B ⊃ K
2.   A / S   2.   ~ ~B / K
3.   ~ ~ A   DN 2   3.   ~ ~B ⊃ K   DN 1
4.   S   MP 1, 3 4.   K   MP 2, 3

So, to emphasize a point that needs emphasizing, two tildes "cancel each other" out only in case the first applies *directly* to the second, with no intervening parenthetical device.

Notice that English grammar allows the use of the double negative. No rule of grammar is violated in the following conversation:

Ann: You are not happy.
Bob: It is not the case that I am not happy.

De Morgan's Rule

In Chapter 13 we saw that any sentence ~ (**P** & **Q**) is equivalent to the corresponding sentence ~ **P** v~ **Q**. (To say "Ann and Bob are not both home" is equivalent to saying "Either Ann is not home or Bob is not home.") We also saw that any sentence ~(**P** v **Q**) is equivalent to the corresponding sentence (~ **P** & ~ **Q**). (To say "It's not the case that either Ann or Bob is home" is equivalent to saying "Ann is not home and Bob is not home.") The corresponding rule is named after Augustus De Morgan, the first logician to use the rule in a modern system of logic, although it was known to William of Ockham some 500 years earlier.

Let us now employ DM within a proof. Consider the following argument:

1.   (A & B) v ~(~E v ~F)
2.   (~A v ~ B)
3.   F ⊃ (A v E)   / E v (A v S)

This argument is valid. However, using only the eight inference rules, it cannot be proved valid. This is where the replacement rules are indispensable. Notice that line 2 displays a DM pattern. By applying DM to line 2, we can derive:

4.   ~(A & B)   DM 2

In this case, we swapped ~(A & B) for ~A v ~B in accord with the DM rule. Notice that this formula, ~(A & B), is the negation of the left disjunct of line 1. This allows us to break line 1 down by DS:

5.   ~(~E v ~F)   DS 1, 4

Because line 5 instantiates one of the DM forms, we next apply DN and DM to it and replace it with:

6.   (E & F)   DN, DM 5

This is fortunate, for now line 6 can be broken down by Simp:

7.   E   Simp 6
8.   F   Simp 6

Next, notice that lines 3 and 8 instantiate the premise section of MP. This gives us:

9.   A v E   MP 3, 8

Now we can use comm to turn this into:

10. E v A   Comm 9

Using add, we move S into place:

11 (E v A) v S   Add 10

Finally, we use association to shift the parentheses over and derive our conclusion:

12. E v (A v S)   Assoc 11

Remember that you may shift the parentheses by assoc only if the formula is wedges all the way across, or ampersands all the way across, and the parentheses that shift are not encumbered by a tilde. Thus, assoc cannot be applied to this formula: ~(A v B) v G.

The Distribution Rule

This interesting rule has two parts, as summarized here.

Distribution (Dist)

Anywhere in a proof, a formula **P** v (**Q** & **R**) may replace or be replaced with the corresponding formula (**P** v **Q**) & (**P** v **R**).

Anywhere in a proof, a formula **P** & (**Q** v **R**) may replace or be replaced with the corresponding formula (**P** & **Q**) v (**P** & **R**).

Distribution reflects the fact that any sentence **P** v (**Q** & **R**) is equivalent to the corresponding sentence (**P** v **Q**) & (**P** v **R**) and any sentence **P** & (**Q** v **R**) is equivalent to the corresponding sentence (**P** & **Q**) v (**P** & **R**). (This can be confirmed in an eight-row truth table.) The following proof employs distribution at its first step:

1. A v (B & C)
2. (A v B) ⊃ E / E
3. (A v B) & (A v C)   Dist 1
4. A v B   Simp 3
5. E   MP 2, 4

This proof used dist on line 3 to replace A v (B & C) with (A v B) & (A v C).

In the next proof, at step 3, a line of the form **P & (Q v R)** replaces a corresponding line of the form **(P & Q) v (P & R)**:

1. (A & B) v (A & C)
2. A ⊃ E / E
3. A & (B v C)   Dist 1
4. A   Simp 3
5. E   MP 2, 4

Notice that when we apply the distribution rule to a sentence, the main operator switches from the ampersand to the wedge or from the wedge to the ampersand.

Math Connection

The distribution rule in logic is very similar to the distributive rule in arithmetic, which may be put this way:

$$a \times (b + c) = (a \times b) + (a \times c)$$

For example, $3 \times (7 + 4) = (3 \times 7) + (3 \times 4)$. Some students use their knowledge of the math form of distribution to more easily remember the logic form of the rule.

Again, there is an interesting logical connection between the logic and math versions of this rule, involving what is called Boolean algebra, but any discussion of that matter would take us beyond elementary logic and into advanced logic.

History Note

The distribution rule was first used in logic during the Middle Ages

---

Exercise 20.1   Using any of the eight inference rules plus any of the first five replacement rules, supply justifications for the following:

1.
   1. A v (B & C)
   2. (A v B) ⊃ S
   3. ~ S v (Q v R) / R v Q
   4. (A v B) & (A v C)

5. A v B
6. S
7. ~~S
8. Q v R
9. R v Q

2.
1. (A v B) v C
2. ~ B & R
3. A ⊃ F
4. C ⊃ S / ~ ~ (F & S)
5. (B v A) v C
6. B v (A v C)
7. ~ B
8. A v C
9. F v S
10. ~ ~ (F v S)

3.
1. ~ (A v B)
2. ~B ⊃ Z
3. H ⊃ ~ Z
4. ~ H ⊃ (Q & R) / ~ (~ Q v ~ R)
5. ~ A & ~ B
6. ~ B
7. Z
8. ~ ~ Z
9. ~ H
10. Q & R
11. ~ (~ Q v ~ R)

4.
1. H & (S v G)
2. (~ H v ~ S)
3. G ⊃ P / P
4. (H & S) v (H & G)
5. ~ (H & S)
6. H & G
7. G
8. P

5.

    1. A & B
    2. A ⊃ S
    3. S ⊃ Q
    4. (Q v P) ⊃ H
    5. ~ H v T / T
    6. A
    7. S
    8. Q
    9. Q v P
   10. H
   11. ~~H
   12. T

Exercise 20.2   Use the inference rules and the first five replacement rules to prove the following valid.

1.

    1. (A v B) ⊃ ~ E
    2. B v (G v A)
    3. ~ G / ~ E

2.

    1. (H ⊃ S) v ~ R
    2. (A v B) v Q
    3. ~ B & ~ S
    4. (A v Q) ⊃ R / ~ H

3.

    1. [(A v B) v C] ⊃ S
    2. B v (A v C)
    3. S ⊃ Q / Q

4.

    1. (A v B) ⊃ G
    2. R & H
    3. ~ (~ A & ~ B) / G

5.

    1. ~ (A v B)
    2. ~ B ⊃ E
    3. E ⊃ S / S

6.
1. A v (B & C)
2. (A v C) ⊃ ~ S
3. H ⊃ S / ~ H

7.
1. (H & S) v (H & P)
2. H ⊃ (G v M) / G v M

8.
1. A & (B v C)
2. (A & B) ⊃ H
3. (A & C) ⊃ O / H v O

9.
1. ~ (~ A v ~ B)
2. B ⊃ H
3. H ⊃ S / S

10.
1. (R ⊃ S) v ~ G
2. ~ ~ G
3. (R ⊃ S) ⊃ ~ ~ P
4. H ⊃ ~ P / ~ H

11.
1. R ⊃ ~ (H v B)
2. H v (A & B)
3. S ⊃ R / ~ S

12.
1. (G ≡ H) v ~ F
2. ~ (A v ~ F)
3. (G ≡ H) ⊃ P / P

13.
1. ~ (R & S)
2. ~ R ⊃ Q
3. ~ S ⊃ Z
4. ~ Q
5. Z ⊃ (A ≡ B) / A ≡ B

14.
1. (P ⊃ Q) & (R ⊃ S)

2. $(Q \lor S) \supset {\sim} H$
3. $P \lor (R \& B) \,/\, {\sim} H$

15.

1. ${\sim} R \supset {\sim} S$
2. ${\sim}{\sim} S$
3. ${\sim}{\sim} R \supset H$
4. $(H \supset A) \& (Z \supset O) \,/\, A \lor O$

16.

1. $A \lor (B \& C)$
2. ${\sim} B$
3. ${\sim} A \lor E \,/\, E$

17.

1. $S \supset {\sim} P$
2. $(P \& S) \lor (P \& F) \,/\, F$

18.

1. ${\sim} ({\sim} H \& E)$
2. $A \& (B \& E) \,/\, H \lor S$

19.

1. ${\sim} A$
2. $(A \& B) \lor (H \& S) \,/\, S$

20.

1. $H \supset S$
2. $K \supset H$
3. ${\sim} (A \lor S) \,/\, {\sim} (K \lor A)$

21.

1. $A \lor (W \& U)$
2. $(A \lor W) \supset {\sim} (U \lor C)$
3. $(A \& {\sim} C) \supset (E \& {\sim} F)$
4. $F \lor ({\sim} O \supset {\sim} M)$
5. $M \,/\, O$

22.

1. ${\sim} A \supset (C \& Z)$
2. ${\sim} B \supset (Z \& H)$
3. ${\sim} (A \& B)$
4. $Z \supset {\sim} (O \lor E)$
5. $I \supset E$
6. $C \supset I \,/\, H$

23.

    1.   (A & B) v (W & E)

    2.   B ⊃ ~E

    3.   ~E v ~W

    4.   (E &W) v O

    5.   (A & B) ⊃ X / X & O

24.

    1.   H v E

    2.   ~H & ~E / Z

25.

    1.   ~ ~K

    2.   ~(A & B) & ~(E & F)

    3.   (H & K) ⊃ [(A & B) v (E & F)] / ~ H

26.

    1.   H ⊃ (E & P)

    2.   A v (B & ~C)

    3.   A ⊃ ~E

    4.   ~C ⊃~P / ~H

27.

    1.   ~ (A & B)

    2.   ~ A ⊃ (P & O)

    3.   ~ B ⊃ (O & S) / O

The Transposition Rule

Any sentence **P ⊃ Q** is equivalent to the corresponding sentence ~ **Q ⊃ ~ P**. This gives us our next replacement rule.

The Transposition Rule

A formula **P ⊃ Q** may replace or be replaced by the corresponding formula ~**Q** ⊃ ~**P**.

Here are some examples of the inferences allowed by this new rule:

1. A ⊃ B	1. S ⊃ G	1. (A & B) ⊃ (H v E)	1. ~O ⊃ ~K
2. ~B ⊃ ~ A	2. ~G ⊃ ~S	2. ~(H v E) ⊃ ~(A & B)	2. K ⊃ O

In each case, the second sentence was derived from the first by an application of transposition. The following proof employs transposition:

1. E ⊃ (A ⊃ B)
2. (~B ⊃ ~A) ⊃ S
3. (E ⊃ S) ⊃ H   / H
4. (A ⊃ B) ⊃ S   Trans 2
5. E ⊃ S   HS 1, 4
6. H   MP 3, 5

Here is one way to remember this rule: The antecedent and consequent of a conditional can "trade places" as long as each loses a tilde or each gains a tilde in the process.

The Implication Rule

A sentence **P ⊃ Q** is equivalent to the corresponding sentence ~**P** v **Q**. (This can easily be confirmed on a truth table.) This is the basis of our next replacement rule, the implication rule.

> ### The Implication Rule (Imp)
>
> Anywhere in a proof, a formula **P ⊃ Q** may replace or be replaced with the corresponding formula ~ **P** v **Q**.

In each of the following examples, the second sentence was derived from the first sentence in accord with the implication rule.

| 1. A ⊃ B | 1. ~E v S | 1. H ⊃ G | 1. ~ F v P |
| 2. ~A v B | 2. E ⊃ S | 2. ~H v G | 2. F ⊃ P |

So, when the operator is either a horseshoe or a wedge, you may negate the left side and change the horseshoe to a wedge or the wedge to a horseshoe, provided that you leave the right side as it is.

Here is a proof requiring implication:

1. A ⊃ (G ⊃ E)
2. (E v ~ G) ⊃ S / A ⊃ S
3. A ⊃ (~ G v E)   Imp 1
4. A ⊃ (E v ~ G)   Comm 3
5. A ⊃ S   HS 2, 4

This proof could have been worked this way as well:

1. A ⊃ (G ⊃ E)
2. (E v ~ G) ⊃ S / A ⊃ S
3. (~ G v E) ⊃ S   Comm 2
4. (G ⊃ E) ⊃ S   Imp 3
5. A ⊃ S   HS 1, 4

The Exportation Rule

A simple truth-table test will show that any sentence **(P & Q) ⊃ R** is equivalent to the corresponding sentence **P ⊃ (Q ⊃ R)**. In accordance with this, we have the exportation rule.

The Exportation Rule (Exp)

Anywhere in a proof, a formula **(P & Q) ⊃ R** may replace or be replaced with the corresponding formula **P ⊃ (Q ⊃ R)**.

In each of the following examples, the exportation rule has been applied to the first sentence to derive the second sentence.

1. (A & B) ⊃ E   1   [(H v S) & G)] ⊃ M
2. A ⊃ (B ⊃ E)   2.   (H v S) ⊃ (G ⊃ M)

The following proof employs exportation:

1. A ⊃ (B ⊃ S) / B ⊃ (A ⊃ S)
2. (A & B) ⊃ S   Exp 1
3. (B & A) ⊃ S   Comm 2
4. B ⊃ (A ⊃ S)   Exp 3

The Tautology Rule

Any sentence **P** is equivalent to the corresponding sentence **P v P**, and any sentence **P** is also equivalent to the corresponding sentence **P & P**. Thus, the tautology rule, summarized in the following box, is certainly valid.

The Tautology Rule (Taut)

Anywhere in a proof, a formula **P** may replace or be replaced with the corresponding formula **P** v **P**.

Anywhere in a proof, a formula **P** may replace or be replaced with the corresponding formula **P** & **P**.

Here is a proof employing this new rule:

1. A ⊃ (S ⊃ G)
2. A v A
3. S v S / G & G
4. A   Taut 2
5. S   Taut 3
6. S ⊃ G   MP 1, 4
7. G   MP 5, 6
8. G & G   Taut 7

At line 4, A v A was replaced with A, and A was later used to derive S ⊃ G. At line 5, S v S was replaced by S, and this was used to derive G. Tautology then allowed us to replace G with G & G.

The Equivalence Rule

We have reached our last replacement rule. The following two principles are the basis of the replacement rule for the triple bar: Any sentence **P** ≡ **Q** is equivalent to the corresponding sentence (**P** ⊃ **Q**) & (**Q** ⊃ **P**). Any sentence **P** ≡ **Q** is equivalent to the corresponding sentence (**P** & **Q**) v (~**P** & ~**Q**). The Equivalence rule reflects both principles:

The Equivalence Rule (Equiv)

Anywhere in a proof, a formula **P** ≡ **Q** may replace or be replaced with the corresponding formula (**P** ⊃ **Q**) & (**Q** ⊃ **P**).

Anywhere in a proof a formula **P** ≡ **Q** may replace or be replaced with the corresponding formula (**P** & **Q**) v (~**P** & ~**Q**).

The following inferences are among those permitted by the equivalence rule:

1.	A ≡ B	1.	A ≡ B	1.	D ≡ K
2.	(A ⊃ B) & (B ⊃ A)	2.	(A & B) v (~A & ~ B)	2.	(D ⊃ K) & (K ⊃ D)

The following proof uses our last replacement rule.

1. A ≡ B
2. ~B / ~A
3. (A ⊃ B) & (B ⊃ A)   Equiv 1
4. A ⊃ B   Simp 3
5. ~A   MT 2, 4

Do We Really Need Replacement Rules?

The replacement rules are certainly more complicated than the rules of Chapters 18 and 19. In addition, they can sometimes be more difficult to work with. However, without them, our proof system is limited, for many valid arguments cannot be proved valid without the replacement rules. For one example, using only the rules of Chapters 18 and 19, we could not construct a proof of the following extremely simple and obviously valid argument:

1. (A v B) ⊃ C
2. (B v A) / C

Notice that MP does not apply directly to lines 1 and 2 of this argument, for line 2 is not the antecedent of line 1. To prove this argument valid, we must employ the commutative rule. Two alternative proofs are possible:

I.
1. (A v B) ⊃ C
2. (B v A) / C
3. A v B   Comm 2
4. C   MP 1, 3

II.
1. (A v B) ⊃ C
2. (B v A) / C
3. (B v A) ⊃ C   Comm 1
4. C   MP 2, 3

Proving Invalidity?

You probably noticed that we only use natural deduction to prove arguments valid; we do not use natural deduction to prove arguments *invalid*. Suppose an argument is invalid and we want to demonstrate the fact to someone. In that case, we turn to the method of truth tables (Chapters 15–18). An argument is easily shown to be invalid using the method of truth tables. For arguments containing many letters, the partial table is the most efficient method. In this sense, truth tables and natural deduction complement each other within a system of logic.

Exercise 20.3   Using any of the inference and replacement rules, fill in the justifications for the following.

1.

    1.   J ⊃ I

    2.   (~I ⊃ ~J) ⊃ S

    3.   (S v H) ⊃ [(A & B) ⊃ C]

    4.   A / ~C ⊃ ~B

    5.   ~I ⊃ ~J

    6.   S

    7.   S v H

    8.   (A & B) ⊃ C

    9.   A ⊃ (B ⊃ C)

    10.   B ⊃ C

    11.   ~C ⊃ ~B

2.

    1.   J ≡ I

    2.   (J ⊃ I) ⊃ W

    3.   (~J v ~I)

    4.   W ⊃ S / S & (~J & ~I)

    5.   (J ⊃ I) & (I ⊃ J)

    6.   J ⊃ I

    7.   W

    8.   S

    9.   (J & I) v (~J & ~I)

    10.   ~(J & I)

    11.   ~J & ~I

    12.   S & (~J & ~I)

3.

    1.   A ⊃ B

    2.   E ⊃ B

    3.   ~(~A & ~E)

    4.   B ⊃ G / G

5. A v E
6. B v B
7. B
8. G

4.
1. ~S ⊃ S
2. ~S v G
3. G ⊃ ~(J v I)
4. ~J ⊃ Z / Z
5. S v S
6. S
7. ~~S
8. G
9. ~(J v I)
10. ~J & ~I
11. ~J
12. Z

5.
1. A ⊃ B
2. (~A v B) ⊃ J
3. H ⊃ ~J
4. ~H ⊃ I
5. (I v I) ⊃ (S v S) / S
6. ~A v B
7. J
8. ~~J
9. ~H
10. I
11. I v I
12. S v S
13. S

Exercise 20.4   Use any of the replacement and inference rules to prove the following.

1.
1. H ⊃ ~S
2. (~H v ~S) ⊃ F
3. F ⊃ B / B

2.
1. ~ A ⊃ B
2. A ⊃ E
3. B ⊃ S
4. (E v S) ⊃ X / X

3.
1. J ⊃ I
2. (~ I ⊃ ~ J) ⊃ S
3. F ⊃ ~ S / ~ F

4.
1. H ⊃ S
2. ~ J ⊃ ~ S / H ⊃ J

5.
1. ~ (A & ~ B) ⊃ C
2. A ⊃ B
3. H v ~ C / H

6.
1. A ⊃ B
2. A ⊃ ~ B
3. ~ A ⊃ G / G

7.
1. (J v J) ⊃ S
2. J & F / S

8.
1. A ⊃ (B ⊃ C) / B ⊃ (A ⊃ C)

9.
1. H ⊃ (A ⊃ E)
2. (E v ~ A) ⊃ S / H ⊃ S

10.
1. (A & E) ⊃ S
2. (E ⊃ S) ⊃ F / A ⊃ F

11.
1. ~ J v I
2. ~ I v J / J ≡ I

12.
1. B ≡ G
2. (B & G) ⊃ Z
3. (~ B & ~ G) ⊃ Z / Z

13.

    1.   J ≡ I

    2.   ~ (J & I) / ~ J & ~ I

14.

    1.   A ⊃ (B & C)

    2.   B ⊃ (C ⊃ S) / A ⊃ S

15.

    1.   (A ⊃ B) & (E ⊃ B)

    2.   ~ (~ A & ~ E) / B

16.

    1.   ~ [(J ⊃ I) & (I ⊃ J)]

    2.   (A & S) ⊃ (J ≡ I)

    3.   A / ~ S

17.

    1.   (A ⊃ B) ⊃ [(T v I) & (H ≡ J)]

    2.   (T v I) ⊃ [(H ≡ J) ⊃ X] / (A ⊃ B) ⊃ X

18.

    1.   A ⊃ (B & E) / (A ⊃ B) & (A ⊃ E)

19.

    1.   H ⊃ ~ H

    2.   ~ (H & S) ⊃ G / ~ (H v ~ G)

20.

    1.   A ⊃ B

    2.   A ⊃ ~ B / ~ A

21.

    1.   P ⊃ [(Q v R) v S]

    2.   [(S v Q) v R] ⊃ (U & T)

    3.   ~ (T & U) / ~P

22.

    1.   (~P ⊃ R) & (Q ⊃ ~S)

    2.   (R & ~S) ⊃ T

    3.   ~T / P v ~Q

23.

    1.   ~(P ⊃ Q) v (R v S)

    2.   (~T v U) ⊃ ~(R v S)

    3.   [(P ⊃ Q) ⊃ ~(~T v U)] ⊃ ~V / ~(V & W)

24.
1. A ≡ ~B
2. ~A ⊃ (C & E)
3. A ⊃ ~ E / B ≡ E

25.
1. (J ⊃ I) ⊃ W
2. W ⊃ ~ W / J

26.
1. P & Q
2. P ⊃ ~~R
3. Q ⊃ S
4. ~R v M
5. P ⊃ T / (M & S) & T

27.
1. R v (P v S)
2. T & ~K
3. ~(~ T v K) ⊃ ~R
4. (S ⊃ Q) & ~Q / P

28.
1. (W v E) v O
2. (E v O) ⊃ (A ⊃~ B)
3. ~(W v O)
4. E ⊃ B / ~(A & U)

29.
1. A ⊃ B
2. ~A ⊃ (D ⊃ ~L)
3. ~~E & D
4. O ⊃ L
5. B ⊃ ~E / ~O

30.
1. J ⊃ (S & H)
2. W ⊃ (~S & ~H)
3. J v W / H ⊃ S

31.
1. O ⊃ (B v C)
2. D v ~(B v C)
3. ~O ⊃ (E & W)

    4. E ⊃ ~H

    5. ~D & (G & Z) / (W & G) & ~H

32.

    1. A ⊃ (B ⊃ C)

    2. ~(A & ~B)

    3. B ⊃ (C ⊃ O) / (A & C) ⊃ O

33.

    1. A = B

    2. A v B / A

34.

    1. A = B

    2. A ⊃ (B ⊃ Z)

    3. ~(A v B) ⊃ Z

    4. ~Z v ~J / (A & B) ⊃ ~J

35.

    1. (A ⊃ B) ⊃ G

    2. (I ⊃ B) ⊃ ~ G / ~ B

36.

    1. (J ⊃ I) ⊃ (I ⊃ J)

    2. (J ≡ I) ⊃ ~(A & ~B)

    3. I & A / A & B

Exercise 20.5   Prove these ancient Stoic arguments valid.

1.

    1. P ⊃ (P ⊃ Q)

    2. P / Q

2.

    1. P ⊃ P

    2. ~P ⊃ P / P

3.

    1. P ⊃ Q

    2. P ⊃ ~Q / ~P

4.

    1. (P & Q) ⊃ R

    2. ~R

    3. P / ~Q

Derived Rules of Inference

A *derived rule of inference* is a rule formed by abbreviating a sequence of lines in a proof. Our proof system does not need any additional rules, for it is complete in the following precise sense: Every valid truth-functional argument can be proved valid in the system as it is. (For more on logical "completeness," see Appendix B on Metalogic at the back of the book.)

A derived rule serves only one purpose: It allows us to construct a proof that is shorter than it otherwise might be. Derived rules are therefore always redundant: When we prove something using a derived rule, we could have proved the same thing using other rules instead. Economy is a derived rule's only reason to be; it earns its keep simply by the shortcuts it makes possible. Consider the following proof:

1. ~(P ⊃ Q) / P & ~Q
2. ~(~P v Q)   Imp 1
3. ~~P & ~Q   DM 2
4. P & ~Q   DN 3

This proof shows that from a statement of the form ~(P ⊃ Q) a statement of the form **P & ~Q** can be validly derived. It follows that this *derived* inference rule is a valid rule:

From a statement of the form ~(P ⊃ Q) you may infer a statement of the form **P & ~Q**.

Exercise 20.6   Show that each of the following derived rules is valid.

1.
  1. Given a compound sentence of the form **P ⊃ Q**
  2. Given the corresponding sentence **P ⊃ R**
  3. You may infer the corresponding sentence **P ⊃ (Q & R)**

2.
  1. Given a compound sentence of the form **P ⊃ Q**
  2. Given the corresponding sentence **R ⊃ S**
  3. Given the corresponding sentence ~Q v ~S
  4. You may infer the corresponding sentence ~P v ~R

3.
  1. Given a compound sentence of the form **P ⊃ Q**
  2. Given the corresponding sentence **Q ⊃ R**
  3. Given the corresponding sentence **R ⊃ S**
  4. You may infer the corresponding sentence **P ⊃ S**

4.

    1.   Given a compound sentence of the form **P ⊃ Q**

    2.   Given the corresponding sentence **Q ⊃ R**

    3.   Given the corresponding sentence ~**R**

    4.   You may infer the corresponding sentence ~P

5.

    1.   Given a compound sentence of the form **P ⊃ Q**

    2.   Given the corresponding sentence **Q ⊃ R**

    3.   Given the corresponding sentence **R ⊃ S**

    4.   You may infer the corresponding sentence ~**S ⊃ ~P**

Exercise 20.7   Using other rules of inference, show that *absorption* is a valid rule and provide an example of the argument form in everyday English: From a sentence of the form **P ⊃ Q** you may infer the corresponding sentence **P ⊃ (P & Q)**

Redundancy

Literally an infinite number of valid inference rules exist—more than anyone could write down in a lifetime, or in a thousand lifetimes. Most, however are redundant. A rule R is redundant in a system of logic if it can be excused and everything we might prove using the rule R can be proved using other rules of the system. For example, disjunctive syllogism is redundant in our system, for we could place DS on leave, and in place of it, we could always get by this way:

    1.A v B

    2. ~A

    3. ~~A v B   DN 1

    4. ~A ⊃ B   Imp 3

    5. B   MP 2, 4

We could have reached B directly, using DS. However, a combination of imp, DN, and MP also does the trick. DS is thus redundant in relation to imp, DN, and MP.

Exercise 20.8   Using other rules of inference in each case, show that each of the following rules is redundant in our system.

    1.   MP

    2.   MT

    3.   DS

4. HS

5. CD

Concluding Reflection: On the "Formal" Nature of Truth-Functional Logic

Recall the distinction between a natural language and an artificial language: A *natural* language is a general tool of communication that is typically taught to people from birth. In contrast, an *artificial* language, such as musical notation, is constructed by a group of people to simplify the expression of a limited body of information. In logical theory, the distinction between natural and formal languages is closely related to the distinction between formal and informal logic. In *formal* logic, the focus is on argument forms or structures rather than on specific arguments expressed within a natural language. Because argument forms are more efficiently expressed in symbols rather than in the words of a natural language, formal logic employs an artificial symbolic language. This is why formal logic is also sometimes called *symbolic logic*. Truth-functional logic is one branch of formal logic because truth-functional logic focuses on abstract forms of reasoning rather than on specific arguments expressed within a natural language. This focus on form rather than content is why truth-functional logic employs a formal symbolic language.

In contrast, *informal* logic is so named because the focus is not on the formal aspects of reasoning. This leaves the nonformal aspects of reasoning, which puts the focus on arguments expressed within a natural language context. This is why the arguments of everyday currency get the spotlight on the informal side of logic; this is also why informal logic largely avoids the need for a formal symbolic language.

Each side of logic has its advantages. By studying abstract, content-free argument forms, we can analyze patterns of reasoning common to many arguments across many natural languages—universal patterns we might not notice if the arguments were to be left within a natural language. On the other hand, when we study arguments in their natural language habitat, immersed in the currency of everyday discussion, we might learn more about applying logical principles to the real world. Both formal and informal logic have much to teach us.

Before the nineteenth century, logicians used few symbols in their theorizing. However, as we have seen, in the late nineteenth century Gottlob Frege introduced the first symbolic artificial language for logical theory, complete with a syntax and semantical theory. Frege's "formal" language allowed logicians to simplify expressions of extremely complex ideas, and this in turn led to enormous advances in logical theory. Incidentally, the new symbolic logic, invented by Frege in the nineteenth century, also greatly advanced our understanding of language and also laid the conceptual foundations of computer science. Thus, formal logical languages play a role in both linguistics and in computer science. So, as abstract and theoretical as it might seem, formal truth-functional logic has indeed made a difference.

Appendix 20.1   An Axiomatic Presentation of TL

The notion of an axiom system was introduced in Unit Two. Recall that an axiom system is composed of axioms, definitions, rules of inference, and theorems. The axioms are the unproven starting points of the system, usually asserted as self-evident. The theorems are statements deduced from the axioms using the definitions and rules of inference. Each theorem in a standard axiom system follows from one or more axioms by valid, gap-free, deductive reasoning, via one or more definitions and one or more inference rules. Modern logicians generally avoid the axiomatic approach and instead develop logic as a system of natural deduction, as we have done here. The main reason natural deduction is usually preferred to the axiomatic approach is that axiom systems are so cumbersome, so much harder to work with.

In their now-classic little primer, *Introduction to Symbolic Logic* (New York: The Free Press, 1960), Basson and O'Conner presented modern logic axiomatically. Their compact system employs a language similar to our TL and rests on four axioms, four rules of deduction, and three definitions. The interested reader is invited to take the system for a test drive right here. Basson and O'Conner use capital letters P, Q, and R as metalinguistic variables ranging over the sentences of their system's language, which are all expressed with lowercase letters. I am translating some parts of their system into our current terminology.

Axioms

A1. $(p \lor p) \supset p$

A2. $q \supset (p \lor q)$

A3. $(p \lor q) \supset (q \lor p)$

A4. $(q \supset r) \supset [(p \lor q) \supset (p \lor r)]$

Gloss. These are the starting points of the system, the basis upon which all else will be proved. Using truth tables, it can be proved that each axiom is a truth-functional tautology. Each axiom is thus a necessary truth.

Transformation Rules

Rule of Detachment. From a wff $P \supset Q$, and another wff corresponding to P, you may infer the corresponding wff Q. (This is modus ponens.)

Rule of Uniform Substitution. Any wff may be substituted for any sentence variable throughout an expression.

Gloss. The replacement must be made uniformly throughout the whole expression. For example, starting with A1, substituting the wff "p & q" for the variable p yields the formula:

$$[(p \& q) v (p \& q)] \supset (p \& q)$$

Rule of Substitution by Definition. In any axiom or theorem, you may substitute for any *part* of the formula any expression that is equivalent to it by definitions 1 through 3.

Gloss. Notice that each of the transformation or inference rules is truth-preserving: If the formula to which the rule is applied is true, the formula deduced must also be true.

Definitions

Definition 1. P & Q is definitionally equivalent to ~(~P v ~Q).

Definition 2. P ⊃ Q is definitionally equivalent to ~P v Q

Definition 3. P ≡ Q is definitionally equivalent to (P ⊃ Q) & (Q ⊃ P).

For example, starting with the formula derived earlier, we can reach the following formula by substituting ~(~p v ~q) for p & q on the basis of Definition 1:

$$[~(~p v ~q) v ~(~p v ~q)] \supset ~(~p v ~q)$$

Finally, a sample proof:

1. (p v p) ⊃ p   A1
2. (~p v ~p) ⊃ ~p   1 (~p/ p)
3. (p ⊃ ~p) ⊃ ~p   2, Def 2

Line 1 is axiom 1. On line 2 we uniformly substituted ~p for p by applying the rule of uniform substitution to line 1, replacing p with ~p, as indicated by the expression ~p/ p. Line 3 is the result of applying definition 2 to line 2, replacing the

~p v ~p part with p ⊃ ~p according to the second definition. Thus, (p ⊃ ~p) ⊃ ~p is a theorem of the system.

Metalogical properties of the system. It can be proved that the axioms of this system are independent. This means it is not possible to derive one of the axioms as a theorem on the basis of the other axioms. It can also be proved that the system is complete. Roughly, a system of logic is complete if it proves all you would want it to prove. It can be proved that any truth-functional tautology can be proved in the system. It can also be proved that any truth-functionally valid argument can be proved valid in the system.

In addition, it can be shown that every theorem of the system is a tautology. Roughly, since every axiom is a tautology, and since every definition expresses a necessary truth, and since the rules of inference are truth-preserving, it follows that every theorem is a tautology. Because there are an infinite number of tautologies, that is a lot of theorems! See Appendix B at the back of the book for more about the metatheory of truth-functional logic.

21 Truth-Functional Deduction Part 4 « « « « «

Indirect and Conditional Proof

Inference rules may be simple or complex. A *simple rule of inference* states that from a sentence or sentences of such and such a form, you may infer a sentence of a certain form. The rules we have employed so far have all been simple rules in this sense. A *complex rule of inference* allows us to write a formula of such and such a form in a proof if previously in the proof we have already derived a formula of a certain form.

A proof inside of a proof is called a *subordinate proof*. When a proof is carried out inside a proof, the lines of the subordinate proof are indented, and the larger proof is called the *superordinate proof*. This chapter adds two complex rules of inference to our system, both requiring subordinate proofs: indirect proof and conditional proof.

Indirect Proof

When an attorney suspects that a witness for the opposing side is lying, the attorney will probably ask the witness lots of detailed questions during cross-examination. If the witness contradicts himself, the members of the jury will naturally (and rightly) conclude that at least part of his testimony is not true. If at one point in the questioning Joe Doakes says one thing, and at another point says or implies the logical opposite, at least one of his claims is not true. "I was in France at the time of the crime" and "I have never been to Europe" cannot both be true. Mothers have been known to employ the same logic:

Mom: Where have you been, Billy?
Billy: I was over at Joe's house.
Mom: What did you do there?

Billy: We swam in their pool.

Mom: But they took their pool out over a year ago. Do you want to tell me where you *really* have been?

Socrates used this form of reasoning on his interlocutors when he felt they were seriously in error and needed a "wake-up call," as we saw in Unit One, Chapter 6. The Socratic elenchus began with Socrates asking the other person, "So you believe such and such, do you?" After the other persons answered "Yes," Socrates would continue: "But you also believe so and so, don't you?" Of course, this would be something that could not rationally be denied. It would also be something that contradicted the person's errant belief. In this way, the other person would come to see that although he thought he had the truth, at least two of his beliefs stood in logical contradiction. It followed that at least one of the beliefs in question must go.

The trial attorney, the mother, and Socrates himself were all employing the basic logic of indirect proof, which we now state in a more formal way. Suppose you want to prove some claim **P**, on the basis of certain premises—call them A, B, and C. Begin your proof by assuming the *logical opposite* of the claim you wish to prove. The logical opposite of a sentence **P** is the corresponding sentence ~**P**, and the logical opposite of a sentence ~**P** is the corresponding sentence **P**. So, because we want to prove **P**, we assume ~**P**. Next, demonstrate that this assumption, ~**P**, combined with the stated premises, implies a self-contradiction. (Recall that a **self-contradiction** is any statement conjoined to its negation, so A & ~A, B & ~B, ~C & C, ~D & D, etc., are all self-contradictions.) Now, it is an accepted principle of logic that whenever a set of statements implies a self-contradiction, the members of the set cannot all be true. Thus the premises and the assumption—since they imply a self-contradiction—cannot all be true. Therefore, assuming the premises are all true, it follows that the assumption, ~**P**, must be false. It follows that **P**—the claim we originally sought to prove—must be true, because **P** is the logical opposite of the assumption and the opposite of false is true. In other words, it follows that **P** must be true if the premises A, B, and C are true. This is certainly valid reasoning.

In the Middle Ages logicians in Europe named this method of proof **reductio ad absurdum proof** (Latin: "reduction to absurdity"). When it had been shown that an opponent's statement logically implies a self-contradiction, it was said that his position had been "reduced to an absurdity." Today this method is also called **indirect proof** because, in such a proof, the conclusion is derived indirectly, by first deriving a contradiction from the negation or denial of the conclusion and then inferring the conclusion from that. In mathematics this form of proof is usually called *proof by contradiction*.

The Rule of Indirect Proof

The following inference rule reflects the reductio ad absurdum (indirect proof) method.

The Rule of Indirect Proof (Concise Version)

Anywhere in a proof, to prove a sentence, you may indent and assume the logical opposite of the sentence you seek to prove. If you succeed in deriving a self-contradiction, then you may end the indentation and infer the original sentence you sought to prove.

The Rule of Indirect Proof (Detailed Version)

Anywhere in a proof, to prove a sentence, you may do the following:

1. Indent and assume the opposite of the sentence you seek to prove, writing AIP (assumption for indirect proof) as justification. The **opposite of a formula P** is the corresponding formula ~P; the opposite of a formula ~P is the corresponding formula **P.**
2. Using the assumption plus any lines that are available, derive a self-contradiction.
3. End the indentation and draw a vertical line in front of the indented steps (to mark them off from the other lines). On the next line assert the sentence that you sought to prove. (This is called *discharging* the assumption.) As a justification, write IP (indirect proof) and cite the indented lines.

Proviso. The indented lines are called an *indirect proof sequence*. Once an assumption has been discharged and the conclusion has been derived, the indented lines in the indirect proof sequence may no longer be used to derive future lines in the proof. In other words, once the assumption has been discharged, the indented lines are no longer "available"—they are out of the game.

The indirect proof rule may be abbreviated thusly:

IP (Abbreviation)

To prove **P**: Indent, assume the opposite of **P**, derive a self-contradiction, end the indentation, assert **P**.

The proviso is very important. Always keep in mind that when an assumed premise is discharged and the indirect proof sequence has been concluded, the indented lines may no longer be used in the proof. Otherwise, invalid inferences may result, for the indented lines do not themselves actually follow from the premises.

Let us now apply the indirect proof rule (IP) to the following argument:

1. ~A ⊃ ~H
2. H v G
3. G ⊃ H / A

Our first step is to indent and assume the negation of our conclusion. The negation of A is ~A. So, we indent and assume ~A:

4.   ~A   AIP

Next, we can apply MP to lines 1 and 4 to derive ~H:

5.   ~ H   MP 1, 4

Now, we apply DS to lines 2 and 5 to bring down G:

6.   G   DS 2, 5

Applying MP to lines 3 and 6, we derive H:

7.   H   MP 3, 6

Conjoining 5 and 7 produces:

8.   H & ~H   Conj 5, 7

But this is a self-contradiction, that is, a sentence of the form **P** & **~P**. Because we have derived a self-contradiction, we "dis-indent" and assert our original conclusion:

9. A   IP 4–8

We began at line 4 by assuming the opposite of our conclusion. From that, we used the rules to derive H & ~ H, which is a self-contradiction. Because our assumption implied a contradiction, we discharged that assumption and inferred its opposite, which was the conclusion we originally sought to prove. The justification for line 9, "IP 4–8," is to be interpreted as saying, "We applied the IP rule on the basis of lines 4 through 8."

Understand that in this proof, the indented lines 4 through 8 do *not* follow from the premises; they merely follow from the assumption, which itself does not follow from the premises. However, for reasons given earlier, line 9 *does* follow from the premises—that's what the indirect proof sequence establishes.

In the following indirect proof, the conclusion we seek to prove is A v B. Because the method requires that we assume the opposite of our conclusion, our assumed premise will be ~ (A v B).

1.   (A v B) v ~G
2.   G v R
3.   R ⊃ G / A v B
4. | ~ (A v B)   AIP
5. | ~G   DS 1, 4
6. | R   DS 2, 5
7. | G   MP 3, 6
8. | G & ~ G   Conj 5, 7
9.   A v B   IP 4–8

At line 8, we derived a self-contradiction, G & ~G. So, we dis-indented, moved to line 9, and wrote down our original conclusion, A v B. In the following example, we begin, as usual, by assuming the opposite of our conclusion.

1.   J ⊃ (B & I)
2.   B v (J & I)   / B
3. | ~B   AIP
4. | J & I   DS 2, 3
5. | J   Simp 4
6. | B & I   MP 1, 5
7. | B   Simp 6
8. | B & ~ B   Conj 3, 7
9.   B   IP 3–8

History Note

The indirect proof method was known as *apagoge* in ancient times, according to the Harvard logician W. V. O. Quine.[1]

---

[1] I have drawn many of my short "history notes" from W. V. O. Quine, *Methods of Logic*, 3rd ed. (New York: Holt, 1972).

Exercise 21.1   Use the indirect proof method to prove the following:

1.
    1. J v (I & E)
    2. J ⊃ E / E

2.
    1. (H v B) ⊃ (A & E)
    2. (E v S) ⊃ (G & ~ H) / ~ H

3.
    1. (~J v I) ⊃ (A & B)
    2. (A v Z) ⊃ (B ⊃ J) / J

4.
    1. A v (L & P)
    2. A ⊃ L / L

5.
    1. ~B ⊃ C
    2. C ⊃ B / B

6.
    1. G ⊃ ~ N
    2. ~ A
    3. ~ G ⊃ A / ~ N

7.
    1. ~~M ⊃ (N ⊃ O)
    2. ~O ⊃ (M ⊃ N)
    3. ~ M ⊃ O / O

8.
    1. (~~A & ~ A) ⊃ (A & ~A)
    2. A ⊃ B
    3. ~B / ~ A

9.
    1. A
    2. A ⊃ B
    3. (A & B) ⊃ K
    4. K ⊃ G / G

10.
    1. (A v B) ⊃ (G & W)
    2. ~G / ~A

11.

    1.   (P ⊃ ~ R) & (Q ⊃ S)
    2.   (~R ⊃ T) & (S ⊃ ~ U)
    3.   (T ⊃ ~X) & (~U ⊃ Y)
    4.   P & Q   / ~X & Y

12.

    1.   ~X ⊃ (B ⊃ W)
    2.   X v B
    3.   B ⊃ ~W
    4.   X ⊃ O / X & O

Exercise 21.2   This is an advanced exercise. Examine the summary of Anselm's ontological argument in Chapter 35. As best you can, translate the argument into statements of TL, in such a way that the argument is truth-functionally valid and can be proved valid using the method of indirect proof. With the argument in a truth-functional format, prove it valid using the method of indirect proof. What does this establish? If the argument is valid, does it follow that the conclusion is true?

Conditional Proof

We sometimes reason this way in everyday life: Someone makes a claim. Suppose they claim that the hamburgers at the local burger joint are not really made from beef at all. Rather, they insist, the patties are a specially flavored concoction made out of processed seaweed. We might reason in response, if that is true, then *if* we test their patties for the presence of proteins specific to meat, then the test will come out negative.

Notice that in this example, the argument does not conclude that something is actually the case. Rather, it ends with a hypothetical or conditional assertion: If such and such is the case, *then* so and so is the case. This is essentially the reasoning known in logic as **conditional proof**. Let us proceed in steps.

Suppose you are given the following argument:

    1.   A ⊃ B
    2.   A ⊃ C / A ⊃ (B & C)

You might show this is valid, in English, by reasoning informally as follows. If we assume A is true, then given the premise A ⊃ B, it follows that B must be true (by MP). It also follows, if A is true and given the premise A ⊃ C, that C must be true (by MP). So, given the premises, if we assume A is true, then B and C must be true, too. But that is the same as saying that if the premises are true, then if A is true then B and C are true. But that is the same as saying that if the premises are true then A ⊃ (B

& C) must be true. And A ⊃ (B & C) is the argument's conclusion. So if the premises are true, then the conclusion must be true. This informal reasoning shows that the argument is valid. The conditional proof rule (CP) incorporates this general pattern of reasoning.

The Rule of Conditional Proof (Concise Version)

To prove a sentence of the form **P ⊃ Q**, anywhere in a proof you may indent and assume the sentence **P**. If you succeed in deriving, from it and the premises of the superordinate proof, the corresponding sentence **Q**, then you may end the indentation and infer the corresponding sentence **P ⊃ Q**.

The Rule of Conditional Proof (Detailed Version)

If, at any point in a proof, you wish to derive a conditional **P ⊃ Q**, you may do the following:

1. Indent and assume the antecedent of the conditional you seek to prove, writing ACP (assumption for conditional proof) as justification.
2. Using this assumption plus, if needed, any available lines occurring earlier, derive the consequent of the conditional.
3. Draw a vertical line in front of the indented steps (to mark them off from the other lines). The indented lines constitute a conditional proof sequence.
4. End the indentation and infer the conditional whose antecedent is the assumption with which you began the conditional proof sequence and whose consequent is a line in that sequence. As a justification, write CP (for conditional proof) and cite the line numbers of the indented lines within the sequence. The completion of this step is called "discharging the assumption."

Proviso. Once an assumption has been discharged and the conditional has been derived, the indented lines in the assumption's conditional proof sequence are no longer "available" to be used in justification of further lines in the proof. Once you disindent, the indented lines are out of the game.

The conditional proof rule can be abbreviated as follows:

CP (Abbreviation)

To prove a sentence of the form **P ⊃ Q**: Indent, assume **P**, derive **Q**, end the indent, and assert **P ⊃ Q**.

Once again, the proviso is important. When an assumed premise is discharged and the conditional proof sequence has been concluded, the indented lines may no longer be used in the proof. Otherwise, invalid inferences may result, for the indented lines do not themselves follow from the premises.

Let us now apply our new rule. In the following proof, we need to derive H ⊃ G. Employing the conditional proof strategy, we first indent and assume H. We then derive G. After this, we disindent, and we infer H ⊃ G according to the CP rule.

1. (H v S) ⊃ (~E & B)
2. E v G   / H ⊃ G
3. | H ACP
4. | H v S Add 3
5. ~E & B | MP 1, 4
6. ~E | Simp 5
7. | G DS 2, 6
8. H ⊃ G   CP 3–7

Notice that we began by assuming the antecedent of the conditional we were seeking to prove. We then applied addition and added S to derive the antecedent of line 1. This allowed us to break up line 1 and derive ~E & B. We then applied simp and derived ~E, which allowed us to infer the consequent of the conditional we were trying to prove. At step 8, we discharged our assumption and inferred the conditional whose antecedent was our assumption and whose consequent was the last line reached within the conditional proof sequence.

History Note

The conditional proof entered modern logic in 1929 in the work of the Polish logician Alfred Tarski and in 1930 in the work of the French mathematician Jacques Herbrand.

Understand that in the preceding proof, lines 3 through 7 do not follow from the premises; they merely follow from the assumption, which itself does not follow from the premises. However, for reasons given earlier, line 8 does follow from the premises—that's what the conditional proof sequence establishes.

Here is another example:

1. A ⊃ J
2. A ⊃ (J ⊃ T) / A ⊃ T

3.		A	ACP
4.		J ⊃ T	MP 2, 3
5.		A ⊃ T	HS 1, 4
6.		T	MP 5, 3
7.	A ⊃ T	CP 3–6	

Here is a more complicated CP:

1.	(W & M) ⊃ (W ⊃ H)		
2.	H ⊃ D		
3.	M / (W & K) ⊃ D		
4.		W & K	ACP
5.		W	Simp 4
6.		W & M	Conj 3, 5
7.		W ⊃ H	MP 1, 6
8.		H	MP 5, 7
9.		D	MP 2, 8
10.	(W & K) ⊃ D	CP 4–9	

It is extremely important that you remember this: You are not allowed to end a proof on an indented line. That is, the assumption of a conditional or an indirect proof sequence must be discharged before a proof is ended. So, the last line of a proof can never be an indented conditional or indirect proof sequence line. If you could legally end a proof on an indented line, without discharging the assumption, you could derive any arbitrary conclusion from any premise.

For example, consider the following English argument:

1. George Costanza is neurotic.
2. If Wyoming is a city, then Seattle is a state.
3. Therefore, Seattle is a state.

In TL, using obvious abbreviations, this is:

1. G
2. W ⊃ S / S

Now, the following would be a correct proof if you were allowed to end a conditional proof (or an indirect proof) without discharging your assumption, as in this incorrect conditional proof:

1. G
2. W ⊃ S / S
3. | W   ACP
4. | S   MP 2, 3

This argument is obviously invalid. We were able to construct a "proof" of it only because we ended on an indented line.

Proving Triple Bar Formulas

The conditional proof rule can also be used to prove formulas of the form **P ≡ Q**. The following proof employs two conditional proofs, one right after the other, before closing with a triple bar:

1. A ⊃ (B ⊃ C)
2. O & B
3. C ⊃ G
4. G ⊃ Z
5. ~Z v A / A ≡ G
6. | A   ACP
7. | B ⊃ C   MP 1, 6
8. | B   Simp 2
9. | C   MP 7, 8
10. | G   MP 3, 9
11. A ⊃ G   CP 6–10
12. | G   ACP
13. | Z   MP 4, 12
14. | ~~Z   DN 13
15.   A   DS 5, 14
16. G ⊃ A   CP 12–15
17. (A ⊃ G) & (G ⊃ A)   Conj 11, 16
18. A ≡ G   Equiv 17

Exercise 21.3   Use conditional proof to prove each of the following:

1.
    1.   A ⊃ (B & C) / A ⊃ C
2.
    1.   J / I ⊃ I

3.
    1. J ⊃ (I ⊃ W)
    2. (I ⊃ W) ⊃ (I ⊃ S) / J ⊃ (I ⊃ S)

4.
    1. (A & B) ⊃ C
    2. A ⊃ B / A ⊃ C

5.
    1. ~ I v Z
    2. Z ⊃ A / I ⊃ (Z & A)

6.
    1. (J v I) ⊃ S
    2. A ⊃ J / A ⊃ (S v T)

7.
    1. (J v I) ⊃ (A & B)
    2. (B v E) ⊃ (O & S) / J ⊃ O

8.
    1. H ⊃ (S & L)
    2. ~ L v I
    3. X ⊃ ~ I
    4. ~ X ⊃ B / H ⊃ B

9.
    1. A ⊃ J
    2. A ⊃ (J ⊃ B)
    3. J ⊃ (B ⊃ T)/ A ⊃ T

10.
    1. J ⊃ (I ⊃ W)
    2. S ⊃ (W ⊃ B)
    3. (I ⊃ B) ⊃ (H v ~ S) / (J & S) ⊃ H

11.
    1. A ⊃ B / A ⊃ [(B v S) v G]

12.
    1. E ⊃ A / (E & O) ⊃ A

13.
    1. (P v Q) ⊃ (R & S)
    2. (S v E) ⊃ F
    3. (E v G) ⊃ (Z & H)
    4. (Z v M) ⊃ W / E ⊃ W

14.
    1.   A ⊃ B
    2.   B ⊃ R / A ⊃ (R v X)

Appendix 21.1   Advanced Techniques

How to Build a "Nested" Proof

The conditional proof rule and the indirect proof rule allow you to construct a conditional proof or an indirect proof inside another conditional or indirect proof. That is, you may construct a conditional proof within a conditional proof, an indirect proof within an indirect proof, a conditional proof within an indirect proof, and an indirect proof within a conditional proof. An indented proof within an indented proof is called a **nested proof**. Because nested proofs can get complicated, there are rules to guide us. First, to make matters more precise, let us say that the scope of an assumption consists of the assumption itself along with all of its indented sentences. One conditional or indirect proof sequence lies inside the scope of another if its assumption is within the scope of the other proof sequence. When constructing nested proofs, you must obey the following rules:

1. You may not discharge an assumption unless all other assumptions within the assumption's scope have been discharged.
2. Every assumption must be discharged before a proof is completed.

Here is an example of a nested conditional proof:

1.   G ⊃ (F ⊃ H) / F ⊃ (G ⊃ H)
2. | F   ACP
3. | G   ACP
4. | F ⊃ H   MP 1, 3
5. | H   MP 2, 4
6. | G ⊃ H   CP 3–5
7.   F ⊃ (G ⊃ H)   CP 2–6

    Notice that the conclusion of this argument is a conditional whose antecedent is F and whose consequent is (G ⊃ H). Notice further that the consequent (G ⊃ H) is itself a conditional. At line 2 we assumed the antecedent of the conclusion. At 3 we assumed the antecedent of the *consequent* of the conclusion; that is, we assumed the antecedent of (G ⊃ H). At this point we had a conditional proof within a conditional proof.

We then completed the inner conditional proof sequence, discharged our assumption, and closed it off. This gave us what we were after when we started the first conditional proof. So we completed the outer conditional proof sequence and closed it off.

Concerning the preceding nested proof, the first of the two rules given earlier shows that you cannot end the first conditional proof sequence—the sequence whose assumption is F—and discharge its assumption until the conditional proof within has been completed and its assumption has been discharged. The second rule simply reminds you that you cannot end a proof on an indented line; all assumptions must be discharged before you derive the final conclusion.

Consider the following nested proof:

1. $G \supset (B \lor {\sim}A)$
2. $E \lor {\sim}B \: / \: {\sim}E \supset (G \supset {\sim}A)$
3. ${\sim}E$ ACP
4. ${\sim}B$ DS 2, 3
5. G ACP
6. $B \lor {\sim}A$ MP 1, 5
7. ${\sim}A$ DS 4, 6
8. $G \supset {\sim}A$ CP 5–7
9. ${\sim}E \supset (G \supset {\sim}A)$ CP 3–8

While we are deriving lines inside the inner conditional proof sequence, we can use lines from the outer conditional proof sequence, for its assumption has not yet been discharged. Thus, at step 6 in the immediately preceding proof, we can appeal to steps 1 through 5 if we need to. However, once the inner proof sequence has been closed off and its assumption has been discharged, we cannot appeal to or cite lines from within its "region"—lines 5 through 7—as we continue on in the outer conditional proof sequence. Thus, after step 8, we cannot derive lines from lines 5 through 7 as we go about finishing the rest of the proof. Similarly, after step 9, if we were to make further inferences, we could not appeal to any of the lines within the outer conditional proof—lines 3 through 8—to derive further lines in the proof.

Generally, you will need to "nest" two conditional proofs if the conclusion you seek to prove is a conditional whose consequent is itself a conditional; in other words, if the sentence is of the form **P** $\supset$ (**Q** $\supset$ **R**). In such a case, the consequent of the conditional you are seeking to prove will itself contain an antecedent and consequent. To use a nested proof to derive a formula of this form, do the following:

1. Indent and assume the antecedent, **P**, of the whole conditional.
2. Indent again and assume the antecedent, **Q**, of the conditional constituting the consequent of the whole conditional.

You may also nest an indirect proof sequence within a conditional proof sequence or a conditional proof sequence within an indirect proof sequence. The rules allow both types of proofs. Here is an indirect proof nested within a conditional proof:

1. L ⊃ [~M ⊃ (N & O)]
2. ~N & P / L ⊃ (M & P)
3. | L   ACP
4. | ~M ⊃ (N & O)   MP 1, 3
5. | ~M   AIP
6. | N & O   MP 4, 5
7. | N   Simp 6
8. | ~N   Simp 2
9. | N & ~ N   Conj 7, 8
10. | M   IP 5–9
11. | P   Simp 2
12. | M & P   Conj 10, 11
13. L ⊃ (M & P)   CP 3–12

Nonstandard IP and CP Proofs

If you closely examine the rules for CP and IP, you will notice that the assumption for an indented sequence does not have to be the first line following the premises, and the conclusion established at the end of an indented sequence need not be the last step in a proof. For example, in the next proof, HS is applied *before* the IP sequence begins:

1. A ⊃ B
2. B ⊃ E
3. (A ⊃ E) ⊃ R
4. G v ~ R / G
5. A ⊃ E   HS 1, 2
6. | ~ G   AIP
7. | ~R   DS 4, 6
8. | R   MP 3, 5
9. | R & ~R   Conj 7, 8
10. G   IP 6–9

Thus, the assumption for an IP (or a CP) does not have to be the first step in a proof. In the following proof, the conclusion established by IP is not the conclusion of the proof. Rather, IP is used to derive E, and E is then used to derive the argument's conclusion:

1. H v E
2. H ⊃ E
3. E ⊃ S / S
4.   ~E   AIP
5.   ~H   MT 2, 4
6.   E   DS 1, 5
7.   E & ~ E   Conj 4, 6
8. E   IP 4–7
9. S   MP 3, 8

Thus, the IP sequence does not have to yield the last line of a proof; it may be used to derive an intermediate step. Also, the indirect proof rule may be used more than once in a single proof:

1. (~W v ~ E) ⊃ ~ E
2. (~E v W) ⊃ B
3. B ⊃ ~ B / W
4.   ~E   AIP
5.   ~E v W   Add 4
6.   B   MP 2, 5
7.   ~B   MP 3, 6
8.   B & ~B   Conj 6, 7
9. E   IP 4–8
10.   ~W   AIP
11.   ~W v ~ E   Add 10
12.   ~E   MP 1, 11
13.   E & ~ E   Conj 9, 12
14. W   IP 10–13

Notice that at line 10 of this proof, the assumption made at line 4 has already been discharged. (It was discharged at line 9.) This means that lines 4 through 8 are no longer available for use; they are now out of the loop, so to speak, and cannot be referred to in justification of any future lines. Thus, after line 9, no justification should refer to lines 4 through 8. Also, at line 10, notice that a whole new indirect proof is started.

Turning to a conditional proof, the assumption for a conditional proof sequence does not have to be the first line after the premises. In the following proof, the conditional proof sequence begins in the middle of the proof:

1. B v (B ⊃ C)
2. (B ⊃ C) ⊃ H
3. H ⊃ A
4. A ⊃ S / ~B ⊃ S
5. (B ⊃ C) ⊃ A   HS 2, 3
6. (B ⊃ C) ⊃ S   HS 4, 5
7. | ~ B   ACP
8. | B ⊃ C   DS 1, 7
9. | S   MP 8, 6
10. ~B ⊃ S   CP 7–9

Furthermore, the conditional established at the end of a conditional proof sequence need not be the last line of the proof. In the following proof, the conclusion is not a conditional, and the conditional proof sequence in the argument's proof is not used to derive the conclusion of the argument. Rather, the conditional proof is used to derive a formula in the middle of the proof, and this intermediate step is then used to derive the conclusion of the argument.

1. G v B
2. (~A ⊃ E) ⊃ ~ G
3. A v D
4. D ⊃ E
5. B ⊃ W   / W
6. | ~ A   ACP
7. | D   DS 3, 6
8. | E   MP 4, 7
9. ~ A ⊃ E   CP 6–8
10. ~G   MP 2, 9
11. B   DS 1, 10
12. W   MP 5, 11

Exercise 21.4   Nested proofs are recommended or required on the following problems:

1.

     1. J ⊃ (I ⊃ W)
     2. W ⊃ (I ⊃ S) / J ⊃ (I ⊃ S)

2.
   1.   A ⊃ (B ⊃C)
   2.   (C v H) ⊃ K / A ⊃ (B ⊃ K)

3.
   1.   A ⊃ (B & E) / (J ⊃ A) ⊃ (J ⊃ E)

4.
   1.   A ⊃ (B ⊃ J)
   2.   A ⊃ (I ⊃ ~ X)
   3.   X ⊃ (B v I) / A ⊃ (X ⊃ J)

5.
   1.   H ⊃ (S & T)
   2.   B ⊃ (A & G) / (T ⊃ B) ⊃ (H ⊃ G)

6.
   1.   A ⊃ B
   2.   (A & B) ⊃ I
   3.   (H & I) ⊃ S / A ⊃ (H ⊃ S)

7.
   1.   {[(P v Q) & (P v R)] & (P & R)} ⊃ T / P ⊃ (R ⊃ T)

8.
   1.   B ⊃ (W & ~D)
   2.   (W & O) ⊃ ~E
   3.   F ⊃ (D v E) / O ⊃ (B ⊃ ~F)

9.
   1.   H / A ⊃ (B ⊃ A)

10.
   1.   W ⊃ X
   2.   X ⊃ (N ⊃ M)
   3.   ~W ⊃ (I & T) / W ⊃ (N ⊃ M)

11.
   1.   (O & D) ⊃ W
   2.   (~B & D) ⊃ (O ⊃ E)
   3.   ~D ⊃ F / (O & ~F) ⊃ (W v E)

Glossary

Conditional proof A proof in which you indent, assume the antecedent of a conditional, deduce the consequent of the conditional, end the indentation and assert the conditional.

Indirect proof A proof in which you indent, assume the opposite of the formula you seek to prove, deduce a self-contradiction, end the indentation, and assert the conclusion you originally sought to prove. Usually called *proof by contradiction* in mathematics.

Nested proof A conditional or indirect proof inside another conditional or indirect proof.

Opposite of a formula The opposite of a sentence **P** is the corresponding sentence ~**P**, and the opposite of a sentence ~**P** is the corresponding sentence **P**.

Reductio ad absurdum proof An indirect proof.

Self-contradiction A statement of the form **P** &~ **P** or ~**P** & **P**.

22 Premise-Free Proofs « «

A **premise-free proof** is a natural deduction proof that begins with no premises at all and reaches a conclusion nevertheless. How can a proof exist with no premises? The idea sounds impossible! Indeed it does at first. Examine the following proof carefully:

To be proved: $[(A \supset B)\ \&\ A] \supset B$

1.	$(A \supset B)\ \&\ A$	ACP
2.	$(A \supset B)$	Simp 1
3.	A	Simp 1
4.	B	MP 2, 3
5.	$[(A \supset B)\ \& A] \supset B$	CP 1–4

This is a perfectly legal proof. Notice that the proof began at step 1 with no premises at all. It began with nothing but an assumption (an assumption is not a premise). The conditional proof rule allows us "anywhere in a proof" to indent, assume a formula, and write as justification "ACP." That is just what we did. We assumed $(A \supset B)$ & A, and then we proceeded to deduce, on the basis of only that formula, B (at step 4). At step 5, the assumed premise was discharged, after which it was out of the game. In accord with the conditional proof rule, we then ended the indent and asserted the conditional formed by joining our assumption, $(A \supset B)$ &A, to the last line of the indented subproof, B, using the horseshoe. The conclusion was thus derived using no premises at all, a "premise-free" proof.

Theorems and Tautologies

A formula that can be derived using no premises at all, thus on the basis of a premise-free proof, is called a **theorem** of our system. Thus, the preceding proof proved that [(A ⊃ B) &A] ⊃ B is a theorem of TD. However, no ordinary formulas of TL are theorems in our system. Every theorem of TD has a very important logical property. As usual, the explanation requires some setting up. To begin with, recall that a **tautology** is a sentence that is true in all possible cases, false in none. A tautology is necessarily true—true in such a way that it cannot possibly be false. In Chapter 15 we learned to use a truth table to show that a given sentence is a tautology. If every cell under the formula's main connective shows true, then the single formula on top of the table is a tautology.

In the branch of logic called **metalogic**, the "logic of logic," it has been rigorously proved that any formula derived on the basis of a premise-free proof in TD must be a tautology. (Metalogic is treated in Appendix B at the end of the book.) In other words, it has been proved that every theorem of our system is a tautology. Thus, in addition to the method of truth tables, a premise-free proof can also be used to demonstrate that a formula is tautological. A comparison of the two methods shows that natural deduction is the more efficient (less time consuming) method of the two.

FOR THOSE INTERESTED

Here is a nontechnical, informal metalogical argument for the claim that every theorem of TD is tautological. A natural deduction proof demonstrates that the conclusion at the end of the proof must be true if the premises are true. Now, if a proof begins with no premises at all, and any assumptions made are discharged, the proof demonstrates that the conclusion is true absolutely (i.e., regardless of anything else), and not just true on the condition that certain listed premises are true. In other words, the conclusion must be true no matter what premises are true (i.e., no matter what is the case). For we could add any number of premises to a premise-free proof, even contradictory premises, and the proof would still go through (because it would not even use the premises). It follows that any sentence proved on the basis of a premise-free proof *must* be a sentence that is true no matter what premises are true. But that means the sentence proved by a premise-free proof is true no matter what is the case. But a sentence that is true "no matter what" is a tautology. Thus, any sentence derived on the basis of a premise-free proof is a tautology.

It has also been proved in metalogic that every truth-functional tautology is a theorem of our system. The proof is fascinating, but it is a matter best taken up in an advanced course in logical theory—a course in the "metatheory" of logic.

Logical Truths

Recall that tautologies are also called **logical truths** because they can be shown true using only the abstract procedures of logical theory, without investigating the material universe; that is, without relying on empirical statements, without using our senses to probe the physical world. In an earlier chapter, we used truth tables to prove sentences tautological. But when we are evaluating long sentences, the corresponding truth tables can become enormous. Now we see that natural deduction can also be used to show that some sentences are tautological or logically true, and in a less time-consuming way.

Examples

Here are a few more premise-free proofs:

1. | J   ACP
2. | J v B   Add 2
3. J ⊃ (J v B) CP 1–2

This proves that J ⊃ (J v B) is a theorem and thus also a tautology. Here is another example:

1. | [(A v B) & ~A]   ACP
2. | A v B   Simp 1
3. | ~A   Simp 1
4. | B   DS 2, 3
5. [(A v B) & ~A] ⊃ B   CP 1–4

Because we derived [(A v B) & ~A] ⊃ B without using any premises, this proves that the formula is a theorem and thus a tautology.

A Nested Premise-Free Proof

Nested proofs were introduced in Appendix 21.1. Let us use the technique of nested proofs to prove that:

$$[J \supset (B \supset R)] \supset [(J \supset B) \supset (J \supset R)]$$

is a theorem and thus a tautology. Notice that this formula is a conditional whose antecedent is itself a conditional and whose consequent is itself a conditional as well. Indeed, the consequent of the antecedent is itself a conditional, and the antecedent and consequent of the consequent are each also conditionals. That's a lot of conditionals. This is the clue that suggests we'll be building a nested proof. When you begin a proof such as this, proceed in two steps:

1. Set up the overall structure of the proof.
2. Fill in the structure.

To set up the overall structure, you must arrange the assumed premises in the proper order. Let us first assume the antecedent of the formula as a whole:

1.	$J \supset (B \supset R)$	ACP

Next, assume within this sequence the next antecedent; that is, the antecedent of the whole formula's consequent:

1.	$J \supset (B \supset R)$	ACP
2.	$(J \supset B)$	ACP

Within this nested sequence, assume the last antecedent:

1.	$J \supset (B \supset R)$	AP
2.	$(J \supset B)$	ACP
3.	J	ACP

You now have the proof's overall structure worked out. The completed proof follows:

1.	$J \supset (B \supset R)$	ACP
2.	$(J \supset B)$	ACP
3.	J	ACP
4.	$B \supset R$	MP 1, 3
5.	B	MP 2, 3
6.	R	MP 4, 5
7.	$(J \supset R)$	CP 3–6
8.	$(J \supset B) \supset (J \supset R)$	CP 2–7
9.	$[J \supset (B \supset R)] \supset [(J \supset B) \supset (J \supset R)]$	CP 1–8

The nested proof method is often required when proving theorems in our system.

Exercise 22.1   Construct premise-free proofs for the following tautologies.

1. [(A v B) & ~A] ⊃ B
2. [(J ⊃ I) & (I ⊃ I)] ⊃ (J ⊃ I)
3. A ⊃ [(A ⊃ B) ⊃ B]
4. (A ⊃ B) ⊃ [(A & E) ⊃ (B & E)]
5. [(A ⊃ B) & (A ⊃ I)] ⊃ [A ⊃ (B & I)]
6. A ⊃ [(B & ~B) ⊃ K]
7. {[(A ⊃B) & (B ⊃ C)] & ~C} ⊃ ~A
8. { [(A ⊃ B) & (H ⊃ K)] & (~B v ~ K)} ⊃ (~A v ~H)
9. [(P v Q) v ~R] ⊃ [P v (~~Q v ~R)]
10. (P ⊃ P) v (P ⊃ Q)
11. (P ⊃ P) v [(P ⊃ ~Q) v ~P]
12. J ⊃ [~(~A v ~B) ⊃ (A & B)]
13. [~(~A & ~B) & ~ (A v B)] ⊃ I
14. (A ≡ B) v ~ (A ≡ B)
15. (A ⊃ B) v ~ (A ⊃ B)
16. G ⊃ [(A ≡ B) v ~ (A ≡ B)]
17. ~K ⊃ [(A ⊃ B) v ~ (A ⊃ B)]

Other Uses of Natural Deduction

Earlier in this unit we used truth tables to show that two sentences are inconsistent. This question might have arisen: Can we also use natural deduction to show that a set of sentences is inconsistent? The answer is yes. To prove that a set of two or more sentences is inconsistent using natural deduction, we derive a contradiction from the set. Because only a contradiction follows logically from a contradiction, this proves that the set of sentences is self-contradictory. To show that a single (complex) sentence is a contradictory, we derive a contradiction from it.

Likewise, earlier we used truth tables to show that two formulas are equivalent. Can this be accomplished with natural deduction in place of tables? Again, the answer is yes. To show that two sentences are equivalent using natural deduction, we derive the first from the second, and then the second from the first. Because two sentences are equivalent if they imply each other, this proves that the two are equivalent.

Glossary

Logical truth A statement that can be known on the basis of logical theory alone, without investigating the physical world.

Metalogic The logic of logical systems.

Premise-free proof A proof that uses no premises.

Tautology A sentence that is true in all possible circumstances, false in none.

Theorem A formula that can be proved true without the use of premises.

Theorem of TD A sentence that can be proved with a premise-free proof in the system TD.

INTERLUDE

Philosophy of Logic

Philosophy of logic is the philosophical investigation of fundamental questions that naturally arise when we think about logical theory and its implications. Throughout this book we have been speaking of things called propositions (or statements) and of propositions or statements being true or false. Such talk is unavoidable in logical theory. A theory of logic that contained no mention of propositions or truth and falsity, or their equivalents, would be a strange creature indeed. However, profound questions arise when we think about what we mean when we talk about these things. What *is* a proposition or a statement? And what is it for a proposition, or anything for that matter, to be true or false? Finally, how can something be necessarily true or false? These are among the most fundamental questions raised in philosophy of logic. It seems we have found our entry point into the field. Let us begin with the nature of the proposition. Truth will be probed second.

What are the Bearers of Truth?

When someone says "That's true," or "Your premise is true," what is it that is said to be true? The speaker is attributing truth to something. What is the object that is being called true? And when someone says "That's false," what is it that is false? What is it that is true (or false) when something is true (or false)?

Suppose someone walks up to you and for no apparent reason says, "That's purple." You might naturally respond, "*What* is purple?" In other words, what is the thing that is supposedly purple? Now, imagine that someone says, "The moon has craters," and you reply, "That's true." When you say "That's true" or "That's false," *what* is true or false? In other words, what is it that is true or false? What are you attributing truth (or falsity) to? Truth and falsity seem to be characteristics of something. Of what? Logicians put the question this way: What are the "bearers" of truth and falsity?

A number of theories have been proposed, but not all answer the question satisfactorily. Let us examine a few of the important theories on the nature of the bearer of truth. In the case of each one, opposing arguments will be presented. As we move from one theory to the next, the discussion will be dialectical in nature. As you think about each theory and the arguments against it, it will be up to you to decide which theory provides the most reasonable answer to the question under discussion.

The Belief Theory

So, what is it that is true when something is true? One suggestion that seems plausible initially is called the belief theory: It is the beliefs in people's minds that are the bearers of truth and falsity. On this view, if Pat says, "The moon has mountains," and someone replies, "That's true," the thing that is true is Pat's belief. According to the belief theory, it is Pat's belief—a psychological state or component of his mind—that is the thing that is true. This belief arose in Pat's mind at a certain time, was caused by certain things he saw and heard, and it will cease to exist at some moment in time.

The belief theory seems, at first glance, to provide a plausible answer to our question. After all, we do sometimes say things like "Her belief turned out to be true." However, the belief theory seems to conflict with several things we know about belief and truth. Consider the following argument.

We learn in elementary mathematics that there are an infinite number of positive whole numbers. Mathematicians study the properties of these numbers, prove theorems about them, and so on. However, corresponding to each of these numbers is the truth that that particular number has a successor, and corresponding to each there is also the falsehood that that particular number has no successor. Because there are an infinite number of positive whole numbers, and because each has associated with it at least one truth and at least one falsehood, it follows that there are an infinite number of truths and also an infinite number of falsehoods.

An infinite series of truths:

1 has a successor
2 has a successor
3 has a successor
. . . and so on

An infinite series of falsehoods:

1 has no successor
2 has no successor
3 has no successor
. . . and so on

Unfortunately, this conclusion seems fatal to the belief theory, for in all of history, only a finite number of persons have lived, and each has had a finite number of beliefs. Even if each person acquires a billion beliefs every billionth of a second, each person still acquires, in the course of a lifetime, a finite number of beliefs. This means that a finite number of belief states—the entities referred to by the belief theory—are available to serve as the bearers of truth and falsity. Because there exist an infinite number of truths and an infinite number of falsehoods, it follows that there are more truths and falsehoods than there are belief states. But beliefs can't be the things that are true and false if there are more truths and falsehoods than there are beliefs. There are simply not enough beliefs to serve as truth-bearers. Belief states, therefore, cannot be that which is true or false.

Another argument also seems to count against the belief theory. Billions of years ago, before anyone was around to have any beliefs, it was true that water is composed of hydrogen and oxygen. It simply makes no sense to suppose that it became true that water is composed of hydrogen and oxygen only when, in 1793, Henry Cavendish made his famous discovery and became the first human being to believe that water is composed of hydrogen and oxygen. Rather, this truth was discovered in 1793, when it was first believed. It was true that water is composed of hydrogen and oxygen long before it was believed to be true. Similarly, billions of years ago, before anyone had any beliefs about the matter, it was false that water freezes at 10,000 degrees Celsius. It makes no sense to suppose that this became false only when the corresponding mistaken belief formed in someone's mind. So it seems that truth and falsity may exist independently of, or in the absence of, human belief. This gives us further reason to reject the belief theory, for if truths and falsehoods may exist in the absence of any human beliefs, then that which is true must be something other than a belief.

The reasoning against the belief theory can be generalized to support the conclusion that the bearer of truth cannot be any sort of mental or psychological entity existing in the mind. Consider the following argument:

1. There are an infinite number of truths and falsehoods.
2. Only a finite number of people have ever lived, and each has had only a finite number of beliefs, thoughts, and other mental states.
3. Therefore, the bearers of truth and falsity are not beliefs, thoughts, or any other mental states.
4. So, the things that are true and false are entities that exist independently of—separate from—the human mind.

If this argument is sound, then the bearers of truth and falsity must be nonmental, nonpsychological entities of some sort.

If you are convinced that the bearer of truth is a belief, or some kind of mental state, and you wish to defend your theory, there are several ways you might argue. You might try producing an argument for the claim that there does not exist an infinity of truths. Your argument would attack a crucial premise in the reasoning against the belief theory. Alternatively, you might try producing an argument that there does exist an infinity of beliefs. This argument would attack a different premise in the reasoning against the belief theory. Or you might develop an argument for the claim that there were no truths in existence before human believers existed. Here you would have to explain, for example, in what sense it was not true 5 million years ago that water is H_2O, and you would want to explain how something like this became true when the relevant belief formed in someone's mind.

The Sentence Theory

If the truth-bearer is not a belief or a mental entity, what is it? What is that which is true? According to another proposal, the truth-bearer is a sentence. This suggestion also seems plausible at first glance. We naturally say things such as "That sentence is true," or "That sentence seems false." However, this suggestion faces a problem. The word *sentence* is ambiguous; two senses of the word must be distinguished. Consider the following box.

> Aristotle is a logician.
> Aristotle is a logician.

How many sentences does the box contain? If you answered that it contains two sentences, then you were thinking of what philosophers call sentence tokens. These are the individual physical sentences in front of you, the marks on paper, composed of ink, with a certain size, shape, location, and so on. If you answered that the box contains just one sentence that has been written twice, you had in mind what philosophers call the sentence type. The box "contains" just one sentence type, although it contains two *instances* or *tokens* of that type. The relation between a sentence type and a sentence token is analogous to the relation between a sentence form and its instances.

Here is another example to help you grasp the distinction between a sentence token and a sentence type. Suppose 100 people are each asked to write their favorite sentence on a scrap of paper. Suppose they each wrote down the same sentence. In this case, we would have 100 scraps of paper and 100 sentence tokens, but only one sentence type. The 100 written sentences are all the same sentence by virtue of being 100 tokens of the same type.

Now, a physical entity is an entity that is composed of matter, that occupies a volume of space, and that has a position in space and time. We detect physical entities with our five physical senses and with physical instruments such as microscopes and telescopes. The sentence token is a physical entity. It is composed of ink or some other writing material, it occupies a volume of space, it reflects light, it has a physical location, and so on. In addition, it came into existence at a specific moment in time (when it was written). The sentence type, however, is not a physical entity. The type is what philosophers call an *abstract entity*. This is an entity that is not composed of material particles, does not occupy a volume of space, does not have a location in space and time, and is not detected by the five physical senses. Although they cannot be detected using the five physical senses, abstract entities are such that they can be thought of and understood by the mind.

Are there such things as abstract entities? Do abstract entities really exist? *Absolute materialism* is the view that absolutely nothing exists except particles of matter and objects composed of particles of matter. If you hold this view, then you won't accept the existence of abstract entities such as sentence types. If you agree with absolute materialism and deny that abstract entities exist, and if you also suppose that the truth-bearer is a sentence of some sort, then you will want to postulate that it is the sentence *token* that is the bearer of truth. Call this suggestion the sentence token theory.

Are physical sentence tokens the bearers of truth? This suggestion seems plausible at first. After all, we do sometimes say things like "That sentence is true" or "That sentence is false" while pointing at a sentence token, such as a sentence written on a piece of paper or on a blackboard. However, the sentence token theory faces a major objection. We have already argued that there exist an infinite number of truths as well as an infinite number of falsehoods. The truth-bearers, whatever they are, must therefore be available in infinite number. But only a finite number of sentence tokens have ever been written down, printed, or produced in any way, counting all cultures, all language systems, and all times. Even if each person in the world had been writing a billion sentence tokens every billionth of a second, that would still add up to a finite number of sentence tokens. That implies that there are more truths and falsehoods than there are sentence tokens. Consequently, whatever the bearers of truth and falsehood are, it seems they are not sentence tokens.

However, if you are convinced that the bearer of truth is a physical sentence token and you wish to defend the sentence token theory, you might argue that only a finite number of truths exist. This would undermine a key premise of the argument against the sentence token theory. Also, you might try explaining the sense in which the first production of a sentence token brought the first truth into existence, and how it could be that there would be no truths at all if we were to erase or destroy all sentence tokens.

The argument given earlier against the sentence token theory can be generalized to support the conclusion that the bearer of truth is not any sort of physical entity. Consider the following argument:

1. An infinite number of truths and falsehoods exist.
2. No physical object that could plausibly be construed to be the truth-bearer and falsity-bearer exists in infinite numbers.
3. Therefore, the bearers of truth and falsity are not any sort of physical object.

As a result of reasoning along these lines, many philosophers argue that we have good reason to suppose that truth-bearers are neither belief states nor sentence tokens. They are neither mental nor psychological objects, nor are they physical or material objects. What, then, are the bearers of truth and falsity? From here, philosophers divide into two schools of thought. Some argue that the bearers of truth and falsity are sentence types. Others argue that the bearers of truth and falsity constitute a unique kind of abstract object, a kind of abstract entity that is not a sentence type and indeed is not sentential or linguistic at all. Let's look briefly at the reasoning for these two schools of thought.

The Sentence Type Theory

According to some philosophers, although the truth-bearer is obviously not in any case a belief in the mind or a physical sentence token, it does make sense to say that the sentence type is that which is true. However, a problem immediately arises if we simply say that the sentence type, by itself, is the truth-bearer. Suppose that at noon, Pat says,

> I am hungry.

Abstracted from the context of utterance, the sentence type in this case seems to have no truth-value at all. This suggests that a sentence type by itself—that is, abstracted from its context of utterance—cannot plausibly be said to be that which is true or false.

In response to this line of argument, proponents of the sentence type theory amend their account by supposing that it is not the pure sentence type alone that is the thing that is true or false. Rather, it is the sentence type with its context of utterance built into it that is true or false. The suggestion is that the sentence type's context must be built into it in such a way that the sentence can be fully understood when abstracted from its context of utterance. The following example should illustrate the procedure. Assuming Pat's last name is Smith, Pat's sentence, with context built in, becomes:

> Pat Smith is hungry at noon on August 17, 1982.

Interpreted in this way, the sentence type in this case can plausibly be said to be true. It is such "context-free" sentence types—sentences with their context built in—that are proposed, then, as the bearers of truth and falsity. Call this account the sentence type theory. One virtue of this theory is that attributions of truth and falsity are explained in terms of familiar entities, namely, context-free sentences, which are themselves parts of a language.

Propositions as *Sui Generis* Abstract Entities

Some philosophers reject the previous theories we have surveyed and argue that the truth-bearer is an entity that can be expressed by a sentence but that is neither mental, physical, nor sentential in nature. On this view, the truth-bearer is a *sui generis* abstract entity—an entity that is like nothing else on the list of proposed truth-bearers. What reasons exist for such a view? We will look at two lines of reasoning.

First of all, three sentences, drawn from three different languages, can express the same (one) truth. For example, consider the following three sentences, drawn from three different languages, and suppose each to be an accurate translation of the other two:

1. The moon has craters.
2. La luna tiene cráteres.
3. Maraming maliliit na bulkau sa buwan.

One thing seems obvious. Among the three sentences, only one truth is expressed. But what is this one thing that is true here? That which is true cannot, it seems, be the individual sentences themselves, for there are three sentences and one truth. And the truth-bearer cannot be a part of one language either, for our example displays three language systems but only one truth. This is puzzling. Many philosophers believe we can make sense of the example if we suppose that:

1. All three sentences express, in different ways, one and the same truth.
2. This truth-bearer, although it can be expressed within each language, does not itself belong to any one language.

If this is an adequate explanation, then it seems that the thing that is true can't be a component of a language. Therefore, it seems plausible to suppose that the truth-bearer must be a nonsentential and indeed a nonlinguistic entity of some sort.

Another line of reasoning for the claim that truth-bearers are nonlinguistic entities begins with some thoughts about our prelinguistic ancestors who lived tens of thousands of years ago. Lacking a language, they did not write, speak, or understand any sentences of any language. This is because a sentence is a part of a language, and if one is to understand or use a sentence, one must understand the grammar and semantics of the language to which the sentence belongs. However, although our prelinguistic ancestors understood no sentences, they must have had beliefs. To survive, they must have believed certain things about the world. And sometimes, that which they believed was true, and other times, that which they believed was false. Now, this argument continues, that which was believed—whether true or false—couldn't have been sentences of any kind. Remember that these individuals had no language and so were incapable of understanding any sentences, token or type. It seems to follow that whatever the objects of their beliefs were, they were not sentences or components of a language. This is another reason to suppose that the truth-bearer is a nonsentential and nonlinguistic entity.

Someone might object to this line of reasoning as follows: A being could not possibly have a belief without also having a language. Consequently, our prelinguistic ancestors had no beliefs and therefore knew no truths. But this objection faces a problem. If our prelinguistic ancestors had no beliefs, then how and why would they go on to eventually develop the communication systems we call languages? Specifically, why and how would they finally come to use a sentence that we would translate as, say, "Mastodons live by the river," unless they first believed that mastodons lived by the river?

Which of the theories just canvased makes the most sense to you? To accommodate as many viewpoints as possible on the nature of the truth-bearer, and to avoid as much as possible taking sides on a controversial issue, let us at this point introduce a special terminological convention. Let us use the term *proposition* to stand for whatever it is that is the bearer of truth. So, a proponent of the belief theory might interpret the word *proposition* as another term for belief; an advocate of the sentence type theory might treat the word *proposition* as just another term for sentence type; and so on.

The last two theories surveyed—the sentence type theory and the *sui generis* theory—both hold that the truth-bearer is an abstract entity. The difference between the two is that according to the sentence type theory, the truth-bearer is a sentential abstract entity, whereas the *sui generis* theory holds that the truth-bearer is a nonsentential abstract entity. Propositions, understood as abstract entities, seem to be a mysterious type of object. Although they are not physical and consequently occupy no location in physical space, our minds nevertheless comprehend them. After all, we think about various propositions, we believe them true or false, and we form various other judgments about them. This raises the question: How do our minds become aware of or "grasp" abstract entities? How are propositions accessible to our thought? Furthermore, how do such nonphysical objects fit into the modern scientific worldview, a view that seems to see everything as composed of purely physical parts? Anyone who believes in the existence of abstract entities faces this difficult line of questioning. Some philosophers argue that this difficulty makes it very hard to believe that there really are such things as abstract entities. Can we really accept a theory that posits such mysterious objects of thought? Let's explore this question for a moment.

Theoretical Entities

Philosophers who hold that a proposition is an abstract entity consider propositions to be *theoretical entities*. A theoretical entity is an object that cannot be seen or directly detected, but that, for theoretical reasons, we suppose must exist. Everyone has heard of the theoretical entities that physicists study, particles such as the electron, the proton, the neutron, and the quark. Consider, for example, the particles physicists call quarks. Physicists tell us that inside each proton and neutron are three quarks. What is the nature of a quark? Nobody knows for sure. What do they look like? They can't be seen or directly detected. Physicists still know very little about the sorts of properties they supposedly possess. Quarks are at this point mysterious objects. How do we know they even exist? Our best theories of the proton and neutron tell us there must be three particles inside each proton and neutron. These particles have been named quarks. In other words, quarks are referred to in our explanations of certain things. So, although they can't be seen, reference to them helps explain various phenomena observed in the laboratory. According to most physicists, this is good reason to suppose that such objects truly exist.

In general, if reference to a theoretical object helps make sense of some facet of the world, this constitutes a reason to suppose the theoretical object exists. Thus, one reason we suppose that electrons exist, to take another example from physics, is that although no one has ever seen one, we need to refer to electrons if we are to explain such things as the operation of a battery, the flash of a lightning bolt, or the effect of a magnet. This is the form of reasoning known as *inference to the best explanation* (see Chapter 33).

When we use the term *proposition*, we are simply assigning a name to the theoretical objects, whatever they are, that are true or false, just as the physicist assigns the term *quarks* to the mysterious objects inside protons and neutrons. We assign names to theoretical entities so that we can refer to them. Philosophers who believe propositions are abstract entities argue that we need to refer to propositions, conceived as abstract entities distinct from sentence tokens, to explain or make sense of certain of our linguistic activities, specifically our attributions of truth and falsity. If reference to abstract objects helps make sense of our world, then this is good reason to suppose such objects exist. So, one reason for supposing that there are such things as propositions—understood as abstract objects—is that reference to them helps explain or make sense of our attributions of truth and falsity. Physicists and philosophers both posit theoretical entities to make sense of the world.

Propositions, understood as abstract entities, can be compared to a similar type of abstract entity studied by mathematicians: numbers. Perhaps the comparison will prove illuminating. We all think in terms of these abstract mathematical entities, and we refer to them daily. But just what is a number?

Mathematicians distinguish numbers from numerals. Numerals, like sentence tokens, are physical marks on paper, blackboards, computer terminals, and so on. They are composed of molecules of graphite, ink, chalk, or other writing compounds. Because it is physical, a numeral has a size, a shape, a location, an age, a weight, and other physical properties. Numbers, on the other hand, are simply not physical objects. The number three, for instance, which has been studied since ancient times, does not reflect light, is not located at some point in space, is not composed of molecules of some substance, and has no size, shape, weight, or age. If someone were to claim that the number three is a physical object, we could ask such questions as these: Where is it located?" How much does it weigh? How tall is it? or How old is it? There is general agreement among mathematicians that the number three is not located somewhere on Earth or in outer space.

Numerals are said to express numbers. For example, the numerals 3 and III each express the number three. The number itself is distinct from the numerals that express it, for in this example, there are two numerals but only one number is expressed.

Mathematicians distinguish the number—an abstract entity—from the physical numerals that express it. Similarly, philosophers who believe propositions are abstract entities distinguish between the proposition and the sentence token that expresses the proposition. The distinction between numbers and numerals is therefore analogous to the distinction between propositions and sentence tokens, and the relationship between numbers and the numerals that express them is analogous to the relationship between propositions and the sentence tokens that express them.

Philosophers who accept the existence of propositional abstract objects address the following question to those who doubt the existence of such objects: If we can accept the existence of an infinity of abstract objects in mathematics called numbers, then why should we balk at accepting an infinity of similar abstract objects in logic, objects we're calling propositions.?

Nevertheless, not all philosophers think of propositions as abstract entities. If you are convinced that a proposition is not an abstract entity, then interpret the term *proposition* in the light of your favored account. Although our discussion will not officially take sides on the question of the nature of a proposition, our wording will sometimes distinguish between sentence tokens and propositions. The reader who believes that sentence tokens are the bearers of truth and falsity can simply ignore the distinction.

Exercise 1

Part I
Fill in the blanks with either *numeral* or *number* in such a way that the sentences all express truths.

1. The _____ on the computer screen is a pretty shade of blue.
2. We painted a new _____ on the airplane.
3. Twice the _____ four is the _____ eight.
4. That _____ five is shorter than that _____ seven.

5. The _____ 10 is half the _____ 20.
6. You write a _____ 21 by placing a _____ 2 beside a _____ 1.
7. Many symbols can be used to refer to the _____ three.
8. The cookie is in the shape of a _____ two.

Part II

Fill in the blanks with either *sentence token* or *proposition* in such a way that the sentences all express truths.

1. Your _____ is hard to read.
2. The first _____ you wrote is messier than the second one.
3. That _____ is very hard to believe.
4. $2 + 2 = 4$ is a _____ of English and expresses a true _____.
5. The _____ "Pat is older than Jan" means the same as the _____ "Jan is younger than Pat."
6. It is possible to see a _____ but nobody can see a _____.
7. That _____ is written in yellow.
8. A _____ has a shape but a _____ has no shape.
9. That _____ is exactly two feet long.

What Is Truth?

"What is truth?"   *–Pontius Pilate*

An even more fundamental question arises when we ask about truth itself. If something is true, what does its truth consist in? What *is* truth? This is the second of our two questions: What is it for a proposition to be true? What characteristic does a true proposition have that makes it a true proposition (rather than a false one)? Let's begin with a specific example. Suppose someone says, "The cat is on the mat." We have already seen that in such a situation, truth is being attributed not to the sentence spoken, but to the proposition expressed by the sentence. So the question is this: What do we mean when we say that the proposition expressed by this sentence is true? Well, the following seems to be common sense. If the cat is actually on the mat, then the proposition expressed by "The cat is on the mat" is a true proposition. And if the cat is not actually on the mat, then that proposition is a false proposition. More formally:

> The proposition expressed by "The cat is on the mat" is true if and only if the cat is on the mat; the proposition is false if and only if the cat is not on the mat.

Reflecting on the matter, it looks as if truth involves a relation between two separate things. On the one hand, there is a proposition. A proposition in effect makes a claim about the way the world is; it specifies a way the world may be. On the other hand, there is the way the world really is, independent of, or separate from, what the proposition claims. When the proposition's claim or specification of the world corresponds to the way the world is, the proposition is true. When the proposition's claim or specification of the world does not correspond to the way the world is, the proposition is false.

Here are some examples of sentences expressing propositions that "correspond" to or "specify" the way things are:

The Moon has more than one crater.

$1 + 1 = 2$

Here are some examples of sentences expressing propositions that do not "correspond" to or "specify" the way things are:

The sun is smaller in diameter than the Earth.

$1 + 2 = 406$

After thinking about these rather obvious examples, do you see the common-sense way in which a proposition can correspond or fail to correspond to the way the world is?

If you are puzzled by the relationship between a proposition and the world, consider for a moment the relation between a map and the world. A map also specifies a way the world is; it makes a claim about the world. The map is "correct" just in case the way the world is corresponds to or fits the map's claim or specification; the map is incorrect otherwise. In this way, maps are somewhat like propositions.

And so, according to these considerations, truth is a property that a proposition has just in case it corresponds to the way the world is. Truth, in short, is correspondence with reality. This account of truth goes back at least to Aristotle, the first to state it in written form, and is known as the *correspondence theory of truth*. Thus, in *Metaphysics*, the first text on the subject, Aristotle puts the correspondence theory this way:

> To say of what is that it is not, or of what is not that it is, is false, while to say of what is that it is, and of what is not that it is not, is true. (*Metaphysics* 1011b25)

The correspondence account of truth has been accepted by most philosophers throughout history as providing the best explanation of the matter. We have been assuming this theory in this book.

Objections to the Correspondence Theory

Not all philosophers find the correspondence theory satisfactory. Some object by raising questions that they claim the theory has no answers to. If the theory cannot answer the questions, then it is not an adequate explanation. For instance, what is the nature of the correspondence relation between a proposition and the world? It can't be a *physical* relationship, for on the most reasonable theory, propositions are not physical objects located in space–time, and so are not physically related to anything. The correspondence relation isn't pictorial, as when a map corresponds to some portion of the world by picturing that portion of the world, for propositions surely don't *picture* what they correspond to. In what sense, then, does a proposition *correspond*? Can it be made precise?

Here is another question for the correspondence theory. Consider the proposition expressed by "The moon has mountains." To what does this proposition correspond? To the world as a whole? Or to just the moon? Or only to the moon's mountains? Here is one more question, which you can puzzle over on your own. Consider a negative proposition:

Santa Claus does not exist.

To what does this proposition correspond?

Of course, philosophers of logic have developed answers to these questions, and the theories proposed are fascinating, although we cannot go further into the issue here. Most philosophers throughout history have found the correspondence theory of truth to be "self-evident" or in some way intellectually indispensable. Nevertheless, two alternative theories have won a small amount of support in certain parts of the philosophical world: the coherence theory of truth and the pragmatic theory of truth.

The Coherence Theory of Truth

According to the coherence theory of truth, to say that a proposition is true is to say that it belongs to a coherent system of propositions. What is this? Very roughly, a group of propositions is said to be coherent if the propositions belonging to the group are (a) consistent, and (b) they stand in certain explanatory relations to one another, which means they form an explanation. Thus, on a coherence theory, truth is a relation between propositions, and not, as in the theory of Aristotle, a correspondence relation between a proposition and the world.

The coherence theory of truth has its roots in the view—held by the philosophers in the idealist school of thought—that at bottom, reality consists of minds and thoughts in minds, and nothing more. It would be desirable to explain further why some philosophers hold a coherence theory of truth. However, the issue is deep and difficult and simply cannot be summed up in a few words. Any fair attempt at a summary would take us beyond the scope of an introductory logic text.

The coherence theory has always faced an objection that many philosophers find decisive. It is possible to specify two opposing systems of propositions, such that each system is coherent, yet such that one contradicts the other. Because the two systems are contradictory, they cannot both be true. If this is correct, then a system of propositions can be coherent yet fail to be true. The conclusion of this line of reasoning is that truth is not the same thing as coherence.[1]

The Pragmatic Theory of Truth

A second alternative to the correspondence theory is the pragmatic theory of truth. According to this proposal, advanced by philosophers in the school of thought known as pragmatism, to say that a proposition is true is to say that it is useful. Truth, on this view, is identified with usefulness. Very roughly, a proposition is useful if our knowledge of it can serve a human interest.

The pragmatic theory of truth has its roots in the pragmatic theory of meaning. That theory explains the meaning of a sentence in terms of the use to which the sentence is put. It would be desirable to explore this interesting theory further here, but doing so would take us beyond the scope of an introductory symbolic *logic* book.

The pragmatic definition of truth also faces an objection that many philosophers find decisive. Surely there are propositions that are useful to some people, yet they are clearly false propositions. For instance, Hitler's racial theories were useful to him and his fellow Nazis in their quest for power, yet those theories were certainly false. If this is right, then truth and usefulness would seem to be two separate concepts.[2]

One Caveat

We have been speaking here of the nature of truth itself, not of how people find the truth. These are two separate matters. The correspondence theory is a theory about the nature of truth; it tells us what truth consists in. If one wants to know how to go about finding the truth, one is asking a question about evidence, about what sorts of things indicate that we have found truth. It is important to keep these two things separate. We have been discussing the nature of truth, not how one finds the truth. A theory of the nature of truth belongs to the branch of philosophy called *metaphysics*, the study of the most fundamental aspects of reality, whereas a theory of evidence belongs to the branch of philosophy called *epistemology*, the study of the nature of knowledge.

---

[1] See Nicholas Rescher, *The Coherence Theory of Truth* (London: Oxford University Press, 1970).

[2] See William James, *Essays in Pragmatism* (New York: Macmillan, 1948), and *The Meaning of Truth* (Ann Arbor: University of Michigan Press, 1970).

Necessary Truth?

Throughout this book we distinguish necessary truth from contingent truth. A proposition is necessarily true if it is true and could not possibly be false, whereas a proposition is contingently true if it is true but could have been false if circumstances had been sufficiently different. However, the following objection often occurs to people when they are first introduced to the idea of a necessary truth. One often hears the following argument, or one very much like it:

> It seems that there are no necessary truths; any truth could have been false. Take $1 + 1 = 2$ as an example. Perhaps on other planets or in other possible worlds, mathematicians speak the truth when they say "It's false that $1 + 1 = 2$." Perhaps there are worlds where people speak the truth when they say "Not all triangles are three-sided." And similarly for each of the so-called necessary truths you have listed. Each *could be* false. Therefore, *necessary* truth does not exist.

In response to this argument, let us first try to understand the "possibilities" referred to. So we ask:

> How do you make sense of the possibility in which people speak the truth when they say, "It's false that $1 + 1 = 2$" or "Not all triangles are three-sided"?

And the usual reply to this question goes along the following lines:

> Well, I'm thinking of planets or worlds in which the sentence "$1 + 1 = 2$" means something different from what it means in our world, and the term *triangle* has a meaning that is different from its meaning in our world. That is why in those other worlds they say things like "It's false that $1 + 1 = 2$" and "Not all triangles are three-sided."

The error in this line of thought is not difficult to detect. The argument under consideration confuses sentences with the propositions those sentences express. When we say that it is necessarily true that $1 + 1 = 2$, we do not mean to say that the sentence "$1 + 1 = 2$" is a necessary truth. Nor do we mean to say that the sentence "$1 + 1 = 2$" has the same meaning in every world or situation. Surely, that sentence has different meanings in different worlds or places. But this just means that the sentence "$1 + 1 = 2$" is used in different worlds to stand for different propositions. This does not imply that the proposition we express with the sentence has different truth-values in different worlds. When we say that it is necessarily true that $1 + 1 = 2$, we mean that the unique proposition—the proposition expressed by the sentence "$1 + 1 = 2$" as we use that sentence—is necessarily true. Which unique proposition is that? It's the one we typically have in mind when we use that sentence with its standard meaning, the meaning established by the linguistic practices and conventions of our linguistic community. Once given a specific meaning, our sentence "$1 + 1 = 2$" expresses a specific proposition, a proposition about numbers. Now, it is that *proposition* that is true in every possible circumstance or world.

How then do we make sense of planets or worlds where mathematicians speak the truth when they say "$1 + 1 = 2$ is false"? The only way to make sense of such a possibility is to suppose that these are situations—worlds—in which the sentence "$1 + 1 = 2$" has a different meaning from the meaning we typically give it and so expresses a different proposition, a proposition that is false. Thus, in the worlds under consideration, those mathematicians are not attributing falsity to the proposition we have in mind when we say "$1 + 1 = 2$." Rather, they are attributing falsity to the proposition they have in mind when they use those words.

What proposition are they thinking of? To answer this, we would have to be able to translate their sentences into our sentences. Suppose that when they say "$1 + 1 = 2$," they are expressing the same proposition we express with $2 + 2 = 7$. Then, assuming they mean by "it's false that" what we mean when we say "it's false that," it follows that when they say "It's false that $1 + 1 = 2$" they are attributing falsity to the proposition we refer to when we say "$2 + 2 = 7$." And we're in agreement on the falsity of *that* proposition! None of this contradicts the plain fact that as we use the sentence, $1 + 1 = 2$ expresses a necessarily true proposition.

Of course, we can redefine terms and coin new meanings, but our listener won't understand us unless we use the standard meanings as we construct our new definitions. If we are going to successfully communicate, the meanings of the words we use must be consistent throughout the discourse. That's enough food for thought for now.

Unit 4

Predicate Logic

The following argument is valid, yet neither truth-functional logic alone nor categorical logic alone can prove it valid:

1. All bulldogs are cute and sweet.
2. If something is cute and sweet, then it is lovable.
3. Etta is a bulldog.
4. So, Etta is either lovable or obstreperous.

The reason neither truth-functional nor categorical logic can prove this argument valid is that neither system has the symbols to represent, or capture, the logical form that makes this a valid argument. This argument does contain elements that categorical logic likes, for instance, subject and predicate terms standing for categories of things, and quantifiers standing for numbers of things. It also contains truth-functional operators: just ripe for truth-functional logic. The problem is it's a mix, a composite, a hybrid of two different logical systems. This example suggests that a bigger system of logic is needed—a "combo" system combining both categorical and truth-functional logic.

However, the problem goes deeper than this. The following argument cannot be proved valid even using a combination system of categorical and truth-functional logic, yet it is valid:

1. Everybody is loved by somebody or other.
2. If there is nobody who is not loved by someone or other, then it is not the case that the world is as bad as some people have said that it is.
3. Therefore, the world is not as bad as some people have said that it is.

The problem is that the logical form that makes this a valid argument contains elements that would not be recognized even by a combination of Aristotle's categorical logic and truth-functional logic. This example suggests that an even more robust system of logic is needed, a super-duper system that combines both categorical and truth-functional logic *and* that also goes beyond them.

Such a system of logic, known today as *predicate logic* (and sometimes called *quantificational logic*) was discovered in 1879 in Germany by a little known but brilliant mathematician, who was also a logician and a philosopher. Actually, we already met this individual. Gottlob Frege (1848–1925) was introduced in the last unit as the founder of modern truth-functional logic. Frege is also the founder of the new system of logic that combines categorical and truth-functional logic and then transcends them both: predicate logic, the subject of this unit. No wonder Frege is often called the founder of modern logic.

Predicate Logic
Version 1.1 ‹‹ ‹‹ ‹‹ ‹‹ ‹‹ ‹‹ ‹‹

Frege Unites Categorical and Stoic Logic

Product Description

- Creator: German mathematician and logician Gottlob Frege
- Release Date: 1879
- Distinctions: Modernization and expansion of Aristotle's categorical logic
- Also known as: Quantificational logic
- Bonus Feature: Includes integrated truth-functional logic pack
- Advertisement: This system completes classical logic.

Historical Introduction: Who's on First? Math or Logic?

As we saw in the last unit, by the middle of the nineteenth century, mathematicians and logicians were pondering this question: What is the relationship between mathematics and logic? Some argued that mathematics is an outgrowth of pure logic. Others argued that logic is an outgrowth of pure math. The German mathematician Gottlob Frege developed the first formal logical language (a close cousin of which we learned in the last unit) as part of his quest to prove once and for all that mathematics is, in reality, just a branch of logic. To recap, Frege attempted to construct an axiom system in which (a) all the axioms and definitions would be drawn from pure logic alone, with no mathematics present in the foundation; and (b) all mathematical truths would be logically deduced, step by step, from the axioms and definitions alone, using precisely defined rules of logical inference. Such a proof would show that *logicism* is true—the claim that mathematics is a branch of pure logic.

We also saw in the last unit that many theoretical roadblocks stood in the way. For one thing, no sufficiently rigorous theory of mathematical proof existed. In addition,

Frege found that even the most elementary theorems of arithmetic and geometry could not be expressed within the existing language of logic: Neither the symbols of Aristotle's categorical logic nor those of the Stoics' truth-functional logic were up to the job. The first step in Frege's grand project was therefore the construction of a new symbolic language for logic. We studied a simplified version of the first half of that language in the last unit: the language TL.[1] In this unit we learn the rest of it: the language of predicate logic, to be named here PL.

Frege's Life Work Is Ruined by a Barber

Frege's life project, the reduction of all of mathematics to logic, failed in the end. On June 16, 1902, a letter arrived in the mail from Bertrand Russell, a young, unknown logician at the University of Cambridge in England. Russell had read the first volume of Frege's attempted reduction of math to logic, and he had a question. One of the crucial steps in Frege's proof was a principle from the mathematical theory known as set theory, stating that a set exists for any group of objects satisfying any stated condition. Russell asked Frege, "Is there a set whose members are all and only those sets that are *not* members of themselves?" What an interesting question! Sets are abstract mathematical objects. Most sets are not members of themselves, for instance the set of all mathematicians. But some sets *are* members of themselves, for instance the set of all nonmathematicians (since a set is not a mathematician) or the set of all abstract objects (since a set is an abstract object). According to this crucial premise in Frege's proof, there should exist a set having as members all sets that are not members of themselves. Call this set S. Russell's great question was: Is S a member of itself?

When Frege attempted to answer Russell, he discovered that he contradicted himself either way he turned. If he answered, "Yes, S is a member of itself," then S is one of those sets that are *not* members of themselves. If he answered, "No, S is not a member of itself," then S is one of those sets that are not members of themselves, and so it *is* a member of itself. In other words, if S is a member of itself, then it must not be a member of itself; if S is not a member of itself, then it must be a member of itself. A self-contradiction whichever way you turn! Fatal flaw.

With one carefully posed question, Russell had shot down Frege's grand project, his life's work. Frege's axioms contained a hidden contradiction. As a result, although Frege could prove the truths of arithmetic on the basis of his axioms, any and every other statement could be proved true, because (as we saw in Unit Three) *every*

---

[1] The language TL, and the language we meet in this unit, PL, are close cousins of the logical language Bertrand Russell and Alfred North Whitehead developed in their monumental work, *Principia Mathematica*, published in three volumes between 1910 and 1913. Although they were building on the formal logical language and system first developed by Frege, the formal language invented by Russell and Whitehead in this work was easier to read, easier to write, and became the standard in logic for these reasons.

statement logically follows from a self-contradiction. The lesson was clear: If there is an axiom system capable of systematizing all (and only) the truths of arithmetic, it has not yet been discovered. Within 30 years, another previously unknown logician would make his mark in history by rigorously proving that the dream is logically unattainable. Mathematics and logic will *never* be fully axiomatized, not because nobody is smart enough to do the job, but because the goal is logically impossible. For more on this remarkable development, see Appendix C on Kurt Gödel at the back of the book.

The Barber Paradox

Russell's question is sometimes put in more mundane terms. Suppose there is a village, and in this village there lives a barber who shaves all those, and only those, who do not shave themselves. Does the barber shave himself? A contradiction follows either way you turn: If the barber *does* shave himself, then it follows he does *not* shave himself (as he shaves only those who do not shave themselves). If he does *not* shave himself, then it follows he *does* shave himself. This version of Russell's paradox is sometimes called the barber paradox.

Frege spent years attempting to repair his proof, but each patch failed—the contradiction remained. Logicism—the theory Frege tried to prove—has no adherents in logic or mathematics today. However, Frege's life work was not totally in vain. The symbolic logical language and system of logical proof that he developed in his attempt to reduce math to logic was such a revolutionary advance in its own right that it became the foundation of all future research in logic, and the logic of Frege is considered the beginning of modern logic. In short, his systematization of logic was a smash hit. It is time to learn the rest of that language, albeit using a more "student-friendly" system of notation.

Grammar and Elementary Symbolizing

As usual, we must begin with some elementary grammar. Every sentence is either singular or general. A **singular sentence** says something about one specifically identified thing. "John is happy" is a singular sentence. Any sentence that is not singular is a **general sentence**. "Someone is happy" is an example of a general sentence. Next, every sentence can be divided, or "parsed," into a subject and predicate. The subject part states what the sentence is about, while the predicate part says something about that which is denoted or referred to by the subject part.

Singular Sentences

The subject part of a singular sentence always contains a singular term, and the predicate part always contains one or more general terms. A **singular term** is a word or phrase that denotes (refers to) one specifically identified thing. Two types of singular terms will concern us: proper names and definite descriptions. **Proper names**, such as "John F. Kennedy," "Barack Obama," and "The Space Needle," pick out one specifically identified thing by naming it. **Definite descriptions**, such as "the 20th President of the United States" or "the first person to walk on the moon," single out one specifically identified thing by describing it in definite terms. A singular term is such that it only applies to one specific thing. We use a singular term to refer to one thing so that we can say something about it.

A **general term** is a word or phrase representing an attribute (i.e., a quality, property, or characteristic) that can be said of, or applied to, more than one thing. The word *red*, for example, is a general term because it can be applied to many different things (fire engines, candy canes, apples, rubies, etc.)—its application is not limited to one specific thing. A general term represents, or stands for, a characteristic, attribute, or property that many different things could have in common.

In a singular sentence, the subject part is a singular term—either a proper name or a definite description—referring to one specific thing, and the predicate part contains one or more general terms that say something about the entity designated by the subject part. Consider the following examples:

1. Herman Snodgrass is obnoxious.
2. Rita's favorite bike is blue.
3. The tallest building in Chicago has more than 90 floors.

Each of these three complete sentences identifies a specific thing via the subject clause and then says something about that specific thing via the predicate clause. The subjects in these sentences are, in order:

1. Herman Snodgrass
2. Rita's favorite bike
3. The tallest building in Chicago

Note that the first subject (Herman Snodgrass) is a proper name; the other two are definite descriptions. The predicate expressions in these three sentences are, in order:

1. _____ is obnoxious.
2. _____ is blue.
3. _____ has more than 90 floors.

The blank placed at the beginning of each predicate expression represents the place where a singular term would be inserted if we wanted to fill in the rest of the sentence. The blank is therefore a "placeholder" for a subject term.

Variables and Constants

The next step is to specify symbols that will abbreviate singular sentences. We begin with the predicates. Notice that a predicate expression is not a complete sentence in its own right; it lacks a subject part. A predicate expression alone, with the blank attached to it where a subject term would go, is called an **open sentence** because it contains an opening where a subject expression could be placed. Because it lacks a subject term, an open sentence does not designate a specific individual and therefore does not make a claim that is either true or false. Open sentences therefore do not have truth-values.

An open sentence, however, can be turned into a complete sentence by adding an appropriate subject clause. When we do so, we produce what is called a *substitution instance* of the open sentence. The substitution instance is a complete sentence (thus it is not open), and it has one of the two truth-values. The sentence "John is happy," for example, is a substitution instance of the open sentence "_____ is happy."

To represent predicate clauses (i.e., open sentences), we begin by introducing variables x, y, and z ranging over individual things. As you know, a **variable** is a symbol standing for anything from a group of things. The group of things is called the domain of the variable, and the variable is said to range over its domain. You are probably familiar with the variable x in mathematics and with the way it is used in mathematical sentences such as the following: "If x is any positive integer, x^2 is also a positive integer." Here the variable x ranges over all the positive integers. The sentence says, in effect, "Pick any positive integer, and call it x. Now, if you square x, the result will also be a positive integer."

If the domain of a variable is not stated, we assume the variable ranges over all things in the entire universe, and we call this domain the *universal domain*. We can also specify a restricted domain for a variable by saying something like, "Let the variable x range over all animals," or "Let the variable y range over all rational numbers," or "Let the domain be all plants," and so on. The following predicate expressions or open sentences use variables as placeholders for the missing subject expressions:

1. x is tall.
2. x is blue.
3. y has more than 90 floors.

Notice that in each case, the variable marks the opening, or gap, where a singular term would be added so as to complete the sentence. In effect, the variable serves as a placeholder marking the spot where the subject is inserted. The variable holds a place open for a subject term. In the case of each of these open sentences, it makes no difference whether we use as a variable x or y or z—the choice of variable is completely arbitrary.

Next, we introduce capital letters A, B, . . . Z, called *predicate constants*. These symbols will stand in for predicate expressions such as "is obnoxious," "is blue," "is happy," "is the oldest person in the room," and so on. Recall that, unlike a variable, a **constant** is a symbol standing for one specifically identified thing. Thus, a constant does not range over a domain. Each predicate constant abbreviates or stands in for one specified predicate expression.

Putting this all together, we symbolize an open sentence, for example, "_____ is happy," in two steps: First we mark the opening or hole by writing down a variable. Second, we represent the predicate by writing down a predicate constant. The international convention in logic is that we place the predicate constant before the variable:

Hx

where H is a predicate constant standing for the predicate "is happy," and the variable x marks the spot where a subject term would go. The open sentences "_____ is tall" and "_____ has more than 90 floors" are symbolized similarly:

1. Tx where T abbreviates the predicate "is tall."
2. Hx where H abbreviates the predicate "has more than 90 floors."

Notice that in each case we chose a predicate constant that reminds us of the predicate it abbreviates.

When a variable in an open sentence is replaced by a singular term, the result is a substitution instance of the open sentence. For example:

Open sentence	Three different substitution instances
1. Cx	Cj, Ck, Cl
2. Lx	La, Lb, Lc
3. Wy	Wa, Wb, Wc

A specific thing is said to "satisfy" an open sentence just in case replacement of the variable in the open sentence with a singular term designating that thing results in a substitution instance that expresses a true proposition. For example, if we let Tx abbreviate x is tall, then Kobe Bryant satisfies this open sentence, because the substitution instance Tk, with k abbreviating Kobe Bryant, expresses a truth. However, Jerry Maren, the actor who played the Lollipop Kid in the Wizard of Oz, does not satisfy this open sentence, because he is not tall. The concepts of substitution instance and satisfaction will come into play shortly: Tj is not true.

Symbolizing Singular Sentences

To symbolize complete singular sentences rather than open sentences, we need an additional symbol. Individual constants are lowercase letters a, b, c, . . . w abbreviating or standing for singular terms, either proper names or definite descriptions. For example, we can abbreviate the proper name "Herman Snodgrass" using the individual constant h, we can abbreviate the definite description "Rita's favorite car" with the constant r, and so on.

To symbolize a singular sentence, we replace the subject part with an individual constant, we replace the predicate part with a predicate constant, and as is the custom, we place the predicate constant to the *left* of the individual constant. To abbreviate the sentence "Joe is tall," for example, we place the predicate constant T (for "is tall") to the left, and next to it we place a lowercase j standing for the singular term Joe: Tj. The complete abbreviations of three singular sentences follow:

Sentence	Abbreviation
1. Herman Snodgrass is obnoxious.	Oh
2. Rita's favorite bike is blue.	Br
3. The tallest building in Chicago has more than 90 floors.	Mt

The formula "Oh" says that the individual represented by the constant h has the property represented by the predicate constant O. That is, Herman Snodgrass has the property of being obnoxious, or more simply, Herman Snodgrass is obnoxious. We naturally speak of properties as if they are "shared" by individuals. For instance, the property, represented in English by "is tall," and represented in our symbols by the open sentence Tx, is shared by a number of individuals, namely, by all those who are tall.

Truth-Functional Combinations of Singular Sentences

Truth-functional combinations of singular sentences also count as singular sentences. The abbreviations of the following examples should be fairly obvious:

English sentence	Symbolic equivalent
McCoy is Irish or Scotty is Irish.	Im v Is
If Spock is logical, then Spock is not emotional.	Ls ⊃ ~Es
It's not the case that Kramer is employed.	~Ek
It's not true that both Niles and Frasier are dandies.	~(Dn & Df)

Study these examples carefully and note the close connection between English and our new logical language PL.

We now have predicate constants standing for general terms, individual constants standing for singular terms, and variables ranging over domains. These are among the many innovations introduced into logic by Frege in his groundbreaking book published in 1879—the book that gave birth to modern symbolic logic. That book, one might add, has perhaps the most imposing title of any logic text ever published: *Begriffsschrift, eine der arithmetischen nachgebildete Formelsprache des reinen Denkens (Concept-Script: A Formal Language for Pure Thought Modeled on that of Arithmetic)*. How would you like that title for your class text?

Exercise 23.1   Symbolize the following singular sentences in PL. Use obvious abbreviations.

1. Grandpa Munster banks at the blood bank.
2. Wimpy likes hamburgers and Popeye likes spinach.
3. The starship *Enterprise* has 21 decks and it also has a complement of 72 officers and 428 enlisted crew members.
4. Jethro Bodine wants to become a "double-nought" spy and Granny cooks possum stew.
5. If Moe is happy , then Curly is happy and Larry is happy.
6. If Aristotle was the greatest logician of antiquity, then Chrysippus was the second greatest.
7. Gottlob Frege was a logician and a mathematician.
8. It is not the case that Stilpo of Megara was a poet.
9. It is not the case that if Frege lectures on logic then Russell will attend.
10. It is not the case that Blipo the barber is working today.
11. Alice is lost and the Queen of Hearts is not very nice.
12. The first man on the moon was an American astronaut.
13. It is not the case both that Socrates was a sophist and Socrates was a true philosopher.
14. This is not true: If Socrates was born in Athens then Aristotle was born in Athens.
15. Chrysippus is not a singer and he is not an artist.
16. Spock is logical and he is in control of his emotions. It is not the case that Spock lacks emotions; he has emotions but he subjects them to rational self-control.
17. If it is not the case that Plato is a philosopher, then it is not the case that Aristotle is a philosopher.
18. The earth is not a star and Pluto is not an asteroid.

Symbolizing General Sentences

Any sentence that is not singular is general. General sentences fall into two groups: universal sentences and existential sentences (also called "particular" sentences). **Universal general sentences** make a claim about all things or about all the members of a group of things without naming, definitely describing, or specifically identifying something. **Existential** (or **particular**) **general sentences** make a claim about some members of a group, where *some* means "at least one" or (equivalently) "one or more"— without employing a proper name, definite description, or specific identification.

The subject part of a universal general sentence typically contains a quantity word indicating universality: *all*, *no*, *every*, or some related term. The subject part of an existential general sentence typically contains a quantity word indicating *some* or *at least one* or a related expression.

Universal General Sentences

Suppose Joe says, "Everything is good." Perhaps Joe belongs to the Optimists' Club and has a positive attitude about everything in the universe. How can we represent his statement symbolically? One idea that first comes to mind is this: Let G abbreviate the predicate phrase *is good*, let e abbreviate *everything*, and then put the two together:

Ge

However, this won't do. The problem is that the word *everything* has been symbolized with an individual constant—e. This would be fine if the word *everything* were to be a singular term. (Individual constants such as e may *only* be used to abbreviate singular terms; i.e., terms that refer by name or definite description to one specifically identified item.) But the word *everything* is not a singular term, for a singular term is always either a name or a definite description used to single out *one* specifically identified thing. The word *everything* certainly does not do this. Of course, we could use the constant e to abbreviate a definite description such as "Ernest's bowling ball" or a proper name such as "Eddie." Thus, in place of "Ernest's bowling ball is good" we could write Ge, and to abbreviate "Eddie is good" we could write Ge. But the constant e cannot be used for the term *everything* because that word is not a singular term. We are back to where we started. How shall we abbreviate "Everything is good"?

We could try this:

Gx

This literally says, "x is good." However, this is just an open sentence; it is therefore not about anything, and it is certainly not a complete sentence with a subject and a truth-value. The sentence "Everything is good" surely says more than this. The sentence "Everything is good" claims that the predicate "is good" applies to, or characterizes, everything in the universe. In short, this won't do.

It is time for an entirely new approach. When an open sentence applies to an object, or characterizes it, we say that the open sentence "is true of" the object; we also say the object "satisfies" the open sentence. For example, on June 26, 2011, the open sentence "_____ is the President of the United States" is true of Barack Obama; it characterizes him (because he is president on that date). Alternatively, we could say that, on the same date, Barack Obama satisfies the open sentence "_____ is the President of the United States." Using this terminology, we can say the sentence "Everything is good" asserts that each and every thing in the universe satisfies the open sentence "x is good." In other words, it claims that the open sentence Gx is true of each thing in the universe. Here is one final way to put it: "Everything is good" claims that each and every thing in the universe has the property of being good.

Next, to properly symbolize our sentence in the style of Frege, we shall proceed by a series of paraphrases. First, let us paraphrase "Everything is good" into:

Every thing is such that it is good.

Next, let us paraphrase this by replacing the word *thing* with the variable x, since the variable x functions in our system the way the word *thing* functions in English:

Every x is such that it is good.

Because the pronoun *it* relates back to the variable x in the subject clause, let us also replace *it* with x:

Every x is such that x is good.

Next, the predicate expression "x is good" is abbreviated Gx. (We have already seen the rationale for this.) Finally, the quantifier word *every* will be abbreviated using the symbol (x). This symbol, called a *universal quantifier*, is to be understood as saying: "Every x is such that." Putting this all together, the thesis "Every x is such that x is good" can be abbreviated as follows:

(x) Gx

Assuming the universal domain, this is read as, "Every x in the universe is such that x is G" or "For all x, x is G." Literally, this expression claims that the open sentence "is good" applies to, or is true of, or characterizes, each and every thing in the universe. In other words, each thing in the universe satisfies the open sentence "x is good." That is how we say, in modern predicate logic, "Everything is good." This formula can be understood in various equivalent ways:

1. For every x, it is the case that x is good.
2. Every x satisfies "x is good."
3. Every x satisfies "Gx."
4. For all x: x is good.
5. For all x: Gx.
6. Everything is good.
7. All things are good.

We can also use y or z as individual variables. So "Everything is good" might just as well be symbolized with the y or with the z variable. It's your call which variable to use. Thus, either:

(y) Gy

or

(z) Gz

would suffice to symbolize the claim at hand. The symbols (x), (y), and (z) are all universal quantifiers.

It might help to think of the first part of the sentence, (x), as the subject clause telling you what the sentence is about and to think of the second part of the sentence, Gx, as the predicate part saying something about that which is referred to by the subject part. In this case, the (x) tells you the sentence is going to say something about each and every thing in the entire universe, and the Gx part says, of each thing referred to in the subject part, that it is good.

Pessimistic Pete (so named because for him the glass is always half empty) holds the opposite view. A member of the Pessimists' Club, his motto is, "Everything is not good." In our new language:

(x) ~Gx

Now let us symbolize a universal sentence that has a more complex structure: "All dogs have fleas." How should this be symbolized? One suggestion that first comes to mind is this. Let F abbreviate the predicate "has fleas," and let d abbreviate "all dogs."

Fd

However, this doesn't work. An individual constant such as d may only be used to abbreviate a singular term—either a proper name or a definite description. The expression "all dogs" is neither the proper name of one specific thing nor a definite description singling out one specific thing. It is not a singular term, and we cannot abbreviate it using an individual constant such as d. Of course, if a specific dog named Dave has fleas, then we could abbreviate "Dave has fleas" with Fd, but we can't abbreviate "All dogs have fleas" this way.

We shall again work through a series of paraphrases to reach the proper symbolization. Let us first paraphrase "All dogs have fleas" into:

Every dog is such that it has fleas.

Next, this is equivalent to:

Every thing such that it is a dog is also such that it has fleas.

Replacing the word *thing*, and the pronouns that refer back to it, with x, this in turn may be rewritten as:

Every x such that x is a dog is such that x has fleas.

This may be abbreviated:

Every x such that Dx is such that Fx.

where Dx abbreviates "x is a dog" and Fx abbreviates "x has fleas."

Before we make the next paraphrase, it will be helpful if we perform a brief thought experiment. Afterward, the next move will make more sense. Suppose the Ace Widget Corporation has hundreds of computers, some of them made by the XYZ Company and some made by that company's rival. Now imagine that the president of Ace Widgets, eager to impress visiting dignitaries from XYZ, says, "Pick any company computer in our office at random: If it is an XYZ computer, then it is certain to be brand new." Doesn't this *if–then* sentence say, in effect, that *all* XYZ computers (in the office) are brand new? Think about it: The only way the boss could be *certain* that *any* randomly picked XYZ computer is brand new would be if he knew that *all* the XYZ computers in the office are brand new.

After reflecting on this example, consider the next step in this series of paraphrases. We earlier paraphrased:

Every thing that is a dog is such that it has fleas.

as:

> Every x such that Dx is such that Fx.

Now, we will say instead:

> For any and every x you might pick, *if it is a dog, then it has fleas.*

That is:

> For every x: if Dx then Fx.

In other words, for anything you might pick, if it happens to be a dog, then it has fleas. That is one way to indicate that all dogs have fleas. Finally, using the universal quantifier, this may be abbreviated:

> (x) (Dx ⊃ Fx)

This expression can be understood in a number of logically equivalent ways:

1. For every x, if x is a dog, then x has fleas.
2. For any x, if x is a dog, then x has fleas.
3. For every x, if x satisfies "x is a dog," then x satisfies "x has fleas."
4. For every x, if x satisfies Dx, then x satisfies Fx.
5. For all x, if x is a dog, then x has fleas.

Again, it might help to think of the first part of the sentence, the universal quantifier (x), as the subject clause telling you what the sentence is about, and to think of the second part of the sentence, (Dx ⊃ Fx), as the predicate part saying something about that which is referred to by the subject part. In this case, the (x) tells you the sentence is going to say something about each and every thing in the entire universe, and then the (Dx ⊃ Fx) part says, *of each and every thing referred to in the subject part,* that *if* it is a dog, then it has fleas. The universal quantifier here operates like a mathematical function applying (Dx ⊃ Fx) to each and every thing in the universe, saying of each thing in the universe, "If it is a dog, then it has fleas."

Symbolizing Existential General Sentences

An existential general sentence says something about some unnamed members of a group, without using a proper name, definite description, or specific identification. Now, how shall we symbolize an existential sentence such as "Some things are green"?

One suggestion that comes to mind is to let the letter s abbreviate "some things" and to let G abbreviate the predicate "is green":

Gs

But this won't work. The letter s is an individual constant; therefore, it can only be used to abbreviate a singular term, either a proper name or a definite description. But the word *some* is not a singular term, for it does not single out one specifically identified item for discussion. The word *some* cannot be represented by an individual constant such as s.

So we are back to our original question: How shall we abbreviate "Some things are green"? Again, we shall proceed through a series of paraphrases. Because *some* means "at least one," our sentence may be written "At least one thing is green." This can be paraphrased as:

At least one thing is such that it is green.

Substituting a variable x for the word *thing*, we can rewrite this as:

At least one x is such that it is green.

If we replace the pronoun *it* with the variable it relates to, we produce:

At least one x is such that x is green.

Now, we already know how to abbreviate "x is green." This is symbolized Gx. We'll abbreviate the quantifier phrase "at least one" (meaning *some*) with the symbol (∃x), known as an existential quantifier. Putting this together, we produce:

(∃x) Gx

which can be read:

There is at least one x such that Gx.

Our new formula says that there is at least one thing, call it x, and Gx is true of it. In other words, at least one thing is green. Here is still another way to put it: At least one thing satisfies the open sentence Gx. We can understand this formula in various alternative, but equivalent, ways.

1. There exists at least one x such that "x is green" applies to it, or is true of it.
2. For at least one x: it is green.

3. There exists at least one x such that x satisfies "x is green."

4. Some x are such that they satisfy "x is green."

5. Something is green.

6. At least one thing is green.

7. There exists at least one green thing.

Think of the first part of the sentence, (∃x), as the subject clause telling you what the sentence is about, and think of the second part of the sentence, (Gx), as the predicate part saying something about that which is referred to by the subject part. In this case, the (∃x) tells you the sentence is going to say something about *one or more* unnamed, unidentified things, and the Gx part says, of each thing referred to in the subject part, that it is green. As you symbolize existential sentences, keep in mind that in logic, the word *some* means the same as "at least one."

History Note

The backward ∃ symbol was introduced into logic in 1895 by the mathematician Peano.

Next, consider a more complicated, existentially quantified sentence, "Some cars are noisy." How shall we put this into symbols? First, let us paraphrase:

There is at least one noisy car.

This is equivalent to:

There exists at least one thing such that it is a car and it is noisy.

That is:

There exists at least one x such that x is a car and x is noisy.

Letting Cx abbreviate "x is a car," and letting Nx abbreviate "x is noisy," this sentence goes into symbols easily:

(∃x)(Cx & Nx)

Think of the first part of the sentence (∃x) as the subject clause telling you what the sentence is about, and think of the second part of the sentence, (Cx & Nx), as the predicate part saying something about that which is referred to by the subject part. In this case, the (∃x) tells you the sentence is going to say something about one or more unnamed, unidentified things, and then the (Cx & Nx) part (the predicate part) says, of each thing referred to in the subject part, that it is a car and it is noisy. Incidentally, there is nothing wrong with writing this sentence as:

(∃x)Cx & Nx

No ambiguity results if we leave off the second pair of parentheses.

We now have identified two types of subject clauses:

1. Those containing the quantifier *all* or an equivalent.
2. Those containing the quantifier *some* or an equivalent.

Sentences with a subject phrase of the first type are called *universal quantifications* (They can also be called *universal sentences*.) Sentences with a subject phrase of the second type are called *existential quantifications*. (They may also be called *existential sentences*.) Existential sentences are also called *particular sentences*.

EXISTENTIAL OR PARTICULAR?

The term *existential* in logic arises in this way. As we saw in Unit Two, Aristotle assumed that the subject terms of all universal statements refer to actually existing things. To interpret universal sentences in this way is to take the Aristotelian standpoint. Modern logic, following the groundbreaking work of George Boole in the nineteenth century, dispenses with this assumption and does *not* assume that the subject terms of every universal sentence always refer to actually existing things. (This was explained in Chapter 9.) Thus, on the modern, or "Boolean," interpretation of universal sentences, we do not suppose the universal sentence "All perfect squares are four-sided figures" implies the actual existence of perfect squares or that the universal sentence "All dodos are mammals" logically implies the actual existence of dodos. Rather, we understand these universal sentences to be saying, "*If* something is a perfect square, then it has four equal sides" and "*If* something is a dodo then it is a mammal." Both of these statements would be true even if no perfect squares exist and no dodos exist. The Boolean standpoint thus does not assume that universal sentences assert the existence of things corresponding to their subject terms. Modern logicians argue that this is in accord with the way universal sentences are used in science and in many other contexts: A physicist who says, "All bodies moving at the speed of light have infinite mass" is not saying that there actually *are* any such bodies. A farmer who says, "All trespassers will be shot" is not claiming any such individuals actually exist (and are about to be shot). On the other hand, when we say something like "Some cats are orange," whether we assume the Aristotelian or the Boolean standpoint, we *are* making a claim about the actual *existence* of something, for in this case we are saying that at least one cat does exist (and that it is orange). This is why sentences about "some" members of a group are called existential—they assert existence. They are also called particular sentences because they make a claim that could apply to *part* of a group.

Exercise 23.2   Using your understanding of commonsense grammar, translate the following sentences into the symbols introduced so far in this chapter.

1. All human beings are intrinsically valuable creatures.
2. Some human beings are interested in poetry and some human beings are not,
3. All things that are made of matter are tangible.
4. All atoms are cloud-like entities.
5. All visible things are material things.
6. All persons are immaterial souls animating material bodies.
7. Every person possesses dignity and equal moral worth.
8. Every human being deserves to be treated respectfully.
9. All animals are fully conscious beings possessing wills of their own; they are not merely instinct-driven machines. (Hint: You could translate this as two separate sentences.)
10. No unelected dictators are worthy of the power they wield. (Hint: Try translating this as: Every unelected dictator is unworthy of the power he wields.)

The Formal Language PL

Everything has been stated informally so far, without complicated rules and such, which is fine at the beginning because too many formal rules at first can make learning a new branch of logic harder and more daunting than it needs to be. However, now that you have the basics down, it is time to follow Frege (and his mathematical instincts) and specify all of this in a more systematic and precise way, in terms of what modern logic calls a formal language. Recall from Chapter 12 that a language can be specified, or defined, in terms of two things: its syntax and its semantics. The *syntax* of a language is the vocabulary and the rules of grammar for the language. The *vocabulary* of a language is the symbols one uses to form expressions in the language, and the *rules of grammar* state how the elements of the vocabulary can be combined to create properly formed expressions. The *semantics* of a language assigns meanings or objects to the well-formed expressions of the language.

Recall also the distinction between a natural and a formal language. A *natural language* is one that is usually learned at birth and that serves as a general tool of communication. English, Spanish, Japanese, and Swahili are examples. Natural languages have huge vocabularies and very complex rules of grammar and normally take years to learn. In contrast, a *formal language* is defined in formal terms by a group of specialists for the purpose of communicating a limited, specific body of information. Musical notation, electronics diagrams, architectural blueprints, and mathematical equations are formal languages.

Frege's great accomplishment was the invention of the first fully formal logical language. We have already learned (in Chapter 12) a simplified version of (a close cousin of) the first part of his language, TL, the fragment designed for the precise expression of the principles of truth-functional logic. The rest of Frege's new language was designed for the precise expression of the principles of predicate logic, also called quantificational logic. Our version of the complete language shall be named PL (for predicate language). In some texts, this language is named QL for quantificational language. PL includes TL in the sense that the syntax and semantics of TL are included as part of the syntax and semantics of PL. As computer scientists might put it, TL is "resident within" PL.

Syntax of PL

Vocabulary

Sentence constants:	A, B, C, . . . Z
Predicate constants:	A′, B′, C′, . . . Z′
Individual constants:	a, b, c . . . w, a′, b′, c′, . . . w′
Individual variables:	x, y, z, x′, y′, z′ . . .
Sentence operators:	v & ∼ ⊃ ≡
Quantifier symbols:	(x) (y) (z) (∃x) (∃y) (∃z)
Parenthetical or grouping indicators:	( ) [ ] { }
The identity operator:	=
The iota symbol:	i

The prime marks (′) on the predicate constants are needed to distinguish predicate constants from sentence constants in our formal vocabulary. However, when actually symbolizing predicates in "real life," we will normally omit the prime marks and simply use the capital letter alone as an abbreviation of a predicate constant. (In other words, a predicate constant without a prime is technically an abbreviation of a predicate constant.) In most contexts, it will be easy to distinguish the two types of constants because a sentence constant stands alone and a predicate constant is paired with one or more individual constants. Also, we will normally use only x, y, and z as variables, but in a situation where more than three different variables are needed, we can add prime marks to generate up to six different variables.

Rules of Grammar

In the following statement of PL's grammar, **c** and **d** are metalinguistic variables ranging over individual constants of PL, **v** is a metalinguistic variable ranging over variables of PL, and bold-faced **A** is a metalinguistic variable ranging over monadic and relational predicates of PL. Boldfaced **P** and **Q** serve as metalinguistic variables ranging over well-formed formulas or "wffs" of PL.

1. Any sentence constant is a wff.
2. Any n-place predicate followed by n individual constants is a wff.
3. If **P** is a wff, then ~**P** is a wff.
4. If **P**, **Q** are wffs, then (**P** & **Q**), (**P** v **Q**), (**P** ⊃ **Q**), (**P** ≡ **Q**) are wffs.
5. If **P** is a wff containing a constant **c**, and **v** is a variable that does not appear in **P**, then (**v**) [**P** with **c**/**v**] and (∃**v**) [**P** with **c**/**v**] are wffs, where [**P** with **c**/**v**] abbreviates sentence **P** with one or more occurrences of **c** replaced uniformly by **v**.
6. If **c** and **d** are individual constants, then (**c** = **d**) is a wff.
7. **A**(iv)(**A**v) is a wff, **A**(iv)(**A**vv) is a wff, and so on.

Any formula that can be constructed by a finite number of applications of these rules is a sentence, or wff of PL. Nothing else is a sentence or wff of PL. The identity operator (=) is not introduced until Chapter 25. The iota will appear in Chapter 30.

Now, if you compare the syntax for PL with the syntax for TL, you will notice that any wff of TL counts as a wff of PL, although not every wff of PL will count as a wff of TL. In this sense PL "contains" TL, and we may say that PL is more comprehensive than TL. One more point: Recall the difference between an object language and a metalanguage. In this context, English is the metalanguage and PL is the object language.

Quantifier Scope and the Meaning of "Overlapping"

We now have six quantifiers. In a sentence containing just one quantifier, the scope of the quantifier is the quantifier itself plus the expression enclosed in parentheses to the quantifier's immediate right. In the following, the scope of each quantifier is underlined:

$$\underline{(x)(Fx \supset Gx)} \quad \underline{(x)Fx \supset Gx} \quad \underline{(x)(Fx)} \supset Sa \quad \underline{(x)(Fx)} \supset \underline{(\exists x)(Hx)} \quad \underline{(x)Fx} \supset \underline{(x)Hx}$$

Notice that as far as scope is concerned, a quantifier functions exactly as if it were a tilde. In other words, the scope of a quantifier is just what the scope would be if the quantifier were to be removed and replaced with a tilde.

A quantifier is said to "bind" the variable it contains plus any occurrences of that variable that lie within the quantifier's scope. Thus, in the following sentence, the quantifier binds all three variables:

$$(x)\ (Fx \supset Gx)$$

If a variable is not bound by a quantifier, it is a "free" variable. In each of the following, the variable x is bound by the universal quantifier and the variable y is a *free* variable.

$$(x)\ (Fx) \supset Gy \qquad (x)\ (Fx \supset Gx)\ v\ Sy$$

Any quantified sentence that contains one or more free variables is an open sentence. Recall that open sentences, expressions such as Fx or Hxy, contain no subject terms and so do not express claims about things. It therefore makes no sense to ask, concerning an open sentence, "Is it true or false?" This is why open sentences do not have truth-values.

A sentence that is not open is said to be closed. To turn an open sentence into a closed sentence, one or the other of two things must be done: (a) the variables must be replaced by constants, or (b) each variable must be bound by an appropriate quantifier, that is, by a quantifier that contains the same variable. Unlike open sentences, closed sentences represent claims that are either true or false, and so every closed sentence has a truth-value.

Translating Common Types of General Sentences

In Unit Two we examined categorical logic, the first branch of logic systematically developed and taught in the classroom. The author of the first textbook of categorical logic, Aristotle, focused on the logic of categorical sentences asserting that all, or some, or no members of a group or category of things either belong to, or do not belong to, another group. For example, "All cats are mammals" is a categorical sentence. It asserts that all the members of the category named "cats" belong to the category named "mammals." Let us follow in Aristotle's footsteps and begin by translating traditional categorical sentences, the same type of sentence Aristotle studied when he was developing the first systematic branch of logic in history.

The material at this point will be a little repetitive if you studied Unit 2 (categorical logic) because the information in that unit is not presupposed by this unit. A categorical sentence is *universal* if it asserts something about *all* the members of a group, and it is *existential* if it asserts something about *some* of the members of a group, where *some* means one or more. (As previously noted, *existential categorical sentences* are also called *particular categorical sentences* because they say something that could be true of *part* of a group.) In addition, a categorical sentence is *affirmative* if it asserts that all, some, or no things in one group *belong* to a second group, and it is *negative* if it denies membership in a group. This gives us four different types of categorical sentences: universal affirmative, universal negative, existential affirmative, and existential negative.

Universal Affirmative

The standard form for a universal affirmative is the following:

All _____ are _____.

where the blanks are filled in with the names of groups or categories. For example, "All dogs are animals" is a universal affirmative. The name that fills in the first blank, in this case, *dogs*, is called the *subject term* and the name that fills in the second blank, in this case, *animals*, is called the *predicate term*. The word *all* is called a *quantifier word* because it states a quantity. The word *are* is called a *copula* because it joins, or couples, the subject to the predicate. Thus:

All	**dogs**	**are**	**animals.**
↑	↑	↑	↑
Quantifier	subject term	copula	predicate term

We can interpret such a sentence in two different but equivalent ways. We may read it as saying that every member of the group named by the subject term ("dogs") belongs to the group named by the predicate term ("animals"). We can also interpret it in terms of things having or not having a property (i.e., an attribute or characteristic), in which case we read it as saying this: Every thing that has the property of being a dog also has the property of being an animal.

We have already seen how to symbolize this type of sentence. We paraphrase a sentence such as "All whales are mammals" into "Every thing that is a whale is such that it is a mammal," which is to say "Every x such that x is a whale is such that x is a mammal." In other words, "For every x, if x is a whale, then x is a mammal." This goes straight into PL as (x) (Wx ⊃ Mx), which says: For any x, if x is a whale, then x is a mammal. That is how we express, within PL, the universal affirmative claim that all whales are mammals.

Various alternative, but equivalent, ways exist by which to express a universal affirmative sentence in English. For example, instead of saying, "All whales are mammals," we could just as well say any of the following:

1. Whales are mammals.
2. Any whale is a mammal.
3. A whale is a mammal.
4. Every whale is a mammal.

These are all symbolized as:

(x)(Wx ⊃ Mx)

Universal Negative Sentences

The standard form for a universal negative sentence is No _____ are _____, where the first blank is filled in with the name of a group of things and the second blank holds the name of a group of things; for example, "No dogs are reptiles." Such a sentence denies that any of the members of the group named in the subject part belong to the group named in the predicate part. In other words, it denies that any members of a specified group have a certain property. But to deny that any of the members of a group have a certain property is to assert that *none* of the members of the group have the property. This is why the standard form for a universal negative begins with the quantifier word *No*. Examples of this type of sentence include the following:

No birds are reptiles.
No rocks are living things.
No horses are winged creatures.
No Vulcans are illogical creatures.

Let us symbolize the first example. Notice first that:

No birds are reptiles

is equivalent to:

All birds are nonreptiles.

That is, "No bird has the property of being reptilian" is equivalent to "All birds have the property of being *non*reptilian." Thus, we could also represent the standard form of a universal negative as:

All _____ are not _____.

Let us therefore paraphrase the first example:

For every x, if x is a bird, then x is not reptilian.

In symbols, this is simply:

(x) (Bx ⊃ ~Rx)

Notice that universal negatives are symbolized exactly as we symbolized universal affirmatives except for the addition of a suitably placed negation operator.

Existential Affirmative Sentences

An existential affirmative sentence is used to assert that some (i.e., at least one) of the members of a group of things belong to another group of things, in other words, that some of the members of a group of things have a certain property or characteristic. The standard form of such a sentence is:

Some _____ are _____.

where each blank is filled in with an expression referring to a group of entities. One of the sentences we examined earlier, "Some cars are noisy," is an example of this type of sentence. Other examples include the following:

Some trees are poplars.
Some horses are pets.
Some comedians are funny people.

To translate the second example into symbols, we can again think through a series of paraphrases. First, "Some horses are pets" is equivalent to:

At least one thing is such that it is a horse and it is a pet.

That is:

At least one x is such that x is a horse and x is a pet.

Letting Hx abbreviate "x is a horse" and letting Px abbreviate "x is a pet," this translates into symbols as:

(∃x) (Hx & Px)

The first of the three existential affirmatives thus goes into symbols as follows:

Some trees are poplars.
(∃x) (Tx & Px)

Another Word of Caution

Some people, after using horseshoes when symbolizing universal quantifications, attempt to use a horseshoe when symbolizing existential affirmatives. For instance, they might symbolize "Some trees are maples" with (∃x) (Tx ⊃ Mx). This is not an accurate symbolization. Let us see why. The formula (∃x) (Tx ⊃ Mx) literally says:

There is at least one x such that *if* x is a tree, then x is a maple.

Now, reflect on the meaning of this sentence. Notice that this is *not* equivalent to "Some trees are maples." For one reason, "Some trees are maples" asserts the existence of at least one maple tree, whereas the suggested translation, with its *if–then*, construction, does not assert the existence of any maple tree. (Remember that in modern logic an *if–then* or hypothetical sentence does not assert the actual existence of anything.) Rather, the sentence in effect asserts that either a non-tree exists or a maple tree exists. The sentence "There is an x such that *if* x is a tree, then x is a maple" therefore does not assert the actual existence of a maple tree; the sentence could be true even though no maple trees actually exist. Thus, the expression (∃x) (Tx ⊃ Mx) does not accurately capture the *existential* meaning of "Some trees are maples." Although there are exceptions, the main connective of an existential sentence is typically not a horseshoe. Better in this case to write (∃x) (Tx & Mx).

Lesson: There are rare exceptions, but it is *not* recommended that you combine an existential quantifier and a horseshoe.

Existential Negative Sentences

An existential negative sentence is used to claim that some of the members of one group do not belong to a second group, that is, that some members of a group do not have a certain property. The standard form of such a sentence is:

Some _____ are not _____.

For example:

1. Some students are not Republicans.
2. Some basketball players are not stamp collectors.
3. Some trees are not maples.

These existential negatives are symbolized exactly as we symbolized existential affirmatives, except for the addition of an appropriately placed negation operator:

1.	Some students are not Republicans.	(∃x) (Sx & ~Rx)
2.	Some basketball players are not stamp collectors.	(∃x) (Bx & ~Sx)
3.	Some trees are not maples.	(∃x) (Tx & ~Mx)

The following list sums up this discussion. S represents the subject term and P represents the predicate term of a categorical sentence. Since the Middle Ages, the four categorical forms have been assigned as names the letters of the vowels A, E, I, and O as follows:

A: Universal affirmative   All Ss are Ps   (x) (Sx ⊃ Px)
E: Universal negative   No Ss are Ps   (x) (Sx ⊃ ~Px)
I: Existential affirmative   Some Ss are Ps   (∃x) (Sx & Px)
O: Existential negative   Some Ss are not Ps   (∃x) (Sx & ~ Px)

Exercise 23.3   Translate the following sentences into PL:

1. All the members of the Seattle Musicians Union are fine artists.
2. No cats are fully morally responsible creatures.
3. Some human beings are not members of the community of law-abiding persons.
4. All unelected dictators are human rights violators.
5. Some logicians are Stoic philosophers.
6. All sane human beings are morally responsible creatures.
7. All angels are creatures capable of dancing on the head of a pin.
8. Every dog is a mammal.
9. No birds are mammals.
10. Some entertaining magicians are professors of the humanities.
11. No sophists are members of the Anti-Sophist Club.
12. Every member of the Pro-Logic Society of Seattle is a logical individual.

Swap It Out: Trade One Quantifier for Another

Sentences that contain a universal quantifier can be translated into sentences containing an existential quantifier, without loss of meaning, and vice versa. The rules that govern the translations are based on the following general principles:

- If all individuals have a certain property, then it is not the case that some individual does *not* have the property.
- If it is false that all individuals have a certain property, then it must be that some individual does *not* have the property.
- If some individuals have a certain property, then it must be false that all individuals do *not* have the property.
- If it is false that some individuals have a certain property, then it must be that all individuals do *not* have the property.

With these principles in mind and assuming a universal domain, let us begin with a simple example that we have already symbolized, the motto of the Optimists' Club, "Everything is good." By the first principle, this is logically equivalent to "Not even one thing is not good." Because "Everything is good" is symbolized with (x) Gx and "Not even one thing is not good" is symbolized as ~(∃x) ~Gx, it follows that (x) Gx is equivalent to ~(∃x)~ Gx.

Next, notice that by these principles, "Something is good," symbolized (∃x)Gx, is equivalent to "It is not the case that everything is not good," which is symbolized ~(x)~Gx. Thus, (∃x) Gx may be expressed equivalently as ~(x)~Gx.

Similarly:

It is not the case that at least one thing is good

is equivalent to:

All things are nongood.

That is:

~ (∃x) Gx is equivalent to (x) ~Gx.

And

It is not the case that all things are good

is equivalent to:

At least one thing is nongood.

That is:

~(x) Gx is equivalent to (∃x) ~Gx.

These general principles are all summed up in the following simple algorithm. To "swap out" a quantifier:

1. Trade one quantifier for the other.
2. Negate each side of the quantifier.
3. Cancel out any double negatives that result.

Following these rules, ~(x)Fx changes into (∃x) ~Fx, (∃x)Gx changes into ~(x)~Gx, ~(∃x) Ox changes into (x) ~Ox, and so on.

Application to Categoricals

Following the preceding algorithm, we can switch quantifiers in categorical sentences while preserving the original meaning, as long as we make some adjustments in the grammatical structure of the sentences at the same time. Study these examples carefully:

1. **Universal affirmatives.** "All As are Bs" is equivalent to "There does not exist an A that is a non-B." For example, "All aardvarks are brown" is equivalent to "There does not exist an aardvark that is not brown." Thus:

   (x) (Ax ⊃ Bx) is equivalent to ~(∃x)(Ax & ~Bx)

2. **Universal negatives.** "No As are Bs is equivalent to "There does not exist an A that is a B." For example, "No aardvarks are brown" is equivalent to "There does not exist an aardvark that is brown." Thus:

   (x) (Ax ⊃ ~ Bx) is equivalent to ~(∃x)(Ax & Bx)

3. **Existential affirmatives.** "Some As are Bs is equivalent to "It's not the case that all As are non-B." For example, "Some aardvarks are brown" is equivalent to "It is not the case that all aardvarks are nonbrown." Thus:

   (∃x) (Ax & Bx) is equivalent to ~(x) (Ax ⊃ ~ Bx)

4. **Existential negatives.** "Some As are non-B" is equivalent to "It's not the case that all As are B." For example, "Some aardvarks are not brown" is equivalent to "It is not the case that all aardvarks are brown." Thus:

   (∃x)(Ax & ~Bx) is equivalent to ~(x)(Ax ⊃ Bx)

In sum, A, E, I, and O categorical sentences can be symbolized using either universal or existential quantifiers. In the following, S represents the subject term and P the predicate term.

A: (x)(Sx ⊃ Px)	or equivalently	~(∃x)(Sx & ~Px)
E: (x)(Sx ⊃~ Px)	or equivalently	~(∃x)(Sx & Px)
I: (∃x)(Sx & Px)	or equivalently	~(x)(Sx ⊃ ~ Px)
O: (∃x)(Sx & ~ Px)	or equivalently	~(x)(Sx ⊃ Px)

Exercise 23.4   Symbolize each of the following sentences twice, first using a universal quantifier, then using an existential quantifier. For example, "All bats are cute": (x) (Bx ⊃ Cx), ~ (∃x) (Bx & ~ Cx)

1. All books are valuable.
2. No mammals are reptiles.
3. Some dogs are friendly.
4. Some dogs are not friendly.
5. It is not the case that something is right.
6. It is not the case that something is not right.
7. Something is good.
8. Something is not good.
9. All things are good.
10. It is not the case that all things are good.
11. All members of the Martin van Buren street gang are toughies.
12. It is not true that everything is desired.

Translating Sentences Containing Multiple Adjectives

Adjectives typically translate into symbols as predicate constants. For instance, "All old werewolves are gruesome" is symbolized as:

(x)[(Ox & Wx) ⊃ Gx]

where Ox abbreviates "x is old," Wx abbreviates "x is a werewolf," and Gx abbreviates "x is gruesome." This formula reads "For all x, if x is O and x is W, then x is G."
Consider the following sentence:

All Stoics are logical and in control of their emotions.

If we let Sx abbreviate "x is a Stoic," Lx abbreviate "x is logical," and Cx abbreviate "x is in control of his or her emotions," this translates thus:

(x) [Sx ⊃ (Lx & Cx)]

This says, "For any x, if x is a Stoic, then x is logical and x is in control of x's emotions."
Here are a few more examples:

All friendly old cats purr.
(x)[(Fx & (Ox & Cx)) ⊃ Px]

This says, "For any x, if x is friendly, x is old, and x is a cat, then x purrs."

> Some fish are blue and orange.
> (∃x)(Fx & (Bx & Ox))

This says, "For some x, x is a fish, and x is blue and x is orange."

> Some tall, sleepy giraffes are cute.
> (∃x)[(Tx & (Sx & Gx)) & Cx]

This says, "For at least one x, x is tall, and x is sleepy and x is a giraffe, and x is cute."

As the preceding sentences demonstrate, we usually choose predicate constants that remind us of the English adjectives they abbreviate. Study these examples carefully and note the close connection between English and our formal logical language.

"Hybrid" Sentences

Consider this sentence:

> If everyone cheers, then someone will boo.

Notice that *everyone* is not a singular term, and neither is *someone*. Therefore, this sentence cannot be symbolized as Ce ⊃ Bs. This is actually a compound sentence consisting of two separate general sentences joined in the middle by a truth-functional operator (the *if–then* connective). This sentence is thus a "hybrid" containing both quantificational and truth-functional elements. The two component sentences, each a general sentence in its own right, are:

> Everyone cheers.
> Someone will boo.

These two independent sentences are linked by the *if–then* operator:

> If   [Everyone cheers] then   [Someone will boo].

Symbolized, "Everyone cheers" becomes:

> (x)(Px ⊃ Cx) (This says: For any x, if x is a person, then x cheers.)

"Someone will boo" becomes:

(∃x) (Px & Bx) (This says: There is at least one x such that x is a person and x boos.)

Joining these two sentences, each a separate general sentence in its own right, by the *if–then* connective ⊃ produces the proper symbolization:

(x)(Px ⊃ Cx) ⊃ (∃x) (Px & Bx)

Does "Nessie" Exist? Symbolizing Existence

Sentences that assert and deny the existence of things are symbolized with the help of the existential quantifier. Let us consider for a moment the case of the Cadborosaurus, the "sea monster" species said to live in Loch Ness, Scotland (the so-called Loch Ness Monster). Suppose someone asserts the following:

There exists at least one Cadborosaurus.

It is standard to symbolize this as (∃x) Cx, which says, "There exists at least one x such that x is a Cadborosaurus." Of course, if we wish to use the variable y, the symbolization is (∃y) Cy. Notice that the notion of *existence* is captured in predicate logic by the existential quantifier, not with a predicate. Thus, we do *not* symbolize "A Cadborosaurus exists" with "Ec." Likewise we would *not* symbolize "Nessie exists" with "En." Make sure you see why this is the case before you move on. This is important, because many people, when first learning PL, want to use a predicate constant (usually E) instead of a quantifier to translate an existence claim, and as we have just seen, this is not the way we do it.

Lesson: Existence is normally expressed in predicate logic with an existential quantifier rather than a predicate. To say that a goat exists, we write (∃x) Gx rather than Eg.

PHILOSOPHICAL MOMENT

There is an interesting debate in the philosophy of logic over the question of the proper way to symbolize "exists," that is, over the proper way to represent existence in formal logical symbolism. Is existence a *property* of a thing? When an object exists, is existence one of its properties? If so, isn't existence better expressed with a predicate constant?

(continued)

Or is existence something else? If so, is existence, whatever it is, best expressed using a quantifier? Surprisingly, this quite ethereal question lies at the heart of one of the most famous philosophical arguments for God's existence ever devised, the ontological argument. Indeed, the author of that argument, Saint Anselm (1033–1109), was the first to introduce our present question into logic, the question of how to represent existence within a system of logic. See Chapter 35 for a summary of Anselm's famous argument.

Next, suppose someone else says:

Cadborosauri do not exist.

This person means the following: There are no Cadborosauri. In other words, it is not the case that there are Cadborosauri. A denial of existence, which is what this is, is symbolized as a negated existential:

~(∃x) Cx

This says, "It is not the case that there is at least one x such that x is a Cadborosaurus."

If we switch quantifiers per the translation scheme introduced earlier, this may also be expressed as:

(x) ~ Cx

which abbreviates "For each and every x, x is not a Cadborosaurus"; in other words, "Each and every thing in the universe is not a Cadborosaurus."

Let us consider a "hybrid" sentence that combines the singular and the general. Suppose old Captain Jack has been searching Loch Ness for a Cadborosaurus for 50 years. If one is finally discovered, Captain Jack, the Cadborosaurus hunter, will surely be happy. In English, this is:

If at least one Cadborosaurus exists, then Captain Jack will be happy.

How shall we symbolize this? First, this sentence is a compound of two embedded sentences. More specifically, this is a conditional sentence with an antecedent and a consequent. So the first thing to keep in mind is that when we translate the sentence into a formula, the main connective should be a horseshoe. Second, the antecedent of the conditional is a general or quantified sentence ("At least one Cadborosaurus exists") and the consequent is a singular sentence ("Captain Jack will be happy"). In symbols, with obvious abbreviations, the sentence thus becomes:

(∃x) (Cx) ⊃ Hc

What Is a "Bat-Rat"?

Consider the sentence "Bats and rats are mammals." At first glance, the proper symbolization would appear to be (x) [(Bx & Rx) ⊃ Mx], where Bx says x is a bat and Rx says x is a rat. However, consider what this formula literally says: For any and every x, if x is *both a bat and a rat at the same time*, then x is a mammal. In other words, all "bat-rats" are mammals! Of course, this is probably not what was intended by the speaker of the English sentence. There is no such thing as a bat-rat. The correct formula is:

(x) [(Bx v Rx) ⊃ Mx]

This says, for any x, if x is *either a bat or a rat*, then x is a mammal. Notice that we used a wedge to capture the idea that bats *and* rats are all mammals. This sentence could also have been broken into two parts and symbolized as a conjunction of two universal affirmatives:

(x) (Bx ⊃ Mx) & (x)(Rx ⊃ Mx)

This says, "All bats are mammals and all rats are mammals."

Exclusive Sentences: The "Only" Way to Go

Sentences containing *only* can be difficult to symbolize. Perhaps this is because the logic of such sentences is confusing at first glance. Let us abbreviate the certainly false sentence "Only politicians are honest." Notice that this is *not* equivalent to saying "All politicians are honest." Rather, this is to say:

The only persons who are honest are politicians.

Another way to put this is:

All honest persons are politicians.

Paraphrased, this becomes:

For any x, if x is honest, then x is a politician.

With H abbreviating "is honest" and P abbreviating "is a politician," this is:

(x) (Hx ⊃ Px)

Notice that the claim that all honest persons are politicians does not imply that all politicians are honest. (Compare: That all bachelors are males does not imply that all males are bachelors.) In symbols, "All politicians are honest" would look like this:

(x) (Px ⊃ Hx)

A sentence of the form "Only so and sos are such and such" is called an *exclusive sentence* because it indicates that the predicate term applies exclusively to the things designated by the subject term. Notice that when we symbolized the exclusive sentence earlier ("Only politicians are honest"), we used a horseshoe and we reversed the positions of the subject and predicate terms as they had appeared in the English sentence.

Here is another example. The exclusive sentence "Only boaters are happy with the new regulations" is equivalent to "The only people happy with the new regulations are boaters." In PL:

(x) (Hx ⊃ Bx)

where Hx abbreviates x is a person who is happy with the new regulations and Bx abbreviates x is a boater. Here is a more complicated case:

Only teachers with certification were hired.

That is:

All who were hired were teachers who had certification.

We paraphrase this:

For any x, if x was hired, then x was a teacher and x had certification.

In symbols:

(x)[Hx ⊃ (Tx & Cx)]

Exceptive Sentences

An *exceptive sentence* is best symbolized as a conjunction of two sentences. For example, consider "All except truckers are happy with the new freeway." This is equivalent to the following conjunction: "All nontruckers are happy with the new freeway, and no truckers are happy with the new freeway." In symbols, with obvious abbreviations, this conjunction is:

(x) (~Tx ⊃ Hx) & (x) (Tx ⊃ ~ Hx)

The Blues Brothers Wreck a Relative Clause

Consider the following sentence:

Any person who likes the Blues Brothers movie has a wacky sense of humor.

How shall we capture the relative clause, "who likes the Blues Brothers movie"? First, let us paraphrase the whole sentence:

Every x such that x is a person and x likes the Blues Brothers movie is such that x has a wacky sense of humor.

This is equivalent to:

For every x, *if* x is a person and x likes the Blues Brothers movie, then x has a wacky sense of humor.

If we let Px abbreviate "x is a person," Lx abbreviate "x likes the Blues Brothers," and Hx abbreviate "x has a wacky sense of humor," this becomes:

(x)[(Px & Lx) ⊃ Hx]

And there you go.

Exercise 23.5

Part 1
Symbolize the following in PL. Use obvious abbreviations or state what abbreviates what.

1. No old and gray books are interesting.
2. Some books are long and dull.

3. If Elaine dances, then everyone will laugh.

4. If all are happy, then Newman will be happy.

5. Some movies are philosophical and some movies are not.

6. Dragons do not exist.

7. All aardvarks as well as tapirs are mammals.

8. At least one nondetectable strain of the AIDS virus exists.

9. Only the brave are free.

10. There is a very old blue car in the garage.

11. Every human being is deserving of respect and equal treatment.

12. Not all Klingons are bad.

13. Any hot dog with peanut butter on it is a tasty treat.

14. Some people are either overly busy or too preoccupied.

15. Anyone who likes the Marx Brothers and the Three Stooges has good taste in humor.

16. Not every philosophy book is a good read.

17. Everything is temporary and perishable.

18. Everything that exists is inherently good.

19. All things are either material or nonmaterial.

20. Nothing is bad.

Part 2

The following sentences are different. Hint: In each case, the main operator is *truth-functional*.

1. Either all things are material or all things are nonmaterial.

2. If someone claps, then someone will boo.

3. If Elaine dances, then everyone will stare.

4. If all human beings have the right to be free, then Stalin and Hitler were moral monsters.

5. All minds are immaterial and all bodies are material.

Glossary

Categorical sentence A general sentence that asserts that all or some members of a group have or lack a specified property. A categorical sentence is universal if it asserts something about all the members of a group, and it is existential if it asserts something about some of the members of a group. A categorical sentence is affirmative if it asserts that things have a certain property, and it is negative if it denies that things have a certain property. Thus, there are four different types of categorical sentences: universal affirmative, universal negative, existential affirmative, and existential negative.

Constant A symbol that stands for a specifically identified thing. In quantificational logic, individual constants such as a, b, and c are symbols that abbreviate singular terms, and predicate constants are symbols such as A, B, and C that abbreviate predicates.

Definite descriptions Descriptions that refer by unique description to one specific thing.

Existential general sentence A sentence that makes a claim about some members of a group, where *some* is understood as meaning "at least one."

General sentence A sentence that makes a claim about some or all members of a group.

General term A term that can be used to characterize a general category of entities, or things, that have a property in common. Unlike a singular term, a general term can be applied to many things, and it represents a property that many things could have in common.

Open sentence An incomplete sentence that is lacking a subject expression and that has a space where a subject expression can be placed.

PL An artificial symbolic language for predicate logic, also called quantificational logic.

Proper names Capitalized names that refer by name to one specific thing.

Quantificational argument An argument whose validity or invalidity is due to the arrangement of quantifiers and the units to which these attach.

Singular sentence A sentence that makes a claim about one specifically identified thing.

Singular term An expression that refers to or describes one specifically identified thing.

Universal general sentence A sentence that makes a claim about all of the members of a group.

Variable In PL, a symbol such as x, y, or z that serves as a placeholder for individual constants. A variable in predicate logic performs the function that is performed by the word *thing* within English.

24 Predicate Logic Version 1.2 « « « « « « «

It's All About Relationships

Relational vs. Monadic Predicates

It is only with the addition of relational predicates that predicate logic begins to go beyond the traditional categorical logic of Aristotle. The predicates we have examined so far have been monadic, or one-place, predicates. A *monadic* predicate is used to say something about one thing; in other words, it attributes a property or characteristic to *one* thing. In the sentence "Joe is happy," the predicate "is happy" is monadic. A *relational* predicate is used to assert that a *relationship* exists between two or more things. These are all relational predicates:

_____ knows _____
_____ is older than _____
_____ is taller than _____
_____ bought a gift from _____ and gave it to _____

Notice that these expressions are written as open sentences. In addition, notice that each one has two or more holes or blanks where a subject term is to be inserted. To turn one of these dyadic predicates into a complete sentence, we must insert singular terms into each blank, as in the following examples.

Pat knows Chris.
Pat is older than Chris.
Pat is taller than Chris.
Jane bought a gift from Ed and gave it to Chris.

Relational open sentences are symbolized just as we symbolized monadic ones, except for the addition of additional variables representing the additional blanks. Thus:

_____ knows _____	x knows y	Kxy
_____ is older than _____	x is older than y	Oxy
_____ is taller than _____	x is taller than y	Txy
_____ bought a gift from _____ and gave it to _____	x bought a gift from y and gave it to z	Bxyz

In each case, to form the open sentence we used variables in place of the blanks. If we next substitute names for the variables, we produce the following substitution instances of these open sentences:

Kpc "Pat knows Chris."
Opc "Pat is older than Chris."
Tpc "Pat is taller than Chris."
Bjec "Jane bought a gift from Ed and gave it to Chris."

Notice that we place the relational predicate constant to the left and the singular terms to the right in order of their appearance in the sentence we are symbolizing. When a relational predicate relates two things, it is a **dyadic** ("two-place") predicate. Relational predicates relating two or more things are *polyadic* ("many-place") predicates.

How to Combine Quantifiers and Relational Predicates

Let us consider a sentence that combines a single quantifier with a dyadic predicate. How about, "Jan knows everybody"? We proceed by paraphrases. First, this is equivalent to:

For all x such that x is a person, Jan knows x.

This may be paraphrased as:

For all x, if x is a person, then Jan knows x.

If we now abbreviate Jan with j, Jan knows x with Kjx, and x is a person with Px, our sentence may be symbolized as:

(x) (Px ⊃ Kjx)

Consider next the sentence, "Fred knows somebody." We may paraphrase this as:

There exists at least one x such that x is a person and Fred knows x.

In symbols this is:

(∃x)(Px & Kfx)

where Kfx abbreviates the predicate "Fred knows x" and Px abbreviates "x is a person."

Now, compare "Fred knows somebody" with "Somebody knows Fred." The sentence "Somebody knows Fred" is equivalent to:

There exists at least one x such that x is a person and x knows Fred.

In symbols this becomes:

(∃x) (Px & Kxf)

where Kxf abbreviates "x knows Fred." Notice the difference in meaning between Kfx and Kxf in the last two PL sentences. Here they are again for comparison:

Fred knows somebody.   (∃x)(Px & Kfx)
Somebody knows Fred.   (∃x) (Px & Kxf)

In the following examples, Txy abbreviates "x is taller than y," and the other abbreviations are obvious:

All brontosauri are taller than Pat.   (x)(Bx ⊃ Txp)

The formula reads, "For any x, if x is a brontosaurus, then x is taller than Pat."

Pat is taller than all brontosauri.   (x)(Bx ⊃ Tpx)

The formula reads, "For any x, if x is a brontosaurus, then Pat is taller than x."

Not all brontosauri are taller than Sam.   ~(x)(Bx ⊃ Txs)

The formula reads, "It is not the case that for any x, if x is a brontosaurus, then x is taller than Sam."

Any and Every

It is interesting that in some cases the terms *any* and *every* function quite differently when on the level of surface grammar they appear to serve the same meaning. In the following example, the two words function in unison:

Wimpy likes *every* hamburger.   (x)[Hx ⊃ Lwx]

This says, "For every x, if x is a hamburger, then Wimpy likes x."

Wimpy likes *any* hamburger.   (x)[Hx ⊃ Lwx]

This says, "For every x, if x is a hamburger, then Wimpy likes x."
However, here *every* and *any* function in opposing ways:

Wimpy does not like every hamburger.   ~ (x)[Hx ⊃ Lwx]

This says. "It is not the case that for every x, if x is a hamburger, then Wimpy likes x."

Wimpy does not like any hamburger.   (x)[Hx ⊃ ~ Lwx]

This says, "For every x, if x is a hamburger, then Wimpy does not like x."
The last two symbolized sentences obviously do not carry the same meaning. In the first case, there may be some hamburgers Wimpy likes; in the second case, the hamburger king likes no burger at all. This shows that "surface grammar" can in some cases be deceiving. This exercise also demonstrates the power of logical symbolism. After translating language into symbols, we sometimes see things we might not otherwise have noticed

Random Examples

Let us examine a few more translations:

Everybody loves Raymond.   (x)(Px ⊃ Lxr)

The formula reads, "For every x, if x is a person, then x loves Raymond."

Not everybody knows Fred.   ~(x)(Px ⊃ Kxf)

This reads, "It is not the case that for every x, if x is a person, then x knows Fred."

Fred doesn't know anybody.   ~ (∃x)(Px & Kfx)

The formula reads, "It is not the case that there is an x such that x is a person and Fred knows x."

Fred doesn't know everybody.   ~(x)(Px ⊃ Kfx)

This reads, "It is not the case that for every x, if x is a person, then Fred knows x."

Nobody knows Fred.   (x) (Px ⊃ ~Kxf)

This reads, "For any x, if x is a person, then x does not know Fred." Notice that this could also be symbolized:

~(∃x) (Px & Kxf)

This formula reads, "It is not the case that there is an x such that x is a person and x knows Fred."

Reflexive Sentences

"Narcissus loves himself" is an example of a reflexive sentence, a sentence that states a relation something has to itself. Let's look at some examples of singular reflexives with their proper symbolizations.

Sentence	Translation in PL
Susan is proud of herself.	Pss

Here P stands for the two-place predicate "_____ is proud of _____" and s abbreviates "Susan." Thus "Pss" indicates that Susan is proud of Susan.

Joe is as tall as himself.   Tjj

Here T stands for the two-place predicate "_____ is as tall as _____" and j abbreviates "Joe." Thus "Tjj" says that Joe is as tall as Joe.

General Reflexives

Psychological egoism (from the Latin word for "I," *ego*) is the theory that every human being, without exception, is by nature selfish. The claim is that everyone is "hard-wired" by nature or by evolution to always be selfish. If psychological egoism is true, then each of us, in each of our acts, is ultimately motivated by self-interest alone. Each of us is always out for "number one," even when it appears otherwise, and we cannot do otherwise. If this view of human nature is true, then the following formula is true:

(x) (Px ⊃ Cxx)

Letting C stand for "cares only about," this says, "For any x, if x is a person, then x cares only about x." However, although the view has been advocated and defended by numerous philosophers and others down through the ages, including apparently President Abraham Lincoln, many philosophers have argued that psychological egoism is a false view of human nature. The critics of this view claim that the following better expresses the truth about human nature:

~(x) (Px ⊃ Cxx)

A few more examples and you will be set. Socrates was famous for saying, "Know thyself." Surely some have followed his advice.

Somebody knows himself.   (∃x)(Px & Kxx)

This reads, "There is at least one x such that x is a person and x knows x." In other words, someone knows himself (or herself, as the gender is not indicated). Perhaps it would be a better world if everyone followed his advice.

Everybody knows herself.   (x)(Px ⊃ Kxx)

This reads, "For every x, if x is a person, then x knows x." In other words, every person knows herself (or himself).

Exercise 24.1   Symbolize the following in PL.

1. Pam is taller than Sue but Sue is older than Pam.
2. Archie Bunker does not like any "liberal."
3. Archie Bunker does not like every liberal.
4. Wimpy, the hamburger man, respects himself.
5. Someone knows himself.
6. Everybody knows Bill Gates.
7. All elephants are larger than Nathan's pet mouse.
8. Lorraine likes any horse.

9. Somebody knows Katie.
10. Matt is a friend of Elliot's.
11. Everything with caffeine in it is liked by Elmer.
12. Sam dislikes somebody.
13. Sam dislikes everybody.
14. Socrates knows himself.
15. Nobody knows Jay.
16. Jay knows nobody.
17. Pat is taller than any aardvark and is shorter than any elephant.
18. Any human being is more valuable than that hundred-dollar bill you are holding in your hand right now.
19. Socrates was the teacher of Plato, Plato was the teacher of Aristotle, and Aristotle was the teacher of Theophrastus.

Overlapping Quantifiers

Recall that the scope of a quantifier is the same as if it (the quantifier) were a tilde. If one quantifier appears immediately to the right of another quantifier, as in the formula (x) (y) Fxy, the scope of the first quantifier is that quantifier itself plus the scope of the second quantifier. In such a case, the quantifiers are **overlapping quantifiers**. When quantifiers overlap, each quantifier "binds," or links to, only the matching variable(s) within its scope. Thus, in the preceding sentence with overlapping quantifiers, the variable y in the Fxy part is bound only by the second quantifier (y), and the variable x is bound only by the first quantifier (x). With that over with, let's translate some "big ideas" from the history of philosophy and see how their overlapping quantifiers go into symbols.

Example 1: Is it true that everything has a cause? Some philosophers have argued for the principle of universal causation, which states that everything has a cause. The universe, they argue, is a deterministic system that functions according to precise and rigid universal laws, and this means that nothing happens without a preexisting cause that causes it to happen. The principle is not to be confused with the claim that there is one thing (e.g., God) that is the universal cause of everything else. The principle of universal causation claims that each thing has some cause or other, not that there is one thing that is the cause of all things. Thus, although each thing has a cause, the cause of one thing might be different from the cause of another thing, and so on. To begin with, let us state the principle this way: Everything is caused by something or other. This can be paraphrased:

For every x, there exists at least one y such that y is the cause of x.

In other words, for every thing x, there is something y such that y is x's cause. Now, if we let Cyx abbreviate y causes x (or y is the cause of x), the principle of universal causation goes into symbols:

(x) (∃y) Cyx

This reads, "For every x, there is at least one y, such that y is the cause of x." Note that it does not logically follow from this that some *one* thing (such as God) exists and is the universal cause of everything. It might be true that there is one thing that is the cause of all things, but further argument would be needed to prove this claim true.

Example 2: Is there a universal cause? Philosophers from the time of Plato (428–348 BC), and even before him, have produced philosophical arguments for the claim that God exists. Of course, other philosophers have criticized these arguments and have argued for the nonexistence of God. Suppose now we consider "Something causes everything." This sentence is primarily about a something, and so it should begin with an existential quantifier. The sentence can be paraphrased:

There exists a y such that for every x in the universe, y is the cause of x.

In other words, there exists some one thing y and y is itself the cause of everything. In this case, the sentence asserts the existence of a cause of the universe, a creator of the cosmos. In symbols, this translates as:

(∃y) (x) Cyx

This reads, "There is some thing y, and for every x, y is the cause of x." Notice that the last two formulas match except for the order of the quantifiers. As we have seen, these two sentences have two distinct meanings. In general, when universal and existential quantifiers appear next to each other in a formula, the order of the two quantifiers affects the meaning of the sentence. We'll come back to this point later on.

Example 3: Is everything active? Consider the claim, "Everything causes something or other." Call this the principle of universal activism. To translate this sentence we begin by noting that it is primarily claiming something about everything, and so its symbolization should begin with a universal quantifier. This sentence says that for every x, there is at least one y such that x causes y. In other words, for anything whatsoever, there exists something or other that it causes. But this need not be the same y in each case (hence the "or other" in the formulation of the claim). That is, each thing causes something, but it doesn't follow from this that one thing exists that is itself caused by everything. If we let Cxy abbreviate x causes y, the sentence goes into symbols as (x) (∃y) Cxy.

Example 4: Is there one big universal result? Suppose someone claims, "Something is caused by everything." Call this the principle of the big result. I am not aware of a school of philosophical thought specifically associated with this idea, but someone might argue that the whole universe is headed for one big train wreck in the end, and that would do as an example. To represent this idea we simply rearrange the order of the quantifiers in the previous formula, leaving the rest the same:

(∃y) (x) Cxy

This says, "There is at least one y such that for every x, x causes y." In other words, something is caused by everything. Thus we see again that when a sentence has both a universal and an existential quantifier, the order in which the quantifiers appear can make quite a difference.

It will be helpful to remember this: If a multiply-quantified sentence is primarily about everything, as in examples 1 and 3, then its symbolization starts off with a universal quantifier. If it is primarily about something, as in examples 2 and 4, then its formula starts off with the existential quantifier. In most cases, when an existential quantifier appears first, followed by a universal quantifier, the sentence asserts that at least one thing stands in a relation to all things. When a universal quantifier appears first, followed by an existential quantifier, the sentence asserts that for each and every thing, some entity stands in a relation to that thing.

"What Are You Talking About?"
Shrinking the Universe (of Discourse)

A variable (x, y, or z) is said to "range" over a domain. Recall that the **domain of a variable** is the set of things the variable can take as values, where the values of a variable are just the things represented by the singular terms that can replace the variable in a sentence. When we specify the **universe of discourse** for a sentence containing a variable, we are stating the domain of the variable; that is, we are specifying what it ranges over. When the domain of a variable is everything in the universe, we call this the **universal domain**. If the domain is a set of things within the universe, for instance, if the domain is all cats, we call this a *restricted domain*.

We have been presupposing the universal domain in all that we have done so far. That is, we have been assuming that our variables range over all things in the universe. For the following examples, it will simplify things greatly if we stipulate a restricted domain, a restricted universe of discourse. To see how a restricted domain can simplify the expression of some things, compare the following two symbolizations of the same English sentence. First, assuming an unrestricted universe of discourse, that is, the universal domain, the sentence:

All persons have rights.

goes into symbols as:

(x)(Px ⊃ Rx)

This says, "For any x in the entire universe, if x is a person, then x has rights." The Stoic philosophers of ancient Greece were the first thinkers in history to state *philosophical* arguments for the basic idea underlying this claim. If we now stipulate that the domain is persons, in other words, that the variable x ranges only over persons, then "All persons have rights" can be symbolized as:

(x) Rx

Because the variable now ranges only over persons, the universal quantifier (x) is telling us that the sentence is only about all persons, and so the sentence (x) Rx in effect says, "For all persons, each has rights." Notice that in this case we dispense with the "Px" part of the formula.

In contrast, if we assume the universal domain, then the sentence (x) Rx says that all things in the entire universe have rights. For another example, if we stipulate that our domain is all and only Vulcans, then "All Vulcans have hidden emotions" may be symbolized (x)(Hx) with the understanding that x ranges only over Vulcans and Hx abbreviates "x has hidden emotions."

For the following, assume the domain is persons. Consider this sentence:

Someone knows someone.

To symbolize this, let us paraphrase it into an appropriate form. First, "someone knows someone" is equivalent to:

For some x and for some y, x knows y.

In symbols, this is abbreviated thus:

(∃x) (∃y) Kxy

where Kxy abbreviates "x knows y." (Remember that we are assuming the variables range only over persons.) Next, consider the following:

Everyone knows everyone.

Another way to put this is:

For every x, and for every y, x knows y.

In PL, this becomes:

(x) (y) Kxy

If a sentence contains two universal quantifiers in a row, or two existential quantifiers in a row, we can switch the order of the adjacent quantifiers without altering the meaning of the sentence. For example, "Someone knows someone" can be symbolized by either:

(∃x)(∃y)(Kxy)

or

(∃y)(∃x)(Kxy)

Both say the same thing. And "Everyone knows everyone" may be symbolized by either:

(y)(x)(Kxy)

or

(x)(y)(Kxy)

In general, if a sentence contains two universal quantifiers—each with a different variable attached—or two existential quantifiers with different variables, the order of the adjacent quantifiers makes no difference. However, as we saw earlier, when two quantifiers appear next to each other in a sentence, and one is universal and the other is existential, the order of the two quantifiers affects the meaning of the sentence. Changing the order of the quantifiers changes the meaning of the sentence.

History Note

The notion of a universe of discourse goes back to 1846 and the writings of DeMorgan.

Universal Love, the 1960s, and All That

Let us now sum this up by symbolizing some sentences about people, assuming the domain of our variables is limited to human beings. Consider first a principle made famous in a 1965 song by that former Rat-Packer, the one and only Dean Martin:

Everybody loves somebody (sometime).

This goes into symbols through the following series of paraphrases:

Every x is such that x loves someone.
Every x is such that there is someone such that x loves this someone.
Every x is such that there is some y such that x loves y.
(x) (∃y) Lxy

Consider next, "Someone loves everyone." This sentence says that there is someone who is such that no matter whom you pick, this someone loves the one you picked. Paraphrasing, this is "There is at least one x such that for any y, x loves y." In PL:

(∃x) (y) Lxy

Notice the difference between the following two sentences.

1. Everyone is loved by someone (or other).
2. Someone loves everyone.

The two have different meanings. Sentence 1 says that no matter whom we pick, someone loves that person. But sentence 2 says that someone—a very special someone—exists who, no matter whom we pick, loves the person we pick. This someone is a saint.

Sentence 1 is a universal statement, because it is primarily about all persons. But sentence 2 is an existential statement, because it is primarily about this one special someone. Consequently, sentence 1 begins with a universal quantifier and sentence 2 begins with an existential quantifier:

1. (x)(∃y) Lyx
2. (∃y)(x) Lyx

Study the following examples carefully. Remember that the domain is limited to people.

English	Symbolization
Somebody is known by everybody.	(∃y) (x) Kxy
Everybody knows somebody or other.	(x) (∃y) Kxy
Everybody is known by somebody or other.	(y)(∃x) Kxy

This discussion is summed up in the following list:

English	Formula	Image
Everyone loves everyone.	(x) (y) Lxy	The 1960s
Everyone loves someone.	(x)(∃y) Lxy	Dean Martin
Everyone loves himself.	(x) Lxx	Egoism
Someone loves everyone.	(∃x) (y) Lxy	Mother Teresa
Someone loves someone.	(∃x) (∃y) Lxy	Romeo and Juliet
Someone loves himself.	(∃x) Lxx	Narcissus
Everyone is loved by someone.	(x) (∃y) Lyx	A soap opera
Someone is loved by everyone.	(∃x) (y) Lyx	Mickey Mouse

Exercise 24.2   Symbolize the following in PL. Assume the domain is all human beings.

1. There is a person who is universally respected.
2. There is a person who respects everybody.
3. Everybody respects someone or other.
4. There's a person whom everyone respects.
5. Some people do not know anybody.
6. If everybody knows somebody, then somebody knows everybody.
7. If someone helps someone, then God is pleased.
8. Nobody who loves someone is all bad.
9. Anyone who loves no one is to be pitied.
10 Someone is not known by anyone.

Appendix 24.1   Advanced Topic: Properties of Relations

Many logic teachers do not cover the ideas in this section, preferring to reserve them for an advanced logic course. However, the concepts are accessible from where we are now, and they are interesting in their own right. Many deep philosophical arguments—about the existence and nature of God, free will, the nature of consciousness, and such things—employ premises that can be seen to be making claims about the properties of relations between things once those premises are translated into the symbols of PL. So let's have a look.

You already know that the sentence "Julie is older than Peter" is abbreviated in PL with "Ojp" where O represents the two-place relation of "being older than," the constant j abbreviates "Julie," and the constant p abbreviates "Peter." The sentence asserts the existence of a *relation* between Julie and Peter. Relations are abstract enough, but even more abstract is the fact that relations between things have properties of their own, and the proper analysis of complicated arguments, such as those mentioned earlier, often depends on which properties it is correct to suppose a particular relationship actually has. Here we examine three especially important properties of relations: transitivity, symmetry, and reflexivity.

Transitivity

A relation is **transitive** just in case if one thing bears the relation to a second thing, and the second thing bears the relation to a third thing, the first *must* bear the relation to the third. In other words, if A has the relation to B, and B has the relation to C, then A must have the relation to C. The relation of "being older than" is therefore transitive, for if A is older than B, and B is older than C, A must be older than C. In general, for any two-place relation R, R is transitive if and only if:

$$(x) \, (y) \, (z) \, [(Rxy \, \& \, Ryz) \supset Rxz]$$

This says, "For any x, for any y, and for any z, if x has relation R to y, and y has R to z, then x has R to z." A relation is *intransitive* just in case if one thing bears the relation to a second and the second bears the relation to a third, the first cannot possibly bear the relation to the third. The relation of "being the grandmother of" is intransitive, for if one person is the grandmother of a second person, and the second is the grandmother of a third person, the first person cannot possibly be the grandmother of the third. In general, for any two-place relation R, R is intransitive just in case:

$$(x) \, (y) \, (z) \, [(Rxy \, \& \, Ryz) \supset {\sim}Rxz]$$

This says, "For any x, for any y, and for any z, if x has relation R to y, and y has R to z, then x does not have R to z. Relations that are neither transitive nor intransitive are *nontransitive*. The relation "is a friend of" is an example of a nontransitive relation, for if Betty is a friend of John and John is a friend of Susan, it does not follow that Betty and Susan must be friends and it does not follow that they must not be friends. Other examples of nontransitive relations are "admires," "is jealous of," "loves," and "gave money to."

Examples of transitive relations are "is the same weight as," "owns more cars than," "has a larger hat size than," and "received more votes than." Examples of intransitive relations are "is exactly 10 years older than," "ate exactly twice as many hamburgers as," and "owns one more car than."

Symmetry

A relation is **symmetrical** just in case if one thing has the relation to a second thing, the second thing has that relation to the first thing. In other words, if A has the relation to B, then B has the relation to A. For example, the relation "is the same age as" is symmetrical, for if one thing is the same age as a second thing, then the second thing is the same age as the first. Other examples of symmetric relations are "is married to," "lives in the same city as," "is a cousin of," "is the same height as," and "is a friend of." In general, for any two-place relation R, R is symmetrical if and only if:

$$(x) (y) (Rxy \supset Ryx)$$

This says, "For any x and for any y, if x has the relation R to y, then y has R to x. A relation qualifies as *asymmetrical* just in case if one thing has that relation to a second, the second cannot possibly have that relation to the first. For example, "is taller than" is asymmetrical, for if one person is taller than a second, the second must *not* be taller than the first. Other asymmetrical relations include "is older than," "is father of," "is mother of," and "is east of." In general, a relation R is asymmetrical if and only if:

$$(x) (y) (Rxy \supset {\sim} Ryx)$$

This says, "For any x and for any y, if x has the relation R to y, then y does not have R to x.

If a relation is neither symmetrical nor asymmetrical, it is *nonsymmetrical*. Thus, "knows the name of" is nonsymmetrical, for if one person knows the name of a second person, it doesn't follow that the second knows the name of the first, and it also doesn't follow that the second does *not* know the name of the first. Other examples of nonsymmetrical relations are "is a sister of," "painted a picture of," "admires," and "greeted."

Reflexivity

A relation is **reflexive** if and only if the following is the case: If one thing has the relation to something or something has the relation to the first thing, then the first thing has that relation to itself. For example, the relation "belongs to the same church as" is reflexive, for if Clyde belongs to the same church as Bonnie, Clyde belongs to the same church as himself. Other examples of reflexive relations are "weighs as much as," "went to the same school as," "is as tall as," and "has the same parents as."

In general, a relation R is reflexive just in case:

(x) [(∃y) (Rxy v Ryx) ⊃ Rxx]

This says, "For any x, if x has the relation R to something y or if something y has the relation R to x, then x has relation R to itself." A relation is *irreflexive* if and only if nothing has the relation to itself. Thus, "is older than" is irreflexive, for nothing could possibly be older than itself. In other words, a relation R is irreflexive just in case:

(x) ~ Rxx

Other examples of irreflexive relations are "is a brother of," "is older than," "weighs more than," and "owns more pencils than." If a relation is neither reflexive nor irreflexive, it is *nonreflexive*. The relations "gave a present to," "looked at," "sang to," and "likes" are examples. As you might have guessed, the logical principles of relations are employed heavily in the advanced branch of logic known as metalogic, the logic of logic. See Appendix B at the back of the book for more about this fascinating branch of our subject.

Exercise 24.3   Instructions are given in context.

1.   List additional examples of relations that are:

a.	transitive	f.	nonsymmetric
b.	intransitive	g.	reflexive
c.	nontransitive	h.	irreflexive
d.	symmetric	i.	nonreflexive
e.	asymmetric		

2.   Classify as transitive, symmetric, and so on. (Note: Each relation will possess more than one of the properties covered in this section.)

a.	is south of	g.	has more stamps than
b.	is the sister of	h.	borrowed a book from
c.	is at least 10 pounds heavier than	i.	is not taller than
d.	is proud of	j.	went to the circus with
e.	is a relative of	k.	is acquainted with
f.	is the boss of	l.	is identical with

Glossary

Domain of a variable The set of things the variable can take as values. The values of a variable are just the entities represented by the singular terms that can replace the variable. The domain of a variable is also known as the universe of discourse for the sentence containing the variable.

Dyadic (or "two-place") predicate A predicate phrase that contains two blanks and is typically used to represent a relation between two things.

Monadic (or "one-place") predicate A predicate phrase that contains one blank and is used to attribute a property to just one thing.

Overlapping quantifier One quantifier appearing within the scope of another quantifier.

Psychological egoism The theory that every human being, without exception, is hard-wired to always be motivated by self-interest and by nothing else.

Reflexive relation A relation that possesses the following feature: If A has the relation to B or B has the relation to A, then A has that relation to itself.

Symmetrical relation A relation that possesses the following feature: If one thing has the relation to a second thing, the second thing has that relation to the first thing.

Transitive relation A relation that possesses the following feature: If one thing bears the relation to a second thing and the second thing bears the relation to a third thing, the first must bear the relation to the third.

Universal domain Everything in the universe. When the domain is everything in the universe, the domain is unrestricted or universal.

Universe of discourse The collection of things that the sentence or sentences are making a claim about. Essentially, the things we are talking about on an occasion.

The simple little word *is* has a surprising number of different uses and meanings in the English language. Sometimes we use the word *is* to attribute a characteristic, or property, to something, as when we say, "That flower *is* a beautiful shade of red." This is called the *predicative* use of "is." (Note that we use a predicate constant when we express this meaning of the word *is*, symbolizing the sentence: Rt) In some contexts we may use *is*, or a variation of the verb, to assert existence, as when someone says, "God is." This is the *existential* use of the word. (As you know from Chapter 23, we use an existential quantifier, rather than a predicate constant, to express existence, that is, to express this meaning of the verb *to be*.) We may also use *is* to say something like this: "Robert Allen Zimmerman, born in Duluth, Minnesota on May 24, 1941, *is* Bob Dylan, the composer of such songs as 'Like a Rolling Stone' and 'Thunder on the Mountain.'" In logic this *is* is called the "is of identity." This one little word will be our focus for the rest of this chapter.

When we say that Robert Allen Zimmerman *is* Bob Dylan, we are claiming that the individual from Duluth Minnesota, named Robert Allen Zimmerman, is *one and the same individual* as the famous singer, songwriter, and poet known as Bob Dylan. In other words, Robert Zimmerman and Bob Dylan are one and the same person, not two different persons. This identity is true, by the way.

An interesting example of the "is of identity" concerns the heavenly object known to ancient astronomers as the Evening Star. In ancient times, the term the *Morning Star* had one meaning, and the term the *Evening Star* carried another meaning because it was thought that the two names referred to two different stars. (After all, the two objects appeared in different parts of the sky at different times.) However, astronomical observations eventually proved that the two terms actually refer to one and the same individual object, namely, the planet Venus. Thus, through observation, it was discovered that:

The Morning Star *is* the Evening Star

expresses a true proposition. In other words, the Morning Star and the Evening Star are not two different entities, they are one and the same entity. Here are additional examples of the *identificational* use of *is*:

Taiwan is Formosa.
Muhammad Ali is Cassius Clay.
Olympia is the capital of Washington State.
Richard Starkey is Ringo Starr.

Quantitative vs. Qualitative Identity

It is important not to confuse the concept of identity just explained with the concept of similarity. In everyday speech, we might point to two coffee cups and say that they are "identical." But we would normally *not* mean by this that the two cups are one and the same cup; rather, we would normally mean that the two cups, although two separate cups, look exactly alike, in other words, they have the same characteristics or properties. This would be a case of two different cups with similar characteristics. Two separate coffee cups, no matter how similar in appearance, could never be identical in the sense defined earlier; that is, they could never be *one and the same* cup. To distinguish these two very different uses of the word *identical*, logicians distinguish between quantitative identity and qualitative identity. If x and y are two different things but have all their characteristics in common, they are qualitatively identical. Because the two coffee cups look exactly alike, they are *qualitatively* identical. If x and y are *not* two different things but are in reality one and the same thing, then we say they are *quantitatively* identical. Because our discussion focuses on quantitative identity, let us now assume that by *identity* we mean quantitative identity unless otherwise specified.

The Identity Operator

We are finally ready to introduce the symbol we shall use for the *is* of identity. We will abbreviate the open sentence "_____ is identical with _____" as x = y. Likewise, we will abbreviate "_____ is *not* identical with _____" as ~(x = y). A sentence such as "Mark Twain is identical to Samuel Clemens" would go into symbols as m = s.

Symbolizing with the Identity Sign

Numbers of Things

The identity operator allows us to abbreviate certain types of sentences that previously could not have been accurately symbolized. In particular, we can capture sentences asserting specific quantities of things. In the following, assume the domain is restricted to persons. Consider:

There are at least two musicians.

Without the identity sign, one might try symbolizing this as:

(∃x) (∃y) (Mx & My)

That is, for some x and for some y, x is a musician and y is a musician. However, this won't do, for it is possible that in this case x and y stand in for the same person, in which case it is possible, given the symbolism under consideration, that only one musician exists. That is, if only one musician were to exist, (∃x) (∃y) (Mx & My) would nonetheless be true. This attempted symbolization therefore fails to capture the meaning of the sentence at hand. Similarly, suppose we know that:

(a)   Someone in the house is an electrician.

and

(b)   Someone in the house is a truck driver.

It does not necessarily follow that two different persons are in the house; perhaps the two occurrences of the variable word *someone* refer to one and the same person. The solution is to symbolize "There are at least two musicians" as follows:

(∃x) (∃y) [(Mx & My) & ~(x = y)]

This reads, "There is an x and there is a y, and x is a musician and y is a musician, and it is not the case that x is the same individual as y." Now, if it is *not* the case that x is the same individual as y, then x and y must be two different individuals, which guarantees that there are at least two musicians.

Next, consider:

There are at least three musicians.

(∃x) (∃y) (∃z) {[Mx & (My & Mz)] & [~(x = y) & [~(y = z) & ~(x = z)]]}

That's a lot of parentheses! This reads, "There exists at least one x, there exists at least one y, and there exists at least one z such that x is a musician, y is a musician, and z is a musician, and x is not identical with y, y is not identical with z, and x is not identical with z." Now, if x is not the same individual as y, then x and y must be two different individuals; if y is not the same individual as z, then y and z must be two different individuals; and if x is not the same individual as z, then x and z must be two different individuals. This guarantees that there exist at least three musicians.

Suppose we wish to abbreviate the following:

There exists at most one Creator.

The symbolization (assuming an unrestricted domain) is:

(x) (y) [(Cx & Cy) ⊃ (x = y)]

According to this, for any x and any y, if x is a creator and y is a creator, then x is identical with y. This guarantees that there do not exist two *different* creators, which is to say that at most one Creator exists.

And to symbolize:

There exist at most two Creators.

we need:

(x) (y) (z) {[(Cx & Cy) & Cz] ⊃ [[(x = y) v (x = z)] v (y = z)]}

This reads, "For any x, for any y, and for any z, if x is a creator, y is a creator, and z is a creator, then either x is the same individual as y or x is identical with z or y and z are one and the same individual. This guarantees that at most two Creators exist.

Next, here is a slightly different construction:

There exists exactly one Creator.

This becomes:

(∃x) (y){Cx & [Cy ⊃ (y = x)]}

This means, "There is an x, and x is a Creator, and for any y, if y is a Creator, then y is the same entity as x."

To simplify things a bit now, in the next abbreviation let us leave out some of the parentheses in the long conjunctive clause. To translate:

There exist exactly two Creators

we may write:

(∃x) (∃y) (z) {[Cx & Cy & ~(x = y)] & [Cz ⊃ (z = x) v (z = y)]}

This reads, "There exists at least one x, there exists at least one y, and for any z, x is a creator, y is a creator, and it is not the case that x is identical with y (so x and y are two different entities), and if z is a creator, then z is identical with x or z is identical with y. This guarantees that exactly two Creators exist. How about a translation for "Exactly three Creators exist"? You don't want to see it.

Exceptive Sentences

We can also use the identity sign to abbreviate *exceptive* statements. Here is the first of several examples:

Rita is happier than anyone else except Joe.

In PL, this may be rendered:

(x) {[Px & ~(x = r) & ~(x = j)] ⊃ Hrx}

This says, "For any x, if x is a person and x is not Rita and x is not Joe, then Rita is happier than x." Notice that we had to say that x is not Rita to avoid self-contradiction. (Can you explain why a self-contradiction would have resulted otherwise?) Next:

Everyone is happy except me and my monkey Jim.

In PL, this is:

(x) [Px & ~(x = j) & ~(x = m)] ⊃ Hx] & (~Hm & ~Hj)

where j abbreviates the monkey and m abbreviates "me." Note that we are simplifying things a bit by leaving out a pair of brackets within the triple conjunction. The symbolized sentence says, "For any x, if x is a person and x is not Jim and x is not me, then x is happy; and in addition, I am not happy and Jim is not happy." Here is another example:

Rodney Dangerfield is the only person who respects Rodney Dangerfield.

If the constant r designates Rodney Dangerfield and Rxy abbreviates "x respects y," this goes into PL as:

Rrr & (x) [~(x = r) ⊃ ~ Rxr]

This says, "Rodney respects himself and for any x, if x is not Rodney, then x does not respect Rodney."

Superlatives

The identity sign also comes into play when we symbolize superlative statements. For instance:

Rita is the loveliest meter maid.

(x) {[Mx & ~ (x = r)] ⊃ Lrx} & Mr

where Mx abbreviates "x is a meter maid," Lxy abbreviates "x is lovelier than y," and r designates Rita. This PL sentence says, "For each x, if x is a meter maid and x is not Rita, then Rita is lovelier than x, and Rita is a meter maid." (Why did we have to add that Rita is a meter maid?)

In his famous *ontological argument* for the existence of God, Saint Anselm (1033–1109) claimed to prove with deductive certainty the existence of a greatest possible being. His claim in PL could be rendered this way, assuming the universal domain:

(∃x) [Gx & (y) ~(y = x) ⊃ Gxy]

In words, there is an x such that x is great, and for any y, if y is not x, then x is greater than y. Certainly a superlative claim. See Chapter 35 for a symbolized version of Anselm's famous argument.

Definite Descriptions

Recall that a *definite description* is a singular term that purports to refer to one specifically identified thing by describing it rather than by using a proper name. "The first car I ever owned" and "the President of the United States" are definite descriptions, because in each case only one definite entity is picked out for discussion. We can use the identity sign to represent definite descriptions in PL. Let us translate: "The President of the United States is a Democrat." Using obvious abbreviations, we write:

(∃x) [[Px & (y) [Py ⊃ (x = y)]] & Dx]

This says, "There is an x, and x is President of the United States, and if anything in the universe is President, it is x, and in addition, x is a Democrat." The first part of the PL sentence, up to "and x is a Democrat," states that there is only one thing that is President of the United States, and then the last clause adds that this one thing is a Democrat. To translate "My car is a blue Chevrolet Corvair," we may write:

(∃x) [[Mx & [(y) (My > (y = x)]] & (Bx &Cx)]

Assuming reasonable abbreviations, this says, "There is an x, and x is my car, and if anything in the universe is my car, it is x, and in addition, x is blue and x is a Chevy Corvair."

Introducing the Iota Symbol

There is a simpler way to translate definite descriptions. We can translate them using the iota symbol. As usual, we proceed in steps. Any definite description breaks down into two parts. One part is a descriptive phrase describing a thing, and the second part asserts that this description refers descriptively to just one specific thing. Consider the following definite description: "the inventor of bifocals." In this description, the expression "inventor of bifocals" constitutes the descriptive phrase and the definite article "the" tells us that the descriptive phrase describes just one thing. First, the description may be paraphrased as:

(a) The thing which the description "the inventor of bifocals" describes

This is logically equivalent to:

(b) the x which is such that x invented bifocals

Consider next the descriptive phrase within (b), namely, the words "x invented bifocals." This part may be abbreviated with the open sentence Ix, which produces:

(c) the x which is such that Ix

The final step in this process is to abbreviate the phrase "the x which is such that." The convention in logic is to represent this phrase using the ninth letter of the Greek alphabet, the iota, inverted and placed in front of the variable x, with the whole enclosed within parentheses. For typographical reasons, we shall use the lower case i as our "iota"—there is hardly an iota of difference between the two characters anyway. The expression thus produced, (ix), is called a *descriptive operator*. If we combine the descriptive operator with an open sentence, we generate a formula called a *descriptor*. The following descriptor fully abbreviates our definite description:

(ix)(Ix)

This is read as, "The x which is such that x invented bifocals."

There are a couple things to keep in mind as you work with this new symbol. First, a descriptor simply abbreviates a definite description. As such, it is a type of singular term. Thus, a descriptor does not represent a complete sentence and so does not represent something that is either true or false. It merely represents the subject of a sentence. Second, it follows from this that the descriptive operator is not a quantifier, for when this operator is attached to an open sentence, the result does not express a sentence that is either true or false.

In PL the descriptor is used as if it were an individual constant. For example, if we abbreviate "x is a philosopher" with "Px" and the name "Anselm" with the constant "a," the sentence "Anselm is a philosopher" goes into symbols simply as: Pa. However, we can identify Anselm more specifically. He is probably best known as the author of *Proslogion*, a book in which he first put forward the ontological argument for God's existence. If we paraphrase "The author of the *Proslogion*" as "The x such that x authored the *Proslogion*," then the corresponding descriptor is: (ix)(Axp). This reads: "The x which is such that x authored the *Proslogion*." The sentence "The author of the Proslogium is a philosopher" may now be abbreviated: P(ix)(Axp). Notice that the upper case P is a predicate constant standing for "is a philosopher," while the lower case p is an individual constant standing in for the *Proslogion*. The only change from Pa to P(ix)(Axp) is that the constant a was replaced with (ix)(Axp).

Consider next the sentence: "The most decorated soldier of World War II is Audie Murphy." In order to abbreviate this we will need both a descriptor and an identity sign. First, we can abbreviate "Audie Murphy" with the constant a, and we can abbreviate "the most decorated soldier of World War II" with (ix)(Mx). Next, we place the identity sign between these two terms: (ix)(Mx) = a.

Does France Have a Bald King?

Definite descriptions generally function syntactically as if they were individual constants. A fascinating problem arises, however, when we consider nonreferring definite descriptions, that is, descriptions that do not describe any existing individual thing. Consider an example first discussed by Bertrand Russell:

(a)   The present King of France is bald.

This is abbreviated:

    B(ix)(Kx)

where "Kx" abbreviates "x is presently King of France" and "Bx" abbreviates "x is bald."

Does this express a truth or a falsehood? Since France has no King, B(ix)(Kx) surely doesn't express a truth. However, suppose we say that the sentence expresses a falsehood. This seems to imply that France does have a King, but a King who is not bald. The problem is that it doesn't seem right to assign truth to the sentence, but it doesn't sound right to assign falsity to it, either.

One solution to this dilemma is to suppose that the sentence has no truth-value; it expresses neither truth nor falsity. As satisfactory as this solution sounds at first, the adoption of this solution raises a whole new set of problems. All of our definitions of validity, inconsistency, and so on have presupposed the law of excluded middle, i.e., the principle that every sentence is true or false. If we were to drop this assumption and allow that some sentences lack a truth-value, we would have to rewrite all of our logical definitions. The result would be a radical change in our logical principles, a far more complex set of definitions, and a less intuitive semantical theory.

Bertrand Russell developed a solution that is widely regarded as the best resolution of the difficulty. What are the truth-conditions of sentence (a)? In order for (a) to express the truth, Russell argued, three conditions must obtain:

1. At least one person is presently King of France.
2. At most one person is presently King of France.
3. Whoever is presently King of France is bald.

If we observe our world, we see that the first condition does not obtain. So, the truth-conditions of sentence (a) do not obtain and the sentence must therefore be assigned the truth-value false. Thus, on Russell's view, (a) has the same truth conditions as, and is therefore equivalent to, the following:

$$(\exists x)[(Kx \ \& \ Bx) \ \& \ (y)(Ky \supset (y = x)]$$

where "Kx" abbreviates "x is presently King of France" and "Bx" abbreviates "x is bald."

In sum, according to Russell's solution, a sentence containing a definite description and purporting to attribute a property to a uniquely described thing is assigned the truth-value false when either (i) the description fails to refer to anything, or (ii) the thing referred to lacks the property attributed to it. Enough with the symbolizing. With our new symbolic logic in hand, we are ready to put it to work proving arguments valid.

Exercise 25.1   Symbolize the following in PL as accurately as you can, assuming the universal domain.

1. At least two sasquatch exist.
2. Exactly two sasquatch exist.
3. At least three sasquatch exist.
4. Exactly three sasquatch exist.
5. Exactly one sasquatch exists.
6. At least one abominable snowman exists.
7. Jones is taller than anyone else in the world.
8. Jan is the oldest person in the United States.
9. Bill is richer than everyone else except Sam.

10. The X car is the most expensive car in the world.
11. World War II was the deadliest war in human history.
12. There is a being who is greater than all other beings.
13. Billy the Kid is William Bonney.
14. The Beatles were the greatest rock band of all times.
15. Muhammad Ali is the greatest boxer of all.
16. God is that being than which a greater is not possible.
17. It is not the case that Billy the Kid was the greatest outlaw of all.
18. The greatest rocker of all time was either John Lennon or Elvis Presley.

In this chapter, five new deduction rules are added to the truth-functional deduction rules. The new rules will thus work in tandem with the truth-functional rules of Unit Three. The combination of truth-functional and quantificational rules produces a powerful system of natural deduction. Our first rule governs inferences that run from a universal general sentence to an *instantiation* of that sentence.

Universal Instantiation

A wff of PL is called a **universal quantification** if and only if it begins with an unencumbered universal quantifier and the scope of the quantifier is the *entire* wff. A universal quantifier is "unencumbered" if no tilde has been applied to it. In the following examples, the universal quantifier is not encumbered and its scope spans the whole sentence:

(x)Fx   (y)~Fy   (z)Fz   (x) (Fx ⊃ Gx)   (x) (Mx v ~Mx)

These sentences are therefore "universal quantifications." In contrast, the following quantifier is "encumbered" with a tilde: ~(x)Fx. And the scope of the following quantifier does *not* span the whole formula: (x)(Fx) v (Ga & Ha). Therefore, these last two sentences are *not* universal quantifications.

Now, if we remove the quantifier from a universal quantification and uniformly replace each occurrence of the variable it binds with a constant or descriptor, we produce an "instantiation" (or "substitution instance") of the universal quantification. For example, suppose we begin with the universal quantification:

(x) (Wx ⊃ Mx)

If we remove the quantifier and in place of each occurrence of the variable we uniformly place the constant n into the formula, we get this substitution instance:

Wn ⊃ Mn

We are now ready for our first inference rule for predicate logic.

The Universal Instantiation Rule (UI)

From a universal quantification, you may infer any instantiation, provided that the instantiation was produced by uniformly replacing each occurrence of the variable that was bound by the quantifier with a constant.

In each of the following cases below, the second line was derived from the first by an application of UI:

1. (x)Fx	1. (x)(Fx ⊃ Gx)	1. (x) ~ Fx	1. (x) ~ (Fx ⊃ Gx)	1. (x) Fx
2. Fa	2. Fc ⊃ Gc	2. ~Fs	2. ~(Fb ⊃ Gb)	2. Fe

In each of these examples, the first sentence is a universal quantification and the second sentence is an instantiation of the universal quantification. In each example, the second sentence was derived from the first by performing two steps: First, the quantifier was removed from the first sentence, and then each occurrence of the variable was uniformly replaced by a constant. Since you may infer any instantiation, you may instantiate using *any* constant.

This is important: The replacement must be uniform, meaning all across the line. Notice, for example, that in the second and fourth instantiations just shown, the same constant is used all the way across the formula. Thus, the following inference, from 1 to 2, is an incorrect application of UI because the constant has not been replaced *uniformly*:

1. (x)(Fx ⊃ Gx)
2. Fa ⊃ Gb   (Illegal instantiation)

Here is a natural deduction proof employing UI:

1. (x)(Fx ⊃ Gx)
2. (x)(Gx ⊃ Hx) / Fs ⊃ Hs
3. Fs ⊃ Gs   UI 1
4. Gs ⊃ Hs   UI 2
5. Fs ⊃ Hs   HS 3, 4

The first step in this proof was the application of UI at line 3. We stripped the quantifier off line 1, we uniformly replaced the variable with the constant s, and we wrote the result on line 3. Then, at line 4 we applied UI to the formula on line 2. Again, we removed the quantifier from line 2 and replaced the variable with s to produce line 4. One application of UI can employ the same constant used in a previous application, if needed. In this case, we had to use the same constant on lines 3 and 4 to set things up for an application of HS on line 5. If we had instantiated with s on line 3 and then with, say, b on line 4, we would have derived two formulas that would not fit the HS rule, namely:

3. Fs ⊃ Gs   UI 1
4. Gb ⊃ Hb   UI 2

Keep this in mind: UI can only be applied to a line that begins with an unencumbered universal quantifier whose scope is the whole line. In other words, UI may only be applied when the line starts with a universal quantifier, the universal quantifier has no tilde over it, and the scope of the quantifier is the whole rest of the line. Thus, UI may *not* be applied to a line that looks like this:

~(x)(Fx ⊃ Gx)

Nor to one that looks like this:

(x)(Fx) ⊃ (x)(Gx)

UI cannot be applied to these sentences because in each case the scope of the universal quantifier fails to cover the entire sentence. Accordingly, the following inferences from 1 to 2 are not permissible:

1. ~(x) (Fx ⊃ Gx)   1. (x) (Fx) ⊃ (x) (Gx)
2. ~(Fa ⊃ Ga)   (illegal)   2. Fa ⊃ Ga   (illegal)

Justification. Why is UI valid? A universal quantification makes a claim about everything in the universe of discourse. For instance, (x) Gx says that all things have the property designated by the predicate G. Therefore, if a universal quantification is true, its claim is true of each and every thing in the universe of discourse. Therefore, it is true of each and every instantiation. It will therefore be true of a, b, c, and so forth. But let us linger on this last point for a moment. Suppose someone writes: (x) (Hx ⊃ Jx). The claim is that *everything in the universe* that is H is also J as well. Therefore, we may validly apply this to the case of anything whatsoever, thus, to the case of some individual a. Thus, we may infer that if a is H then a is J: Ha ⊃ Ja. Certainly if *everything* that is H is J, then if a is H then a is J, no matter who or what individual a is. Likewise, we may validly infer that Hb ⊃ Jb. Certainly if everything that is H is J, then if b is H then b is J, no matter who or what individual b is, and so forth down the line.

Existential Generalization

Suppose a sentence of PL contains no quantifiers and one or more constants. If we prefix to this an existential quantifier, uniformly replacing one or more occurrences of a constant occurring in it with the variable occurring in the existential quantifier, the result is called the **existential generalization** of the sentence. In each of the following examples, the sentence below is an existential generalization of the sentence on top:

Fa	~Hb & ~Rb	Gs v Fs	Gw
(∃x) Fx	(∃x) (~Hx & ~Rx)	(∃y) (Gy v Fy)	(∃x) Gx

We are ready for our next rule.

The Existential Generalization Rule (EG)

From a sentence containing an individual constant, you may infer any corresponding existential generalization, provided that (a) the variable used in the generalization does not already occur in the sentence generalized upon, and (b) the generalization results by replacing at least one occurrence of the constant with the variable used in the generalization, with no other changes being made.

In each of the following examples, the second sentence was derived by applying EG.

1. Fa	1. ~Fb	1. Fc	1. Fd v Hd
1. (∃x) Fx	2. (∃x) ~Fx	2. (∃x) Fx	2. (∃x) (Fx v Hx)

The following proof employs EG:

1.   (∃x) (Fx) ⊃ (x) (Hx ⊃ Gx)
2.   Fa
3.   Hs / Gs
4.   (∃x) Fx   EG 2
5.   (x) (Hx ⊃ Gx)   MP 1, 4
6.   Hs ⊃ Gs   UI 5
7.   Gs   MP 3,6

At line 4 in this proof, we applied EG to line 2. The existential quantifier was added, and the constant a (from line 2) was replaced by the variable x. The formula thus produced at line 4, namely (∃x) Fx, is the antecedent of line 1. This fact allowed us to apply modus ponens to lines 1 and 4 to derive line 5. At the next line, we applied UI to line 5 and removed the quantifiers. Notice that we employed the constant s on the applications of UI. This allowed us to make the MP "move" on line 7.

Justification. Why is this rule valid? A sentence containing an individual constant asserts that one specific thing, named by the constant, has a certain property. The existential generalization of the sentence asserts the weaker claim that *something or other* has the property. Certainly if a specific individual designated by a singular term has a certain property, it logically follows that *something* has that property. For example, from "Gottlob is a logician," it certainly follows that *something* is a logician. From "The Space Needle is yellow," it certainly follows that something is yellow.

Existential Instantiation

If a wff begins with an unencumbered existential quantifier whose scope is the entire wff, the wff is called an **existential quantification**. Each of the following sentences is an existential quantification:

(∃x) (Hx)

(∃x) (Jx v Gx)

Each of the following is *not* an existential quantification:

~(∃x) (Hx)

(∃x) (Jx v Gx) & Ka

The first is not an existential quantification because the line starts with a tilde; the second is not an existential quantification because, although the line starts with an unencumbered quantifier, the scope of the quantifier is not the *whole* line.

Next, if the existential quantifier is removed from an existential quantification and each of the variables bound by that quantifier is uniformly replaced by a constant, the result is an instantiation or substitution instance of the existential quantification. For example, suppose we begin with this existential quantification:

(∃x) (Wx v Mx)

If we remove the quantifier and in place of each occurrence of the variable we uniformly insert the constant n into the formula, we get the following instantiation:

Wn v Mn

The existential instantiation rule follows.

The Existential Instantiation Rule (EI)

From an existential quantification, you may instantiate using any constant, provided that (a) each occurrence of the variable bound by the quantifier in the existential quantification is uniformly replaced with a constant and no other changes are made, and (b) the constant used in place of the variable is completely new to the proof, meaning it does not appear anywhere else in the argument. Thus, the constant used does not appear in a premise, in a previous line, in the present line, or in the conclusion.

Special Restriction for Relational Sentences. The following may not make sense at the present moment, but when we do proofs containing relational predicates in Chapter 29, the following additional restriction on EI will be required: When applying EI to an existential quantification containing one or more relational predicates, do not use a constant if the constant already appears in the existential quantification.

Here are some applications of EI. In each case, the second sentence was derived from the first by applying EI.

1. $(\exists x)\ Fx$ 1. $(\exists x)\ (Hx\ \&\ Gx)$ 1. $(\exists x)\ {\sim}Jx$
2. Fa 2. $Ha\ \&\ Ga$ 2. ${\sim}Jb$

In each of these cases, the first sentence is an existential quantification and the second sentence is an allowed instantiation of the existential quantification. Remember that each occurrence of the variable must be replaced uniformly when the instantiation is written.

Caution! When you employ this rule, it is crucial that you instantiate *only* with a constant that does not appear anywhere else in the proof. In order to see why we must impose this restriction, consider what we could do if the restriction were to be dropped. Suppose the restriction is dropped and we can apply EI using any constant we wish, including one already in the premises, one already in the conclusion, and one used in a previous instance of EI. In such a case, the three following invalid arguments could easily be "proved" valid:

Argument 1

There is a millionaire.
So, Pat is a millionaire.

If we could apply EI with any constant, we could use EI to prove this argument valid in one step:

1. (∃x) Mx / Mp
2. Mp   EI 1 (Incorrect)

Argument 2

1. There exists an octogenarian.
2. There exists a teenager.
3. So, there exists someone who is both a teenager and an octogenarian.

If we could apply EI using any constant, we could instantiate twice with the same constant and prove this argument valid:

1. (∃x) Ox
2. (∃x) Tx / (∃x) (Ox & Tx)
3. Oa   EI 1 (Incorrect)
4. Ta   EI 1 (Incorrect)
5. Oa & Ta   Conj 3, 4
6. (∃x)(Ox & Tx)   EG 5

Argument 3

1. Bob is an octogenarian.
2. Something is a teenager.
3. So, Bob is a teenager.

Again, if we could use any constant when applying EI, we could construct the following proof:

1. Ob
2. (∃x) Tx / Tb
3. Tb   EI 2 (Incorrect)

    Each of these three arguments is invalid, of course. And each proof involves a violation of EI's restrictions. Thus, in the first, we instantiated the existential quantification using a constant appearing in the conclusion. In the second, we instantiated using a constant that had been used in a previous existential instantiation. In the third, we instantiated using a constant that appears in the premises. To avoid invalid inferences such as the three just shown, we must make sure that when we apply EI, we use a constant that does not violate EI's restrictions.

The following proof employs a correct application of EI:

1. (x)(Fx ⊃ Gx)
2. (∃x)Fx / (∃x) Gx
3. Fv   EI 2
4. Fv ⊃ Gv   UI 1
5. Gv   MP 3, 4
6. (∃x)Gx   EG 5

Apply EI before UI. Notice that in this proof we deployed EI *before* we applied UI. When you are building a proof, and you will be employing both EI and UI, you will usually want to apply EI before you apply UI, or else you might paint yourself into a corner that you cannot get out of. Recall that you are allowed to instantiate with *any* constant when applying UI. However, when you apply EI you are only allowed to use a constant completely *new* to the proof. Thus, if you apply UI first and instantiate with a constant, when you next apply EI you will have to instantiate with a constant new to the proof, in which case you will not be able to coordinate the formulas gotten by EI and UI; that is, you will not be able to set them up so that they have the same constant. But there will be many times when you will want the formula derived by UI to have the same constant as that found in the formula derived by EI. Experience will confirm this. Therefore, when you will be applying both UI and EI in the same proof, it is best to apply EI before applying UI.

Justification. Sometimes we must reason about an unidentified, unnamed individual. We know the individual exists, but we do not know his or her name. In such cases, we sometimes call the person "John Doe." For example, suppose the police learn that a tall, red-headed man robbed a bank, but they do not know his name. (He did not leave a card.) To talk about the robber more efficiently, they assign him a temporary name—usually "John Doe." They know John Doe has a real name, they just do not know it *yet*. When we apply EI in a proof and use a constant that is *completely new to the proof*, we are using the constant somewhat the same way we use the name "John Doe" in real life when we reason about an unidentified individual. We are simply assigning an unused name to an unnamed individual, so that we may more easily reason about that individual. EI is surely a valid rule of inference.

Universal Generalization

If we start with a sentence containing one or more constants and no quantifiers, and then uniformly replace each occurrence of a constant in the sentence with a variable bound by a universal quantifier, the result is the **universal generalization** of the sentence.

| 1. Fa | 1. Fb ⊃ Hb | 1. ~(Fd & Gd) |
| 2. (x)Fx | 2. (y)(Fy ⊃ Hy) | 2. (x) ~(Fx & Gx) |

In each of these cases, the second sentence is a universal generalization of the first sentence. We can now formulate our fourth rule.

The Universal Generalization Rule (UG)

From a sentence containing a constant, one may infer the corresponding universal generalization, provided that (a) the constant is uniformly replaced by a variable and no other changes are made, (b) the constant generalized upon does not appear in any premise of the argument, (c) the constant was not introduced into the proof by EI, (d) the variable you use in the generalization does not already appear in the sentence from which you are generalizing; and (e) the constant does not appear in any assumed premise that has not already been discharged.

Special Restriction. Again, the following may not make sense at the present moment, but when we do proofs containing relational predicates in Chapter 29, the following additional restriction on UG will be required: Do not apply UG to a constant when that constant appears in a relational sentence along with a constant that was introduced into the proof by EI.

Our new rule is used in the following proof:

1.	(x)(Gx)	
2.	(x)(Cx) / (x)(Gx & Cx)	
3.	Ga	UI 1
4.	Ca	UI 2
5.	Ga & Ca	Conj 3, 4
6.	(x)(Gx & Cx)	UG 5

Justification. This rule reflects a valid form of reasoning frequently employed in mathematics. Arguments in geometry, for example, often begin with a diagram and a statement such as, "Let figure ABC be any triangle." A deductive chain of reasoning is then applied to triangle ABC and something is proven about it. This fact about triangle ABC is then generalized to all triangles; that is, it is asserted as true of all triangles and not just for the particular triangle ABC. Why is this reasoning valid? It is valid because no special assumptions are made in the proof concerning triangle ABC, assumptions that would differentiate ABC from any other triangle. It follows that if something is proven about ABC, without making any assumptions that would distinguish ABC from any other triangle, then what is true of ABC is true of all triangles, thus the fact proven about ABC will be true of *any* triangle and not just of ABC. In other words, it will be true of triangles in general. If the proof had contained special assumptions about ABC, assumptions distinguishing ABC from other triangles, such as an actual measurement of its angles or sides, the proof would only establish something about ABC, not about triangles in general. But because we knew nothing about ABC that would distinguish it from any other triangle, what we proved about it would be true of all other triangles.

Now, if we correctly apply UG to a statement, the statement we are applying the rule to can only be one that was derived by UI. It is therefore saying something about *all* things, not just about some things. What is true in the case at hand must therefore be true in all like cases. Therefore, after we have finished reasoning about what this case represents, we are justified in generalizing our results to everything and asserting that what is true in the case at hand is true of all like things. UG is certainly a valid rule. Examine the following proof closely:

1. $(x)(Fx \supset Gx)$
2. $(x)(Gx \supset Sx)$
3. $(x)(Sx \supset Rx) / (x)(Fx \supset Rx)$
4. $Fa \supset Ga$ UI 1
5. $Ga \supset Sa$ UI 2
6. $Sa \supset Ra$ UI 3
7. $Fa \supset Sa$ HS 4, 5
8. $Fa \supset Ra$ HS 6, 7
9. $(x)(Fx \supset Rx)$ UG 8

Here are further examples of our new rules. In the next problem, we begin by removing the universal quantifier. We then apply a truth-functional rule and end by attaching the existential quantifier:

1. $(x)(Hx \supset Bx)$
2. $Hg / (\exists x) Bx$
3. $Hg \supset Bg$ UI 1
4. Bg MP 2, 3
5. $(\exists x) Bx$ EG 4

We instantiated premise 1 using the constant g. It is not a coincidence that this is the same constant that appears in line 2. We could have used any constant when we instantiated line 1, but if we had instantiated line 1 using a constant other than g, we could not have applied modus ponens to lines 2 and 3. We chose the constant g with the next step in mind. Next, examine the first line of the following argument:

1. (∃x) (Jx) ⊃ (x) (Kx ⊃ Lx)
2. Jb & Kb / Lb

This is important. Because line 1 does not begin with a quantifier with a scope that extends over the entire line, we cannot instantiate line 1. Neither UI nor EI applies in such a case. Therefore, our only hope is to break line 1 up into its two quantified components. Here are the steps:

3. Jb   Simp 2
4. (∃x) Jx   EG 3
5. (x) (Kx ⊃ Lx)   MP 1, 4

In these steps, we derived the antecedent of line 1 and brought down 1's consequent by modus ponens. Now we can instantiate line 5 and get rid of its quantifier:

6. Kb ⊃ Lb   UI 5
7. Kb   Simp 2
8. Lb   MP 6, 7

We instantiated line 6 with the constant b so that we could apply modus ponens later in the proof.

In the previous proof we used something derived from line 2 to break up line 1. The following argument calls for the same strategy:

1. (x) (Bx ⊃ Gx) ⊃ (∃x) (Ax & Hx)
2. (x) (Bx ⊃ Hx) & (x) (Hx ⊃ Gx) / (∃x) Hx

This is very important. Because line 1 contains two quantified formulas joined by a horseshoe, we cannot instantiate; that is, we cannot apply either UI or EI to it. Remember, you cannot apply UI to a line unless the universal quantifier sits at the start of the line and has the entire rest of the line as its scope. Our first job is to somehow break line 1 up into parts that can be instantiated. We therefore begin with the only move available—we simplify line 2:

3. (x) (Bx ⊃ Hx)   Simp 2
4. (x) (Hx ⊃ Gx)   Simp 2

Next, we remove the quantifiers:

5. Ba ⊃ Ha   UI 3
6. Ha ⊃ Ga   UI 4

Notice that these two lines fit the requirements for the hypothetical syllogism rule. Thus:

7. Ba ⊃ Ga   HS 5, 6

From this, we derive the antecedent of 1:

8. (x) (Bx ⊃ Gx)   UG 7

Now we can bring down the consequent of 1:

9. (∃x) (Ax & Hx)   MP 1, 8

Finally:

10. Av & Hv   EI 9
11. Hv   Simp 10
12. (∃x) Hx   EG 11

An Alternative System of Proof

In recent years, many logicians have come to favor a slightly different method of proof for predicate logic. The differences between the approach they favor and the rules of deduction presented so far in this book are very interesting. Both methods lead to exactly the same logical results in the end, that is, both prove exactly the same arguments valid; however, the path to the final destination takes some different turns along the way. Using the new approach, favored by logicians such as Patrick Hurley, some of the steps in a legal proof will contain open sentences; whereas no open sentences appear in any of the proofs licensed by the stricter, more traditional rules. The alternative system of proof requires only three small changes in our deduction rules.

In the alternative approach, the UI rule is written to allow instantiation with any constant *or any variable.* Thus, in the alternative system, in addition to any of the usual instantiations using constants, one may deduce Fx ⊃ Hx from (x) (Fx ⊃ Hx) by Universal Instantiation, and so on.

Second, two words are added to the rule for Existential Generalization, allowing you to apply EG to a sentence containing no quantifier and "one or more constants *or variables.*" Finally, the UG rule is rewritten to apply only to sentences containing no quantifiers and no constants, thus guaranteeing that you universally generalize only upon variables introduced through UI. Existential Instantiation and Quantifer Exchange are unchanged. The new or alternative rules look like this:

Alternative Universal Instantiation Rule ("UI-A")

For example:

1. (x)Fx	1. (x)(Fx $\supset$ Gx)	1. (x) Fx	1. (x) (Fx $\supset$ Gx)
2. Fa	2. Fc $\supset$ Gc	2. Fx	2. Fx $\supset$ Gx

Justification. Why allow universal instantiation with variables? Advocates argue as
follows: A universal quantification makes a claim about everything in the universe of
discourse. For instance, (x) Gx says that all things have the predicate G. Therefore, if
a universal quantification is true, its claim is true of each and every thing in the universe of discourse. Therefore it will be true of a, b, c, and so forth, *and of any x, y, or z
in play as well.* Suppose we instantiate using a variable instead of a constant, and infer
instead: Hy $\supset$ Jy. Some logicians balk at this instantiation, since it produces an open
sentence and open sentences are neither true nor false. But we can lighten up a bit
and treat an instantiation with a variable, in a case like this, as saying: If an unnamed
y is H then it is also J. In other words, we are letting our variable serve here as a stand-
in for anything and everything in the universe of discourse. Another way to put this:
In this context, the variable y is serving as a stand in for anything randomly selected
from the universe of discourse. Interpreted in this way, Hy $\supset$ Jy simply reflects the
fact that if anything is H then it is also J.

Alternative Existential Generalization Rule ("EG-A")

Alternative Universal Generalization Rule ("UG-A")

The rules of the alternative system are clearly valid. In addition, argue their advocates, they are easier to use. Those favoring the stricter, more traditional system observe, however, that the new rules result in the appearance of open sentences on some lines of a proof, and open sentences, they point out, are neither true nor false. Is this the logical equivalent of "You say tomato, and I say toma*h*to?" Or is there a reason to favor one system of rules over the other? You decide!

Quantifier Exchange: Our One Replacement Rule

The previous four rules all applied to *whole* lines of a proof, never to part of a line, even if the part is well-formed. The next rule is different. It is a replacement rule, which means (you will recall) that it can be applied to a well-formed *part* of a line or to a *whole* line. (Inference rules and replacement rules all fall within the broader category of "natural deduction" rules.) In Chapter 23 we saw how to exchange one quantifier for another while keeping the meaning the same. That discussion is the logical basis for the following replacement rule.

The Quantifier Exchange Rule (QE)

If **P** is a wff of PL containing either a universal or an existential quantifier, **P** may be replaced by, or may replace, a sentence that is exactly like **P** except that one quantifier has been switched for the other in accord with the following steps:

1. Switch one quantifier for the other.
2. Negate each side of the quantifier.
3. Cancel out any double negatives that result.

For example, if we apply QE to "(x)~ Fx" we get this: ~(∃x) Fx. And if we apply QE to "(∃x) Fx" we get this: ~(x) ~ Fx. Notice that if we apply QE to a quantifier that has one tilde on one side, we switch quantifiers and "flip" the tilde over to the other side; if a quantifier has no tildes, we add a tilde to each side; and if a quantifier has a tilde on both sides, it loses both tildes. There is a pattern to this madness!

In each of the following examples, the second sentence was derived from the first by applying QE:

1.	(x) Fx	1.	~(x) Fx
2.	~(∃x) ~ Fx	2.	(∃x)~ Fx

1.	~(x) (Fx v Gx)	1.	~(y) ~ Hy
2.	(∃x) ~(Fx v Gx)	2.	(∃y) Hy

The following proofs illustrate our new rule.

1. (x) (~Hx) ⊃ (x) (Fx ⊃ Gx)
2. ~(∃x)Hx
3. Fa   / (∃x) Gx
4. (x) ~Hx   QE 2
5. (x) (Fx ⊃ Gx)   MP 1, 4
6. Fa ⊃ Ga   UI 5
7. Ga   MP 3, 6
8. (∃x) Gx   EG 7

Notice that we could not apply UI to line 1 because line 1 does not start with an unencumbered universal quantifier whose scope is the whole line. We had to take a different tack. On line 4 we applied QE to line 2: We went to line 2, flipped the tilde over to the other side, switched quantifiers, and this gave us line 4. But this matched the antecedent of line 1. When a line of a proof matches the antecedent of a conditional, this suggests MP. Thus, at the next step, we applied MP to lines 1 and 4. This allowed us to "break up" line 1. We brought down the consequent of line 1. The rest of the proof opened up from there. Here is another use of QE:

1. (∃x) (Fx) ⊃ (∃x) (Gx)
2. (x)~ Gx   / (x) ~Fx
3. ~ (∃x) Gx   QE 2
4. ~ (∃x) Fx   MT 1, 3
5. (x)~ Fx   QE 4

Notice again that an instantiation rule cannot be applied to line 1. We cannot apply EI to line 1 because the line does not start with an unencumbered quantifier whose scope is the whole line. QE was the only rule applicable at the start of this proof. So we applied QE to line 2 and generated line 3. But line 3 is the negation of the consequent of line 1. This is what suggested MT. When you have a line that is the negation of the consequent of a line, MT can always be applied to bring down a new line—the negation of the antecedent of the line. Once we had line 4, the solution was obvious: We used QE to make a "quantifier trade." We flipped the tilde over the top of the quantifier, traded quantifiers, and this produced the conclusion.

With five new quantifier rules now on the table, it is time to reveal the name of our new natural deduction system. Its name is **QD** (for quantificational deduction). QD consists of two parts:

1. The language PL, which includes TL.
2. All the truth-functional deduction rules of Unit Three plus all the quantificational deduction rules in this and in succeeding chapters.

Because the language PL includes the language TL, we say that TL is "resident within" PL. Likewise, because QD includes the rules of truth-functional deduction, we may say that TD is resident within QD.

Definitions. A *proof in QD* may be defined as "a sequence of sentences of PL, each of which is either a premise or an assumption or follows from one or more previous sentences according to a QD deduction rule, and in which (a) every line (other than a premise) has a justification, and (b) any assumptions have been discharged." An argument is valid in QD if and only if it is possible to construct a proof in QD with premises that are the premises of the argument and with a conclusion that is the conclusion of the argument. An argument is invalid in QD if and only if it is not valid in QD. Where **P** is a well-formed formula of PL, a proof with a last line that is **P** and that contains no premises is a premise-free proof of **P**. If a premise-free proof of **P** can be constructed in QD, **P** is a theorem of QD. In this case, **P** is also called logically true, or quantificationally true because P can be proved true using only the methods of quantificational logic, without investigating the physical world.

Exercise 26.1 Using truth-functional inference rules and the four new quantifier rules, supply the missing justifications for the following proofs.

   1.

       1. (x) [Fx ⊃ (Gx & Sx)]
       2. (x)[(Gx & Sx) ⊃ (Hx v Rx)] / (x)[Fx ⊃ (Hx v Rx)]
       3. Fa ⊃ (Ga & Sa)
       4. (Ga & Sa) ⊃ (Ha v Ra)
       5. Fa ⊃ (Ha v Ra)
       6. (x)[Fx ⊃ (H x v Rx)]

   2.

       1. (x) [Px ⊃ (Sx v Hx)]
       2. (∃x)(Px & ~ Sx) / (∃x) (Px & Hx)

3. Pc & ~ Sc
4. Pc
5. Pc ⊃ (Sc v Hc)
6. Sc v Hc
7. ~ Sc
8. Hc
9. Pc & Hc
10. (∃x) (Px & Hx)

3.
1. (∃x) (Fx) ⊃ (x) (Ax ⊃ Bx)
2. Fc
3. Ag / (∃y) (By)
4. (∃x) (Fx)
5. (x) (Ax ⊃ Bx)
6. Ag ⊃ Bg
7. Bg
8. (∃y) (By)

4.
1. (x) (Hx) ⊃ (x) (S x ⊃ Px)
2. ~ (x) (Sx ⊃ Px)
3. ~ (x) (Hx) ⊃ (x) (Mx) / (x) (Mx)
4. ~ (x) (Hx)
5. (x) (Mx)

Exercise 26.2   Using truth-functional rules and the four new quantifier rules, supply proofs for the following valid arguments.

1.
1. (x) (Wx ⊃ Sx)
2. (x)(Sx ⊃ Px) / (x) (Wx ⊃ Px)

2.
1. (x) (Hx ⊃ Jx)
2. (∃x) (Hx) / (∃x) (Jx)

3.
1. (x) (Sx ⊃ Gx)
2. Sa / Ga

4.
1. (x) (Ax ⊃ Bx)
2. ~ Bc / ~ Ac

5.
1. (x) (Mx)
2. Hg / Hg & Mg

6.
1. (∃x) (Fx & ~ Mx)
2. (x) (Fx ⊃ Hx) / (∃x) (Hx & ~ Mx)

7.
1. Sa ⊃ (x) (Fx)
2. Ha v Sa
3. ~ Ha
4. (x) (Fx ⊃ Gx) /(x) (Gx)

8.
1. (x) (Hx & S x)
2. (∃x) (Hx) ⊃ (∃x) (Gx) / (∃x) (Sx) & (∃x) (Gx)

9.
1. (x)(Hx) ⊃ (∃x)(Sx)
2. (x) (Fx) v (x)(Hx)
3. ~ (x) (Fx) / (∃x) (Sx)

10.
1. (x) (Ax ⊃ Bx)
2. (x) (Jx ⊃ Fx)
3. (x) (Ax v Jx) / (x) (Bx v Fx)

11.
1. (x) (Ax ⊃ Bx)
2. (x) (Ax) / (x) (Bx)

12.
1. (x) (Hx ⊃ Gx)
2. (x) (~ Gx) / (x) (~ Hx)

13.
1. (x) (S x) ⊃ (x) (Gx)
2. ~(x) (Gx) / ~ (x) (Sx)

14.
1. (∃x) (Bx) ⊃ (x) (Hx ⊃ G x)
2. Bb & Hb / Gb

15.

    1.   (x) (Fx ⊃ Sx)

    2.   Fa & Fb / Sa & Sb

16.

    1.   (x) (Hx ⊃ Qx)

    2.   Ha v Hb / Qa v Qb

17.

    1.   (∃x) (Sx) ⊃ (x) (Hx ⊃ Gx)

    2.   Sp & Hp / Gp

18.

    1.   (∃x) (Fx) ⊃ (x) (Sx)

    2.   (∃x) (Hx) ⊃ (x) (Gx)

    3.   Fs & Hg / (x) (Sx & Gx)

Exercise 26.3   Using truth-functional inference rules, truth-functional replacement rules, and the four new quantifier rules, supply proofs for the following valid arguments:

1.

    1.   (x) {Sx ⊃ [Px & (Bx & Qx)]}

    2.   (∃x) (Sx) / (∃x)(Px & Qx)

2.

    1.   (x) (Ax v ~ Bx)

    2.   Hs / (∃x) [(Hx & Ax) v (Hx & ~ Bx)]

3.

    1.   (∃x) (Jx) ⊃ (x) (Hx v Sx)

    2.   (x) (Fx v ~ Sx)

    3.   (x) (Jx) / (∃x)(Hx v Fx)

4.

    1.   (x) [Hx ⊃ (Sx v Gx)]

    2.   ~ Sb & ~ Gb / ~ Hb

5.

    1.   (∃y) (Sy & H y)

    2.   (x) [(Gx v Rx) ⊃ ~ S x] / (∃x)(~ Gx)

6.

    1.   (x) [Hx ⊃ (Bx & Wx)]

    2.   (∃y) (~ By) / (∃z) (~ Hz)

7.

    1.   (x) [Hx ⊃ (Sx v Gx)]

    2.   (∃y) (~ Sy & ~ Gy) / (∃x)(~ Hx)

8.

    1.   (∃x) (Gx) ⊃ (x) (Hx ⊃ Sx)

    2.   (∃x) (Gx v Sx)

    3.   (x)(Sx ⊃ Gx) / (x)(~ G x ⊃ ~ Hx)

Exercise 26.4   Using truth-functional inference rules, truth-functional replacement rules, the four new quantifier rules, and the quantifier exchange rule, supply proofs for the following valid arguments.

1.

    1.   ~ (x) (Sx) / (∃x) (~Sx v Px)

2.

    1.   (x) [(Bx v Cx) ⊃ Wx]

    2.   ~ (x) (Hx v ~ Bx) / (∃x) (Wx)

3.

    1.   (x) (Hx) ⊃ (∃x)(Sx)

    2.   (x) (~ Sx) / (∃x)(~ Hx)

4.

    1.   (∃x) (~ Hx) v (∃x)(~ Sx)

    2.   (x) (Sx) / ~(x) (Hx)

5.

    1.   ~ (∃x) (Ax) / (x)(Ax ⊃ Bx)

    (∃x) (~ Jx)

10.

    1.   ~ (∃x) (Mx & ~ Gx)

    2.   ~ (∃x) (Mx & ~ Jx) / (x)[Mx ⊃ (Gx & Jx)]

11.

    1.   (x) [(Px & Qx) ⊃ Rx]

    2.   ~ (x) (Px ⊃ R x) / (∃x) (~ Qx)

12.

    1.   (∃x) (~ Hx) ⊃ (x) (Ax ⊃ Bx)

    2.   ~ (x) (Hx v Bx) / (∃x) (~ Ax)

13.

    1.   (x) (Fx ≡ Gx)

    2.   (x) (Gx ⊃ Hx)

    3.   (∃x) (Fx v Gx)/ (∃x) (Fx & Hx)

14.

    1.   (x) [Wx ⊃ (Fx v Gx)]

    2.   (x) {Gx ⊃ [Hx ⊃ (Ix ≡ Jx)}

    3.   (x) (Wx v (Hx & Ix)

    4.   (x) Wx

    5.   (x) [Mx ⊃ (Wx & Hx)] / Wa & (Fa v Ga)

15.

    1.   (∃x) Ax ⊃ (∃x) Hx

    2.   (∃x) Bx ⊃ (∃x) Gx

    3.   ~(∃x) (Hx) / ~(∃x) (Ax & Bx)

16.

    1.   (∃x) Ax ⊃ (∃x) Hx

    2.   (∃x) Bx ⊃ (∃x) Gx

    3.   (∃x) (Ax & Bx) / (∃x) (Ax & Bx)

Exercise 26.5   As we saw in Unit Two, Aristotle proved a number of categorical argument forms valid on the basis of a deductive system. This exercise includes 14 categorical syllogisms first proved valid by Aristotle, along with the names they were assigned during the Middle Ages. Translate each one into PL and then prove each valid using our modern deduction system. For example:

Barbara

1.   (x) (Mx ⊃ Px)

2.   (x) (Sx ⊃ Mx) / (x) (Sx ⊃ Px)

3.	$Mc > Pc$	UI 1
4.	$Sc > Mc$	UI 2
5.	$Sc > Pc$	HS 3, 4
6.	$(x) (Sx > Px)$	UG 5

Name	Logical Form	Traditional Abbreviation
1. **Barbara**	AAA-1	All M are P; all S are M. So all S are P.
2. **Celarent**	EAE-1	No M are P; all S are M. So no S are P.
3. **Darii**	AII-1	All M are P; some S are M. So some S are P.
4. **Ferio**	EIO-1	No M are P; some S are M. So some S are not P.
5. **Cesare**	EAE-2	No P are M; all S are M. So no S are P.
6. **Camestres**	AEE-2	All P are M; no S are M. So no S are P.
7. **Festino**	EIO-2	No P are M; some S are M. So some S are not P.
8. **Baroco**	AOO-2	All P are M; some S are not M. So some S are not P.
9. **Darapti**	AAI-3	All M are P; all M are S. So some S are P.
10. **Disamis:**	IAI-3	Some M are P; all M are S. So some S are P.
11. **Datisi**	AII-3	All M are P; some M are S. So some S are P.
12. **Felapton**	EAO-3	No M are P; all M are S. So some S are not P.
13. **Bocardo**	OAO-3	Some M are not P; all M are S. So some S are not P.
14. **Ferison**	EIO-3	No M are P: some M are S. So some S are not P.

Glossary

Existential generalization of a singular sentence The sentence that results if we begin with a singular sentence that contains one or more constants and then prefix to this an existential quantifier and uniformly replace one or more occurrences of a constant with the variable occurring in the existential quantifier.

Existential quantification A sentence of PL that begins with an existential quantifier whose scope is the entire formula.

Instantiation (or substitution instance) of an existential quantification The formula that results if the existential quantifier is removed from an existential quantification and each of the variables bound by that quantifier is uniformly replaced by a constant.

Instantiation (or substitution instance) of a universal quantification The formula that results if you remove the quantifier from a universal quantification and uniformly replace each occurrence of the variable it binds with a constant.

QD The name of the deductive system presented in this chapter.

Singular sentence of PL A sentence of PL containing no quantifiers and no variables.

Universal generalization of a singular sentence The formula that results if we take a singular sentence containing one or more constants and prefix to it a universal quantifier term, and uniformly replace each occurrence of a constant in the sentence with the variable contained in the quantifier.

Universal quantification A sentence of PL that begins with a universal quantifier with a scope that covers the entire sentence.

27 A Semantical Theory for Predicate Logic ≪ ≪ ≪

The Notion of an Interpretation

Recall that a language can be specified or defined in terms of its syntax and its semantics. A formal syntax for truth-functional logic was stated in Chapter 12, and a formal semantics for truth-functional logic was specified in Chapter 16. We have already specified the syntax for predicate logic—the vocabulary and rules of grammar of PL. The addition of a formal semantical theory in this chapter completes the definition. As you might expect, the semantical basis of predicate logic is a bit more complicated than the semantical basis of truth-functional logic. The semantics for predicate logic is normally specified using the notion of an *interpretation*. Suppose **P** is a wff of PL containing one or more predicates, one or more variables, and one or more individual constants. An **interpretation** of **P** is a specification of three things:

1. The universe of discourse or domain over which the variables of **P** range.
2. The individual objects of the domain designated by each of the constants occurring in **P**.
3. The properties or relations designated by the predicate constants in **P**.

For example, consider this sentence of PL: (x) (Rx ⊃ Bx). One interpretation is this: Let the domain be trees, let Rx abbreviate "x is a redwood," and let Bx abbreviate "x is beautiful." On this interpretation, the sentence says that all redwood trees are beautiful. Because of the way the world actually is, we say the sentence is "true on this interpretation." However, on the following interpretation, the sentence (x) (Rx ⊃ Bx) is obviously false: Let the domain be animals, let Rx abbreviate "x is a reptile," and let Bx abbreviate "x is blue." On this interpretation, the sentence expresses the (false) claim that all reptiles are blue.

We may also specify an interpretation for an argument expressed in PL. For example, here is a set of three PL sentences and an interpretation:

Argument

1. (x)(Bx ⊃ Gx)
2. (x)(Gx ⊃ Px) /(x)(Bx ⊃ Px)

Interpretation:

Domain: animals
Bx: x is a bird
Gx: x is graceful
Px: x is peaceful

On this interpretation, the argument in English is:

1. All birds are graceful.
2. All graceful things are peaceful.
3. Therefore, all birds are peaceful.

Here is another PL argument with an interpretation:

1. (x) Fx
2. (x)Gx / (x) (Fx & Gx)

Let the domain be the universe, let Bx abbreviate "x is beautiful" and Gx abbreviate "x is grand." On this interpretation this argument reads:

1. Everything is beautiful.
2. Everything is grand.
3. Therefore, everything is beautiful and grand.

Interpretations of multiply quantified sentences typically involve relations between individual things. For example:

Sentence: (x) (∃y) (Gxy)
Interpretation: Let the domain be the rational numbers, and let Gxy abbreviate x is greater than y.

On this interpretation, the sentence says that for every rational number x, there is at least one number y such that x greater than y. In other words, for every rational number, there is a number less than it. Notice that this sentence expresses a true proposition on this interpretation. However, consider another interpretation of the same formula:

Domain: human beings

Gxy: x is the grandmother of y

On this interpretation, (x) (∃y) (Gxy) expresses the claim that for every person x, there is a person y such that x is the grandmother of y. In other words, every person is a grandmother to someone. The sentence is obviously false on this interpretation.

Here is an interpretation of a *set* of sentences:

1. (x)(Ax v Bx)
2. (∃x)(Ax) & (∃y)(By)
3. (∃x)(∃y)(Gxy)

Interpretation:

Domain: the real numbers

Ax: x is positive

Bx: x is negative

Gxy: x is the square root of y

On this interpretation, the three sentences read:

1. Every real number is either positive or negative.
2. There exists at least one positive number and there exists at least one negative number.
3. Some number is the square root of another number.

All three sentences are true on this interpretation. However, consider another interpretation of the same set of sentences:

Domain: subatomic particles

Ax: x is a lepton

Bx: x is a gauge boson

Gxy: x is the antiparticle of y

On this interpretation, the three sentences read:

1. Every subatomic particle is either a lepton or a gauge boson.
2. There exists at least one lepton and there exists at least one gauge boson.
3. Some particle is the antiparticle of another particle.

All three sentences do not together come out true on this interpretation, because of course not all subatomic particles are either leptons or gauge bosons.

Notice that an uninterpreted PL sentence (i.e., a PL formula prior to interpretation) is serving as a sentence form rather than a sentence constant. And an interpretation of a sentence in predicate logic is the analogue in predicate logic of a row of a truth table in truth-functional logic.

What if *Nothing* Exists?

We are almost ready to specify a formal semantics for PL. However, an interesting qualification must first be stated. In the clauses to follow, we must exclude from consideration an empty universe of discourse—a universe containing no individual things. It is assumed that every universe of discourse contains at least one individual thing. Why? If empty universes are not excluded from the semantical theory of predicate logic, absurd consequences will follow. Most important, argument forms that seem clearly valid will turn out to be invalid, a result it is certainly wise to avoid. However, because this issue is properly taken up in metalogic, rather than in an introduction to logic, we do not take it any further here.

A Semantical Theory for Predicate Logic

Using the idea of an interpretation, and assuming the qualification just specified , we can now state a precise semantical basis for predicate logic in the form of the following definitions.

- A sentence of PL is a *logical truth* if and only if it is true on every interpretation.
- A sentence of PL is a *logical falsehood* if and only if it is false on every interpretation.
- An argument in PL is *valid* if and only if there is no interpretation on which its premises would be true and its conclusion false.
- An argument in PL is *invalid* if and only if there exists at least one interpretation on which the premises would be true and the conclusion would be false.

- Two sentences of PL are equivalent if and only if there is no interpretation that would make one true but the other false.
- One sentence of PL implies a second if and only if there is no interpretation on which the first is true and the second is false.
- Two sentences of PL are consistent if and only if there is at least one interpretation on which both are true; otherwise, they are inconsistent.

If you will look back at the formal semantics for truth-functional logic, you will notice that interpretations in predicate logic are analogous to truth tables in truth-functional logic: Interpretations and truth tables play similar roles in their respective semantical theories. As you might suspect, just as truth tables can be used in truth-functional logic to show that a truth-functional argument is invalid, interpretations can be used in predicate logic to show that a predicate logic argument is invalid.

History Note

The argument for excluding the empty universe from the semantics for languages like PL goes back to 1939 and the writings of Hilbert and Ackerman.

Using Interpretations to Show Invalidity

In everyday life, we sometimes use an analogy to show someone that his or her argument is invalid. For example, suppose Joe argues, "Because all squares have four sides, it follows that all four-sided figures must be squares." In reply, someone might say, "Joe, that's like arguing that because all dogs are mammals it follows that all mammals must be dogs." Now, this second argument is similar *in form* to Joe's argument, yet this second argument is obviously invalid, for it has a true premise and a false conclusion. When Joe sees the analogy or similarity between the form of his argument and the form of this obviously invalid one, he might agree that his argument is invalid. As we saw in Unit Two, this method of showing an argument "formally invalid" is sometimes called **refutation by logical analogy**.

So, to show someone that his or her argument has an invalid form, cite an argument that has exactly the same form but that also has obviously true premises and a false conclusion. Because the new argument is obviously invalid (it actually has true premises and a false conclusion), then an argument with exactly the same form is arguably invalid as well, which suggests that the person's original argument is invalid. This suggests one way to show that a quantified English argument is invalid: Symbolize the argument in PL, and then specify an *interpretation* that makes the premises obviously true and the conclusion obviously false. This will show that the argument's form is invalid. The logical response, of course, will be either to revise the argument or reject it. For example, consider the following English argument:

1. Everything has a cause.
2. Therefore, something causes everything.

In PL, assuming the universal domain, this is:

1. (x) (∃y) Cyx
2. Therefore, (∃y) (x) Cyx

Now, let us specify an interpretation for this PL argument. Let the domain be persons and let Cyx abbreviate "y is the mother of x." On this interpretation, the argument symbolizes:

1. Every person has a mother.
2. Therefore, there is someone who is the mother of everyone.

This argument is clearly analogous to the previous English argument. The two arguments have exactly the same logical form (since they are both interpretations of the same argument form). But the second argument has a true premise and a false conclusion and is therefore obviously invalid. Because this invalid argument has the same form as the original argument, the original argument has an invalid form; it has been shown to be "formally invalid."

For another example, suppose Joe gives an argument that goes into symbols this way:

1. (∃x) Fx
2. (∃x) Gx / (∃x) (Fx & Gx)

We can show Joe that his argument's form is invalid by presenting the following interpretation:

Domain: mammals
Fx: x is an elephant
Gx: x is a lion

On this interpretation, the argument is:

1. There exists at least one elephant.
2. There exists at least one lion.
3. Therefore, there exists a beast that is both a lion and an elephant. (Perhaps a "liophant.")

According to this interpretation, the argument has true premises and a false conclusion. Yet it has the same logical form as Joe's original argument. Hopefully, after seeing this, Joe will revise his case. Or drop it.

Recall that a **counterexample** to an argument is a description of a possible circumstance in which the premises would be true and the conclusion would be false. This interpretation also constitutes a counterexample to Joe's argument, for the interpretation shows us the possibility that his argument has true premises and a false conclusion. This method is thus sometimes called refutation by counterexample, because it involves showing an argument invalid by producing a counterexample to the argument.

Let us examine one more example. Consider this argument:

1. (x) (Fx ⊃ Gx)
2. (x) (Fx ⊃ Hx) /(x) (Gx ⊃ Hx)

And consider this interpretation:

Domain: automobiles
Fx: x is a Model T
Gx: x is a Ford
Hx: x is black

On this interpretation, the argument reads:

1. All Model Ts are Fords.
2. All Model Ts are black.
3. Therefore, all Fords are black.

Now, this argument might seem valid at first glance, but here is an analogous argument:

1. All sound arguments are valid.
2. All sound arguments have true premises.
3. So all valid arguments have true premises.

True premises and a false conclusion. Surely an invalid form! One more example is irresistible. Consider the following symbolized argument:

1.   (x) [(Ax v Bx) ⊃ Fx]
2.   (∃x) (Ax & Fx)
3.   (∃x) (Bx & Fx) / (x) (Fx ⊃ (Ax v Bx))

The following interpretation shows the possibility of true premises with a false conclusion:

Domain: cars

Ax: x is a Nova

Bx: x is an Impala

Fx: x is a Chevrolet

Both premises are true on this interpretation, yet the conclusion is obviously false, for according to this interpretation, the conclusion says that anything that is a Chevrolet is a Nova or an Impala. The argument's form is clearly invalid.

Here is another way to understand this method. In the case of a valid argument, it is not possible that the premises are true and the conclusion is false, no matter what is the case, no matter how the world might be or might have been. Therefore, even if the world contained fewer things, the argument would still be valid. When we state an interpretation for an argument, we are creating a model universe—a shrunken universe containing fewer things than the universe in which we live. We then use our model universe to show that it is possible the argument in question could have true premises and a false conclusion, which shows that the argument is invalid. Thus, almost like a mad scientist, we show an argument to be invalid by creating a model universe on paper—in which the premises are true and the conclusion is false. If the argument is invalid in the smaller universe, it must be so in the larger universe as well.

Predicate Logic and Truth Tables

If you read the section in Unit Three on truth tables, you might have noticed just now an analogy between the truth-table test for validity in truth-functional logic and the method of interpretations stated here for predicate logic. In the present branch of logic, producing an interpretation for a predicate argument showing that the argument could have true premises and a false conclusion is the analogue to showing an argument invalid in truth-functional logic by exhibiting a row on a truth table on which the premises all are true and the conclusion is false. An interpretation (in predicate logic) is thus like a row of a truth table (in truth-functional logic). There are no truth tables in predicate logic, however, for logicians have proved (in the branch of logic known as metalogic) that if predicate logic with relational predicates were to have something like truth tables, the "predicate" tables would have to contain an infinite number of rows. Too many even for a lifetime devoted to logic. See Appendix B on metalogic at the back of the book for the fascinating details.

Exercise 27.1 Specify an interpretation showing that each of the following PL argument patterns is invalid.

1. (x) (Ax ⊃ Bx) / (x) (Bx ⊃ Ax)
2. (x) (Ax ⊃ Bx)
   (x)(Bx) / (x) Ax
3. (x)(Ax ⊃ Bx)
   (x) ~ Ax / (x) ~Bx
4. (x) (Ax ⊃ Bx)
   (∃x) Ax / (x) Bx
5. (x) (Ax v Bx)
   (x) Ax / (x) Bx
6. (x) (Ax ⊃ Bx) / (x) (Bx ⊃ Ax)
7. (x) (Ax ⊃ Bx) / (x) (~ Ax ⊃ ~ Bx)
8. (x) (Ax ⊃ Bx)
9. (∃x) Bx / (x) Ax
10. (∃x) Ax
    (∃x) Bx / (∃x)(Ax & Bx)
11. (∃x) (Ax v Bx)
    (∃x) Ax / (∃x) Bx

The Monadic Predicate Test

If a quantificational argument contains *only* monadic predicates, it is possible to translate the argument into a purely truth-functional form containing no quantifiers. Once this is accomplished, a straight truth-functional test for validity can be performed. Thus, for a limited class of quantified arguments, namely, monadic predicate arguments, truth-functional decision procedures exist. Let us proceed in stages.

Suppose we have a quantified formula such as (x) Fx. Assume that the variable x ranges over a finite domain, one consisting just of the objects a, b, c, d, and e. When we say that *every x is F*, we are saying that each and every member of the domain has the property represented by F, which is to say:

Fa & Fb & Fc & Fd & Fe

So, assuming a three-member domain consisting of just the individuals a, b, and c, we may translate (x) Fx into:

Fa & Fb & Fc

Call this truth-functional formula a *truth-functional expansion* of the quantified formula.

Next, suppose instead *that at least one* member of the same domain is F. That is, assume (∃x) Fx. It follows that at least one of a, b, or c is characterized by F. In symbols, this is:

Fa v Fb v Fc

Consequently, assuming this three-member domain, (∃x) Fx may be translated into the following truth-functional expansion:

Fa v Fb v Fc

Consider two more cases for a three-member domain:

Formula   Expansion
(x)(Fx ⊃ Gx)   (Fa ⊃ Ga) & (Fb ⊃ Gb) & (Fc ⊃ Gc)
(∃x)(S x & Hx)   (Sa & Ha) v (Sb & Hb) v (Sc & Hc)

In metalogic, a general theorem has been proved for quantificational arguments, although we won't provide the metaproof here. That principle is this: Suppose a quantificational argument contains no relational predicates, and suppose it contains n different monadic predicates. Given that the number of monadic predicate letters in the argument is n, if there exists no interpretation yielding true premises and a false conclusion for a domain of 2^n objects or individuals, then the argument is valid.

This result makes possible a decision procedure, a mechanical test, for any quantificational argument containing only monadic predicates. For any such argument, we simply go to the case of a 2^n universe or domain, where n stands for the number of monadic predicates in the argument, we construct the appropriate truth-functional expansions, and we mechanically test for validity using the methods of truth-functional logic.

However, it has also been proved in metalogic that there exists no such mechanical procedure for quantificational arguments containing two-place or higher predicates. This is not to say that a decision procedure for such arguments hasn't been discovered. Rather, it has been proved that no such procedure exists.

Let us now test a monadic predicate argument for validity using the method of truth-functional expansions. Consider the following argument:

1. (∃x) (Sx & Px)
2. (∃x) (~ Sx & Px)
3. So, (x) (Px)

The test for validity requires a truth-functional expansion in a domain of 2^n individuals, where n represents the number of different monadic predicates appearing in the argument. Because the argument contains two such predicates, the domain must contain four individuals. The argument's truth-functional expansion for a four-member universe is:

Premise 1:   (Sa & Pa) v (Sb & Pb) v (Sc & Pc) v (Sd & Pd)
Premise 2:   (~Sa & Pa) v (~ Sb & Pb) v (~ Sc & Pc) v (~ Sd & Pd)
Conclusion: Pa & Pb & Pc & Pd

A *partial truth-table test* (explained in Unit Three) on these expansions would prove that the argument is invalid. If Sa, Pa, and Pb are assigned T, and Sb and Pc are assigned F, then the premises are true and the conclusion is false. This shows that the argument is invalid.

Here are two more examples. Consider the argument:

1. (x) ~ (Hx & ~ Rx) / (x) ~ (Rx & ~ Hx)

The premise expansion is:

~(H a & ~ Ra) & ~ (Hb & ~ Rb) & ~ (Hc & ~ Rc) & ~ (Hd & ~ Rd)

The conclusion's expansion is:

~ (Ra & ~ Ha) & ~ (Rb & ~ Hb) & ~ (Rc & ~ Hc) & ~ (Rd & ~ Hd)

If on a partial table Ha, Hb, Hc, and Hd are assigned F, and Ra, Rb, Rc, and Rd are assigned T, then the premise is true and the conclusion false, which shows that the argument is invalid.

Consider next:

1. (∃x) (Hx & Gx) / (x) (Hx & Gx)

The premise expansion is:

(Ha & Ga) v (Hb & Gb) v (Hc & Gc) v (Hd & Gd)

The conclusion's expansion is:

(Ha & Ga) & (Hb & Gb) & (Hc & Gc) & (Hd & Gd)

If Ha is assigned T, Ga is assigned T, and Hb and Gb are assigned F, then the premise is true and the conclusion is false.

Exercise 27.2 Construct truth-functional expansions showing that the following arguments are invalid.

1. (∃x) (Ax & Px) / (x) (Ax & Px)
2. (∃x) (Ax & Jx) / (∃x) (Ax & ~ Jx)
3. (x) Hx / (∃x) (Hx & Gx)
4. (x) (Ax ⊃ Bx) / (x) (Bx ⊃ Ax)
5. (x) (Ax ⊃ Bx) / (x) (~Ax ⊃ ~ Bx)
6. (x) (Ax ⊃ Bx)
    (∃x) Bx / (∃x) Ax
7. (x) (Ax ⊃ Bx)
    (x) (Bx ⊃ Cx)/ (x) (Cx ⊃ Ax)
8. (x) (Ax ⊃ Bx)
    Ba   /Aa
9. (∃x) (Hx & Ix)
    (∃x) (Ix & Gx) / (∃x) [Hx & (Ix &Gx)]
10. (x) (Ax ⊃ Bx)
    (x) (Hx > Bx) / (x) (Ax ⊃ Hx)
11. (∃x) Ax
    (∃x) Bx / (∃x) (Ax & Bx)
12. (x) (Ax ⊃ Bx)
    (∃x)Ax / (x) Bx

Glossary

Counterexample to a PL argument An interpretation under which the premises of the argument are true and the conclusion false.

Interpretation of a PL sentence A specification of three things: (a) the universe of discourse or domain over which the variables of the sentence range, (b) which individual objects of that universe of discourse are designated by each of the constants occurring in the sentence, and (c) which property or relation is designated by each predicate constant occurring in the sentence.

Refutation by logical analogy To show that a particular argument is formally invalid, produce an argument that has exactly the same logical form as the original argument but that also has obviously true premises and a false conclusion. Because the second argument is obviously invalid, and because it displays the same logical form as that displayed by the first argument, the form in question must not be a valid form. This way of showing an argument formally invalid is also sometimes called refutation by counterexample because the logically analogous yet invalid argument is a counterexample to the original argument.

Conditional and Indirect Predicate Proofs « « « « « « « « « «

We begin this primarily technical chapter with proofs containing no overlapping quantifiers. The first example employs the conditional proof rule.

1. (∃x)(Gx) ⊃ (y) (Gy ⊃ Jy) / (x) (Gx ⊃ Jx)
2.   Ga   ACP
3.   (∃x) Gx   EG 2
4.   (y) (Gy ⊃ Jy)   MP 1, 3
5.   Ga ⊃ Ja   UI 4
6.   Ja   MP 2, 5
7. Ga ⊃ Ja   CP 2–6
8. (x) (Gx ⊃ Jx)   UG 7

This is an interesting proof. Study it carefully. Notice that UG was applied (on line 8) only *after* the assumed premise was discharged. This follows the last clause of the UG rule. We could not have generalized before the CP assumption had been discharged. If this proof puzzles you, think of it this way. The premise says that if at least one thing x exists and is a G, then all things x that are G are also J. The conclusion says in effect that anything that is a G is also a J; in other words, there are no things x that are G that are not J. Given the premise, wouldn't it be impossible that there is a G that is not a J? Can you explain why? (Hint: Assume there is a G that is not a J. Given the premise, what follows?)

Next, consider this argument:

1. (x) (Ax ⊃ B x) / (x)(Ax) ⊃ (∃y) By
2. | (x)(Ax)   ACP
3. | Ac   UI 2
4. | Ac ⊃ Bc   UI 1
5. | Bc   MP 3, 4
6. | (∃y) By   EG 5
7. (x) (Ax) ⊃ (∃y) By   CP 2–6

Here we assumed the antecedent of the conclusion, (x) (Ax), derived the consequent of the conclusion, (∃y) By, and asserted the conclusion after disindenting. The following proof employs the indirect proof rule:

1. (x) (Ax ⊃ Dx)
2. (∃x)Ax / (∃x) Dx
3. | ~ (∃x)Dx   AIP
4. | (x) ~ Dx   QE 3
5. | Av   EI 2
6. | Av ⊃ Dv   UI 1
7. | Dv   MP 5, 6
8. | ~Dv   UI 4
9. | Dv & ~ Dv   Conj 7, 8
10. (∃x)Dx   IP 3–9

Adding Truth-Functional Replacement Rules to the Mix

The following indirect proof cleverly uses DeMorgan's rule at line 7.

1. ~(∃x)Bx / (∃x)(~Bx v Hx)
2. | ~(∃x)(~Bx v Hx)   AIP
3. | (x) ~ (~Bx v Hx)   QE 2
4. | (x) ~ Bx   QE 1
5. | ~Bd   UI 4
6. | ~(~Bd v Hd)   UI 3
7. | ~~(~ ~ Bd & ~ Hd)   DM 6
8. | ~~Bd & ~ Hd   DN 7
9. | ~~Bd   Simp 8

10.	Bd	DN 9
11.	Bd & ~Bd	Conj 5, 10
12.	(∃x) (~ Bx v Hx)	IP 2–11

This proof also employs the ever-popular DeMorgan rule:

1.	(x) (Ax ⊃ Gx)	
2.	(x) (Bx ⊃ Ax)	
3.	(x) ~ (Dx & ~ Bx) / (x) (Dx ⊃ Gx)	
4.	Da	ACP
5.	~(Da & ~ Ba)	UI 3
6.	~~ (~ Da v ~~ Ba)	DM 5
7.	~Da v ~~ Ba	DN 6
8.	~Da v Ba	DN 7
9.	~~Da	DN 4
10.	Ba	DS 8, 9
11.	Ba ⊃ Aa	UI 2
12.	Aa ⊃ Ga	UI 1
13.	Ba ⊃ Ga	HS 11, 12
14.	Ga	MP 10, 13
15.	Da ⊃ Ga	CP 4–14
16.	(x) (Dx ⊃ Gx)	UG 15

Here is a pretty complex indirect proof:

1.	(x) ~ (Cx & ~ Bx)	
2.	(x) ~ (Bx & ~ Ax) / (x)~ (Cx & ~Ax)	
3.	~(x)~ (Cx & ~ Ax)	AIP
4.	(∃x) (Cx & ~Ax)	QE 3
5.	Cv & ~ Av	EI 4
6.	~ (Cv & ~ Bv)	UI 1
7.	~(Bv & ~Av)	UI 2
8.	~~(~ Cv v ~~ Bv)	DM 6
9.	~Cv v Bv	DN 8 (twice)
10.	~~(~Bv v ~~ Av)	DM 7
11.	~Bv v Av	DN 10 (twice)

12.	Cv	Simp 5
13.	~~Cv	DN 12
14.	Bv	DS 13, 9
15.	~~ Bv	DN 14
16.	Av	DS 15, 11
17.	~Av	Simp 5
18.	Av & ~Av	Conj 16,17
19. (x)~ (Cx & ~ Ax)		IP 3–18

Using Premise-Free CP and IP Proofs to Prove Theorems

Recall that a theorem is a formula that can be proved true using a "premise-free" proof, a proof of a conclusion that uses no premises at all. It has been proved (in metalogic) that every theorem of QD is a tautology. Recall that a tautology is a statement that is true no matter what is the case, a statement true in all possible circumstances. Tautologies are said to be "logically true" because we can prove them true using purely abstract, logical procedures, without relying on scientific experiments or empirical observations of the physical world.

So, if a quantified formula can be proved true using a premise-free proof, it is a logical truth of predicate logic or quantificational logic. It is also said to be "quantificationally" true. Let us now prove that the formula (x) (Fx) ⊃ (∃x) (Fx) is logically true. A premise-free proof must start, of course, with either a conditional proof assumption or an indirect proof assumption:

1.	(x)Fx	ACP
2.	Fa	UI 1
3.	(∃x)Fx	EG 2
4. (x)(Fx) ⊃ (∃x)(Fx)		CP 1–3

The formulas (∃x) (Ax ⊃ Ax) and (x) (Ax ⊃ Ax) are each obviously logically true. Notice how similar their premise-free proofs are:

1.	~ (∃x)(Ax ⊃ Ax)	AIP
2.	(x) ~(Ax ⊃ Ax)	QE 1
3.	~(Aa ⊃ Aa)	UI 2
4.	~(~Aa v Aa)	Imp 3
5.	~~ Aa & ~Aa	DM 4
6.	Aa & ~Aa	DN 5
7. (∃x)(Ax ⊃ Ax)		IP 1–5

1.		~(x)(Ax ⊃ Ax)	AIP
2.		(∃x) ~ (Ax ⊃ Ax)	QE 1
3.		~ (Av ⊃ Av)	EI 2
4.		~(~Av v Av)	Imp 3
5.		~~Av & ~Av	DM 4
6.		Av & ~Av	DN 5
7.	(x)(Ax ⊃ Ax)		IP 1–6

Exercise 28.1   Use either the conditional proof rule or the indirect proof rule as you prove each of the following.

1.
   1.   (x) (Ax ⊃ ~ Bx)
   2.   (x) [Bx ⊃ (Hx & Ax)] / (∃x)(~ Bx)

2.
   1.   (Ax) (Hx ⊃ Sx)
   2.   (x) (Sx ⊃ Gx) / (x) [Hx ⊃ (Sx & Gx)]

3.
   1.   (x) [Ax ⊃ (Bx & Cx)] / (x) (Ax ⊃ Cx)

4.
   1.   (x)[Ax ⊃ (Bx v Cx)] / (∃x) (Ax) ⊃ (∃x) (Bx v Cx)

5.
   1.   (x) (Hx ⊃ Qx)
   2.   (x) (Hx ⊃ Rx) / (x) [Hx ⊃ (Qx & Rx)]

6.
   1.   (x) [Hx ⊃ (Qx & Sx)]
   2.   (x) [Px ⊃ (Rx & Mx)] / (x)(Sx ⊃ Px) ⊃ (x)(Hx ⊃ Mx)

7.
   1.   (x)[P x ⊃ (Hx & Qx)] / (x)(Sx ⊃ Px) ⊃ (x) (Sx ⊃ Qx)

8.
   1.   (x) ~ (Hx & ~ Bx)
   2.   (x) ~ (Bx & ~ G x) / (x) ~ (Hx & ~ Gx)

9.
   1.   (x) [(Fx v Gx) ⊃ Px]
   2.   (∃x) (~ Fx v Sx) ⊃ (x)(Rx) / (x) (Px) v (x) (Rx)

10.
   1.   (∃x) (Px) v (∃x)(Qx & Rx)
   2.   (x) (Px ⊃ Rx) / (∃x) (Rx)

11.

    1.   (∃x) (Fx) ⊃ (x) (Gx ⊃ Sx)

    2.   (∃x) (Hx) ⊃ (x) (~ Sx) / (x) [(Fx & Hx) ⊃ ~ Gx]

12.

    1.   (x) (Jx ⊃ Px)

    2.   (x) (Hx ⊃ Mx) / (∃x) (Jx v Hx) ⊃ (∃x)(Px v Mx)

13.

    1.   (x) [(Hx v Px) ⊃ Qx]

    2.   (x) [(Qx v Mx) ⊃ ~Hx] / (x) (~ H x)

14.

    1.   (∃x) (Qx) ⊃ (x)(Sx)

    2.   Qa ⊃ ~ Sa / ~ Qa

15.

    1.   (∃x) (Px v Jx) ⊃ ~ (∃x) (Px) / (x) (~ Px)

16.

    1.   (∃x) (Hx) ⊃ (∃x) (Sx & Fx)

    2.   ~(∃x) (Fx) / (x) (~ Hx)

17.

    1.   (∃x) (Sx) ⊃ (∃x)(Hx & Jx)

    2.   (x) (Fx ⊃ Sx) / (∃x) (Fx) ⊃ (∃x) (Hx)

18.

    1.   (∃x) (Px) ⊃ (∃x) (Qx & Sx)

    2.   (∃x) (Sx v Hx) ⊃ (x) (Gx) / (x) (Px ⊃ Gx)

Exercise 28.2   Prove the following logical truths.

    1.   (x)[(Hx v Px) v ~ Px]

    2.   (x)(Px v Qx) v (∃x)(~Px v ~ Qx)

    3.   ~ (x)(Ax & Bx) ⊃ (∃x)(~Ax v ~ Bx)

    4.   (∃x) (Px) v (x) (~ Px)

    5.   (x) (Px) ⊃ ~ (∃x) (~ Px)

    6.   ~ (∃x) (Px & ~P x)

    7.   (∃x) (Fx & Gx) ⊃ [(∃x) (Fx) & (∃x) (Gx)]

    8.   [(x) (Fx) & (x) (Gx)] ⊃ (x) (Fx & Gx)

    9.   (x) (Sx) v (∃x)(~ Sx)

    10.   (x) [(Sx & Hx) ⊃ (Sx v Hx)]

11. (x) (Hx) ⊃ (∃x) (Hx)

12. (x)(Sx ⊃ Px) ⊃ [(∃x)(Sx) ⊃ (∃x)(Px)]

Putting QD on a Diet: A Reduced Set of Quantifier Rules

We have been working with truth-functional rules, five quantifier rules, plus CP and
IP. However, all the valid arguments that can be proved valid with the rules we have
been employing can also be proved valid using a reduced set of rules, namely, the set
that results if we drop EG and UG. However, if we drop these rules and work with
the simpler system, the proofs become more complex and in many cases more difficult to complete. In most cases, we are forced to employ IP. For example, compare
the following two proofs. The first proof employs UG:

1. (x) Gx
2. (x) Sx   / (x) (Gx & Sx)
3. Ga   UI 1
4. Sa   UI 2
5. Ga & Sa   Conj 3, 4
6. (x) (Gx & Sx)   UG 5

The second proof of the same argument employs IP *in lieu of* UG:

1. (x) Gx
2. (x) Sx   / (x) (Gx & Sx)
3. | ~ (x) (Gx & Sx)   AIP
4. | (∃x) ~ (Gx & Sx)   QE 3
5. | ~ (Gv & Sv)   EI 4
6. | ~ Gv v ~ Sv)   DM 5
7. | Gv   UI 1
8. | ~~ Gv   DN 7
9. | ~ Sv   DS 6, 8
10. | Sv   UI 2
11. | Sv & ~ Sv   Conj 9, 10
12. (x) (Gx & Sx)   IP 3–11

Notice that it takes a bit more work to derive the same result when we use IP
in lieu of UG, but both proofs "work"; that is, both proofs succeeded in proving the
argument valid. Here is one more example. The next proof employs UG:

1. (x)(Fx ⊃ Gx)
2. (x)(Gx ⊃ Sx) / (x)(Fx ⊃ Sx)
3. Fc ⊃ Gc   UI 1
4. Gc ⊃ Sc   UI 2
5. Fc ⊃ Sc   HS 3,4
6. (x) (Fx ⊃ Sx)   UG 5

Now, if we drop UG from our kit of rules, we can still prove the argument valid, but we must use IP:

1. (x)(Fx ⊃ Gx)
2. (x)(Gx ⊃ Sx) / (x)(Fx ⊃ Sx)
3.   ~ (x)(Fx ⊃ Sx)   AIP
4.   (∃x)~ (Fx ⊃ Sx)   QE 3
5.   ~ (Fv ⊃ Sv)   EI 4
6.   ~ (~ Fv v Sv)   Imp 5
7.   ~ ~ Fv & ~ Sv   DM 6
8.   Fv & ~ Sv   DN 7
9.   Fv ⊃ Gv   UI 1
10.   Gv ⊃ Sv   UI 2
11.   Fv   Simp 8
12.   ~ Sv   Simp 8
13.   Gv   MP 9, 11
14.   ~ Gv   MT 10, 12
15.   Gv & ~ Gv   Conj 13, 14
16. (x)(Fx ⊃ Sx)   IP 3–15

Exercise 28.3   Symbolize the following arguments and then prove each valid using natural deduction.

1. Every cat is a mammal. No fish is a mammal. So no fish is a cat.
2. No cat is a reptile. Some pets are reptiles. So some pets are not cats.
3. Some cats are orange. Every cat is a mammal. So some mammals are orange.
4. Every dog is a mammal. No airplane is a mammal. If no airplane is a dog, then no airplane barks at cats. So no airplane barks at cats.

5. Every musician is an artist. Every artist is a dreamer. Some high school dropouts are musicians. So some high school dropouts are dreamers.

6. Charlie's car has a personality. Anything that has a personality is a person. So Charlie's car is a person.

7. Cats and dogs reason, learn, and love. Any creature that reasons, learns, and loves possesses an immortal soul and goes to be with God when it dies. Therefore, cats and dogs possess immortal souls and will go to be with God when they die.

8. Anyone who loves hamburgers isn't a vegetarian. Wimpy loves hamburgers. So Wimpy isn't a vegetarian.

9. Each event in one's life possesses eternal significance. A person's birth is one event in his or her life. So, a person's birth is an event of eternal significance.

10. Every hamburger sold by Dag's has Dag's special sauce on it. No other burger joint puts Dag's special sauce on its burgers. The burger Joe is eating does not have Dag's special sauce on it. Therefore, the burger Joe is eating is not a Dag's burger.

11. No member of the Revolutionary Communist Party is a Republican. Some Marxists are members of the Revolutionary Communist Party. So, some Marxists are not Republicans.

12. All who hang out at the Hasty Tasty admire Mao Tse-tung. All who admire Mao Tse-tung belong to the Progressive Labor Party. Stephanie does not belong to the Progressive Labor Party. So Stephanie does not hang out at the Hasty Tasty.

13. Anyone who frequents the Blue Moon Tavern reads the *Helix*. If Deane sells the Helix, then Deane reads the *Helix*. Deane sells the *Helix* but doesn't frequent the Blue Moon. (He only goes in there once in a blue moon.) So some who read the *Helix* don't frequent the Blue Moon.

14. Dragons live forever. Nothing that lives forever is to be feared. Puff is a dragon. So, Puff is not to be feared.

15. All songs written by either Lennon or McCartney are rock 'n' roll songs. Therefore, there is no song written by Lennon or McCartney that is not a rock 'n' roll song.

16. If that piece of varnished sewer sludge is a work of art, then anything is a work of art. That piece of varnished sewer sludge is a work of art. So this glazed pile of dead bugs is a work of art.

17. If rocking horse people eat marshmallow pies, then newspaper taxis are waiting to take you away. If the girl with kaleidoscope eyes meets you, then

rocking horse people eat marshmallow pies. The girl with kaleidoscope eyes will meet you. So newspaper taxis are waiting to take you away. (Do you need to use quantifiers to prove this valid?)

18. Either all things are created by God, or all things are material. If all things are material, then life has no transcendent meaning. If God does not exist, then it's not the case that all things are created by God. So if God does not exist, then life has no transcendent meaning. (Do you need to use quantifiers to prove this valid?)

19. Any senator or House member is a member of Congress. No anarchist is a member of Congress. George is an anarchist. So George isn't a senator.

Proofs containing adjacent or "overlapping" quantifiers and relational predicates require special care. We must add or remove the quantifiers one at a time, being careful to follow the corresponding inference rule to the letter (literally). Study the following example:

1. (∃x)(∃y) (Ax & Bxy) / (∃x)Ax
2. (∃y) (Aa & Bay)   EI 1
3. Aa & Baw   EI 2
4. Aa   Simp 3
5. (∃x)Ax   EG 4

In this proof, at line 2, when we applied EI to line 1, we began by stripping away from line 1 the first existential quantifier (∃x); then we uniformly replaced the variable x with the constant a all through the formula. Notice that on this move we did not touch the other quantifier (∃y). Next, at line 3, we applied EI to line 2, removing the other quantifier, (∃y), and replacing the variable y with the constant w. Notice that we used a constant new to the proof here. The rest of the proof was simple.

Further Examples

Here is another example of a proof containing overlapping quantifiers:

1. (x)(y) Kxy / Kab
2. (y) Kay   UI 1
3. Kab   UI 2

At line 2, we applied UI to line 1 and removed only the universal quantifier (x) and the x variable, instantiating with the constant a (thus replacing x with a). Notice that we left the y variable and its quantifier untouched. Then, at line 3, we applied UI to line 2 and removed the (y) quantifier, instantiating y with b.

Here are some further examples for your inspection:

1. (x) (∃y) (Kxy)
2. (∃y)(Kay) ⊃ Ga / Ga
3. (∃y) Kay   UI 1
4. Ga   MP 2, 3

1. (∃x) (∃y) (Fxy) / (∃y) (∃x) (Fxy)
2. (∃y) Fay   EI 1
3. Faw   EI 2
4. (∃x) Fxw   EG 3
5. (∃y) (∃x) (Fxy) EG 4

1. (x)(y) (Hxy)   / (y) (x) (Hxy)
2. (y) Hay   UI 1
3. Hab   UI 2
4. (x) Hxb   UG 3
5. (y)(x) Hxy   UG 4

The last two proofs illustrate a point made in Chapter 24, namely, that when two quantifiers of the same type appear next to each other, their order doesn't affect the truth-value of the sentence. However, as we also saw in Chapter 24, if universal and existential quantifiers appear next to each other, the order cannot arbitrarily be altered, for the order affects the truth-value of the sentence. That is, (x) (∃y) (Fxy) does not imply (∃y) (x) (Fxy).

Here is an interesting proof:

1. (x) (y) (Fxy ⊃ ~ Fyx)
2. (∃x) (∃y) Fxy / (∃x) (∃y) ~ Fyx
3. (∃y) Fay   EI 2
4. Faw   EI 3
5. (y) (Fay ⊃ ~ Fya) UI 1
6. Faw ⊃ ~Fwa   UI 5
7. ~ Fwa   MP 4, 6

8. (∃y) ~ Fya   EG 7
9. (∃x) (∃y) ~ Fyx   EG 8

When you work with sentences containing overlapping quantifiers—sentences in which one quantifier appears within the scope of another quantifier—you apply the quantifier exchange rule in the usual way. The following proof illustrates the proper procedure:

1. ~ (x) (∃y) (Hxy) / (∃x) (y) (~ Hxy)
2. (∃x) ~ (∃y) (Hxy)   QE 1
3. (∃x) (y) ~ (Hxy)   QE 2

Notice that as the tilde passes over each quantifier, it converts the quantifier it passes over into the opposite quantifier. Here is a proof that combines QE with IP:

1. (x) (∃y) (Axy) ⊃ (x)(∃y) Gxy
2. (∃x)(y) ~ Gxy   / (∃x)(y) ~ Axy
3. | ~ (∃x)(y) ~ Axy   AIP
4. | (x) ~ (y) ~ Axy   QE 3
5. | (x) (∃y) Axy   QE 4
6. | (x) (∃y) Gxy   MP 1, 5
7. | (y) ~ Gay   EI 2
8. | (∃y) Gay   UI 6
9. | Gaw   EI 8
10. | ~ Gaw   UI 7
11. | Gaw & ~ Gaw   Conj 9, 10
12. (∃x)(y) ~ Axy   IP 3–11

Notice that we applied EI before we applied UI. The first application of EI, at line 7, replaced the variable x with the constant a. Next, at line 8, we applied UI and again instantiated with a. At line 9, we again applied EI, but this time we used a new constant—w. The next application of UI also used w. This allowed us to derive the contradiction at line 11.

The following proof uses the CP strategy:

1. (x) (∃y) (Fxy) / Pa ⊃(∃y) Fay
2. | Pa   ACP
3. | (∃y) Fay   UI 1
4. Pa ⊃ (∃y) Fay   CP 2–3

We began this proof by assuming the antecedent of the conclusion. At line 3, UI was applied to line 1: The universal quantifier was stripped away and the x variable was replaced by the constant a. This produced the consequent of the conclusion. We discharged our assumption and asserted the conclusion by CP.

Application: The Logical Properties of Relations

In Appendix 24.1 we examined the properties of reflexivity, transitivity, and symmetry. Let's put our understanding of transitivity to work. Suppose we wish to prove valid the following argument.

1. Carol's car is heavier than Pete's car.
2. Pete's car is heavier than Katie's car.
3. So Carol's car is heavier than Katie's car.

If we let c designate Carol's car, p designate Pete's car, and k designate Katie's car, this argument goes into PL as:

1. Hcp
2. Hpk / Hck

The English argument is obviously valid. However, the argument as expressed in PL cannot be proved valid with our rules. The problem is that the argument is only valid if we assume that being "heavier than" is a transitive relation and add this to the argument. We subconsciously add this assumption to the English version of the argument when we evaluate it, which is why the English version seems obviously valid even though the PL version cannot be proved valid. Let us fix up the PL translation by adding to the argument a premise stating that "heavier than" is a transitive relation:

1. Hcp
2. Hpk
3. $(x) (y) (z) [(Hxy \ \& \ Hyz) \supset Hxz]$ / Hck

The third premise says that if one thing is heavier than a second thing, and if the second thing is heavier than a third thing, the first is heavier than the third. In other words, the third premise says that "heavier than" is transitive. Now, with the assumption added, the argument can be proved valid.

4. $(y) (z) [(Hcy \ \& \ Hyz) \supset Hcz]$ UI 3
5. $(z)[(Hcp \ \& \ Hpz) \supset Hcz]$ UI 4

6.	(Hcp & Hpk) ⊃ Hck	UI 5
7.	(Hcp & Hpk)	Conj 1, 2
8.	Hck	MP 6, 7

The following "Andy of Mayberry" argument provides another illustration involving multiple quantification:

> Goober knows who Betty is. Betty does not know who Goober is. So it's not the case that if one person knows another, then the second person knows the first person.

In PL, this is represented as follows (assuming a domain limited to persons):

1. Kgb
2. ~Kbg / ~(x) (y) (Kxy ⊃ Kyx)

The proof shows that "knows" is not symmetrical.

1.	Kgb	
2.	~Kbg / ~ (x) (y) (Kxy ⊃ Kyx)	
3.	$\vert$ ~ ~ (x) (y) (Kxy ⊃ Kyx)	AIP
4.	$\vert$ (x) (y) (Kxy ⊃ Kyx)	DN 3
5.	$\vert$ (y) (Kgy ⊃ Kyg)	UI 4
6.	$\vert$ Kgb ⊃ Kbg	UI 5
7.	$\vert$ Kbg	MP 1, 6
8.	$\vert$ Kbg & ~ Kbg	Conj 2, 7
9.	~ (x) (y) (Kxy ⊃ Kyx)	IP 3, 8

Exercise 29.1

Part A
Prove the following arguments valid.

1.

1. (x) (y)(Hxy ⊃ ~ Hyx)
2. (∃x) (∃y) (Hxy) / (∃x) (∃y) (~ Hyx)

2.

1. (∃x) (y) (Sxy) / (y) (∃x) (Sxy)

3.
1. (x)(Fx ⊃ Bx)
2. (x) (∃y) (Sxy v ~ Bx) / (∃x) (∃y) (Sxy v ~ Fx)

4.
1. (∃x) (y) (Lxy) / (∃y) (x)(~Lxy)

5.
1. (x) (∃y) (Sx & Py) / (∃y) (∃x) (Sx & Py)

6.
1. (x) (∃y) (Jx v Ry) / (∃y) (∃x) (Jx v Ry)

7.
1. (x) (∃y) (Hxy) ⊃ (x) (∃y) (Sxy)
2. (∃x) (y) (~Sxy) / (∃x) (y)(~ Hxy)

8.
1. (∃x) (y) (Pxy ⊃ Sxy)
2. (x) (∃y) (~ Sxy) / ~ (x) (y) (Pxy)

9.
1. (Ex)(y) Mxy / (x) (∃y) (Myx)

10.
1. (x) (y) [(Wx & Lxy) ⊃ Lya]
2. (x) (y) (Lxa ⊃ Lxy) / (x) (y) [(Wx & Lxy) ⊃ Lyx]

11.
1. (x) (∃y) (Px ⊃ Wy) / (x) (Px) ⊃ (∃y) (Wy)

12.
1. (∃x) (∃y) (Kxy) / (∃y) (∃x)(Kxy)

13.
1. (∃x) (y) (~Kyx v ~(Kxy) / ~(x) (Kxx)

14.
1. (x) (y) (Lxy) / (∃x)(∃y) (Lxy)

15.
1. (∃y) Fyy
2. (∃x) (z)Gxz / (∃x) (∃y) [(Gyx) & Fxx]

16.
1. (x) (y) (Bxy > Ayx)
2. (x) Bxx / (∃ x) (∃ y) (Axy)

Part B

Symbolize the following arguments, and then prove each valid in QD. Add a premise if you believe an argument is enthymematic.

1. Every material thing has a cause. Not everything has a cause. Therefore, at least one nonmaterial thing exists.

2. Every person loves that which he or she makes. Each person makes his or her own enemies. So each person loves his or her enemies.

3. Everything has a cause. If the universe has a cause, then a Creator of the universe exists. So a Creator of the universe exists.

4. Everything has a cause. If God exists, then something does not have a cause. (Note: God would not have a cause.) So God does not exist.

5. Every human being is a moral agent. Every moral agent possesses a natural right to equal concern and respect. Therefore, every human being is to be treated with concern and respect.

6. Everyone respects somebody or other. If there is somebody who is old, then there is somebody who is young. Jose respects only people who are old. So somebody somewhere is young.

30 The Summit: Predicate Logic with Identity « « « ‹

When we add natural deduction rules for the identity operator to all the previous logical machinery, we reach the summit of standard "first-order" predicate logic, the completion of the system. This is as far as the system goes. There is one qualification before we begin. A system of logic is "first-order" if its quantifiers range only over individuals. The quantifiers in a "second-order system" of logic are allowed to range over properties of individuals and sets of individuals. The quantifiers in our system range only over individuals. Our system (QD) is therefore a first-order system of logic. Second-order systems of logic are typically studied only in advanced courses in symbolic logic. When we add rules for the identity operator to our system, it is properly called "first-order predicate logic with identity."

The Identity Operator

The identity operator (=) was introduced in Chapter 25. When x and y are in reality just one and the same thing and not two different things we say that x is **identical** to y or x is "identical with" y and we write "x = y." For example, Mark Twain, the author of *Huckleberry Finn*, is identical to Samuel Clemens, meaning they are one and the same person, not two different persons. To say this in PL, we might write m = s. It is time to add to our system deduction rules for the identity operator.

The First Rule of Identity: The Principle of Self-Identity

The first rule of identity arises out of the necessary truth about identity known as the Principle of Self-Identity.

The Principle of Self-Identity

Each thing is identical with itself.

In PL:

(x) (x = x)

Surely this needs no argument; certainly it is necessarily true. (How could something possibly *not* be identical to itself?) Our first deduction rule for identity reflects this principle:

The Self-Identity Rule (SI)

At any step in a proof, you may assert (x) (x = x).

After you apply this rule in a proof, you have a line that reads "(x) (x = x)." What do you do with this? In the usual case, you will next instantiate the line, using UI and a specially chosen constant. For instance, if the constant you choose is c, then instantiation will give you c = c. From there, you will use the quantifier rules to reach your conclusion. Here is a simple little argument that only a philosopher would love.

1. Bob is happy.
2. Therefore, Bob is identical with himself.

1. Hb / b = b
2. (x) (x = x)   SI
3. b = b   UI 2

We actually reason this way in everyday life, whether we are aware of it or not. For instance, at a party, Bob is being annoying and obnoxious. Sue says, "Bob is being annoying and obnoxious." Rita replies, "Bob is Bob."

The Second Rule of Identity: Leibniz's Law

The next principle of identity is known as the **principle of the indiscernibility of identicals**. It is also known in philosophy as **Leibniz's law**.

For any x and for any y, if x is identical with y, then whatever is true of x is true of y and whatever is true of y is true of x.

For instance, as you know, Robert Allen Zimmerman is identical to Bob Dylan. The principle says that *if* it is the case that Robert Zimmerman *is* Bob Dylan, then anything true of Robert Zimmerman is also true of Bob Dylan, and vice versa. So, if it is true that Robert Zimmerman formed a band in high school called The Golden Chords, then it is also true that Bob Dylan formed a band in high school called The Golden Chords, and so on. Logicians call this principle Leibniz's Law because Gottfried Leibniz (1646–1716), the great German logician and mathematician, was the first to formulate it and employ it in a system of logic. Leibniz's principle, which seems most certainly to be a necessary truth, gives rise to the following deduction rule.

The Indiscernibility of Identicals Rule (Leibniz's Law or LL)

If **c** and **d** are two constants in a proof and a line of the proof asserts that the individual designated by **c** is identical with the individual designated by **d**, you may carry down and rewrite any available line of the proof replacing any or all occurrences of **c** with **d** or any or all occurrences of **d** with **c**. A line of a proof is "available" unless it is within the scope of a discharged assumption.

This rule can also be expressed informally as follows:

Given an identity statement asserting that the constants **c** and **d** designate the same individual, one constant may replace the other in any available line.

And more formally:

Given that $\quad$ **c** = **d**
Given that $\quad$ **P**
Infer: $\quad$ **P** [**c** // **d**]

where **P** is an available line of the proof containing one or more occurrences of one of the constants and **P** [**c** // **d**] is exactly like **P** except that one or more occurrences of **c** have been replaced with **d** or one or more occurrences of **d** have been replaced with **c**.

Incidentally, Leibniz's Law must not be confused with a related principle, the Principle of the Identity of Indiscernibles. The two principles look deceptively similar

As noted, the introductory predicate logic you have been learning is a first-order system of logic, for its quantifiers range only over individual things. If we were to add to our system quantifiers that range over properties or attributes of individuals, then we would have second-order predicate logic. The principle of the indiscernibility of identicals (Leibniz's law) cannot be fully expressed in first-order predicate logic with identity because its expression requires quantifiers that range over properties or attributes. Let us now specify a universal quantifier (**P**) that says, "For all properties or attributes **P**," where **P** is a variable ranging over properties and attributes of individual things. Using this second-order notation, Leibniz's law may be put this way:

$(x) (y) (P) [(x = y) \supset (Px \equiv Py)]$

This reads, "For any individual thing x, and for any individual thing y, and for any property or attribute **P**, if x is identical with y, then any property possessed by x is also possessed by y and any property possessed by y is possessed by x." In other words, if x and y are one and the same thing and not two different things, then any property possessed by x is possessed by y and vice versa. This symbolized sentence does not belong to our present system, QD, of course, because QD is a first-order system of logic and so does not include second-order notation.

(and have similar-sounding names) but one is clearly necessarily true, whereas the other is very debatable. In second-order predicate logic with identity, the **principle of the identity of indiscernibles** reads:

$(x) (y) (P) [(Px \equiv Py) \supset (x=y)]$

This reads, "For any individual thing x, and for any individual thing y, and for any property or attribute **P**, if it is the case that any property **P** possessed by x is also possessed by y and any property **P** possessed by y is also possessed by x, then x is identical with y." In other words, "For any x, and for any y, and for any property or attribute **P**, if it is the case that x and y have all their properties in common, then x is identical with y, that is, x and y are one and the same thing, not two separate things."

Logicians agree that Leibniz's law, the principle of the indiscernibility of identicals, is necessarily true; however, they do not agree on the second principle, the identity of indiscernables. (Note how the names of the principles differ.) Counterexamples have been given to the second principle and a good case has been made for the claim that the identity of indiscernables is *not* necessarily true. (Here is a hint: Is it logically possible that there is an x and a y, and x and y possess all their properties in common [i.e., they have all the same properties], yet x is not the same entity as y because x exists in one world and y exists in a separate world, in a world distinct from the world in which x exists?)

Here is an example of Leibniz's law at work:

1.	(x) (Ax ⊃ Bx)	
2.	At	
3.	(x) [Bx ⊃ (x = g)] / Ag & Bg	
4.	At ⊃ Bt	UI 1
5.	Bt	MP 2, 4
6.	Bt ⊃ (t = g)	UI 3
7.	t = g	MP 5, 6
8.	Ag	LL 2, 7 (note: g replaced t)
9.	Bg	LL 5, 7 (note: g replaced t)
10.	Ag & Bg	Conj 8, 9

When we use LL, we may, if we wish, replace only *some* occurrences of a constant. For example:

1.	a = b / b = a	
2.	(x)(x = x)	SI
3.	a = a	UI 2
4.	b = a	LL 1, 3

In this proof, the identity statement on line 1 gives us the right, via Liebniz's law, to replace b with a or a with b, on any line. Therefore, we derived line 4 by replacing only the left-side occurrence of a in 3 with b.

Here is another argument highlighting Leibniz's law:

Robert Zimmerman was a singer and Ed Sullivan was not a singer. Robert Zimmerman is Bob Dylan. So, Ed Sullivan is not Bob Dylan.

The argument is simple, but the proof is instructive. Using obvious abbreviations, validity is established via the method of indirect proof as follows.

1. Sz & ~Ss
2. z = d / ~ (s = d)
3. | ~ ~ (s = d)   AIP
4. | (s = d)   DN 3
5. | Sz   Simp 1
6. | ~ Ss   Simp 1
7. | Sd   LL 2, 5
8. | ~ Sd   LL 4, 6
9. | Sd & ~ Sd   Conj 7, 8
10. ~ (s = d)   IP 3–9

The Mind–Body Problem

An argument given by the French philosopher René Descartes (1596–1650), the founder of modern philosophy, can be proved valid using the rules for identity. In one of the most seminal works in the history of philosophy, *Meditations on First Philosophy*, Descartes argues roughly as follows:

1. My brain state has the physical property of being extended in space.
2. My mental state does not have the physical property of being extended in space.
3. Therefore, my mental state is not identical to my brain state.

From here, Descartes goes on to argue for the view known in philosophy as *mind–brain dualism*, which is the claim that the mind is an immaterial thing, and the brain is a material or physical thing, and thus that mind and brain are two different things, not one and the same thing. On the basis of this argument or one very close to it, Descartes argued that a living human being is essentially an immaterial soul joined to a material body, with the soul serving as the seat of consciousness and the locus of personal identity. His root argument can be rendered in PL if we let b stand for my brain state, m for my mental state, and P for the physical property of having an extension in space; that is, the property of occupying a region of space.

1. ~Pm
2. Pb / ~(m = b)

The proof follows:

3. | m = b   AIP
4. | ~Pb   LL 1, 3
5. | Pb & ~Pb   Conj 4, 5
6. ~(m = b)   IP 3–5

Of course, Descartes's argument did not go unchallenged. Other philosophers have argued, contra Descartes, that the mind does have physical properties, including extension in space. The view that the mind and the brain are one and the same (physical) object is called in philosophy the *mind–brain identity theory*. It is a variant of the view known as materialism, the view that everything in existence is made of matter. According to materialism, matter is all that exists; no immaterial things such as God, angels, souls, and so on, exist. Descartes replied to his critics, and other philosophers have defended his position as well. The debate continues today; indeed, it is one of the most exciting areas of contemporary philosophy. It is called the mind–body problem.

The Third Rule of Identity: The Symmetry of Identity

Certainly if a is identical with b, then b is identical with a. The principle needs no defense; it is self-evident. To use the language of Chapter 24, identity is a **symmetrical relation**. This gives rise to the following handy little rule.

Symmetry of Identity Rule (Sym)

Given a formula **c** = **d**, you may infer the corresponding formula **d** = **c** where **c** and **d** are variables ranging over constants of PL.

For example:

1. a = b
2. b = c
3. c = d / d = a
4. a = c   LL 1, 2
5. a = d   LL 4, 3
6. d = a   Sym 5

The Nature of Identity: Proving the Properties of the Identity Relation

Reflexivity, transitivity, and symmetry were defined in Appendix 24.1. We can now use our natural deduction rules to rigorously prove that the identity relation is reflexive, transitive, and symmetrical. The proofs are all premise-free.

Reflexivity

First, identity is a **reflexive relation;** that is, each and every thing is identical with itself. The proof is short:

1.	$\sim(x)\ (x = x)$	AIP
2.	$(x)\ (x = x)$	SI
3.	$(x)(x = x)\ \&\ \sim(x)(x = x)$	Conj 1, 2
4.	$(x)(x = x)$	IP 1–3

Symmetry

The identity relation is symmetrical; that is:

$$(x)(y)[(x = y) \supset (y = x)]$$

This says, "For any x and for any y, if x is identical with y then y is identical with x." The proof is indirect:

1.	$\sim(x)(y)[(x = y) \supset (y = x)]$	AIP
2.	$(\exists x)\ \sim(y)\ [(x = y) \supset (y = x)]$	QE 1
3.	$(\exists x)\ (\exists y)\ \sim[(x = y) \supset (y = x)]$	QE 2
4.	$(\exists y)\ \sim[(v = y) \supset (y = v)]$	EI 3
5.	$\sim[(v = w) \supset (w = v)]$	EI 4
6.	$\sim[\sim(v = w)\ v\ (w = v)]$	Imp 5
7.	$\sim \sim (v = w)\ \&\ \sim(w = v)$	DM 6
8.	$\sim \sim (v = w)$	Simp 7
9.	$\sim(w = v)$	Simp 7
10.	$v = w$	DN 8
11.	$\sim(v = v)$	LL 9, 10
12.	$(x)\ (x = x)$	SI
13.	$v = v$	UI 12
14.	$(v = v)\ \&\ \sim(v = v)$	Conj 11, 13
15.	$(x)(y)[(x = y) \supset (y = x)]$	IP 1–14

Notice the neat way that the tilde shuffles over the quantifiers in steps 2 and 3 of the proof, changing each one as it moves along. Imagine trying this in a natural language!

Transitivity

The identity relation is also a **transitive relation.** That is:

$$(x)\ (y)\ (z)\ \{[(x = y)\ \&\ (y = z)] \supset (x = z)\}$$

This says, "For any x, for any y, and for any z, if x is identical with y and y is identical with z, then x is identical with z." The proof is again premise-free and indirect:

1.	$\sim$(x) (y) (z) {[(x = y) & (y = z)] $\supset$ (x = z)}	AIP
2.	($\exists$x) $\sim$ (y)(z){[(x = y) & (y = z)] $\supset$ (x = z)}	QE 1
3.	($\exists$x) ($\exists$y) $\sim$ (z){[(x = y) & (y = z)] $\supset$ (x = z)}	QE 2
4.	($\exists$x) ($\exists$y) ($\exists$z) $\sim$ {[(x = y) & (y = z)] $\supset$ (x = z)}	QE 3
5.	($\exists$y) ($\exists$z) $\sim$ {[(v = y) & (y = z)] $\supset$ (v = z)}	EI 4
6.	($\exists$z) $\sim$ {[(v = w) & (w = z)] $\supset$ (v = z)}	EI 5
7.	$\sim$ {[(v = w) & (w = c)] $\supset$ (v = c)}	EI 6
8.	$\sim$ {$\sim$ [(v = w) & (w = c)] v (v = c)}	Imp 7
9.	$\sim$ $\sim$ [(v = w) & (w = c)] & $\sim$ (v = c)	DM 8
10.	[(v = w) & (w = c)] & $\sim$ (v = c)	DN 9
11.	(v = w) & (w = c)	Simp 10
12.	$\sim$ (v = c)	Simp 10
13.	v = w	Simp 11
14.	w = c	Simp 11
15.	v = c	LL 13, 14
16.	(v = c) & $\sim$ (v = c)	Conj 12, 15
17.	(x) (y) (z) {[(x = y) & (y = z)] $\supset$ (x = z)}	IP 1–16

Exercise 30.1   Using the identity rules plus any of the other rules, prove each of the following arguments valid.

1.
    1. Aa $\supset$ Ha
    2. $\sim$ Ha
    3. a = b / $\sim$ Ab

2.
    1. Hc $\supset$ Kc
    2. Md $\supset$ Nd
    3. Hc & Md
    4. c = d / Kd & Nc

3.
    1. Aa $\supset$ Ha
    2. $\sim$ (Ab $\supset$ Hb) /$\sim$ (a = b)

4.
    1. (x) (Ax $\supset$ Px)
    2. (x) (Px $\supset$ Hx)
    3. Aa & $\sim$ Hb /$\sim$ (a = b)

5.

    1.   Ab ⊃ Bb

    2.   Rd ⊃ Sd

    3.   Ab & Rd

    4.   b = d / Bd & Sb

6.

    1.   (x) (Ax ⊃ Wx)

    2.   Aa

    3.   Ab ⊃ ~Wb / ~ (a = b)

Exercise 30.2   Symbolize the following arguments, and then derive the conclusions by natural deduction. The identity rules will be needed.

1. If Jim is sick, then the store will be closed. Sue's husband is sick. Jim is Sue's husband. Therefore, the store will be closed.

2. Jim is either an adult or he is a minor. If Jim is a minor, then he cannot enter the contest. Betty's nephew is not an adult. Jim is Betty's nephew. Therefore, Jim cannot enter the contest.

3. Bob Zimmerman is a Boeing machinist and Bob Dylan is not a machinist. Bob Dylan is identical with Robert Zimmerman. So, Bob Zimmerman is not identical with Robert Zimmerman.

4. The car in the garage is green. Jim's car is not green. So, Jim's car is not the car in the garage.

5. Meg's movie is exciting. The movie on the screen is not exciting. Therefore, the movie on the screen is not Meg's movie.

6. There are at least two persons in the quad. Joe is the only male in the quad. Therefore, at least one person in the quad is not male.

7. Every mind lacks mass. Every hunk of matter has mass. My brain is a hunk of matter. Therefore, my mind is not my brain.

8. Joe's uncle is identical to Sue's boss. Sue's boss is Catholic. So Joe's uncle is Catholic.

9. Jose's brother is identical to Sue's husband. Sue's husband is not a Republican. So Joe's brother is not a Republican.

10. Ann's mother is identical to Rita's best friend. Rita's best friend is identical to Joe's sister. Joe's sister is not a gardener. Therefore, Ann's mother is not a gardener.

11. All electrons have a negative charge. This mystery particle, which we have named particle m, does not have an electric charge. Therefore, particle m is not an electron.

12. All rhythm and blues bands include a sax. The Wired band does not include a sax. Any band that is not a rhythm and blues band is not a band that will be playing at the House of R & B. Therefore the Wired band is not playing at the House of R & B.

Glossary

Identity To say that x is identical with y is to say that x and y are one and the same entity.

Leibniz's law The principle stating that for any x and for any y, if x is identical with y, then whatever is true of x is true of y and whatever is true of y is true of x.

Principle of the Identity of Indiscernibles The principle stating that if x and y have all the same properties, then x and y are one and the same thing and not two different things. More technically, for any individual thing x, and for any individual thing y, and for any property or attribute P, if it is the case that any property P possessed by X is also possessed by y and any property P possessed by y is also possessed by x, then x is identical with y.

Principle of the Indiscernibility of Identicals The principle stating that if x is identical with y, then whatever is true of x is true of y and whatever is true of y is true of x.

Principle of Self-Identity The principle stating that each thing is identical with itself.

Reflexive relation A relation that possesses the following feature: If one thing (A) has the relation to something (B) or B has the relation to A, A has that relation to itself.

Symmetrical relation A relation that possesses the following feature: If one thing has the relation to a second thing, the second thing has that relation to the first thing.

Transitive relation A relation that possesses the following feature: If one thing bears the relation to a second thing and the second thing bears the relation to a third thing, the first must bear the relation to the third.

Unit 5

Informal and Inductive Logic

It is time to recall the distinction drawn in Unit One, between formal and informal logic. Formal logic focuses on the abstract patterns or *forms* of correct reasoning. The spotlight is on form rather than content. If you have been reading this book diligently from the first page, you deserve a medal. You have also been exposed to three branches of formal logic: categorical, truth-functional, and predicate logic. As stated in Unit One, informal logic studies the nonformal aspects of reasoning—those parts of the reasoning process that cannot accurately be translated into the abstract symbols used in formal logic. This is why the nonformal branches of logic for the most part eschew special symbols. Inductive logic, the study of the standards of correct inductive reasoning, is primarily informal. In this unit we explore three important branches of logic that are nonformal: the art of defining words, informal fallacies, and inductive reasoning.

31 The Art of Definition « « « « « « « « •

Have you ever been in the middle of an argument with someone when you suddenly realize that the other person does not understand what you are saying? I do not mean they are not listening. They just don't understand what you are saying. As the prison warden said to Cool Hand Luke in the classic movie of the same name, "What we have here is a failure to communicate."

Presenting an argument is a form of communication. Thus, when we reason with others, our argument will get nowhere if the process of communication breaks down. If two people are trying to reason with each other, and one person attaches one meaning to a key word and the other person attaches a different meaning to it, neither will really understand what the other is saying. In such a case, we say the two people are "talking past each other." They might be reasoning with each other, but their words are passing like ships in the night.

A **definition** is an explanation of the meaning of a word or phrase, and a precise definition is a detailed explanation of the meaning of a word or phrase. When words are not defined adequately, they are not understood, and when this happens, communication breaks down. This is why it is always a good idea to define your words at the start of an argument, so that your words and the words of the other person don't pass like ships in the night. This is also why logical theory is concerned with the nature of definition. Reasoning breaks down when words are not well-defined.

There are many different ways to state a definition. Here are several examples displaying several common formats:

- By *inductive argument* I shall mean "an argument that aims to show that its conclusion is probably true though not certainly true."
- The word *true* means "corresponds to reality."
- Let the word *justice* mean "each person gets his or her due."

- Determinism is the view that every event, including the occurrence of each human action, is caused to occur by preexisting conditions.
- "Square" = df. "A four-sided, closed, plane figure with four equal sides and four equal angles."

In a definition, the word (or phrase) to be defined is called the **definiendum**, and the word (or phrase) doing the defining is called the **definiens**.

Ambiguity and Vagueness

Ambiguity and vagueness are two of the most basic obstacles to successful communication and effective argumentation. A good definition removes vagueness and ambiguity as much as possible. A word is **vague** if it has borderline cases. A **borderline case** for a word is a case where we are not sure whether or not the word applies. For example, the word *rich* is vague. Certainly the word *rich* applies to Bill Gates, the founder of Microsoft, and surely it does *not* apply to most college students. But there are borderline cases where we are just not sure whether the word applies or does not apply. (Can you think of a borderline case for the term *rich*?) A vague word or phrase that has borderline cases is said to have "fuzzy boundaries of application." The problem with a vague word is not that the word lacks a meaning; the problem is that we are not clear on the *limits* of the word's meaning. That is, in some cases we are not sure if the word applies. To remedy vagueness, we clarify the meaning by providing a more precise definition, one that will make a decision in the borderline cases. Vagueness becomes a problem in the midst of reasoned argument when it short-circuits the reasoning process: Reasoning with vague terms can be like trying to pick pieces of eggshell out of a bowl of beaten eggs—it is hard to get a firm hold on anything.

In contrast, a word is **ambiguous** within a particular context if it can be interpreted in two or more different ways in that context. Ambiguity is a concern in logic because it, too, can sidetrack or short-circuit the reasoning process. For instance, reasoning is thrown off track when a crucial word in an argument is used with one meaning in one place and then with a different meaning in another place, and in addition, the switch in meaning is not signaled and the shift affects the correctness of the reasoning process.

In the *Analects*, the Chinese philosopher Confucius says of the "superior" man, "He hates those who advertise the faults of others. He hates those who abide in lowliness and slander the great." Fine. But what does "lowliness" mean here? Is it a reference to socioeconomic status? Or moral status? Lowliness in terms of what measure? And what does "great" mean? Does it refer to those with power? Or those who are wise? Exactly who is Confucius talking about here? It would seem that both ambiguity and vagueness are present in this example, but surely nothing that a good definition or two couldn't remedy.

Two Types of Disagreement

The presence of ambiguity and vagueness can give rise to disagreements that are more verbal than real. In some cases, we agree on the meanings of the words we are using, but we disagree on the facts of some matter. Person A claims that average household income has gone down over the past ten years, whereas person B claims it has risen. This is a real, or factual, disagreement. In other cases, two or more people *seem* to be disagreeing about the facts of the matter, but the dispute is merely verbal in nature. Without either party realizing it, one party is using a word in one way, to mean one thing, and the other party is using the same word to mean something else entirely. The two are not even talking about the same thing! To settle a factual disagreement, we need to investigate the facts of the matter. To settle a verbal disagreement, we need to agree on the meanings of the words we use. In other words, we need to define our terms.

Types of Definitions

Just as there are many ways to remove ambiguity and vagueness as much as possible, there are many different types of definitions. Here are five of the most common:

1. Sometimes we use a definition to explain the commonly understood meaning of a word or phrase—the meaning that is typically provided in a dictionary or "lexicon." This common or "dictionary" meaning is called the **lexical meaning** and this type of definition is called a **lexical definition**.

2. Sometimes we formulate a definition to give a word or phrase a brand new meaning, independent of current usage. When we do this, we are "stipulating" a new meaning, and the definition is called a **stipulative definition**. For example, as computers rose to prominence, we needed a word to describe those who break into computer systems, and the word *hacker* acquired a new meaning. In one episode of *Seinfeld*, someone gave Elaine a gift, and Elaine realized that the gift was actually something she had given the person the year before. Jerry invented a new word to describe such a person: a "regifter," someone who saves a gift and gives it to someone else as a gift later on (and thus avoids the trouble of buying a gift). Jerry coined a new word and stipulated its new meaning.

3. Sometimes a definition contains a theory about the nature of something. For example, during the nineteenth century, the British physicist James Clerk Maxwell proposed and confirmed the theory that light is in reality an oscillating electromagnetic field traveling through space. Maxwell's theory helped us understand the nature of light and at the same time provided what we call a *theoretical* meaning for the word *light*. In the eighteenth century, Count Rumford discovered that heat is the motion (mean kinetic energy) of molecules. Rumford's discovery provided a *theoretical* account of the nature of heat, and it also provided a theoretical meaning for the word *heat*. Definitions that provide theoretical meanings are called **theoretical definitions**.

Definitions in science are often theoretical definitions because they draw on scientific theory to characterize the nature of things. For example, when the astronomer defines the morning star as "Venus when seen in the morning sky," we are given a new, theoretical way of understanding the morning star. When heat is defined as "the motion of molecules," we are given a theory as to the nature of heat. Theoretical definitions provide us with a theoretical picture of a part of our world, and this deepens our understanding of the world.

4.   A definition in which the main purpose is to remove vagueness is called a **precising definition.** Legislative bodies frequently construct this type of definition to clarify the meaning of a term in a law. For instance, suppose a new city ordinance forbids loud noise after 9 p.m. But what constitutes loud noise? Calling the cat? Starting up the car for a late-night trip to the store for munchies? As a result, a precising definition might be added to the ordinance: "Loud noise shall be defined as any sound that exceeds 100 decibels for more than 10 seconds."

A precising definition aims to combat vagueness. However, in constructing a precising definition, we are not free to make up just any meaning we wish. The definition should remain in line with ordinary usage, yet it should add enough precision to help us decide borderline cases. Precising definitions thus differ from stipulative definitions in that a stipulative definition does not have to remain in line with established usage.

Our courts of law have had to formulate precising definitions for terms such as *obscenity, free speech,* and *sexual harassment.* Currently, our society is attempting to make the meaning of the word *death* more precise. We are also debating the meaning of marriage.

5.   Sometimes people develop definitions primarily to influence our attitudes, positive or negative, toward something, and to persuade us of something. When someone formulates a **persuasive definition,** he or she hopes that the definition will call up a favorable or an unfavorable attitude toward what the word stands for. For example, someone opposed to abortion might define abortion as "the killing of a defenseless human being," whereas a proponent of abortion rights might define abortion as "a woman choosing to have something done to her body."

The Two Main Methods of Definition

Most definitions of a word or phrase accomplish their primary task of explaining meaning either by referring in some way to the extension of the word (or phrase) or by stating the word's intension. The **extension** of a word or expression, also called the **denotation** of the word or expression, is all those entities to which the word or expression can truly be applied. For instance, the extension (or denotation) of the word *city* includes Seattle, Los Angeles, Portland, Boston, and so on. In other words, the word *city denotes* Seattle, Boston, Portland, and so on. The extension of the term *rock band* includes the Beatles, the Animals, the Doors, Cream, and so on.

The **intension** of a word or expression, also called the **connotation** of the word or expression, is those features, properties, characteristics, or attributes that an entity must have for the word or expression to truly apply to it. In other words, the intension (or connotation) of a word is the properties that determine whether an entity is a member of the class of entities *denoted* by the word. Still another way to put this would be as follows: The intension of a word is the set of properties that determines whether or not an entity belongs in the extension of the word or phrase. For instance, the intension of the word *square* includes "closed figure with four equal angles," "figure with four equal sides," "plane figure," and so on. Here is yet another way to put the point: The connotation, or intension, of a word is the properties that determine whether the word applies or not in a given case.

It is interesting that some words have an intension but no extension, such as *unicorn*, *Leprechaun*, and *Santa Claus*. Also, two different words can have the same intension. For example, *car* and *automobile*. If two words have the same intension, they have the same extension, of course.

Extensional Definitions

Extensional, or **denotative, definitions** assign meaning to a word or phrase by giving *examples* of what the word or phrase denotes or applies to. In other words, they define a word by citing things from the word's extension. There are two common types. If you explain the meaning of a word by pointing at an example, you are giving an *ostensive* (from the Latin word *ostens* for "display") or demonstrative definition. For instance, you might say, "Circuit means this" as you point at a circuit. If you explain a meaning by listing or "enumerating" members of a term's extension, you are giving an *enumerative* definition. For example, you might say, "*Comedian* means a person such as John Candy, Groucho Marx, or Bob Hope."

Intensional Definitions

An **intensional**, or **connotative, definition** assigns meaning by indicating the qualities or attributes a word or phrase connotes. That is, it lists the properties that an entity must have if the word or phrase is to apply correctly to it. There are two common types. If you define a word by stating a synonym, you are giving a synonymous definition. In other words, the definiendum is defined in terms of one word or phrase that connotes the same attributes. For example, the word *physician* means "medical doctor," the word *adage* means "proverb," and so on.

To analyze something is to break it down into its parts. An **analytical definition** explains the meaning of a word by breaking the meaning down into its constituent concepts. This involves specifying the characteristics possessed in common by those items to which the word or phrase applies. For example, a mathematician might define a square as "a closed figure with four equal sides and four equal angles" because all squares have this set of features in common. A chemist might define an *acid* as "a substance that increases the hydrogen-ion concentration of water." In another example, *bachelor* means "unmarried adult male."

Two Types of Meaning

Corresponding to these two very general types of definition, extensional and intensional, it is possible to distinguish two types of defined meaning.

The **extensional**, or **denotative, meaning** of a term consists of the class of objects to which the term may correctly be applied. In other words, the extensional meaning is the members of the class denoted by the term. This collection is, of course, the "extension," or denotation, of the term.

The **intensional**, or **connotative, meaning** of a term consists of the qualities or attributes the term connotes. In other words, the objects in a term's extension have common attributes or characteristics that lead us to apply the term to them, and this collection of attributes or properties, shared by all and only those objects in a term's extension, is the intension, or connotation, of the term.

Advice When Constructing Definitions

Rules for Extensional Definitions

Common sense guides us when we construct extensional or denotative definitions. Choose items from the extension that are known by your audience, avoid esoteric examples, choose items that are representative of the extension and not exceptional, and so on.

Rules for Intensional Definitions

Things are not as simple when we are constructing intensional definitions. Guidance is in order, for there are a number of pitfalls to be avoided, not all of them obvious. Here are some commonly accepted rules that can help you construct effective intensional definitions.

Rule 1. An intensional definition should be neither too narrow nor too broad. If a definition is too narrow, it applies to too little; if a definition is too broad, it applies to too much. If the definition is neither too narrow nor too broad, it gives the necessary and sufficient conditions for applying the term.

For example, the following definition of baseball is too broad: "Baseball is a game commonly played on a large athletic field." (So is football.) On the other hand, the following definition is too narrow: "Art is anything painted on canvas." (Aren't there forms of art that do not involve paint?)

Rule 2. This rule is related to the first. An intensional definition should convey the essential properties connoted by the word or phrase. Essential properties are those characteristics or attributes that an entity cannot lack and still remain part of the extension of the word (or phrase). For instance, suppose someone defines a clock as "a mechanism for telling time that contains gears, springs, and cogs, and has 12 numbers on its face." The problem with this definition is that these properties (having gears, springs, hands, and such) are not *essential* features of a clock, for digital clocks are clocks, but they lack springs and gears. Because this definition cites nonessential features, it leaves out many clocks. It misses the target. The following definition does not violate this rule: "A triangle is a closed, planar figure that has three sides and three angles." Definitions in mathematics typically cite only essential properties.

Rule 3. Intensional definitions should be positive rather than negative. For example, suppose someone attempts to define a computer by saying that a computer is a machine that is *not* powered by water, is *not* made entirely of glass, and is *not* typically larger than a television set. This definition conveys little understanding of what a computer is, for many items besides computers fit this definition. This is inevitable when you try to characterize something using only negative terms. It is true that an aardvark, for instance, is not a duck, is not a cat, and so on. However, that does not tell you much about what it *is*. Usually, definitions in terms of negatives convey little understanding.

Rule 4. Intensional definitions should avoid vague, obscure, ambiguous, or figurative language. For example, suppose someone defines a television set as "gin and tonic for the brain." This figurative language provides little in the way of understanding for someone who does not already know what a television set is. Or imagine that someone defines love as "a big smiley face in the garden of life." This image would apply to much more than just love. The German philosopher Martin Heidegger once defined truth as "the dissimulation of the dissimulated." This definition explains the obscure in terms of the more obscure, and sheds little light on the nature of truth.

Rule 5. Intensional definitions should avoid language that manipulates the emotions and attitudes. For example, someone who defines socialism as "a system in which an all-powerful government dominates all aspects of society" is hoping that the proposed definition will cause negative feelings toward socialism, but the definition does not adequately explain what the word *socialism* actually means.

Here is one final bit of advice with respect to our current subject. When you present an argument to others, think about the words you are using, and ask yourself if your words are going to be understood. If they are ambiguous or vague, if it is likely they will not be understood, or if it is likely they will create the wrong impression, then take the time to define your words so that they will adequately carry your point across to the other person. Effective definition is one of the keys to effective argument, if you know what I mean.

Exercise 31.1   Instructions are given in context.

1. In one *Seinfeld* episode, Jerry's stereo wasn't working and Kramer came up with a scheme to acquire a new stereo for free: He would break the stereo into pieces, and Jerry would take it to the post office and tell them it had broken during shipment. It wouldn't cost the taxpayers anything, Kramer argued, because the post office would simply treat it as a "write-off." Jerry looked at Kramer and said, "What is a write-off?" When Kramer frowned and shrugged his shoulders, Jerry said, "You don't even know what a write-off is." What type of definition did Kramer need? Explain your answer.

2. The definition Isaac Newton formulated in the seventeenth century helps us understand the concept of physical force: "Force equals mass times acceleration" ($F = M \times A$). What type of definition is this?

3. Fred wants to go to Burger King with Sue for their tenth anniversary dinner, and Sue wants to go to Wendy's. In the middle of intense negotiations, Sue says to Fred, "Now you're just quibbling." Fred says, "I'm what?" What type of definition does Fred need?

4. Give an original example (i.e., an example not discussed in this book) of each of the following kinds of definition.
   a. Lexical
   b. Theoretical
   c. Precising
   d. Stipulative   ,
   e. Persuasive

5. Give an original example of a vague word and explain why the word is vague.

6. Give an original example of an ambiguous use of a word and explain why the word is ambiguous in that context.

7. Make up a stipulative definition to introduce a new term and explain why your definition would be useful.

8. Write a precising definition for each of the following. If you think your definition is inadequate, explain why it is inadequate.
   a. Old person
   b. Cool person

   c. Rich person

   d. Conservative

   e. Liberal

   f. Rock 'n' roll

   g. Cold weather

   h. Poverty

9. Write a persuasive definition for each of the following.

   a. Socialism

   b. Capitalism

   c. Religion

   d. Communism

   e. Intellectual

   f. Racism

   g. Prejudice

   h. Altruism

   i. Selfishness

10. Determine whether the following definitions are lexical, stipulative, precising, theoretical, or persuasive.

   a. *Decadent* means in a state of decline or decay.

   b. *Cursory* means hasty, superficial, and not thorough.

   c. A star is a large ball of hot, burning hydrogen gas.

   d. *Cool* shall mean below 60 degrees and above 40 degrees Fahrenheit.

   e. Let's say a "plate scraper" is a person who finishes every bit of food on his plate and obnoxiously scrapes the plate with his fork to make sure he's gotten virtually every molecule of food.

   f. *Jeopardy* means danger or risk of loss or injury.

   g. A fanatic is a person possessed by an irrational zeal, especially for a ridiculous religious or political cause.

   h. A juggernaut is something that draws blind and destructive devotion, or to which people are ruthlessly sacrificed.

   i. A gene is a portion of a DNA molecule.

   j. By the term *capitalism* I shall mean a system in which people have the freedom to make their own economic decisions without the government telling them what to do.

   k. An ingrate is an ungrateful person.

   l. *Frank* means open and sincere in expression, undisguised, and straightforward.

m. *Capacious* means "able to contain a large quantity."

n. An anomaly is a deviation from the normal order.

o. *Ancillary* means "subordinate."

p. *Worker* means "person who is oppressed by a capitalist."

q. *Capitalist* means "person whose act of saving creates jobs for others and benefits society."

r. *Pulsar* means "dense neutron star with a high rate of spin."

Exercise 31.2   In each of the following cases, determine whether the definition is an intensional definition or an extensional definition.

1. A mother is a female parent.

2. Courage: Seattle School Superintendent John Stanford battling cancer.

3. *Sulky* means "sullen."

4. A substance is soluble if it dissolves when it is placed in water.

5. A politician is someone such as Richard Nixon, Bill Clinton, or Patty Murray.

6. Substance X is harder than substance Y: X can be used to scratch Y but Y cannot be used to scratch X.

7. *Classy*: Buddy Love in the Jerry Lewis movie *The Nutty Professor*.

8. A groovy person is someone like Austin Powers, the international man of mystery.

9. Negative liberty is the absence of aggressive, forceful interference in one's life.

10. *Sphere* means "set of points in three-dimensional space equidistant from one point."

Exercise 31.3   Which of the rules of definition is violated in each of the following?

1. A mind is a terrible thing to waste.

2. God is that which is not material, not limited, and not visible.

3. A protester is someone who protests.

4. A depressant is not a stimulant.

5. A soul is a nonmaterial substance that has no weight, physical size, or physical shape.

6. Time is an old gypsy man ceaselessly moving from one stop to the next.

7. A human being is a carnivorous animal.

8. Rock music is music that is not jazz, not country, not classical, and not blues.

9. *Religious* means obsessively concerned with things that don't really matter.

10. *Peace* means the absence of war.

Exercise 31.4 The following definitions are from State of Washington, Initiative Measure 1163. In each case, what type of definition are the citizens being asked to consider?

1. For purposes of this section, the "fair market value" of distribution rights as to a particular brand means the amount that a willing buyer would pay and a willing seller would accept for such distribution rights when neither is acting under compulsion and both have knowledge of all facts material to the transaction.

2. "Terminated distributor" means a distributor whose agreement of distributorship with respect to a brand of spirits or malt beverages, whether oral or written, has been terminated, canceled, or not renewed.

3. "Terminated distribution rights" means distribution rights with respect to a brand of malt beverages which are lost by a Initiative Measure.

Glossary

Analytical definition A definition that explains the meaning of a word by breaking the meaning down into its constituent concepts.

Ambiguous A word within a particular context that can be interpreted as having two or more meanings in the given context.

Borderline case A case where we are not sure whether the word applies or does not apply.

Connotation (or intension) The features or attributes something must have for a word or expression to correctly apply to it.

Definiendum The word (or phrase) to be defined.

Definiens The word (or phrase) doing the defining.

Definition An explanation of the meaning of a word or phrase.

Denotation (or extension) All those entities to which a word or expression can truly be applied.

Extensional (or denotative) definition A definition that assigns meaning to a word or phrase by giving examples of what the word or phrase denotes.

Extensional (or denotative) meaning The class of objects to which the term may correctly be applied; that is, the members of the class that the term denotes.

Intensional (or connotative) definition A definition that assigns meaning by indicating the qualities or attributes a word or phrase connotes, that is, by listing the properties that an entity must have if the word or phrase is to apply to it.

Intensional (or connotative) meaning The qualities or attributes the term connotes, that is, the common attributes or characteristics that lead us to apply the term.

Lexical definition A definition that reports a word's commonly understood meaning.

Lexical meaning The commonly understood meaning of a word or phrase.

Precising definition A definition that provides a more precise meaning for a word that formerly had a vague but established meaning. The more precise meaning provides additional guidance as to how the word is to be applied in various borderline cases.

Persuasive definition A definition that aims to influence attitudes.

Stipulative definition A definition that constitutes a new meaning for a word or phrase.

Theoretical definition A definition that characterizes the nature of something. Such a definition provides a theoretical picture of an entity, or a way of understanding the entity.

Vague A word that has borderline cases.

32 The Informal Fallacies « « « « « « « « «

The jawbone of an ass is just as dangerous a weapon today as in Sampson's time.

—*Richard Nixon*

Have you ever had this happen? You are in the middle of an argument, making what seems to be a perfectly good point, when the other person shouts at you, "That's a fallacy!" What does he or she mean? Sometimes people use the word *fallacy* to refer to a mistaken belief. However, more often the word is used to refer to an error in reasoning. In logic, a **fallacy** is often defined more specifically as an error in reasoning that nevertheless might appear to many to be correct reasoning. Fallacies are thus deceptive in the sense that they might *appear* correct even though in reality they are examples of bad reasoning. (The word *fallacy* actually stems from the Latin verb *fallere*, which means "to deceive.") In other words, fallacies are a species of intellectual trickery—they can be psychologically persuasive even though they are logically in error.

Logicians distinguish two general types of fallacy. **Formal fallacies** are errors in reasoning that can be completely defined in terms of their form or abstract logical structure, without reference to the content or subject matter of the reasoning. The flaw lies in the general form of the reasoning rather than in the content. In Unit Three we looked at two of the most common formal fallacies, affirming the consequent and denying the antecedent. In contrast, **informal fallacies** are errors in reasoning that are *not* simply due to the pure logical form of the argument (hence they are "informal"). In the case of an informal fallacy, one must examine the actual content of the reasoning to find the error because the problem is not a matter of pure logical form alone.

Aristotle, the founder of logic, was the first to write a systematic study of informal logical fallacies. His book, *On Sophistical Refutations*, thus launched the branch of logical theory that we are about to enter. This is one more reason he deserves the title that history has bestowed on him, founder of logic. "That some reasonings are genuine," he wrote, "while others seem to be so but are not, is evident." Aristotle catalogued a number of different types of informal fallacies; since his day logicians have catalogued many, many more. Hundreds are listed on the websites featured later.

In this chapter, we are going to take a brief look at the nature of the informal fallacy by analyzing several representative examples. The fallacies that follow were chosen because they are common errors and because each is easily recognized. A complete list of all possible informal fallacies has probably never been written, and, if it were to be written, would probably take up thousands of pages. One caveat is in order, however, before we begin our survey of informal fallacies. In many, if not most, instances, a "real-life" fallacy will fit more than one of the definitions that follow. That is, in many cases one person will categorize a given fallacy one way, as an example of one type of fallacy, whereas another person will place it under another heading. In many cases, both persons will be right. The distinctions between the various fallacies are, in many cases, fuzzy.

What's with Those Latin Names?

You will notice in a moment that many of the fallacies have Latin names. For instance, the "argument against the man" is known as the *argumentum ad hominem* fallacy. During the Middle Ages, when logic was one of the core subjects taught in the universities and cathedral schools of Europe, Latin was the universal language of scholars and virtually all research was conducted in Latin. As a result, many of the fallacies were assigned Latin names. Many of these quaint names remain in use. For most fallacies, it is common practice to give both the English name and the traditional Latin name.

Fallacies of No Evidence

Fallacies of no evidence traditionally are fallacies that present no evidence whatsoever for their conclusion.

The Argument Against the Person: *Argumentum Ad Hominem*

An ad hominem argument (Latin: "against the man") occurs when someone attacks a person's character, or the person's circumstances, or the person's associates, rather than the person's reasoned argument, and then concludes on this basis alone that the person's argument has been refuted. This happens all the time in politics. A political figure gives an argument for some controversial bill, for instance, and then opponents attack the person's character, associates, or circumstances, rather than his actual reasoning in favor of the bill. This type of behavior is a fallacy because personal matters such as these, by themselves, are irrelevant to the validity or strength of the person's argument. They are also logically irrelevant to the truth or falsity of the conclusion the person being attacked may be supporting. A bad person can still give a good argument, and someone in a bad circumstance or someone who has some bad friends might still be right about *some* things. The mere fact that someone has been bad or has bad friends does not mean his or her *argument* must be bad! When someone gives an argument for a claim, an honest concern for truth requires that the argument be judged on its logical merits, apart from the arguer's character, circumstances, associates, and other logically irrelevant matters.

If you attack a person's argument by attacking his or her character, you commit what logicians call an *abusive ad hominem*. If you attack a person's argument by attacking his or her circumstances, you commit a *circumstantial ad hominem*. If you attack an argument by attacking the arguer's associates, that is a "guilt by association" fallacy. In each of these cases, of course, the fallacious arguer thinks that he has defeated the person's argument, but all he has done is attack the person (or the person's circumstances or associates). Not good.

There are many ways to attack a person's character and thus to commit an abusive ad hominem fallacy; one is especially worth mentioning. The *Tu Quoque* (Latin: "You too" or "You're another") is a wonderful variant of the abusive ad hominem. Suppose a mother is lecturing her teenage son on the dangers of drugs, and the son says, "Why should I listen to you? You took drugs when you were my age"; in other words, "You, too." The implication is that the mother's reasoning is bad because she doesn't (or didn't at one time) live up to the advice she is giving.

Essentially, the Tu Quoque attempts to discredit a person's argument by charging the person with hypocrisy or inconsistency. "Look who's talking" is another way to express a Tu Quoque. "Your momma" is another. The Tu Quoque is a fallacy because what a person does with her personal life is logically irrelevant to the logical connection between the premises and the conclusion of her argument. A hypocrite can still give a good argument. An inconsistent person might still reason well, at least on some matters. A doctor who smokes can still present a good argument against smoking. Of course, although the fact that someone does not practice what he or she preaches is logically irrelevant to the value of the person's argument, it can nevertheless be psychologically persuasive.

Here is an example of the guilt by association fallacy. Professor Jones is giving a lecture on the Constitution and someone says, "Her argument is a bunch of nonsense. Did you know she associates with right-wing extremists?" By attacking the professor's associates, the speaker supposes that the audience will reject the professor's argument. This fallacy owes some of its psychological power to our tendency sometimes to judge people by the friends they make. However, even someone who has associates we do not like could give a good argument nevertheless. Again, the argument a person is giving ought to be judged on its logical merits, on the evidence offered, and not on such logically irrelevant matters as the company they keep.

Suppose Joe Blow, a rich industrialist, gives an argument in favor of lower taxes. In response, someone says, "His argument is nonsense. He stands to gain if tax rates are lowered." This is a circumstantial ad hominem fallacy. The fact that he will gain if tax rates are lowered has nothing to do with the evidential connection between the premises and the conclusion of Joe's argument. His reasoning needs to be judged in terms of its logical merits and not in terms of his personal circumstances. Just because someone stands to gain from a measure does not in itself prove that his or her argument is a bad argument. A person who stands to gain if the conclusion of his argument is accepted might still be giving a good argument. For example, Martin Luther King stood to gain if some of his arguments were accepted, but that does not prove that his arguments were bad arguments!

In sum, the key feature of all forms of ad hominem argumentation is that the ad hominem arguer attempts to discredit someone's argument by personally attacking the *arguer* rather than the person's *argument*. Although this can be psychologically persuasive, it is logically fallacious, for even if the person being attacked is a bad person, a bad person can sometimes give a good argument. This cannot be emphasized too many times: An argument needs to be considered on its own logical merits, apart from the personal characteristics, associates, or circumstances of the arguer.

Exceptions to the Rule

Having said that, there are exceptions to the rule. Here is an interesting one. In a court of law, if the reliability of a witness is at issue, then the witness's character, associates, or circumstances might be logically relevant. For example, if a witness has a disreputable character, is a known liar, has a strong motive to lie, or is being coerced by someone, and so on, the jury might then have good reason to doubt the person's testimony. The attack, in a court of law, on a witness's character, associates, or circumstances might, in some cases, not be a *fallacious* ad hominem at all.

The Appeal to the People (*Argumentum ad Populum*)

People sometimes think differently when they are in a crowd. When alone or with a few friends they might be very rational, but in a crowd they could become excited and give in to irrational urges while caught in the grip of tangled emotions. The appeal to the people fallacy attempts to arouse and use the emotions of a group, or crowd, to win acceptance for a conclusion. It relies on the psychological fact that individuals often want to join in the enthusiasm of a crowd, and it encourages people to give in to such feelings rather than to think logically.

Because most of us need some form of peer approval, the idea of being a part of the group can also motivate us to accept a group conclusion. This strategy is a fallacy, for the mere fact that the group favors a conclusion is not, by itself, a logically relevant reason to accept the conclusion as true or right. Groups are not always right.

For example, a television ad shows a group of teenagers all wearing a particular brand of sunglasses. In the background a voice says, "Everyone is wearing Brand X sunglasses. Don't you want to be part of the action?" The implicit argument here is this: Because the group is wearing these, you ought to wear them.

Or an ad says, "Polls show that Senator Smith will be elected by a landslide, so join the Senator's party and be on the winning side." This type of ad populum argument is also known as the bandwagon argument because it (figuratively speaking) presents a bandwagon full of people and asks the listener to jump on and party with everyone else.

The ad populum is also known as the *appeal to the gallery* because of the way some politicians have been known to use the technique during legislative debates. Instead of reasoning with their fellow legislators in the legislative chamber, they speak to the visitors watching the proceeding from the gallery of the legislative building. They hope that if their fellow legislators hear the people in the gallery cheering and clapping, this, rather than the evidence and reasons, will decide their vote. Politicians who use this technique are called *demagogues*.

The many versions of the ad populum fallacy share a common structure: "Join in with everyone else; accept my conclusion so that you will be part of the group." This is a fallacy because the mere fact that a group favors something does not, by itself, show that what the group favors is right or is true. Groups are sometimes way off track, and their beliefs are sometimes wildly mistaken.

The Appeal to Pity (*Argumentum ad Misericordiam*)

The appeal to pity fallacy attempts to evoke the emotion of pity from the audience (the reader or listener) and then to use that pity to manipulate the audience into a desired conclusion. Attorneys have been known to use this strategy. For instance, an attorney whose client is charged with armed robbery might play up his client's unfortunate childhood in hopes that the jurors will feel so sorry for the defendant that they will be lenient. This is an appeal to pity.

The ad misericordiam argument is a fallacy because it treats pity as the only relevant factor to take into account in reaching the conclusion, ignoring logical factors that could be relevant. Of course, we do sometimes take pity into account, but only along with other logically relevant factors.

The Fallacy of Irrelevant Conclusion (*Ignoratio Elenchi*, "Ignorance of the Proof")

In the fallacy of irrelevant conclusion, someone puts forward premises in support of a stated conclusion, but the premises actually support a different conclusion instead of the stated conclusion, although the presenter does not realize it. For instance, suppose the senate is debating a bill that would place laptop computers in every public school classroom. Senator Smith is supposed to present an argument for the bill.

"Our children are our most precious investment," the senator begins. "The public schools help prepare the next generation for responsible adulthood. Only a scrooge would oppose children. Therefore we must pass this bill."

The senator is supposed to be arguing in favor of a bill that would place laptops in schools, but his premises are actually directed at a completely different conclusion, namely, the generally accepted conclusion that public schools are a good thing. His premises do nothing to show that schools will actually do a better job if classrooms have laptops. The senator is "arguing beside the point." This is an ignoratio elenchi.

An ignoratio elenchi succeeds in being psychologically persuasive by manipulating the audience's favorable emotions, which are directed toward the conclusion the speaker wants accepted. In the preceding case, the senator's speech evokes positive emotions in support of children and public schools, and then attempts to subtly slip this positive approval over to the laptop bill—without actually giving an argument for the laptop bill. If everyone is vigorously nodding their heads in approval at the mention of public education and the welfare of children, they might still be nodding their heads when the senator mentions the laptop bill.

Sometimes, an ignoratio elenchi is simply the lazy way out. For instance, suppose Representative Jones is scheduled to argue in favor of a bill that would increase federal funding for public housing. However, Jones hasn't done her homework and doesn't have any facts at hand. What does she do? She talks about the general human need for decent housing, and tells an emotional story about her own poverty-stricken childhood in a house with no indoor plumbing. This is an ignoratio elenchi, for it completely ignores the key issue: Will this particular bill actually provide decent housing? Is there a better way to help the poor, or is this the most effective use of scarce resources? Presumably, everyone agrees that decent housing is needed and that it is a good thing—but that is not the point at issue. The point at issue is whether or not this particular bill is justified. The congresswoman's speech is supposed to prove one thing (that this particular bill is needed) but is instead directed at a different thing (that decent housing is a good thing). Her argument misses the point.

Begging the Question (*Petitio Principii*, "Postulation of the Beginning")

Someone "begs the question" if they present an argument for a conclusion and their argument in some way employs the conclusion they are trying to support as a *premise* in support of itself. Here is a glaring example:

Joe: God exists.
Fred: Why believe that?
Joe: Because God exists.

Because Joe has not given Fred an independent reason to believe in God, he is in effect "begging" Fred to accept the conclusion as a favor. Joe hasn't done the hard work of producing a solid logical argument, but he wants the same result. He wants something for nothing. Notice that although a question-begging argument does not give anyone who doubts its conclusion a good reason to believe its conclusion, a question-begging argument is technically valid if construed as a deductive argument. Can you explain why?

Of course, few people are so misguided that they will simply place the conclusion word-for-word into the premises in this way. Usually, an arguer (perhaps unconsciously) rephrases the conclusion and then uses the rephrased conclusion as a premise in support of itself. Because it has been rephrased, it might not be obvious that the conclusion is doing double duty as a premise. Here are some examples:

- He is angry right now. How do I know? Because right now he is mad.
- Free trade is a good thing, for the unimpeded flow of products is a good thing.
- Liberty is good, for freedom is a good thing.
- Nobody has free will, for real choice doesn't exist.

The most deceptive form of this fallacy occurs when someone gives an argument containing a premise that logically presupposes the conclusion. To explain this we must first clarify the nature of a presupposition. Suppose someone says, "The king of the United States has issued a proclamation." This sentence cannot be true unless there is actually a king of the United States. So, anyone asserting or accepting the sentence must take it for granted that the United States has a king. The sentence therefore presupposes that the United States has a king. In general, one sentence **S** presupposes a sentence **P** if it is the case that anyone asserting or accepting **S** must take it for granted that **P** is true. Now, consider the following argument for God's existence:

1. The Bible says God exists.
2. The Bible is inspired by God.
3. Anything inspired by God is true.
4. Therefore, God exists.

Notice that the second premise cannot be true unless God exists. To grant the truth of this premise is *already* to suppose God exists. The premises therefore presuppose the conclusion. This argument "begs the question." Because nobody would accept the premises unless the person already accepted the conclusion, the argument begs us to take for granted what it is supposed to prove.

An argument that begs the question is also called a *circular argument*. The following argument begs the question by arguing in a circle:

Ed: Why do you believe Pat is trustworthy?
Ned: Because Sue is trustworthy, and Sue told me Pat is trustworthy.
Ed: But why do you believe what Sue says?
Ned: Because Rita is trustworthy, and she told me that Sue is trustworthy.
Ed: But why do you believe what Rita says?
Ned: Because Fred is trustworthy, and Fred says that Rita is trustworthy.
Ed: But why do you believe what Fred says?
Ned: Because Pat is trustworthy, and Pat says that Fred is trustworthy.

Notice that the premises form a chain that circles back on itself and ends where it began. This argument "begs" the point at issue, which is: Why believe Pat is trustworthy? In the end, we are asked to believe Pat is trustworthy because . . . Pat is trustworthy. Of course, if the circle is long enough, the listener (and the arguer) might not notice that the argument is circular, or that the question has been begged.

The Red Herring Fallacy

In the red herring fallacy, the arguer diverts attention from his or her opponent's argument by changing the subject and then drawing a conclusion about the new subject. For instance, suppose an American company has been accused of selling products made by slave labor in the country of Ruritania. In the middle of the heated press conference, the CEO says, "Our company is a large donor to Amnesty International. Why, last year we gave $25,000." The CEO has changed the subject, and the argument is now completely off track. By switching the subject to the donations, he has introduced a "red herring" into the argument.

To introduce a red herring into an argument is to change the subject in the middle of the argument, derailing the train of reasoning and diverting attention from the point at issue. The fallacy might have gotten its name from a tactic used to train hunting dogs. As the dogs are running down a trail attempting to track a rabbit, drag a strong-scented red herring across the trail to throw them off track. Most of the dogs will follow the herring's scent and lose the rabbit; only the best dogs will stay with the original scent. In the context of an argument, a "red herring" throws us off the scent, by throwing the argument off track.

Why would someone introduce a red herring into an argument? Perhaps the person knows he or she is losing the argument and wants to change the subject to another issue. Perhaps the person feels uncomfortable with the point at issue and unconsciously wants to change the topic. Also, an arguer might innocently interject a red herring into an argument thinking (mistakenly) that it is a pertinent point. However, in most cases, the herring is presented in an attempt, conscious or unconscious, to avoid a conclusion.

The Genetic Fallacy

When we explain the origin (the "genesis") of a thing, we have given a genetic explanation. The genetic fallacy is committed when someone attacks a viewpoint by disparaging the view's origin rather than the argument for the view. Often this involves attacking the way in which the view was initially acquired. In short, the origin of the view is attacked rather than the evidence for the view, and then this alone is offered as a reason to reject the view.

For example, during the heyday of Soviet communism, communist economists would argue against modern, neoclassical economic theory by pointing out that it originated in the minds of "bourgeois" or "capitalist" economists, that is, economists who taught at universities in the capitalist world. These universities and their highly paid professors, Soviet communists claimed, were "hired prize fighters" of the ruling capitalist class. So, they suggested, because modern economic theory originated in the capitalist class, modern economic theory is false. This line of thought commits a genetic fallacy. Modern economic theory, as taught in any university, should be evaluated on the basis of the evidence for it, and on the basis of the logic and arguments offered for and against various competing theories. To simply dismiss it on the basis of its origin (genesis) is to dismiss it for a logically irrelevant reason. Similarly, during the 1930s, Soviet biologists argued against Darwin's theory of evolution (and in favor of Lysenko's theory) because Darwin was a "bourgeois" or "capitalist" scientist and thus must be wrong about the nature of evolution. This was another genetic fallacy.

One more example is in order. Some have argued against the truth of religious belief by arguing that (a) religious beliefs originate in a fear of the unknown, and (b) this fear produces a desire to have some higher power protect us from unknown (and possibly dangerous) forces. It is argued that if this psychological condition is the source of religious belief, then the claim that God exists is refuted. This argument is also a case of the genetic fallacy. The premises of the argument are logically irrelevant to the conclusion, for even if religious belief does usually originate in a fear of the unknown, this fact alone would not show at all that religious belief is false. There are serious and deep philosophical arguments for the existence of God, developed by such philosophers as Plato, Aristotle, Anselm, Aquinas, Descartes, Locke, Leibniz, Kant, and others, and in contemporary times, by such logicians and philosophers as Kurt Gödel, Richard Swinburne, Alvin Plantinga, Robert Adams, and many others. A reasonable person would have to carefully consider these arguments, on their own merits, including the criticisms that have been made *and the responses to the criticisms*, before concluding with logical justification that God does not exist.

The Appeal to Ignorance (*Argumentum ad Ignorantium*)

In the appeal to ignorance fallacy, someone argues that a proposition is true simply on the grounds that it has not been proven false. For example, suppose a believer in UFOs argues, "It is reasonable to believe in UFOs because nobody has proven there aren't any." Or, "I believe in astrology; after all, it has not been disproved."

We must here state a qualification. In some cases, *if* something were true, evidence of its truth would exist and be known. In such a case, the absence of evidence for the proposition is indeed evidence of its falsity. For instance, a teacher might argue, "If an elephant were in this classroom, we would be very much aware of it. So, because we have no evidence of an elephant in this classroom, there probably isn't one here." This is not a fallacious appeal to ignorance.

Courts of law present another typical exception. In a court of law, the defendant is considered innocent until proven guilty. In the absence of admissible evidence of the defendant's guilt, he or she is indeed considered not guilty. This inference, that the defendant is not guilty because he has not been proven guilty, is not a fallacious argument—assuming the legal principle that a person is legally innocent until proven guilty in a court of law. Notice that we have not been defining these fallacies in terms of pure, abstract logical form alone; content and context matter. That is why these are the "informal" fallacies.

The Straw Man Fallacy

Sometimes, when person A criticizes person B's argument, person A first summarizes B's argument because B's argument is too long to present in full. After summarizing the argument, A then criticizes the summarized version of B's argument, rather than B's original argument, and then concludes that B's *original argument* has been refuted. The straw man fallacy is committed when (a) A's summary of B's argument is not a fair representation but instead is a weakened, exaggerated, or distorted version of B's original argument; (b) A attacks only this unfairly summarized version of B's argument (instead of B's original argument); and (c) A concludes that B's *original argument* has been refuted. Not a fair fight.

Poisoning the Well

Poisoning the well occurs when an arguer uses emotionally charged language to bash an argument or position before arguing against it. In other words, you bias the audience against the opposing view before the argument even begins. For instance, at the start of a lecture on the nature of capitalism, suppose an economist begins, "What can we say about this selfish, inhumane system known as capitalism?" Right away, before any evidence has been given, the audience is given a negative image of capitalism. The system won't stand a chance during this lecture. Or, at the start of a lecture on communism, suppose the speaker begins, "What can be said in defense of these violent, bloodthirsty communists?" For the rest of the lecture, people will have this negative image in mind.

Here is an especially tricky version of this fallacy: In a debate, one debater says, "My opponent cannot handle the truth, so after I make my next point, she will certainly object." This "poisons the well," for after the point is made, the opponent is going to be in a real bind. If she objects, as she must, it will look as if she is confirming her opponent's prediction. If she does not object, it will look as if she is conceding the point. Either way, she will lose. (The best response in such a case is to point out the nature of the fallacy before giving a response to it.)

Fallacies of Little Evidence

Fallacies of little evidence traditionally are fallacies that present little evidence whatsoever for their conclusion; moreover, any evidence that is presented is flawed evidence.

The Fallacy of Weak Analogy

In the fallacy of weak analogy, an analogical argument is presented, but the analogy is not strong enough to support the conclusion. (The next chapter discusses the nature of analogical argument in detail.) Consider the following example:

> We must force people to believe in the true religion, just as we must force a
> suicidal person away from the edge of a cliff.

Now, most of us agree that a suicidal person might rightly be forced away from the edge of a cliff. However, this argument is fallacious, for there is little similarity—analogy—between forcing a suicidal person away from the edge of a cliff and forcing someone to believe the "true" religion. In the face of weak analogies, we sometimes say, "You're mixing apples with oranges."

During the Vietnam War, when student radicals protested both the war and capitalism, I once heard a speaker from the Progressive Labor Party (a pro-Mao group) argue that we shouldn't criticize Mao Tse-tung for having killed millions of political opponents while building his communist society in China, for "you have to break a few eggs in order to make an omelet." His argument was apparently that just as there's nothing wrong with breaking a few eggs to make an omelet in the morning, there's nothing wrong with killing a few million political opponents to build a communist society. His argument was fallacious because killing human beings isn't very much like breaking a few eggs for your morning omelet. Is it?

The Fallacy of Accident

Most general principles or rules are not meant to be applied in *literally* every case; there are usually exceptions. In this fallacy, a general rule or principle is applied in a situation, but the rule was not intended for the situation; the situation is an accepted *exception* to the general rule. For example, we all know that one must not shout "Fire!" in a crowded theater. The reason is that someone might get trampled to death. However, in the following situation, Joe is definitely taking the rule too far:

> Jefferson High is putting on its annual play, *Don't Shout "Fire" in a Crowded Theater*. The purpose of the play is to explain to everybody the dangers of shouting "Fire!" in a crowded theater. It is the final night of the play, everyone is in a festive mood, and the theater is crowded. The climactic moment occurs when one of the characters in the play, Rita Schmuck, stands in the middle of the stage and shouts "Fire!" It is all part of the plot, but her shining moment in high school play history is ruined when Joe Blow stands up and, at the top of his lungs, shouts, "Hey, you are not allowed to shout 'Fire' in a crowded theater!" Joe has committed the fallacy of accident. The rule was not meant to be applied in such a case; the case is an accepted exception!

The No True Scotsman Fallacy

Some fallacies have cute names. In this fallacy, a person arbitrarily defines away any possibility of counterevidence to his own pet theory, thus ensuring that his theory will never be refuted, as illustrated in the following dialogue.

Joe: No true Scotsman is Catholic. They are all Protestant.
Rita: But our friend Scotty McCoy is Catholic, and he is a Scot.
Joe: Scotty is Catholic? Then he's no true Scotsman! For a *real* Scot would not be Catholic!

No possible evidence is going to shake Joe's belief that no Scot is a Catholic; he will go on believing this for the rest of his life.

The Appeal to Questionable Authority (*Argumentum ad Verecundiam*)

Sometimes we base a conclusion on the testimony of a recognized authority on some subject, and this is not always a bad thing to do; for instance, "That chemical is a poison, for Dr. Brown says so, and he's a recognized expert on poisons." This type of reasoning can produce a strong argument if the authority is trustworthy and if the authority knows a lot about the matter at issue. In such a case, the authority has credibility and the reasoning is certainly not fallacious. However, if someone attempts to support a claim by appealing to an authority when the authority is not trustworthy, or when the authority is ignorant on the subject at hand, or when the authority is prejudiced, or when the authority is unqualified to speak on the matter (e.g., the issue lies outside her field of competence), or when the authority has a motive to lie, then the *ad verecundiam* fallacy is committed. Advertising sometimes involves an ad verecundiam fallacy. For example:

> Ashley Greene says I should buy brand X bread, therefore, brand X it is.

> Kobe Bryant says brand X cereal is healthy. So, I am going to buy it.

These are ad verecundiam fallacies, for the famous personalities just mentioned are not experts or authorities on food.

However, the following two arguments avoid the ad verecundiam fallacy because Ashley Greene does know a lot about acting and Kobe Bryant knows a lot about basketballs:

> Ashley Greene endorses the Ace School of Acting, so that is a good reason to attend the school.

> Kobe Bryant says Wilson makes good basketballs. So their basketballs are probably pretty good.

The Fallacy of Hasty Generalization

Archie Bunker: You can't trust any of them type of people.
Michael (Meathead): How do you know, Archie?
Archie Bunker: When I was a kid, a family of them lived down the street and they was all no good.

Archie has jumped to a conclusion a little too quickly here. Certainly more evidence is required before asserting such a conclusion. This is an example of hasty generalization.

The False Cause Fallacy

False cause fallacies are grouped into two important types, both known by their Latin names. In a *post hoc ergo propter hoc* ("after this, therefore because of this") fallacy, someone concludes that A caused B simply on the grounds that A happened before B. For example, suppose that every time Joe plays pickle ball, he eats an apple before the game. Most of the time, his team wins. He concludes that eating the apple magically helps his team win. This is a post hoc fallacy, because the mere fact that B happened after A does not prove that A *caused* B.

In a *non causa pro causa* ("not the cause for the cause") fallacy, someone claims that A is the cause of B, when in fact (a) A is not the cause of B; but (b) the mistake is not based merely on one thing coming after another thing. One version of this fallacy is the fallacy of accidental correlation. Someone concludes that A is the cause of B simply on the grounds that A and B are correlated. For example, at ocean beaches and lakes there is a statistical correlation between ice cream sales and drownings. When ice cream sales are up, so are drownings, and when they are down, so are drownings. Suppose someone argues, on the basis of this correlation alone, without any additional evidence, that ice cream sales cause people to drown. This would be the fallacy of accidental correlation. We should not conclude, from the correlation alone, that ice cream sales cause drownings (nor that drownings cause ice cream sales). Investigation would reveal that there is a third factor at work, a factor behind both ice cream sales and drowning, an underlying factor causing both ends of the correlation: the presence of sunshine. Sunshine encourages people to swim and it also encourages people to eat ice cream.

> **Lesson:** The mere fact that A and B are correlated over time does not *alone* show that A caused B or that B caused A. It might be that one is the cause of the other, or it might be that a third factor is the cause of both.

In other cases, the non causa pro causa fallacy might involve an oversimplified claim of causation. Usually this happens when someone selects and focuses on one cause out of many causal factors, and then treats this as the *sole* cause, ignoring other relevant factors. For example, a riot occurs on a college campus and several fraternity members are involved. The police chief ignores all other factors and focuses blame only on the fraternity brothers. This would be a fallacy if other factors and individuals were ignored in a "rush to judgment." A theory that assigns all blame to one factor is sometimes called a *silver bullet theory*. It might also be called a *magic bullet theory*.

The Slippery Slope Fallacy

In the slippery slope fallacy, also known as the domino argument, someone objects to a position P on the grounds that P will set off a chain reaction leading to a bad result; however, no good reason is given for supposing the chain reaction leading to the bad result will actually occur. Metaphorically, the idea is that if we adopt a certain position, we will start sliding down a slippery slope and we won't be able to stop until we slide all the way to the bottom (where the bad result lies in wait). Thus, it is better to not take the first step. A popular form of this reasoning is expressed in the adage, "Give 'em an inch and they'll take a mile."

For example, at a meeting of the Social Sciences division of Harmony Community College, the classified staff asks if classified employees can have their own coffee-break room. But the economics professor, Professor McScrooge, argues, "If we give them their own room, the next thing you know, they'll be asking for their own exercise room, then they'll want a sauna, then a hot tub, and a tanning salon, then a day spa, and before you know it, they will be working about two hours per day." This is an unwarranted slippery slope.

The slippery slope fallacy has also been called the fallacy of the camel's back because it reminds us of the old story of the straw that broke the camel's back. The president of the Society for the Prevention of Cruelty to Camels argues thus: We cannot place even one straw on a camel, for if we are justified in adding one straw on his back, we are justified in placing a straw on top of the first straw, and if we are justified in adding the second straw, we are justified in adding a straw on top of that, and so on, and we won't be able to stop until we eventually place "the straw that breaks the camel's back." But it is wrong to hurt an animal. So, not even one straw can be placed on a camel's back.

The Fallacy of False Dilemma

In the fallacy of false dilemma, someone assumes that only two alternatives exist with respect to some matter, rules out one of the two, and then concludes in favor of the other alternative, when in fact more alternatives exist but they haven't been considered. Here are some examples:

> You either hate America or you love her. You obviously don't love America, so you hate America.

> Either we see the movie or we stay home. You obviously don't want to stay home. So let's see the movie.

> Everyone is either an agent or a victim. You are not an agent, so you must be a victim.

The Fallacy of Suppressed Evidence

When the arguer leaves out evidence that would count heavily against the conclusion of his or her argument, the fallacy of suppressed evidence is committed. For example:

> Car salesman: This car was driven by a little old lady who only drove it to church on Sundays. It's a great buy! (The rest of the story: Her grandson has been driving it for the past year and has totaled it twice.)

> Politician: I voted for bill X. (Unstated fact: He voted against it on ten previous votes and only voted for it this time because of the upcoming election.)

The Fallacy of Special Pleading

In the fallacy of special pleading, an arguer applies a principle to someone else's case but makes a special exception for her own case. For example, an official of political party X argues, "The other party takes special-interest money, so join our party instead." What the official doesn't mention is that her party also takes special-interest money. Or a communist activist argues against a right-wing dictator, saying of the dictator, "He jails and tortures his political opponents and outlaws political dissent." What he does not mention is that communist dictators do the same thing.

Fallacies of Language

The informal fallacies placed in the category of **fallacies of language** involve a serious misuse of language.

The Fallacy of Equivocation

The fallacy of **equivocation** begins when the arguer uses a particular word or phrase with one meaning at one place in an argument and then uses the same word or phrase with another meaning later in the argument. A fallacy results if the premises are true on one interpretation of the word but not on the other, and the conclusion follows only from the other meaning. We do not normally allow the meaning of a word or phrase to shift within an argument. If the listener fails to notice the shift in meaning, she might unwittingly accept the conclusion when she actually should not. For example, the following (silly) argument commits the fallacy of equivocation:

> Sugar is an important chemical constituent of your body, so, eating candy and food that is loaded with sugar can't harm your body.

This is a fallacy because the form of sugar that is a key chemical constituent of your body is different from the form of sugar in a candy bar. The premise is talking about one kind of sugar and the conclusion is talking about a different kind, although the listener might not realize it. The premise is true if "sugar" means one thing, and the conclusion is true if "sugar" means something else. The meaning of the word *sugar* must shift if the argument is to have both a true premise and a true conclusion. Without such a shift, either the argument has a false premise or it is invalid. That's equivocation.

When someone gives an argument, we normally suppose his or her words retain a constant meaning throughout. In the case of equivocation, if someone thinks that the conclusion is actually proven by the premise, the person has not noticed the shift in meaning. Consider this argument:

1. A person ought to do what is right.
2. I have a right to eat unhealthy foods.
3. So, I ought to eat unhealthy foods.

The shift in meaning occurs with the word *right*. That which is "right" is one thing, but a "right" possessed by a person is another thing entirely. If *right* is given a constant meaning throughout the argument, the argument is faulty. Someone would consider the conclusion proven only if she did not notice that the meaning has shifted. Having noted the meaning shift, she would also note that the premise and the conclusion are really talking about two different things. If the meaning of *right* is not allowed to shift during the argument, either the argument has a false premise or it is invalid. Notice that in a fallacy of equivocation, the two meanings must be closely related if the shift in meaning is to fool anyone. Here are a few more examples of the fallacy:

1. Only man is rational.
2. No woman is a man.
3. So, no women are rational.

1. The legislature can revoke laws.
2. The law of gravity is a law.
3. So, the legislature can revoke gravity and we'll all be able to float through the air.

1. You believe in the miracles of modern science.
2. So you do believe in miracles.
3. You should therefore believe in the miracles of the Bible.

The Fallacy of Amphiboly

A sentence is amphibolous if (a) it can be interpreted in more than one way, and (b) because of the grammatical structure of the sentence, it is unclear which meaning is intended. An example of **amphiboly** is the following sentence, which appeared at the start of a newspaper article: "Police went to the home where they shot the entire family." Did the police kill everyone? Here is another example. Captain Spaulding, the great African explorer, once described an encounter with an elephant thus: "The other morning I got up and shot an elephant in my pajamas." (However, after saying this, he removed the amphiboly by adding, "How he got in my pajamas I'll never know!")

In an amphibolous argument, a premise or conclusion is ambiguous because of its grammatical construction. One interpretation makes the statement true, the other makes it false. If the ambiguous statement is interpreted one way, the premises are true but the conclusion is false. If the ambiguous statement is interpreted the other way, the premise is false but perhaps the conclusion is true. The meaning must shift if the argument is to go from a true premise to a true conclusion. Now, when someone gives an argument, we normally suppose his or her words retain a constant meaning throughout the whole process. Either way we interpret the ambiguous sentence, the argument is defective.

Here is an example. Imagine that a person's legal will states, "I leave my car and my dog to Ann and to Bob." The attorney concludes that Ann gets the car and Bob gets the dog. Or, Jethro Bodine is on his way to Greenwich Village to have a look at the Empire State Building. Why does he expect to find it there? He gives this argument: "The tour guide said that standing in Greenwich Village, the Empire State Building could easily be seen. The Empire State Building therefore must be in Greenwich Village."

A famous example of amphiboly is found in Herodotus's *Histories*. Croesus, the King of Lydia, was thinking of going to war against Cyrus, the king of the Persians. Because the Oracle of Delphi was known to be wise, Croesus asked the oracle, "Should

I go to war?" The oracle replied, "If Croesus goes to war with Cyrus, he will destroy a mighty kingdom." Croesus went to war, certain of victory. However, he was defeated by Cyrus. After the battle, Cyrus spared Croesus's life, and Croesus asked the Oracle for an explanation. The reply was as brief as the original revelation: "In going to war, you did indeed destroy a mighty kingdom: your own."

The Fallacy of Composition

In the fallacy of composition, someone assumes, without justification, that what is true of a *part* of a whole must also be true of the *whole*. For example, after learning about the individual members of a string quartet, someone reasons:

> Each member of the quartet is a good musician, so, the quartet as a whole must be a good string quartet.

The problem is that although each individual member might be a good musician, it could be that the quartet as a whole might not be very good. Perhaps they won't play well together.

Suppose A, B, and C are reporters who have never met each other. The news editor reasons as follows:

> A is a happy person. B is a happy person. C is a happy person. So, if we put them all together on assignment overseas, they will make a happy team.

The problem is that each person might individually be happy, but when combined in a group, the individuals might not be happy at all. Similarly, someone might argue the following:

> Each of these basketball players is an excellent athlete, so, the team must be an excellent team.

Each player might indeed be excellent, but they might function poorly together as a group.

Advertisers sometimes encourage people to commit the fallacy of composition when they divide a large price into many small monthly payments and then focus only on the size (not the number) of the monthly payments. For instance, after watching an ad on TV, Pat thinks, "That huge exercise set is only $19.95 per month. That's not very much for such a big piece of equipment. Maybe we'd better buy it."

The Fallacy of Division

The fallacy of division is the logical reverse of the composition fallacy. In this fallacy, someone assumes, without justification, that what is true of the *whole* must be true of the *parts*. Here are some examples.

- Wilbur is on vacation and sees the biggest hotel he has ever seen in his life: "Wow. The hotel is huge, so the rooms must be big rooms."
- Fonebone buys an expensive new car. When the door handle breaks, he reasons: "This car is expensive, so each part must be expensive."
- The average household has 1.6 cars. So the Jones household must have 1.6 cars.
- Self-identified liberals earn 6% more than self-identified conservatives. Joe is an outspoken conservative and Jan is a proud liberal, so Jan must make 6% more than Joe.

In these cases, someone is assuming that because the whole has a particular property, each part must have that property as well. This is the fallacy of division.

Exercise 32.1   For each fallacy listed, make up an argument that commits the particular fallacy. Provide some context for each argument.

1. The petitio principii fallacy
2. The red herring fallacy
3. The argumentum ad misericordiam fallacy
4. The abusive ad hominem fallacy
5. The circumstantial ad hominem fallacy
6. The Tu Quoque fallacy
7. The genetic fallacy
8. The ad populum fallacy
9. The argumentum ad baculum
10. Poisoning the well
11. The argumentum ad ignorantium
12. The Ignoratio elenchi fallacy

Exercise 32.2   Identify the fallacy in each of the following.

1. A mom tells her child why the child should not take drugs, and this is the reply: "But you took drugs as a kid, so why should I listen to your argument?"
2. That book was written by a radical, atheist, communist sympathizer. Don't buy it.
3. A scientist who works at the Tobacco Institute, an industry-funded research think tank, argues that cigarettes are actually good for you. A critic counters, "That's a bunch of baloney. Do you know where he works? The

Tobacco Institute. Look who is paying the salaries of their researchers. They probably got a raise for saying cigarettes are healthy."

4. Joe says, "Hydrogen burns." Pete replies, "No it doesn't. Give me an argument." Joe responds, "Okay. Hydrogen is combustible, therefore, it burns."

5. The world is good because it was made by a good God. How, you ask, do we know God is good? Look at this world! It is such a good place that the God who made it must be good.

6. If you are a true-blue, loyal American, you will support this candidate.

7. If I don't earn at least B in this class, my parents won't pay for school and I'll be kicked out of the house. I think I should be allowed to do extra credit.

8. Logic is absolutely necessary for organized thinking. Anyone who wants to think in an organized way must study logic.

9. Mafia goon: It would be smart to buy our protection policy. It's only $200 a month, and it will save you thousands of dollars a month in damage to your facility.

10. I really think Joe should get the job. He lost all his money investing in a fraudulent land deal, his kids are hungry, and his wife will leave him if he doesn't find work soon.

11. Fred says we should increase spending on welfare. But he is a welfare caseworker who makes his living dispensing welfare money to poor people. Can't you see he is advocating this because he will benefit? His argument should be rejected.

12. You should read the new novel, *Love on Main Street*. It's a bestseller, and everyone will be talking about it at lunch next week.

13. Our company stands accused of polluting the river, but the Army Corps of Engineers has been causing all sorts of damage to the river for decades.

14. Nobody has ever proven UFOs don't exist, so we must suppose the sightings are legitimate.

15. I am sure he respects me, because he told me so, and he wouldn't lie to someone he respects.

16. You say your bird can sing, but no bird can sing. So your bird doesn't sing.

17. We criticize the Soviets for repressing freedom of speech, but we don't allow people to yell "Fire!" in a crowded theater.

18. Dr. Smith says smoking is bad, but he chain-smokes, so his arguments are no darned good.

19. Professor Levy's argument for increasing teacher pay is not worth listening to. She's a teacher, so she'll benefit from such a policy.

20. The African diplomat has no business criticizing America for its race relations. Africa has intertribal conflicts so severe that literally millions of Africans have been killed by other Africans just in the past few decades.

21. That man's argument against rent control is faulty—he's a landlord who will benefit if rent control is not instituted.

22. That man's argument for rent control is faulty—he's a renter who will benefit if rent control is instituted.

23. Nobody has ever proven that a fetus has rights. So a fetus does not have rights.

24. Nobody has ever proven that there is no such thing as ESP. So, ESP is a real phenomenon.

Exercise 32.3   For each of the following fallacies, make up an argument that commits the particular fallacy listed. Provide some context for each argument.

1. The ad verecundiam fallacy
2. The fallacy of false dilemma
3. The fallacy of weak analogy
4. The fallacy of accident
5. The fallacy of hasty generalization
6. The fallacy of post hoc ergo propter hoc
7. The fallacy of non causa pro causa
8. The fallacy of special pleading
9. The straw man fallacy
10. The fallacy of suppressed evidence
11. The slippery slope fallacy

Exercise 32.4   Identify the fallacy in each of the following.

1. Doctor Smith is a hypocrite, for he kills rats in his laboratory, and doctors take an oath to protect life.
2. It is apparently okay to speed, for ambulances can speed.
3. Professor McOrnery: I do not allow any questions in class. Here is why: If I allow one student to ask a question, someone else will have a question; if someone else asks a question, another will, and pretty soon I'll be doing nothing but answering questions.
4. We should not have a student government at this school. After all, at home, we do not allow teenagers to run the family.

5. Actor Joe Blow says nuclear power is dangerous. So, it is dangerous.

6. Watching television cannot be harmful to children. After all, it keeps them out of mischief—when they are watching it, they aren't out on the street.

7. I always rub my lucky quarter before a game. Most of the time I win after I do that. It brings me good luck.

8. Drinking milk with bourbon cures the flu. Every time I've had the flu, I drink milk mixed with bourbon, and my condition improves within a day or two.

9. It doesn't matter that you had to stop on the way to rescue someone who was drowning. You promised to meet me for coffee at six, you're late, and one should not break one's promises.

10. America. Love it or leave it. You won't love it, so, you should leave it.

11. There are only two types of people in this world: Those who work and those who sponge off those who work. So people who don't work are sponges.

12. You are either for us or agin' us. You aren't for us, so, you're agin' us.

13. Because it is right to speak the truth, it is right to tell Martha that she looks ridiculous in that dress, even if this is her 80th birthday.

14. We have to buy a car. We'll buy either an expensive one or a cheap one. We can't afford to buy an expensive one, so we'll buy that cheap one for $500.

15. The Constitution guarantees freedom of speech. Therefore, it was okay that we broke into the meeting and began screaming obscenities at the top of our lungs.

16. I'll never go to another doctor. I've been to two, and they didn't help me at all.

17. Tests on Mr. Brown have not found any physical cause of his illness, so it must be psychological.

18. It's against the law to cut someone with a sharp instrument. Dr. Verrier, the heart surgeon, should be arrested.

19. The Constitution guarantees the free exercise of religion. Our religion, which is a revival of the Aztec religion and practices mass human sacrifice, should therefore be protected by law.

20. I ate your sandwich at noon and I got sick at three, so your sandwich made me sick.

21. It is illegal to go through a red light, so that ambulance should get a ticket for going through that light.

22. Either you support welfare or you want the poor to die. You wouldn't want the poor to die, so you must support welfare.

23. Four local teenagers were arrested for selling drugs. Teenagers are nothing but a bunch of drug-crazed thugs.

24. Animal-rights activists say dogs and cats have rights. But if we grant them that premise, the next thing they'll argue is that birds, trees, fleas, and mosquitoes have rights, and mosquito spray will become an illegal substance. We therefore must not agree that dogs and cats have rights.

25. The larger the city, the more churches. The larger the city, the more prostitution. So, churches cause prostitution.

26. Humans are similar in many ways to cows and chickens: similar hearts, similar lungs, and so on. Humans have a right to life. So cows and chickens do, too.

27. The constitution guarantees freedom of speech, so I was within my rights telling this little old lady I would sell her the Brooklyn Bridge for $1,000.

Exercise 32.5 For each fallacy here, make up an argument that commits the particular fallacy listed. Provide some context for each argument.

1. The fallacy of equivocation
2. The composition fallacy
3. The fallacy of amphiboly
4. The fallacy of division

Exercise 32.6 Name the fallacy in each of the following.

1. Modern societies have conflicts. So the people within them must have conflicts.
2. Our team is strong. Pat is on our team, so, Pat must be strong.
3. This house must have a huge living room, for look how big the house is!
4. The company has performed poorly, so, the employees must have performed poorly.
5. Chemists have studied free radicals. John is a chemist, so, John has studied free radicals.
6. Captain Spaulding, the great African explorer, got up in the morning and saw an elephant in his pajamas. So elephants wear pajamas.
7. The Bullitt Foundation is generous, so the people working there are generous.
8. The party was wild. Joe was at the party. So Joe was wild.

9. The consumer price index rose last month, so that stereo you are going to buy has gone up in price over the past month.

10. College grads earn 30% more than high school grads, so, Pat must earn 30% more than Jan, for Pat went to college and Jan only went through high school.

11. Each person in that mob is a decent person who normally wouldn't hurt anyone, so, the mob won't hurt anyone.

12. This first chapter is long, so the book must be long.

13. A slice of stale bread is better than nothing. Nothing is better than God. A slice of stale bread is better than God.

14. Pete removed his computer from the shipping crate and threw it in the garbage. He must not have liked the computer, because he threw it away.

15. Encouraging people to take the bus won't cut down on energy use, for a bus uses more energy than a car.

16. Because salt is not poisonous, the constituents of salt, sodium, and chlorine, are not poisonous.

17. Father to son: "It's wrong to steal." Son: "But Dad, you watch baseball and they steal bases."

18. If we really believed in liberty, we would tear down all the prisons, for prisoners don't have liberty.

19. It is morally right to give food to starving families. Our family is always starving by the time we sit down at the table. Therefore, people should give our family food.

20. Every item of clothing she is wearing is in style. Therefore, her outfit is in style.

21. Nobody can read all of Shakespeare in a day, so, nobody can read *Hamlet* in a day, because it is part of Shakespeare's works.

22. America is a wealthy nation, so, Jim, who is an American, must be wealthy.

23. I can lift each individual part of my car, so, I can lift my whole car.

24. America is 10% atheist. So, your family of 10 must contain one atheist.

25. Half of America is Protestant and half is Catholic. So Sue must be half Protestant and half Catholic.

26. Every member of the Young Democrats Club is under 20. So the club must be under 20 years old, and it was founded less than 20 years ago.

27. Each brick in that house weighs less than 10 pounds, so the house weighs less than 10 pounds.

28. There are more cats than dogs, so cats consume more food than dogs, therefore Felix the cat eats more than Abner the dog.

29. Water will quench your thirst. Water is composed of hydrogen and oxygen. So hydrogen will quench your thirst.

30. The average family has 2.3 children. So the Smith family must have 2.3 kids.

Glossary

Amphiboly A sentence is an amphiboly if (a) it can be interpreted in more than one way, and (b) because of the grammatical structure of the sentence, it is not clear which meaning is intended.

Equivocation The act of using a word in one sense in one part of an argument and in another sense in another part of the argument. A word is used equivocally in a passage if it has one meaning in one place but a different meaning in another place.

Fallacies of language Informal fallacies that involve a misuse of language.

Fallacies of no evidence Informal fallacies that present no evidence whatsoever.

Fallacies of little evidence Informal fallacies that present some evidence, but the evidence is too little or is flawed in some way.

Fallacy A defective argument that nevertheless can appear to some to be a correct argument.

Formal fallacies Arguments that contain errors that are due to the form or abstract logical structure of the argument alone. The flaw can be defined without reference to the content or context of the argument.

Informal fallacies Arguments that contain flaws that are not simply due to the abstract logical form of the argument. To determine the flaw we must look at the content and context of the argument.

33 The Varieties of Inductive Reasoning « « ‹

Recall the distinction between inductive and deductive reasoning. A deductive argument aims to show that its conclusion must be true. In contrast, an inductive argument is intended only to show that its conclusion is probably true, not that its conclusion must be true or is guaranteed. A deductive argument has an air of definiteness—the premises, it is claimed, guarantee the conclusion. If the premises are true, it is claimed, we can be certain the conclusion is true. On the other hand, inductive arguments claim no such certainty or finality—they leave open the possibility that the conclusion might be false and only claim the conclusion is probably true. However, although the conclusion of an inductive argument might not be conclusively shown, it can nevertheless be made probable, likely, or plausible, and on that ground might be reasonable to accept.

In this chapter, we examine five very common types of inductive reasoning: analogical arguments, enumerative induction, inference to the best explanation, the confirmation and disconfirmation of hypotheses, and the standard scientific tests for the causes of things. Almost all inductive reasoning in science, in the courtroom, and in everyday life falls into one of the argument types that we examine in this chapter.

Analogical Reasoning

An **analogy** is a resemblance or similarity between two things. To draw an analogy between X and Y is to cite respects in which the two are similar. Here's an example of an analogy: Ollie's symptoms are similar to Mollie's symptoms. Both have no appetite, both have a temperature of 101 degrees, both feel nauseated, and both have red splotches on their faces.

An **analogical argument** begins with the assertion that two or more things, call them A and B, have many features in common. After asserting an analogy between A and B, the arguer claims that A has a particular feature X and that B is not known *not* to have the feature. The conclusion will be that B probably also has the feature X. The driving idea is that if A and B are alike in many other ways, they are probably alike with respect to the additional feature X. In short, an analogical argument infers an additional similarity from an already established similarity.

To go back to our example, suppose that after Ollie and Mollie compare their symptoms (no appetite, temperature, red splotches, etc.), Ollie goes to the doctor and is diagnosed with chicken pox. Mollie might naturally conclude that she probably also has chicken pox. Why? Because her symptoms are similar. The fact that Mollie has the same symptoms as Ollie is a good reason to suppose that the cause of her symptoms is probably the same as the cause of Ollie's. This would be an example of analogical reasoning. More formally, Mollie's reasoning can be put this way:

1. Ollie has no appetite, has a temperature of 101 degrees, feels nauseated, and has red splotches on his face.
2. Mollie has no appetite, has a temperature of 101 degrees, feels nauseated, and has red splotches on her face.
3. Ollie's symptoms are caused by chicken pox, and we have no reason to suppose Mollie does not have the pox.
4. Therefore, Mollie's symptoms are probably also caused by chicken pox.

Let us now put this into more formal terms. An analogical argument takes the following general form:

1. A has attributes or characteristics a, b, c, d, e, f.
2. B has attributes or characteristics a, b, c, d, e, f.
3. A also has attribute x.
4. B is not known *not* to have attribute x.
5. So B probably also has attribute x.

Analogical argumentation is an extremely common type of reasoning. In each of the following cases, analogical reasoning is employed.

Monkeys have hearts that are similar to human hearts. Drug X successfully treated heart disease in monkeys. Therefore, drug X will probably treat heart disease in humans.

In the summer of 1964, a bunch of kids went down to the local record store to buy the new Beatles album, *A Hard Day's Night*. They reasoned: The last two Beatles albums were great. *A Hard Day's Night* is a Beatles album, so it probably will be great, too.

Evaluating Analogical Arguments

Analogical arguments, like all inductive arguments, come in degrees: Some are stronger than others and some are weaker. Remember that a strong inductive argument has this feature: If the premises are true, then the conclusion is probably true. In the case of some inductive arguments, the premises, if true, make the conclusion extremely probable. In the case of others, they do not. We judge the strength of an analogical argument on the basis of the following criteria:

1. Generally, the more characteristics in common between the things compared, the stronger the analogy, and thus the stronger the argument.
2. Generally, the more relevant the similar characteristics are to the characteristic mentioned in the conclusion, the stronger the argument.

Comment. What makes a similarity a *relevant* one? There are two ways in which a similarity could be relevant. A characteristic can be *causally* relevant, or it can be *statistically* relevant. In the case of a causally relevant factor, there is a cause-and-effect connection between the possession of the attribute mentioned in the premise and the possession of the characteristic mentioned in the conclusion. In the case of a statistically relevant factor, there is a statistical relationship between the possession of the attribute mentioned in the premise and the possession of the characteristic mentioned in the conclusion.

3. The larger the number of primary analogates, the stronger the argument.

Comment. The **primary analogates** are the objects being compared that appear only in the premises; the **secondary analogate** is the object that also appears in the conclusion. Suppose Rita is trying to decide if she should buy a slice of pizza at Pete's Pizza Place. She reasons, "I know two people who said Pete's has great pizza. Because this is a slice of Pete's pizza, it will probably also be good." This argument is a fairly strong analogical argument. But suppose we alter the argument by changing the premise to "I know six people who said Pete's makes great pizza." The argument now contains six primary analogates, and is obviously stronger.

4. The more diverse or heterogeneous the primary analogates, the stronger the argument, provided that the diversity concerns features unrelated to the feature cited in the conclusion.

Comment. The more diverse the primary analogates, the more likely the pattern is not accidental and thus the more likely the pattern is not unrepresentative of the larger group of things.

5. The larger the number of relevant dissimilarities, the weaker the argument. (This is called the degree of disanalogy.)

Comment. Of course, *irrelevant* dissimilarities do not weaken an argument.

6. Generally, all else being equal, the more specific and definite the conclusion, the weaker the argument; the more general the conclusion, the stronger the argument.

Comment. For example, the conclusion that Jane's car will get exactly 24 miles per gallon is more specific than the prediction that her car will get 20 to 30 miles per gallon. The conclusion that Pete will arrive between 8:00 and 8:15 p.m. is more definite than the prediction that he will arrive between 8:00 and 10:00 p.m. Why is an argument stronger the less specific its conclusion, all else being equal? The more specific the conclusion, the more possible circumstances there are in which the conclusion turns out to be false. But the more circumstances there are in which it turns out to be false, the more chances there are for it to be false and thus the "easier" it is for it to come out false. All of this makes for a weaker argument. Thus, the more general the conclusion (i.e., the less specific or definite the conclusion), the stronger the argument, all else being equal.

For example, consider the following argument:

1. We tested the Jeep six times and got the following results, each on a tank of gas: 28.2 mpg, 28.9 mpg, 26.2 mpg, 24.9 mpg, 29.7 mpg, and 28.6 mpg.
2. Therefore, the Jeep will probably get between 28 and 29 mpg on our next trip.

This is a pretty strong argument. However, if we remove the conclusion and swap it for the following conclusion, the argument is even stronger:

3. Therefore, the Jeep will probably get between 25 and 30 mpg on our next trip.

Analogy and Legal Reasoning

Arguments in courts of law are often analogical. In many types of cases, a judge must follow precedent when issuing a decision. The *Encyclopedia Britannica* defines a legal precedent as "a judgment or decision of a court that is cited in a subsequent dispute as an ... analogy to justify deciding a similar case or point of law in the same manner."[1]

---

[1] Precedent. In Encyclopedia Britannica *Encyclopedia Britannica Ultimate Reference Suite*. (Chicago: Encyclopedia Britannica, 2011).

When a judge makes a decision based on precedent, he or she looks at how similar (analogous) cases in the past were decided and then rules in the same way. The decision in the similar case is treated as a rule to be followed in the case at hand. An attorney in such a case might argue that the present case is analogous to a particular case X—a case that was decided in a way that the attorney believes would be favorable for his or her client, of course. In such a case, the argument would be analogical:

1. Case A was decided in such and such a way.
2. The present case is very similar, for the following reasons . . .
3. Therefore, the present case should be decided in such and such a way as well.

No wonder the Law School Admissions Test (LSAT) includes a big section on analogical reasoning.

Enumerative Induction

Imagine that a rock band has moved into the house next door. Every Wednesday night for the first month they play their music from 6 p.m. until 11 p.m. The bass amp is so powerful it rattles every dish in your house; the singing is so loud your dog howls, and the lead guitarist is so loud it makes your ears hurt. Now it is the first Wednesday of the second month, and it is your turn to host the monthly meeting of your chess club. You conclude that the band next door will be playing again tonight and that the club members will not be happy. Your reasoning is as follows:

1. The band practiced Wednesday night four weeks ago.
2. The band practiced Wednesday night three weeks ago.
3. The band practiced Wednesday night two weeks ago.
4. The band practiced Wednesday night one week ago.
5. Therefore, they will probably practice this Wednesday night.

This is an **enumerative induction**. In such an argument, the premises list or enumerate information about a series of individuals or cases, a pattern is observed, and then a conclusion is drawn that extends the pattern to other individuals, cases, or to a whole group of things. Essentially, this kind of inductive argument begins with a series of observations or cases and then extends the series to new (unobserved) cases. The reasoning is inductive in nature because the argument claims only that the premises make the conclusion probable.

In some enumerative inductions, the premises are about individuals, and the conclusion is about a group as a whole, as in the following argument about cats:

1. Purr Kitty is a cat and likes fried chicken.
2. Baby is a cat and likes fried chicken.
3. Worty is a cat and likes fried chicken.
4. Jinx is a cat and likes fried chicken.
5. Orangie is a cat and likes fried chicken.
6. Therefore, probably all cats like fried chicken.

In some enumerative inductions, the premises provide a listing of cases, but the conclusion is not about all of a group; rather, it is about the next case or the next individual we expect to observe. For instance, someone reasons as follows:

1. The first skateboard rider I saw wore baggy pants.
2. The second skateboard rider I saw wore baggy pants.
3. The third skateboard rider I saw wore baggy pants.
4. The fourth skateboard rider I saw wore baggy pants.
5. Therefore, the next skateboard rider I see will probably be wearing baggy pants.

In some enumerative inductions, the premises are about classes or groups of individuals, and so is the conclusion:

1. All observed tabbies like fried chicken.
2. All observed calicos like fried chicken.
3. All observed Siamese cats like fried chicken.
4. All observed Manx cats like fried chicken.
5. So, probably all cats like fried chicken.

Statistical induction is a special type of enumerative induction. Consider the following example:

We interviewed 100 students at random at the Student Union Building and 80% said they approved of the job the president is doing. We made sure that our sample included students from every group on campus. Therefore, probably 80% of all students on campus approve of the job the President is doing.

Here is one way to state the general form of a statistical induction:

1. N percent of a sample of a group of things have the property P.
2. Therefore, probably N percent of all the members of the group have property P.

The observed members of a group constitute a *sample* of the group if the number observed is less than the group as a whole. In a statistical induction, the premises present information about a sample of a group. On the basis of this, the argument concludes something about the larger group.

The following factors determine the strength of enumerative and statistical inductions.

1. **Sample size**. Generally, the larger the sample is in relation to the group as a whole, the more likely it is that the sample is representative of the group as a whole, and thus the stronger the argument.
2. **Sample variation**. Generally, the more varied or heterogeneous the sample items, the more likely it is that the sample is representative of the group as a whole, and thus the stronger the argument.
3. **Randomness**. Generally, the more random the sample, the stronger the argument.

If a sample is unrepresentative of the whole population, it is a **biased sample**. For example, suppose a group conducts a poll to see how many people in the city of Seattle still believe in God. Five hundred people are interviewed, and 99% say they still believe in God. However, the interviews were all conducted at six Catholic churches after Mass one Sunday. The group concludes that probably 99% of all *Seattleites* believe in God. The people surveyed were Catholics coming out of church, but the conclusion made a claim about all of Seattle. Certainly this is a most unwarranted conclusion. The following argument is stronger:

1. 1,000 people from all walks of life were interviewed.
2. 90% said they believe in God.
3. The interviews were conducted all over the city, at all times of the day, and we made sure that people were chosen randomly and broadly from every age group, ethnic group, and so on.
4. Therefore, probably 90% of all Seattleites believe in God.

In this second argument, the sample is larger, it is more varied, and the members of the sample are chosen in a more random manner. This results in a stronger inductive argument.

Exercise 33.1   Instructions are given in context.

1.   Joe is 55 years old, is 100 pounds overweight, and eats a fast-food diet that includes three Big Macs every day for lunch and usually something like pizza, fish and chips, or deep-fried burritos for dinner each day. Pete is 56, is 108 pounds overweight, and eats a fast-food diet that includes three Whoppers every day for lunch and usually something like a 6-pack of corn dogs, a large plate of deluxe nachos, or a large bag of Cheetos for dinner. Joe just had a heart attack. Therefore, Pete probably will have a heart attack.

   a.   List several irrelevant dissimilarities that would have no bearing on the argument.

   b.   List several additional relevant similarities that would strengthen the argument.

   c.   Change the conclusion so that the argument is weaker.

   d.   Change the conclusion so that the argument is stronger.

   e.   Add a premise that makes the argument stronger.

   f.   Add a premise that makes the argument weaker.

2.   Consider this simple argument: "Professor Smith's Introduction to Logic course last fall was extremely dry and extremely boring. So, his class this fall will be like the previous one—extremely dry and extremely boring." How do the following additional facts bear on this reasoning? Do they make the argument stronger? Weaker? Or do they leave the strength of the argument unaffected? Consider each additional fact separately.

   a.   His class last fall met in room 1408 and this fall it will also meet in 1408.

   b.   Last year's class met on Wednesdays and this year's class will also meet on Wednesdays.

   c.   Last year's class used the text written by Professor Smith himself. So will this year's class.

   d.   Last year's class was held just after lunch. This year's class is at 8:30 in the morning.

   e.   Last year, Professor Smith was going through a divorce. This year, he is through with the divorce and is into the swinging singles scene.

   f.   His class last year was small. His class this year is a large class.

   g.   Since last year, Professor Smith has experienced a religious conversion.

   h.   This year the class will use a new textbook.

   i.   Last year, Smith did not know how to dance. This year Smith is taking swing dancing lessons.

j. We change the conclusion to: His class this year will be very dry and very boring.

k. We change the conclusion to: His class this year will be at least somewhat dry and boring.

3. Brigit has decided to buy a new TV. She reasons: "Susan's RCA has an excellent picture, and Bob's RCA has an excellent picture. So, the RCA that is on sale will have an excellent picture, just like the others." Now, how do the following additional facts bear on the argument? Do they make the argument stronger? Weaker? Or do they leave the strength of the argument unaffected? Consider each additional fact separately.

   a. Brigit lives far out in the country, but Susan and Bob live in the city.

   b. Brigit will watch only what her antenna picks up, but Sue and Bob watch only cable.

   c. Brigit knows three others who own RCA TVs, and all three report good picture quality.

   d. Brigit knows three others, each with RCA TVs, each from a different part of the country, and all report good picture quality.

   e. Brigit revises her conclusion. She concludes that her new set will have at least a decent picture.

   f. The set Brigit plans to buy is like Bob's and Susan's only in two respects: It has the same color cabinet and the same size screen; it turns out not to be an RCA.

   g. Bob and Sue bought their TVs on a Sunday; Brigit plans to buy hers on a weekday.

4. Spuds Fish and Chips, a Seattle "institution" since the 1950s, has decided it needs to hire a new fish buyer. Smith, with a master's degree in fish buying from the University of Washington, is offered the job. Spud's CEO reasons: "The last time we hired a buyer from the UW fish-buying program, he increased business 10% (because he selected such good fish). So Smith should similarly increase business 10% as well." Now, how do the following additional facts bear on the argument? Do they make the argument stronger? Weaker? Or do they leave the strength of the argument unaffected? Consider each additional fact separately.

   a. The previous fish buyer had formerly worked for Skippers Fish and Chips (another Seattle institution) where he had also increased business 10%. However, this will be the new buyer's first job.

   b. Smith previously worked for Ivar's Fish and Chips, where he was fired for buying rotten fish.

c. The old buyer was a philatelist; Smith's hobby is ping pong.

d. The earlier buyer was a workaholic, but the new buyer is a member of Workaholics Anonymous and claims he is a recovering workaholic.

e. Graduates of the UW fish buying program tend to be successful fish buyers.

f. The CEO revises his conclusion to "Smith will likely increase sales by at least 5%."

g. The CEO revises his conclusion to "Smith at least will likely not cause business to drop."

5. Consider this argument: "The Lancaster New Grand Theater is showing a Charlie Chaplin film. I've seen four Charlie Chaplin films and loved all of them. So, I'll love this one just as much." Which of the following, if added to the argument, increase the argument's strength, which decrease it, and which leave it unaffected?

a. All four Charlie Chaplin films that I've seen were comedies; this new film is not a comedy.

b. All four of the previous Charlie Chaplin films were directed by the same director, but this new film has a new director.

c. One of my favorite actors, Joe Blow, was in all four previous Charlie Chaplin films, but he is not in this new one.

d. I saw all four previous films on Wednesdays; this film will be shown on a Saturday.

e. The previous four were watched in a small theater, this will be watched in a large theater.

f. We change the conclusion to "I'll at least like this next film."

6. Here is another short argument: "I've taken three classes from Professor Jones. All were interesting. So, I expect his next course to be like the others—interesting." Which of the following, if added to the argument, increase the argument's strength, which decrease it, and which leave it unaffected?

a. The three previous classes were all in ancient philosophy; this next class is modern philosophy.

b. The previous three were ancient, medieval, and modern philosophy.

c. The previous three classes were all ancient philosophy, which is his specialty. The next class is existentialism, a field he says he dislikes.

d. We change the conclusion to "This class will at least not be boring."

e. All three of the previous classes were in the morning; this next class will be in the evening.

7. Another short argument: "We've always stayed at Bob Newhart's Inn the past 10 years. Each time was wonderful. We expect this visit to be like the others—wonderful." Which of the following, if added to the argument, increase the argument's strength, which decrease it, and which leave it unaffected?

   a. The previous visits were in the fall; this visit will be in the summer.

   b. The Inn has a new manager.

   c. In previous visits, our room had a balcony; this time it is a ground floor room.

   d. On previous visits, we flew; this time we are driving.

   e. The previous visits were three in the fall, three in the winter, and four in the spring.

   f. We change the conclusion to "This visit will at least be tolerable."

   g. They've painted the rooms since we were last there.

   h. On previous visits, our rooms have been in the north section, the south section, the east section, and the west section.

8. One of the most often-discussed philosophical arguments for the existence of God is the teleological argument. In *Dialogues Concerning Natural Religion*, the Scottish philosopher David Hume (1711–1776) summed up the analogical version of the argument in the following words. Evaluate the argument using the principles pertaining to analogical induction.

   > Look round the world: contemplate the whole and every part of it: You will find it to be nothing but one great machine, subdivided into an infinite number of lesser machines, which again admit of subdivisions, to a degree beyond what human senses and faculties can trace and explain. All these various machines, and even their most minute parts, are adjusted to each other with an accuracy, which ravishes into admiration all men, who have ever contemplated them. The curious adapting of means to ends, throughout all nature, resembles exactly, though it much exceeds, the productions of human contrivance; of human designs, thought, wisdom, and intelligence. Since therefore the effects resemble each other, we are led to infer, by all the rules of analogy, that the causes also resemble; and that the Author of Nature is somewhat similar to the mind of man; though possessed of much larger faculties, proportioned to the grandeur of the work, which he has executed. By this argument . . . do we prove at once the existence of a Deity, and his similarity to human mind and intelligence.

Exercise 33.2   Instructions are given in context.

1. The Bards, a Seattle rock band, need a new sound system. The system must handle four singers, and it must be powerful enough to fill up a school gym. Friends in another band, the Jimmy Hannah and the Dynamics, have a brand Z sound system that works well, so the Bards decide to buy a brand Z system. They reason that the brand Z sound system worked fine for the Dynamics, so it will probably work fine for the Bards. For each additional item below, would the addition of the item strengthen the argument, weaken the argument, or leave the strength of the argument unchanged? Consider each addition separately from the rest.

   a. The Dynamics regularly play in school gyms.

   b. The Bards know another band that uses and likes the same brand sound system.

   c. The Dynamics have used their sound system in many different settings and it has always worked well.

   d. The conclusion is changed to: "The sound system will work perfectly."

   e. The conclusion is broadened to: "The sound system will be adequate although not always perfect."

   f. The Bards play rock 'n' roll, but the Dynamics actually play only new wave polka music at senior centers.

2. On a visit to the Kingdom of Ogg on the Isle of Grog, all 10 adults observed at dinner drank coffee with their meal. The conclusion drawn is that all adult Oggians drink coffee with dinner. Does the suggested alteration strengthen the argument, weaken it, or does it leave the argument unchanged? Consider each alteration independently of the others.

   a. All 10 observed adults were adult men.

   b. Five of 10 adults were women and five were men.

   c. All Oggians were observed on a Sunday.

   d. We change the conclusion to: "All Oggians drink coffee."

   e. The 10 adults were observed over a period of seven different days.

   f. All of the adult men observed wore unusually long beards, whereas no other Oggians wore beards.

   g. We change the conclusion to: "All adult Oggians drink coffee with their meals."

   h. We change the conclusion to: "All Oggians drink coffee with their dinners."

i. We change the conclusion to "Many Oggians drink coffee with their dinners."

3. You take your car to Latka's Total Car Care on three different occasions, and each time your car is fixed. You conclude that this time your car will again be fixed. Does the alteration strengthen or weaken the original argument? Or does it leave the argument's strength unaffected?

   a. The earlier three visits were for transmission work; this one is for body work.

   b. The shop has a new manager.

   c. You have actually taken your car in eight times.

   d. The earlier visits were for mechanical work, but this time the problem is electrical.

   e. The earlier visits were for your Ford Escort; this time you have a new car, a Jeep.

   f. The earlier visits were for 1960s models; now you have a 1998 model.

   g. You conclude instead that your car will probably be returned in absolutely perfect condition.

   h. You conclude instead that you will probably be satisfied.

4. You buy four sandwiches at Doug's Deli and all four are awful. A week later, you decide to go back, but you figure that the next sandwich you buy will probably also be awful. Does the alteration strengthen or weaken the original argument? Or does it leave the argument's strength unaffected?

   a. All four awful sandwiches were made by the same guy.

   b. The four awful sandwiches were made by four different employees.

   c. All four were bought on a Sunday; this visit will be on a Tuesday.

   d. All four were ham, this will be turkey.

   e. You conclude instead that the next sandwich won't be good.

   f. The four awful sandwiches were made by Doug himself.

   g. The four awful sandwiches were made by a new employee.

   h. The Health Department has since inspected and fined Doug's Deli.

5. One hundred college students from four colleges were surveyed, and 90% approved of the president's performance. Does the alteration strengthen or weaken the original argument? Or does it leave the argument's strength unaffected?

   a. The colleges were all Catholic colleges.

   b. Actually, only 10 students were surveyed.

   c. 1,000 students were surveyed.

d. All students surveyed were Capricorns.

e. All surveyed had grades of 3.8 or above.

f. Ninety percent of those surveyed said they regularly read novels.

g. Those surveyed were freshmen, sophomores, juniors, and seniors.

h. Those surveyed were seniors only.

i. Those surveyed were from large cities only.

j. Those surveyed were from the South only.

k. Those surveyed were from all regions of country.

l. All those surveyed like Mars bars.

m. We change the conclusion to: "Exactly 90% approve."

n. We change the conclusion to: "At least 70% approve."

o. We change the conclusion to: "The majority approve."

6. Consider this argument: "All my cats like fried chicken. So, all cats like fried chicken." Does the alteration strengthen or weaken the original argument? Or does it leave the argument's strength unaffected?

a. I actually only have one cat.

b. I have seven cats.

c. All my cats are Manx cats.

d. One is a calico, one is a rag-doll cat, one is Siamese, and one is a tabby.

e. All my cats were strays.

f. I lied. I have no cats.

g. I've always been allergic to cats.

h. I change the conclusion to: "Most cats like fried chicken."

i. I change the conclusion to: "Most cats like chicken."

j. I change the conclusion to: "Most cats like meat."

k. I change the conclusion to: "Most cats like fried food."

7. Your school's football team has played 10 games so far this season and has won 9. You conclude that it will probably win the next game. Does the alteration strengthen or weaken the original argument? Or does it leave the argument's strength unaffected?

a. It rained hard during the other 10 games. Sun is forecast for this game.

b. The next team you play has only played one game this year.

c. You won four games instead of nine.

d. Your star quarterback broke his leg snowboarding.

e. The next team has played 20 games and won 20.

f. The previous 10 games were at home, but the next is across the state.

g. The previous five games were all against the same team.

h. The next team you will play won every game by at least a 20-point margin.

i. Your team has new uniforms.

8. Pete and Sally have flown from Kodiak to Seattle 10 times. Each trip has taken three hours. They conclude that the next flight will probably also take three hours. Does the alteration strengthen or weaken the original argument? Or does it leave the argument's strength unaffected?

a. Actually, Pete and Sally have made more than 100 trips, each lasting three hours.

b. Actually, they've only made a total of four trips.

c. They conclude instead that the next flight will take at least three hours.

d. They conclude instead that next flight will take at least two and one-half hours.

e. They conclude that the next trip will take three to five hours.

f. The previous flights were on Alaska Airlines; the next flight is on a new airline.

g. The previous flights were in winter, but the next flight will be in summer.

h. Meals were served on all previous flights. The next flight will have no meals.

i. The previous flights were all on 727s, and the next flight will be on a 747.

j. The previous flights had strong headwinds; this flight will have no headwind.

Explanatory Reasoning or "Inference to the Best Explanation"

An act of "explanatory reasoning" occurs when we begin with one or more facts in need of explanation and then decide what to infer by thinking about what would *best explain* those facts. In philosophy, an argument made up of explanatory reasoning is usually called an **inference to the best explanation**. The American logician Charles Sanders Peirce (1839–1914), the first to systematically analyze this general form of reasoning, called the arguments that instantiate it *abductive* arguments. Here we shall call all such arguments *explanatory arguments*. An explanatory argument typically takes the following form:

1. Begin with one or more facts in need of explanation.

2. Critically examine as many plausible potential explanations as possible (where a *potential* explanation is one that, if true, would explain the facts in

question and a *plausible* explanation is one that is consistent with existing, well-established theories and general background information).

3. Rank one explanation as the "best" explanation on the basis of the standard measures (explanatory scope, simplicity, internal and external consistency, etc.) explained later.

4. Conclude that the explanation ranked as the best explanation is probably true.

We often give explanatory arguments in everyday life. For example, Jan comes home hungry and finds that the leftover meatloaf is gone. She reasons, "My roommate Joe is a vegetarian. My roommate Sue is also a vegetarian. The cat would eat it, but he can't get into the refrigerator. However, my roommate Chris absolutely loves meatloaf, and he came home late last night, too. The best explanation is therefore that Chris ate the leftover meatloaf. So, that is probably what happened."

Arguments given in the courtroom also often take the form of an explanatory argument or inference to the best explanation. For instance, in the "trial of the century," prosecuting attorneys Christopher Darden and Marcia Clarke argued that the best explanation of the sum of the physical evidence, more than 400 pieces in all, was that O. J. Simpson committed murder. For example, blood drops very closely matching the blood of both victims and of O. J. were found *inside* his locked car the very morning of the murder. On the other hand, defense attorney Johnnie Cochran argued that the best explanation of the evidence is that Detective Mark Fuhrman and others in the Los Angeles Police Department framed Simpson for the crime. "If the glove does not fit, you must acquit!" he famously stated. As a result of the back-and-forth arguments, the jury decided that it had grounds for reasonable doubt.

Scientific arguments often take the form of an inference to the best explanation. For example, at the beginning of the twentieth century, physicists who relied on Newtonian physics couldn't explain certain atomic phenomena. When Einstein put forward the special theory of relativity in 1905, it became clear to physicists that Einstein's theory offered the best explanation of the phenomena in question. The reasoning in favor of the theory is complicated, but the fact that it provided the best explanation of the phenomena in question was the reason physicists concluded that Einstein's special theory is the correct explanation. That is, the fact that the Special Theory provided the best explanation gave physicists a very good reason to suppose it *true*. In science, as well as in the courtroom and in everyday life, the fact that a hypothesis provides the best explanation of a phenomena is generally considered a good reason for accepting the hypothesis as true.

Of course, one way to critique or object to an explanatory argument is to come up with a better explanation and an argument for the claim that the new explanation *is* better. Another way to critique an explanatory argument is to show that plausible hypotheses have been overlooked.

What Makes One Explanation Better than Another?

No set of universally agreed on criteria exists that determines in a precise way which explanation is best. The evaluation of an explanation and the comparison of rival explanations is an inexact science, so to speak. However, certain criteria are widely accepted. When we evaluate potential explanations and compare rival explanations, we often apply the following criteria.

1. A good explanation is internally consistent. An *internally consistent* explanation contains no self-contradictory elements.

2. A good explanation is externally consistent. An *externally consistent* explanation does not contradict already established facts and already proven theories.

3. A good explanation explains the widest possible range of relevant data. The wider the range of relevant data explained, the greater is the explanation's *explanatory scope*.

4. In the case of empirical explanations, a good explanation should be testable, and one explanation is better than a rival explanation if it passes more tests and passes tests that its rival does not pass. The more tests an empirical explanation passes, generally the better the explanation.

5. If two potential explanations explain the same range of data and are otherwise equal, except that one explanation is simpler than the other, the simpler explanation is preferable. One explanation is simpler than another if it makes fewer assumptions, refers to fewer explanatory entities, or contains fewer explanatory principles.

The fourth criterion requires some explanation. What is an empirical explanation and how do we "test" an empirical hypothesis? First, an empirical hypothesis is one that can be tested on the basis of observation, that is, on the basis of things we detect using one or more of our physical senses (sight, hearing, taste, touch, smell). We test empirical hypotheses all the time in everyday life, as a matter of common sense. For example, suppose that 18-year-old Bobby believes that if he asks Suzie to the prom, she will turn him down. "She positively hates me," he keeps saying. One day, his buddy says to him, "Why don't you ask her?" What a brilliant idea. For that would be one way to find out if the hypothesis is true or is likely true. Bobby's problem is that he assumes Suzie doesn't like him, but he hasn't tested his hypothesis.

Scientists also test hypotheses, and when they do so, they use the same common-sense logic. This is why Albert Einstein once wrote that science is "nothing more than a refinement of everyday thinking." Boiled down to essentials, the test of an empirical hypothesis involves five steps:

Step 1. We encounter a fact in need of explanation.

Step 2. A hypothesis is proposed that, if true, would explain the fact.

Step 3. We ask: If the hypothesis is true, what other facts about the world can we expect to observe using our senses? That is, what observational facts does the hypothesis imply or predict?

Comment. The prediction needs to be something *other than* what the hypothesis was introduced to explain or else it is obviously of little evidential value. Furthermore, the prediction must be an *observable* event or phenomenon, something we can detect with our senses (seeing, touching, hearing, tasting, or smelling) or with our senses augmented by instruments (microscopes, telescopes, binoculars, Geiger counters, etc.).

Step 4. We "test" the hypothesis by looking to see if the predicted phenomenon is observed. If it is, the prediction has "come true." If it is not, the prediction has failed to come true.

Step 5. We accept, reject, or revise the hypothesis on the basis of such observations. If the predicted phenomenon is observed, that is evidence in support of the hypothesis. If the predicted observation is not observed, that is evidence against the hypothesis.

When the predicted phenomenon is observed, we say that the hypothesis has been "confirmed." It is important to keep in mind, however, that this reasoning is inductive, not deductive. When the predicted phenomenon is observed, that does not show that the hypothesis *must* be true; the evidence only makes the hypothes *probable* to some degree. The more times a hypothesis is confirmed, the higher the probability it is true. Thus, confirmation is never an "all-or-nothing" affair, and a theory is never guaranteed to be true. Confirmation is always a matter of degree. Likewise, when the predicted observation is not observed, we say that the hypothesis has been "disconfirmed." The evidence makes it probable to some degree that the hypothesis is false. The more times a hypothesis has been disconfirmed, the more likely it is false. The evidence makes it probable to some degree that the hypothesis is false. The process by which a hypothesis is shown to be probably true is called the **process of confirmation**. The process by which a scientific hypothesis is shown to be probably false is called the **process of disconfirmation**.

Regarding criterion 5, sometimes called the **principle of economy** or the principle of simplicity, consider the following brief example. Suppose a criminologist examines a crime scene and finds 60 shoe prints, all made by size 12 Ace brand tennis shoes. Several hypotheses suggest themselves: Perhaps one person wearing size 12

Ace shoes left all the prints. Perhaps two persons, each wearing identical Ace shoes, left the prints. Perhaps three persons, each wearing identical Ace shoes, left the prints, and so on. If each hypothesis is equally consistent with the evidence, the principle of simplicity says that the simpler hypothesis is preferable. In this case, the simpler hypothesis is the "one person" theory, because it posits one person, whereas the others posit multiple persons.

The principle of economy was first explicitly formulated in the fourteenth century, by the philosopher William of Ockham (c. 1285–1347), who put the principle this way: "What can be explained with fewer terms is explained in vain with more." This is usually interpreted to mean that if we are choosing between two competing explanations of a phenomenon, and both equally explain the data, the simpler explanation—the explanation postulating fewer explanatory entities or explanatory principles—is rationally preferable. This principle is sometimes called *Ockham's razor*, in honor of its author, because it requires that we "shave" our explanatory theories down to a minimum of entities and a minimum of complexity.

Some philosophers have given the following argument argued in support of Ockham's razor. Suppose two potential explanations explain the same phenomena equally, but one explanation is simpler than the other. If we adopt the more complicated explanation, then we postulate additional explanatory entities with no gain in explanatory power. As a result, we take on an increased risk of error compared to the adoption of the simpler explanation (because we might be wrong about the extra explanatory entities) with no compensating gain in explanatory power. The extra, unnecessary elements in a hypothesis thus increase the possibility of falsehood with no balancing gain in explanatory power. Thus, if we adopt Ockham's razor as a general explanatory policy, and always strive to eliminate unnecessary explanatory elements, it follows that *in the long run* we will minimize the risk of error with no loss in explanatory power. Less chance of error, with just as many things explained in the end is not a bad bargain.

Exercise 33.3   Choose one of the following questionable claims. Research the item and provide an inference to the best explanation for the conclusion that the story is a myth, or else an inference to the best explanation backing the story up.

1. Cressie is said to be a giant freshwater eel inhabiting the waters of Crescent Lake, Newfoundland. Photos exist of the alleged creature.
2. People claim to have pictures of ghosts.
3. Pictures exist of alleged UFOs.
4. Psychics such as Sylvia Browne allegedly possess paranormal powers. Browne was a weekly guest on the Montel Williams show.

Exercise 33.4   Instructions are given in context.

1. Construct an inference to the best explanation argument in support of each of the following claims. (Some of these might require some research on your part.)

   a. The Earth is round.
   b. Caffeine is a stimulant.
   c. Oswald did it alone.
   d. Oswald didn't do it alone.
   e. O. J. did not do it.
   f. O. J. did it.
   t. Elvis is still alive.
   h. Elvis is no longer alive.
   i. UFOs are visitors from another planet.
   j. UFOs are not from another planet.

2. Suppose someone is very mad at you. Give an inference to the best explanation in support of your claim that the person is feeling angry.

3. Give an inference to the best explanation argument for the claim that your teacher is a conscious, living being rather than a nonliving, computerized robot.

4. Pick a story from *The Adventures of Sherlock Holmes*, find an inference to the best explanation ("It's elementary, my dear Watson"), and explain Holmes's reasoning.

5. Pick an episode of a TV detective story (or pick a detective movie) and summarize an inference to the best explanation argument employed by the detectives.

6. Evaluate the following inference to the best explanation: On our recent trip to Minnesota we noticed that most of those riding motorcycles do not wear a helmet. We never saw anyone getting ticketed for not wearing a helmet. Several times we saw the police pass by a motorcyclist who was not wearing a helmet without stopping them. The best explanation is that Minnesota does not have a law requiring that motorcyclists wear a helmet. Therefore, probably, Minnesota does not have a law requiring motorcyclists to wear a helmet.

Exercise 33.5   Explain why this is not an empirical explanation: The roof of this building is being held up by an invisible gremlin.

Semmelweiss Discovers the Germ: The Logic of Confirmation and Disconfirmation Illustrated

The logic of confirmation and disconfirmation are both illustrated in an interesting and often retold episode from the history of science, the discovery of the cause of "childbed fever" by Hungarian-born doctor Ignaz Semmelweis (1818–1865). While working at Vienna General Hospital during the 1840s, Semmelweis found that the mortality rate in the maternity division was unusually high. Many women who gave birth in that division came down with puerperal or "childbed" fever, and a large percentage died from the disease. However, the death rate in the first maternity division was almost three times as high as the rate in the second maternity division. Semmelweis began searching for the cause.

One widely accepted hypothesis was that something was being transmitted through the air. However, Semmelweis rejected this hypothesis by reasoning that if an airborne epidemic were the cause of the disease, it would affect both divisions equally, and it would also affect the city of Vienna. Yet no epidemic of childbed fever was detected outside the hospital's maternity division, and furthermore the two divisions had very different disease rates.

This reasoning can be put in the form of the following argument:

1. If the airborne epidemic hypothesis is true, then the disease would affect both divisions equally, and it would also affect the larger city. (This is the predicted observation.)
2. The disease does not affect both divisions equally and does not affect the larger city. (The prediction, in other words, is false.)
3. So, probably the hypothesis is false.

The evidence, in this case, disconfirms the hypothesis; that is, it gives us reason to suppose the hypothesis is probably false.

Semmelweis considered, tested, and rejected many other hypotheses. For instance, someone proposed that overcrowding was the cause of the illness. However, Semmelweiss investigated and found that the second division was actually more crowded than the first division (primarily because women were trying to avoid the first division). Disconfirmation again:

1. If overcrowding is the cause, then the first division should be more crowded than the second division. (This is the prediction.)
2. The first division is not more densely crowded. (The predicted observation is not observed.)
3. Therefore, probably, the hypothesis is false.

One of the hypotheses tested by Semmelweis is especially interesting. When a patient in the hospital's sickroom was dying, a priest, accompanied by an altar boy ringing a bell, would arrive to administer the last rites of the Catholic Church. Because of the layout of the hospital, the priest walked through the first division but not through the second division. The hypothesis was this: Perhaps the fear caused by the appearance of the priest caused the women in the first division to contract the fever. To test this hypothesis, Semmelweiss had the priest change his route. The change had no effect on the mortality rate. Thus, against the hypothesis, one could reason: If the hypothesis is correct, changing the priest's route should change the mortality rate. Changing the route did not change the rate. The hypothesis is probably false.

At one point in the process, Semmelweis noticed that women in the first division delivered their babies while lying on their backs, whereas in the second division they delivered while lying on their sides. Perhaps, he wondered, the position during birth was the cause of the illness. So Semmelweis had the two divisions switch their procedures. However, changing the procedures did not affect the mortality rate at all. If the hypothesis were correct, changing the delivery positions should have changed the mortality rate. False again.

One day, one of the anatomy teachers accidentally cut himself with a scalpel while performing an autopsy at the hospital. The professor soon became extremely sick, and, as he lay dying, showed the symptoms of childbed fever. Semmelweis formulated a new hypothesis: Perhaps some agent from the cadaver in the autopsy room was the cause of childbed fever. After investigating the matter, he discovered that doctors would routinely perform autopsies on dead bodies, wash their hands, and go immediately into the first maternity division to deliver babies and treat patients. The women in the second maternity division, on the other hand, were taken care of by midwives rather than by doctors, and the midwives did not perform autopsies.

Semmelweis hypothesized that the soaps being used after the autopsies did not remove the infectious agent from the hands of the doctors. To test his hypothesis, he had the doctors wash with a solution of chlorinated lime, a far more powerful cleaning agent, before they treated the women in the first division. The first division's mortality rate quickly plummeted. Semmelweis now had an argument in favor of a hypothesis:

1. If this new hypothesis is true, washing with chlorinated lime should cut the mortality rate in the first division.
2. Washing with chlorinated lime did indeed cut the mortality rate.
3. Therefore, the hypothesis is probably true.

The evidence in this case "confirms" the hypothesis; that is, it gives us reason to suppose the hypothesis is probably true. The claim is not that the evidence proves the hypothesis with certainty, or that the hypothesis *must* be true. Rather, the claim is that the observations make the hypothesis likely, make it probable.

Confirming a Hypothesis

Where H stands for the hypothesis being tested and P stands for an observational prediction derived from the hypothesis:

1. If H is true, then P will be observed.
2. P is observed.
3. Therefore, probably, H is true.

Case Study: Confirming the "Sea of Air" Hypothesis

It has been known since ancient times that if you want to drain liquid from one end of a barrel, you must have an opening at the other end. Children are aware of a similar phenomenon: If you suck some liquid up a straw and quickly place your thumb over the end of the straw, the liquid won't drain out.

From ancient times until the seventeenth century, this phenomenon was explained by the "full universe" hypothesis, an idea originated by the ancient Greek philosopher Aristotle. According to this hypothesis, nature is a "plenum"—a completely full thing. Indeed, nature is so full that it will not allow a vacuum to form. The central slogan of the full universe hypothesis was "nature abhors a vacuum." Evidence that supported this hypothesis included an experiment with a keg of water. Every time people tried to make liquid flow out of the bottom of a keg without a hole in the top, it was observed that unless the hole at the bottom is large enough to admit air, nothing will flow out of the keg. If the hole is big enough to admit air, then water flows out. On the other hand, if even a small hole is cut in the top of the keg, then the water readily flows out the bottom hole. All of this is exactly what the full universe hypothesis predicts, of course, and the whole thing is also easily explained on the full universe hypothesis. If water were to escape without admitting any air into the keg, then a vacuum would form inside the keg where the water had been. But according to the hypothesis, nature is a plenum and will not allow a vacuum to form. Hence, nature will not let the water flow out unless the hole at the bottom is big enough to let air in as the water flows out—or unless a hole is cut in the top of the keg.

The evidence therefore seemed to support the full universe, or plenum, hypothesis. Supporters of the full universe hypothesis reasoned that because nature abhors a vacuum, it won't allow the liquid to escape unless a hole is cut in the top of the keg.

However, in the seventeenth century, during the rise of modern science, observations were made that seemed to contradict the full universe hypothesis. For example, in approximately 1641, an interesting experiment was performed in Rome. A glass container was attached to the top of a 40-foot pipe that had been strapped upright to a tower. The whole tube was then filled (from the top) with water. The bottom of the tube had a valve that opened and closed. With the tube full and the top sealed shut, the valve at the bottom was opened and water rushed out, creating a vacuum in the top of the tube.

It began to look as if something was wrong with Aristotle's full universe theory. Galileo's student, Evangelista Torricelli (1608–1647), began searching for a better theory. He noticed that a suction pump, which uses a piston to draw water out of a well, could raise water only 33 feet above the surface of the well. In 1642, in a stroke of genius, Torricelli came up with a hypothesis that would explain this puzzling fact. He hypothesized that the earth is surrounded by a "sea of air." This sea of air actually has weight, just as a sea of water has weight. Torricelli further reasoned that if the sea of air has weight, it should exert pressure ("air pressure") on all objects within it—just as water exerts pressure ("water pressure") on anything submerged in it. This pressure on the surface of the well must be what pushes the water up the pipe when the suction pump's piston is raised. Furthermore, the height of the column of water in the suction pump must be related to the total pressure of the air.

This hypothesis suggested an interesting test. Torricelli reasoned that because mercury is 14 times heavier than water, the sea of air ought to hold up only a 29-inch column of mercury (because it holds up a 33-foot column of water). If a tube of mercury is sealed at one end, and inverted, and the open end is placed in a bowl of liquid mercury, some of the mercury in the tube should flow out and into the bowl, but the weight of the sea of air ought to push down on the surface of the bowl of mercury with enough force to hold the rest of the mercury in the inverted tube, thus creating a vacuum inside the tube. An equilibrium should be reached where the weight of the mercury in the tube is equal to the weight of the sea of air pressing down on the bowl. With this reasoning, Torricelli derived an exact prediction from his sea of air hypothesis: The weight of the atmosphere should support a 29-inch column of mercury in an inverted tube, with the rest of the tube a vacuum. This prediction was easily verified.

There was an unanticipated side effect of the experiment. The device, Torricelli realized, could measure fluctuations in atmospheric pressure, thus predicting the weather. Torricelli had invented the mercury barometer.

After reading about Torricelli's sea-of-air hypothesis, French philosopher Blaise Pascal (1623–1662) realized another implication of the hypothesis: Just as water pressure diminishes as you ascend from the bottom of a lake toward its surface, air pressure should diminish if we ascend to the surface of the sea of air. Consequently, Pascal argued that if Torricelli's hypothesis is true, air pressure must decrease at higher altitudes, because at a higher altitude one is closer to the surface of the sea of air, and less air presses down. The following prediction was consequently derived from Torricelli's hypothesis: The height of a mercury column in an inverted tube should decrease as the device is carried up a mountain.

In 1648, Pascal had his brother-in-law, Perrier, perform the experiment. While the "Torricelli barometer" was carried up a mountain, an identical barometer on the ground (a control) was watched continuously. The device on the ground never changed, but the device that was carried up the mountain behaved as predicted. At the top of the mountain, the column of mercury in the barometer had dropped. The experiment was repeated five times while the observer at the bottom of the mountain watched the control tube. Each time, the same result was observed.

Case Study: Disconfirming the Caloric Hypothesis

If two material objects are brought together, and one has a higher temperature, the two will eventually reach the same temperature. It seems common sense to suppose some sort of fluid substance flows from the warmer to the cooler object, just as water flows from a higher level to a lower level. In the Middle Ages, this phenomenon was explained by the caloric hypothesis. According to this hypothesis, heat is an invisible substance, called *caloric*, that tends to flow from the warmer to the cooler body. Caloric theory seemed to answer many questions about heat. It explained why two bodies reach a temperature equilibrium, it explained why bodies expand when heated, and so on. (Bodies supposedly expand as they fill with caloric substance.)

However, contradictory evidence began to mount. For instance, according to the caloric hypothesis, a quantity of red-hot iron should weigh more than an equal quantity of cold iron (because the hot iron is full of caloric). But after careful measurements, it was found that hot metal weighs no more than cold metal. This evidence *disconfirmed* the caloric hypothesis.

Count Rumford (1753–1814) was supervising the boring of cannon for the British Artillery when he noticed that hot chips of metal fell off the boring tip. Rumford asked a simple question: Where does the heat come from? The borer had no fire or obvious source of heat. Furthermore, the heat generated by the borer seemed to be inexhaustible. So, Rumford reasoned, heat cannot possibly be a material substance, because matter cannot be created out of nothing. Heat could only be particles in motion, given the way it is generated and communicated. More precisely, material objects are made of many small particles—atoms and molecules—moving in many directions, at many different speeds, and heat is the average motion or mean kinetic energy of these particles. Rumford's hypothesis is now known as the kinetic theory of heat.

Exercise 33.6   Instructions are given in context.

1. Write a short paper on an episode from the history of science. Identify (a) the problem under investigation, (b) the hypothesis or hypotheses formulated, (c) the implications drawn from the hypothesis or hypotheses, (d) the test procedure used, and (e) the result.

2. Write a short paper on a hypothesis formulated by Sherlock Holmes in one of the stories by Arthur Conan Doyle. Include the problem under investigation, the hypothesis or hypotheses, the implications drawn, the test procedures, and the result.

3. Watch an episode of a contemporary detective show or an old show such as *Dragnet, Colombo, Magnum P.I., The Rockford Files*, and so on, and explain the hypothetical reasoning employed to solve the problem.

4. Find an account of a specific line of scientific research in the newspaper, a magazine, or a science book. Analyze the logical structure in terms of the steps discussed in this chapter.

5. Take a *CSI* case and analyze the hypothetical reasoning in terms of the steps outlined in this chapter.

6. According to advocates of the phlogiston theory, oils are almost pure phlogiston. Why do you think they supposed this?

7. Formulate a hypothesis that can be confirmed or disconfirmed by observation evidence. Give two observation statements. One of these should be an observation statement that would confirm the hypothesis if the observation statement were to be true; the other should be an observational statement that would disconfirm the hypothesis if the observation statement were to be true.

8. List confirming evidence for the following hypotheses:
    a. The Earth is spherical.
    b. The Earth rotates on its axis.
    c. Electricity is a form of energy.
    d. Stars are extremely far away.

Logic in the Laboratory: "Mill's Methods"

When a group of people all come down with the same illness, scientists from the health department often are called in to track down the likely cause. For example, a few years ago, a number of people in Washington State got sick, and several died. In their search for the cause of the illness, scientists quickly learned that all the victims had eaten the same food at the same fast-food restaurant. Eventually, the deaths were traced to a particular strain of *E. coli* bacteria in undercooked hamburgers.

When scientists track down the *causes* of things, the procedures they use are often based on a set of principles first formulated by British philosopher John Stuart Mill (1806–1873) in his *System of Logic* published in 1843. These principles, now known as **Mill's methods**, state procedures for identifying the probable causes of things. Most of the principles are common sense. However, before we survey Mill's methods, we must first clarify the concept of a cause.

Cause and Effect

One of the key objectives of "causal" investigation is to discover, for a specified effect, the conditions under which the effect will occur and the conditions under which the effect will not occur. Likewise, a key question of causal reasoning is this: Under which conditions will the effect occur and under which conditions will the effect be absent? Thus, philosophers have found it illuminating to analyze causes in terms of underlying or antecedent conditions, and specifically in terms of two types of antecedent or underlying conditions: necessary conditions and sufficient conditions. We already encountered these terms in Chapter 13. To recap, a **necessary condition** for some circumstance or effect E has the following feature: In the absence of this condition, E cannot occur. In other words, this condition must be present for E to occur. Let us state this more formally: N is a necessary condition for effect E if the following is true:

- E will not be present unless N is present.
- In the absence of N, E will not be present.
- Without N, E won't occur.
- E cannot occur when N doesn't hold.

For example, the presence of oxygen is a necessary condition for the operation of a gasoline engine, reaching age 18 is a necessary condition for voting in the United States, and a bachelor's degree is usually a necessary condition for entering graduate school.

A **sufficient condition** for an effect E has a different feature: When the sufficient condition is present, E must occur. For instance, standing openly in the rain is a sufficient condition for getting wet, and drinking six tequila sunrises is (for most people) a sufficient condition for getting drunk. More formally, S is a sufficient condition for effect E if the following are true:

- If S is present, E will occur.
- If S is present, E is certain to occur.
- In presence of S, E is certain to occur.
- E must occur when S holds.

Mill's methods are commonsense guides for discovering the causally necessary and sufficient conditions for things.

Mill's Method of Agreement

Suppose you and two of your friends eat lunch in the school cafeteria. Later in the afternoon, all three of you begin getting sick. By 3:00, you are in and out of the restroom every few minutes. What made you sick? That is, what is the cause of your illness? Suppose the following list shows what you each ate:

You	Friend 1	Friend 2
2 burritos	3 cheeseburgers	2 fish burgers
1 large fry	2 orders of onion rings	1 large nachos
1 taco	2 tacos	1 taco

What would you conclude is the probable cause? If you concluded that the cause is in the tacos, you probably followed a logical process known as Mill's **method of agreement.**

Notice in the list shown that the taco is the only antecedent factor always present when the effect (sickness) is present. From this, we naturally conclude that the cause of the sickness is probably in the tacos. The basic idea here is that the probable cause of the effect E (the illness) is to be found in the one antecedent condition common to each case where the effect E is present.

The method of agreement requires that we draw up a list of possible causes. We use our commonsense knowledge of cause-and-effect connections to identify the various possibilities. After this, we look for one antecedent causal factor common to all cases of the effect in question. This common factor, if found, is identified as the probable cause or as part of the cause. Note that the conclusion is not that the condition singled out *must* be the cause; the conclusion is only that this is probably the cause (or is part of the cause).

Mill put the method into these terms:

> If two or more instances of a phenomena under investigation have only one circumstance in common, the circumstance in which alone all the instances agree, is the cause (or effect) of the given phenomenon.

The method of agreement identifies a probable necessary condition of an effect. The reasoning underlying the method is that if an antecedent condition is absent when the effect is present, the condition cannot be a necessary condition for the effect and can thus be crossed off the list of suspected necessary conditions. After a variety of underlying antecedent conditions have been crossed off the list, the remaining condition that is present in all cases in which the effect is present is probably a necessary condition of the effect. The instances, or cases, examined must all be alike in terms of the presence of the effect under investigation, and they should differ as much as possible in all other respects.

Mill's Method of Difference

Suppose Jan and Pat both have lunch at the school cafeteria. Later on, in biology class, Jan gets sick, but Pat feels fine. The following list gives the relevant information.

Student	Foods eaten	Effect
Jan	A B C D E F	Sick
Pat	A B C D E	Not sick

Jan and Pat ate the same lunch except for one item. Food F is the obvious suspect. Why? It is the factor present when the effect (the sickness) is present and absent when the effect is absent, and the two cases are otherwise similar in all relevant respects. We naturally conclude that food F probably caused the sickness.

This reasoning embodies Mill's **method of difference**. According to this method, if an effect E is present in one case, and a *closely similar case* doesn't exhibit E, we look for the difference between the cases. The probable cause of the effect E is the circumstance or condition present when E occurs and absent when E doesn't occur, provided that the cases compared are otherwise alike in all or nearly all relevant respects. The one way in which the two cases differ is therefore the suspected cause. This, in its essentials, is Mill's method of difference.

Mill stated the method of difference as follows:

If an instance in which the phenomenon under investigation occurs, and an instance in which it does not occur, have every circumstance in common save one, that one occurring only in the former, the circumstance in which alone the two instances differ is the effect, or the cause, or an indispensable part of the cause of the phenomenon.

In general, the information for applying the method of difference will fit into a list somewhat like the following:

Case	Antecedent conditions	Event for which a cause is sought
1	abcw	E
2	abc	E does not occur

Therefore, condition w is probably the cause of E.

Unlike the method of agreement, the method of difference identifies a probable *sufficient* condition of an effect. (The method of agreement identifies a probable necessary condition.) The reasoning underlying the method of difference is as follows: If a condition is present when the effect did not occur, that condition cannot be a sufficient condition of the effect, and can therefore be eliminated from the list of suspected sufficient conditions. After a variety of possibilities have been eliminated, the condition that is present when the effect is present and absent when the effect is absent is probably a sufficient condition for the effect. The instances or cases being compared should be as much alike as possible, except for the effect under investigation.

For another example, suppose researchers are testing the effects of a drug. They begin with, let us suppose, 100 rats. The rats are divided into two identical groups, each consisting of 50 rats. Both groups receive the same food and live in the same conditions. Both groups of rats are alike in every respect. Now, drug D is administered to the rats in one group (the test group) and no drug is administered to the rats in the other group (the control group). The two groups are now similar except for the one difference: Only the test group received the drug. Suppose the rats in the test group act nervous, whereas the rats in the control group do not. The conclusion is that the drug probably causes nervousness. The drug is the only difference, and this is evidence in support of the claim that the drug is the cause of the nervousness. The difference is the factor present when the effect is present and absent when the effect is absent.

In science, the method of difference is often implemented in the form of what is called a **controlled experiment**. In such an experiment, scientists search for the cause of a particular effect. Two groups of individuals are formed: the test group and the control group. The two groups must be extremely similar except for the following difference: Only the test group has or is given the factor suspected to be the cause of the effect. The control group is similar to the test group except that it lacks the factor under investigation; that is, the suspected cause. After investigating the differences, a list similar to the following is constructed:

Case	Antecedent Factors	Effect is
1	ABCDJ	Present
2	ABCE	Absent
3	ABCD	Absent
4	ABCG	Absent

Factor J is the suspected cause, because it is the only factor that has the following feature: The effect occurs when it is present, and is absent when it is absent.

In the nineteenth century, Louis Pasteur hypothesized that vaccination with anthrax virus makes an animal immune to anthrax disease. Reluctantly, Pasteur performed the following experiment. He had one group of animals vaccinated with the anthrax vaccine while the vaccine was withheld from a second, nearly identical group. He then administered a fatal dose of anthrax germs to each group. The vaccinated animals didn't contract the disease, but the others did. This was evidence that the vaccination does indeed confer immunity to the disease. Pasteur employed Mill's method of difference.

The tests to find the cause of lung cancer employed the method of difference. Groups of smokers were compared with various groups of nonsmokers who were otherwise extremely similar to the smokers. The only discernible difference between the groups being compared was the practice of smoking. The groups of smokers had significantly higher rates of lung cancer, which was then attributed to the only difference: smoking.

The method of difference is also common sense. For instance, a cook wonders, "What difference will it make if I leave out ingredient X when I bake these scones?" So he bakes two batches of scones. The batches are similar except for one difference: One batch contains ingredient X, and the other does not. He notes the difference the absence of X makes. If the scones with X have property P, and the scones without X lack property P, he concludes that ingredient X probably causes the scones to have property P.

What Is a Double-Blind Experiment?

Suppose we are to use Mill's method of difference to test a new diet drug. Here is one way to reduce the possibility of error to a minimum. We select two large groups of people, alike in every way, except that one group (the test group) will get the drug and the second group (the control group) will not get the drug. The control group will only be given a placebo. However, to make sure people's *expectations* won't influence the outcome, nobody in either group will know which group is getting the drug and which group is getting the placebo. So, nobody will know whether the pill he or she is given is the drug or the placebo. However, this is not enough. It is still possible that the researchers administering the pills might tip people off as they are conducting the experiment, perhaps even unintentionally (e.g., by giving unconscious cues to people as they hand out the pills). A "double-blind" setup will prevent this by keeping everyone in the dark, not just those being tested: Those handing out the real pills and the placebo pills won't know which pill is which, and each person in each group will not know whether he or she is in the control group or the test group. This provides less chance for the mind to play tricks on the body. Ours is a double-blind test.

In sum, according to the method of difference, if there is some antecedent phenomenon, B, present when phenomenon A is present and absent when A is absent, and the two cases are alike in every other relevant respect, then we may conclude that A and B are causally related; that is, that B is probably the cause of A.

Let us now compare the two methods. The method of agreement is aimed at the identification of a necessary condition for an effect E, and it bids us search for the common factor in all cases of E. The common factor, if found, is cited as the probable cause or as part of the cause. On the other hand, the method of difference is aimed at the identification of a sufficient condition for an effect E, and it directs us to choose as cause the one respect in which a case where the effect E occurs differs from an otherwise relevantly similar case where E is absent.

Mill's Method of Concomitant Variation

Suppose a direct relationship is discovered between eating food X and stomach cancer. People who eat food X tend on average to develop stomach cancer. People who do not eat food X tend on average not to develop stomach cancer. The rate of stomach cancer varies in a regular way with the eating of food X. The more of X that a person eats, the more likely it is that he will get stomach cancer. We would conclude from this that a causal connection *probably* (but not necessarily) exists between eating food X and stomach cancer. Because some people who have stomach cancer do not eat food X, and some people who eat food X do not have stomach cancer, we would not conclude that eating food X is the *only* cause of stomach cancer, but we would conclude that it is probably part of the cause or is connected with the cause.

Mill's **method of concomitant variation** looks for changes in one phenomenon that vary with or correspond to (are concomitant with) changes in a second phenomenon. If the measured change in the one varies along with the measured change in the second, this is evidence that the two phenomena are *probably* causally related: One of the two probably causes the other, or some third factor is the cause of both.

The method of concomitant variation is often used in everyday life as well as in the laboratory setting. For instance, suppose a community college district discovers a correlation between changes in enrollment and changes in the unemployment index: When unemployment goes up, enrollment goes up; when unemployment goes down, enrollment goes down. The district officials conclude that unemployment is one of the causes of college enrollment.

Mill expressed the method of concomitant variation this way:

> Whatever phenomenon varies in any manner whenever another phenomenon varies in some particular manner, is either a cause or an effect of that phenomenon, or is connected with it through some fact of causation.

However, a word of caution: The mere fact that two phenomena are correlated does not prove with certainty that they are causally related. Ice cream sales at the beach and drownings are statistically correlated, in the sense that ice cream sales at beachfront parks are higher in the summer than in the winter and so are drownings. However, this does not prove that eating ice cream causes people to drown. Common sense suggests that there is probably a third factor driving both ice cream sales and accidents in the water.

The Joint Method of Agreement and Difference

The joint method of agreement and difference simply combines both methods. Suppose we first use the method of agreement to find a factor that is probably a necessary condition of an effect E. We decide that X is probably a necessary condition for effect E. Next, we deploy the method of difference and look for evidence that X is a sufficient condition for E. This, in brief, is the joint method of agreement and difference.

Mill's Method of Residues

Suppose a farmer is trying to figure out what is causing a loss of pressure in his well. He figures the cause is either factor A, factor B, factor C, or factor D. These are the only possible sources. Let us suppose that after much investigation he determines that 10% of the loss is due to factor A, 20% is due to factor B, and 20% is due to factor C. He stops and concludes that the remaining 50% of the loss must be due to factor D. The farmer has just employed Mill's method of residues.

In general, if we know that (a) A, B, and C are causal conditions responsible for effects X, Y, and Z, and (b) A is found to be the cause of X, and (c) B is found to be the cause of Y, we can conclude that that C, the residual factor, is probably the cause of Z. This is common sense again.

Exercise 33.7   In each case, which of Mill's methods is being used?

1. To test the quality of a new transmission additive, a company buys two identical cars, one red, the other blue. The red car gets the new additive and the blue car gets no additive. At the end of the test, they take apart the transmissions and measure the wear and tear. The red car has significantly less wear. The mechanics conclude that the additive reduced wear and tear on the transmission.

2. A Martian lands, sees a car for the first time, and wants to figure out what makes the car speed up and slow down. He gets in, manages to start the engine, and then starts pushing buttons and turning the steering wheel. Finally, because he is on a level street, he notices a perfect correlation between the position of the gas pedal and the speed of the car: The closer the pedal is to the floor, the faster the car goes; the further the pedal is from the floor, the slower the car's speed. The Martian concludes that pushing on the gas pedal causes the car to speed up and slow down.

3. Six pupils are extremely poor readers. The teacher investigates the background of each student and finds that each comes from a different family, each has a different socioeconomic background, and each had attended a different previous school. However, all six lacked phonics instruction. The teacher concludes that phonics instruction causes good reading.

4. Many XYZ computers keep getting returned for repairs. The company looks into the matter and finds that the computers that are returned were produced in different years and were sold in different areas. Finally, it is found that all were sold in areas with very high humidity. The company concludes that highly humid air damages something in the computers.

5. A department store manager notices a statistical relationship between the local employment rate and the shoplifting rate in her store. As the employment rate increased, the theft rate decreased, and vice versa. The manager concludes that unemployment is part of the cause of shoplifting.

6. A patient developed an allergic reaction. When she eliminated foods x, y, and z from her diet, the reaction ended. She then added the foods back one at a time. When she began eating food y, milk products, the reaction reappeared. She concluded that the reaction was caused by milk products.

7. A doctor is treating five cancer patients. The only common factor is that all five were employed by the XYZ chemical company in a division producing a chemical defoliant. The doctor concludes that the defoliant caused the cancer.

8. The Smith family moves from city A to city B and discovers that their clothes are cleaner. Yet they are using the same soap and the same washing machine. They conclude the change must be due to the water.

9. Two bushes are covered with aphids. The gardener sprays one with chemical X and leaves the other unsprayed. The next day, the aphids are gone from the sprayed bush, but they remain on the unsprayed bush. The gardener concludes that chemical X killed the aphids.

10. Tax revenues are down. The city council wants to know the cause. Their economist discovers that some of the decline is due to the economic downturn, and some is due to the increase in the interest rate. The economist concludes that the remaining decline must be due to increased cheating on taxes.

11. A resort is testing a new bass plug. The manager gives the new plug to 6 of 12 fishermen. The six with the new plug all used different gear, and all caught fish. The other six fishermen didn't catch any fish. The manager concludes that the bass plug works.

12. A psychiatrist has 10 patients unable to sustain prolonged and meaningful relationships with men. All 10 have different backgrounds, all have different religious beliefs, all have different jobs, and so on. However, all the patients had in common the lack of a male parent figure during childhood. The psychiatrist concludes that this is part of the cause of the problem.

13. A metallurgist tries adding five different chemicals to a metal while attempting to produce a new alloy. All the added chemicals that contain chemical X produce an alloy that is resistant to corrosion. The other chemicals fail to produce a corrosion-proof alloy. The metallurgist concludes that chemical X makes the alloy resistant to corrosion.

14. During late 1940s a number of men from different parts of the country developed the same eye disease. Investigators discovered that all had worked in nuclear energy projects during World War II and all had been exposed to neutron beams. The investigators concluded that the cancer was caused by the neutron beams.

15. During the late nineteenth century, scientists searched for the cause of rickets (a bone disease). At first rickets was thought to be due to poverty because many of those who had rickets were poor. Consequently, malnutrition was investigated as a possible cause. But then it was discovered that wealthy people often had rickets as well. Finally, a common factor was found: a lack of sunlight. The conclusion was therefore that rickets is caused by a lack of sunlight.

16. After Randy adjusts the timing belt on his car, installs new tires, and puts in a new carburetor, he notices that his car gets better gas mileage. Obsessed with finding the cause, he does three things. First, he puts the old carburetor back in and drives the car for a week, carefully recording the

gas mileage each day. Next, he puts the old tires back on and drives the car for another week, again carefully recording the gas mileage each day. Finally, he puts the timing belt back to its old setting and again drives the car for a week, carefully recording the gas mileage each day. He decides the increased gas mileage is due to the new carburetor.

17. In 1854, John Snow sought the cause of cholera. He discovered that all areas of London had approximately the same frequency of cholera except for one area, which had a very low level of the disease. On investigation, it turned out that the drinking water for this one area was supplied by a company that used drained water that had no sewage in it. However, the water for the other areas of London was contaminated by raw sewage. Snow consequently proposed that cholera is caused by fecal contamination of drinking water.

18. Dr. Christian Eijkman sought the cause of the disease beriberi. He observed that hens in the courtyard of an asylum where he worked acted like the humans who had the disease. Could it be, he wondered, that the same cause was at work in both humans and chickens? Further investigation revealed that in prisons where prisoners were fed polished rice, there were high rates of beriberi. In these prisons, the chickens were also fed polished rice. But in prisons with unpolished rice, there were few cases. So polished rice was present when the disease was present, and absent where the disease was absent. Eijkman could find no other relevant difference. He concluded that the beriberi disease is caused by the diet of polished rice. (Technically, the disease is caused by a dietary deficiency of B-complex vitamins. Whole grains provide this vitamin, but when rice is polished, the polishing process removes some of the outer hull, and the outer hull contains much of the vitamin content.)

19. People used to think that maggots came from within meat. In the nineteenth century, Pasteur performed the following test of the theory. He boiled meat broth in a flask to kill the bacteria; then he sealed the container and let it sit for an extended time. When he examined it later, the broth remained free of bacteria. However, meat broth that had been exposed to the air became covered with bacteria and soon started to decay. His conclusion was that the bacteria came from the air rather than from within the meat broth.

20. A group of patients with disease x are all found to have one thing in common (other than x): a dietary deficiency of vitamin z. Next, the patients are given vitamin z and one by one their symptoms all clear up. The doctor concludes that the condition is caused by a lack of vitamin z.

Exercise 33.8   How would you investigate the situation, if you were to use Mill's methods?

1. A disproportionately large number of athletes are enrolled in Professor Smith's class. Why?
2. Joe has occasional stuttering attacks. Why?
3. The divorce rate rose during the 1980s, and then fell during the 1990s. Why?
4. Business at Pink's Hot Dogs rose during August and then declined during September. Why?
5. You and four coworkers get sick after lunch. Why?
6. You plant six rose bushes. Three grow and three die. Why?
7. You bake cherry pie three times, and twice the pie turns out lousy. Why?
8. Two singers in a chorus get sore throats. Why?
9. Two people on a group camping trip become sick. Why?
10. Sometimes the latte you order is good, and sometimes it is not good. Why?
11. Every time you get busy, you get sick. Why?

Glossary

Analogical argument An argument in which we (a) assert an analogy between two things or kinds of things, A and B; (b) point out that A has a particular feature and that B is not known not to have the feature; and (c) conclude that B probably also has the feature.

Analogy A resemblance or similarity between two or more things.

Biased sample A sample of a larger population that is unrepresentative of that larger population.

Controlled experiment An experiment in which a cause of an effect is sought and in which the following occurs: (a) two groups of individuals are compared; (b) the two groups are extremely similar except for the following difference: one group, called the test group, has or is given the factor suspected to be the cause of the effect, and the other group, called the control group, is similar to the test group except that it lacks the factor under investigation, or the suspected cause; and (c) the method of difference is employed to determine the probable cause.

Enumerative induction Argument in which premises about observed individuals or cases are used as a basis for a generalization about unobserved individuals or cases.

Hypothesis An explanation offered for a phenomenon.

Hypothetico-deductive method The method used in the sciences to confirm and disconfirm theories.

Inductive argument An argument that claims, explicitly or implicitly, that if the premises are true the conclusion is probably true, although it might nevertheless be false.

Inference to the best explanation A type of argument that (a) cites one or more facts that need explanation, (b) canvasses possible explanations, (c) puts one explanation forward as the best explanation, and (d) concludes that that explanation is probably the correct (or true) explanation.

Mill's methods A set of principles first formulated by British philosopher John Stuart Mill (1806–1973) in his *System of Logic* published in 1843. These principles are used when seeking to determine the probable cause of a circumstance or effect.

- **Joint method of agreement and difference** The combined use of both the method of difference and the method of agreement.
- **Method of agreement** The method for determining a probable cause that comprises the following steps. (1) Draw up a list of possible causes. (2) Look for one causal factor common to all cases of the effect. (3) Select this as the probable cause or as part of the probable cause.
- **Method of concomitant variation** The method for determining a probable cause that is based on the following general principle: If changes in one phenomenon accompany or correspond to (are concomitant with) changes in a second phenomenon, and if the magnitude of the change in the one varies along with the magnitude of the change in the second, the two phenomena are probably causally related—either one of the two probably causes the other, or some third factor is probably the cause of both.
- **Method of difference** The method for determining a probable cause that comprises the following steps. (1) Examine a case where an effect E occurs and a similar case where E does not occur. (2) Choose as the probable cause the one respect in which the case where the effect E occurs differs from the case where E is absent.
- **Method of residues** This method is based on the following general principle: If we know that (a) A, B, and C are causal conditions responsible for effects X, Y, and Z; and (b) A is found to be the cause of X; and (c) C is found to be the cause of Y, we can figure that B, the residual factor, is probably the cause of Z.

Necessary condition A condition for some circumstance or effect E that has the following feature: In the absence of this condition, E cannot occur; that is, this condition must be present if E is to occur.

Observational prediction A prediction about the results of observations that can be made, where the observation can concern facts related to the past, present, or future.

Primary analogates In an analogical argument, the objects being compared that appear only in the premises.

Principle of economy If two potential hypotheses explain the same range of data and are otherwise equal, except that one hypothesis is simpler than the other, the simpler hypothesis is preferable. One hypothesis is simpler than another if it makes reference to fewer entities or contains fewer explanatory principles or explanatory elements. Also known as Ockham's razor.

Process of confirmation The process by which a scientific hypothesis is shown to be probably true.

Process of disconfirmation The process by which a scientific hypothesis is shown to be probably false.

Secondary analogate In an analogical argument, the object that appears in the premises and also appears in the conclusion.

Sufficient condition A condition for an effect E that has this feature: When the sufficient condition is present, E must occur. The sufficient condition S for an effect E is the condition such that it is all that is required for E to occur.

34 Elementary Probability Theory « « «

As you know, one major difference between deduction and induction is that inductive strength is a matter of degree, whereas deductive validity is an absolute, all-or-nothing feature of an argument. Any deductive argument is either valid or not valid—there are no degrees of validity and no valid argument is more valid than another.

When students are first introduced to the concept of inductive strength, they often want to know if the degree of inductive strength can be measured or calculated. Unfortunately, logicians have not yet discovered a standard of measurement that will measure degrees of probability in *all* inductive arguments. However, in some special, restricted contexts, the degree of probability can be assigned a number. The standard principles we use to assign numerical probabilities, in these special contexts, are the subject of the branch of inductive logic known as probability theory, also called *statistics*. Ironically, the methods are very formal, even mathematical in nature, although they are part of inductive logic, which itself is one of the nonformal branches of logical theory.

The Classical Theory of Probability

In the seventeenth century, French philosopher and mathematician Blaise Pascal (1623–1662), along with Pierre Fermat (1601–1665), developed the first systematic theory of probability, now known as the **classical theory of probability**. Pascal and Fermat sought an exact method of measuring the odds in games of chance. Suppose two assumptions can reasonably be made:

1. All possible outcomes can be counted.
2. Each outcome is equally likely.

Then, according to the classical theory, the probability of an event E occurring is:

$$P(E) = \frac{f}{T}$$

where P(E) abbreviates the probability of event E occurring, f is the number of favorable outcomes, and T is the total number of possible outcomes.

For example, suppose you reach into a perfectly shuffled poker deck and draw a card at random. What is the probability that the card drawn is a queen? Because the deck contains 52 cards, the total number of possible outcomes is 52. The deck contains four queens, so there are four "favorable" outcomes among the possible outcomes. Therefore, assuming it's reasonable to suppose that all possible outcomes have been counted and that each is equally likely, the probability of drawing a queen from a shuffled poker deck is 4/52 or 1/13. In other words:

1. You just reached into a perfectly shuffled poker deck and drew a card at random.
2. Therefore, the card drawn is a queen.

The probability that the conclusion is true, given the premise, is exactly 4/52.

Exercise 34.1   Use the classical theory to compute the probabilities of the following events.

1. A six-sided die is rolled and comes up with a 4.
2. A six-sided die is rolled and lands showing an odd number.
3. A card drawn from a poker deck is red.
4. A book of 165 pages is opened and a page is selected at random. The page selected is page 55.
5. A car is selected at random from a car lot containing 400 cars. The car chosen is car number 33.
6. A bird drops its payload randomly on a crowd of 250 people. Ed is in the crowd, and it is Ed who has to go home and wash his hair.
7. A six-sided die is rolled and it comes up with a 6 or 1.
8. A six-sided die is rolled and it comes up with a 1, 2, or 3.
9. Three hundred forty students are enrolled in a Philosophy 100 class at the University of Ruritania, including student Herman Snodgrass. The professor will call on one student randomly this morning and ask him or her to explain the philosophical significance of Gödel's proof. What is the probability Herman gets put on the spot?
10. A card is drawn from a regular poker deck and the card is a king.

The Relative Frequency Theory of Probability

During the eighteenth century, mathematicians in England developed a theory of probability that could be used to calculate rates on life insurance policies. Whereas Pascal and Fermat were concerned with the odds at the roulette table and other organized games of chance, these mathematicians were concerned with more practical questions, such as questions relating to the emerging institution of life insurance. For instance, what is the probability that a 30-year-old person in good health will live to be 60? The problem in such a case was that when trying to figure a person's probable life span, the two assumptions required by the classical theory simply could not be made. (Given any 30-year-old, there is no way to count all the possible outcomes of the person's life; there is no way to determine how many of these are favorable to the person living 60 years; and there is no reason to suppose each outcome is equally likely.)

The solution was the **relative frequency theory of probability**. On this theory, the probability of an event E, when E belongs to a category of events that occur again and again, is:

$$P(E) = \frac{f_0}{T_0}$$

where f_0 is the number of observed favorable outcomes and T_0 is the total number of observed outcomes.

Suppose we wish to know the probability that a 30-year-old in good health will live to be 40. Using this theory of probability, we would observe a large group of 1,000 healthy 30-year-olds. If, 10 years later, 950 are still alive, then the probability that a healthy 30-year-old will live to be 40 is 95%.

Rules of the Probability Calculus for Compound Events

The classical and relative frequency theories were developed to assign probability values to single events. Another problem within probability theory is this: Once probabilities have been assigned to single events, how are we to assign probabilities to *compound* arrangements of events? For example, we earlier used the classical theory to assign a probability to the event of drawing a queen on one draw from a shuffled poker deck. What is the probability that someone draws two cards in a row and both are queens? To determine such a compound probability, we need a set of principles known as the *probability calculus*.

If the occurrence of an event E has no effect on the occurrence of an event E', then E and E' are called independent events. For example, if someone draws a card and replaces it before drawing a second card, the first draw has no effect on the second draw and so the two draws are independent events. If two events cannot both occur at the same time, the two events are called *mutually exclusive* events. For example, if a normal coin is tossed, it's not possible that it will come up both heads and tails at the same time, and so the heads outcome and the tails outcome are mutually exclusive events.

In the following, let x and y be variables ranging over events, and let P(x) abbreviate the probability of event x occurring. We briefly examine seven fundamental rules of the probability calculus.

The Necessity Rule

The probability of an event that necessarily must happen is, by convention, 1. Thus:

If x necessarily must happen, then P(x) = 1

For example, the probability that it will either snow tomorrow or it will not snow tomorrow is exactly 1.

The Impossibility Rule

The probability of an event that necessarily cannot happen is 0. Thus:

If x necessarily cannot happen, P(x) = 0.

For example, the probability that it will snow tomorrow in Atlanta at noon and yet *not* snow tomorrow in Atlanta at noon is 0. Contradictions always have a probability of zero.

The Restricted Conjunction Rule

This principle is used to compute the probability of two events occurring together when the two events are independent of each other. If x and y are independent events, then the probability that x and y both happen is equal to the probability of x multiplied by the probability of y. That is:

$$P(x \text{ and } y) = P(x) \times P(y)$$

where x and y are independent.

Here is an example. We have already seen that the probability of drawing a queen from a shuffled poker deck is 1/13. What is the probability of drawing a queen on the first draw, and then, after placing that card back in the deck, drawing a queen again on the second draw? According to the restricted conjunction rule, the probability is figured this way:

P(queen 1 and queen 2) = P(queen 1) times P(queen 2)
= 1/13 × 1/13 = 1/169

where queen 1 abbreviates "a queen is drawn on the first draw" and queen 2 abbreviates "a queen is drawn on the second draw."

For another example, what is the probability that you toss two quarters in the air and both land tails up? Because the first toss has no effect on the second toss, the two events are independent. The probability of a fair coin landing tails is obviously 1/2. So, the probability that both land on tails is calculated as follows:

$$P(\text{tails 1 and tails 2}) = P(\text{tails 1}) \text{ times } P(\text{tails 2})$$
$$= 1/2 \times 1/2 = 1/4$$

What is the probability of rolling two threes with a standard pair of dice? Because each die has six sides, the probability that a single die is rolled and comes up three is 1/6. As the outcome of one die's roll doesn't affect the outcome of the other's roll, the probability that a pair of dice comes up two threes is calculated according to the restricted conjunction rule as follows:

$$P(\text{three 1 and three 2}) = P(\text{three 1}) \text{ times } P(\text{three 2})$$
$$= 1/6 \times 1/6 = 1/36$$

The General Conjunction Rule

This rule is used to compute the probability of two events occurring together in cases where the two events are not independent:

$$P(p \text{ and } q) = P(p) \times P(q \text{ given that } p \text{ occurred})$$

For example, what is the probability of drawing two cards in a row without replacing any cards drawn, and both are aces? The probability that the first card is an ace is, of course, 4/52. The probability that the second card is an ace—given that the first card was an ace and was not replaced—is 3/51, for at the second draw, only three aces remain. The probability of drawing two aces in a row without replacement is therefore:

$$P(\text{ace 1 and ace 2}) = P(\text{ace 1}) \times P(\text{ace 2 given ace 1})$$
$$= 4/52 \times 3/51 = 12/2{,}652 = 1/221$$

The general conjunction rule may also be used if the two events are independent. In such a case, the value of $P(q \text{ given } p)$ will be the same as $P(q)$. So, when the two events are independent, the general conjunction rule gives the same result as the restricted conjunction rule.

Exercise 34.2   Suppose a bowl contains eight apples, three oranges, and six peaches.

1. What is the probability of drawing at random two apples in a row with replacement? What is the probability of drawing two apples in a row without replacement?
2. What is the probability of randomly drawing an orange and then a peach, with replacement? What is the probability of drawing an orange and then a peach without replacement?

The Restricted Disjunction Rule

This rule is used to compute the probability that one or the other of two events occurs when the two events are mutually exclusive. The rule is:

$$P(p \text{ or } q) = P(p) + P(q)$$

For example, what is the probability of drawing just one card from a poker deck, and the card is either a jack or an ace? The probability that a drawn card is an ace is 4/52. The probability that a drawn card is a jack is also 4/52. Therefore, the probability that a single card drawn is either a jack or an ace is:

$$P(\text{jack or ace}) = P(\text{jack}) + P(\text{ace})$$
$$= 4/52 + 4/52 = 8/52 = 2/13$$

Exercise 34.3   A bowl contains eight grapes, five cherries, and three hamburgers.

1. What is the probability that someone randomly selects one item from the bowl and the item is either a grape or a cherry?
2. What is the probability one item is randomly drawn and it is not a grape?

Combining the Rules

Let us now use the restricted disjunction rule in combination with the restricted conjunction rule. Assume we are reaching into the bowl just mentioned in Exercise 34.3. What is the probability of randomly drawing either a grape or a cherry and then, after replacing what was drawn, drawing again either a grape or cherry? That is, what is the value of:

$$P[(\text{grape or cherry})1 \text{ and } (\text{grape or cherry})2]$$

The probability of drawing either a grape or a cherry on a single draw is, according to the restricted disjunction rule:

$$P(\text{grape or cherry}) = P(\text{grape}) + P(\text{cherry})$$
$$= 8/16 + 5/16$$
$$= 13/16$$

According to the restricted conjunction rule, the probability that this happens twice is calculated by multiplying the probability of the first by the probability of the second. We may now insert this into the format required by the restricted conjunction rule as follows:

$$P[(\text{grape or cherry})1 \text{ and } (\text{grape or cherry})2]$$
$$= P(\text{grape or cherry})1 \times P(\text{grape or cherry})2$$
$$= (8/16 + 5/16) \times (8/16 + 5/16)$$
$$= 13/16 \times 13/16$$

The General Disjunction Rule

This rule is used to compute the probability that one or the other of two events occurs, whether or not the two events are mutually exclusive events. In this discussion, we limit ourselves to the simpler case in which the two events are independent. The rule in this case is:

$$P(p \text{ or } q) = P(p) + P(q) - P(p \text{ and } q)$$

Because p and q are independent, this is equal to:

$$P(p \text{ or } q) = P(p) + P(q) - [P(p) \times P(q)]$$

What is the probability of drawing at least one ace on two draws from a deck of cards, with replacement? That is, what is the probability of drawing either an ace on the first draw, on the second draw, or on both draws—with replacement? Notice that this is an inclusive disjunction of events. Because the events are not mutually exclusive, the restricted disjunction rule does not apply and we must use the general disjunction rule. According to that rule, in this case:

$$P(\text{ace 1 or ace 2}) = P(\text{ace 1}) + P(\text{ace 2}) - P(\text{ace 1 and ace 2})$$
$$= (4/52 + 4/52) - (4/52 \times 4/52)$$

What is the probability of getting tails on either or both of two tosses of a quarter? According to the general disjunction rule:

$$P(\text{tails 1 or tails 2}) = P(\text{tails 1}) + P(\text{tails 2}) - P(\text{tails 1 and tails 2})$$
$$= (1/2 + 1/2) - (1/2 \times 1/2)$$
$$= 1 - 1/4$$
$$= 3/4$$

For one more example, what is the probability of getting at least one 3 when rolling a pair of 10-sided dice, where the sides are numbered 1 through 10? The general disjunction rule tells us:

$$P(\text{three 1 or three 2}) = P(\text{three 1}) + P(\text{three 2}) - P(\text{three 1 and three 2})$$
$$= (1/10 + 1/10) - (1/10 \times 1/10)$$
$$= (1/10 + 1/10) - 1/100$$
$$= 19/100$$

Exercise 34.4   You have been blindfolded and placed in front of two buckets of hot, greasy burgers. The first bucket contains three hamburgers, four cheeseburgers, and five fish burgers. The second bucket contains two hamburgers, three cheeseburgers, and six fish burgers.

1. You are to reach into the first bucket and pull out two burgers in a row, without replacement. You are next to reach into the second bucket and do the same thing. If one or more of the buckets yields first a cheeseburger and then a fish burger, you win the grand prize. (You get to eat the burgers you pull out!) What is the probability that you will win? That is, what is the probability you will draw first a cheeseburger and then a fish burger from one or the other or from both of the buckets? (Hint: You will have to combine both the general conjunction and general disjunction rules.)

2. Assume you have in front of you the two buckets of burgers from the previous problem. What is the probability of drawing one burger from each bucket, getting either a cheeseburger or a fish burger? That is, what is the probability that either the first bucket yields either a cheeseburger or a fish burger or the second bucket yields either a cheeseburger or a fish burger? (Hint: You will have to use both the general disjunction and the restricted disjunction rules.)

The Negation Rule

The negation rule is used to compute the probability of an event when the probability of the event *not* happening is known. The rule is:

$$P(p) = 1 - P(\text{not } p).$$

The proof of this rule is fairly simple. According to the restricted disjunction rule:

$$P(p \text{ or not } p) = P(p) + P(\text{not } p)$$

Because either p or else not p must happen, Rule 1 tells us:

$$P(p \text{ or not } p) = 1$$

Therefore:

$$1 = P(p) + P(\text{not } p)$$

If we subtract P (not p) from each side, we get:

$$1 - P(\text{not } p) = P(p).$$

For example, what is the probability of tossing two dimes and getting tails on at least one? The probability of this not happening is the probability of getting heads on both tosses, which is $1/2 \times 1/2 = 1/4$. So the probability of at least one tail on two tosses is:

$$1 - 1/4 = 3/4.$$

Exercise 34.5   Figure the following probabilities, assuming an ordinary deck of cards and an ordinary pair of dice, and so forth.

1. P(6 or 2 on a single roll of a die)
2. P(heads on four successive tosses of a coin)
3. P(king or ace on one draw)
4. P(at least one king or queen on two draws, with replacement)
5. P(two kings in two draws) if:
   a. The first card drawn is replaced.
   b. The first card is *not* replaced.

Exercise 34.6   If a pair of dice is rolled, what is the probability that the points add up to:

1. 3?
2. 4?
3. 5?
4. 6?

Exercise 34.7   Imagine two bowls of marbles. One has three green, six blue, and seven yellow marbles, and the other has two blue, four green, and five yellow marbles. If a single marble is drawn from each, what is the probability that:

    1.   Both are the same color?

    2.   At least one is blue?

    3.   One is blue and the other is green?

    4.   At least one is either blue or yellow?

    5.   Both are green?

Exercise 34.8   Imagine a jar containing five purple, six orange, and seven gold marbles. If two marbles are drawn without replacement, what is the probability that:

    1.   Both are the same color?

    2.   Both are gold?

    3.   Both are orange?

    4.   The marble drawn is either gold or it is not gold.

    5.   The marble drawn is either black or it is not black.

    6.   Either the marble drawn explodes or it does not explode.

Bayes's Theorem

This theorem of probability theory, named after its discoverer, the Reverend Thomas Bayes (1702–1761), an English theologian and mathematician, is used to measure the degree of support conferred on a hypothesis by the empirical (observational) evidence that has been offered in support of it. **Bayes's theorem** rests on the elementary rules of probability calculus and can be derived from them in several different ways. Here is one proof.

Let H be a variable ranging over hypotheses. Let E be a variable ranging over statements that summarize the evidence for a given hypothesis. At each step in the deduction, we assume that in addition to the evidence that might be in play, we are also relying on neutral background knowledge. This consists of our general knowledge of the world before we have the evidence in question; in other words, what we know about the world independently of the evidence at issue. According to the conditional rule:

$$P(H/E) = \frac{P(H \text{ \& } E)}{P(E)}$$

This says, "The probability of a hypothesis H given the evidence for it, E, equals the probability of the conjunction of the hypothesis and the evidence offered for it, divided by the probability of just the evidence alone."

Next, because truth-table analysis can easily show that any statement E is logically equivalent to [(E & H) v (E & ~H)], we may replace one with the other anywhere in the formula:

$$P(H/E) = \frac{P(H \ \& \ E)}{P[(E \ \& \ H) \ v \ (E \ \& \ \sim H)]}$$

The restricted disjunction rule allows us to replace P[(E & H) v (E & ~H)] with P(E & H) + P(E & ~H):

$$P(H/E) = \frac{P(H \ \& \ E)}{P(E \ \& \ H) + P(E \ \& \ \sim H)}$$

Applying the commutation rule turns this into:

$$P(H/E) = \frac{P(H \ \& \ E)}{P(H \ \& \ E) + P(\sim H \ \& \ E)}$$

Last, by three applications of the general conjunction rule, we arrive at a common way of expressing Bayes's theorem:

Bayes's Theorem

$$P(H/E) = \frac{P(H) \times P(E \ / \ H)}{[P(H) \times P(E \ / \ H)] + [P(\sim H) \times P(E \ / \ \sim H)]}$$

P(H) represents the prior probability of H (also called the intrinsic probability of H). This is the probability of H before considering the evidence E and assuming only neutral background information. In other words, this is the probability that H is true, based only on our general knowledge of the world prior to, or independent of, our knowledge of E. E represents the empirical evidence offered for H. P(E/H) represents the probability that the evidence would exist given the truth of the hypothesis. P(E /~H) represents the probability that the evidence would exist given the falsity of the hypothesis.

Bayes's formula tells us that the probability that the hypothesis (H) is true, given the evidence E, assuming only neutral background knowledge, is equal to the prior probability of H times the probability of E given H, divided by the values in the denominator of the formula.

Application

Suppose a patient has symptoms S1, S2, and S3, pointing to a particular disease D, and the doctor decides that *either* the patient has the disease, which happens to be a serious one, or the patient has some minor infection that will go away by itself in time. Thus, the hypotheses H and ~H are jointly exhaustive and mutually exclusive; that is, these are the only two possibilities and it is one or the other and not both. Thus:

H: The hypothesis that the patient has disease D.
~H: The hypothesis that the patient does not have disease D.

Next, suppose the doctor administers a test for the disease, and the patient tests positive for the presence of disease D. The evidence in this case is the positive test result:

E: The test is positive.

Next, let us suppose that prior to giving the test, the doctor knows two things:

- Patients with symptoms S1, S2, and S3 have the disease in 30% of all cases.
- 90% of patients with D test positive for it.

Thus, given just the background evidence, we have the prior probability of H:

$$P(H) = 3/10$$

That is, given background knowledge and the initial symptoms, the chance the patient has D is 30%. By the negation rule, because H and ~H are mutually exclusive and jointly exhaustive:

$$P(\sim H) = 7/10$$

In addition, because people who have D test positive in 90% of cases, we also have this piece of the puzzle:

$$P(E/H) = 9/10$$

Assuming that people who do not have D test positive in 10% of the cases, we also have:

$$P(E /\sim H) = 1/10$$

Finally, we plug these numbers into Bayes's theorem. What is the final percentage? Given that the test is positive, what is the probability that the patient has the disease? The calculation is left to the astute reader.

Bayes's Theorem and Relative Estimates of Probability

Exact numerical probabilities are not required when using Bayes's theorem; relative estimates of probability can be used instead and often are. Suppose a box of jewels has been stolen from the Gottrocks' residence and the police have a suspect. Joe Doaks was seen running from the scene of the crime hiding something under his coat. In addition, his fingerprints were found at the scene of the crime. These facts are suspicious, given that Doaks does not know the Gottrocks. Furthermore, Doaks, let us suppose, has been convicted of burglary seven times in the past. To make matters worse for Doaks, he also lives 10 miles from the scene of the crime. The hypothesis under consideration is this:

H: Joe Doaks stole the jewels.

The direct evidence is summarized in statement E:

E: Joe was seen running from the Gottrocks' home hiding something under his coat and his fingerprints were found at the scene of the crime.

Using Bayes's theorem, investigators might reason this way. If Doaks did *not* commit the crime, then the probability that E exists is very low, given neutral background knowledge (i.e., our general knowledge of the world independent of the evidence). That is, if he did not commit the crime, it is quite unlikely he would be seen running from the house, and hiding something under his coat, or that he would have left his fingerprints at the house, and so on, at the exact time the jewels were stolen. Thus:

$$P (E/ \sim H \& k) = \text{very low}$$

where k represents our neutral background knowledge. In addition, the investigative team might argue that the prior probability of H is significantly higher than the prior probability of E, given only neutral background knowledge. That is:

$$P (H/k) > P (E/k)$$

Finally, the investigative team might argue, again on the basis of common sense, that the probability of E, given that H is true, is quite high:

$$P (E / H \& k) = \text{very high}$$

Thus:

$$P (E / H \& k) > P (E / \sim H \& k)$$

Given these purely relative values, it follows from Bayes's theorem that the evidence in this case makes it probable that Doaks stole the jewels. We may also convert our relative probabilities into plausible numerical values, plug these into the theorem, and then estimate the probability on a numerical basis as well. For example, the following two estimates seem plausible:

$$P(E/\sim H \& k) = .1$$
$$P(E/H \& k) = .9$$

Either way, when we "weigh" the probabilities on the scale of Bayes's theorem, the evidence points to the probable truth of the hypothesis. In other words, we have a strong inductive argument for the conclusion that Doaks stole the jewels. Do you agree?

Glossary

Bayes's theorem A formula for estimating the probability that a hypothesis is true given the evidence for the hypothesis.

Classical theory of probability The theory developed by French philosopher and mathematician Blaise Pascal along with Pierre Fermat. The first systematic theory of probability.

Relative frequency theory of probability The theory developed by mathematicians in England during the eighteenth century to assess probabilities in actuarial cases such as estimating life expectancies for various groups of people.

Unit

6

Modal Logic

Our tour through the many branches and worlds of logical theory ends in this unit with a brief look at modal logic, the logic of possibility and necessity. Exciting research is being conducted right now in this fascinating branch of our subject.

35 Elementary Modal Logic ≪ ≪ ≪ ≪ ≪ ≪ ≪

One of the most fundamental distinctions of all, drawn at the very dawn of philosophy in the sixth century BC, is that between necessary and contingent truth. The earliest philosophers of the Western tradition, known as the "pre-Socratics" because they lived in the era before Socrates, noticed a fundamental difference between the truth of a mathematical theorem such as the Pythagorean theorem and the truth of a more mundane proposition such as the statement that Zeno has a beard. A mathematical theorem is not only true, it is true in a necessary sort of way, for it is true and cannot possibly be false without self-contradiction. On the other hand, a mundane truth such as that Zeno has a beard, may be true, but the proposition could have been false without any self-contradiction—as it would have been if Zeno had chosen to shave the day before. Unlike a proven mathematical theorem, which is true come what may, the truth of the statement ("Zeno has a beard today") is therefore contingent on Zeno and what he decides to do. Thus the ancient distinction between two fundamentally different "modes" of truth and falsity: necessity and contingency. We first examined this distinction in Chapter 6.

Modal logic is the study of the modes of truth and falsity and their relationship to reasoning. Founded by Aristotle in the fourth century BC, this is one of the most active fields of logic today—exciting research is being carried out by logicians and philosophers all over the world in this specialized branch of logic. The first part of this chapter concerns the formal language of modal logic; the second part covers modal natural deduction. As usual, we begin with precise definitions.

Semantics and Symbols for Modal Logic

Basic Definitions

Recall that in logic anything short of self-contradiction counts as **logically possible**, no matter how improbable, unlikely, or bizarre it is. If something is not self-contradictory and does not imply a self-contradiction, it counts as logically possible. Logic thus employs the word *possible* with the broadest available meaning. As we saw in Chapter 6, a proposition expressed by a declarative sentence is a **necessarily true proposition** if it is true in all possible circumstances, false in none, where a possible circumstance is any noncontradictory state of affairs. Thus, a proposition is necessarily true if and only if it is not logically possible that it is false. Parallel to this, a proposition expressed by a declarative sentence is a **necessarily false proposition** if it is false in all possible circumstances, true in none. In other words, a proposition is necessarily false if and only if it is not logically possible that it is true. We will look at examples in a moment.

A proposition that is neither necessarily true nor necessarily false is **logically contingent**. Thus, a proposition is logically contingent if there is at least one possible circumstance in which it is, or would be, true *and* there is at least one possible circumstance in which it is, or would be, false.

Finally, a proposition is a **possibly true proposition** if it is true in at least one possible circumstance, and it is a **possibly false proposition** if there is at least one possible circumstance in which it is false. A number of interesting propositions follow from our definitions:

- Every necessarily true proposition is also possibly true.
- It is not the case that every possibly true proposition is necessarily true. (Some possibly true propositions are necessarily true, but some possibly true propositions are contingent and thus *not* necessary.)
- Every necessarily false proposition is also possibly false.
- It is not the case that every possibly false proposition is necessarily false. (Some possibly false propositions are necessarily false, but other possibly false propositions are contingent and thus not necessary.)
- Every contingent proposition is both possibly true and possibly false.
- Every necessary truth is a noncontingent proposition.
- Every necessary falsehood is a noncontingent proposition.

Symbols

Let **P** be a proposition, and let the symbol □, called "box," stand for the sentence operator "It is necessarily true that . . ." If **P** is a necessarily true proposition, we write □**P**, which says, "It is necessarily true that **P**." Thus, when we prefix □ to a sentence, we assert that the sentence to which it is applied expresses a necessary truth. The formula □P, pronounced "box P," may also be read, "Necessarily, it is true that P" or more simply, "P is necessarily true." It can also be read as saying, "In all possible circumstances, P is true." Notice that the box symbol is a *monadic* sentence operator—a connective or operator operating on or connecting to—one sentence so as to produce a compound sentence. Thus, the box symbol will function syntactically the same way a tilde functions.

It is necessarily true that   2 + 2 = 4.
Operator ↑   ↑ Embedded sentence

Because ~P indicates that P is false, if we want to say that P is *necessarily* false, we simply place the box in front of ~P and write □~P. This formula, pronounced "box not P," may be read, "Necessarily, it is false that P," or "It is necessarily false that P," or more simply, "P is necessarily false." It can also be read as, "In all possible circumstances, P is false" or "P is false in all possible circumstances."

Let the symbol ◇, called "diamond," stand for the sentence operator "It is possibly true that . . ." If P is a possibly true proposition, we write ◇P. This says, "It is possibly true that P." Thus, when we prefix ◇ to a sentence, we assert that the sentence to which it is applied expresses a possible truth. The formula ◇P, pronounced "diamond P," may also be read, "Possibly, it is true that P," or more simply, "P is possibly true." It can also be read as, "In at least one possible circumstance, P is, or would be, true." Like box, diamond is a monadic sentence operator producing a compound sentence when it is applied. Thus, the diamond, like the box, will function syntactically the same way a tilde functions.

Because ~P says that P is false, if we want to say that P is *possibly* false, we simply place diamond in front of ~P and write ◇~P. This formula, pronounced "diamond not P," may be read, "Possibly, it is false that P," or "It is possibly false that P," or more simply, "P is possibly false." It can also be read as saying, "In at least one possible circumstance, P is false."

The symbol ▽ (called *nabla*) stands for the sentence operator "It is contingent that . . ." When we apply ▽ to P, we are saying that P expresses a contingent proposition. In other words, we are saying that P is, or would be, true in at least one possible circumstance *and* that P is, or would be, false in some possible circumstances. Thus, ▽P indicates that there is at least one possible circumstance in which P is true *and* there is at least one possible circumstance in which P is false. Nabla also functions syntactically the way tilde functions, namely, as a monadic operator.

If we want to say that it is false that P is contingent, we simply place a tilde in front of nabla and write ~▽P. This says, "It is false that P is contingent." If it is false that P is contingent, then P is *noncontingent*. Thus, the formula may also be read as indicating that **P** is noncontingent. Note that if some proposition **P** is non-contingent, then **P** must be either necessarily true or else necessarily false. Can you explain why?

The next two operators are both dyadic (two-place) operators. Recall from Chapter 6 that a proposition **P** "implies" a proposition **Q** if and only if it is not possible that **P** is true but **Q** is false. In other words, there are no possible circumstances in which **P** would be true and at the same time and in the same circumstances **Q** would be false. In modal logic, to indicate that **P** logically implies **Q**, we write **P** → **Q**. The symbol →, called *arrow*, indicates the relation of **implication**. Notice that → does not mean the same as ⊃. The two symbols have completely different meanings. The meaning of → is *modal* in nature, whereas the meaning of ⊃ is *truth-functional* in nature. The meaning of ⊃ is defined on a finite, four-row truth table; the meaning of → cannot be defined on a truth table or on *any* finite array of values.

Recall from Chapter 6 that two propositions are equivalent if and only if they imply each other. In other words, there are no possible circumstances in which one is true while the other is false; their truth values match in any and every possible circumstance. In modal logic, to indicate that **P** and **Q** are equivalent, we write **P** ↔ **Q**. The symbol ↔ is called *double arrow* and indicates the relation of mutual implication or equivalence. Notice that ↔ does not mean the same as ≡. Again, the two symbols have completely different meanings. The meaning of ↔ is modal in nature, whereas the meaning of ≡ is truth-functional in nature. The meaning of ≡ is defined on a finite, four-row truth table; the meaning of ↔ cannot be defined on a truth table or on any finite array of values. Table 35.1 summarizes these symbols and their meanings.

TABLE 35.1 A Summary of the Modal Symbols

Symbol	Name	Meaning
□	Box	Necessity
◇	Diamond	Possibility
▽	Nabla	Contingency
→	Arrow	Implication
↔	Double arrow	Equivalence

History Note

Recall the ancient debate over the nature of the conditional, explained in Chapter 10. The Megarian logician Philo argued for a truth-functional interpretation of *if, then* sentences: A conditional is only false when the antecedent is true and the consequent is false; it is true in every other case. His teacher Diodorus, on the other hand, argued that a conditional is only true when it is *not possible* the antecedent is true and the consequent is false. In other words, argued Diodorus, an if, then sentence is true only when it is the case that if the antecedent is true the consequent *must* be true. Now we can more fully see the difference between the two positions: Philo was arguing for a truth-functional interpretation of the conditional, whereas Diodorus was arguing for a *modal* interpretation. Horseshoe captures Philo's truth-functional interpretation; the arrow of modal logic captures the interpretation favored by his teacher. A conditional sentence symbolized with the horseshoe and whose truth conditions are given by the truth table for horseshoe, is called a "material" conditional. A conditional sentence symbolized with the arrow and whose truth conditions are those associated with the arrow is called a "strict" conditional. Thus, the material conditional is truth-functional in nature, the strict conditional is modal in nature. The crows no longer need caw about the nature of the conditional.

Examples

It is time for examples. The following sentences, if given their standard meanings, all express necessary truths.

1. $2 + 2 = 4$
2. All triangles have three sides.
3. All bachelors are unmarried.
4. If something is red, then it is colored.
5. Either Garth Brooks is over 30 or it is not the case that Garth Brooks is over 30.
6. Nothing is both red all over and green all over at the same time.
7. If A is taller than B, and B is taller than C, then A is taller than C.

Given the standard meaning that our linguistic community attaches to each of these sentences, each expresses a unique truth. In each case, there are no consistently describable circumstances in which the proposition expressed would be false. Thus, each expresses not just a truth but a *necessary* truth.

The following sentences, given their usual meanings, all express necessary falsehoods.

1. Vinegar is an acid, and it is not the case that vinegar is an acid.
2. Japan is an island, and it is not the case that Japan is an island.
3. $1 + 1 = 64$
4. Some triangles have 17 angles.

5. All squares have 22 sides.

6. In Australia, there are two brothers and each is older than the other.

7. There is a man who is older than all men.

Given the standard meaning that we attach to each of these sentences, each expresses a necessarily false proposition. For in each case, there are no consistently describable circumstances in which the proposition expressed would be true.

The following sentences express logically contingent propositions.

1. The average price of butter lettuce on June 28, 2011, is 98 cents a head.

2. Bob Dylan performed in Santa Monica, California, in July 2007.

3. The average temperature in Seattle in 2010 was 62 degrees.

4. The Beatles sold 4 million albums in 1967.

5. Donovan wrote "Mellow Yellow" in 1965.

6. Crosby, Stills, Nash, and Young performed at Woodstock.

7. Ringo Starr performed at Chateau Ste. Michelle on July 31, 2010.

The propositions expressed by these sentences are contingent because, in each case, whether the proposition is true or false depends on circumstances. In each case, the proposition is true in some possible circumstances, but false in others.

The following sentences express possibly true propositions.

1. In 1862 someone, somewhere, ate three apples for lunch on a bright summer day.

2. At least two people read *Catcher in the Rye* at the Woodstock festival in 1969.

The following sentences express possibly false propositions.

1. In 1862 someone, somewhere, ate five apples for lunch on a bright summer day.

2. At least one person read *Catcher in the Rye* at the Woodstock festival in 1969.

What Is a Modal Argument?

A **modal argument** is an argument that has the following two properties: (a) it contains modal operators, and (b) its validity or invalidity depends only on the formal arrangement of its modal operators. Many of the most interesting arguments in the history of philosophy—arguments about free will, the existence and nature of God, the nature of consciousness, fatalism, the soul, social justice, and more—are modal arguments. The analysis and evaluation of modal arguments is obviously the central task of modal logic. Several classic arguments will be examined later, after a little more logical machinery is in place.

The Formal Language ML

As you know by now, a language is specified in terms of its syntax and its semantics. It is time to specify the syntax for a formal language of modal logic. The language will be called ML (for modal language).

Vocabulary for ML

1. Sentence constants: A, B, . . . Z.
2. Sentence operators
    Monadic operators: ~ □ ◇ ▽
    Dyadic operators: & v ⊃ ≡ → ↔
3. Grouping devices
    Parentheses: ( ) Brackets: [ ]
    Braces: { }

Rules of Grammar for ML

M1. Any sentence constant alone is a sentence of ML.
M2. If **P** is a sentence of ML, then ~ **P**, □ **P**, ◇ **P**, ▽ **P** are sentences of ML.
M3. If **P** and **Q** are sentences of ML, then (**P** & **Q**), (**P** v **Q**), (**P** ⊃ **Q**), (**P** ≡ **Q**), (**P** → **Q**), (**P** ↔ **Q**) are sentences of ML.

Any expression that contains only items drawn from the vocabulary of ML and that can be constructed by a finite number of applications of the rules of grammar M1 through M3 is a sentence, or well-formed formula, of ML. Nothing else counts as a sentence of ML.

You might have noticed that the syntax for ML is exactly the same as the syntax for TL except that the modal operators have been added to the lists of monadic and dyadic operators. Thus, any sentence that is a wff of TL will automatically count as a wff of ML, although it is not the case that any wff of ML will count as a wff of TL. The truth-functional language TL is thus resident within ML.

You might also have noticed that ML does *not* include PL, the language of predicate logic. If we were to include PL in ML, we would have what is called quantified modal logic. This branch of our subject is best reserved for an advanced text in logical theory; the conceptual and philosophical problems that arise when quantifiers and modal operators are combined in one logical system are fascinating, but they are also extremely difficult and call for some very advanced theoretical work indeed. Propositional modal logic nicely rounds out an introductory study of logical theory.

Modal Operators Need Scope, Too

When symbolizing sentences containing modal operators, it is important to pay attention to the scopes of the modal operators. The box, diamond, and nabla are monadic operators. The scope of one of these three operators will always be exactly what the scope would be if the operator were to be a tilde. The arrow and double arrow operators are dyadic. Their scopes will always be the same as if they were ampersands, wedges, or horseshoes.

Translation: Aristotle's Principles

Aristotle, the founder of logic, wrote the first treatise containing a theoretical discussion of modal logic; in this sense he is the founder of modal logic, in addition to being the founder of logical theory in general. We find the following modal principles in his treatise *De Interpretatione*:

- The necessary is that which cannot possibly be otherwise.
- The possible is that which is not necessarily not otherwise.

Therefore:

- "It is necessarily so" is equivalent to "It is not possibly not so."
- "It is not necessarily so" is equivalent to "It is possibly not so."
- "It is possibly so" is equivalent to "It is not necessarily not so."

These are among the Aristotelian principles traditionally represented on the "modal square of opposition." Let us symbolize each within our new language, ML. Suppose A is some proposition-expressing sentence, and assume the Aristotelian modal principles stated above. To say, "In every possible circumstance, A is true," in other words, to say that A is a necessary truth, is equivalent to saying, "There's not even one possible circumstance in which A is false." Thus:

□ A is equivalent to ~◇ ~ A

Next, to say, "There's a possible circumstance in which A is true," in other words, to say that A is possibly true, is equivalent to saying, "It's not the case that in every possible circumstance A is false." Therefore:

◇ A is equivalent to ~ □ ~ A

Next, to say, "There's no possible circumstance in which A is true," in other words, to say that A is impossible, is equivalent to saying, "In every possible circumstance A is false." Therefore:

~ ◇A is equivalent to □ ~ A

Finally, the expression "It's not the case that in every possible circumstance A is true," in other words, to say that A is not a necessary truth, is equivalent to saying, "There's at least one possible circumstance in which A is false." Consequently:

~ □ A is equivalent to ◇ ~ A

With these principles in mind, suppose we want to translate a formula containing a box into an equivalent formula that contains a diamond, or vice versa. For that, we use the following rule.

The Diamond Exchange Rule (DE)

1. Add a tilde to each side of the box or diamond.
2. Change the box to the diamond or the diamond to the box.
3. Cancel out any double negatives that result.

For example, let us translate ~ □A into a formula containing the diamond, without loss of meaning. Here are the three steps:

1. Add a tilde to each side of the box or diamond: ~ ~ □ ~ A
2. Change the box to the diamond or the diamond to the box: ~ ~◇ ~ A
3. Cancel out any double negatives: ◇~ A

Thus, we transformed ~ □ A into the logically equivalent formula ◇~ A.

Sentence	Symbolization
1. It is necessarily true that Fermat's Last Theorem is true.	□ F
2. It is not necessarily true that electrons are lighter than protons.	~□ E
3. It is necessarily false that an omnipotent zombie exists.	□ ~O
4. It is not necessarily false that robot zombie bats inhabit Mars.	~□ ~R
5. It is possibly true that Fermat's Last Theorem is true.	◇ F

6. It is not possibly true that electrons are lighter than protons.   ~◇ E
7. It is possibly false that an omnipotent zombie exists.   ◇ ~O
8. It is *not* possibly false that robot zombie bats inhabit Mars.   ~◇ ~R
9. It is contingent that some mountains have snowy tops.   ∇M
10. It is not contingent that 4 + 4 = 8.   ~∇F
11. It is contingent that some mountains do not have snowy tops.   ∇~M
12. It is necessary that it is contingent that some mountains have snowy tops.   □∇M
13. It is necessary that it is possible that some trees have bird nests.   □◇T
14. It is contingent that it is possible that water freezes.   ∇◇W
15. It is necessary that it is a necessary truth that Fermat's Last Theorem is true.   □□F
16. It is possible that it is a possible truth that snow is white.   ◇◇S
17. It is necessary that it is necessarily false that all triangles have two sides.   □□~A
18. All triangles have three sides strictly implies that 2 + 2 = 4.   A →T
19. The falsity of 1 + 1 = 3 strictly implies the falsity of 2 + 2 = 6.   ~O →~S
20. If P is necessarily true then P is possibly true.   □P →◇P

Exercise 35.1   Let S be the proposition that Shoreline Community College (SCC) has a volleyball team. Translate the following into ML.

1. In every possible circumstance SCC has a volleyball team.
2. There is no possible circumstance in which SCC has a volleyball team.
3. In every possible circumstance it is false that SCC has a volleyball team.
4. It is false that in every possible circumstance SCC has a volleyball team.
5. Not every possible circumstance is one in which SCC has a volleyball team.

Exercise 35.2   Symbolize the following in ML, using obvious abbreviations.

1. It is not a necessary truth that protons are heavier than electrons.
2. It is a contingent truth that a universe actually exists.
3. It is impossible that 2 + 2 = 99.
4. It is necessarily false that some triangles have seven sides.
5. It is possible that Bill Gates retires, but it is also possible that he doesn't.
6. Necessarily, it is false that the square root of two is rational.
7. It is necessarily true that the derivative of a constant is zero.
8. It is not possible that it is not true that 2 + 2 = 4.

9. It is not possible that it is true that $2 + 2 = 7$.

10. Necessarily, if the universe was created, then God exists.

11. It is false that it is contingent that $2 + 2 = 4$.

12. Necessarily, either the universe will expand forever or it will not expand forever.

13. Either it is necessary that the universe will expand forever or it is necessary that the universe will not expand forever.

14. Either it is a necessary truth that the universe was created or it is not a necessary truth that the universe was created.

15. Either it is necessary that the universe was created or it is necessary that the universe was not created.

16. If materialism is true, then it is necessarily true that God does not exist.

17. If it is necessarily true that God exists, then it is necessarily true that materialism is false.

18. If it is necessarily true that the universe will expand forever, then it is not possible that God exists.

19. If God exists, then it is a necessary truth that God exists.

20. If God does not exist, then it is a necessary truth that God does not exist.

21. If God does not exist, then it is not possible that God exists.

22. If it is possible that the universe was created, then it is possible that God exists.

23. If it is possible that nothing exists, then it is contingent that the universe exists.

Modal Operators Are Not Truth-Functional

Philosophers and logicians have encountered many difficulties in developing an adequate semantical theory for modal logic in the years since Aristotle stated the first modal principles on record. Although the semantics for truth-functional logic, and the semantics for predicate logic, were both completed during the first half of the twentieth century, a formal and complete semantical theory for modal logic wasn't developed until the late 1950s, by a young logician named Saul Kripke (b. 1940). If the modal operators had been truth-functional in nature, constructing the semantics of modality would have been as easy as drawing up a few new truth tables. Unfortunately, the semantics for the modal operators cannot be defined in terms of truth-functions, on truth tables, for the fundamental modal concepts are not truth-functional in nature. Essentially, this is because the truth-value of a sentence that has as its main operator a modal operator is *not* a function of just the truth-value (or values) of its component (or components) alone. That is, when the main operator is a modal operator, there is no determinate or functional relationship between *just* the truth-values of the components and the truth-value of the compound as a whole.

For example, suppose we know that a proposition A is false. Given just this information, what is the truth-value of □ A? In this case □ A must be false. However, suppose all we know is that A has the truth-value true. Given just this information, what is the truth-value of □ A? There's no way to tell from this information alone. In some cases, a sentence A will be true when □ A is true, and in other cases a sentence A will be true but □ A is false. Given just the information that some sentence A is true, nothing determinate follows regarding the truth-value of □ A. Thus, no purely truth-functional relationship exists between A's truth and the truth value of □ A. Therefore, although we can fill in the second row of the table for □ A, we cannot fill in the first row of the truth table. In other words, the truth-value of □ A is not a function of the truth-value of A alone. The most we can do, if we try to state a general truth table for □ **P**, is this:

P		□	**P**
T		?	T
F		F	F

The function is incomplete; it has a gap. A similar argument can be given for each of the other modal operators, showing that none of the modal operators is truth-functional in nature. In sum, if we were to try to specify truth tables for any of the modal operators, in each case we find rows that cannot be filled in. Thus, the modal operators are not truth-functional in nature, that is, no truth-functions exist that can be associated with the modal operators.

Formal Semantics for ML

The American philosopher and logician C. I. Lewis (1883–1964) did pioneering work in modal logic during the 1920s and 1930s and is considered the founder of modern modal logic. Lewis developed a number of formal systems of modal logic, each designed to represent a different way of interpreting the modal operators. He also investigated the theoretical properties of these systems (known as the "Lewis systems") and mapped out their interrelationships. However, most logicians at the time rejected modal logic for one main reason: Lewis was not able to provide an adequate semantical basis for modal logic. That development would not occur until the late 1950s, when Saul Kripke borrowed a concept from the German philosopher Leibniz (1646–1716) and produced the first complete formal semantics for modal logic. *Kripke semantics*, as it is sometimes called, has become the standard semantics for modal logic, and indeed for all research in the advanced, cutting-edge areas on the frontiers of logical theory.

Leibniz had asked this question: Before God created the material universe, did he have a choice as to which world to create? Did God face an abstract array of many **possible worlds**—each one not yet real or actual—and then it was a matter of deciding which possible world to "actualize" or bring into existence? The question is fascinating, whether or not one believes in God. Is the universe we live in the *only* way a universe or "world" could possibly be? Or are there other ways a world could be, other possible worlds, and the universe in which we live is just one universe out of many possible universes? If so, what distinguishes the universe in which we live from the many possible universes that could have existed instead? Does our universe have a special property, "actuality," that the others, being merely possible, lack? Do nonactual possible worlds exist in some nonactual "limbo," waiting in the wings for their turn to "be" or to become real? What is the difference between possibility and actuality?

Kripke employed the Leibnizian concept of a "possible world" to specify a semantical theory for modal logic. The semantics he developed has become the standard in the field. What do modal logicians have in mind when they speak of a possible world? Let us approach their idea in stages. Our planet orbits a star that sits about 20,000 light years from the edge of an enormous disk-shaped collection of stars called the Milky Way galaxy. Our galaxy, which contains more than 100 billion stars, is located near the edge of a swarm of about two dozen galaxies, each with billions of stars, each trillions of miles apart. This cluster of galaxies, called the Local Group, is part of a "supercluster" of galaxies—a gigantic cluster of clusters of galaxies. Beyond our supercluster lie neighboring superclusters containing billions of additional galaxies.

When we speak of "our world," let this refer to everything in the universe, no matter how far away in space and no matter how far away in time. So the term *our world* means "the entire universe." Now, consider this statement: Our world might have been different from the way it actually is. Instead of containing as many galaxies as it actually contains, it might have contained only half as many, a fourth as many, twice as many, and so on. Instead of containing protons, neutrons, and electrons, it might have contained other kinds of particles. Furthermore, it seems plausible to suppose that the laws of nature (the physical laws studied in physics, chemistry, etc.) might have been different from what they are. Cosmologists plug alternative laws of nature into their computer models of the universe and produce a picture of what the universe would have been like if the laws of physics had been different. And the alternatives are seemingly endless. Moreover, you might have grown up in a different city, you might have slept an hour longer this morning, and so on.

Just consider the sequence that begins thus: The universe might have contained exactly 1,000 galaxies, it might have contained exactly 1,001 galaxies, it might have contained exactly 1,002 galaxies, it might have contained exactly 1,003 galaxies . . . . So, it seems there are infinitely many "ways things might have been."

These infinitely many ways things might have been constitute an infinite number of ways a world could be. Furthermore, had one of these other ways been real or actual, the actual world—the way things actually are—would itself have been just another way things might have been. Consequently, the actual world—the universe we actually inhabit—also represents a way a world could be. Let us call each of these ways that things might have been or might be a *possible world*. These infinitely many ways that things might have been or might be constitute an infinity of possible worlds—an infinity of ways a world could be.

However, there seems to be one major difference between the actual world we inhabit and all the other possibilities: All the other possible worlds are nonactual possible worlds; the world we inhabit is the only *actual* world. A few philosophers disagree with this last statement, but the absolute difference between the actual and the merely possible seems to be firmly rooted in common sense.

It is important to emphasize that other possible worlds are not distant planets or galaxies or universes far away in space. Remember that anything, no matter how far away in physical space–time, counts as part of what we are defining as the actual world. So, other possible worlds are not located "out there" in physical space. They are merely possibilities, not actualities.

Now, using the notion of a possible world, and letting **P** and **Q** be any proposition-expressing sentences, a simplified version of the standard semantical theory for propositional modal logic can be stated.

Semantics for ML

- A proposition **P** is necessarily true if and only if it is true in all possible worlds.
- A proposition **P** is necessarily false if and only if it is false in all possible worlds.
- A proposition **P** is possibly true if and only if it is true in at least one possible world.
- A proposition **P** is possibly false if and only if it is false in at least one possible world.
- A proposition **P** is contingent if and only if it is true in some possible worlds and it is false in some possible worlds.
- An argument is valid if and only if there are no possible worlds in which its premises would be true and at the same time its conclusion would be false.
- An argument is invalid if and only if there is at least one possible world in which its premises would be true and at the same time its conclusion would be false.

- **P implies Q** if and only if there are no possible worlds in which P is true and Q is false.
- **P** and **Q** are equivalent if and only if there are no possible worlds in which they differ in truth-value.
- **P** and **Q** are consistent if and only if there is at least one possible world in which they are both true.
- **P** and **Q** are inconsistent if and only if there is not at least one possible world in which they are both true.

Exercise 35.3   True or false?

1. Every possibly true proposition is also possibly false.
2. Every necessarily true proposition is possibly true.
3. Every necessarily false proposition is possibly false.
4. Every possibly true proposition is necessarily true.
5. Every necessary truth is possibly false.
6. Every contingent proposition is possibly false.
7. Every possibly true proposition is also contingent.
8. Every true proposition is necessarily true.
9. Every necessarily true proposition is true.
10. Every necessarily false proposition is false.
11. Every necessarily true proposition is contingent.

Exercise 35.4   Symbolize each of the following and indicate in each case whether the sentence is true or false.

1. If A is true, then either A is necessarily true or A is contingent.
2. If A is necessarily true, then it's not possible that A is false.
3. If A is contingent, then it's not possible that A is false.
4. If A is true, then it's not possible that A is false.
5. If A is contingent, then either A is possibly true or A is possibly false.
6. If A is possibly true, then A is either necessarily true or contingent.
7. If A is necessarily false, then A is not contingent.
8. If A is false, then A is not necessarily true.
9. If A is necessarily false, then A is not possibly true.
10. If A is true, then A is not necessarily false.
11. If A is contingent, then A is not necessarily true.
12. If A is contingent, then A is possibly true.

Exercise 35.5 True or false?

Part I

1. If proposition A is actually true and proposition B is actually true, then A and B must be consistent.
2. If A and B are both necessarily false, then A and B must be consistent.
3. If A is necessarily false and B is necessarily true, then A must imply B.
4. If A is actually false and B is actually false, then A and B must be inconsistent.
5. A necessary truth is consistent with any contingent proposition.
6. If A is necessarily true and B is contingent, then B must imply A.
7. If A and B are both necessarily true, then A and B must be consistent.
8. If A and B are both necessarily true, then A and B must be equivalent.
9. If A and B are both necessarily false, then A and B must be equivalent.
10. If propositions A and B are both contingent, then A and B must be equivalent.
11. If propositions A and B are both contingent, then A and B must be consistent.

Part II
Symbolize the same statements in ML.

Five Modal Principles

Many (but not all) modal logicians agree that the following principles of modality express necessary truths. Most modal logicians find the first three principles to be self-evident; however, the fourth and fifth principles are the subject of much debate in modal logic.

Modal Principle 1: If **P** is a truth-functional tautology, then **P** is necessarily true.

Reasoning: If a sentence **P** is a truth-functional tautology, the final column of **P**'s truth table contains all Ts. Because collectively the rows of a truth table represent all possibilities, it follows that **P** is true in all possible circumstances or possible situations. Consequently, every truth-functional tautology is a necessary truth.

Modal Principle 2: If **P** is necessarily true, then **P** is actually true as well.

Reasoning: If **P** is necessarily true, **P** is true in every possible circumstance or possible situation. It would follow that **P** is true in the actual circumstance. So, if **P** is necessarily true, **P** is actually true as well. Every necessary truth must be actually true as well.

Modal Principle 3: If **P** is necessarily true, and **P** implies **Q**, then **Q** is also necessarily true.

Reasoning: Suppose that **P** is necessarily true and that **P** implies **Q**. Because **P** is necessarily true, **P** is true in every possible circumstance. Because **P** implies **Q**, there is no circumstance in which **P** is true and **Q** is false. It follows that **Q** must be true in every possible circumstance as well. For if there were to be even one circumstance in which **Q** is false, that would be a circumstance in which **P** is true and **Q** is false, which would mean, contrary to our assumption, that **P** does not imply **Q**. Here is another way to put the principle: Whatever is implied by a necessary truth is itself also necessarily true.

Modal Principle 4: If **P** is necessarily true, then **P** is necessarily necessarily true.

Reasoning: It would seem that if **P** is true in a circumstance—call it circumstance 1—then in every circumstance it's true that **P** is true in circumstance 1. Suppose **P** is true in all possible circumstances. It would seem that from the perspective of any circumstance, it is true that **P** is true in every circumstance. So, if **P** is true in every circumstance, then in every possible circumstance it must be true that **P** is true in every circumstance. That is, if it is necessarily true that **P**, it is necessarily true that **P** is necessarily true.

Comment. Some philosophers dispute this principle, although we shall not enter into that debate in this text. Principle 4 amounts to the claim that the necessity of a proposition is itself a matter of necessity. That is, it is not a contingent matter if P is a necessary truth; rather, if P is necessarily true, it is *necessary* that P is necessarily true.

Modal Principle 5: If P is possibly true, then P is necessarily possibly true.

Reasoning: Suppose that a sentence **P** is possibly true. That is, suppose **P** is true in at least one possible circumstance. It would seem that from the perspective of any circumstance, it's true that there is a circumstance in which **P** is true. But then it seems plausible to suppose that in every possible circumstance, it's true that there is a possible circumstance in which **P** is true. So, if **P** is possibly true, then it's necessarily true that **P** is possibly true.

Comment. Some philosophers dispute this principle as well, although we shall not enter into that discussion here. According to principle 5, possibility is also a matter of necessity: If it is true that in at least one circumstance **P** is true, then it is the case that in all circumstances it is true that in at least one circumstance **P** is true.

These five principles of modality can be abbreviated and expressed more formally as follows:

MP 1: If P is tautological, then $\Box$ P

MP 2: $\Box$ P $\rightarrow$ P

MP 3: [$\Box$ P & (P $\rightarrow$ Q)] $\rightarrow$ $\Box$ Q

MP 4: $\Box$ P $\rightarrow$ $\Box$ $\Box$ P

MP 5: $\Diamond$ P $\Box$ $\Diamond$ P

Systems of Modal Logic

A number of different natural deduction systems of modal logic have been developed, each with a different set of natural deduction rules based on a different set of fundamental modal assumptions. Each system constitutes a unique way of representing formally what we believe about the modal operators and modal reasoning. Many modal logicians and philosophers argue that all five of the modal principles above are necessarily true. Consequently, the deduction rules they specify for modal logic are all logical consequences of modal principles MP1 through MP 5. C. I. Lewis named the system of modal logic that is based on all five of the modal principles the system S5. Some philosophers dispute the truth of the fifth modal principle and accept only the first four principles. (We shall not enter into this debate here.) Accordingly, they specify natural deduction rules that are designed to reflect only principles MP1 through MP4. Lewis named the system of modal logic that is based on the first four of the modal principles S4.

Although philosophers do not all agree on which system best represents the correct logic of possibility and necessity, the system S5 is probably the most widely used formal system of modal logic. The system S5 is "stronger" than the system S4 in the sense that any argument that can be proven valid using S4 rules can also be proven valid using S5 rules, but not vice versa. So, many arguments that can be proven valid in S5 cannot be proven valid in S4. Another way to put this is to say that S5 "contains" S4 or that S4 is "resident within" S5.[1]

S5 Natural Deduction

The System S5D

An S5 natural deduction system is a natural deduction system that includes (a) a modal language, (b) all of the truth-functional deduction rules, and (c) rules for handling the modal operators. In addition, such a system is designed to reflect all five of

[1] For further information on modal logic, see James W. Garson, *Modal Logic for Philosophers.* (Cambridge: Cambridge University Press, 2006).

the principles of modality presented, MP1 through MP 5. Let us now learn a simpli-fied, incomplete, miniversion of an S5 natural deduction system. The name of our system is S5D (for S5 natural deduction). Perhaps after learning to use it, you will want to apply it to some modal proofs of your own creation. S5D incorporates all the rules of truth-functional deduction. (Thus, TD is resident within S5D.) In addition to the rules of the system TD, the following rules are added.

The Box Removal Rule (BR)

From a sentence □**P**, you may infer the corresponding sentence **P**.

The Possibility Introduction Rule (PI)

From a sentence **P**, you may infer the corresponding sentence ◇ **P**.

Modal Modus Ponens (MMP)

From a sentence **P** → **Q** and the corresponding sentence **P**, you may infer the cor-responding sentence **Q**.

Modal Modus Tollens (MMT)

From a sentence **P** → **Q** and the corresponding sentence ~**Q**, you may infer the corresponding sentence ~**P**.

Modal Hypothetical Syllogism (MHS)

From a sentence **P** → **Q** and the corresponding sentence **Q** → **R**, you may infer the corresponding sentence **P** → **R**.

The Contingency Rule (C)

From a sentence ∇**P**, you may infer the corresponding sentence ◇ **P** & ◇ ~**P**.

The Diamond Exchange Rule (DE)

A diamond may be traded for a box, or vice versa, if at the same time you add a tilde to each side of the operator, canceling out any double negatives that might result.

Our seven modal deduction rules can now be abbreviated as follows.

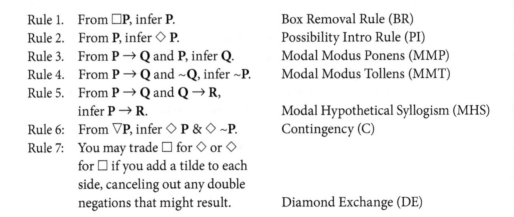

Rule 1. From □P, infer **P**.   Box Removal Rule (BR)
Rule 2. From **P**, infer ◇ **P**.   Possibility Intro Rule (PI)
Rule 3. From **P** → **Q** and **P**, infer **Q**.   Modal Modus Ponens (MMP)
Rule 4. From **P** → **Q** and ~**Q**, infer ~**P**.   Modal Modus Tollens (MMT)
Rule 5. From **P** → **Q** and **Q** → **R**,
        infer **P** → **R**.   Modal Hypothetical Syllogism (MHS)
Rule 6: From ∇**P**, infer ◇ **P** & ◇ ~**P**.   Contingency (C)
Rule 7: You may trade □ for ◇ or ◇
        for □ if you add a tilde to each
        side, canceling out any double
        negations that might result.   Diamond Exchange (DE)

An infinite number of symbolized modal arguments can be proven valid using just this limited set of S5 deduction rules. More than enough for a lifetime of proofing. It is time for applications. Here are two modal proofs. Study them carefully.

1.

1.	A → B	
2.	B → C	
3.	(A→C) → □ G /~□ ~ G	
4.	(A → C)	MHS 1, 2
5.	□ G	MMP 3,4
6.	G	BR 5
7.	◇G	PI 6
8.	~ □ ~G	DE 7

2.

1.	A → B		
2.	~B		
3.	~A→ ◇C		
4.	◇C ⊃ □ ~H		
5.	H v O	/ ◇ O	
6.	~A		MMT 1, 2
7.	◇ C		MMP 3, 6
8.	□ ~H		MP 7, 4
9.	~H		BR 8
10.	O		DS 5, 9
11.	◇ O		PI 10

More Definitions

The system of modal logic consisting of (a) the language ML, and (b) the rules of S5D natural deduction, is named the **system S5D**. A **proof in S5D** may be defined as "a sequence of formulas of ML that is such that every formula is either a premise, or an assumption, or follows from previous formulas by an S5D rule, in which every line that is not a premise is justified and every assumption has been discharged." An argument is **valid in S5D** if and only if it is possible to construct a proof in S5D whose premises are the premises of the argument and whose conclusion is the conclusion of the argument. Any argument that is valid in S5D may also be said to be "S5 valid." Now it is time to go to work.

Exercise 35.6   Prove these arguments valid using S5D.

1.
    1.   ◇ (H & S) ⊃ G
    2.   ~R
    3.   R v (H & S) / G

2.
    1.   R → M
    2.   H & R / M v G

3.
    1.   ~H
    2.   S → H
    3.   ◇ ~ S ⊃ R / R v ◇ M

4.
    1.   H → G
    2.   G → (M & N)
    3.   [H → (M & N)] ⊃ S / S

5.
    1.   ~R
    2.   R v (A ⊃ B)
    3.   (A ⊃ B) ⊃ (P → Q)
    4.   Q → L / P → L

6.
    1.   ◇A → □ ◇ S
    2.   A / ◇ S

7.
    1.   □R
    2.   R ⊃ G
    3.   ~G v M / ◇ M

8.
    1.   □ A → ◇ B
    2.   H ⊃ ~ ◇B
    3.   ~ H ⊃ G
    4.   ~ G / ~ □ A

9.

    1.   F → (□A & □B)

    2.   G ⊃ F

    3.   H & G / (□A & □B)

10.

    1.   G → ◇M

    2.   H & (G & R)

    3.   ◇M ⊃ A / ◇A

11.

    1.   M v (H & W)

    2.   M → ~ G

    3.   □(G & S)

    4.   ◇W ⊃ □B / A ⊃ B

12.

    1.   □(A ⊃ ◇B)

    2.   H v A

    3.   ~ (F v H) / ◇B

13.

    1.   □(A ⊃ B)

    2.   B ⊃ G

    3.   ~ G v S

    4.   ~ (S v R) / ◇ ~ A

14.

    1.   □(A v B)

    2.   B ⊃ H

    3.   ~ R & ~ H / A

Advanced Modal Deduction

If we add the following rules to S5D, we get S5D+, an augmented and advanced system of modal deduction based on the five modal principles, MP1 through MP5. Using this system, some extremely complex modal arguments can be proven valid, and some of the most fascinating arguments in the history of philosophy can be explored in depth and with rigor.

The Possibility to Necessity Rule

Surprisingly, under certain special conditions an inference from pure logical possibility to strict logical necessity is valid. As usual, some setup is necessary. First, a formula **P** of ML is *modally closed* just in case every sentence letter *within* **P** appears within the scope of a modal operator. Thus, each of the following sentences is modally closed:

$$E \rightarrow A \qquad \Box(A \& B) \qquad \Diamond(H \vee G) \qquad \nabla(A \vee B) \qquad \Diamond P \& \Diamond Q$$

Notice that in each of the first four cases here, the scope of the modal operator takes in the whole sentence, not just part of the sentence. In the fifth case, each letter (P, Q) lies within the scope of a modal operator. Each of the following is not modally closed:

$$\Box A \vee B \qquad A \vee \Box B \qquad \Diamond P \supset Q \qquad (A \rightarrow B) \& G$$

Each of these formulas is not modally closed because the scope of the modal operator is not the whole sentence. Remember that the scope of a box or diamond is exactly the same as if the symbol were a tilde, and the scope of an arrow or double arrow is the same as if the symbol were a horseshoe. In the first sentence, the scope of the box does not extend to the B. In the second sentence, the scope of the box does not cover the A, and so on.

Second, it can be rigorously proven that every modally closed sentence of ML expresses a noncontingent proposition, assuming the semantics for S5. In other words, if a sentence of ML is modally closed, the sentence expresses a necessary truth, or it expresses a necessary falsehood. Still another way to put this is as follows: If a sentence of ML is modally closed, the truth-value of the proposition expressed is invariant across all possible worlds. This fact is a logical consequence of the five principles of modality, although it will not be demonstrated here.

Possibility to Necessity (PN) Rule

From a line of the form:

$$P \rightarrow Q$$

and a corresponding line:

$$\Diamond P$$

you may infer □**Q**, provided that the formula that instantiates **Q** is a modally closed formula.

Here is a more earthy way to put this instruction: From a line of the form **P** → **Q**, and a line that is the same as the **P** part of the **P** → **Q** except that it has a diamond attached to it, we may infer a line that is the same as the **Q** part of the **P → Q** except that it has a box added to it (provided that the formula instantiating **Q** is a modally closed formula). Here is an example of this interesting rule:

1. A →□E
2. ◇ A
3. □□ E   PN 1, 2

At line 3, we were allowed to apply the PN rule because the formula following the arrow on line 1, namely, the formula □E, is modally closed. The formula □E is modally closed because every letter within it (there is only one letter within it) lies within the scope of a modal operator, in this case the operator being □.

If this rule does not seem valid to you, consider the following line of reasoning. Suppose P strictly implies Q. Suppose Q is a modally closed formula. Suppose P is possibly true. It follows that there is at least one possible world, call it world w, in which P is true. Since P strictly implies Q, it must be that Q is true in world w as well. So there is a world in which Q is true. Q is therefore possibly true. But Q is modally closed, so it is a noncontingent proposition. Since Q is noncontingent, its truth-value must be invariant across all possible worlds. If Q is possibly true, and its truth-value is invariant across all possible worlds, it must therefore be necessarily true.

The following proof employs PN:

1. A →◇ H
2. J ⊃ A
3. J & G
4. □◇ H → D / D
5. J   Simp 3
6. A   MP 2, 5
7. ◇ A   Poss 6
8. □◇ H   PN 1, 7
9. D   MMP 8, 4

Notice that we were allowed to apply the "P to N" rule to lines 1 and 7 because (a) on line 1, the formula is of the form **P → Q**, (b) the formula instantiating **Q** in line 1 is indeed modally closed (that formula is ◇H), and (c) line 7 is a possibilization of the **P** part of the **P → Q** on 1, namely, it is ◇A.

The Necessitation Rule

The next rule is easy to work with, even though the explanation is a bit complicated. According to the third of the five principles of modality, MP3, whatever logically follows from a necessary truth is itself a necessary truth. That is:

$$[\Box\, P\, \&\, (P \rightarrow Q)] \rightarrow \Box\, Q$$

Assuming this principle, suppose we begin a line of reasoning with one or more modally closed formulas and, using only valid rules of inference, derive a formula **P** from them. Remember that a modally closed formula is always noncontingent. Its truth-value is therefore invariant across all possible worlds. Also keep in mind that only a necessary truth logically follows from a necessary truth. Now, if the modally closed formulas we began with are true, they must be necessarily true, for a modally closed formula is true in *all* circumstances if it is true in even *one* circumstance. It follows that **P** must be necessarily true, since **P** follows from one or more modally closed formulas, each assumed true and each of which is necessarily true if true at all. This logic is incorporated into our next rule, the necessitation rule. As usual, some setup is required before the rule can be stated.

First of all, a formula that appears as a whole line of a proof is "reiterated" if it is copied from an earlier line and entered as a later line in the proof. Now, suppose that at some point in a proof you indent, number one or more new lines, and bring down or *reiterate* one or more modally closed lines, and derive from just those reiterated lines a sentence **P**. (Such a sequence of indented lines is called a *necessitation subproof*.) Because **P** has been derived *only* from modally closed formulas, **P** must be necessarily true if the modally closed formulas brought down are true. Of course, these must be true if the premises are true. It follows that we are justified in prefixing a box to **P**. The corresponding rule follows.

The Necessitation Rule (Nec)

At any point in a proof, you may indent and construct a necessitation subproof in which every line is either justified by the reiteration rule (later) or follows from previous lines of the subproof by a valid rule of inference. You may then end the indentation, draw a vertical line in front of the indented lines (to mark them off from the rest of the proof), write down any line derived within the subproof, and prefix a box to that line. (As justification, write "Nec" and the line numbers of the subproof.)

Reiteration (Reit)

You may reiterate into a necessitation subproof any entire line of the proof, provided that the entire line is brought in, the entire line consists of just one modally closed formula, and the formula does not lie within the scope of a discharged assumption or a terminated necessitation subproof. (As justification, write "Reit" and the formula's original line number.)

This rule sounds complicated, but it is actually quite easy to apply. Here is a simple example to begin with:

1. $\Box(A \rightarrow B)$
2. $\Box(B \rightarrow R)$ /$\Box(A \rightarrow R)$
3. $\quad\quad\quad$ $\Box(A \rightarrow B)$ $\quad\quad$ Reit 1
4. $\quad\quad\quad$ $\Box(B \rightarrow R)$ $\quad\quad$ Reit 2
5. $\quad\quad\quad$ $A \rightarrow B$ $\quad\quad\quad$ BR 3
6. $\quad\quad\quad$ $B \rightarrow R$ $\quad\quad\quad$ BR 4
7. $\quad\quad\quad$ $A \rightarrow R$ $\quad\quad\quad$ MHS 5, 6
8. $\Box(A \rightarrow R)$ $\quad\quad$ Nec 3–7

Notice that after completing a necessitation subproof, we mark the indented lines off as in a conditional or indirect proof.

A necessitation subproof serves to demonstrate that a particular formula follows validly from only modally closed premises. When we have derived a formula within a necessitation subproof, we have shown that it follows from modally closed formulas. Because modally closed formulas are necessarily true if true at all, and because only necessary truths follow from necessary truths, any formula derived within such a subproof must be necessarily true if the premises it is derived from are true. We are therefore justified in prefixing a box to any formula so derived. This is clearly a valid rule of inference. The following proof contains another necessitation subproof:

1. $\Box(A \vee B)$
2. $\Box(\sim A \And \sim R)$
3. $\Box(\sim B \vee S)$ /$\Box(S \vee R)$
4. $\quad\quad\quad$ $\Box(A \vee B)$ $\quad\quad\quad$ Reit 1
5. $\quad\quad\quad$ $\Box(\sim A \And \sim R)$ $\quad\quad$ Reit 2
6. $\quad\quad\quad$ $\Box(\sim B \vee S)$ $\quad\quad$ Reit 3
7. $\quad\quad\quad$ $A \vee B$ $\quad\quad\quad\quad$ BR 4
8. $\quad\quad\quad$ $\sim A \And \sim R$ $\quad\quad\quad$ BR 5
9. $\quad\quad\quad$ $\sim B \vee S$ $\quad\quad\quad$ BR 6
10. $\quad\quad\quad$ $\sim A$ $\quad\quad\quad\quad\quad$ Simp 8
11. $\quad\quad\quad$ B $\quad\quad\quad\quad\quad\quad$ DS 7, 10
12. $\quad\quad\quad$ $\sim \sim B$ $\quad\quad\quad\quad$ DN 11
13. $\quad\quad\quad$ S $\quad\quad\quad\quad\quad\quad$ DS 9, 12
14. $\quad\quad\quad$ $S \vee R$ $\quad\quad\quad\quad$ Add 13
15. $\Box(S \vee R)$ $\quad\quad$ Nec 4–14

Exercise 35.7   Construct proofs for the following arguments. The necessitation rule is recommended on these problems.

1.
   1. □ (A v B)
   2. □~ B
   3. □A ⊃ □E / E

2.
   1. □(H ⊃ S)
   2. □(S ⊃ R)
   3. □(H ⊃ R) ⊃ G / ◇G

3.
   1. □(~R ⊃ S)
   2. □(~S v G)
   3. □[(R v G) ⊃ H]
   4. ~□H v S / S

4.
   1. □(A ⊃ B)
   2. □(~ B v ~ A)
   3. G ⊃ ~ □ ~ A / ~G

5.
   1. □(P & Q)
   2. □(Q ⊃ S) / □ S

6.
   1. □(H ⊃ S)
   2. □(S ⊃ P)
   3. □[□ (H ⊃ P) ⊃ G] / □ (M ⊃ G)

7.
   1. P → Q
   2. □ P / □Q

8.
   1. □(A ⊃ B)
   2. □(B ⊃ ~C) / ~ ◇ (A & C)

9.
   1. □(A ⊃ B) / □A ⊃ □B

10.
   1. □A & □B / □(A & B)

11.
  1. $\Box$ [(P & Q) & R] / $\Box$ P & ($\Box$Q & $\Box$R)

12.
  1. $\Diamond$A / $\Box$ $\Box$ $\Diamond$ A

13.
  1. $\Box$ A / $\Box$ $\Box$ A

14.
  1. $\Diamond$ A / $\Box$ $\Diamond$ A

15.
  1. $\Box$ A / $\Diamond$ $\Box$ $\Box$ A

16.
  1. A $\rightarrow$ B
  2. B $\rightarrow$ C
  3. $\Box$ ~C / $\Box$ ~A

Application to Philosophy: Anselm's Ontological Argument

Logicians teaching at the universities of Europe during the medieval period were especially interested in modal logic. Consequently, a great deal of advanced research in this branch of our subject was conducted during the Middle Ages. Indeed, there are scholars today who spend their entire academic careers probing medieval modal logic. One reason medieval logicians were so interested in modal logic is that they were keenly interested in arguments for and against the existence of God, immortality, the soul, free will, and the claims of the Christian church. Arguments about such matters are always modal in nature, dealing as they inevitably must with matters of logical possibility, necessity, and eternity. Certainly one of the most intriguing of all the modal arguments produced during this era is the famous ontological argument for the existence of God, first proposed by Saint Anselm (1033–1109), one of the greatest of the medieval philosophers. Few arguments in the history of philosophy have sparked as much discussion or inspired as much important philosophical research.

According to his biographer, the initial idea for the ontological argument came to Anselm late one night during evening prayers in the form of the following thought: The concept of God is the concept of a being so great, so perfect, that nothing could even *possibly* be greater or more perfect. In the terminology of possible worlds semantics (or "possible worlds talk"), this thought is: If God exists, God is not just the greatest or most perfect being in the *actual* world, God is the greatest *possible* being, the most perfect being there could possibly be.

The point is not obvious at all. God is usually thought of as the greatest or most perfect actual being. The concept of the greatest *possible* being is a different idea altogether. For example, in his heyday, Muhammad Ali was the greatest boxer in the actual world, but he certainly was not the greatest boxer *possible*. We can easily imagine a boxer who would have been taller, stronger, faster, and better in every way. Ali might have been the greatest *actual* boxer, but he was not the greatest *possible* boxer. Anselm was the first philosopher, as far as we know, to draw the modal distinction between the greatest actual being and the greatest possible being, and then to construct a modal argument for the existence of God on the basis of the distinction. But this is getting ahead of the story.

Anselm now had a strict philosophical definition of God: God is understood as *that than which a greater or more perfect is not possible*. But a definition is not an argument. All that seems to follow at this point is that *if* God exists, then God is the greatest, most perfect being possible. The hypothetical statement ("If God exists, God is the greatest being possible") is about a *possibility*, and as everyone knows, just because something is possible doesn't entail that it is real or actual. Lots of things are possible but not actual (e.g., Santa Claus).

While meditating on the concept of God, another idea seemed to be forcing its way into his mind: Absolute, unsurpassable greatness or perfection necessarily includes *existence*. For it seems that a being could not be unsurpassably great or absolutely perfect while being nonexistent or imaginary. The great French philosopher René Descartes (1596–1650), the founder of modern philosophy, would later make the same point by arguing that the idea of unsurpassable greatness includes existence just as the idea of a triangle includes the idea of three-sidedness. Just as one cannot consistently conceive of a triangle that lacks three sides, Descartes argued, one cannot consistently conceive of an unsurpassably great being *lacking* real existence.

This idea seemed extremely attractive to Anselm, from a purely logical point of view, but he kept rejecting it as fallacious. Absolute, unsurpassable greatness or perfection is one thing, he thought, and real existence is another thing entirely. Surely there is no purely logical bridge linking the two ideas. And so Anselm resisted the inference from greatest possible to real. However, the more he thought about it, the more the inference seemed logically necessary: Absolute, unsurpassable perfection logically includes existence. After concluding that it does, the argument reached its conclusion: An unsurpassably perfect being is not only possible—it must actually exist. For it would be contradictory to suppose that an unsurpassably perfect being lacks existence, just as it would be contradictory to suppose that a triangle lacks three sides.

Anselm published his philosophical "discovery" in 1078, in a book titled *Proslogion* (Latin: "an address"). In the preface Anselm explained that his argument is written for one who is "striving to elevate his own mind to the contemplation of God." Here is one way to summarize Anselm's argument:

1. Whether or not one believes in God, God is understood as "that being a greater than which is not possible."

2. Let us assume, for the sake of argument, that God, as defined, does not exist.

Comment. This is Anselm's AIP—his assumption for indirect proof.

3. It follows that God is just a figment of our imagination, a mere idea in our minds, an imaginary, nonexistent being, like the tooth fairy or Santa Claus.

Comment. In other words, God exists as a subjective idea in our minds, but does not exist as a really existing object, as an entity existing in reality, independently of our minds.

4. However, it is greater, all else being equal, to really exist, that is, to exist *both* as an idea thought of in the mind and as an object existing independently of the mind, in reality, that is, in the real world outside the mind.

5. It is even greater to exist *necessarily* rather than to exist in a merely contingent sort of way.

Comment. Modal logicians say that a being exists *necessarily* if it exists independently of changing circumstances, and they say that a being exists *contingently* if its existence depends on circumstances.

6. Therefore, supposing that God does not really exist, supposing that God is just a figment of our imagination, it follows that we can consistently conceive of a being greater than God is, namely, a being just like God in every way, but in addition existing in reality as well, and moreover existing *necessarily* and not merely contingently. This would be a being existing not just as a subjective idea in the mind, but existing in objective reality as well, outside the mind, and indeed independently of all changing circumstances.

7. But this is a contradiction. For it is contradictory to suppose there could be a being greater than that than which a greater is not possible.

Comment. The claim here is this: Our assumption logically implies a contradiction. If this is right, then the assumption has been "reduced to absurdity." If so, then by the principle of indirect proof, Anselm is justified in his conclusion.

8. Therefore, God, understood as that than which a greater is not possible, must truly exist.

What an intriguing argument! In philosophy, an **ontological argument** is one that claims to deduce the existence of God from a purely logical analysis of the concept of God. Although the complex logical structure of Anselm's argument—the first ontological argument in recorded history—cannot fully be represented within the elementary modal logic of this chapter, we can use our modal language to translate a close cousin of the argument. Letting G stand for the proposition that God, understood as the greatest possible being, actually exists, here is one way to render this fascinating modal argument:

1. $G \rightarrow \Box G$
2. $\sim G \rightarrow \Box \sim G$
3. $\Diamond G / G$
4. $\qquad \sim G$ AIP
5. $\qquad \Box \sim G$ MMP 2, 4
6. $\qquad \sim\Box \sim G$ DE 3
7. $\qquad \Box \sim G \ \& \sim\Box \sim G$ Conj 5, 6
8. G   IP 4–7

Of course, every philosophical argument faces philosophical objections; it is the nature of the subject.

Objections to the Argument

Guanilo's Parody

Shortly after Anselm published his argument, Guanilo, a monk from a nearby monastery, wrote a rebuttal. Guanilo's argument took the form of a *parody* of Anselm's argument. What is this? Basically, a *parody* of an argument X is an argument that has the same logical structure as the target argument X while reaching an absurd conclusion on the basis of that common structure. In other words, Guanilo attempted a refutation by logical analogy. Here is one way to summarize Guanilo's ingenious reply to Anselm.

1. The same form of argument employed by Anselm can be used to reach a ridiculous conclusion. Let us define *Lost Island* as "that island a greater than which is impossible." In other words, Lost Island is the greatest island there could possibly be.
2. But unsurpassable greatness necessarily includes existence, for something cannot be unsurpassably great unless it exists.
3. Therefore, Lost Island, the greatest possible island, must exist. For it would be contradictory to suppose that an island is the greatest possible island but does not exist!
4. Our reasoning started with a plausible premise but reached a ridiculous conclusion. The form of our reasoning must therefore be invalid, as it permits

true premises with a false conclusion. Yet our reasoning has the same logical form as Anselm's argument.

5. Therefore, Anselm's argument is invalid.

Anselm's Reply

In true philosophical fashion, Anselm replied in writing to Guanilo. Here is one way to summarize Anselm's counterargument.

1. The basic form of reasoning of the ontological argument cannot properly be applied to a contingent being, such as an island. The reasoning of the onto-logical argument only produces a valid and sound argument when applied in the case of a possible noncontingent being.

2. For in the case of any contingent being, whether it be actual, or merely pos-sible, there will be possible circumstances in which it exists, and possible circumstances in which it does not exist. Thus, even if a particular contin-gent being is really great in some circumstance, there may well be some circumstance in which it is not so great. Thus, even if we prove that some contingent being must be really, really great, we will still not know whether the circumstance in which it is really great—the circumstance in which it reaches its peak of greatness—is the present circumstance, the actual cir-cumstance in which we live, or whether it is some possible but nonactual circumstance, in which case, the contingent entity does not exist but might have existed. In terms of possible worlds semantics, even if it is proven that some contingent being must be really great, we will still not know whether it attains its possible greatness in a possible but nonactual world, in which case it does not actually exist, or whether it attains its greatness in the ac-tual world, in which case it does exist.

3. Therefore, the reasoning of the ontological argument cannot be properly applied in the case of a contingent being. But an island is most surely a con-tingent being, for it comes into existence at a moment in time, formed by a geological process, it will go out of existence at some moment in time, and it would not exist if conditions had been sufficiently different. Therefore, the parallel argument fails to show that the reasoning of the ontological argu-ment is invalid or that the argument is unsound.

Another Objection

Another way to attack the ontological argument is to argue that the very concept of a greatest possible being is self-contradictory or logically impossible. But if the very concept of God, as defined by Anselm, is self-contradictory, then it is logically impossible that God exists, and one premise of the ontological argument is false. This is a very serious line of attack. If the concept of God is a "contradiction in terms," then not only does Anselm's argument fail, but it is positively *irrational* to believe in God. But is God, defined as the greatest possible being, a logical impossibility? Is there a self-contradiction lurking inside the concept? There are philosophers who argue yes. Here is a summary of one such argument.

> A greatest possible being, if such a being were to exist, would necessarily be all-powerful ("omnipotent"), all-knowing ("omniscient"), and all-good ("omnibenevolent"). Being omniscient, it would know everything. Being omnipotent, it could do anything. But if it knows everything, then there is something it cannot do, namely, get lost. So a being could not possibly be *both* omniscient and omnipotent at the same time. Therefore, it is impossible that a greatest possible being exists, for the concept of such a being contains a self-contradiction.

Of course, there are philosophers who defend the traditional concept of God against the charge of self-contradiction. Unfortunately, we do not have the space to enter the issue here. All we have time for is a little food for thought. However, if one wants to pursue the matter, the great ontological argument debate is still taking place, and not only in monasteries: It can be found all over the Internet. Did you notice the modal nature of the arguments we have been examining?

Appendix 35.1　Two Modal Fallacies for Discussion

The Fallacy of Illicitly Shifting the Necessity Operator

Recall that a fallacy is an error in reasoning. We often express a relation of implication by saying, "If so and so, then it is necessary that such and such." Or we sometimes say, "If so and so, then it must be that such and such." For example, "If Rita gave birth to three children, then it is necessary that Rita is a mother."

Now, this sentence about Rita is ambiguous. On one interpretation, the necessity applies only to the *consequent* of the conditional. According to this interpretation, if Rita gave birth to three children, then *it is a necessary truth* that she is a mother. In other words, given that she gave birth, it is necessarily true that she is a mom. On a second interpretation, the necessity applies to the conditional relationship as a whole, that is, to the *relation* between the antecedent and the consequent, not to the consequent alone. On this interpretation, it is necessary that if Rita gave birth, then she is a mother. On this second interpretation the sentence attributes necessity to the *relation* between the antecedent and the consequent, rather than to the consequent alone. If she gave birth, then it necessarily follows that she is a mother.

How shall we symbolize the two interpretations? On the first interpretation, necessity is attributed to the consequent. The first interpretation should therefore be symbolized R ⊃□ M, with R abbreviating "Rita gave birth to three children" and M abbreviating "Rita is a mother." The second interpretation should be symbolized □ (R ⊃ M). Do you see the difference between the two?

The first interpretation says that if Rita gave birth then it is a necessary truth that she is a mother. So, supposing she did give birth, then necessarily she is a mother, that is, she could not possibly have *not* been a mother. Assuming that if one could not have done otherwise, then one is not acting of one's own free will, this suggests that she did not have children of her own free will. Thus, on this interpretation, one could argue:

1. R ⊃ □ M
2. R   / □ M
3. □ M   MP 1, 2

The conclusion says Rita is necessarily a mother, in which case it seems she could not have done otherwise (than become a mother). Rita apparently lacks free will, at least with respect to having children. However, on the second interpretation, the assertion is something very different, namely, it is necessary that *if* she gave birth, then she is a mother. This interpretation is common sense, and seems to sidestep the free will issue altogether.

An error in modal reasoning occurs when someone transfers the necessity from the conditional as a whole to the consequent alone, without justification. Because logicians in the Middle Ages were deeply interested in modal reasoning, they catalogued numerous modal fallacies, including the fallacy just illustrated. In explaining this fallacy, they distinguished between the following two types of modal sentence:

- The *necessity of the consequence*. This is a sentence asserting the necessity of the relation between antecedent and consequent. In symbols: □ (**P** ⊃ **Q**).
- The *necessity of the consequent*. This is the sentence attributing necessity to the consequent alone. Symbolized: **P** ⊃ □ **Q**.

When engaged in a modal argument with your neighbor, you might want to ask this: Do you mean the necessity of the *consequence*, or the necessity of the *consequent*?

Application: The Sin Argument

Here is an interesting argument from the history of philosophy that commits this fallacy. See if you can pinpoint the problem. (Or, perhaps you might wish instead to defend the argument.) This argument is adapted from an argument that was discussed with gusto in ancient and medieval philosophical circles.

1. Necessarily, if God foreknew that human beings would sin, then human beings would sin.
2. God foreknew that human beings would sin.
3. So, it is necessary that human beings sin.
4. So, when a person sins, he or she sins of necessity.
5. If someone does something of necessity, then he or she could not have done otherwise.
6. If someone does something, and could not have done otherwise, then he or she does not act of his or her own free will.
7. So, human beings never sin of their own free will.

Did you spot the place in this argument where the necessity was shifted from the conditional to the consequent? Was that shift justified? Is this a valid argument? Is it sound?

The "Lazy Argument" for Fatalism

Another interesting argument from the history of philosophy, debated furiously in ancient philosophical circles, is known as the "lazy argument." This argument was offered as a definitive proof that nobody has free will. The argument is interesting because it claims to prove its startling conclusion using purely abstract logical considerations alone, without relying on empirical considerations at all. Here is one way to express the lazy argument:

Take any event in the future, for instance, the next lunch you will eat.

1. It is necessarily true that either you will eat a burrito for that lunch, or you will not eat a burrito for that lunch.
2. Therefore, it is necessarily true that you will eat a burrito for your next lunch, or it is necessarily true that you won't eat a burrito for your next lunch.
3. So, whichever one you do, you will do it of necessity, which means that you couldn't possibly have done anything else.
4. If, in a situation, someone does something, and they couldn't possibly have acted otherwise, then they do not act of their own free will.

5. Therefore, when you eat your next lunch, you will not eat of your own free will.

6. Furthermore, this reasoning applies to each minute and to each second of each day in your future. So each thing you will ever do will be done of necessity (and without free will).

In other words, each time you do something, it will be true that it was *necessary* that you do precisely that thing. Now, you cannot change or prevent what is necessarily true. But if you cannot do otherwise in a situation, then you do not act of your own free will. So, nothing you ever do will be done of your own free will. Because this reasoning can be applied to each event in your future, it follows that your future is predetermined and you do not have free will. But this same reasoning can be applied to each and every person, so it follows that nobody has free will.

Before we analyze this argument, let us put it into symbols, with reference to one particular person, Pat, bearing in mind that the reasoning can be generalized to each and every person. (Thus, Pat will be a stand-in for each and every person, a "John Doe" constant, if you will, for anyone.) Let B abbreviate "Pat's next lunch is a burrito," and let F abbreviate "Pat has free will."

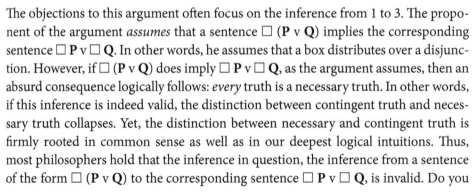

1. □ (B v ~B)   (premise)
2. (□ B ⊃ ~F) & (□ ~B ⊃ ~ F)   (premise)
3. □ B v □ ~B   (inferred from premise 1)
4. ~ F v ~F   (Constructive Dilemma, 2, 3)
5. ~F   Tautology, 4

Now, this argument can be reconstructed for each possible event in Pat's future, and indeed for each possible event in anyone else's future, including yours. The conclusion "logical fatalists" draw from this is that nobody has free will.

An Objection

The objections to this argument often focus on the inference from 1 to 3. The proponent of the argument *assumes* that a sentence □ (P v Q) implies the corresponding sentence □ P v □ Q. In other words, he assumes that a box distributes over a disjunction. However, if □ (P v Q) does imply □ P v □ Q, as the argument assumes, then an absurd consequence logically follows: *every* truth is a necessary truth. In other words, if this inference is indeed valid, the distinction between contingent truth and necessary truth collapses. Yet, the distinction between necessary and contingent truth is firmly rooted in common sense as well as in our deepest logical intuitions. Thus, most philosophers hold that the inference in question, the inference from a sentence of the form □ (P v Q) to the corresponding sentence □ P v □ Q, is invalid. Do you think the "Burrito" argument is valid? Or does it contain a modal fallacy at step 3? If you think the argument is valid, is it sound as well?

Appendix 35.2 The Paradoxes of Implication

The definition of implication in modal logic makes perfectly good sense when we apply it to contingent propositions. For instance, most find it entirely natural to say that the following statement:

Pat is 16.

implies that:

Pat is a teenager.

However, things are different when we apply the definition of implication to noncontingent propositions. When we do, we get genuinely paradoxical results. You can see this for yourself by performing the following simple logical experiment. On one line of a sheet of paper, on the left side, write any sentence that expresses a necessary falsehood. On the right side of the line, write any proposition-expressing sentence of your choice. Let the proposition expressed by the sentence on the left be A, and let the proposition expressed by the sentence on the right be B. Now, ask yourself this question:

Are there any circumstances in which A would be true and B false?

If you think about it, you will see that your answer is no. But, then, according to the definition of implication, A implies B. And if you think about the matter further, you will see that your answer would be the same no matter which necessarily false proposition you represented on the left and no matter what proposition you represented on the right. The general principle in this case is paradoxical:

A necessarily false proposition implies any and every proposition.

That is, any necessarily false proposition implies every proposition. Thus, the proposition that $2 + 2 = 88$ implies the proposition that Kennedy is president. The proposition that $2 + 2 = 88$ also implies the proposition that $1 + 1 = 2$, and so on.

Here is a second logical experiment that will uncover a second paradox. On one line of a sheet of paper, on the left side, write any proposition-expressing sentence. On the right side of the line, write any necessary truth of your choice. Call the proposition expressed by the sentence on the left G and the proposition expressed by the sentence on the right H. Now, ask yourself: Are there any circumstances in which G is true and H is false? The answer is again no. But, then, according to the definition of implication, G implies H. Further reflection shows that the answer is the same no matter which necessary truth you choose and no matter what the other proposition is. The general principle in this case is paradoxical as well:

A necessary truth is implied by any proposition.

That is, any and every proposition implies a necessary truth. For example, the proposition that Jimmy Carter is president implies the proposition that all triangles have three sides. The proposition that $2 + 2 = 1,003$ implies the proposition that $1 + 1 = 2$, and so on.

Most people find these two principles paradoxical, yet the two paradoxes follow from our definition of implication. Consequently, they are called the *paradoxes of implication*.

In everyday life, we often look for the implications of contingent propositions. This is the context in which our intuitions about implication are formed. With contingent propositions, when one proposition implies another, the two always have something to do with each other; the two are *relevant* to each other. For example, that Chris is age 50 implies that Chris is an adult. Notice that both statements are about Chris and both are about age. But when we extend the definition of implication to cases of noncontingent propositions, we get the paradoxical consequences in which one proposition can imply another proposition, even though the first is not about the second, nor is relevant to it in any obvious way. Perhaps this consequence should not be terribly surprising. After all, noncontingent propositions are very different in nature from contingent ones. Why suppose the logic with respect to implication of the one type of sentence will be exactly the same as that of the other? Perhaps the logic of the one category, with respect to implication, is quite different from the corresponding logic of the other.

However, the paradoxes of implication are bothersome. Why isn't the definition of implication altered so as to eliminate these paradoxical consequences? Logicians have found that the definition of implication cannot be altered without resulting in other equally paradoxical logical results. Why not restrict implication to contingent propositions only? The problem with this suggestion is that logic makes extensive use of the implication relations obtaining between noncontingent propositions, and many of these relations make perfectly good sense. For instance, it seems right to say that the fact that all squares have four equal sides *implies* the fact that all squares have more than three sides.

Incidentally, logic is not the only field containing paradoxes. Modern physics contains a number of puzzling and even bizarre paradoxes, including the twin paradox and the clock paradox within relativity theory and the Schrodinger's cat paradox within the theory of quantum mechanics.

We have seen that within truth-functional logic, if we start a natural deduction proof with a contradictory premise, a premise of the form **P** & ~**P**, then any conclusion whatsoever follows. But this is just another way of saying that a contradiction implies any and every proposition. We also saw that we can prove a proposition to be tautological or necessarily true using a premise-free proof. In such a case, no matter what premises we add to the argument, the conclusion still follows, for we can prove the conclusion true without even using the premises. But this is another way of saying that any and every proposition implies a necessary truth. Perhaps in the light of these purely logical considerations, the paradoxes of implication will seem a little less paradoxical.

Appendix 35.3   Logical and Physical Possibility Distinguished

The Leibnizian idea of a possible world allows us to state and clarify an important distinction in modal logic and in philosophy—the classic distinction between *logical* possibility and *physical* possibility. This distinction also plays an important role in modern physics and in the physical sciences in general. We can approach the idea by way of the following question: Could a human being swim the Atlantic Ocean—all 3,000 miles or so of it—in five minutes? It seems, on initial reflection, that such a swim would be impossible. The laws of physics won't allow anyone to swim that far that fast. At the required speed, which would be around 36,000 miles per hour, the friction alone would destroy a human body. And besides, no matter how many cans of spinach a person eats, the human body doesn't have the strength or the stored energy for such a task. So, given the laws of physics and the facts of human biology, that long-distance swim would be impossible.

If you answered "no" to the question about swimming the Atlantic in five minutes, and if you reasoned along the lines just given, you had in mind the kind of possibility termed *physical possibility*. An event is **physically possible** if its occurrence would not violate a physical law of nature, and an event is **physically impossible** if its occurrence would violate a physical law. Physical possibility can now be explained in terms of possible worlds. Consider just those possible worlds that have the same physical laws of nature as does the actual world. Call such worlds physically possible worlds. Now let us say: Something is a physical possibility if and only if there is a physically possible world in which it happens.

To go back to our earlier example, it is not physically possible that someone might swim the Atlantic in five minutes, for there are no physically possible worlds in which someone swims 36,000 miles per hour and so on.

In contrast, consider this: Is it physically possible for someone to win the Washington State Lottery 10 times in a row? Well, such a thing would be extremely improbable, but it would not violate any physical laws of nature. That is to say, in some physically possible worlds a person wins the Washington State Lottery 10 times in a row. Thus, such an event is physically possible, although incredibly improbable. Notice the distinction here between possibility and probability. Some events are physically possible even though they are highly improbable. In short, it is physically possible that someone could win the Washington State Lottery 10 times in a row, but it is physically impossible that someone could swim the Atlantic in five minutes.

The next step in this sequence requires that we broaden our thinking. We are now going to think of possibility in the broadest possible sense of the word. If the laws of nature had been sufficiently different, and if the facts of human biology had been sufficiently different, it would be possible, in some sense, that someone could swim the Atlantic in five minutes. This is an entirely different kind of possibility, corresponding to a much broader sense of the word *possible*. Suppose the physical laws of nature had been *so* different that people could easily swim the Atlantic in five minutes. It seems plausible to suppose that is a way things might have been, for there is nothing self-contradictory in the idea. Therefore, it seems, we're speaking of a possible world. Of course, it's not a physically possible world, but it is a possible world nonetheless, for it's a way things might have been (had they been very, very different). So, there is a possible world in which someone swims the Atlantic in five minutes. In modal logic, if there is even one possible world in which an event occurs, we say the event is logically possible. Thus, although the Atlantic swim is not *physically* possible, it is nevertheless *logically* possible. Logical possibility thus encompasses a broader range of possibilities than is encompassed by physical possibility. Indeed, it encompasses the broadest possible set, the set of all possibilities, period.

This distinction between logical and physical possibility is of such crucial significance in logic and in science that we must examine it more closely for a moment. As we have seen, logicians traditionally use the term *logically possible* for the broadest, most inclusive category of possibilities, the category that includes within itself all possibilities and all kinds of possibilities. So, every possible world counts as a logically possible world. It follows that every physically possible world, that is, every world that contains the same physical laws of nature as the actual world, counts as a logically possible world as well. However, it seems plausible to suppose that some logically possible worlds are not physically possible worlds, for some possible worlds, it would seem, have laws of nature different from those we find in the actual world. (Many works of science fiction are based on just this premise.) Although all physically possible worlds are also logically possible worlds, surely not all logically possible worlds are physically possible worlds.

So, to sum this up, is it possible that someone might swim the Atlantic Ocean in five minutes? There are two answers. It's not physically possible, for in no *physically* possible world does someone swim the Atlantic in five minutes. But such a thing is *logically* possible, simply because in some possible world, someone can swim the Atlantic in five minutes.

Some readers might be puzzled by our talking of events happening "in" various possible worlds. Does such talk really make any sense? What do we mean when we speak of something happening *in* a possible world? Perhaps the following will help make sense of such talk. We readily understand sentences such as these:

In the novel *Robinson Crusoe*, a man is shipwrecked on a deserted island.

In the story of Hansel and Gretel, two children get lost in the woods.

And so it seems that we understand what it is for an event to happen "in" a novel or a story. But a novel or story is essentially a description of a possibility. As such, a novel or story describes a possible world. Therefore, let us think of an event happening "in" a possible world in much the way we think of an event happening "in" a novel, a story, or a movie. The two senses of *in*—the possible worlds *in* and the literary *in*—seem closely analogous, if not identical.

Beam Me Up, Scotty

Here is food for thought. In the original *Star Trek* series, Kirk, Spock, and others would report to the transporter room, where they would be "beamed down" to a strange planet (where all sorts of dangers usually lay in wait). The transporter on the starship *Enterprise* had a "safe beaming range" of 19,500 miles. Is the Enterprise's transporter system (with its redesigned "field generator matrix") *physically* possible? Is it *logically* possible? If you want to pursue these and related questions, an interesting place to begin is Lawrence Krauss's excellent book *The Physics of Star Trek* (New York: Basic Books, 1996).

Glossary

Logically contingent proposition A proposition that is true in at least one possible circumstance and that is also false in at least one possible circumstance.

Logically possible Possibly true.

Modal argument An argument built out of modal sentence operators and the components to which these attach.

Modal logic The study of the modes of truth, especially necessity and possibility, and their relationship to reasoning and argumentation.

Necessarily false proposition A proposition that is false in all possible circumstances.

Necessarily true proposition A proposition that is true in all possible circumstances.

Ontological argument An argument claiming to deduce the real existence of something from an analysis of the mere concept of the thing.

Physically impossible Inconsistent with the actual laws of physics (and of the laws of nature in general) that govern the physical universe.

Physically possible Consistent with the actual laws of physics (and of the laws of nature in general) that govern the physical universe.

Possible world A way the universe might be or might have been.

Possibly false proposition A proposition that is false in at least one possible circumstance or situation.

Possibly true proposition A proposition that is true in at least one possible circumstance or situation.

Proof in S5D A sequence of formulas of ML that is such that every formula is either a premise, an assumption, or follows from previous formulas by an S5D rule, and in which every line that is not a premise is justified and every assumption has been discharged.

System S5D The natural deduction system consisting of (a) the language ML and (b) the natural deduction rules of this chapter.

Valid in S5D An argument is valid in S5D if and only if it is possible to construct a proof in S5D with premises that are the premises of the argument and with a conclusion that is the conclusion of the argument. Any argument that is valid in S5D may also be said to be "valid in S5" or "S5 valid."

A Classical Indian Logic « ‹

Mark Storey, Professor of Philosophy, *Bellevue College, Bellevue, Washington*

Indian logic, or *Nyaya*, is a system of formal logic developed in India sometime between 300 BC and 500 AD. This appendix presents the basic elements of the Nyaya system of Indian logic.

A small handful of philosophy textbooks have been published recently that include passages from Nyaya texts, but no one has offered an introductory presentation of the system that could assist students unfamiliar with classical and medieval Indian philosophy.[1] The purpose of this appendix is to fill that gap.

Introduction

Indian philosophies have their foundation in two important doctrines: *karma* and *samsara*. Early in the history of India and long before the Nyaya systems of proper reasoning were developed in the third and fourth centuries AD, the Indians held these two doctrines as virtually axiomatic. The doctrine of karma holds that all actions must have an effect. For instance, if a rock strikes a window, then an effect must transpire: Most often the glass is broken. So is it with every other physical action. But there are actions that are not physical: words and thoughts. Every word spoken must have an effect. We can readily imagine the effect the words "You are so stupid!" must have when spoken by a parent to a child. The effects of physical actions are made manifest readily enough, but the effects of words and especially thoughts (e.g., desires, beliefs, choices, emotions, attitudes, dreams) often take time to come

---

[1] See, for instance, Daniel Bonevac and Stephen Phillips, *Understanding Non-Western Philosophy: Introductory Readings* (Mountain View, CA: Mayfield, 1993); Koller and Koller, *A Sourcebook in Asian Philosophy* (New York: Macmillan, 1991); Robert C. Solomon and Kathleen M. Higgins, *World Philosophy: A Text with Readings* (New York: McGraw-Hill, 1995).

to light. Karma, according to most Indians, is something like a causal law of nature, and it is affirmed with the degree of certainty accorded the law of gravity.

The word *karma* comes from the Sanskrit verb "kr," which has the double meaning of "to do" and "to make." It is sometimes argued that the doctrine of karma was originally embraced because the concept of doing something (acts, speech, or thought) was identified with the concept of making something: an effect. This historical explanation for the origin of belief in karma is not satisfactory because in French the verb *faire*, in Spanish the verb *hacer*, and in Latin the verb *facere* all mean both "to do" and "to make," yet we do not find the doctrine of karma arising in French-, Spanish-, or Latin-speaking cultures. Thus the double meaning of the verb "kr" is not sufficient to produce this doctrine.

The doctrine of karma is in no straightforward way falsifiable. Indians will point out that the doctrine, if true, explains many otherwise apparently inexplicable phenomena. For example, karma (and the attendant doctrine of *samsara*, or reincarnation) can account for the evil and suffering experienced by apparently innocent victims; it can explain why two children who are brought up in exactly the same way can turn out differently; and it can explain why some people are pig-like in their eating habits or move like cats when they walk. Indians have argued that because the doctrine of karma can explain these and other phenomena, and because there is no evidence to show that the doctrine is false, it is then reasonable to accept the doctrine as true.

In India the doctrine of samsara arises from the doctrine of karma. If you perform actions that must produce karmic results and you die before these results are manifest, then you must be reborn so that in another life these effects can be worked out. Karma will have three kinds of effects on your next life:

1. It will determine the kind of birth you will have. For instance, it will determine whether you will be born male rather than female, and it will determine what caste you are born into: priestly, warrior/prince, landowner/farmer/merchant, or servant. Ideally you want to be born male and in an upper caste so that it will be socially acceptable for you to devote much of your life to seeking release from the causal effects of karma.
2. It will determine the length of your next life.
3. It will determine the quality of experiences (pleasurable or painful) you will have in your next life.

The problem facing you is that in this new life you will be performing more actions. So as effects from past actions are being worked off, you are at the same time doing things (breathing, eating, talking, procreating, thinking) that must result in further effects. Eventually you die, but must be reborn once again so that the effects of *these* actions can be worked out. The cycle of rebirth thus goes on and on. Indian philosophies are primarily directed toward helping people escape this endless cycle of samsara. The goal is known as *moksa*—literally "liberation" or "release"—and once attained, as many Hindu philosophies will claim, your individual soul (*atman*) becomes one with the all-encompassing impersonal cosmos (*Brahman*). In this state the suffering that comes with rebirth is at an end.

Indian philosophies offer an array of suggestions on how to break free from the law of karma and the cycle of samsara. Ascetic traditions have advocated doing as little as possible so that as you work off old karma you do not produce any new karma. They might also advocate performing acts of austerity (e.g., wearing no clothes in cold weather, or standing on one leg for many years) to "burn off" the karmic effects that have attached to your soul. Over the course of many lifetimes, they contend, you will produce a net loss of karma. Once the amount of karma to be worked off is reduced to zero you will achieve moksa. Given the allure of sensual delights found in most earthly lives, this avenue is seldom successful.

Nyaya was developed by a philosopher named Gautama (or Gotama) of Apastamba who lived at some time between the second century BC and the fifth century AD. Not much is known about Gautama except his nickname: Aksapada, which means "the foot-eyed." Nyaya served as a means of reducing the amount of karma to be worked off in this or forthcoming lives. The basic idea behind it is that we should limit our thoughts to ones that are true or properly reasoned. Such thoughts were believed to produce few or no karmic effects that would need to be worked off. A question immediately comes to mind: How can we be sure that our thoughts, or beliefs, are true and properly warranted? This is where the Nyaya system of reasoning comes into play. Nyaya logicians contend that if we reason, argue, and defend ourselves using the logical principles they outline, then we stand the best chance of having only true or properly warranted beliefs.

The word *Nyaya* can be translated as "right reasoning" or "logic." Thus "Nyaya logic" is probably a redundancy. The specific purpose of Nyaya is to give us guidelines for *pramana*: acceptable means of attaining properly justified true beliefs. Within the Nyaya tradition there are generally said to be four types of pramana. *Pratyaksa* are perceptions. These perceptions include seeing something with your eyes. Thus if I see a tree before me and I am in a normal situation, I am justified in believing that there is a tree before me. Along with the other four senses I might perceive something with my mind (the Indian's "sixth sense"). Thus if I "see" with my "mind's eye" that all bachelors are adult unmarried men, then I am justified in believing that all bachelors are adult unmarried men. *Anumana* is proper inference or argumentation. The rules and other guidelines that make up anumana are the subject of this discussion. *Upamana* is analogical reasoning. If I know that a particular dog is a mammal and I one day see or think of a different dog, I can reason by analogy that this second dog—which is relevantly like the first dog—is a mammal also. *Sabda* are authoritative texts that can be appealed to in demonstrating a claim. There of course was debate over the authority of some texts, but the *Vedas*, the *Upanishads*, and the *Bhagavad Gita* were accepted by nearly everyone. (Note: The Buddhists, who adopted the Nyaya guidelines when they were inclined to use logical analysis, were considered heterodoxical by the Hindus because they rejected the authority of these three texts.)

The purpose of Indian philosophical discussion is often different from that of the so-called Western philosophical traditions following Aristotle. Aristotle provides us with the idea that we, as humans, are distinct from other beings due to our rational capabilities. To live the most thriving or flourishing (*eudaimonaic*) human life, we need to develop our distinctive human potential. Because at least part of our distinctive human potential is to use reason, rational discourse and the objects of rational discourse—truths—are inherently valuable to us. Thus we can discuss or contemplate abstract verities, or even the hypothetical nature of unicorns, and in so doing take steps to developing our human nature and becoming fully human. The ancient Chinese philosopher Confucius develops a similar view of the ideal state for humans; he calls it *ren*: being humane or truly human (some translations offer "kind" or "benevolent"). It would be naive, then, to place too much emphasis on the simplistic Western–Eastern philosophical dichotomy. For the Indian philosophers the purpose of philosophical discussion is wholly practical. It is devoted to helping people achieve moksa. Any discussion that does not serve this purpose is counterproductive and will probably result in unwanted karmic effect. Hence the guidelines for proper reasoning demand that all aspects of an argument avoid reference to things that do not exist (e.g., unicorns) and anything else that would detract from the practical task of acquiring only true beliefs.

Since the purpose of Indian argumentation is ultimately to break free from samsara, it is to everyone's advantage that we help one another to reason correctly. To this end a spirit of charity is advocated in Indian logic. If someone offers an argument and there is something improper about it, then if we can we should in charity help the arguer remedy this fault. Ideally we want true beliefs and to use our reasoning powers properly; thus we will charitably help our interlocutor whenever we can so that all of us can benefit from his or her argument. Although there was also a vast tradition of debate in India's history, a tradition in which much time was spent learning rhetorical techniques to *appear* to have the superior position, we here are focusing on the more philosophically reputable Indian tradition of amiably seeking truth about reality over mere opinion about appearance. Thus, rather than being a stickler and emphasizing logical mistakes in an inference, we will enter into a charitable discussion and do what we can to "fix" the inference. If the argument is beyond repair, then we must reject it; but if in charity we can resolve its problems, then we can join ranks so to speak with our interlocutor and be glad of the new truth acquired. Think of an ideal Indian discussion of this type not as an intellectual fight, but as conversation among rational beings sharing a common goal, working together under accepted rules of reasoning, and helping each other to discover the value of a particular line of inference.

Proper Form for Indian Arguments

The Greek philosopher Aristotle (384–322 BC) was the first person we know of in world history to present a systematic form of logic. From his work in logic Western philosophers have accepted the following as a model of good argumentation:

All men are mortal.
Socrates is a man.
Thus Socrates is mortal.

In a similar fashion, the Indian logicians often presented a model argument:

There is a fire on that mountain,
because there is smoke on it,
like a kitchen, and
unlike a lake.

If we were to try to rewrite this argument in the Aristotelian form of a syllogism, it might look something like this:

All things identical to that mountain are smoking things.
Thus all things identical to that mountain are things on fire.

We would note that the major premise is missing ("All smoking things are things on fire"), and we would probably be at a loss as to what to do with the seemingly odd references to kitchens and lakes. Nyaya is similar in some respects to Aristotelian syllogistic logic, yet it makes some additional demands. Before attempting to assess the strength of an Indian argument we first need to understand the form or structure of the Indian argument.

In presenting what I will call the standard Nyaya form of an argument, we will be indebted to Karl Potter's work in Indian logic and epistemology.[2] The standard form as presented here is a compilation of the various demands made by different Nyaya philosophers. Although no one Nyaya philosopher presented his system in exactly this way, the vast majority would probably agree that this presentation is in accordance with the basic principles of proper reasoning as they have developed them.

Many arguments in ordinary discourse are not initially presented in standard form, just as many Western syllogisms are not presented with every premise (as is the case with enthymemes). Our initial task is to rewrite the argument in standard form. It will help us to have an example of a simple argument in mind. Consider the following argument:

---

[2] See Karl Potter, *Presuppositions of India's Philosophies* (Westport, CT: Greenwood, 1963).

```
Dogs are animals,
because dogs are mammals,
like bears, and
unlike rocks.
```

Standard Nyaya form has three parts containing a total of five terms. In our example the three parts are the conclusion ("Dogs are animals"), the premise ("because dogs are mammals"), and the examples ("like bears, and unlike rocks"). The terms are "dogs," "animals," "mammals," "bears," and "rocks." The terms are in plural form so that they refer to classes of things. For example, "dogs" refers to the class of things that are dogs. Terms can be made up of more than one word. "Dogs," "Dogs that are brown," "Dogs that are not brown," "Things other than dogs that are brown," and "Things identical to that puppy in the window" are all acceptable terms because they each pick out a specific class of things. Indian arguments relate one class to another, claiming that one class overlaps, is entirely within, or is entirely outside another class. By presenting or rewriting an argument so that the terms refer to classes of things, specific problems are avoided once the assessment procedure begins. This will be made clearer once we begin working with some arguments.

Each term in an Indian argument has a name. In our example "dogs" is the *paksa* (p), "animals" is the *sadhya* (s), "mammals" is the *hetu* (h), "bears" is the *sapaksa* (sp), and "rocks" is the *vipaksa* (vp). These Sanskrit words refer to a particular term. For instance, *paksa* refers to the first term in the conclusion and in the premise; *sadhya* refers to the second term in the conclusion; and so on.

To test the inference of an argument we need to (a) reformulate it into proper Nyaya form, and (b) test it against five rules of validity.

In rewriting the original argument into standard Nyaya form, be sure to be honest in presenting the argument as the original arguer would. Your goal is to restructure the argument in such a way that the person offering the argument would say, "Yes, that's my argument." The time to "fix" the argument comes later when you begin to assess it. If you alter the content of the argument and then go on to assess it as invalid, you would be guilty of a straw man fallacy. Such an informal fallacy occurs when you misinterpret an argument, show your misinterpreted version to be bad, and conclude that you have shown the arguer's argument to be bad.

Reformulating Arguments into Proper Form

The following are brief guidelines for reformulating an argument into standard Nyaya form. The examples that follow illustrate the procedures.

1. Write the conclusion first, the premise second, the affirmative example third, and the negative example fourth.

2. You can change the wording, but be faithful to the meaning of the original argument.

3. Do not provide missing parts of the argument (e.g., the vipaksa) if the argument does not have them. Your task at this stage is to rewrite the *arguer's* argument, not an improved version.

4. Rewrite each term so that it refers to a class of objects. Plural nouns or noun phrases should be used (e.g., "Dogs are furry" can be changed to "Dogs are furry *things*").

5. Rewrite references to single objects (e.g., Tokyo) in a plural form (e.g., "Cities identical to Tokyo"). This is more important for the terms in the conclusion and premise than it is for the terms in the examples. The arguments we examine later illustrate this point.

6. Rewrite negative statements (e.g., "No pigs are snakes") as logically equivalent affirmative statements (e.g., "Pigs are nonsnakes").

7. Both instances of the paksa should have the exact same wording.

It might seem like a great deal of unnecessary work to rewrite an argument into standard Nyaya form. In a sense, this initial response is justified: It often *is* the most difficult part of a Nyaya analysis of an argument. Keep in mind, however, that if the argument is reworded to fit an artificially specified form, it will then be easier to assess its validity using the rules discussed later. If we did not make the original argument fit the standard form, then the set of rules demonstrating validity would become awkwardly large in number and difficult to apply. Any effort in reformulating the argument will pay dividends once we get to the point of assessing its validity. Once Indian logicians became familiar with the pattern and structure of arguments, however, they could easily dispense with the formal process of analyzing arguments in this conventional form, as can we after we have mastered the basics presented here.

Examples

Let's consider some examples of arguments that need to be rewritten into standard Nyaya form.

1. Every rabbit has fur, because each bunny is a mammal, like dogs.

Conclusion: Rabbits are furry things
Premise: rabbits are mammals
Examples: like dogs.

In this example "rabbit" and "bunny" are most likely referring to the same thing. Context and knowledge of the arguer might be able to tell us this. Since we want each of the paksas to have the exact same wording, we arbitrarily select "rabbit" (or "bunny") for use in both the conclusion and the premise. Keeping in mind that the arguments will be much easier to assess if we formulate them so that the terms are plural, we change "rabbit" to "rabbits." Likewise, we change "mammal" to "mammals." "Has fur" does not refer to a class of things, so we change it to "furry things" ("things that have fur" would also work; there are many possibilities). No vipaksa is offered, so we do not provide one at this point. The person offering this argument should be satisfied with how we have presented it.

2. No cats are fish, thus no cats are sharks, like great white sharks but unlike pencils.

Conclusion: Cats are things other than sharks (or nonsharks)
Premise: cats are things other than fish (or nonfish)
Examples: like great white sharks,
unlike pencils.

This time we needed to rearrange the claims by placing the conclusion first. In the original argument "thus" served as an indicator telling us which claim was the conclusion. In Nyaya standard form the conclusion and premise are affirmative, so we have to reword both claims in this case. "No cats are fish" is negative, but a logically equivalent claim is "[All] cats are nonfish." The pattern of this logically equivalent relationship (known as obversion) is this: "No A are B" is logically equivalent to "[All] A are non-B" (or "A are things other than B"). This relationship of logical equivalence works from the negative statement to the affirmative, as well as from the affirmative to the negative.

3. Tokyo is large, since it is a metropolis, like Kyoto and unlike toy poodles.

Conclusion: Cities identical to Tokyo are large things
Premise: cities identical to Tokyo are metropolises
Examples: like cities identical to Kyoto,
unlike toy poodles.

In this example we took a reference to a single object (Tokyo) and reworded it so that the term picks out a class of things: "Cities identical to Tokyo." Because there is only one such city, the class has only one member in it. Other cities named "Tokyo" would not be identical to the Tokyo referred to in the original argument. The same was done for the sapaksa. Note that both instances of the paksa have exactly the same wording, and that the hetu has been reworded so that it is a plural noun picking out a class of things.

4. An omniscient being does not exist, because he is not apprehended by the senses, like a jar.

Conclusion: Omniscient beings are nonexistent things
Premise: omniscient beings are things not apprehended by the senses
Examples: like jars.

Here we needed to make the paksa plural so that it clearly picks out a class of things, and we used the exact same wording—"omniscient beings"—in both the conclusion and the premise. "[D]oes not exist" does not pick out a class of things, so we changed it to "nonexistent things" ("things that do not exist" would be one of many alternatives). We handled the hetu in a similar fashion.

This last example is found in medieval Indian logic texts. It might or might not be of some satisfaction to students to know that for nearly 1,500 years their peers have been learning this same system of logic.

Exercise   The following are practice problems. Reformulate the following arguments into standard Nyaya form, and underline and label each term. Note that there may be more than one way to word a term.

1. An elm is a plant, because it's a tree, like pines and unlike trucks.
2. The Beatles are musicians because they play musical instruments, like Miles Davis.
3. Since dogs have fur, they are mammals, unlike fish but just like cats.
4. No professional killers are compassionate people. Thus hired assassins are not humane.
5. Denver, Colorado is one mile high. Therefore its elevation is over 2,000 feet.

Answers

1.
Conclusion: <u>Elms</u> (p) are <u>plants</u> (s)
Premise: <u>elms</u> (p) are <u>trees</u> (h)
Examples: like <u>pines</u> (sp) unlike <u>trucks</u> (vp)

2.
Conclusion: <u>The Beatles</u> (p) are <u>musicians</u> (s)
Premise: <u>The Beatles</u> (p) are <u>people who play musical instruments</u> (h)
Examples: like <u>people identical with Miles Davis</u> (sp)

3.

> Conclusion: <u>Dogs</u> (p) are <u>mammals</u> (s)
> Premise: <u>dogs</u> (p) are <u>things with fur</u> (h)
> Examples: like <u>cats</u> (sp) unlike <u>fish</u> (vp)

4.

> Conclusion: <u>Professional killers</u> (p) are <u>people who are not humane</u> (s)
> Premise: <u>professional killers</u> (p) are <u>uncompassionate people</u> (h)

5.

> Conclusion: <u>Cities identical to Denver, Colorado</u> (p) are <u>cities with an elevation of over 2,000 feet</u> (s)
> Premise: <u>cities identical to Denver, Colorado</u> (p) are <u>cities that are one mile high</u> (h)

What we've been calling Nyaya logic is actually a simplified version of Nyaya. Gautama's articulation of the standard Nyaya inference in his *Nyaya Sutra* presents a five-part form consisting of the thesis to be proven, the reason for believing the thesis, an affirmative or negative example (i.e., a sapaksa or vipaska), the application of the reason to the thesis, and a restating of the conclusion with reference to how the reason was thus applied. Various logicians within other traditions—such as Buddhism, Mimamsa, and Jainism—argued that Gautama's standard five-part form was redundant, and that the heart of the inference can be reduced to three parts. To provide a basic introduction to classical Indian logic for beginning philosophy students, we've here explored one simpler three-part form. The core ideas regarding Nyaya's inference are here, and though scholars continue to debate the exact purpose of Gautama's earlier additional parts of the standard form, we can be reasonably sure that it was to follow the accepted debate protocol of the time.

Rules of Validity

There are five rules or tests that an argument must pass for it to be considered valid (i.e., an acceptable line of reasoning). An argument is valid if and only if it passes each of the five rules. If the argument is not valid, it is invalid. An argument might technically be invalid, but if the argument can charitably be fixed, we should do so and, in charity, deem the argument valid.

The first rule is the *Rule of Existence*.[3] Each of the terms found in the argument—the paksa, sadhya, hetu, sapaksa, and vipaksa—must refer to things that actually exist (in the sense that dogs exist but not in the sense that unicorns, Shakespeare's *Hamlet*, and justice as an abstract entity are said to exist). To the Indian concerned with

---

[3] The names of these rules are not drawn from Indian sources; they were suggested by students for ease of learning.

achieving moksa, an argument that appeals to things that do not exist is pointless and is serving no practical purpose. It is to be rejected on this basis alone.

If a class of things is introduced whose existence is debatable (e.g., angels), then the arguer must offer independent support for the existence of at least one member of that class. The interlocutor must not be forced to accept the presupposition of the existence of things referred to in any of the terms.

Recall our original argument:

Conclusion: Dogs are animals
Premise: dogs are mammals
Examples: like bears,
unlike rocks.

The argument satisfies this rule because all the terms—"dogs," "animals," "mammals," "bears," and "rocks"—refer to things that exist.

The second rule is the *Rule of Overlapping Sapaksa*. This rule demands that a sapaksa be offered that refers to a class that has at least one member common to both the sadhya and the hetu. Consider the following argument:

Things identical to this plant are trees,
because things identical to this plant are elms,
like . . . .

The sadhya of this argument is "trees" and the hetu is "elms." Three examples of acceptable sapaksas include "the elms in my backyard," "deciduous trees," and "plants." At least one member from each of these three classes falls within the classes of trees and elms. An example of an unacceptable sapaksa would be "Coke bottles," as a Coke bottle is neither a tree nor an elm.

Sapaksas are offered so that we can see that there really is a relation between the things referred to by the sadhya and the hetu. Thus if something (the paksa) is found in the hetu, we have some reason to believe that it will be found in the sadhya.

Note that if the sapaksa is the same as the hetu, then the sapaksa has no polemical use. For example:

This plant is a tree,
because this plant is an elm, like an elm.

The third rule is *the Rule of Excluded Vipaksa*. This rule demands that a vipaksa be given and that none of the members of the class it refers to fall in the classes referred to by the sadhya or the hetu. For example, consider the paradigm Indian argument:

That mountain is on fire,
because that mountain is smoking,
like a kitchen,
and unlike a lake.

If rewritten in standard Nyaya form, the sadhya is "things on fire," the hetu is "smoking things," and the vipaksa is "lakes." Because the water that makes up a lake neither catches on fire nor smokes, "lakes" properly falls completely outside the sadhya and hetu, and is hence an acceptable vipaksa. Unacceptable vipaksas for this argument include "Forests" and "Kitchens." The former is unacceptable because forests can catch on fire; the latter is unacceptable because Indian kitchens have stoves with fire in them. Kitchens would be said sometimes to fall within the class of things that are on fire. Bathrooms would also be an unacceptable vipaksa, as sometimes they, too, catch on fire (as when a house burns down).

The following two arguments fail the Rule of Excluded Vipaksa:

That mountain is a thing on fire,
because that mountain is a smoking thing,
unlike the <u>sky</u>.

This argument fails the third rule because some skies have smoke.

That mountain is a thing on fire,
because that mountain is a smoking thing,
unlike <u>burning wet leaves</u>.

Here "burning wet leaves" would serve as a sapaksa, but not as a vipaksa. Burning wet leaves are both on fire and are smoking.

The Indians' demand for vipaksas is the hardest for us to understand. Apparently by providing a vipaksa you are showing that your argument is not so broad and general as to make claims that are trivially true. If I offer a premise or infer a conclusion that refers to classes that include everything so that nothing can be found to exist outside those classes and so that a vipaksa cannot be given, then my inference offers no useful information and is thus to be rejected as of no practical use. Arguing about such broad topics is going to produce karmic affects and is thus counterproductive to the process of Nyaya.

The fourth rule is *the Rule of Paksa-in-Hetu*. This rule demands that every member of the paksa is also found in the hetu. If "mammals" is the hetu and "dogs" is the paksa, then the argument passes this rule, as all dogs are mammals. But if the terms are reversed, the argument fails to pass this rule, as it is false that all mammals are dogs. A counterexample should be provided to demonstrate that your criticism of the argument at this juncture is correct. Noting that *cats* are mammals that are not dogs would serve this purpose.

Sometimes when an argument fails to pass the fourth rule, a different hetu can be provided, but you must be careful not to change the argument in such a way that a relevantly different premise is offered. By changing the argument you might be able to offer a valid argument, but it might not honestly be said to be what the original arguer was presenting.

Here is an argument that fails rule four:

> Violent acts are things to be avoided,
> because violent acts are immoral acts.

This argument fails the fourth rule because there are violent acts that are not immoral, such as killing for food, self-defense, and killing a fly. It should be noted, however, that the Indian tradition known as Jainism advocates a total avoidance of violence (the doctrine of *ahimsa*). A Jain would disagree with my claim that killing a fly was not an immoral act.

The fifth rule is the *Rule of Hetu-in-Sadhya*. This rule demands that every member of the hetu also be a member of the sadhya. For example, if the hetu is "dogs" and the sadhya is "animals," then the argument would pass this rule because all dogs are animals. But if the terms were reversed, the argument would be invalid. A counterexample should be offered to demonstrate that your criticism of the argument is justified. "Fish" would serve this purpose because fish are animals without being dogs.

If you can see that the argument fails to pass rule five, yet you cannot think of a specific counterexample, you should at least provide a description of the kind of thing that you believe exists and would serve as a counterexample. For instance, if the hetu was "dogs," the sadhya was "dogs that like to herd sheep," and you could not think of any specific breeds of dogs that do not like to herd sheep, then you could offer the following description: "Dogs that like to chase rats" (e.g., dachshunds).

If rule five is broken, the argument is almost surely going to remain invalid. Any change that would fix the argument would so radically alter it that it would probably not be what the original arguer had in mind.

The following argument does not pass rule five:

> That mountain is a thing that is smoking,
> because that mountain is a thing on fire,
> like kitchens,
> unlike lakes.

This might seem just as valid as the paradigm Indian argument, but the hetu does not fall completely within the sadhya. There can be things that are on fire that might not be smoking, such as a red-hot iron ball or a live coal. Remember, to show that an inference violates rule five, an example of a member of the hetu that is not a member of the sadhya must be suggested.

Conclude your assessment of the argument with a brief discussion of its merits. If the argument fails to pass one or more rules, yet you can in charity fix the argument, then say so. The argument would technically be invalid, but in charity it can be considered valid. If the argument is irreparable, then say so, explaining why you deem it invalid. The assessment of an argument using Nyaya techniques is conversational. You are working with the arguer to try to determine if the conclusion should be embraced. A concluding brief discussion of the merits and faults of the argument is thus in order.

Following are four additional examples of argument assessment. For each argument we will (a) rewrite it in standard Nyaya form; (b) underline and label each term; (c) name each of the five rules of validity and briefly explain why the argument passes or fails each of the rules; (d) if the argument breaks a rule, we will fix it in charity if we can; and (e) briefly explain why the argument should be considered valid or invalid.

1. Colas are beverages, since colas are soft drinks, just as Mountain Dew is, but unlike Coke.

Conclusion: Colas (p) are beverages (s)
Premise: colas (p) are soft drinks (h)
Examples: like Mountain Dew (sp)
unlike Coke (vp)

- Rule of Existence: Pass: Each term refers to something that actually exists.
- Rule of Overlapping Sapaksa: Pass: Mountain Dew is both a beverage and a soft drink.
- Rule of Excluded Vipaksa: Fail: Coke is both a soft drink and a beverage, but in charity we can fix the argument by supplying a different vipaksa: pizza.
- Rule of Paksa-in-Hetu: Pass: All colas are indeed soft drinks.
- Rule of Hetu-in-Sadhya: Pass: All soft drinks are indeed beverages.

This argument is technically invalid because it provided an improper vipaksa, but in charity we can easily fix the problem. The argument can therefore be accepted as valid.

2. All apple trees are plants. Thus apple trees are fruit trees, as are orange trees, but not rocks.

Conclusion: <u>Apple trees</u> (p) are <u>fruit trees</u> (s)
Premise: <u>apple trees</u> (p) are <u>plants</u> (h)
Examples: like <u>orange trees</u> (sp)
unlike: <u>rocks</u> (vp)

- Rule of Existence: Pass: All terms refer to things that actually exist.
- Rule of Overlapping Sapaksa: Pass: Orange trees are both plants and fruit trees.
- Rule of Excluded Vipaksa: Pass: Rocks are neither plants nor fruit trees.
- Rule of Paksa-in-Hetu: Pass: All apple trees are fruit trees.
- Rule of Hetu-in-Sadhya: Fail: Some plants are not fruit trees (e.g., water lilies).

This argument is invalid because it fails rule five. The argument cannot be fixed without revising it in such a way that it would clearly fail to be the original argument.

3.   Canton is in China, hence Canton is in Asia.

Conclusion: <u>Cities identical to Canton</u> (p) are <u>things in Asia</u> (s)
Premise: <u>Cities identical to Canton</u> (p) are <u>things in China</u> (h)

- Rule of Existence: Pass: All terms refer to things that actually exist.
- Rule of Overlapping Sapaksa: Fail: No sapaksa is provided, but in charity we can provide one: The Great Wall of China.
- Rule of Excluded Vipaksa: Fail: No vipaksa is provided, but in charity we can provide one: New York City.
- Rule of Paksa-in-Hetu: Pass: Canton is indeed in China.
- Rule of Hetu-in-Sadhya: Pass: Anything in China would have to be in Asia.

Technically this argument is invalid because both the sapaksa and vipaksa were not provided, but we could easily and charitably fix these omissions, so the argument should be considered valid.

4.   No true artworks are made by nonhumans, because true works of art are things made by rational beings.

Conclusion: <u>True artworks</u> (p) are <u>things made by humans</u> (s)
Premise: <u>true artworks</u> (p) are <u>things requiring rationality for manufacture</u> (h)

- Rule of Existence: Pass: The argument passes assuming that there are true artworks (we shall ignore contemporary discussions proclaiming the death of art).
- Rule of Overlapping Sapaksa: Fail: No sapaksa is given, but in charity one can be provided: Computers.
- Rule of Excluded Vipaksa: Fail: None is provided, but in charity one can be offered: Baby cats (if all things not made by humans are believed to be created in a relevant sense by a divine, rational designer, then perhaps no vipaksa can be offered except God Himself; but if God is believed to be the sum total of all that is [i.e., Brahman], then no vipaksa can be given at all and the argument would fail on that basis).
- Rule of Paksa-in-Hetu: Pass: Acknowledging that there is some debate over whether some nonhuman animals or supernatural beings (should they exist) can create art, still we can reasonably hold that only humans can do so.
- Rule of Hetu-in-Sadhya: Pass: Assuming that only humans are rational, the hetu would fall completely within the sadhya.

This argument is difficult to assess. Given the traditional (and probably naive) view that only humans are rational, and given the view that true artworks require rationality for their production, the argument is best seen as valid.

This last argument illustrates why discussion and explanation are vital parts of the assessment of philosophically interesting arguments. It would be simplistic to offer merely the "correct" answer of "valid" when asked to assess this complex inference.

Informal Fallacies

For Indian logicians the context of an inference is important. The following three informal fallacies are often considered in addition to the five rules of validity. These fallacies pertain to the usefulness and acceptability of an inference in the context in which it is given. The context usually includes a demand for practicality and completeness of inference. These fallacies should be kept in mind as you assess an argument. If the argument violates one of them, it might still be valid, but it will be of little or no polemical use.

1.   Unnecessary inferences. We should avoid trying to prove what has already been proven or what is already agreed on. An argument is guilty of unnecessary inferences if it purports to prove the obvious or what has already been proven. There is nothing really wrong with the argument; it is just a waste of time. Remember that the overriding purpose of Indian philosophical discourse is to achieve moksa. Arguments serving no practical purpose are to be ignored. Obviously for the purpose of an in-

troductory logic class an instructor cannot allow students to charge an argument in a practice or test context with this fallacy, as the content of most of the practice and test arguments is indeed trivial.

2.   Nonidentity of terms. None of the five terms in an inference may be identical with any other. An argument is guilty of nonidentity of terms if two or more of the five terms are the same. "Cats" and "felines" would be the same, although the words are different. They are the same because they specifically refer to the exact same class of things. In rewriting the argument in standard Nyaya form one should select one of these words and use it consistently. "Cats" and "Black cats" are not the same because they pick out different classes of things. Consider, however, the following argument:

> Cats are mammals,
> because cats are mammals.

This argument does not violate the Rule of Hetu-in-Sadhya, but it is guilty of nonidentity of terms (or begging the question or circular reasoning). Although valid, this argument does not help to prove any point.

3. Truncated inferences. Inferences should include all five terms. An argument is guilty of truncated inference if one or more of the five terms is missing. Usually if a term is missing it will be the sapaksa or the vipaksa. In ordinary discourse this is often the case because it is obvious to all that an acceptable sapaksa or vipaksa can be agreed on. It is usually easy in this case to provide one in charity. Occasion for this charity on your part would arise when assessing the argument in light of rules two and three.

Occasionally, however, the presuppositions of the arguer are such that a vipaksa cannot be produced. For example, a pantheist might argue for the following conclusion without giving a vipaksa: "Things identical to God are all things, because . . . , like . . . ." What could be offered as a vipaksa? The vipaksa would have to be outside the class of all things. But what could the pantheist be expected to name? A stickler for Indian logic could say that the pantheist thereby has failed to give an acceptable argument. Cases where a vipaksa cannot possibly be offered are fortunately rare.

Practice Problems

Translate each of the following arguments into standard Nyaya form, label each term, name the five rules of validity and briefly explain why the argument passes or fails each rule. Be charitable whenever possible, and briefly explain why the argument is valid or invalid.

1.   Alligators are animals because they are reptiles, like turtles.
2.   All carnivores with teeth are mammals, since they are all animals.

3. Since three-masted sailing vessels float on the water, they are large ships—a negative example being pieces of cork, and a positive example being small rowboats.

4. Since it is true that fresh green beans are vegetation, it must be the case that they are edible foods for humans.

5. Assuming that no bears are vegetarians, we may infer that they are meat-eaters.

6. All animals are carnivorous since they are mammals.

7. Driving while under the influence of alcohol is wrong because it harms people, unlike compassion.

8. Dogs cause a foul odor, since canines are filthy.

9. Because Senator Jones is a Democrat, she, like any liberal, wants to raise taxes.

10. Spanking children is wrong because it causes pain.

11. All leopards are animals, like lions, but not like rocks.

12. Seattle is not in Peru, given that it is not in South America, as is Lima and unlike New York City.

13. Sam Clemens is Mark Twain, since Sam Clemens is the author of *Huckleberry Finn*.

14. Legalizing euthanasia is wrong because it would lead to genocide, just as it happened in Nazi Germany.

15. Capital punishment is wrong because through it innocent people are killed.

See "Answers to Selected Exercises" at the back of the book for answers to these problems.

B Metalogic: The Logic of Logic « « « « « « « « «

Metalogic (from the Greek word *meta* meaning "after" or "about," literally "about logic") is the logical theory of logical systems. Intuitively, *metalogic* is the "logic of logic." Recall that a formal logical system consists of two parts: (a) a formal language (into which natural language arguments are translated), plus (b) a set of natural deduction rules for proving symbolized arguments valid. In metalogic, logicians prove theorems *about* various formal logical systems. A proof in metalogic, about a system of logic, is called a *metaproof*. A metaproof establishes that a system of logic has a certain logical property. The most important properties that systems of logic can possess are completeness, consistency, decidability, and soundness.

Metatheory of Truth-Functional Logic

The first metalogical proofs about systems of logic appeared in the early twentieth century; thus, metalogic is a late addition to logical theory. Our concern for the moment is the metatheory of truth-functional logic. In 1920, American logician Emil Post rigorously proved that the system of truth-functional logic (a version of which is presented in this text in Unit Three) is complete in the following sense: Every truth-functionally valid argument (every valid argument whose validity is due to the formal arrangement of its truth-functional operators and nothing more) can be proved valid using the rules of truth-functional deduction.

Intuitively, a system of logic is complete if it does everything you want it to do. We want a system of truth-functional logic to prove valid all truth-functional arguments that are indeed valid. Post's metaproof shows that a system of truth-functional logic, expressed in the form of axioms with rules of inference, does just that. There is also a metaproof showing that every argument that can be proved valid in truth-functional logic via natural deduction is also truth-table valid (i.e., can be proven valid on a truth table).

It can also be proved in metalogic that every truth-functional tautology can be proved logically true on the basis of a premise-free proof and that every theorem of truth-functional logic (every sentence proved on the basis of a premise-free proof) is a tautology. Thus every truth-functional tautology is a theorem, and every theorem is a truth-functional tautology. This is remarkable, given that truth-functional logic includes an *infinite* number of theorems.

Post also proved (in 1920) that truth-functional logic is consistent. A system of logic is consistent if it is not possible to derive a contradiction, a statement of the form P &~P, within the system. Intuitively, given a set of axioms generating the whole of truth-functional logic, and a set of inference rules, one cannot derive a contradiction using only the rules of the system applied to the axioms and to what follows from the axioms.

A system of logic is decidable if for any formula expressible within the language of the system, there is an algorithm or effective method for determining whether that formula is a theorem or is not a theorem. In the same year, 1920, Post also proved that truth-functional logic is decidable. In effect, this means that it is possible to specify an algorithm (or "decision procedure") for truth-functional logic, one that has the following property: A digital computer running the algorithm can read any well-formed formula of truth-functional logic and say conclusively whether the formula is a tautology, contradiction, or contingent. It follows that the computer could also apply the algorithm to any truth-functional argument expressible in the language of truth-functional logic and determine whether the argument is valid or invalid. Here is why:

Any argument can be represented as a single conditional, called the argument's *corresponding conditional*, by following two steps: (a) Conjoin all the premises of the argument into one sentence and make this the antecedent of the conditional, and (b) make the conclusion of the argument the consequent of the conditional. The corresponding conditional of an argument will be tautological if and only of the argument is valid. Because every truth-functional argument can be represented as a conditional sentence that is tautological if and only if the argument is valid, it follows from the fact that truth-functional logic is decidable that an algorithm exists for deciding whether any truth-functional argument is valid or invalid.

Finally, truth-functional logic has been proved *sound* in the sense that we can derive a conclusion from premises in our system only if the conclusion validly follows; we can never derive a conclusion from premises if the argument is an invalid one. It follows that all the theorems of truth-functional logic are logically true. The word *sound* actually derives from a German word for "health," *gesund*. Truth-functional logic is sound (healthy) in that its axioms and theorems all are logically true.

Soundness and Completeness Compared

Put in terms of tautologies, completeness means that every truth-functional tautology is a theorem; soundness means that every theorem is a tautology. Notice that if a system of logic is sound, then it is automatically also consistent. Consistency logically follows from soundness. (Can you explain why?) However, the reverse does not hold: Soundness does not logically follow from consistency. The fact that a system is consistent does not imply that it is sound. (Can you explain why?) The metalogical proofs for the preceding claims, and many more, are fascinating; however, they are also extremely complex. Even simplified versions of the actual proofs would take us far beyond the scope of an introduction to logic. Metatheory is best reserved for an advanced text in logical theory.

Metatheory of Predicate Logic

This short excursion into the metatheory of predicate logic will depend on the distinction between a first-order and a second-order system of logic. In a first-order system of logic the quantifiers range over individual things—the things denoted by individual constants. Examples of things denoted by individual constants would be dogs, cats, people, rocks, and so on. In a second-order system of logic, the quantifiers also range over the things denoted by predicate constants, i.e., properties (characteristics, attributes) of things. Examples of properties would be the property of being red (a property possessed by fire trucks but not by crows), the property of being human (a property possessed by you but not by your cat), the property of being older than 70 (a property not possessed by teenagers), and so on. The predicate logic presented in this text is all first-order logic. When we add quantification over predicate constants, the result is a second-order system of logic. Some logicians believe it is logically illegitimate to quantify across properties; others disagree.

In 1915, German mathematician Leopold Löwenheim proved that a first-order system of monadic predicate logic (such as we learned in Unit Four) is *complete* in the sense that every logically valid argument expressible in the system can be proved valid using the rules of the system. Again, intuitively, a system of logic is complete if it does everything you want it to do. We want a system of monadic predicate logic to prove valid all monadic predicate arguments that are indeed valid. Löwenheim's metaproof showed that a first-order system of monadic predicate logic does just that.

In the same year, Löwenheim also proved that every logically valid sentence expressible in the language of first-order monadic predicate logic can be proved logically true with a premise-free proof in the system; thus, every logically true monadic predicate sentence is a theorem of monadic predicate logic. Löwenheim also proved monadic predicate logic consistent: It is not possible to derive a contradiction within the system.

Recall that a system of logic is decidable if it is the case that for any formula expressible within the language of the system, it is possible to prove that the formula is either a theorem or is not a theorem. You guessed correctly: Löwenheim also proved in the same year that monadic predicate logic is decidable.

Finally, monadic predicate logic has been proved *sound* in the sense that (a) a set of axioms and rules of inference can be specified for the system, (b) it can be shown that all the axioms are logically true, and (c) it can be shown that all the rules of inference are valid or "truth-preserving." It follows that all the theorems of monadic predicate logic are logically true.

However, when we add dyadic predicates and overlapping quantification to the system of first-order monadic predicate logic, some of the logical properties of the system change radically. In 1928, German mathematician David Hilbert proved that first-order predicate logic with dyadic predicates and overlapping quantifiers is consistent. Two years later a young, unknown German logician named Kurt Gödel proved the system is complete. But in 1936, American mathematician and logician Alonzo Church proved the system is (surprisingly) undecidable. In his classic textbook on metalogic, Geoffrey Hunter writes:

> Informally, this means that it is possible to program a computer to churn out one by one the theorems of [first-order predicate logic with multiple quantification, etc.] without churning out any nontheorems, and in such a way that any formula that is a theorem will sooner or later . . . be churned out. But . . . it is not possible to do the same thing for the formulas that are not theorems.[4]

Further Results

Things do not go so smoothly when we add quantification over properties to a logical system. Second-order predicate logic has been proved incomplete. This means it contains at least one undecidable proposition P such that P is expressible in the system, but neither P nor ~P can be proved in the system. Second-order predicate logic is thus undecidable. It does not do all that we want it to, and indeed it will never do so—it is inherently incapable of completing itself. In addition, it has been proved that the consistency of second-order system of predicate logic cannot be proved within the system. More bad news for second-order logics.

---

[4] See Geoffrey Hunter, *Metalogic: An Introduction to the Metatheory of Standard First Order Logic* (Berkeley and Los Angeles: University of California Press, 1971, p. 251). In my opinion, this is the best single introduction to the subject.

Gödel's Incompleteness Theorem

No survey of metalogic is halfway complete without some discussion of an individual who has been called the greatest metalogician of the twentieth century. In 1931, Kurt Gödel, then a young, unknown logician teaching at the University of Vienna, proved that any formal system that is consistent and that is powerful enough to prove the truths of arithmetic logically (necessarily) must be incomplete. This means that there must be a formula F, expressible in the system, such that neither F nor ~F can be proved in the system. At the same time, Gödel also proved that the consistency of any such system cannot be proved within the system. Gödel rocked the worlds of both mathematics and logic when he presented the news of his two proofs at a conference of mathematicians, logicians, and philosophers the same year. For it follows from Gödel's now-famous *incompleteness theorem* that no formal axiom system, no matter how complex, will ever be able to generate all the truths of arithmetic. This meant that mathematical truth will never be fully captured in a single formal system. It also followed from his incompleteness theorem that no algorithm will ever generate all the truths of mathematics. Many mathematicians had spent decades searching for a single, complete formalization of all of mathematics. The dream was over. No such system will ever be discovered—not because we aren't smart enough, but because such a system is logically impossible. Something equally dismal followed from Gödel's second theorem: Nobody will ever be able to *prove* that arithmetic is consistent, that is, that it is free of contradiction. Nobody will ever prove it because it logically cannot be proved. For more on Gödel and his accomplishment, see Appendix C.[5]

---

[5] For Gödel's complete proof, see Jean van Heijenoort (ed.), *From Frege to Gödel: A Source Book in Mathematical Logic, 1879–1931.* (Cambridge, MA: Harvard University Press, 2002).

C Gödel's Theorem: The Power of Logic Revealed 《 《 《 《 《 《 《 《 《

As we have seen, metalogic is the "logic of logic"—the logical theory of logical systems. Metalogic is seldom mentioned in introductory logic textbooks because it is the most advanced branch of the subject. This is why we have only briefly looked into the metatheory of truth-functional and predicate logic in passing. Many people are shocked when they first encounter the actual proofs of metalogic. They look extremely forbidding. Their first thought is often "This looks more like math than logic." Their second thought is often "What can this knowledge possibly be good for?" To many, metalogic seems like the twentieth-century equivalent of "angels dancing on the heads of pins"—useless theorizing. These questions, and others like them, lead us naturally to an individual who is probably the greatest metalogician of all time—a man whose life's work exemplifies both the power of logic and its relation to issues that do matter.

On October 9, 1930, a young, unknown logician-mathematician at the University of Vienna stood up at a conference of logicians and mathematicians meeting in Königsburg, Germany, to announce that he had proved a theorem that might be of interest to those present. The logician's name was Kurt Gödel (1906–1978), and the theorem that he announced that day is considered to be one of the greatest discoveries in the history of logic and mathematics. Known as Gödel's *incompleteness theorem*, it was described during a ceremony at Harvard University as "the most significant mathematical truth of the [twentieth] century." At 24, Gödel was approximately the same age Einstein had been when, as an unknown physicist, he too had discovered something that would shake the foundations of his discipline. Years later, at the Institute for Advanced Studies in Princeton, New Jersey, Einstein and Gödel would become close friends. Every night the two walked home together, talking about physics, logic, cosmology, and issues such as the beginning of the universe. Toward the end of his life, when Einstein no longer wanted to go to his office at the Institute, he went in every day anyway, late in the afternoon, just in time to walk home with his best friend, the logician Gödel.

Gödel's 20-page proof of his incompleteness theorem was a solution to a problem in mathematical logic that had eluded everyone. As we have seen, in the nineteenth century, mathematicians in Europe began developing axiomatic systems for various branches of mathematics. As the axiomatic method was extended to more and more areas of mathematics, it began to look as if one day soon, all of mathematics would eventually rest on a solid axiomatic basis. An axiom system for all of math would be a single set of axioms yielding as theorems *all* the truths of mathematics. If that were to be accomplished, then a computing machine, following a single algorithm, could theoretically generate and print every mathematical truth—given enough time and a sufficient quantity of paper.

The future of the axiomatic method for both logic and math looked bright in 1889 when Italian mathematician Giuseppe Peano (1858–1932) developed an axiom system for arithmetic. Some of the brightest minds in mathematics and logic now believed that it was only a matter of time before a single axiom system for all of mathematics would be completed: From one compact set of axioms, mathematicians would then be able to derive, using gap-free, deductive reasoning, all the truths of mathematics. With the whole field systematized, there would be nothing left to prove. In short, by the end of the nineteenth century, an axiom system encompassing all of math had become the "Holy Grail" of mathematics.

However, axiom systems face several problems. The first is the problem of consistency. When you first choose the axioms of a system for a specific subject, you cannot be certain that the system is internally consistent. The reason for this initial uncertainty is that you cannot know at the start all the theorems that will eventually be proved on the basis of the axioms and definitions. Axiom systems can spit out huge numbers of theorems, some of them completely surprising. But if an axiom system is inconsistent, then some part of it contains or implies a contradiction, in which case it is possible to derive two theorems, each contradictory to the other. But as we have seen, if a proof system contains or implies a contradiction, then any statement follows from the axioms, and thus anything (and everything) can be proved. Such a system is worthless; it proves too much.

A "proof of consistency" for an axiom system would demonstrate that the system does not have two theorems such that one contradicts the other; in other words, it would prove that you will never be able to derive a self-contradiction, P & ~P, from the axioms, no matter how many theorems you pull out of the hat. As you would imagine, consistency is a very important property of any axiom system.

Completeness is the second problem facing any axiom system. Roughly, an axiom system is complete if it proves everything you want it to prove. For instance, an axiom system for arithmetic would be complete if it proved all the truths of number theory, leaving nothing out. A system is incomplete if it cannot prove some truths in the region it is supposed to be systematizing.

In 1900, German mathematician David Hilbert (1862–1943) gave a speech to the International Congress of Mathematicians meeting in Paris. In his speech, which has been called the most influential address ever given by a mathematician to other mathematicians, Hilbert listed 23 unsolved problems that, he felt, must be tackled during the new century. One of these was the complete formalization of all of mathematics on a single axiomatic basis. Hilbert's dream was dashed forever on that October day in 1930 when Gödel took the floor to announce his theorem.

In his PhD dissertation the year before, Gödel had proved the completeness of first-order predicate logic: Every logical truth expressible in the language of predicate logic can be proved in the proof system of predicate logic. (We already noted this result in Appendix B). However, on this momentous day, the young logician had another theorem to announce—a truly startling discovery. Gödel had completed a metaproof demonstrating that *any* consistent set of axioms for arithmetic is inherently too weak to prove all the truths of arithmetic. Any axiom system for arithmetic, in other words, must be incomplete. Given any axiom system for arithmetic, there logically *must* be truths of arithmetic that are expressible in the language of the system but that cannot be proved as theorems of the system. This astonishing result became known as *Gödel's first incompleteness theorem*.

But there was more. Gödel had another theorem up his sleeve, a proof equally revolutionary. Gödel's *second incompleteness theorem* states that any axiom system for arithmetic cannot prove its own consistency.

It follows that any axiom system for arithmetic must contain undecidable propositions. An *undecidable proposition* in a system is a proposition which is such that neither it nor its negation can be proved true in the system. Singlehandedly, Gödel had proved that there is a logical limit to the axiomatic method: It cannot even accommodate arithmetic, let alone the whole of mathematics. Mathematics will never be fully axiomatized. As one commentator has put it, "The axiomatic method is not omnipotent." In addition, Gödel had proved that there can never be a proof that mathematics is absolutely free of contradictions. We can never know for certain that mathematics is internally consistent!

In their wonderful book on Gödel's accomplishment, Nagel and Newman call his proof "an amazing intellectual symphony."[1]

---

[1] Ernest Nagel and James R. Newman, *Gödel's Proof* (New York: New York University Press, 1958). See also Peter Smith, *An Introduction to Gödel's Theorems* (Cambridge, UK: Cambridge University Press, 2007).

In a fascinating and touching book on Gödel's life and work, philosopher Rebecca Goldstein calls Gödel's short speech at the Konigsburg conference his "shining hour" and says of it:

> Gödel had not let a single note of his symphonic proof escape until this muted moment in Konigsburg. Such a noiseless, inexpressive exterior enclosing such a swelling mathematical noise. Then, at last, he pronounced one tersely precise sentence . . . on the last day of the conference . . . brought it out with no fanfare, played it barely *pianissimo*. The idiosyncratic "announcement" is congruent with the logician's personality. The concise statement that composed his "shining hour," lasting maybe 30 seconds tops, is meticulously crafted, a miniature masterpiece. It says what it needs to say, and not a word more.[2]

Philosophical Consequences?

Some philosophers have drawn the following lesson from Gödel's celebrated theorems. The human mind can know truths that cannot, even in principle, be derived by any possible computing machine, axiom system, or formal logical procedure. Thus (the argument continues), the human mind is not, and cannot possibly be, a machine, an axiom system, or a formal, algorithm-driven processor embedded in flesh; rather, the human mind transcends all of these things. The famous Oxford University mathematician Roger Penrose, among others, argues for this view or for one similar to it. It would seem to follow, if this interpretation of the implications of Gödel's theorems is correct, and if it is true, that artificial intelligence is impossible; that is, that no computer will ever become functionally equivalent to the human mind. In 1951, Gödel received the first Albert Einstein Award for Achievement in the Natural Sciences. The award was presented by Einstein himself!

---

[2] See Rebecca Goldstein, *Incompleteness, The Proof and Paradox of Gödel* (New York: Norton, 2006, p. 224). This wonderful, touching book, delves into the tragic life as well as the fascinating logic of Gödel; at the same time it also tells the story of logic in the twentieth century.

D Logic and Computers « «

How an Idea in Logic Led to the Digital Computer and Transformed the World

A seminal idea present at the founding of logic in ancient Greece during the fourth century BC connects logical theory with the theory of the digital computer. This idea, embraced from the beginning by both mathematics and logic, is the concept of an algorithm. If you have heard this term before, it was probably in connection with either computers or mathematics. Computer scientist David Berlinski calls the algorithm "the idea that rules the world" because of the central role it plays today in the design and operation of the digital computer. What is an algorithm? As a short, preliminary definition, an *algorithm* is a set of extremely precise, step-by-step instructions for accomplishing a task, structured in such a way that each step is a matter of following a precise rule without employing any creativity or additional information, and such that a definite result is guaranteed in a finite number of steps.

The algorithm is indeed a central idea in computer science today. However, Berlinski's "idea that rules the world" originated not in computer science but in ancient Greek mathematics. And the basic idea of the algorithm was soon adopted by Aristotle, the founder of logic, for use in logical theory from the beginning. The founders of math and logic adopted the idea of the algorithm mainly because they saw that it is a very effective tool if you are building precise and well-integrated systems of thought.

For as we have seen, logicians from the beginning aspired to the precision, rigor, and order of mathematics, which is why many logicians over the years developed algorithms and algorithmic methods for key logical operations. Some logicians, for instance, Leibniz, actually sought to convert *all* of logical theory into a system of precise algorithms. (Other logicians, though, have argued that this is a logically impossible goal. Even logicians disagree sometimes!)

But the historical significance of the algorithm goes far beyond its use in the Ivory Tower academic subjects of mathematics and logic. The algorithm is actually *the* seminal idea in logic that led, through a series of steps, many of which were actually taken by logicians, to the birth of the most complex and powerful tool mankind has ever created, the digital computer. As usual in logic, let us proceed step by step.

What Is a Digital Computer?

A digital computer can be thought of as a very complex input–output device, one that takes in electronic signals as "inputs" and sends out electronic signals as "outputs." There's nothing special or mysterious about an input–output device. A garden hose is also an input–output device: it takes in tap water and outputs garden water. For that matter, an electric stove and an oil furnace are both input–output devices. (What are the inputs and outputs for a stove and a furnace?)

The General Structure of an Input–Output Device

Inputs → Internal Processing → Outputs →

The inputs received by a digital computer are electronic signals submitted by a keyboard or some other inputting device. The output is always electronic signals as well, although these are usually sent through a computer display. Thus, a digital computer can be thought of as a complex input–output device, one that takes as inputs various electronic signals and then operates on those inputs to produce various other electronic signals as outputs.

The "Brains" of a Computer

How does a computer "know" which electronic signals to output for each possible set of inputs it might receive? What controls the internal processing of inputs into outputs so that the "right" outputs are produced? For example, when the following keys are pressed in order: 2, +, 2, =, each one sends its own characteristic *input* into the system. We want the *output* to be the one that causes a 4 to appear on the computer screen. How does the computer "know" in this case to print a numeral 4?

A computer simply follows the rules or instructions it has been given. All a computer ever does is follow, with extreme precision, rules or instructions that have been built into it. A computer never does anything except what a specific rule tells it to do.

The rules or instructions that control the processing of inputs into outputs in a computer are contained in the computer's *software*. So, whenever a computer performs any operation, that is, whenever it processes any inputs into outputs, it is doing nothing more than taking a specific input and generating from that a specific output, based on following a specific rule or instruction contained within its software. That's all a digital computer ever does: follow rules that it has been given.

However, a computer cannot follow just *any* type of rule. Due to the nature of computing, more specifically, due to the nature of *mechanical* computing, only one very special kind of rule is suitable for controlling the inner processes of a computer. What type of rule? Computers can only follow a rule if it is an algorithm. We have already defined the term, now it is time for a more precise explanation.

What Exactly Is an Algorithm?

An algorithm has already been defined as a set of precise, detailed instructions for completing a task or solving a problem. However, unlike most sets of instructions, for instance, the instructions for painting a beautiful picture or making someone feel special on his or her birthday, the instructions making up a genuine algorithm must meet the following very stringent requirements:

1. The instructions must be broken down into a finite number of small, discrete steps, with no gaps.
2. Each individual step must be a matter of following a detailed, precise rule and nothing more.
3. Each rule must be so precise and exact that it can be followed without the use of any creativity and without any extra knowledge, that is, knowledge not explicitly presented or presupposed by the algorithm. As David Berlinski puts it, "No art is needed."
4. The steps in the algorithm are guaranteed to complete the task or to yield a definite solution after a finite number of operations (if the rules are followed exactly).

Doesn't the idea of an algorithm naturally go hand-in-hand with the idea of a system of logic? After all, both are aimed at the same goal: precision of thought. The *idea* of translating an instruction into algorithmic form first arose in the context of ancient Greek mathematics. (Certainly the first algorithms in the historical record appear in connection with the axiom systems of the first theoretical mathematicians writing in ancient Greece.) The second application was in logical theory.[1]

---

[1] The term we use today, *algorithm*, is actually a Latin translation of a term coined during the ninth century by al-Khwarizmi, a Muslim mathematician working at the House of Wisdom in Baghdad, a research institute founded by the caliph. Operating under strict religious authority, the House of Wisdom was given two tasks: first, to import from Byzantium and other Western sources "manuscripts of particularly important works that did not exist in the Islãmic countries," especially ancient Greek mathematical, scientific, and philosophical treatises; and second, using Christian translators, to translate these works for the Muslim world (*Encyclopedia Britannica*, 2006).

Mathematical Algorithms

The method of addition—how to add a column of numbers—is an example of an algorithm, one of many algorithms that you learned in grade school math. Subtraction, division, and multiplication are also algorithmic. Remember how "mechanical" arithmetic was? Here is another algorithm from one of your old math classes, a very simple one from algebra, written in English, for multiplying (a + b) by itself, where a and b are any two real numbers.

Algorithm: To Multiply (a + b) by Itself

Let a and b stand for any two real numbers:

Step 1. Multiply a by itself.
Step 2. Multiply a by b.
Step 3. Multiply a by b again.
Step 4. Multiply b by itself.
Step 5. Add the results of the previous steps.

Precise and exact, isn't it? No gaps, a definite order, discrete steps, no ambiguity, no vagueness, and no art required. It's a bit mechanical, but at least it's *exact*. A student once said to me, "One nice thing about an algorithm is you always know the next step." Incidentally, here is this same algorithm, expressed in *symbols*:

$$(a + b)^2 = a^2 + 2ab + b^2$$

Why Symbols Are Used

Notice that the algorithm takes up much less room when it is expressed symbolically. One line of symbols compared with five lines of English—an 80% savings in terms of space on a page. (And the savings sounds even more impressive if measured in terms of characters: 16 characters in symbols compared with around 125 in English.) Symbolizing saves space and allows us to express a complicated thought in a simpler way. In case you are curious, here is an application of the algorithm for (3 +6):

$$(3 + 6) \times (3 + 6) = (3 \times 3) + (3 \times 6) + (3 \times 6) + (6 \times 6) = 81.$$

Question. Why is the following rule *not* an algorithm: "Apply oils to canvas and paint a pretty picture."

Algorithms Are Input–Output Devices, Too

We earlier characterized a computer as an input–output device operating according to rules specified as precisely defined internal algorithms. At another level, an algorithm itself can also be understood as an input–output device, an *abstract* input–output device, one that takes a specific input and then, based on extremely exact and detailed, gap-free, step-by-step instructions, generates a specific output.

To Recap

To recap, a digital computer cannot follow just any rule or instruction; it can only follow a command that is presented in an *algorithmic* form. Each discrete step in following or "implementing" an algorithm must be a matter of following an extremely simple and very precise rule, using no art or creativity. You could say that all a computer ever does, all day long, is slavishly follow algorithms, one after another.

Why Do Computers Need Their Own Language?

Remember how boring grammar class was in middle school? Well, it turns out that the proper use of language makes a difference; language matters. As we have seen, instructions must be extremely precise and detailed, requiring no creativity or art, if they are to count as algorithms. This means that they must be written in very precise language. An algorithm for a machine will not work if it is not written in unambiguous terminology. That is, a machine will not be able to follow an algorithm if it is not precise enough. This is especially true for the algorithms that direct the workings of a digital computer. An algorithm inside a digital computer will not work if it is not written in extremely precise, unambiguous language or terminology. For computers do not accept ambiguity, and they do not accept vagueness. They demand precision!

This is also why computers do not accept contradictions. For example, you can't tell a computer simultaneously to both add and not to add a given string of numbers. The upshot is that when we communicate with a computer, our communication must be consistent, and it must be very unambiguous and precise, or it won't work.

However, this need for a high degree of precision and consistency raises a major problem: As general tools of communication, natural languages, such as English, Spanish, or French, are simply not precise enough, nor are they unambiguous enough, for expressing the algorithms that direct a digital computer. For this reason, computer scientists had to create special, very precise languages, *programming languages*, to effectively communicate with the hardware, and ultimately the circuits, inside an electronic computer. Programming languages were invented because natural languages are just not precise enough. (And as a general tool of communication, a natural language is also too big a thing to program into a computer; a computer normally doesn't need a language that big.)

Recall that every language can be specified in terms of a syntax and a semantics. The *syntax* of a language includes the vocabulary (the symbols that may be used to form expressions within the language) and the grammar (the rules for building properly formed expressions using the elements of the vocabulary). Remember that an expression in a language is called a well-formed expression (wff) of that language if and only if (a) it is formed only out of the vocabulary elements of the language, and (b) it is formed according to the rules of grammar of that language.

As you can imagine, every programming language, such as Basic, Pascal, or C++, has a very, very precise syntax, and a computer will only respond to program instructions that are properly written within an appropriate programming language. This means that if a computer receives an instruction that is not well-formed, according to the rules of syntax of the programming language in use, it will output something such as "syntax error" and will refuse to execute the instruction!

Thus, you could say that a computer is simply a machine that will do anything you tell it to do, exactly as you tell it, as long as your instructions are presented to it in the form of precise, grammatically correct algorithms written in a sufficiently exact (and appropriate) language. Here's the bottom line: A natural language such as English or French or Swahili is not in itself precise or determinate enough for a computer. Programming languages were invented to give us the necessary precision of expression.

Higher-Order and Lower-Order Computer Languages

Most computer programs are written in what are called higher-order languages, while the actual instructions that physically open and close the thousands of circuits inside a computer are contained in a lower-order language called a *machine language*. The process actually has many levels; the machine language that opens and closes circuits is the lowest-order language of all.

To simplify a bit, the machine language contains the instructions closest to the computer's hardware. These are the instructions that actually physically open and close hundreds of thousands of circuits deep inside the machine. A higher level language such as a programming language contains wffs, or expressions that stand for, or abbreviate, lower-level instructions, which in turn abbreviate lower-level instructions, until the process eventually bottoms out in the machine code that physically opens and closes individual circuits.

Thus, a programmer working in a higher-level language might just type in an instruction that looks like this:

Add (a, b)

This instruction might mean "Add the two numbers a and b." This higher-level command will in turn be automatically translated (by algorithms) into a lower-level command, which will in turn be translated into a lower level yet, until the command eventually becomes machine code that physically opens and closes specific circuits in such a way that the computer correctly "adds" the two numbers and prints or displays their correct sum on the monitor. The programmer knows what he or she wants the computer to do, but the programmer normally does not know the complex machine code that actually makes the circuits turn on and off so as to correctly implement the operation of addition. That is taken care of by deeper algorithms already built into the machine.

What Is a Universal Turing Machine?

Alan Turing (1912–1954), a brilliant British mathematician and logician who used truth-functional logic to help crack Hitler's secret wartime code and thereby saved thousands of allied lives and helped defeat the Nazis during World War II, is one of the founders of information theory and computer science. He is also the originator of one of the fundamental ideas in computing theory, an idea that has since been named after him.[2] In theory, every computer is an *instance* of a Turing machine. What is this? A *Turing machine* can be defined as a purely abstract input–output device, the physical instantiation of which would have the following characteristics:

1. The operation of the device is completely determined by a tape feeding through it.
2. The tape is divided into a series of squares, or cells, each containing a single symbol taken from a finite vocabulary of symbols.
3. Each symbol or combination of symbols represents a specific input or output and completely determines a specific state of the machine.
4. The machine's complete repertoire consists in implementing the following purely mechanical actions: (a) it can move the tape one square ahead, (b) it can scan the tape, one square at a time, (c) it can erase a symbol and print a new symbol in its place, and (d) it can change state as determined by the symbols it recognizes on the tape and the strict rules by which the machine operates.

In addition, each possible state of a Turing machine, as well as each possible sequence of states, can in principle be completely described in terms of the input

---

[2] On the life and work of Turing see Douglas Hofstadter, *Alan Turing: The Enigma* (New York: Walker and Company, 2000).

symbols, output symbols, and corresponding mechanical operations. Thus, if we know the internal rules of a Turing machine, and we know the information about to go into it, we know *exactly* what it is about to do. Its behavior, in other words, is completely predictable.

The behavior of a Turing machine is thus strictly determined by antecedent factors, in such a way that at any moment in time there is only one thing it can possibly do. It can only carry out the operation determined by the symbol on its internal tape at the moment and the exact rules of its program. Nothing else is possible. Its behavior is thus determined, its operation mechanistic.

Notice that the definition of a Turing machine makes no reference to the materials out of which it is made. That is, no reference is made to *what* underlying structure is physically running the program. The nature of a Turing machine is abstract, meaning completely independent of its physical realization. This is why each "program state" of a Turing machine can be defined functionally, in terms of nothing but the role the state plays in the overall operation of the system and its relations to other program states of the machine. A Turing machine can thus be completely described functionally, in terms of the way it functions, without any mention of what it is made of.

Any physical entity that operates like a Turing machine is a physical Turing machine. That is, any physical entity with an operation that can be accurately and completely specified in terms of a Turing machine program is a physical Turing machine. There is a rigorous proof in computing theory for the following thesis: Any operation that a computer can perform can also be performed by a Turing machine with a sufficiently complex program.

A universal Turing machine is a Turing machine that can carry out any specified algorithm. If a task can be specified in terms of an algorithm, a universal Turing machine can carry it out. Computers today are coming closer and closer to the ideal of a universal Turing machine.

Philosophical Interlude: Can Computers Think?

Turing takes up this very question in a now classic paper written in 1950, "Computing Machinery and Intelligence."[3] Turing observes that philosophers traditionally approach the problem by first defining the key words, such as *machine* and *think*. His approach will be different:

> The new form of the problem can be described in terms of a game which we call the "imitation game." It is played with three people, a man (A), a woman

---

[3] A. M. Turing. "Computing machinery and intelligence." *Mind, 59*, 433–460 (1950). See also Charles Petzold, *The Annotated Turing. A Guided Tour Through Alan Turing's Historic Paper on Computability and the Turing Machine* (Indianapolis, Indiana: Wiley Publishing, 2008).

(B), and an interrogator (C). The interrogator stays in a room apart from the other two. The object of the game for the interrogator is to determine which of the other two is the man and which is the woman.

The parties communicate from behind closed doors and by typewritten messages so that the voices and appearances of the parties give the interrogator no clues. Turing now introduces his famous test:

> We now ask the question, "What will happen when a machine takes the part of A in this game?" Will the interrogator decide wrongly as often when the game is played like this as he does when the game is played between a man and a woman? These questions replace our original, "Can machines think?"

Suppose that after exchanging messages with the entity in each room, we cannot tell, based only on the typewritten messages we receive, which communication is from the human being and which is from the machine. In such a case, what reason would we have to suppose that the machine is *not* thinking and that the man is thinking? Only an irrational, prohuman prejudice might prevent us from attributing thought equally to both the man and the machine in this type of case. In short, argues Turing, if something behaves exactly *as if* it is thinking, why not say that it *is* thinking? This thought-experiment is known in the field of artificial intelligence as the *Turing test*.

If a computer can pass the Turing test, does this show that it is thinking? Does Turing's thought-experiment give us a good reason to believe that computers can indeed think? If a machine passes a Turing test, does this prove that the machine is conscious? What do you think?

Are You a Physical Turing Machine?

Determinism is the name of a view in philosophy according to which each and every event in the universe, including the occurrence of each human action, is completely determined by the state of the universe a moment before the event and by the laws of nature. Thus, when an event happens at a moment in time t, nothing but that event could possibly have happened at that moment t, given all the antecedent conditions in play at the time. *Hard determinism* is the name of a philosophical view according to which (a) determinism is true, and (b) that which people call "free will" does not exist. Why does the hard determinist deny the existence of free will? Briefly, it is commonly held that if a person has free will at a moment in time t, and the person does something at that moment, then at t, given all the antecedent conditions in play, the person could have done otherwise. At the moment t, given all antecedent conditions, it was possible for the person to do A, and it was possible for the person to do something else, call it B. Free will is thus commonly understood as the power to do something without being caused or determined by the sum total of all antecedent conditions to do so. But if determinism is true, argues the hard determinist, then at any one moment in time, there is only one thing a person can possibly do at that moment, given the sum total of antecedent conditions; thus, nobody has free will.

Question. Given the ordinary definition of free will just explained, if a human being is a Turing machine, albeit one composed of organic matter, then it would seem to follow that although many of us believe we have free will, nobody really does have free will. If we are Turing machines, then the belief in free will would seem to be just one more idea programmed into our behavior by the universe. Do you agree? Or do you disagree? Can you compose an argument in support of your view on this issue?

John Searle's Chinese Room Thought-Experiment

John Searle, professor of philosophy at Berkeley, has proposed a thought-experiment demonstrating, he claims, that the mere fact that a computer can *behave* exactly the way a thinking being behaves does not show that a computer is conscious or that a computer can think. Imagine that someone who does not understand Chinese is placed in a windowless room. Inside the room are thousands of pages of instructions, written in English, which the person understands. Each instruction tells this person, in so many words, that when a piece of paper with a symbol of such and such a shape is passed into the room under the door, a piece of paper with a symbol of so and so a shape is to be passed back out. Pieces of paper containing Chinese characters are next passed into the room, and the person dutifully passes back pieces of paper containing other Chinese characters, following the instructions written in English. Suppose that the flow of characters going in and out of the room *exactly* simulates an intelligible conversation in Chinese.

The "Chinese room," with the person inside taking in and passing out symbols, thus passes the "Turing test" for understanding Chinese, for its behavior is indistinguishable from the behavior of someone who understands Chinese. The room corresponds to a computer, the person in the room corresponds to the central processor of a computer, and the instructions on paper correspond to the computer's software. If the Turing test is valid, then the Chinese room *understands* Chinese (for it passes the Turing test for understanding Chinese), and those who endorse Turing's position are logically committed to saying that the room is actually a *conscious, thinking* entity.

However, argues Searle, the person inside the room (by hypothesis) does not understand Chinese; indeed, *nothing* in the room understands Chinese. Therefore,

Searle argues, the Chinese room thought-experiment constitutes a counterexample to the Turing test and to any behaviorist argument of the following form:

1. Some computers behave exactly as if they are thinking.
2. If something behaves exactly like a thinking being, then it is a thinking being.
3. Therefore, some computers really do think.

Searle draws the following lesson. Following a program, no matter how accurately, does not give something a conscious, thinking mind. There is more to real consciousness than merely implementing an algorithm. Following an algorithm is one thing; thinking is another thing entirely.

Notice that someone who does not speak Chinese could actually conduct this experiment and replicate the result, verifying that the central processor of a computer, even if it follows the program flawlessly and perfectly simulates the understanding of Chinese, does not really understand the meanings of the symbols it is processing. Who has the better argument? Searle or Turing?

Truth-Functions as Input–Output Devices

Let us now connect this with the truth-functional logic of Unit Three. Recall that an input–output device is any device that takes in inputs of some kind, processes the inputs in some way, and then sends out outputs of some kind, with the outputs related to the inputs by the way the internal processing occurred. Each of the truth-functions can also be understood as an abstract input–output device, with *truth-values* as inputs and outputs rather than electronic signals. For example, the negation operator outputs "true" when the input is false, and it outputs "false" when the input is true:

<u>The complete repertoire of the negation operator</u>

Input (truth-value true) → Processing → Output (truth-value falsity) →
Input (truth-value falsity) → Processing → Output (truth-value truth) →

Notice that negation always takes in *one* single value at a time and outputs one value at a time (for each input). Thus, just as negation is a monadic truth-function, it is a monadic input–output device.

In contrast, the dyadic truth functions (*and*, *or*, etc.) take in truth-values two at a time (i.e., in pairs), but then output (for each input pair) one single truth-value as the product. Thus:

Conjunction (*and*)

If the inputs for P and Q are respectively (T, T) then the output is T.
If the inputs for P and Q are respectively (T, F) then the output is F.
If the inputs for P and Q are respectively (F, T) then the output is F.
If the inputs for P and Q are respectively (F, F) then the output is F.

Disjunction (*or*)

If the inputs for P and Q are respectively (T, T) then the output is T.
If the inputs for P and Q are respectively (T, F) then the output is T.
If the inputs for P and Q are respectively (F, T) then the output is T.
If the inputs for P and Q are respectively (F, F) then the output is F.

Conditional (*if, then*)

If the inputs for P and Q are respectively (T, T) then the output is T.
If the inputs for P and Q are respectively (T, F) then the output is F.
If the inputs for P and Q are respectively (F, T) then the output is T.
If the inputs for P and Q are respectively (F, F) then the output is T.

(Did you notice that these input–output charts directly mirror the corresponding truth tables for the truth-functional operators?)

Valid Arguments as Input–Output Devices

A valid argument form can also be thought of as an abstract input–output device. The difference is that a valid argument form is structured in such a way that if truth is fed into it, carried by true premises, then truth automatically emerges out of it, in a true conclusion. (If falsity is fed into it, there is no telling what might come out.)

In other words, *if* its input is all true premises, then it automatically outputs a true conclusion. Truth in, truth out, guaranteed every time. A valid form is structured so that it cannot possibly, in any circumstance, take in all true premises and then output a false conclusion. It always takes us from truth to truth, never from truth to falsity. Of course, as noted, there's no telling *what* will come out of it if *falsity* is fed into it. All bets are off if that occurs. (Can you explain why?)

Thus, both computers and truth-functions are input–output devices. Of course, as noted, truth-functions are purely *abstract* input–output devices (they are not composed of matter), whereas digital computers are *concrete* (i.e., purely material) input–output devices made of metals, plastics, and other types of matter. But at a very basic level, truth-functions and computers are the same sort of thing.

Valid Argument Forms and Electric Circuits

A valid argument form is like a well-constructed electric circuit with respect to the way it functions: If electricity is fed into one end of an electrical circuit, electricity automatically comes out the other end, and we say that the circuit "conducts" electricity. In the case of a valid argument form, if truth is fed into one end, truth automatically comes out the other end (and we could say that the argument "conducts truth"). Valid argument forms are thus perfect "truth conductors": Truth in, truth out, every time. This is why valid arguments are said to be "truth-preserving." They *preserve* truth in the sense that if a valid argument begins with all true premises, then by virtue of its valid form the conclusion must be true as well: truth in, truth out, guaranteed. Inductive arguments, of course, are not truth-preserving.

Truth-Functions in Algorithmic Form

Because an algorithm is an abstract input–output device taking inputs of some kind, processing them according to precise rules, in a definite order, and then outputting a predetermined result, it should not be surprising that the truth functions can also be expressed as algorithms. Examine the following algorithms for negation and conjunction. Notice the way each precisely captures the input–output structure of the corresponding truth-function.[4]

Negation Algorithm

Letting V(P) stand for the truth-value of P, the negation algorithm can be expressed in four steps.

1. Input V(P).
2. If V(P) = T then output F.
3. If V(P) = F then output T.
4. Stop.

Conjunction Algorithm

The conjunction algorithm takes seven steps:

---

[4] Here I am following the formulation in Morton Schagrin's *Logic. A Computer Approach* (New York: McGraw-Hill, 1985.)

1. Input V(P).
2. Input V(Q).
3. If V(P) = T, then if V(Q) = T go to step 6.
4. Output F.
5. Stop.
6. Output T.
7. Stop.

Project. Devise exact algorithms for the remaining truth-functions.

How an Idea in Logical Theory Led to the Birth of the Computer

There's something machine-like about an algorithm, isn't there? Think about it. Implementing an algorithm is like performing a "rote" calculation over and over again—as in long division or addition. Following an algorithm requires no creativity, no art, no context or undefined information—it's just a matter of boringly following extremely simple and precise mechanical rules, step by step, in a predefined order. It's almost like something a machine could do.

That little thought is the genius idea that arose directly out of logical theory and eventually led, through a series of trial-and-error steps, many of which were taken by logicians, to the birth of the digital computer. Let's look briefly at some of the main steps in this process that began in ancient Athens and ended with the birth, in the twentieth century, of the digital computer.

For the intellectual roots of the process, we have to go back to Aristotle's decision to develop algorithmic methods for reasoning. That little decision meant that Aristotle's successors in logic would be working with an algorithmic system of reasoning for the next 2,000 years.

The next major step didn't occur until the thirteenth century AD, when, one day, an idea popped into the head of a relatively unknown logician (who was also a Catholic priest) in Spain as he sat around pondering Aristotle's algorithms. (We learned some of these in Unit Two.) The logician's name was Raymond Lull, and the idea that occurred to him as he pondered Aristotelian logic was, "Hey, I bet a *machine* could do that."[5]

So he designed a machine that implemented simple logical algorithms, specifically, rules pertaining to categorical reasoning. Basically, by turning dials, the operator would set the machine to record the logical form of the premises, and then the

---

[5] See Martin Gardner, *Logic Machines and Diagrams* (Chicago, University of Chicago Press: 1983.)

machine, following an algorithm, would calculate, and then produce, a valid conclusion. It was rudimentary, but the cat was now out of the bag: If the algorithms are precise enough, and if they are sufficiently mechanical, and if the mechanical art embodied in the machine hardware is advanced enough to follow the algorithms precisely, then a machine can do some of our (rote) reasoning for us.

This, I would argue, was the seed idea for the digital computer, a seminal idea that occurred at an unexpected place and time, when a relatively unknown medieval logician looked at a logical algorithm and asked a very simple question: "I wonder if a machine could do that?" Thus began a long series of attempts at designing and building machines capable of following logical algorithms and thereby performing rote calculations for us. Such machines would do what any machine does, namely, save us time and energy by doing the rote "mechanical" work for us.

After Lull, a long line of logicians and others would try their hands at designing ever more complex computing machines, first for the purpose of testing a chain of logical reasoning to see whether or not it was deductively valid, later for more and more complex operations of thought. Inventors eventually designed machines that would perform, in addition to purely logical operations, rote mathematical calculations.

Finally, starting in the nineteenth century, inventors began designing and building "universal computing machines"—general-purpose machines theoretically capable of doing anything, not just math and logic. Well, not really anything, but anything that can be accomplished by following a sufficiently precise algorithm.

Today these universal computing machines take pictures and record movies, play music, process words, store data, test your blood sugar level, regulate your car's fuel flow, and on and on. We now call these machines digital computers because their electronic circuits ultimately open and close according to a digital machine code.

The first primitive computing machines in history were designed to draw correct logical inferences; they were not created for the mathematical calculations we associate with computers today. The idea of automated logical reasoning came first, then programmed mathematical calculation was added on top of that. The seed idea flowed naturally out of logic. For it is only when propositions and instructions can be expressed in extremely precise symbols that they can be communicated to a mechanical computing device. Put another way, until our thoughts and instructions can be translated into exact symbols, they cannot be "read" by a mechanical device. Once logical ideas were translated into extremely exact symbols, it was only a matter of time before someone would hit on the idea of a machine programmed to draw correct logical inferences mechanically. In this sense, Aristotle can be called the intellectual "godfather" of computer science.

In the fourteenth century, Leonardo da Vinci (1452–1519) designed a computing machine capable of performing logical operations, although he did not actually build the device. Nevertheless, his design was so complete that engineers in the twentieth century built a model based strictly and exactly on his plans—and the machine worked.

In 1623, German astronomer and mathematician Wilhelm Schickard designed and built the Calculating Clock, a machine that has been described as the first real calculator.

In 1632, English mathematician William Oughtred invented the first slide rule, a major advance in the technology of computing because it introduced a much simpler way to add and subtract large numbers (using the recent discovery of logarithms by the Scottish mathematician John Napier).

In 1642, the great French philosopher and mathematician Blaise Pascal designed and built his Pascaline, a machine that has been described as the "first calculator or adding machine to be produced in any quantity" (*Encyclopedia Britannica*, 2006). Pascal built at least 50 of the machines, each capable of performing addition and subtraction. With all calculations performed in the binary, or Base Two, system, the Pascaline was the first machine to do digital arithmetic. And as the *Encyclopedia Britannica* points out, because the Pascaline was also used in business, it was the first business machine in history.

Gottfried Wilhelm Leibniz (1646–1716), a German logician, mathematician, and philosopher perhaps most famous as the codiscoverer (along with Isaac Newton) of calculus, launched an ambitious program in logic during the seventeenth century. His effort deserves special comment. First, Leibniz sought to turn logic into one big algorithm by developing:

1. A comprehensive set of extremely exact algorithmic principles of reasoning.
2. A universal logical language possessing the degree of precision needed to express the precise algorithms of logic.

Together the algorithms and universal language would have the following properties:

1. Any problem involving human reasoning could be precisely translated from any natural language into the unambiguous, clear, and exact terms of the universal logical language, without loss of meaning.
2. By applying the clear, exact, *algorithmic* rules of reasoning of the universal system of reasoning, anyone could, in principle, derive with precision the same correct, exact, and necessary solution, in a finite number of discrete steps.

Leibniz believed that if everyone used the precise reasoning of this system—the *calculus ratiocinator*—then everyone would always reach the same solution to every problem, via the same algorithmic process. If such a system of universal logic were to be used worldwide, Leibniz believed, then human beings would resolve all disagreements amicably and unanimously, with the precision of mathematics, and world peace and universal brotherhood would result. War would end, violence would be a thing of the past . . . all vanquished by pure logical theory. Leibniz's calculus ratiocinator anticipated Turing's concept of a universal Turing machine.

Between 1671 and 1673, Leibniz designed and built a machine that could implement logical algorithms. This was the second part of his overall program. Named the Stepped Reckoner, Leibiniz's machine added, subtracted, and multiplied numbers using the binary system, the system in which his logical algorithms were written.

In the next century, British statesman and scientist Charles Stanhope (1753–1816) designed a logical machine called the Demonstrator (*not* the Terminator). By setting the premises of an argument equal to true, the machine would follow an algorithm and derive a true conclusion. In other words, the machine was "programmed" to draw *valid* logical inferences.

In 1820 French inventor Charles Xavier Thomas de Colmar (1785–1870) built the Arithmometer, which has been called "the first mass-produced calculating machine that could add, subtract, multiply, and divide."

William Stanley Jevons (1835–1882), an English logician and an important economist as well, invented a computing machine that operated on the logical notation invented by English mathematician and logician George Boole (1815–1864). Named the Logical Piano, Jevons's machine was the first mechanical device to solve problems in "Boolean algebra."

Charles Babbage (1791–1871) was Lucasian Professor of Mathematics at the University of Cambridge (the chair once held by Isaac Newton), when he designed and built a computing machine that performed mathematical calculations to eight decimal places. Babbage later designed a machine, the Analytical Engine, capable of making correct calculations to 31 places. This was the first machine in history to be put to work mechanically calculating large mathematical tables. Babbage's machine was programmed with punch cards, and it stored numbers in a memory unit. The modern digital computer was on its way.

The American philosopher and logician Charles Sanders Peirce (1835–1882), one of the founders of the only distinctively American school of philosophy, pragmatism, designed a computing machine for solving logical problems by mechanical calculation.

Throughout the nineteenth century, many other calculating machines were invented and built in Europe, often for use in business. Indeed, calculating machines came into widespread use during this period as one inventor after another worked at mechanizing routine, or "rote," tasks such as adding huge columns of numbers for scientific, business, or actuarial purposes.

In the twentieth century, Vannevar Bush, a Massachusetts Institute of Technology engineer, built the first modern analog computer, in 1930, the Differential Analyzer.

In the late 1930s Howard Aiken at Harvard (working with the IBM company) designed a series of increasingly powerful digital computers, eventually creating the massive Harvard Mark I, a fully electronic digital computer over 50 feet long, weighing 10,000 pounds, and containing close to a million parts.

Finally, not to be overlooked in this survey of landmark steps, is a series of computers built during World War II that includes the Colossus built in England, the Eniac built in the United States, and the computers built by George Stibitz and a team at Bell Laboratories—the first computers that could be operated by multiple users connected to the computer by phone.

In Conclusion

Looking back over this 800-year process, two major steps stand out as revolutionary. First was Lull's discovery, in the thirteenth century, that a machine can implement a logical algorithm. Second was the realization, during the nineteenth century, that a "computing" machine can do more than merely draw valid inferences or "crunch" numbers—it can theoretically do *anything* that can be explained in terms of a sufficiently precise algorithm. These two major steps helped pave the way for the machine that has changed the world: the digital computer. This appendix is my answer to two questions about logic that I am often asked in the logic classroom: Why does all this technical stuff matter anyway? What does this have to do with the "real" world?

Answers to Selected Exercises《《 《 《 《 《 《 《

The order and the quantity of the problems answered vary from exercise to exercise. In addition, selected answers are not provided for every single exercise; some exercises are very short and elementary, while others require creative, individualized answers. In short, some exercises are best left to the student's creative genius.

Exercise 1.2

1. Here is an example of a short argument. My words:

> The classic 1939 movie *The Wizard of Oz* is full of fascinating ironies that give us insight into human nature. Scarecrow believes he has no brain, but he is the one who hatches the brilliant plan to rescue Dorothy from the witch's castle. Tin Man believes he has no heart, but he displays heartfelt feelings all the time and not just when he is awarded his testimonial heart-shaped watch in the end. Lion believes he lacks courage, but he is the one who leads the assault on the witch's castle and defeats the dreaded Winkies. The Winkie soldiers appear to be evil, but once the wicked old witch is dead, they turn out to be nice guys after all. It is a humble little animal, Toto the dog, who shows the characters that the wizard is not really a wizard at all. The wizard professes supernatural powers, but he uses plain common sense to solve the problems in the end. Finally, Dorothy Gale does not believe she has the power to go home, but in the end she discovers that she had the power all along.

Exercise 2.1

1. Premise: "Statistics show . . . drive." Conclusion: "if you are traveling across the country . . . drive." Conclusion indicator: Therefore.

5. Premise: ". . . it takes a worried man . . . song." Premise: "Joe is a very worried man." Conclusion: "Joe could sing this worried song very well." Premise indicators: Because, since. No conclusion indicator.

10. Premise: "According to the view . . . moment." Premise: "However . . . horrific." Premise: "Social . . . hellish." Premise: "If a theory . . . theory." Conclusion: "Simple ethical egoism is an absurd ethical principle." Conclusion indicator: Therefore.

Exercise 2.2
1. Conclusion indicator
5. Premise indicator
10. Conclusion indicator

Exercise 2.3
1. An opinion not an argument.
5. Argument.
10. A story, not an argument.
15. A command, not an argument.

Exercise 2.4
1. Therefore this year's model will probably run poorly.
5. The ABC drink is probably like the XYZ drink and I do not want to be up all night
10. The Daily Flash is still performing.

Exercise 2.5
1. (1) In order for something to come into existence, it must first be *possible* that it come into existence. (2) If absolutely nothing were to exist, then possibilities would not exist, since (3) a possibility is a—something not a nothing. Therefore (4) it is impossible that something come into existence out of sheer, absolute nothingness. Therefore, (5) anything that *begins* to exist has a cause. (6) We know from scientific cosmology that the material universe began to exist a finite time ago. (7) Therefore the material universe has a cause. (8) The cause is always greater than the effect and always precedes the effect. (9) Therefore, the cause of the universe is a supernatural being whose existence precedes the creation of time and space.

   In your diagram, statement 3 supports statement 2. Statements 1 and 2 together support statement 4. Statement 4 supports statement 5. Statements 5 and 6 support statement 7. Statements 7 and 8 support statement 9.

Exercise 3.1

1. Inductive
5. Inductive
10. Deductive

Exercise 3.2

1. Deductive (mathematical structure)
5. Inductive (Predicting the future)
10. Inductive (Citing an authority)

Exercise 4.1

1. Invalid. Given only the information in the premises, isn't it at least *possible* that Chevrolet makes a few purple cars but no purple trucks?
5. Invalid. Given only the information in the premises, isn't it *possible* Bob is not a member of PL; rather, he is studying the writings of Mao while taking a course in Chinese history?
10. Valid. If the premises are true, the conclusion must be true!
15. Invalid. Given only the information contained in the premises, isn't it *possible* Mr. Lauber let his union membership lapse and is no longer a member?
20. Valid. If the premises are true, the conclusion *must* be true. If the premises are true, then Ann cannot be swimming today. For if she were to be swimming today, Bob would be swimming today (for if she swims then he swims); but Bob is not swimming today.

Exercise 4.2

1. Consider this possibility: Chevrolet makes purple cars but does not make any purple trucks.
6. Consider this possibility: Joe has never listened to loud music. His hearing was damaged in a car accident.
11. Consider this possibility: Figure A is a parallelogram, not a square.

Exercise 4.4

1. T
5. T
10. T

Exercise 4.5

1. Black says, "All of us are knaves." This statement is either true or it is false. But it cannot possibly be true, for if it were true, then they would all be knaves,

but then Black would be a knave speaking a true statement! This cannot be right because a knave can never tell the truth. So, Black's statement cannot be true, which means two things: First, it is **not** true that they are all knaves; and second, the statement is false, which means that Black must be a lying knave. Therefore, since they are not all knaves, at least one must be a knight. So, White or Red must be a knight, or both are.

White says, "Exactly one of us is a knight." Suppose White is a knave. If White is also a knave, along with Black, then Red is the only knight (remember: we know there is at least one knight). But this would mean that White, a knave, is telling the truth when he says there is exactly one knight. But a knave couldn't tell the truth, so, White could not be a knave (because if he is a knave, then he is a knave telling the truth, which is impossible). So, White **must** be a knight. Therefore White must be telling the truth when he says there is only one knight. Therefore, there must be only one knight in the group and White must be the only knight. Therefore, Red must be a knave.

5. The sentence "Either I am a knight or I am not a knight" has to be true, because every inhabitant of the island is a knight or a knave. But only a knight could speak a true sentence. So, the attendant must be a knight.

Exercise 4.6
1. Add: Your pet is a reptile.
5. Add: All physical objects are spatial objects.
10. Add: Every particle of matter has mass.

Exercise 5.1
1. False
5. True
10. True

Exercise 5.2
1. Strong
5. Strong
10. Moderately strong but this judgment is certainly debateable. One would like more information before saying with confidence that the argument is strong or weak.

Exercise 5.3
1. This addition would make the argument stronger: The police also found his fingerprints. This addition would make the argument weaker: Someone else confessed to the crime.

5. This addition would make the argument stronger: Music critics are praising the new CD. This addition would make the argument weaker: Lately Lorraine has been saying that she is getting tired of listening to Tiny Tim's music.

Exercise 6.1
1. Consistent
5. Inconsistent
10. Consistent
15. Consistent

Exercise 6.3
1. Yes
5. No
10. No

Exercise 6.4
1. Yes
5. No
10. No

Exercise 6.5
1. Necessary truth
5. Necessary truth
10. Contingent

Exercise 7.1
1. A Universal affirmative
5. I Particular affirmative
10. E Universal negative

Exercise 7.2
Part I: 1. Contraries
Part II: 1. Some Greeks are not religious.

Exercise 7.3
1. F, T, F
5. U, F, U

Exercise 7.4
1. Valid
5. Valid
10. Valid

Exercise 7.5
1. a. All Greeks are Athenians. (Not equivalent)
   b. No Greeks are Athenians. (Equivalent)
   c. Some Greeks are Athenians. (Equivalent)
   d. Some Greeks are not Athenians. (Not equivalent)

Exercise 7.6
1. Invalid
5. Valid
10. Valid

Exercise 7.7
1. a. All drops of seawater are things that are salty.

2. a. All cowardly people are people who are not rational. (Note: We could also translate this as: No cowardly people are rational people.)
3. a. Some people are moral warriors. (We are assuming the original sentence is about people.)
4. a. Some politicians are not honest persons.

Exercise 8.1
1. No philosophers are zombies. All logicians are philosophers. So, no logicians are zombies.

    EAE-1

Exercise 8.2
1. Valid.

Exercise 8.3
1. Valid IAI-4
5. Valid OAO-3
10. Invalid IOO-1

Exercise 8.4
A (1) 1. All wealthy Athenians are voters. 2. No wealthy Athenians are slaves. 3. Therefore, no voters are slaves. B: (1) Invalid.

A (5) 1. Some poets are not farmers. 2. All farmers are logicians. 3. So, some logicians are poets. B: Invalid.

Exercise 8.5
1: 1. No cars are airplanes. 2. No airplanes are vehicles parked in your garage. So, no cars are vehicles parked in your garage. (Spoken to someone with cars in his garage.)

Exercise 8.6
1: 1. Some people are atheists. Some people are devout Muslims. So, some people are both atheist and devoutly Muslim.
5: No middle school students are multi-billionaires. No multi-billionaires are 13-year olds. So no middle school students are 13-year olds.

Exercise 8.7
1. The city-state of Alexia is a tyranny.

Exercise 8.8
1. All jurors are sane persons. All logicians are sane persons. No logicians are whimsical persons. So, jurors are whimsical persons. Invalid.

Exercise 8.9

1. Some S are D. All D are A. All S are G. Therefore, some G are A. Valid.

Exercise 9.1

1. No relations obtain.

Exercise 9.2

1. On the Aristotelian Interpretation: Valid.
5. On the Aristotelian Interpretation: Valid.

Exercise 9.3

1. (from Exercise 8.3)

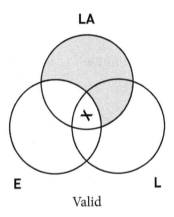

Valid

5. (from Exercise 8.3)

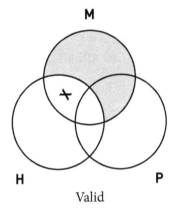

Valid

10. (from Exercise 8.3)

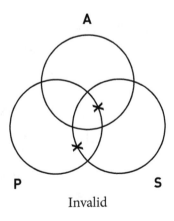

Invalid

15. (from Exercise 8.3)

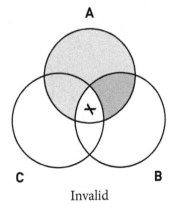

Invalid

20. (from Exercise 8.3)

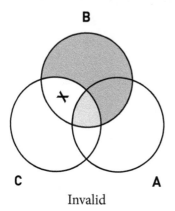

B

C   A

Invalid

25. (from Exercise 8.3)

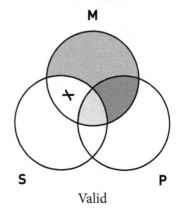

M

S   P

Valid

Exercise 9.4

1. CELARENT:

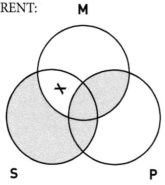

M

S   P

2. FERIO:

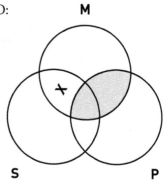

M

S   P

3. DATISI:

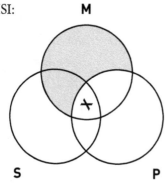

M

S   P

4. FESAPO:

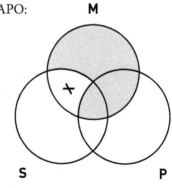

M

S   P

Exercise 10.1

1. Exclamatory
5. Imperative

10. Declarative

15. None of the above. Notice that this sentence refers to itself, and says, of itself, that it is false. Thus if it is true, then it is false, and if it is false, then it is true. Paradox. Logicians call a sentence such as this one "self-referentially incoherent" and debate what kind of sentence it actually is. Many argue that such a sentence is neither true nor false and thus does not count as declarative.

20. Declarative

Exercise 10. 2

1. Simple
5. Compound:
   Operator: It is not the case that . . .
   Embedded: Chrysippus will lecture . . .

10. Compound:
    Operator: It is not the case that . . .
    Embedded: Cleanthes is home.

15. Simple

Exercise 10.3

1. If
5. If
10. and

Exercise 10.4

1. T
5. T
10. F

Exercise 11.1 Part A
Form 1: Arguments 3 and 8 are instances of form 1.

Exercise 11.1 Part B
Be creative!

Exercise 11.2
1. If W, then C. If C, then not-S. If not-S, then not-R. W. Therefore, not R.
5. If S, F. Moreover, S. Therefore, F.

Exercise 11.3

Here is an interesting substitution instance of the modus ponens form: If everything has an ultimate explanation that accounts for its existence and the world is a thing, then there is an ultimate explanation that accounts for the existence of the universe.

Everything has an ultimate explanation that accounts for its existence and the world is a thing. Therefore, there is an ultimate explanation that accounts for the existence of the universe.

Here is a substitution instance of the modus tollens form:

If everything has an ultimate explanation that accounts for its existence and the world is a thing, then there is an ultimate explanation that accounts for the existence of the universe.

It is logically impossible that there is an ultimate explanation that accounts for the existence of the universe. Therefore, the following statement is false: everything has an ultimate explanation that accounts for its existence, and the world is a thing.

Exercise 11.4

1. Modus tollens
5. Not an instance.
10. Modus tollens

Exercise 12.1

Here is an answer for 4:

$\{[\sim(A \text{ v } B) \supset (H \& O)] \equiv L\} \text{ v } G$

Exercise 12.2

1. Well-formed.
5. Well-formed.
10. Not well-formed.
15. Not well-formed.

Exercise 12.3

1. $\sim L \supset \sim M$
5. $N \text{ v } \sim L$
10. $E \& N$

Exercise 12.4

1. ~W ⊃ ~A
5. ~Q v ~P
10. ~S & C
15. E & N

Exercise 12.5

1. Second ampersand from left.
5. Ampersand
10. Second "horse" from left.

Exercise 12.6

1. (R & C) ⊃ (A & U)
5. ~(K v Q)
10. (~M & ~D) & (A v H)
15. (~K & ~Q) ⊃ (~R v ~D)

Exercise 13.1

1. ~(D v F)
5. ~~D & ~~O
10. ~(D v C)

Exercise 13.2

1. (A & B) v D
5. D & (C v O)
10. ~L & M
15. (~A v ~D) v (~T & ~J)

Exercise 13.3

1. F ⊃ (J v B)
5. ~B ⊃ (~C v ~D)
10. (E & R) ⊃ ~(B v D)
17. A ≡ (B & S)

Exercise 14.1

1. False
5. False
10. False

Exercise 14.2

1. Given: A is true and B is false:

   T & F

   F

5. ~ (T & F)

   ~(F)

   T

10. (T v F) v T

    (T) v T

    T

Exercise 14.3

1. T ⊃ T

   T

5. T ⊃ (T ⊃ T)

   T ⊃ (T)

   T

10. ~T ⊃ ~(T ≡ T)

    F ⊃ ~(T ≡ T)

    F ⊃ ~(T)

    F ⊃ F

    T

Exercise 14.5

1. Conjunction
5. Negation
10. Disjunction

Exercise 14.6

1. Conditional
5. Conditional
10. Conditional

Exercise 14.7

1. False (Because one false conjunct is sufficient to make a conjunction false, this sentence must be false, for we know that the left conjunct, C, is false.)

5. True (A look at the truth table for horseshoe reminds us that a true consequent is sufficient, by itself, to make a conditional sentence true. Because we know that the consequent, A, is true, the whole must be true.)

Exercise 15.1

1. This formula is a tautology for its final column, column 4, is all Ts.

[(A	&	B)	⊃	(A	v	B)]
T	T	T	T	T	T	T
T	F	F	T	T	T	F
F	F	T	T	F	T	T
F	F	F	T	F	F	F

5. Tautology again. The final column, column 4, is all Ts.

(A	&	B)	⊃	(A	v	E)
T	T	T	T	T	T	T
T	T	T	T	T	T	F
T	F	F	T	T	T	T
T	F	F	T	T	T	F
F	F	T	T	F	T	T
F	F	T	T	F	F	F
F	F	F	T	F	T	T
F	F	F	T	F	F	F

Exercise 15.2

1. This is a tautological form. Note the final column, column 4.

(P	&	Q)	v	(~	P	v	~	Q)
T	T	T	T	F	T	F	F	T
T	F	F	T	F	T	T	T	F
F	F	T	T	T	F	T	F	T
F	F	F	T	T	F	T	T	F

5. Another tautological form. Note the final column, again column 4.

(P	⊃	Q)	v	(P	&	~	Q)
T	T	T	T	T	F	F	T
T	F	F	T	T	T	T	F
F	T	T	T	F	F	F	T
F	T	F	T	F	F	T	F

Exercise 15.3

1. ~P must be a contradiction. For the truth value of ~P is always the opposite of the truth value of P. But we know that P is always true, so ~P must always be false. This is a sure sign of a contradiction!

10. P v Q must be a tautology. For we know that P is always true, and a disjunction is true whenever one disjunct is true, therefore P v Q must always be true.

Exercise 16.1

1. The argument is invalid, for row 6 shows all true premises and a false conclusion. The relevant columns are 2, 6, and 10, the columns under the main connectives.

(A	v	B)		(B	v	C)	//	(A	v	C)
T	T	T		T	T	T		T	T	T
T	T	T		T	T	F		T	T	F
T	T	F		F	T	T		T	T	T
T	T	F		F	F	F		T	T	F
F	T	T		T	T	T		F	T	T
F	T	T		T	T	F		F	F	F
F	F	F		F	T	T		F	T	T
F	F	F		F	F	F		F	F	F

10. The argument is valid, for no row shows all true premises and a false conclusion.

~	A	⊃	~	B		~	A	//	~	B
F	T	T	F	T		F	T		F	T
F	T	T	T	F		F	T		T	F
T	F	F	F	T		T	F		F	T
T	F	T	T	F		T	F		T	F

Exercise 16.2

1. B ⊃ J

~J / ~B. The argument is valid, for its table contains no row showing true premises and a false conclusion. The relevant columns, of course, are 2, 5, and 8.

B	⊃	J		~	J	//	~	B
T	T	T		F	T		F	T
T	F	F		T	F		F	T
F	T	T		F	T		T	F
F	T	F		T	F		T	F

Exercise 16.3

1. The argument form is valid, for its table contains no row showing true premises and a false conclusion.

P	⊃	(P	⊃	Q)		P	//	Q
T	T	T	T	T		T		T
T	F	T	F	F		T		F
F	T	F	T	T		F		T
F	T	F	T	F		F		F

Exercise 16.4

5. The argument form is valid, for its table contains no row showing true premises and a false conclusion. (Compare columns 2 and 8.)

P	⊃	Q		//	~	Q	⊃	~	P
T	T	T			F	T	T	F	T
T	F	F			T	F	F	F	T
F	T	T			F	T	T	T	F
F	T	F			T	F	T	T	F

Exercise 16.6

1. S ⊃ (~J ⊃ R) // R ⊃ ~J

   Assign T to R, and T to J to make the conclusion false. Assign T to S to make the premise true. This shows that the argument is invalid.

Exercise 17.1

1. The two sentences are equivalent because their final columns match. Compare columns 1 and 8.

~	(P	v	Q)	/	~	P	&	~	Q
F	T	T	T		F	T	F	F	T
F	T	T	F		F	T	F	T	F
F	F	T	T		T	F	F	F	T
T	F	F	F		T	F	T	T	F

Exercise 17.2

1. The two sentences are consistent because on at least one row both show true. Compare columns 1 and 8 on row 4.

~	(P	v	Q)	/	~	P	&	~	Q
F	T	T	T		F	T	F	F	T
F	T	T	F		F	T	F	T	F
F	F	T	T		T	F	F	F	T
T	F	F	F		T	F	T	T	F

Exercise 17.3

1. The first sentence implies the second because there is no row in which the first is true and the second is false. Compare columns 1 and 8 on each row.

~	(P	v	Q)	/	~	P	&	~	Q
F	T	T	T		F	T	F	F	T
F	T	T	F		F	T	F	T	F
F	F	T	T		T	F	F	F	T
T	F	F	F		T	F	T	T	F

Exercise 18.1
1. HS 1, 2
   MP 3, 5
   DS 4, 6
5. MT 3, 4
   DS 2, 5
   MP 1, 6
10. MP 1, 2
    MP 1, 3
    MT 1, 4
15. HS 1, 2
    MP 3, 5
    MT 4, 6

Exercise 18.2
1. 1. (A & B) ⊃ S
   2. H ⊃ R
   3. (A & B) / S
   4. S   MP 1, 3
5. 1. F ⊃ (H & B)
   2. A ⊃ ~(H & B)
   3. A / ~ F
   4. ~(H & B)   MP 2, 3
   5. ~ F   MT 1, 4

10. 1. R ⊃ H
    2. H ⊃ S
    3. S ⊃ G
    4. (R ⊃ G) ⊃ F / F
    5. R ⊃ S   HS 1, 2
    6. R ⊃ G   HS 3, 5
    7. F   MP 4, 6
15. 1. A ⊃ (B ⊃ E)
    2. A
    3. ~ E / ~ B
    4. B ⊃ E   MP 1, 2
    5. ~ B   MT 3, 4
18. 1. A ⊃ B
    2. B ⊃ W
    3. ~ W
    4. J ⊃ I
    5. S ⊃ ~I
    6. ~A ⊃ (J v Z)
    7. S / Z
    8. ~ I   MP 5, 7
    9. ~ J   MT 4, 8
    10. A ⊃ W   HS 1, 2
    11. ~A   MT 3, 10
    12. J v Z   MP 6, 11
    13. Z   DS 9, 12

Exercise 18.3
1. 1. A ⊃ B
   2. A v C
   3. ~ B / C
   4. ~ A   MT 1, 3
   5. C   DS 2, 4
5. 1. R ⊃ A
   2. N ⊃ R
   3. ~A / ~ N
   4. ~ R   MT 1, 3
   5. ~ N   MT 2, 4

13. 1. $M \supset C$
     2. $(M \supset \sim L) \supset (C \supset \sim D)$
     3. $C \supset \sim L / M \supset \sim D$
     4. $M \supset \sim L$ HS 1, 3
     5. $C \supset \sim D$ MP 2, 4
     6. $M \supset \sim D$ HS 1, 5

Exercise 19.1

1. Simp 5
    Add 6
    MP 1, 7
    MP 2, 8
    Add 9
    MP 3, 10
    Add 6
    MP 4, 12
    Conj 11, 13
5. Simp 4
    Add 7
    MP 1, 8
    DS 2, 9
    Add 10
    CD 5, 6, 11

(Notice that 3 was a superfluous premise.)

Exercise 19.2

1. 1. $A \supset B$
    2. $B \supset R$
    3. $\sim R / \sim A \& \sim B$
    4. $\sim B$ MT 2, 3
    5. $\sim A$ MT 1, 4
    6. $\sim A \& \sim B$ Conj 4, 5
5. 1. $B \supset (S \vee R)$
    2. $S \supset J$
    3. $R \supset G$
    4. $H \& B / J \vee G$

5. B   Simp 4
6. S v R MP 1, 5
7. J v G CD 2, 3, 6

7. 1. H v ~ S
  2. [(H v ~S) v G] ⊃ ~M
  3. M v R / R v X
  4. (H v ~S) v G Add 1
  5. ~M   MP 2, 4
  6. R   DS 3, 5
  7. R v X   Add 6

10. 1. A ⊃ (J & S)
  2. B ⊃ F
  3. A
  4. [(J & S) v F] ⊃ G / G
  5. A v B   Add 3
  6. (J & S) v F CD 1, 2, 5
  7. G   MP 4, 6

13. 1. (A ⊃ B) & (A ⊃ C)
  2. A
  3. (B v C) ⊃ Z / Z
  4. A ⊃ B   Simp 1
  5. A ⊃ C   Simp 1
  6. A v A   Add 2
  7. B v C   CD 4, 5, 6
  8. Z   MP 3, 7

15. 1. (A ⊃ B) & (S ⊃ I)
  2. J ⊃ R
  3. (A v J) & (S v E) / B v R
  4. A ⊃ B   Simp 1
  5. A v J   Simp 3
  6. B v R   CD 2, 4, 5

17. 1. S ⊃ [J & (I v S)]
  2. [J v (A & B)] ⊃ (~ N & ~ O)
  3. S & Z / ~N & J
  4. S   Simp 3
  5. J & (I v S) MP 1, 4

6.	J	Simp 5
7.	J v (A & B)	Add 6
8.	~N & ~O	MP 2, 7
9.	~N	Simp 8
10.	~N & J	Conj 6, 9

18.
1.	(A & S) ⊃ Z	
2.	~J ⊃ A	
3.	~J ⊃ S	
4.	~J & B / Z v I	
5.	~J	Simp 4
6.	A	MP 2, 5
7.	S	MP 3, 5
8.	A & S	Conj 6, 7
9.	Z	MP 1, 8
10.	Z v I	Add 9

Exercise 20.1

1. Dist 1
   Simp 4
   MP 2, 5
   DNeg 6
   DS 3, 7
   Comm 8

5. Simp 1
   MP 2, 6
   MP 3, 7
   Add 8
   MP 4, 9
   DNeg 10
   DS 5, 11

Exercise 20.2

5.
1.	~(A v B)	
2.	~B ⊃ E	
3.	E ⊃ S / S	
4.	~A & ~B	DM 1

5. ~B   Simp 4
6. E   MP 2, 5
7. S   MP 3, 6

7. 1. (H & S) v (H & P)
    2. H ⊃ (G v M) / G v M
    3. H & (S v P)   Dist 1
    4. H   Simp 3
    5. G v M   MP 2, 4

10. 1. (R ⊃ S) v ~G
    2. ~ ~ G
    3. (R ⊃ S) ~ ~ P
    4. H ⊃ ~P / ~H
    5. ~ G v (R ⊃ S)   Comm 1
    6. R ⊃ S   DS 2, 5
    7. ~ ~P   MP 3, 6
    8. ~H   MT 4, 7

13. 1. ~ (R & S)
    2. ~R ⊃ Q
    3. ~S ⊃ Z
    4. ~Q
    5. Z ⊃ (A ≡ B) / A ≡ B
    6. ~R v ~S   DM 1
    7. Q v Z   CD 2, 3, 6
    8. Z   DS 4, 7
    9. A ≡ B   MP 5, 8

15. 1. ~ R ⊃ ~ S
    2. ~ ~S
    3. ~ ~R ⊃ H
    4. (H ⊃ A) & (Z ⊃ O) / A v O
    5. ~ ~R   MT 1, 2
    6. H   MP 3, 5
    7. H v Z   Add 6
    8. H ⊃ A   Simp 4
    9. Z ⊃ O   Simp 4
    10. A v O   CD 7, 8, 9

17. 1. $S \supset \sim P$
     2. $(P \& S) v (P \& F) / F$
     3. $P \& (S v F)$ Dist 2
     4. P Simp 3
     5. $\sim \sim P$ DNeg 4
     6. $\sim S$ MT 1, 5
     7. $S v F$ Simp 3
     8. F DS 6, 7

25. 1. $\sim \sim K$
     2. $\sim(A \& B) \& \sim(E \& F)$
     3. $(H \& K) \supset [(A \& B) v (E \& F)] / \sim H$
     4. $\sim [(A \& B) v (E \& F)]$ DM 2
     5. $\sim (H \& K)$ MT 3, 4
     6. $\sim H v \sim K$ DM 5
     7. $\sim K v \sim H$ Comm 6
     8. $\sim H$ DS 1, 7

26. 1. $H \supset (E \& P)$
     2. $A v (B \& \sim C)$
     3. $A \supset \sim E$
     4. $\sim C \supset \sim P / \sim H$
     5. $(A v B) \& (A v \sim C)$ Dist 2
     6. $A v \sim C$ Simp 5
     7. $\sim E v \sim P$ CD 3, 4, 6
     8. $\sim(E \& P)$ DM 7
     9. $\sim H$ MT 1, 8

27. 1. $\sim (A \& B)$
     2. $\sim A \supset (P \& O)$
     3. $\sim B \supset (O \& S) / O$
     4. $\sim A v \sim B$ DM 1
     5. $(P \& O) v (O \& S)$ CD 2, 3, 4
     6. $(O \& P) v (O \& S)$ Comm 5
     7. $O \& (P v S)$ Dist 6
     8. O Simp 7

Exercise 20.3

1. Trans 1

   MP 2, 5

   Add 6

   MP 3, 7

   Exp 8

   MP 4, 9

   Trans 10

5. Imp 1

   MP 2, 6

   DNeg 7

   MT 3, 8

   MP 4, 9

   Add 10

   MP 5, 11

   Taut 12

Exercise 20.4

1. 1. H ⊃ ~S
   2. (~H v ~S) ⊃ F
   3. F ⊃ B / B
   4. ~H v ~S   Imp 1
   5. F   MP 2, 4
   6. B   MP 3, 5

5. 1. ~(A & ~B) ⊃ C
   2. A ⊃ B
   3. H v ~C / H
   4. ~A v B   Imp 2
   5. ~(~ ~A & ~B)   DM 4
   6. ~(A & ~B)   DN 5
   7. C   MP 1, 6
   8. ~ ~ C   DNeg 7
   9. H   DS 3, 8

7. 1. (J v J) ⊃ S
   2. J & F / S

3.   J ⊃ S   Taut 1

4.   J   Simp 2

5.   S   MP 3, 4

10.   1.   (A & E) ⊃ S

     2.   (E ⊃ S) ⊃ F / A ⊃ F

     3.   A ⊃ (E ⊃ S)   Exp 1

     4.   A ⊃ F   HS 2, 3

13.   1.   J ≡ I

     2.   ~ (J & I) / ~ J & ~ I

     3.   (J & I) v (~J & ~I)   Equiv 1

     4.   ~J & ~I   DS 2, 3

15.   1.   (A ⊃ B) & (E ⊃ B)

     2.   ~ (~A & ~E) / B

     3.   ~ ~A v ~ ~E   DM 2

     4.   A v E   DN 3

     5.   A ⊃ B   Simp 1

     6.   E ⊃ B   Simp 1

     7.   B v B   CD 4, 5, 6

     8.   B   Taut 7

20.   1.   A ⊃ B

     2.   A ⊃ ~B / ~A

     3.   ~ ~ B ⊃ ~A   Trans 2

     4.   B ⊃ ~A   DNeg 3

     5.   A ⊃ ~A   HS 1, 4

     6.   ~A v ~A   Imp 5

     7.   ~A   Taut 6

25.   1.   (J ⊃ I) ⊃ W

     2.   W ⊃ ~ W / J

     3.   ~ W v ~ W   Imp 2

     4.   ~W   Taut 3

     5.   ~(J ⊃ I)   MT 1, 4

     6.   ~(~ J v I)   Imp 5

     7.   ~ ~ (~ ~ J & ~ I)   DM 6

     8.   J & ~I   DNeg 7

     9.   J   Simp 8

30.
1. J ⊃ (S & H)
2. W ⊃ (~S & ~H)
3. J v W / H ⊃ S
4. (S & H) v (~S & ~H)   CD 1, 2, 3
5. S ≡ H   Equiv 4
6. (S ⊃ H) & (H ⊃ S)   Equiv 5
7. H ⊃ S   Simp 6

35.
1. (A ⊃ B) ⊃ G
2. (I ⊃ B) ⊃ ~ G / ~ B
3. ~ ~G ~ (I ⊃ B)   Trans 2
4. G ⊃ ~ (I ⊃ B)   DNeg 3
5. (A ⊃ B) ⊃ ~ (I ⊃ B)   HS 1, 4
6. ~(A ⊃ B) v ~ (I ⊃ B)   Imp 5
7. ~(~ A v B) v ~(~I v B)   Imp 6
8. (~ ~A & ~B) v (~ ~I & ~B)   DM 7
9. (A & ~B) v (I & ~B)   DNeg 8
10. (~ B & A) v (~ B & I)   Comm 9
11. ~B & (A v I)   Dist 10
12. ~B   Simp 11

36.
1. (J ⊃ I) ⊃ (I ⊃ J)
2. (J ≡ I) ⊃ ~(A & ~B)
3. I & A / A & B
4. I   Simp 3
5. I v ~J   Add 4
6. ~J v I   Comm 5
7. J ⊃ I   Imp 6
8. I ⊃ J   MP 1, 7
9. (J ⊃ I) & (I ⊃ J)   Conj 7, 8
10. J ≡ I   Equiv 9
11. ~(A & ~B)   MP 2, 10
12. ~A v ~ ~B   DM 11
13. A   Simp 3
14. ~ ~A   DNeg 13
15. ~ ~B   DS 12, 14
16. B   DNeg 15
17. A & B   Conj 13, 16

Exercise 21.1

1. 1. J v (I & E)
   2. J ⊃ E / E
   3. | ~E   AIP
   4. | ~J   MT 2, 3
   5. | I & E   DS 1, 4
   6. | E   Simp 5
   7. | E & ~ E   Conj 3, 6
   8. E   IP 3-7

5. 1. ~B ⊃ C
   2. C ⊃ B / B
   3. | ~B   AIP
   4. | C   MP 1, 3
   5. | B   MP 2, 4
   6. | B & ~B   Conj 3, 5
   7. B   IP 3-6

9. 1. A
   2. A ⊃ B
   3. (A & B) ⊃ K
   4. K ⊃ G / G
   5. | ~G   AIP
   6. | ~K   MT 4, 5
   7. | B   MP 1, 2
   8. | A & B   Conj 1, 7
   9. | K   MP 3, 8
   10. | K & ~K   Conj 6, 9
   11. G   IP 5-10

Exercise 21.3

1. 1. A ⊃ (B & C) / A ⊃ C
   2. | A   ACP
   3. | B&C   MP 1, 2
   4. | C   Simp 3
   5. A ⊃ C   CP 2-4

3. 1. J ⊃ (I ⊃ W)
   2. (I ⊃ W) ⊃ (I ⊃ S) / J ⊃ (I ⊃ S)
   3. | J   ACP

4.   I ⊃ W   MP 1, 3

5.   I ⊃ S   MP 2, 4

6.   J ⊃ (I ⊃ S)   CP 3-5

5.   1.   I v Z

    2.   Z ⊃ A / ~ I ⊃ (Z & A)

    3.   ~I   ACP

    4.   Z   DS 1, 3

    5.   A   MP 2, 4

    6.   Z & A   Conj 4, 5

    7.   ~I ⊃ (Z & A)   CP 3-6

7.   1.   (J v I) ⊃ (A & B)

    2.   (B v E) ⊃ (O & S) / J ⊃ O

    3.   J   ACP

    4.   J v I   Add 3

    5.   A & B   MP 1, 4

    6.   B   Simp 5

    7.   B v E   Add 6

    8.   O & S   MP 2, 7

    9.   O   Simp 8

  10.   J ⊃ O   CP 3-9

12.   1.   E ⊃ A / (E & O) ⊃ A

    2.   E & O   ACP

    3.   E   Simp 2

    4.   A   MP 1, 3

    5.   (E & O) ⊃ A   CP 2-4

Exercise 21.4

1.   1.   J ⊃ (I ⊃ W)

    2.   W ⊃ (I ⊃ S) / J ⊃ (I ⊃ S)

    3.   J   ACP

    4.   I   ACP

    5.   I ⊃ W   MP 1, 3

    6.   W   MP 4, 5

    7.   I ⊃ S   MP 2, 6

    8.   S   MP 4, 7

    9.   I ⊃ S   CP 4-8

  10.   J ⊃ (I ⊃ S)   CP 3-9

5.   1.   H ⊃ (S & T)
     2.   B ⊃ (A & G) / (T ⊃ B) ⊃ (H ⊃ G)
     3. |T ⊃ B   ACP
     4. | |H   ACP
     5. | |S & T   MP 1, 4
     6. | |T   Simp 5
     7. | |B   MP 3, 6
     8. | |A & G   MP 2, 7
     9. | |G   Simp 8
    10. |H ⊃ G   CP 4-9
    11.   (T ⊃ B) ⊃ (H ⊃ G)   CP 3-10

Exercise 22.1

1.   1 |(A v B) & ~A   ACP
     2. |A v B   Simp 1
     3. |~A   Simp 1
     4. |B   DS 2, 3
     5.   [(A v B) & ~A] ⊃ B   CP 1-4

5.   1. |(A ⊃ B) & (A ⊃ I)   ACP
     2. | |A   ACP
     3. | |A ⊃ B   Simp 1
     4. | |B   MP 2, 3
     5. | |(A ⊃ I)   Simp 1
     6. | |I   MP 2, 5
     7. | |B & I   Conj 4, 6
     8. |A ⊃ (B & I)   CP 2-7
     9.   [(A ⊃ B) & (A ⊃ I)] ⊃ [A ⊃ (B & I)]   CP 1-8

Exercise 23.1

1.   Bg (Let B stand for the corny predicate "banks at the blood bank" and let g stand for "Grandpa.")

5.   This compound sentence can be symbolized in two very different ways. Using only truth-functional sentence constants, we can write M ⊃ (C & L), where M stands for "Moe is happy," C stands for "Curly is happy," and so on. Using individual constants and predicate constants, we write Hm ⊃ (Hc & Hl), where the predicate constant H stands for the predicate "is happy," the individual constant m stands for "Moe," and so on. Notice that the second translation,

using the full language of predicate logic, captures more deeply, or in more detail, the underlying logic of the original sentence.

10. ~Wb (Letting b stand in for "Blipo" and letting W abbreviate the predicate "is working today.")

Exercise 23.2
1. (x) (Hx ⊃ Ix)
5. (x) (Vx ⊃ Mx)

Exercise 23.3
1. (x) (Mx ⊃ Fx) This reads, "For any x, if x is a member of the Seattle Musicians Union then x is a fine artist." M is a predicate constant standing for the predicate "is a member of . . ." and F is a predicate constant standing for "is a fine artist."

5. (∃x)(Lx & Sx). This reads, "For some x, x is a logician and x is a Stoic philosopher." L is a predicate constant standing for the predicate "is a logician" and S is a predicate constant standing for the predicate "is a Stoic philosopher."

Exercise 23.4
1. (x) (Bx ⊃ Vx), ~ (∃x) (Bx & ~ Vx)
5. ~(∃x)Rx, (x) ~Rx

Exercise 23.5
1. ~(∃x){ [(Ox & Gx) & Bx] & Ix} This reads, "It is not the case that there is an x such that x is old, x is gray, x is a book, and x is interesting." This sentence could also be symbolized (x)){ [(Ox & Gx) & Bx] ⊃ ~Ix} This reads, "For all x, if x is old, x is gray, and x is a book, then it is not the case that x is interesting."

5. (∃x) (Mx & Px) & (∃x)(Mx & ~Px) This reads, "There is an x such that x is a movie and x is philosophical and there is an x such that x is a movie and x is not philosophical." The predicate constant M stands for the predicate "is a movie" and the predicate constant P stands for the predicate "is philosophical."

10. (∃x) [(Bx & Ox) & Gx] This reads, "There is an x such that x is blue, x is old, and x is in the garage." I gave each adjective ("blue," "old") and "in the garage" a predicate constant to capture all the details of the statement.

Exercise 24.1
1. Tps & Osp Here the individual constant p stands for the proper name "Pam," the individual constant s stands for the proper name "Sue," the relational

predicate constant T stands for the relation "is taller than," and the two-place or relational predicate O stands for the relation "is older than."

5. (∃x) (Px & Kxx) This reads, "There is an x such that x is a person and x knows x." K obviously stands for the two-place relation "knows."

10. Fme Here the relational predicate F stands for the relation "is a friend of," and the individual constants m and e stand for the proper names "Matt" and "Elliot" in that order.

15. (x) (Px ⊃ ~Kxj) This reads, "For any x, if x is a person then x does not know Jay."

Exercise 24.2

1. (∃x) (y) Ryx Here we are assuming that the domain is all persons. This reads, "For some x, and for *every* y, y respects x." In other words, there is some x, and for every y, y respects x. Because the variables range only over people, this tells us there is some person x and everyone respects x.

5. (∃x) (y) ~Kxy We are again assuming that the domain is all persons. This reads, (For some x, and for every y, x does not know y." In other words, there is some x, and for every y, x does not know y. Someone does not know anyone.

Exercise 25.1

1. (∃x) (∃y) [(Sx & Sy) & ~(x = y)] This reads, "There is an x and there is a y, and x is a sasquatch and y is a sasquatch, and it is not the case that x is the same individual as y."

5. (∃x) (y){Sx & [Sy ⊃ (y = x)]} This reads, "There is an x, and x is a sasquatch, and for any y, if y is a sasquatch then y is the same entity as x."

Exercise 26.1

1. UI 1
   UI 2
   HS 3, 4
   UG 5

Exercise 26.2

1.
1.	(x)(Wx ⊃ Sx)	
2.	(x)(Sx ⊃ Px) / (x)(Wx ⊃ Px)	
3.	Wu ⊃ Su	UI 1
4.	Su ⊃ Pu	UI 2
5.	Wu ⊃ Pu	HS 3, 4
6.	(x)(Wx ⊃ Px)	UG 5

5.　　1.　(x) Mx
　　　2.　Hg / Hg & Mg
　　　3.　Mg　　　　　　　　UI 1
　　　4.　Hg & Mg　　　　　Conj 2, 3

7.　　1.　Sa ⊃ (x) Fx
　　　2.　Ha v Sa
　　　3.　~Ha
　　　4.　(x) (Fx ⊃ Gx) / (x) Gx
　　　5.　Sa　　　　　　　　DS 2, 3
　　　6.　(x) Fx　　　　　　MP 1, 5
　　　7.　Fu　　　　　　　　UI 6
　　　8.　Fu ⊃ Gu　　　　　UI 4
　　　9.　Gu　　　　　　　　MP 7, 8
　　10.　(x) Gx　　　　　　UG 9

10.　　1.　(x) (Ax ⊃ Bx)
　　　2.　(x) (Jx ⊃ Fx)
　　　3.　(x) (Ax v Jx) / (x) (Bx v Fx)
　　　4.　Au ⊃ Bu　　　　　UI 1
　　　5.　Ju ⊃ Fu　　　　　UI 2
　　　6.　Au v Ju　　　　　UI 3
　　　7.　Bu v Fu　　　　　CD 4, 5, 6
　　　8.　(x)(Bx v Fx)　　　UG 7

12.　　1.　(x)(Hx ⊃ Gx)
　　　2.　(x)(~Gx) / (x)(~Hx)
　　　3.　Hu ⊃ Gu　　　　　UI 1
　　　4.　~Gu　　　　　　　UI 2
　　　5.　~Hu　　　　　　　MT 3, 4
　　　6.　(x)~Hx　　　　　　UG 5

16.　　1.　(x) (Hx ⊃ Qx)
　　　2.　Ha v Hb / Qa v Qb
　　　3.　Ha ⊃ Qa　　　　　UI 1
　　　4.　Hb ⊃ Qb　　　　　UI 1
　　　5.　Qa v Qb　　　　　CD 2, 3, 4

18.　　1.　(∃x) (Fx) ⊃ (x)(Sx)
　　　2.　(∃x) (Hx) ⊃ (x)(Gx)
　　　3.　Fs & Hg / (x)(Sx & Gx)

4.	Fs	Simp 3
5.	(∃x)Fx	EG 4
6.	(x)Sx	MP 1, 5
7.	Hg	Simp 3
8.	(∃x)Hx	EG 7
9.	(x)Gx	MP 8, 2
10.	Su	UI 6
11.	Gu	UI 9
12.	Su & Gu	Conj 10, 11
13.	(x)(Sx & Gx)	UG 12

Exercise 26.3

1.
1.	(x) {Sx ⊃ [Px ⊃ (Bx & Qx)]}	
2.	(∃x) (Sx) / (∃x) (Px ⊃ Qx)	
3.	Sa	EI 2
4.	Sa ⊃ [Pa & (Ba & Qa)]	UI 1
5.	Pa & (Ba & Qa)	MP 3, 4
6.	Pa	Simp 5
7.	Ba & Qa	Simp 5
8.	Qa	Simp 7
9.	Pa & Qa	Conj 6, 8
10.	(∃x) (Px & Qx)	EG 9

4.
1.	(x) [Hx ⊃ (Sx v Gx)]	
2.	~ Sb & ~ Gb / ~ Hb	
3.	Hb ⊃ (Sb v Gb)	UI 1
4.	~(~ ~Sb v ~ ~Gb)	DM 2
5.	~(Sb v Gb)	DNeg 4
6.	~Hb	MT 3, 5

6.
1.	(x)[Hx ⊃ (Bx & Wx)]	
2.	(∃y) (~By) / (∃z) (~ Hz)	
3.	~Bc	EI 2
4.	Hc ⊃ (Bc & Wc)	UI 1
5.	~Bc v ~Wc	Add 3
6.	~(Bc & Wc)	DM 5
7.	~Hc	MT 4, 6
8.	(∃z) ~Hz	EG 8

Exercise 26.4

1. 1. ~(x)(Sx)/ (∃x)(~Sx v Px)
   2. (∃x)~Sx   QE 1
   3. ~Sd   EI 2
   4. ~Sd v Pd   Add 3
   5. (∃x)(~Sx v Px)   EG 5

5. 1. ~(∃x) (Ax) / (x)(Ax ⊃ Bx)
   2. (x)~Ax   QE 1
   3. ~Au   UI 2
   4. ~Au v Bu   Add 3
   5. Au ⊃ Bu   Imp 4
   6. (x)(Ax ⊃ Bx)   UG 5

7. 1. (x)(Sx & Gx) v (x)(Qx & Hx)
   2. ~(x)(Qx) / (x)(Gx)
   3. (∃x)~Qx   QE 2
   4. ~Qa   EI 3
   5. ~Qa v ~Ha   Add 4
   6. ~(Qa & Ha)   DM 5
   7. (∃x) ~ (Qx & Hx)   EG 6
   8. ~(x)(Qx & Hx)   QE 7
   9. (x)(Sx & Gx)   DS 8, 1
   10. Su & Gu   UI 10
   11. Gu   Simp 11
   12. (x)Gx   UG 12

9. 1. (∃x)(Px v Gx) ⊃ (x)Hx
   2. (∃x)~(Hx) / (x)(~Px)
   3. ~(x)Hx   QE 2
   4. ~(∃x)(Px v Gx)   MT 1, 3
   5. (x)~(Px v Gx)   QE 4
   6. ~(Pu v Gu)   UI 5
   7. ~Pu & ~Gu   DM 6
   8. ~Pu   Simp 7
   9. (x) ~Px   UG 8

Exercise 27.1

1. Domain: Numbers

   Ax: x is even

   Bx: x is rational (On this interpretation, the argument has a true premise but a false conclusion, for although every even number is a rational number, not every rational number is even.)

5. Domain: Persons

   Ax: x is conscious at least once in x's life

   Bx: x has never experienced consciousness

10. Domain: Living beings

    Ax: x is a human

    Bx: x is a martian

Exercise 27.2

1. The premise expansion is (Aa & Pa) v (Ab & Pb)
2. The conclusion expansion is (Aa & Pa) & (Ab & Pb)

   Aa: T   Pa: T

   Ab: F   Pb: F

Exercise 28.1

1.   1. (x)(Ax ⊃ ~Bx)
   2. (x)[(Bx ⊃ (Hx & Ax)] / (∃x)~Bx
   3. | ~(∃x)~Bx   AIP
   4. | (x)Bx   QE 3
   5. | Bp   UI 4
   6. | Bp ⊃ (Hp & Ap)   UI 2
   7. | Hp & Ap   MP 5, 6
   8. | Ap   Simp 7
   9. | Ap ⊃ ~Bp   UI 1
   10. | ~Bp   MP 8, 9
   11. | Bp & ~ Bp   Conj 5, 10
   12. (∃x) ~Bx   IP 3-11

5.   1. (x)(Hx ⊃ Qx)
   2. (x)(Hx ⊃ Rx) / (x)[Hx ⊃ (Qx & Rx)]
   3. | Hu   ACP
   4. | Hu ⊃ Qu   UI 1

	5.	Qu	MP 3, 4
	6.	Hu ⊃ Ru	UI 2
	7.	Ru	MP 3, 6
	8.	Qu & Ru	Conj 5, 7
	9.	Hu ⊃ (Qu & Ru)	CP 3-8
	10.	(x)[Hx ⊃ (Qx & Rx)]	UG 9

7. 1. (x) [Px ⊃ (Hx & Qx)] / (x) (Sx ⊃ Px) ⊃ (x) (Sx ⊃ Qx)

	2.	(x)(Sx ⊃ Px)	ACP
	3.	Su ⊃ Pu	UI 2
	4.	Pu ⊃ (Hu & Qu)	UI 1
	5.	Su ⊃ (Hu & Qu)	HS 3, 4
	6.	~Su v (Hu & Qu)	Imp 5
	7.	(~Su v Hu) & (~Su v Qu)	Dist 6
	8.	~Su v Qu	Simp 7
	9.	Su ⊃ Qu	Imp 8
	10.	(x)(Sx ⊃ Qx)	UG 9
	11.	(x)(Sx ⊃ Px) ⊃ (x)(Sx ⊃ Qx)	CP 2-10

10. 1. (∃x)(Px) v (∃x)(Qx & Rx)

2. (x)(Px ⊃ Rx) / (∃x)(Rx)

	3.	~(∃x)Rx	AIP
	4.	(x)~Rx	QE 3
	5.	~Ru	UI 4
	6.	~Ru v ~Qu	Add 5
	7.	~Qu v ~Ru	Comm 6
	8.	~(Qu & Ru)	DM 7
	9.	(x)~(Qx & Rx)	UG 8
	10.	~(∃x)(Qx & Rx)	QE 9
	11.	(∃x)(Qx & Rx) v (∃x)Px	Comm 1
	12.	(∃x)Px	DS 10, 11
	13.	Pv	EI 12
	14.	Pv ⊃ Rv	UI 2
	15.	Rv	MP 13, 14
	16.	~Rv	UI 4
	17.	Rv & ~Rv	Conj 15, 16
	18.	(∃x)Rx	IP 3-17

13. 1. (x) [(Hx v Px) ⊃ Qx]
     2. (x) [(Qx v Mx) ⊃ ~Hx] / (x) ~ H x
     3. |~(x) ~Hx   AIP
     4. |(∃x)Hx   QE 3
     5. |Ha   EI 4
     6. |(Ha v Pa) ⊃ Qa   UI 1
     7. |Ha v Pa   Add 5
     8. |Qa   MP 6, 7
     9. |Qa v Ma   Add 8
     10. |(Qa v Ma) ⊃ ~ Ha   UI 2
     11. |~Ha   MP 9, 10
     12. |Ha & ~Ha   Conj 5, 11
     13. (x)~Hx   IP 3-12

15. 1. (∃x)(Px v Jx) ⊃ ~(∃x)Px / (x)~Px
     2. |~(x)~ Px   AIP
     3. |(∃x) Px   QE 2
     4. |Pa   EI 3
     5. |Pa v Ja   Add 4
     6. |(∃x)(Px v Jx)   EG 5
     7. |~(∃x)Px   MP 1, 6
     8. |(x)~Px   QE 7
     9. |~Pa   UI 8
     10. |Pa & ~Pa   Conj 4, 9
     11. (x)~Px   IP 2-10

Exercise 28.2

1.   1. |~(x)[(Hx v Px) v ~Px]   AIP
     2. |(∃x)~[(Hx v Px) v ~Px]   QE 1
     3. |~[(Ha v Pa) v ~Pa]   EI 2
     4. |~(Ha v Pa) & ~ ~Pa   DM 3
     5. |~(Ha v Pa) & Pa   DNeg 4
     6. |~(Ha v Pa)   Simp 5
     7. |~Ha & ~Pa   DM 6
     8. |~Pa   Simp 7
     9. |Pa   Simp 5
     10. |Pa & ~Pa   Conj 8, 9
     11. (x)[(Hx v Px) v ~Px]   IP 1-10

5. 1. | (x) Px   ACP
     2. | ~(∃x) ~Px   QE 1
     3.   (x)Px ⊃ ~(∃x)~Px   CP 1-2

7. 1. | (∃x)(Fx & Gx)   ACP
     2. | Fa & Ga   EI 1
     3. | Fa   Simp 2
     4. | Ga   Simp 2
     5. | (∃x)Fx   EG 3
     6. | (∃x)Gx   EG 4
     7. | (∃x)(Fx) & (∃x)(Gx)   Conj 5, 6
     8.   (∃x)(Fx & Gx) ⊃ [(∃x)(Fx) & (∃x)(Gx)]   CP 1-7

10. 1. | ~(x)[(Sx & Hx) ⊃ (Sx v Hx)]   AIP
     2. | (∃x)~[(Sx & Hx) ⊃ (Sx v Hx)]   QE 1
     3. | ~[(Sv & Hv) ⊃ (Sv v Hv)]   EI 2
     4. | ~[~(Sv & Hv) v (Sv v Hv)]   Imp 3
     5. | ~ ~(Sv & Hv) & ~(Sv v Hv)]   DM 4
     6. | (Sv & Hv) & ~(Sv v Hv)   DN 5
     7. | Sv & Hv   Simp 6
     8. | Sv   Simp 7
     9. | ~(Sv v Hv)   Simp 6
    10. | ~Sv & ~Hv   DM 9
    11. | ~Sv   Simp 10
    12. | Sv & ~Sv   Conj 8, 11
    13.   (x)[(Sx & Hx) ⊃ (Sx v Hx)]   IP 1-12

Exercise 28.3

1.   1.   (x) (Cx ⊃ Mx)
     2.   (x) (Fx ⊃ ~Mx) / (x) (Fx ⊃ ~Cx)
     3.   Cu ⊃ Mu   UI 1
     4.   Fu ⊃ ~Mu   UI 2
     5.   ~ ~Mu ⊃ ~Fu   Trans 4
     6.   Mu ⊃ ~Fu   DNeg 5
     7.   Cu ⊃ ~Fu   HS 3, 6
     8.   ~ ~Fu ⊃ ~Cu   Trans 7
     9.   Fu ⊃ ~Cu   DNeg 8
    10.   (x) (Fx ⊃ ~Cx)   UG 9

Exercise 29.1

Part A

1. 1. (x)(y)(Hxy ⊃ ~Hyx)
   2. (∃x)(∃y)(Hxy) / (∃x)(∃y)(~Hyx)
   3. (∃y)Hay   EI 2
   4. Hab   EI 3
   5. (y)(Hay ⊃ ~Hya)   UI 1
   6. Hab ~Hba   UI 5
   7. ~Hba   MP 4, 6
   8. (∃y)~Hya   EG 7
   9. (∃x)(∃y)~Hyx   EG 8

7. 1. (x) (∃y) (Hxy) ⊃ (x) (∃y) (Sxy)
   2. (∃x) (y) (~Sxy) / (∃x) (y) (~ Hxy)
   3. (∃x)~(∃y)Sxy   QE 2
   4. ~(x)(∃y)Sxy   QE 3
   5. ~(x)(∃y)Hxy   MT 1, 4
   6. (∃x)~(∃y)Hxy   QE 5
   7. (∃x)(y)~Hxy   QE 6

12. 1. (∃x) (∃y) (Kxy)/ (∃y) (∃x)(Kxy)
    2. (∃y) Kay   EI 1
    3. Kab   EI 2
    4. (∃x)Kxb   EG 3
    5. · (∃y) (∃x) Kxy   EG 4

Part B

1. 1. (x) (∃y) (Mx ⊃ Cyx)
   2. ~ (x) (∃y) Cyx / (∃x) ~Mx
   3. |~(∃x) ~Mx   AIP
   4. |(x) Mx   QE 3
   5. |(∃x) ~ (∃y) Cyx   QE 2
   6. |(∃x) (y)~Cyx   QE 5
   7. |(y)~Cya   EI 6
   8. |Ma   UI 4
   9. |(∃y)(Ma ⊃ Cya)   UI 1
   10. |Ma ⊃ Cba   EI 9

11.		Cba	MP 8, 10
12.		~ Cba	UI 7
13.		Cba & ~ Cba	Conj 11, 12
14.	(∃x) ~Mx	IP 3-13	

Exercise 30.1

1. 1. Aa ⊃ Ha
   2. ~Ha
   3. a = b / ~Ab
   4. ~Aa   MT 1, 2
   5. ~Ab   LL 3, 4

4. 1. (x) (Ax ⊃ Px)
   2. (x) (Px ⊃ Hx)
   3. Aa & ~ Hb / ~ (a = b)

4.		~ ~ (a = b)	AIP
5.		a = b	DN 4
6.		Aa ⊃ Pa	UI 1
7.		Pa ⊃ Ha	UI 2
8.		Aa ⊃ Ha	HS 6, 7
9.		Aa	Simp 3
10.		Ha	MP 8, 9
11.		~Hb	Simp 3
12.		~Ha	LL 5,11
13.		Ha & ~ Ha	Conj 10, 12
14.	~(a = b)	IP 4-13	

Exercise 30.2

1. 1. Sj ⊃ S
   2. Ss
   3. j = s   / S
   4. Sj   LL 2, 3
   5. S   MP 1, 4

J = Jim; s = Sue's husband ; S = the store will be closed; Sx = x is sick.

Exercise 31.1

4. a. Serendipity is the faculty of making fortunate discoveries by accident. (American Heritage Dictionary)
   b. Sound is vibrations transmitted through an elastic medium.

10.   a.   lexical

      e.   stipulative

Exercise 31.2

1.   intensional

5.   extensional

Exercise 31.3

1.   Too broad. Lots of other things are terrible things to waste.

5.   The definition uses only negative terms to define the soul.

Exercise 32.1

2.   Red herring: Joe has just finished reading *The Black Book of Communism* (Cambridge, MA: Harvard University Press, 1999), a massive work written by French scholars that seeks to add up and document the total number of people killed by communist governments and communist revolutionary movements during the twentieth century. As Joe is in the middle of recounting the numbers of victims attributed to Castro, Ho Chi Minh, and Mao Tse Tung, Joe's friend Che Smith (his parents named him after the famous revolutionary) interrupts him and says, "Someone should write a 'Black Book' of capitalism!" Che has changed the subject and thrown the argument completely off track before Joe has had a chance to complete his train of reasoning.

Exercise 32.2

1.   Tu quoque

4.   Petitio principii

9.   Ad baculum

13.   Red herring

19.   Circumstantial ad hominem

23.   Ad ignorantiam

Exercise 32.3

2.   False dilemma: Either you are liberal or you are conservative. You are not conservative. So, you must be liberal. The problem with this argument is that some people are neither liberal nor conservative; there are other positions on the political spectrum.

Exercise 32.4

1.   Accident

5.   Ad verecundiam

10. False dilemma

13. Accident

16. Hasty generalization

20. False cause

26. Weak analogy

Exercise 32.6

2. Division

6. Amphiboly

11. Composition

17. Equivocation

21. Division

27. Composition

Exercise 33.1

1. a. Joe collects stamps and Pete collects coins. (Our knowledge that this similarity is irrelevant is based on our general background knowledge of cause and effect and the way the world generally works.)

   b. Neither man exercises. (We know that this similarity is relevant on the basis of our general background knowledge of cause and effect and the way the world works.)

   c. Pete will probably have a heart attack within the next 24 hours.

   d. Pete will probably have a heart attack within the next four years.

   e. Pete has recently been experiencing symptoms commonly associated with heart attacks.

   f. Joe's family has a history of heart problems whereas Pete's family does not.

Exercise 33.2

1. a. S

   b. S

   c. S

   d. W

   e. S

   f. W

Exercise 33.7

1. Difference

5. Method of concomitant variation

7. Method of agreement
10. Method of residues
15. Method of agreement
20. Method of agreement and difference

Exercise 33.8

3. Method of concomitant variations: Search for a possible cause that also rose by a similar amount during the 1980s and fell by a similar amount during the 1990s. Use common sense to identify possible causal factors that might fit the bill.

7. Method of difference: What was the difference between the two lousy pies and the one good pie? More specifically, what factor was present in the case of the good pie but completely absent in the cases of the lousy pies?

9. Method of agreement: Search for a common factor. What did they eat? What did they drink?

Exercise 34.1

1. One chance in six, or 1/6.
5. One chance in 400, or 1/400.

Exercise 34.5

1. 1/3

Exercise 35.1

1. □S
5. ~□S

Exercise 35.2

1. ~□P
5. ◇B & ◇~B
10. U → G
15. □C v □~C
19. G →□G

Exercise 35.3

1. F
5. F

Exercise 35.4

1. A → (□A v ∇A) This is true.
5. ∇A → (◇A v ◇~A) This is true. (Remember that the wedge represents an inclusive or.)

10. A → ~ □~A This is true.

Exercise 35.5

1. T
5. T
10. F

Exercise 35.6

1.

1. ◇ (H & S) ⊃ G
2. ~R
3. R v (H & S) / G
4. H & S   DS 2, 3
5. ◇ (H & S)   PI 4
6. G   MP 1, 5

5.

1. ~R
2. R v (A ⊃ B)
3. (A ⊃ B) ⊃ (P → Q)
4. Q → L / P → L
5. (A ⊃ B)   DS 1, 2
6. (P → Q)   MMP 3, 5
7. P → L   MHS 4, 6

12.

1. □(A ⊃ ◇ B)
2. H v A
3. ~ (F v H) / B
4. (A ⊃ ◇ B)   BR 1
5. ~F & ~H   DM 3
6. ~H   Simp 5
7. A   DS 2, 6
8. ◇B   MP 4, 7

Exercise 35.7

1.

1. □(A v B)
2. □~ B
3. □A ⊃ □E / E

		$\Box(A \lor B)$	Reit 1
4.		$\Box(A \lor B)$	Reit 1
5.		$\Box \sim B$	Reit 2
6.		$A \lor B$	BR4
7.		$\sim B$	BR 5
8.		A	DS 6, 7
9.	$\Box A$		Nec 4–8
10.	$\Box E$		MP 3, 9
11.	E		BR 10

5.

1.	$\Box(P \& Q)$		
2.	$\Box(Q \supset S) \,/\, \Box S$		
3.		$\Box(P \& Q)$	Reit 1
4.		$\Box(Q \supset S)$	Reit 2
5.		$P \& Q$	BR 3
6.		$Q \supset S$	BR 4
7.		Q	Simp 5
8.		S	MP 6, 7
9.	$\Box S$		Nec 3–8

10.

1.	$\Box A \,\&\, \Box B \,/\, \Box(A \& B)$		
2.	$\Box A$		Simp 1
3.	$\Box B$		Simp 2
4.		$\Box A$	Reit 2
5.		$\Box B$	Reit 3
6.		A	BR 4
7.		B	BR 5
8.		$A \& B$	Conj 6, 7
9.	$\Box (A \& B)$	Nec 4–8	

Appendix A. Classical Indian Logic

1. Conclusion: <u>Alligators</u> (p) are <u>animals</u> (s)

   Premise: <u>alligators</u> (p) are <u>reptiles</u> (h)

   Examples: like <u>turtles</u> (sp)

   Rule #1: Pass.

   Rule #2: Pass.

   Rule #3: Fail: no vp, but in charity . . . Coke bottles.

Rule #4: Pass.

Rule #5: Pass.

Technically the argument is invalid because it fails to pass rule three, but in charity the argument can be fixed; it is valid.

3. Conclusion: <u>Three-masted sailing vessels</u> (p) are <u>large ships</u> (s)

Premise: <u>three-masted sailing vessels</u> (p) are <u>things that float on water</u> (h)

Examples: like <u>small rowboats</u> (sp) unlike <u>pieces of cork</u> (vp)

Rule #1: Pass.

Rule #2: Fail: the sp does not fall within the s, but . . . tugboats.

Rule #3: Fail: the vp does not fall outside the h, but . . . lead bars.

Rule #4: Pass (ignoring sunken vessels and those in dry dock)

Rule #5: Fail: e.g., pieces of Styrofoam.

This argument is invalid because it fails rule five; its failure to pass rules two and three can in charity be ignored.

5. Conclusion: <u>Bears</u> (p) are <u>meat-eaters</u> (s)

Premise: <u>bears</u> (p) are <u>things other than vegetarians</u> (h)

Rule #1: Pass

Rule #2: Fail: no sp, but in charity . . . lions.

Rule #3: Fail: no vp, but in charity . . . deer.

Rule #4: Pass.

Rule #5: Fail: rocks, for instance, are things other than vegetarians yet not meat-eaters. An additional, and rather obvious, assumption would need to be agreed on: Either bears eat meat or bears eat vegetation (or they eat both).

Technically, the argument is invalid because it fails rules two and three, but these problems can be charitably remedied. Its failure of rule five is more of a problem. If it is assumed that bears can eat only meat or vegetation, then the argument can in charity be considered valid.

Index

Correspondence theory of truth,
15, 462
objections to, 463
Counterexample
defined, 66
method of, 66, 158
use in categorical logic, 158
Critical thinking
defined, 37
not all negative, 39
relation to level one and level two thinking,
37
relation to logic, 38
Socrates and, 40
Socratic method and, 40
why needed, 39

D
Decision procedure (algorithm), 332
Declarative sentence, 34
Deduction
common errors in, 366ff., 394ff.
common forms of, 49ff.
contrasted with induction, 83
defined, 43
Definiendum, 600
Definiens, 600
Definite description, 472
Definition
defined, 13, 599
lexical, 601
persuasive, 602
précising, 602
relation to reasoning, 599
stipulative, 601
theoretical, 601
Denying the antecedent (fallacy), 244, 355
Descartes, René, 719
Digital computer
algorithms and, A-30ff.
defined, A-29
logic and, A-29ff.
programming languages and, A-32ff.
Turing machines and, A-34
Determinism, A-36
Diodorus, 694ff.
Disagreement
types of, 601
verbal vs. real, 601

Disconfirmation, process of, 653ff.
Dodgson, Charles Lutwidge, 202
Alice in Wonderland and, 202
logic and, 202ff.
Domain (of a variable), 514
Double-blind experiment, 666
Dylan, Bob, 588

E
Economy, principle of, 653
Elenchus (Socratic), 86
Enthymemes
categorical syllogisms and, 160
defined, 25–26
valid arguments and, 74
Enumerative induction, 640
Equivalence
defined, 92
relation to deductive validity, 93
Existential
defined, 484
relation to particular, 484
Existential generalization
of a singular sentence, 536
Existential quantification, 537
Existential viewpoint, 171
Explanation
rational, 10
rational distinguished from mythical, 9–10
Explanatory reasoning
criteria for evaluating, 650
defined, 650
Extension (denotation) of a word, 602
Extensional definition, 603
Extensional definitions, rules for, 604
Extensional meaning, 604

F
Falsity
defined, 15
Fallacy
Aristotle and, 611–612
defined, 611
formal and informal distinguished, 611
informal, 611ff.
Latin names of, 612
Fallacies of language
amphiboly, 627–628
composition, 628

Performative sentence, 34
Philo of Megara, 228, 694ff.
Philonian conditional, 228, 694ff.
    vs. theory of Diodorus Cronus, 228, 694ff.
Philosopher, defined, 8
Philosophy
    birth of, 9
    defined, 9–10
    distinguished from myth, 9–10
Philosophy of logic, 452ff.
PL
    general sentence of, 477ff.
    interpretation of an argument in, 557
    interpretation of a sentence in, 556
    interpretations and invalidity, 560
    introduced, 485
    semantics for, 559–560
    singular sentence of, 471ff.
    syntax for, 486
    translation into, 488ff.
Plato, 9
Plato's Academy, 9
Possibility
    defined, 60–61
    logical, 60
    physical vs. logical, 729ff.
Post, Emil, 289, A-19ff.
Potter, Karl, 737
Pragmatic theory of truth, 464
Predicate logic
    birth of, 469
    introduced, 468
    also called quantificational logic, 468
Predicates
    Monadic, 506
    Relational, 506
Predicate term, 106
Premise indicator word
    defined, 17
    examples of, 18
Pre-Socratics, 691
Principia Mathematica, 470
Probability calculus
    Bayes's theorem, 684ff.
    general conjunction rule, 679
    general disjunction rule, 681
    impossibility rule, 678
    introduced, 677
    necessity rule, 678

    negation rule, 682
    restricted conjunction rule, 678
    restricted disjunction rule, 680
    rules of, 677ff.
Programming languages, 764ff.
Proof
    conditional, 433ff.
    contradiction, by, 166
    indirect, 166, 427ff.
    natural deduction system in, 366
    nested, 439
    premise-free, 446ff.
    reductio ad absurdum, 428
Puzzles (truth-functional), 299ff.

Q
QD
    conditional proof in, 572ff.
    defined, 548
    indirect proof in, 572ff.
    introduced, 548
    premise-free proof in, 572ff.
    proof in (defined), 548
    proofs with overlapping quantifiers in, 579ff.
    reduced set of rules for, 575
Quantificational (predicate) logic
    alternative rules for, 544ff.
    contrasted with categorical logic, 468ff.
    existential generalization, 536ff.
    existential instantiation, 537ff.
    inference rules of, 533ff.
    introduced, 468
    quantifier exchange, 546ff.
    universal generalization, 540ff.
    universal instantiation, 533ff.
Quantifier
    categorical logic in, 106
    existential, 482
    overlapping, 487, 512
    predicate logic in, 478ff.
    scope of, 487
    universal, 478
Quine, W.V.O., 431

R
Reasoning
    correct vs. flawed, 4
    deductive, 6
    deductive vs. inductive, 6, 42ff.

Reasoning (*continued*)
  defined, 3
  inductive, 6
Refutation by logical analogy and PL, 560
Relations
  proofs of logical relations, 582
  properties of, 518ff.
  reflexivity, 519
  symmetry, 519
  transitivity, 519
Relative frequency theory of probability, 677
Replacement method, 295
Replacement rules (truth-functional)
  association rule, 400
  commutation rule, 398
  defined, 397
  De Morgan's rule, 402
  distribution rule, 404
  double negation rule, 401
  equivalence rule, 413
  exportation rule, 412
  implication rule, 411
  tautology rule, 412
  transposition rule, 410
Russell, Bertrand, 251n, 470

S
Samsara, A-1ff.
Second order and first order systems
        contrasted, 586
Second order system of logic, 586, 589
Self-contradiction
  defined, 61
  modal logic and, 691
Semantics (formal)
  of modal logic, 704
  of predicate logic, 559ff.
  of truth-functional logic, 331
Semmelweis, Ignaz, 656
Sentence
  categorical, 50
  compound, 216
  conditional, 51
  declarative, 34
  embedded, 216
  exclamatory, 34
  form, 51
  general, 471, 477ff.
  hypothetical, 51

  imperative, 34
  interrogatory, 34
  operator (connective) in, 217
  performative, 34
  simple, 216
  singular, 471ff.
  token, 454
  type, 456
Sentence theory, 454
Sentence token, 455
Simplicity, principle of, 653
Socrates, 40
Socratic method, 40
Software, 761
Some, defined, 105
Sorites
  defined, 112, 162
  test for validity and, 163–164
Square of Opposition, 113
Square of Opposition (relations on)
  contradiction, 113
  contrariety, 114
  subalternation (subimplication), 114
  subcontrariety, 114
  superalternation (superimplication) 114
  undetermined, 117
Statement
  defined, 34
Statistical induction, 641ff.
Stoa poikile, 212
Stoic school of philosophy, 211ff.
  birth of truth-functional logic and, 213ff.
  demise of, 244
  philosophy of, 364–365
Subject term, 106
Sufficient condition, 279
SUN (mnemonic device), 281
Syllogism
  categorical, 50
  defined, 50
  disjunctive, 51
  hypothetical, 51

T
Tarski, Alfred, 435
Terms
  general, 472
  singular, 471
Thales, 9

9 780199 890491